Thomas Nicho

The Pedigree of the English People

Thomas Nicholas

The Pedigree of the English People

Reprint of the original, first published in 1874.

1st Edition 2024 | ISBN: 978-3-36884-834-7

Verlag (Publisher): Outlook Verlag GmbH, Zeilweg 44, 60439 Frankfurt, Deutschland
Vertretungsberechtigt (Authorized to represent): E. Roepke, Zeilweg 44, 60439 Frankfurt, Deutschland
Druck (Print): Books on Demand GmbH, In de Tarpen 42, 22848 Norderstedt, Deutschland

THE PEDIGREE

OF THE

ENGLISH PEOPLE.

Ἐκ δὲ τῶν εἰρημένων τεκμηρίων, ὅμως τοιαῦτα ἄν τις νομίζων μάλιστα ἃ διῆλθον, οὐχ ἁμαρτάνοι· καὶ οὔτε ὡς ποιηταὶ ὑμνήκασι περὶ αὐτῶν, ἐπὶ τὸ μεῖζον κοσμοῦντες, μᾶλλον πιστεύων, οὔτε ὡς λογογράφοι ξυνέθεσαν ἐπὶ τὸ προσαγωγότερον τῇ ἀκροάσει, ἢ ἀληθέστερον, ὄντα ἀνεξέλεγκτα, καὶ τὰ πολλὰ ὑπὸ χρόνου αὐτῶν ἀπίστως ἐπὶ τὸ μυθῶδες ἐκνενικηκότα· εὑρῆσθαι δὲ ἡγησάμενος ἐκ τῶν ἐπιφανεστάτων σημείων, ὡς παλαιὰ εἶναι, ἀποχρώντως.

Thucydides.

Wir tragen die Lasten unserer Väter, wie wir ihr Gutes empfangen haben.

Novalis.

BRITAIN
during the
SAXON HEPTARCHY

SCOTIA

NORTHUMBRIA

STRATHCLYDE

GERMAN

OCEAN

IRELAND

IRISH SEA

Wall of Antoninus

Firth of Forth

Firth of Clyde

Solway Firth

I. of Man

Lindisfarne I.

R. Tyne

York

Humber

R. Mersey

R. Dee

WALLIA

Offa's Dyke

Shrewsbury

R. Severn

MERCIA

EAST ANGLIA

Menevia

R. Wye

Gloucester

Bristol

Bristol Channel

ESSEX

London

Thames

Canterbury

KENT

Dover

SUSSEX

WESSEX

Winchester

Boulogne

CORNWALL

R. Exe

Exeter

R. Tamar

I. of Wight

ENGLISH CHANNEL

FRANCE

Judd & Co. Lith, Doctors Commons, London.

British Ethnology.

THE PEDIGREE

OF

THE ENGLISH PEOPLE:

AN ARGUMENT, HISTORICAL AND SCIENTIFIC,

ON THE

Formation and Growth of the Nation;

TRACING RACE-ADMIXTURE IN BRITAIN FROM THE EARLIEST TIMES, WITH
ESPECIAL REFERENCE TO THE INCORPORATION OF

The Celtic Aborigines.

BY

THOMAS NICHOLAS M.A., Ph.D., F.G.S.

[FOURTH EDITION.]

London:
LONGMANS, GREEN, READER, AND CO.,
PATERNOSTER ROW.

1874.

[ENTERED AT STATIONERS' HALL.]

LONDON: JUDD AND CO., PHŒNIX PRINTING WORKS, DOCTORS' COMMONS, E.C.

PREFACE.

The Question Stated: The Course of the Argument.

The early annals of Britain and the Race relations of the English People are in our day gaining increasing attention. The liberalizing influence of science has relaxed many sturdy prejudices, and its light has so far dispelled historic superstitions, that a chance of obtaining a hearing is now afforded even when cherished national beliefs are sought to be dislodged.

The Author is not aware that the main positions he has laid down have ever been expressly advocated by any of our historians. The ground, it is true, is old, and the materials, always in great part at hand, have of late been much increased by the quarrying of our public archives; but no structure has hitherto been planned and reared.

A presumption lies against the soundness of all

innovating ideas. The popular theory, believed in from the time of Gildas, that the English nation is the proper descendant of the Anglo-Saxons, is "in possession," and enjoys all the force of an article of national faith. Whoever, therefore, wishes to show that a moiety, perhaps the greater part, of the subjects of the early Anglian and Saxon kingdoms must have been of the "British" race, and not men who had come over in small open boats from the barren shores of the Baltic; and that subsequent changes during long ages of immigration, conquest, revolution, brought no substantial ethnical change upon the people of Britain, must, of course, give his Reasons.

Notwithstanding the freedom now professedly conceded to scientific inquiry, the Author advances his Faith and his Reasons with a measure of diffidence. Of their truth and solidity he entertains no question, although he has written throughout as an inquirer and student. But the inveteracy of national sentiments, long dominant, and supposed to favour national heraldic fame, is proverbial. When learned men accommodate their teaching to the popular apprehension, instead of guiding and correcting it, that man who thinks it his duty to put in a word for a neglected Truth, has perhaps not a pleasant prospect: he must seek comfort by an appeal from Tradition to Fact, and go on, saying, with Galileo Galilei, *E pur se muove !*

The OBJECT of the work is to trace, step by step, that process of *race-amalgamation* which has issued

in the compound people called English, maintaining
special reference throughout to the proportion of that
people's descent from the Celtic inhabitants of Britain
usually called the " Ancient Britons."

The latter term, when used in this volume, signifies
the different tribes, clans, or nations inhabiting Britain
at the time of the Roman invasion, and their descendants; and the " English People " means the great
body of the English nation proper in Great Britain
and its dependencies.

The course of the ARGUMENT proceeds thus :—It is
first shown that the numerous tribes found by the
Romans in possession of the British Isles, were all
presumably of what is called the Celtic race, and
presented only such dissimilarities as would arise from
separation into independent clans or States—dissimilarities, indeed, which marked them on the Continent
as well as in Britain, as partly proved by recent discoveries of Gaulish inscriptions which seem to reveal
dialectic varieties in the Celtic language of Ancient
Gaul similar to those which still distinguish the Cymro
from the Gael. Although among these numerous
tribes, the *Cymry* may rightfully claim pre-eminence,
as that branch of the family which both sustained
the heaviest shock from the Teutonic invasion, and
tinged most deeply the new race with Celtic blood—
the Gaels having from remote ages pushed their way
northwards, and into Ireland—the term " Ancient
Britons " cannot be confined to them, but must be

made to comprehend Belgæ, Lloegrians, Brython, Gaels or Gwyddyls, Picts, Scots, &c.; in short, all the early Celtic inhabitants of Britain and Ireland. The amount of Celtic blood, therefore, which, from whatever tribe, and in whatever age, has entered into the English people *in the British Isles*, is taken as the measure of their derivation from the Celtic Aborigines, or Ancient Britons.

The object of introducing a sketch of the *general condition of the Britons* before the Roman invasion has been twofold: first, the supplying the general reader with information expurgated from myth and tradition, in a field of history little traversed ; and, secondly, the constructing of a subsidiary argument, *à priori*, from the improbability of a people such as were the Britons being dislodged wholesale by the kind of people who became their subduers.

Stress is laid, not only on the substantial *oneness*, but also on the *number*, *distribution*, and *intellectual advancement* of the Ancient British populations. From all these would arise their fitness to assert their place, as history proves them to have done, as against both Romans and Anglo-Saxons.

The testimony of history, both direct and negative, is carefully employed ; and, when corroboratory to this, but never when contradictory of it, even the voice of legend and tradition (as in the case of the *Triads*) is with proper caution listened to.

The researches of modern writers—German, French and English—in Ethnology, Philology, Physiology, are then taken into account; and it is believed that as the result, the mixed and largely *Celtic* character of the English nation is demonstrated from the point of view and the use of evidences sanctioned by the most recent labours of science.

From a conviction of the importance of the argument from *Philology*, though with a consciousness of its great liability to abuse, the chapter on that subject has been prepared with laborious care. The Tables given are the fruit of an analysis of the modern Dictionary and of early English for which the author alone is responsible. There has never before been an attempt to distinguish with something approaching to precision that class of Celtic words which the English must have derived *directly* from the Celtic tongues, and *in Britain*. And yet this class alone can have a legitimate bearing upon the question.

The result of a careful and rigorous application of the arguments, inductive and deductive, drawn from the various fields of evidence, has been a conviction more clear and positive than the writer, when some years ago he resolved to investigate the subject, had himself anticipated, that the English people embraces a much larger infusion of Ancient British blood than English historians have been accustomed to recognise, and that some of the most valuable attributes, physical, intellectual, and moral, of the " True Briton," are owing to this fact.

The aim throughout has been to produce, on however small a scale, a contribution to genuine *history* and *ethnology*. The author is not ambitious of gaining a name for bold hypotheses. Conjectures, except as means for unravelling the entanglements of facts, are an inpertinence in history. Of theories respecting the inhabitants, language, and literature of Ancient Britain, we have had more than sufficient. Too free a reliance on legend, fanciful ethnology, ingenious theory, has estranged scholarly men in England from the study of the Ancient British Annals, and the Celtic Tongues; and it is only by the adoption of a sober and painstaking method of treatment, such as will promote knowledge, and satisfy sound judgment rather than national vain-glory, that we can hope to regain for it the attention it deserves. By the accumulation and careful induction of *facts*, and by the adoption of the best established views in *ethnology*, the writer has endeavoured to contribute to the establishment of a truth in our national history hitherto unaccountably neglected. Opinion on this subject is gradually changing. Among our most accomplished English annalists, Turner, Palgrave, and Kemble; and among ethnologists and philologists, Prichard, Latham, Stokes, and Garnett, have done much to prepare the way for its candid investigation.

The author has to acknowledge his great obligations to Professor Max Muller, M.A., of Oxford, to Dr. R. G. Latham, F.R.S., to Dr. S. Davidson, to Dr. Rowland Williams, and to the Rev. E. Mellor,

A.M., for valuable criticisms on the work in MS., and suggestions which have contributed in no small degree to its improvement; and the list of Authors appended, together with the numerous references throughout, will show to what extent he has availed himself of the best sources and authorities, ancient and modern, and of the most recent scientific research.

Part I. is to be understood as INTRODUCTORY ; *the main Argument is embodied in the succeeding parts.*

The less accurate orthography, Celtic rather than Keltic, is followed in deference to prevailing custom. Until the hard sound of *c* before *e* and *i*, as well as before *a, o*, and *u*, in words of Latin and Greek origin, is restored in practice, or the place of *c* filled by *k* in our classical scholarship, it is hardly worth while making an exception in the single case of the word Celt and its associates. The same rule would apply to *Cicero, Cecrops, Cimbri, Cilicia*, in all of which the *c* should, in strictness, be sounded like *k*. German scholars, like those of some other continental countries, are led by the analogy of their own language to the more accurate pronunciation of the classical tongues. The English, who in this and other matters are slow to adopt the linguistic reforms pleaded for by Professor Blackie, have unfortunately an impediment to rational usage sanctioned by the rules of their own orthoëpy.

LONDON, *January*, 1868.

PREFACE TO THE THIRD EDITION.

—◆—

THE work having been out of print for nearly three years, the present Edition, long promised, and already in great measure ordered, is brought out to meet the public demand.

Two causes more especially operated in exhausting the Second Edition : one, the increased interest of late created in the history and languages of the Celtic race, and the early Annals of Britain; the other, an unsuccessful attack made upon the book in the Court of Chancery, contributing, perhaps unintentionally, to make it more widely known, and to give its argument a character for independence and originality which it might not otherwise so indisputably possess.

The author has no reason to complain of the reception given the work by the critical journals. At home, along with a generous estimate of the production as a whole, despite its defects, a readiness has been shewn to consider, *de novo*, the race composition of the English people, and in the main to approve the doctrine pleaded for in these pages. On the Continent, reviews of a commendatory kind have appeared in several journals. Our men of science, from their own independent points of view, are gradually rejecting the old opinions. *Ex. gr.* Professor Huxley says emphatically :—" In Britain, the Teutonic dialects have overpowered the pre-existing forms of speech, and the people are vastly less 'Teutonic' than their language." Of the practice "of speaking of the present inhabitants of Britain as an 'Anglo Saxon' people," he says, "it is, in fact, just as absurd as the habit of talking of the French people as a 'Latin' race, because they speak a language which is in the main derived from Latin.'"[1] Many other declarations of like nature might be adduced, shewing the tendency of candid opinion guided by recent enquiry.

This edition is the result of careful revision and the addition of much new matter. The Section on Gildas, otherwise unaltered, is supplemented with what is believed to be an exposure of a *fraud*, or *blunder*, on the part of the writer who goes under that name, of no little significancy in early English History (pp. 219-224). The Section on the ethnological effects of the Norman Conquest has been re-written and considerably amplified.

The author, who was attacked by a severe illness while the work was printing, wishes to acknowledge with especial thanks the kind and valuable assistance rendered him by the Rev. Robert Gwynne, B.A., in collating and verifying authorities, correcting the press, and making a complete *Index*.

LONDON, *Christmas Day*, 1873.

[1] *Critiques and Addresses*, pp. 176, 177. London, 1873.

PREFACE TO THE FOURTH EDITION.

———◆———

THIS Edition is a reprint, without much alteration, of the Third Edition, for which the work had been carefully revised throughout.

LONDON, *May* 1, 1874.

MAPS AND DIAGRAMS.

Note on the Anglo-Saxon Map.

THE Anglo-Saxon Kingdoms were very unsettled in boundary, and some of them of very short continuance. They were a *Heptarchy* after Northumberland (A.D. 655) became one kingdom—an *Octarchy*, as long as its two divisions, Deira and Bernicia (old Celtic names), formed separate sovereignties—a period of less than a hundred years. The Western side, containing Strathclyde, Wales, and Cornwall, coloured uniformly on the Map, never formed part of the Heptarchy, or Octarchy, unless we except the southern end of Strathclyde, for a time usurped by Bernicia. Wessex—on some maps erroneously made to include Cornwall—at no time ruled beyond the river Tamar, and Cornwall only fell under direct English rule after the absorption of the Anglo-Saxon States in united *England*. The chief towns, or capitals, of several of the states of the Heptarchy cannot be well distinguished; and it may be questioned whether these ever possessed a settled local government, their existence being only prolonged by an incessant state of war.

CONTENTS.

---◆---

PART I.

INTRODUCTORY.

CHAPTER I.

NATIONAL ORIGIN.

CHAPTER II.

THE ANCIENT BRITONS—THEIR ETHNOLOGICAL AFFINITIES—THEIR STATE OF CULTURE.

PART II.

THE INVASIONS OF BRITAIN—THE ELEMENTS OF AD-
MIXTURE OF RACE ACCUMULATING.—ADMIXTURE
COMMENCING.

CHAPTER I.

CHAPTER II.

CHAPTER III.

CHAPTER IV.

PART III.

THE ARGUMENT FOR ADMIXTURE OF RACE — THE
QUESTION: "TO WHAT EXTENT IS THE ENGLISH
NATION OF CELTIC ORIGIN?" DISCUSSED.

CHAPTER I.

THE HISTORICAL ARGUMENT.

CHAPTER II.

THE EVIDENCE OF PHILOLOGY.

CHAPTER III.

THE EVIDENCE OF TOPOGRAPHICAL AND PERSONAL NAMES.

CHAPTER IV.

CHAPTER V.

NOTE ON AUTHORITIES AND OTHER WORKS CONSULTED.

THE succeeding list of Authors is furnished for the benefit of students in British Ethnology, and embraces such works only as bear more or less directly upon the general subject and collateral matters, and are most easily accessible. Its perusal will at once shew that researches into Ethnology and the nearly-related subjects of comparative Philology and Physiology are of modern date, and that the Germans have far outstripped the English in them all. This remark applies with special emphasis to the study of the Celtic languages and race—subjects which, on many accounts, might be expected to prove of interest to English enquirers.

ORIGINAL AUTHORITIES AND OTHER WORKS CONSULTED.

ADELUNG, J. C. und Vater: *Mithridates ; oder Allgemeine Sprachenkunde.* 4 vols. Berlin, 1806-1817.

AKERMAN, J. Y.: *Ancient Coins of Cities and Princes.* Lond. 1841.

AMMIANI MARCELL.: *in Monumenta Hist. Brit.* Lond. 1848.

ANGLO - SAXON CHRONICLE: in *Monumenta Hist. Brit.* Lond. 1848.

ARNDT, C. G. von: *Ueber den Ursprung &c, der Europäischen Sprachen.* Frankft. 1818.

ARNOLD, Dr. T.: *Hist. of Rome.* 3 vols. Lond.

ARNOLD, Dr. T.: *Lectures on Modern History.* Lond. 1843.

BARTH, C. KARL: *Ueber die Druiden der Kelten.* Erlangen, 1826.

BEDDOE, J., M.D.: *on Permanence of Anthrop. Types.* Memoirs of Anthrop. Soc. of Lond. 1865. *On Head Forms of West of England. On Prevalence of Dark Hair in England.* Anthrop. Rev. 1865-6.

BETHAM, Sir W.: *Etruria Celtica.* 2 vols. 8vo. Dublin, 1842.

BETHAM, Sir W.: *The Gael and Cymbri.* 8vo. Dublin, 1834.

BENDER. Dr. J.: *Die Deutschen Ortsnamen.* 8vo. Siegen, 1846.

BLACKSTONE: *Commentt. on Laws of Engl.*, by Stephens. 4 vols. 1863.

BLUMENBACH, J. FRIED.: *Decades Craniorum.* Göttingen, 1828.

BOPP, Dr. FRANC.: *Glossarium Comparativum Linguae Sanscritae.* Ed. Tertia. Berol. 1867.

BOSWORTH, Dr. J., F.R.S.: *Dictionary of Anglo-Saxon Lang.* 8vo. Lond. 1848.

BOSWORTH, Dr. J.: *Origin of English, Germanic, &c., Languages.* 8vo. Lond. 1848.

BRANDES, K.: *Das Ethnograph. Verhält. der Kelten und Germanen.* Leipzig, 1858.

BUCKLE, H. T.: *History of Civilization in England.* 2 vols. 8vo. Lond. 1857.

BUNSEN, Baron C. C. Jos., D.D., D. Ph., &c.: *Philosophy of History.* Lond. 1850.

BUNSEN, Baron C. C. Jos., D.D., D. Ph. &c.: *Results of Recent Egyptian Researches in reference to Ethnology.* Rep. of British Association, 1847.

CAESARIS, JUL.: *Opera Omnia; Commentarii.* Ed. Var.

Cambro-Briton. 3 vols. 8vo. Lond. 1819-1822.

CAMDEN, W.: *Britannia.* Gough's Ed. 4 vols. fol. Lond. 1806.

CHALMERS, G.: *Caledonia.* 3 vols. 4to. Lond. 1810, &c.

Camden Society: The Publications of, but chiefly *A Dialogue between the Soul and the Body. Political Songs;* Temp. Henry III. and Edward I. Edited by T.Wright, M.A.

CHAUCER, GEOFF. : *Poetical Works.* Ed. by Bell. 8 vols. Lond. 1856.

COLERIDGE, HERBERT : *Dictionary of Oldest Words in the English Language.* Lond. 1863.

CONSTANTIUS, PRESBYTER : *Life of St. Germanus,* in " Acta Sanctorum." Vol. vii.

COURSON, AUREL. DE : *Histoire des Peuples Bretons.* 2 vols. Paris.

Crania Britannica: by Dr. B. Davis, and Dr. J. Thurman. Lond. 1856-65.

DARWIN, C.: *Origin of Species.* 8vo. Lond. 1860.

DAVIES, ED.: *Celtic Researches, &c.* 8vo. Lond. 1804.

DAVIES, Rev. J.: *Races of Lancashire, &c.,* Trans. Phil. Soc. Lond. 1855.

DE BELLOQUET, ROGET : *Ethnogénie Gauloise, &c.* 8vo. Paris, 1858.

Dictionary of Greek and Roman Antiquities. By Dr. Smith. 2nd edition. Lond. 1848.

Dictionary of Greek and Roman Biography and Mythol. By Dr. Smith. 3 vols. Lond. 1849, &c.

DIEFENBACH, Dr. LORENZ: *Celtica,* P. I. et II. 2 vols. 8vo. Stuttgart, 1850, &c.

DIEFENBACH, Dr. LORENZ: *Origines Europææ.* 8vo. Frankfort-a-M. 1861.

DIEZ, FRIEDERICH : *Etymological Dictionary of the Romance Lan-*
guages. Transl. by S. C. Donkin, B.A., London. 1864.

DIODORUS SIC.: in *Monument. Hist. Brit.* Rolls Office. Lond. 1848.

DION CASSIUS : in *Monument. Hist. Brit.* Rolls Office. Lond. 1848.

Domesday Book : Ed. by Sir H. Ellis. 4 vols. fol. Lond. 1783-1816.

DONALDSON, Dr. J. W.: *Varronianus.* 8vo. Lond. 1852.

DONALDSON, Dr. J. W.: *On English Ethnography.* Camb. Essays, 1851.

Dosparth Edeyrn Davod Aur : Ed. Rev. J. Williams Ab. Ithel. Llandovery, 1856.

DUCANGE, C. DUFR.: *Glossarium Med. et Inf. Latinitatis.* 7. vols. Paris, 1840, &c.

EBEL, Dr. HERMANN : *Celtic Studies.* By Prof. W. K. Sullivan, Ph. D. Lond. 1863.

EDWARDS, MONS. W. F. : *Des Caractères Physiologiques, &c.* Paris, 1829.

Encyclopædia Britann. : 8th ed. Various Articles.

ELLIS, GEORGE : *Early Metrical Romances.* 3 vols. 8vo. Lond. 1805-1818, &c.

ERSCH UND GRUBER : *Allegemeine Encyklopædie, &c.* 122 vols. Leipzic.

ESQUIROS ALPHONSE : *L'Angleterre et la Vie Anglaise.* Paris, 1859.

EVANS, JOHN, F.R.S., F.G.S., F.S.A.: *The Coins of the Ancient Britons.* 8vo. Lond. 1864.

EWALD HEINRICH VON : *Geschichte des Volkes Israel.* 3 vols. Göttingen, 1843.

FERGUSON, ROB.: *The Northmen in Cumberland, &c.* Lond. 1856.

FÖRSTEMANN, E.: *Die Deutschen Ortsnamen.* Nordhausen, 1863.

GARNETT, Rev. RICH., M.A.: *Philo-*

logical Essays. 8vo. Lond. 1859.

GILDAS: *Hist. in Monumenta Hist. Brit.* Lond. 1848.

GIBBON, EDW.: *Decline and Fall of Rom. Emp.* 8 vols. Lond. 1838.

GOBINEAU, Comte A. de.: *Sur l'Inégalité des Races Humaines.* Paris, 1850.

GRIMM, JACOB: *Deutsche Grammatik.* 4 vols. Göttingen, 1822, &c.

GUEST, Dr. E.: *On English Rhythms.* Lond. 1850.

GUEST, Dr. E.: *On Gentile Names.* Phil. Proceedings, vol. 1.

HARDY, Sir T. DUFFUS: *Descript. Catalogue of Materials relating to the History of Great Britain, &c.* Rolls' Office. Lond. 1862-5.

HALLIWELL, J. O.: *Dictionary of Archaic and Prov. Words.* 2 vols. Lond. 1860.

HALLAM, HENRY: *State of Europe during Middle Ages.* 3 vols. Lond. 1829.

Havelok the Dane. Ed. by Sir F. Madden, for Roxburgh Club.

HAWKINS, ED.: *Silver Coins of England.* Lond. 1841.

HERODOTUS: *Hist.* Ed. Bekker, 1845, and in *Mon. Hist. Brit.*

HOLTZMANN, ADOLF: *Keltan und Germanen.* 4to. Stuttgart. 1855.

HOVEDEN, ROGER DE: *Ex Scriptor. post Bedam.* By Saville. 1591.

HUMBOLDT, W. Von: *Prüfung der Untersuch, &c.* Berlin, 1821.

HUXLEY, Prof. T. II.: *Elements of Compar. Anatomy.* Lond. 1864.

HUXLEY, Prof. T. H.: *Critiques and Addresses.* London, 1873.

Iolo MSS., The: Pub. by Welsh MSS. Society. Lond. 1848.

KEMBLE, J. M.: *Codex Diplomaticus Ævi Saxon.* 5 vols. Lond. 1845.

KEMBLE, J. M.: *The Saxons in England.* 2 vols. Lond. 1849.

KINGSLEY, Rev. C.: *The Roman and the Teuton.* 8vo. Lond. 1864.

King Alysaunder. In Weber's Romances. Vol. 1.

KNOX, Dr. ROB.: *The Races of Men.* 8vo. Lond. 1862.

LAING, S., and HUXLEY, Prof. T. H.: *Pre-historic Remains of Caithness.* Lond. 1866.

LAPPENBERG, J. M.: *Hist. of Eng. under Anglo-Sax. Kings.* 2 vols. 8vo. Lond. 1845.

LAPPENBERG, J. M.: *Hist. of Eng. under Anglo-Norman Kings.* 8vo. Lond. 1854.

LATHAM, Dr. R. G.: *The English Language.* 4th Ed. Lond. 1855.

LATHAM, Dr. R. G.: *Ethnology of Brit. Islands.* 8vo. Lond. 1852.

LATHAM, Dr. R. G.: *The Nationalities of Europe.* 2 vols. 8vo. Lond. 1863.

LATHAM, Dr. R. G.: *The Germania of Tacitus,* with Dissertt. Lond. 1851.

LATHAM, Dr. R. G.: *Prichard's Celtic Nations,* with supp. chapters. Lond. 1857.

LATHAM, Dr. R. G.: *The Nat. Hist. of the Varieties of Man.* 8vo. Lond. 1850.

Leges Walliea Hoeli Boni, &c. Ed. Wotton. Fol. Lond. 1730.

Leges Walliea. The Ancient Laws and Institutes of Wales. Ed. Aneurin Owen, published by the Record Commission. 1 vol. fol. Lond. 1861.

LEO, Dr. HEINRICH: *Vorlesungen über die Geschichte des Deutschen Volkes und Reiches.* 3 vols. 8vo. Halle, 1854-61.

LEO, Dr. HEINRICH: *Feriengeschriften: Ueber Deutschen und Keltischen.* Halle, 1847-1852.

LEO, Dr. HEINRICH: *Wahle und*

Deutsche. (Kuhn's Zeitschrift.) 1853.

LEWIS, Sir GEO. C.: *on the Romance Languages.* 8vo. Lond. 1862.

LHWYD, ED.: *Archæologia Britannica.* Fol. Oxford, 1707.

LINGARD, Dr. J.: *Hist. of the Anglo-Saxon Church.* 2 vols. 8vo. 2nd. Ed. Lond. 1845.

LOBINEAU, M.: *Histoire de Bretagne.* 8vo. Paris.

LYELL, Sir CHARLES: *Elements of Geology.* 6th Ed., 8vo. Lond. 1865.

LYELL, Sir CHARLES: *On the Antiquity of Man.* 8vo. Lond. 1863.

MACKINTOSH, Rev. J.: *Hist. of England.* 3 vols. 12mo. Lond. 1830.

MATTHEW PARIS: *English History,* by Giles. 3 vols. Lond. 1852.

MARSH, G. P.: *Origin and History of English Language.* 8vo. Lond. 1862.

MEYER, Dr. C.: *On the Study of Celtic Languages.* Rep. of Brit. Assoc. 1847.

Monumenta Historica Britannica: Published by command of Her Majesty. Ed. by H. Petrie and J. Sharp. Introd. and Pref. by G. D. Hardy, Esq. 1 vol. fol. Lond. 1848. Contains, besides Extracts from *Classical Writers:* Bedæ Ven. *Historia Ecclesiastica;* et *Chronicon.* Gildæ Sapientis *de Excidio Britanniæ. Roman Inscriptions in Britain. British Coins. The Anglo-Saxon Chronicle* (in A.-Sax.) Asserii Meneven. *Rer.-Gest. Alfredi Magni.* Ethelwerdi *Chronicorum, lib. quatuor.* Florentii Wigorn. *Chronicon.* Simeonis Dunelm. *Historia,* &c. Henrici Huntendunensis *Historia. L'Estorie des Engles, solum la Trans. G. Gaimar. Annales Cambriæ,* ab A.D. circ. 444, usque ad 1066. *Brut y Tywysogion* (Chronicle of Princes of Wales) &c., &c., &c.

MÜLLER, MAX Prof.: *Lectures on the Science of Language.* Lond. 1862.

Myvyrian Archaiology of Wales. 3 vols. 8vo. Lond. 1801-7.

NAPOLEON BONAPARTE, EMPEROR: *Life of Julius Cæsar.* Vols. i. ii. 8vo. Lond. 1863-1866.

NIEBUHR, B. G.: *Lectures on Ancient Ethnography and Geography.* Lond. 1853.

NIEBUHR, B. G.: *The Hist. of Rome.* Translated by Hare and Thirlwall. 1847-51.

PALGRAVE, Sir FRANCIS: *History of Normandy and Engl.* 2 vols. Lond. 1851-7.

PALGRAVE, Sir FRANCIS: *Hist. of English Commonwealth.* 2 vols., 4to. Lond. 1832.

Penny Cyclopædia (Various Articles).

PERCY, Bishop: *Reliques of Ancient English Poetry.* 3 vols. 8vo. Edinburgh, 1858.

Percy Society: The various Publications of, but chiefly *The Owl and Nightingale.* Ed. by T. Wright, M.A. *The Life and Martyrdom of Thomas Beket.* Ed. by Mr. Black.

PICKERING, Dr. C.: *The Races of Man.* Ed. Dr. J. C. Hall. Lond. 1850.

POUCHET, GEORGES: *Pluralité des Races Humaines.* Paris, 1864.

PHILOLOGICAL SOCIETY: *Transactions and Proceed. of.* 1845-1863.

Pictorial History of England. New Ed. by Chambers. 7 vols. roy. 8vo. Edinburgh, 1855, &c.

Piers Ploughman, Vision of; Creed of. Lond. 1832.

Population Returns, Census of 1861, &c.

POSTE, Rev. BEALE: *Britannic Researches.* 8vo. Lond. 1853.

POTT, Dr. AUG. FRIED.: *Die Personennamen*, &c. 8vo. Leipzig, 1853.

POTT, Dr. AUG. FRIED.: *Indo-Germanischer Sprachstamm*. In Ersch und Gruber's Encyklop. Vol. xviii.

PRICHARD, Dr. J. C.: *Physical Hist. of Mankind*. 4 vols. 8vo. Lond. 1841-47.

PRICHARD, Dr. J. C.: *The Eastern Origin of the Celtic Nations*. Ed. Latham. 8vo. Lond. 1857.

PRICHARD, Dr. J. C.: *The Natural Hist. of Man*. 8vo. Lond. 1843.

PTOLEMÆI, CL.: *Geographia*. In *Monumenta Hist. Brit*.

PUGHE, Dr. W. O.: *Dictionary of the Welsh Language*. Second Edition. Denbigh, 1832.

QUATREFAGES, A. DE: *Unité de l'Espèce Humaine*. Paris, 1861.

RASK, E. C.: *Anglo-Saxon Grammar*. Tr. by Thorpe. Lond. 1865.

RENAN, ERNEST: *De l'Origine du Langage*. 8vo. Paris, 1858.

Reports of Commissioners on Public Records. Lond. var. dates.

REES, Rev. W. J.: *Lives of Cambro-British Saints*. Landovery, 1853.

RETZIUS, ANDERS: *Ethnologische Schriften*. Stockholm. 1864.

Revue Celtique: Ed. by M. Gaidoz, Paris. 1870-74.

ROBERTSON, E. W.: *Scotland and her Early Kings*. 2 vols. 8vo. Edinburgh, 1862.

SCHLEICHER, A.: *Die Sprachen Europas*. 8vo. Bonn, 1850.

SISMONDI, J. C. L. S. de: *Hist. de la Chute de l'Empire Romain, et du Déclin de la Civilisation*. Paris, 1835.

SOUVESTRE, EMILE: *Les Derniers Bretons*. 2 vols. post 8vo. Paris, 1858.

STRABONIS: *Geographia*, in *Monument. Hist. Britannica*.

SUETONII C. TRANQUILL : *Vitæ*. Ibid.

TACITI, C. CORN.: *Opera Omnia*. Ed. Bekkeri, &c. 2 vols. Leipzig, 1831.

TAYLOR, Rev. Is., M.A.: *Words and Places*. Lond. 1864.

THACKERAY, Rev. F., A.M., *Researches into State of Ancient Britain*. 2 vols. 8vo. Lond. 1843.

THIERRY, AMADÉE: *Histoire des Gaulois*. 3 vols. 8vo. Paris, 1844.

THIERRY, AUGUSTIN: *Hist. de la Conquête de l'Angleterre par les Normands*. Paris, 1825. Do. *in Bohn's Libr*. 1856.

THIRLWALL, Dr. CONNOP: *History of Greece*. 8 vols. 8vo. Lond. 1845.

THORPE, BENJ.: *Northern Mythology*. 3 vols. 8vo. Lond. 1851.

THURNAM, Dr. J.: *On Ancient British and Gaulish Skulls*. In Memoirs of Anthropol. Society. Lond. 1865.

TRENCH, ARCHBP.: *On the Study of Words*. Lond. 1853.

TURNER, SHARON: *The Hist. of the Anglo-Saxons*. 3 vols. Lond. 1828.

Types of Mankind: by Nott and Gliddon, Philadelphia, 1854.

VILLEMARQUÉ, Vicomte H. HERSART de la: *Poèmes des Bardes Bretons du VI. Siècle*. Paris et Rennes, 1850. 8vo.

VILLEMARQUÉ, Vicomte H. HERSART de la: *La Legende Celtique en Irlande, en Cambrie, et en Bretagne*, &c. 12mo. St. Brieux, 1859.

VILLEMARQUÉ, Vicomte H. HERSART de la: *Barzaz-Breiz: Chants populaires de la Bretagne*. 8vo. Paris, 1839.

Vocabularies, a Volume of: Vol. I., part of a "Library of National Antiquities." Published under the direction of J. Mayer, Esq., F.S.A., &c., of Liverpool. Ed. by Thos. Wright, M.A. 1857.

Welsh-English Dictionaries: Various.

WHITAKER, Dr. J.: *History of Manchester.* 2 vols. 4to. Lond. 1775.

WHITAKER, T. D.: *History of Whalley.* Fol. Lond. 1818.

WHITAKER, T. D.: *History, &c., of Craven.* 4to. 1805.

WILLIAMS, Ven. ARCHD.: *Essays on Various Subjects.* Lond. 1858.

WILLIAMS, Rev. ROB., M.A.: *Lexicon Cornu-Britannicum.* 1 vol. 4to. Llandovery, 1865.

WILSON, Dr. DANIEL: *Prehistoric Annals of Scotland.* Second Edition. 2 vols. Lond. 1863.

WILSON, Dr. DANIEL: *Physical Char. of Celts.* "Canadian Journal," Nov. 1864.

WINDISCH, ERNST: *Ueber Fick's Vergleich. Wörterbuch d. Indo-German. Sprach.* in Zeitschr. für. vgl. sprachf. xxi. 5.

WORSAAE, J. J. A.: *The Danes and Norwegians in England,* &c. Lond. 1852.

WORSAAE, J. J. A., *Primeval Antiquities of Denmark.* Lond. 1849.

WRIGHT, THOS., M.A.: *Wanderings of an Antiquary,* &c. Lond. 1854.

WRIGHT, THOS., M.A.: *The Celt, the Roman, and the Saxon.* Lond. 1861.

ZEUSS, I. C.: *Grammatica Celtica.* 2 vols. 8vo. 2nd Ed. by Ebel. Berlin, 1871.

ZEUSS, J. C.: *Die Deutschen und die Nachbarstämme.* 8vo. München, 1837.

CORRIGENDA.

Page 23, line 4, for " αὐτόχθονες," read αὐτόχθονες.
" 37, notes at foot, add to each cap. 1.
" 38, line 13, for "Matronn," read Matrona.
" 61, " 4 from bottom, for "v. 10" read v. 12.
" 65, " 6 " for "at" read ad.
" 65, last line, after "money" add note, *De Bell. Gall.* v. 12.
" 71, line 3 from bottom, for "iv. 13" read vi. 14.
" 87, " 8 " for "B.C. 56" read B.C. 54.
" 91, " 4 " for "Nimius" read Nimis.
" 92, " 1 " for "A.D. 137" read A.D. 337.
" " " 13, after "sons" read of.
" 105, note 1, after "invisi," read *De Excid. Brit.* 23.
" 117, " 3, for "successioni" read successione.
" 145, line 3 from top, for "commeatum" read commeatuum.
" 177, " 12 " " for "Reguum" read Regnum.
" 188, " 6 " bottom, for "principium" read principum.
" 381, " 4 " " for "Geo." read Gee.
" 448, " 5 " " for "Wootton's" read Wotton's.

PART I.

Introductory.

The Pedigree of the English People.

CHAPTER I.

NATIONAL ORIGIN.

SECTION I.

The Composite Character of Nations.

THOUGHTFUL students of ethnology, even at a somewhat early stage in their researches, arrive at the conviction that purity of national descent—such purity as would entitle any one nation to pronounce itself entirely distinct in blood from other nations—is a thing impossible. The intermixture of different sections of mankind has been more like that of the waves of the sea than of the river of snow-water passing through the Swiss lake. The race has been so unsettled on the face of the globe—its migrations have been so prolonged and numerous; admixture, through amity, interest, force of conquest, necessity, has in every country so much prevailed—that few nations, even the quiescent races of oriental climes, can predicate of themselves that they belong simply and

C 2

exclusively to this variety or that, or can trace their lineage to a single tribe or family.

Many persons may not readily acquiesce in the conclusion that, by an ordination of Providence, the development of the higher qualities of the race has been made dependent upon this intermixture of blood. But if facts which lie on the field of history do not fully and beyond contradiction justify such an hypothesis, they at least go far to establish its probable truth.

Peoples, in proportion as they have been quiescent, isolated, suspicious of foreign customs and alliances, have in the course of ages given signs of exhaustion, and at length paid the penalty of over-conservatism by decay and extinction. On the other hand, the mightiest nations have been those whose origin is traceable to mixed sources. That combination of noble qualities which culminates in national greatness, is found at the focal point where the varying but still harmonizing attributes of different stocks of the race meet and blend. There seems to be a tendency in prolonged isolation to leave in bolder relief some one or some few of the great qualities of a people, and it is by no means improbable that by a beneficent law of the universe such idiosyncracies are made to disappear, or at least recede, before less marked but more solid qualities. In the Celt we have the fervid impulse ; in the Teuton, patient perseverance : the com- bination of the two forms a completer, stronger personality than either by itself. Aptness to luxuriate in the ideal, and power to embody the ideal in actual form—philosophical meditativeness and practical industry—are oftener found apart than in combination. In China, India, Japan, they are not wedded together. But they are found more or less associated among the more composite peoples of Greece, Rome, Germany, France, England, America. The Jews, the most unmixed people, perhaps, in the civilized world, seem in this, as in other things, to form a strange exception to a general rule. Though deprived of empire, of political unity, of country, they still maintain a vitality and display at times an intellectual energy and practical talent truly marvellous.

But there is one consideration which to some extent accounts for this seeming mystery. The Jews, though unmixed, are not properly isolated. They mingle in the daily life and imbibe the habits and modes of thought of all nations. While fortified by a sense of national unity which no other people enjoy, their intellectual treasury is enriched by the literature of the whole civilized world. An intellectual renovation proceeding from such various sources, and the physical influences of the various climates of the globe, may be sufficient to account for the persistent vigour of the Jewish race, while they also supply a clue to some of its manifest defects.

SECTION II.

The Origin of the Aboriginal British Population Obscure— The Analogy of other Early Nations.

The ethnological tree of England spreads its deeply imbedded roots in forms so tangled and directions so diverse as sorely to perplex the student who would understand the whole history of its growth. The labours of the historian and ethnologist are much of a kind with those of the geologist, who has to search out and classify the formations of many thousand ages. The latter finds the strata upheaved, dislocated, intermixed, presenting sudden faults which break off the thread of evidence, and bringing strange materials from regions wholly unknown, transported by forces enormously surpassing any subject to modern experience. The historian, standing over the field of ancient British history, finds himself in similar plight. He sees before him an unwieldy chaos which he wishes to reduce to some order. Whence came those numerous and busy tribes faintly pictured in the pages of Avienus,[1] Diodorus,[2] Strabo,[3] Cæsar,[4] Tacitus,[5] and in the Welsh *Triads ?* What was the age of their arrival? Which was the first comer, if their arrival was in succession? And which continued to bear the generic designation of the stock, if their arrival was simultaneous? Assuming, as we must at last assume, that they all belonged to what modern ethnologists call the great Indo-European family, and to the Celtic branch of that family, whence the wide varieties of their speech, and the designations whereby in Ireland, Caledonia, and Wales, they have continued to be known?

The same or a similar difficulty besets the ethnologist's path, proceed whither he may in the field of ancient history. Thucydides tells us that Hellas was at first the abode of many tribes; that these tribes were migratory; that the stronger pressed upon and dispossessed the weaker, forcing them into the wilder and remoter parts; that thus the fairer and more fertile regions, such as Thessaly, Bœotia, and most of the Peloponnesus became the theatres of contention, and that Attica, by reason of its poverty, enjoyed greater repose, and thereby grew in strength and importance.[6] But beyond these general facts handed down by tradition from primeval times, Thucydides can give us but little information. When he begins to assign to separate tribes their distinct origin, he at once falls back upon the aid of myth and fable, the story of the Trojan war, of Hellen the son of Deucalion, Minos, &c.[7] The

---

[1] *Ora Maritima, vers.* 94 *et seq.*   [2] Lib. v.   [3] Lib. iii.
[4] *De Bell. Gall., passim.*   [5] *Opera, passim.*
[6] *Thucyd.* i. 2, 3.   [7] *Ibid* i. 3, 4.

Athenians, all account of their ancestry failing them, ingeniously made profit out of the disadvantage, and boasted that they were descendants of neither this man nor that, but οἱ αὐτόχθονες, veritable sons of the soil.[1]

This idea was afterwards, along with many others, borrowed by the Romans. Hence their *indigenæ aborigines*. Horace speaks of the human race issuing out of the earth—"Cum prorepserunt primis animalia terris"—showing that the ancients were not at least inferior to the framers of the extremest "development" doctrine of modern times; only the old Greeks and Romans chose to be considered children direct of "mother earth," rather than those of apes—a pride of ancestry which, though not ambitious, is on the whole worthy of commendation.

An impenetrable veil hangs over the progenitors of the Romans, search for them from what quarter we may. This people, therefore, failing a better account of their own origin, fell back upon the confused and contradictory legend of Æneas and Ascanius conducting, after the fall of Troy, the Trojans into Latium. The Pelasgi, it is likely enough, formed the generic stock whence proceeded the various tribes of Italy, the Sabines, Tyrrhenians, Siculians, Prisci, Sacrani, Umbri, Ligurj; and these, though brethren in blood, indulged in hostile incursions upon each other, as the ancient Britons also did, from motives of jealousy and interest. But of the degrees of their kinship we know little; and still less of the consanguinity of the Pelasgi to the old Etruscans, the probable progenitors of the different tribes of Hellas.[2] The story of Hercules arriving in Latium and slaying the giant Cacus, and the whole account of Romulus and Remus, betray a people as helplessly de-

---

[1] *Herodotus* i, 171.
[2] See Thirlwall's *Hist. of Greece*, i. 2. 8vo. ed.

pendent on fable as were the old *Cymry* in their legends of *Hu Gadarn* and *Prydain ap Acdd Mawr*.

Again, we possess but the most shadowy knowledge of the tribes which wandered up and down the plains of India before they coalesced into the mighty Hindoo race; or of the manner in which the same or related tribes founded the other great empires of the East, of which China forms the chief. How the hordes of the North strove together before joining their rude forces to overwhelm the Western Empire; or how many elements fused with the Franks to found the great empire of Charlemagne, it is easier to imagine than specify. The absence of historic records is cause of all the uncertainty. The mystery which hangs about the early inhabitants of Britain is the product of the same cause. They were here, in all probability, long before the art of writing was known in Europe, and certainly long before the art of writing history was known; and even of the things their wise and learned men did commit to writing after the science of history had been taught them by the Romans, what quantities have been lost it is now impossible to tell.

CHAPTER II.

The Ancient Britons.—Their Ethnological Affinities.—Their State of Culture.

It will be useful, preliminarily to entering upon the argument of this essay, to cast a glance at the ethnological *unity* and the culture of the various tribes and confederacies of tribes known by the generic term "Ancient Britons." We shall thus virtually supply an answer to two pertinent questions :—First : Were all the early inhabitants of Britain substantially of the Celtic race, and of near kinship? Secondly : Were they in culture, power, and general political development such as to be fitted, while beaten in the field, to form a persistent and vital element in the future population of the country?

SECTION I.

Results of Modern Ethnological Research respecting the early Inhabitants of the British Isles.

We are to show in the course of this inquiry how far the English nation has, in the process of crystallizing into form, gathered into its body elements from among the Ancient British race. In order to this we must determine at the outset the meaning of the term "Ancient Britons," either eliminating from the mass some of the "nations" found among the early inhabitants of these islands, or supporting by reliable evidence the hypothesis that all the dwellers in Britain and Ireland when Cæsar arrived were, under different names, substantially one people. The latter alternative shall be our task.

In maintaining this hypothesis, we shall not attempt ignoring the fact that Teutonic settlements had been made on our eastern, and north and south-eastern shores prior to Roman times. Whither did not the pirates and free-booters of the Elbe district and Scandinavia penetrate? Still, the aborigines of Britain were a Celtic people, and our conclusion shall be, that in so far as aboriginal blood has been absorbed in the rearing up of the great community now called the English Nation, so far has the English nation been derived from the Ancient Britons. The hypothesis maintained by some searchers into the pre-historic past that a pre-Celtic wave of population passed over Britain is of no importance here. Again, even though Teutonic blood should be accounted alien to the Celtic, and be allowed in some measure to have mixed with it in Britain in the early ages, still this admixture is demonstrably so light, as in no sense materially to affect the soundness of our conclusion. The kinship of Celts and Teutons, however, and their departure at no *very* remote period from a common centre, is a question of great interest, and must be taken account of, here and there, during the progress of our investigations.

(a). *Preliminary Ethnological Data.*

We are of the opinion that the human race is *one*. This ground is taken not merely on the faith of Scripture, but also as the demonstration of science.[1] It is too dogmatic

---

[1] It is hardly necessary to observe that the most eminent naturalists agree in this opinion, as *ex. gr.* Prichard, Cuvier, Blumenbach, Humboldt, Pickering, Owen, Latham, De Quatrefages.

and too little "scientific," to declare that the nations of the earth, which in mental, moral, and physical constitution possess so much in common, have sprung from different centres and at different epochs. As surely as that "one touch of nature makes the whole world kin," so surely does the universal kinship everywhere develop the same touches of nature.

Among the arguments for the unity of the race, as well as for the near consanguinity of some of its branches, that of *language* is allowed to be one of the most interesting and conclusive. The common possession of the same terms as signs of the same ideas by nations inhabiting widely remote regions, argues relationship; and the more ample the common property, the nearer, presumably, the kinship. A comparison of the various languages spoken in Britain, Ireland, and Gaul in the time of Cæsar, in so far as their elements are now ascertainable, leads infallibly to the conclusion that the tribes and "nations" which spoke them, though torn asunder by dissension, and widely separated by locality, constituted substantially but one people.

Not only is the human race, divided by modern scientific classification into the three varieties—the Mongolian, Negro, and European[1]—proved by its modes of speech to have an organic unity, but the Indo-European class of languages, embracing as chief branches the Sanscrit and the Classic tongues, contains abundance of materials in favour of the comparatively recent origin of man on the earth—recent, we mean, when compared with immeasurable geological periods. Bunsen, one of the most adventurous and untrammelled thinkers of our age, has shown that the Egyptian antiquities and language, and other languages,

---

[1] See Latham's *Varieties of Man*, p. 13 *et seq*. Cuvier's designations are Mongolian, Ethiopian, and Caucasian. Latham prefers the terms Mongolidæ, Atlantidæ, and Japetidæ.

furnish evidence that all the nations, which from the dawn of history to the present time have been the pioneers of civilization in Africa, Asia, and Europe, must have had one beginning.[1] It has taken a long time, doubtless, to separate the one race into sections so unlike ; and again long periods to elaborate the subdivisions of each. But facts carefully compared leave no room to doubt the nature of the process.

(b.) *The remote Relation of Celts and Teutons.*

The family of languages termed Indo-European embraces the Sanscrit, Iranian, Hellenic, Romanic, Slavonic, Teutonic and Celtic. A family likeness exists in all these. As to the *Teutonic* and *Celtic*, it may be argued that the points of analogy between them are few. In one sense they are few ; in another, very numerous. They are amply sufficient to establish a proof of relationship.[2] In a subsequent chapter on *Philology*, many of these points of analogy are brought to view.

It is true that the early relationship of Celts and Teutons is not a question whose treatment is essential to the object of this work—that object being to unfold relationships which arose between a portion of the race named Teutonic, and a portion of the race named Celtic, not in remote, but in historic times, and having as the theatre of their operations the British Isles. We have to show, in short, how far the native, perhaps aboriginal, tribes of these islands have entered into the ancestry of the present British people. To inquire, therefore, into prior relationship between Celts

---

[1] See Bunsen's paper on *Egyptian Researches in Relation to Asiatic and African Ethnology*, read before the British Association at Oxford.

[2] See Prichard's *Eastern Origin of the Celtic Nations*, Latham's ed., 1857. Confer also Schilter's *Thesaur. Antiq. Teuton.*, and Wachter's *Glossarium German., passim*.

and Teutons as members of the great Indo-European family, would only be to take a step in the direction of universal ethnology, which would eventually land us at the universal brotherhood of all men. We must not run into this wide inquiry. Our point of incidence is at a recent stage in the history of mankind, where national distinctions had followed race distinctions, and these had obtained such prominence as to sever into widely-separated sections the originally one family of man. Teutons and Celts, for the objects of this essay, form sufficiently distinct Ethnological stocks, meeting in the course of their migrations in these Western regions as strangers, and more or less coalescing with each other, so as to constitute in process of time one great nation.

It is impossible, however, for the sake of an artificial arrangement, to ignore the fact that, as already intimated, these people, if each followed for itself the line of its descent backwards, would as infallibly as the rays of the sun or the branches of an arterial system, meet at no great distance in a common centre. Their modern coalition is only a new confluence of streams, which not only as tiny rivulets had taken their departure from the same fountain, but had now and then glided closely past each other, and even partly mixed their waters in traversing the continent of Europe. It were utterly irrational and unhistoric to hold absolute distinctness and separate purity of blood as between these divisions of Europeans. They were separated by territory, aggregated by interest, not by difference or community of blood. "Britons, Anglo-Saxons, Danes, and Normans," says Sir F. Palgrave, "were all relations: however hostile, they were all kinsmen, shedding kindred blood."[1]

Where could these races have met before they crossed

---

[1] *English Commonwealth*, i. p. 35.

swords on British ground? The *Cimbri* had once possession
of the Cimbric Chersonese or *Jut*land, and being so near
and in such teeming numbers, had most probably peopled
the same tracts which afterwards yielded the Angles, *Jutes*,
and Saxons, who followed them more as despoilers than
friends to Britain.   Nor is it at all beyond the bounds of
probability that the Britons sent for help to North Germany,
not merely as the wonderful region whence heroic warriors
and fierce sea-rovers in countless myriads issued, but also
as the land which they knew by tradition to have once been
the home of their own ancestors.   Tradition, the memory
of a nation, is wonderfully retentive, and upon the whole
singularly accurate. Commerce, also, had evidently existed
between the two peoples. Saxons had been allowed to
settle in Britain prior to the Roman occupation. The
" Saxon Shore" of the Island on the south (*litus Sax-
onicum*), had most likely derived its name from Saxon
incursions and settlements in those parts.[1]   Names of
places on the opposite shore of the Channel clearly prove
that Teutonic settlement had also been largely effected in
Gaul.

The point of early junction referred to between the
ancestry of Britons and Saxons would form a parallel to
the relation subsisting between the Saxons and Danes of
England and the followers of William at the Conquest, for
these also were in part children of the North of Germany
and of the Scandinavian peninsula. The composition of
the Conqueror's forces, however, is largely dealt with in a
subsequent chapter.

It is curious to notice by the way another antecedent
junction, mentioned by Appian.[2] He says that the Nervii,

---

[1] See Grimm, *Gesch. der Deutsch. Sprache*, p. 625.

[2] *De Reb. Gall.*, iv. 1., 4.

one of the Belgic tribes, were descendants of Cimbri and Teutons. Νέρβιοι ἦσαν δὲ Κίμβρων καὶ Τευτόνων ἀπόγονοι.

The names given by Greek and Roman historians are at times very vague and perplexing. For example, Dion Cassius says that the Greeks called some of the Celts " Germans," and the country they inhabited (Celtica), Germany. Κελτῶν γάρ τινες οὓς δὴ Γερμανοὺς καλοῦμεν, &c.

The opinion held by some accomplished ethnologists, such as Latham,[1] that the " so-called " Cimbri of the Chersonese were not Celts, and that they were not related to the Cymri of Britain, is, we conceive, more ingeniously than soundly advocated. Local names in Jutland, and words in the vernacular of Schleswig and Holstein are found to be Cymric. It is difficult to know why the Chersonese should be called Cimbrica at all, except for the reason that Cimbri abode therein ; and it is impossible to account for the belief of ancient historians that this penin-sula was inhabited by Cimbri unless such was the case.

Equally difficult is it to account for the adoption of the name Cymry or Cymri by the people now represented by the inhabitants of Wales, unless we allow as the reason their relationship to the ancient Cimbri. Not much im-portance can be attached to Zeuss's assertion, that the name is of recent adoption by the Celts of Britain. It may be so, and yet be only a revived ancient name, and revived on the ground of conscious right of consanguinity. The etymology Zeuss gives to Cymro, Cymru, &c., is also fanciful and misleading : " can, in comp. cyn—same as Latin con,

---

[1] See The Germania of Tacitus, Ed. by Dr. Latham, 1851. Append., p. clv. Though in this instance compelled to dissent from Dr. Latham, we are bound to confess to the highest admiration of his various writings. An accomplished modern writer, coupling his works with the late Dr. Donaldson's, speaks of them as " somewhat dangerous." They can only be so as his great erudition enables him but too successfully to advocate a wrong opinion when he happens to adopt it.

and *bro=brog*, land—whence he arrives at the meaning of *indigenous, belonging to the country*.[1]   There exists no ground whatever except fancy for such etymology as this.   The plain account of the name is that it is a modification of Cimbri, just as Cimbri again, according to the testimony of Diodorus, is "a slight modification" of Cimmerii.[2]   He says, "Those [Celts] towards the north and bordering upon Scythia are so exceeding fierce and cruel that, as report goes, they eat men like the Britons who inhabit Iris.   So fierce are they that by some they have been held to be the same with those who in ancient times overran all Asia and were then called *Cimmerii*, but who are now through length of time, with a little alteration, named *Cimbri*."

Be the case as it may with respect to the Cimbric Chersonese, there can be no dispute as to whether the Celts of the continent are found in frequent contact with Teutons. As we have just shown, they are said by Appian to unite with the Teutons in the composition of the people called Nervii, and the name he gives them is *Cimbri*.   Paterculus mentions Cimbri and Teutones together as a "German" people.[3]   Cæsar informs us that they overran Gaul together, and were only put in check by the Belgæ,[4] &c.

That people thus intimately associated should to a great extent become mixed, and their languages in future times exhibit many materials in common—as we find them now to do—is all but unavoidable.

(*c.*)   *The Celtic tribes of ancient Britain—the Cymry, Belgæ, Lloegrians, Brython, Gaels, Picts, Scots.*

Having glanced at the *earlier* relations of the stocks which in conjunction have contributed the main materials

---

[1] Confer Zeuss, *Grammatica Celtica*, 2nd Ed. pp. 206, 207.   [2] *Diod. Sic.*v.2.
[3] Lib. ii. 8, 12.   [4] *De Bell. Gall.* ii. 4.

of the English nation, we now confine our attention to the Celtic tribes of Britain, and their relation to each other. We need not stay to prove that the native population found by the Romans in Britain were Celts. Whatever that term may mean, it is a designation properly applied to them. Very few even among the wildest theorists have denied its correctness, while the united voice of historians, ancient and modern, is in its favour. But while the British aborigines were all Celts, they still presented many diversities. They were divided into several independent sovereignties. They went by different names, and spoke languages which to a stranger might appear to be different. They had arrived in Britain, it cannot be doubted, at different times, and probably at different points of the coast, and from different parts of the continent. Some had come from the north of Germany, some from Belgic, some from Armoric Gaul. Their separation prior to their reunion in Britain may have been very long. The only question we need settle here is whether that separation had been so prolonged as to occasion such diversities in speech and manners, and such intermixtures with other races, as would render it improper to consider them one nation or people, under the common designation "Ancient Britons."

The researches of modern historians unequivocally favour the opinion that under the names of Κελται, Γαλαται, Gauls, Gaels, Gwyddyls, Celts, Cimmerii, Cimbri, Cymry, Brython, Lloegrians, Scots and Picts, only *one race*, under different, tribe or clan divisions, political organizations, and periods of existence, is spoken of, and while different degrees of diversity through shorter or longer periods of estrangement and foreign admixture had intervened, still no such diversity prevailed as would materially affect their *unity* and *integrity*, and hence their classification as *one people*.

D

1. The Κιμμεριοι—we mean the historical Κιμμεριοι, not those of Homer—the Cimmerii, Cimbri (hence Welsh *Cymry*), at one time peopled the valley of the Danube, the shores of the Sea of Azof, the *Crimea* on the *Cimmerian* Bosphorus, and the Chersonesus *Cimbrica* or Jutland. From this last locality it was that they issued forth in such formidable hosts in the second century, B.C., and committed such havock among the Roman armies under Papirius Carbo, Junius Silanus, Cn. Mallius, and Servilius Cæpio, until they were at last (B.C. 101) brought to bay by Marius near Verona, and completely and finally defeated. This great branch of the Celtic race was probably its chief representative in Roman times, but they had brethren in the form of scattered tribes in various parts of the continent of Europe which are occasionally mentioned by ancient historians, both Greek and Roman. These were fragments of the great Celtic stock left behind during migrations, cut off by war, or voluntarily wandering in search of better fortune.

At what time, or from what quarter, the Cimbri (Cymry) came first to Britain it is impossible to ascertain. For the Celtic race, in their westward progress from Asia, Meyer assigns two principal routes, and along one or other of these, and perhaps chiefly by the *northern* (if credit is given to the declarations of the *Triads*), the *Cymry* made their way to their final home. Meyer listens to the intimations, slight as they may be, of history, but mostly relies on the abiding footprints discovered in local names. He traces one route through Syria and Egypt, along the northern coast of Africa, across the Strait of Gibraltar, and through Spain to Gaul, where it separates into three branches, one terminating in the British Isles, the other in Italy, and the third near the Black Sea. The other great stream of migration ran less circuitously and more northwards, through Scythia

SUPPOSED ROUTES OF CELTIC MIGRATION.

in Europe, the shores of the Baltic Sea, Scandinavia or Jutland, Prussia (the supposed *Pwyl* of the Welsh *Triads*), through Northern Germany, the plains of the Elbe (the region of the Saxons), and to Britain across the German Ocean, the "hazy sea," (*Môr Tawch*) of the *Triads*. It is conjectured, moreover, that the stream which came by Africa and Spain was the earliest to reach Britain. They may have been the Gaels. The two routes are roughly represented on the annexed sketch map.

Whatever the origin of the name *Cymry*, and whencesoever the people, it is obvious from the whole tenor of their history that they had from early times obtained a commanding position among the other Celtic tribes of Britain. They seem, by pre-eminence, to have been called by the old ancestral name, *Cimbri*—the name, however, of a section only of the generic stock, the Celtæ (Κελται). While, therefore, all the British Celtic tribes shall be comprehended by us under the term "Ancient Britons," a place of distinction must be accorded the *Cymry* as the strongest, and most persistent in maintaining language, race, and territory, of all their brethren. It may be that this distinction was won at the cost of greater comparative reduction in number than fell to the lot of the more yielding tribes—the Brython, Lloegrians, and Cumbrians. Be this as it may, history presents no section of a people standing forth more conspicuously from the general mass, and solemnizing with more impressive sacrifices at the shrine of home and country. They yielded—but only inch by inch, to a superior foe; and, at the last, an unincorporated remnant scorning surrender, carried away with them, as Æneas did from Troy, their choicest and most valued treasures—their kindred, and their

"... . . sacra . . . . patriosque penates,"

made Wales their chosen land, Mona, as many think, the

sanctuary of their priesthood, and the Snowdon mountains the citadel of their freedom. Their name, language, and honour they have to this day preserved as memorials of their past; and though they have left behind them, engulphed in the great vortex of conquest and incorporation, the greater part of themselves, their brethren of Strathclyde, Cumbria, Cornwall, and the long ago vanished Lloegrians and Brython, they still survive, and constitute a part, not insignificant, not morally or politically unhealthy, but strong, vital, and honourable, of the renowned people of Britain. Their time of painful conflict for independence is past; their time of peace, good government, prosperity is come—of which their good genius long centuries ago might have said :—

> " Revocate animos, moestumque timorem
> Mittite ; forsan et hæc olim meminisse juvabit.
> Per varios casus, per tot discrimina rerum
> Tendimus in Latium ; sedes ubi fata quietas
> Ostendunt."

The " Latium " to which, " through so many perilous adventures," and much against their will, they have been conducted, and where, for 1,900 years at least, they have first found " peaceful settlements," is union with England. And now that they have been taught at last to value peace, let them gird themselves for distinction in a new field—to *them* in modern times perfectly new—the field of the industrial arts, intellectual culture, and political progress. With respect to these things, the people of every civilized country, knowing their story, and holding in honour the honesty and brightness of their nature will say to them :—

> " Durate, et vosmet rebus servate secundis."

2. The *Belgæ*. The opinion has always prevailed, and cannot be invalidated, that Britain was first peopled from

Gaul. A large portion of Gaul, corresponding with modern Belgium and Holland, with portions of Flanders, Picardy, and Normandy, was inhabited by the "Belgæ," and named by the Romans *Gallia Belgica*. Tribes were found in Britain also, whom Cæsar calls *Belgæ*, and gives us to understand that they were of the Belgæ of Gaul. Now it has been a question in ethnology whether the Belgæ of Gaul, and by consequence those of Britain, were Celts (like the Galli in general), or Germans, or a mixture of both. We believe that the Belgæ of Gaul themselves were largely a Celtic people, with an infusion of Germanic blood. There is nothing to be gained to ethnology by denying that the Belgæ of Britain were a branch of those of Gaul. Not only the statements of Cæsar, but the local names on both sides the channel, show that they were one people.

Now the only point material to us in this place is, whether these "Belgæ" were, in the main, a Celtic race. That they had received a Teutonic tinge is admitted; but were they Celtic in the main? They were. And more: they were a branch of the Celts nearly related to the *Cymry*. This is proved by the language they spoke. Strabo was not a careless or incorrect historian, and he not only states that the Celtic name was given to *all* the Gauls,[1] but distinctly affirms that the language spoken by the Celts was, with few variations, the language spoken by the *Belgæ*: "Eadem non usque quaque lingua utantur omnes, sed paululum variata."[2]

The nature of this language may also be learned from the local names, and tribe names, of Belgica. The dwellers on the sea coast opposite Dover were the *Morini* (Welsh, *mór*, sea; Corn., *mór*; Arm., *mór*). Many of the

---

[1] Nomen Celtarum universis Gallis inditum, ob gentis claritatem. Lib. iv.

[2] *Strabo*, lib. iv.

towns of the Belgæ situated on rivers were called by names
commencing with *dur*, the Celtic word for "water," as
*Dur*ocortorum (modern Rheims), *Tur*nacum (Tournay),
*Dur*ocatalaunum (Chalons), (Welsh, *dwr*, water, river).[1]
Others, and their inhabitants, commenced as in Welsh,
Cornish, or Armoric, with *tre*, "abode"; as *Tre*viri,
A*tre*batii, *Tri*casses. Some, again, contained the Celtic
dun (Welsh, *din, dinas,* " a high place of strength," citadel;
Corn., *dun*, a hill), as Viro*dun*um, Lug*dun*um. Others had
the Celtic *caer* (Welsh, *caer*; Corn., *caer*; Arm., *ker*; Irish,
cathir, pronounced *cair*, a "fortress," "city"), as *Caer*esi,
*Cor*tovallum, *Cur*miliaca. Their rivers had the Celtic
avon and *wysg*, as Matro*un*, A*xon*a, S*e*quana.[2]

The Celtic character of tribes whose names, and the
names of whose towns and rivers, contained such elements
—elements observable in the most purely Celtic districts
of Britain—cannot for a moment be questioned. That great
numbers of these people moved across to our island, as
intimated by Cæsar, is obvious. The *Atrebatii* of Belgica
had their counterpart in the *Atrebatii* of Wilts and Berks;
the *Catalauni* in the *Cateuchlani* inhabiting the central
parts north of the Thames, &c. Names of towns and
rivers likewise correspond. As to the language, Sir F.
Palgrave gives it as his opinion that at least one-third of

---

[1] Comp. Part III. chap. iii. sect. 3 (*b*) of this essay.

[2] *Ibid.* It is often said, since the opinion was given by Lhwyd, that
wysg and *esk* can only be derived from the Irish *uisk,* "water," and this
is used as one chief argument for the priority of occupation of Britain
by the Gael. But it is observable that rivers designated by this term
are rapid streams, and we are much inclined to take the word as an
adjective marking this quality. In Welsh, g*wysg*, g*wisgi*, feminine
form *wisgi*, is an adjective signifying quick, brisk, gay, precipitate,
headlong. *Gwysg* also in Welsh signifies "stream," and this is from
g*wy*, water. Moreover, it by no means follows that because this word
uisk or *uisge* is now only found in Irish or Gaelic, that in early ages it
was not also found in Cymric.

the vocabulary of the Cymric consists of roots which it possesses in common with the Belgic.[1]

The Belgæ of Britain, therefore, were of a cognate race with the Cymry, and their presence under a name somewhat non-Celtic disturbs not the substantial unity and integrity of the Ancient Britons.

But we have *historic* as well as philologic testimony respecting the Celtic character of the Belgæ. Out of some fifteen Belgic tribes enumerated by Cæsar, he selects only three or four as distinctively Germanic. To none of the great tribes of Belgica, but only to a few of the more insignificant, does Tacitus attribute a Germanic origin. Such is the case with Strabo. The Galatæ of Asia Minor are allowed to be Celts, but St. Jerome testifies that the Belgic Treviri spoke a language similar to theirs. We have seen (see p. 30) that Appian relates that the *Nervii* —probably the least Celtic of all the Belgic tribes—were a compound of Cimbri and Teutons.

When Cæsar, in giving a general description of the people of Gaul, divides them into three portions, Belgæ, Galli (who called themselves, as he says, "Celtæ"), and Aquitani, and informs us, "Hi omnes in *lingua*, institutis,— legibus, inter se differunt," he gives information which, if taken absolutely, is now allowed by all competent judges to be incorrect, but if taken as a loose and general statement, meaning only that *dialectic* variations, even of a marked character, prevailed, may be received as history. The only difference in language in Belgic and other parts of Gaul, so far as we can judge, was one which may fairly be termed dialectic; and when the same people crossed over to Britain, some from Belgica, some from Lugdunensis (which included Normandy and Brittany) they knew each other as brethren of one stock, and had probably

---

[1] *Engl. Comm.*, i. 27.

fewer differences of speech as a barrier to intercourse, than
would be presented now if Cymry from Wales and Bretons
from Finisterre tried to colonize a new region in concert.

With this view agrees the opinion of the accomplished
Frenchman, M. Emile Souvestre, who, with reference to
Cæsar's " trois grands peuples," says :—" Mais il est clair
que ces trois nations, qui avaient une même origine, les
mêmes institutions politiques, la même religion, parlaient,
à peu de chose près, *la même langue ;* et quand César dit :
' *Hi omnes lingua, institutis, legibus, inter se differunt,*' il faut
traduire ici le mot *lingua* par *dialecte.*" And he then adds
with much force, that if this is not so, then the language
used elswhere by Cæsar, with respect to the German king
Ariovistus, is incomprehensible : " Sans cela, ce que dit le
même César serait incompréhensible, lorsqu'il assure, sans
distinguer entre les *Belges,* les *Celtes,* et les *Aquitaines,*
qu'Arioviste, roi des Germains, avait appris la *langue gauloise* par un long commerce avec ce peuple. Que signifierait
la *langue gauloise* s'il ne s'agissait d'une langue parlée dans
toutes les Gaules ? "[1]

Much can be said in favour of the view that the " Belgæ "
and the " Galli " of Cæsar stood in about the same relation
to each other as the Cymry and the Gaels of to-day, both
as to blood and language. Put into tabular form, they
would stand thus :—

The Ancient Galli	Representatives of the true
The Modern Gaels, or Gwyddyls	" Celtæ. "
The Ancient " Belgæ "	Mixed, but cognate to the
The Modern Cymry	true " Celtæ. "

Cæsar may have meant by Belgæ, Galli, and Aquitani,
the peoples otherwise called Flemings, Gauls proper (*i.e.,*
Celts), and Basques ; or (otherwise named) Cimbri, Celtæ,

---

[1] *Les Derniers Bretons,* i. 141, 142.

and Basques, the two former according to this view being
as distinct in language as the Cymry of Wales and the
Gaels of Ireland are now.[1]

The only effect of this theory would be to widen the
distance in some small degree between the Galli and Belgæ
of ancient times, and between the Gaels and Cymry of
to-day, respectively ; making the Irish and Welsh, though
cognate, to differ, as languages, and not as dialects of the
same language. In fact, Irish would then be to Welsh
what Greek is to Latin, or Sclavonic to Lithuanian.

The opinion that the words of Cæsar, when speaking
of the tribes of Gaul, " Hi omnes in *lingua*, &c., inter se
differunt," refer to a dialectic distinction precisely identical
with that existing between modern Cymric and Gaelic,
seems to be supported by the recent discoveries in the soil
of France of old *Gaulish inscriptions*, which are believed to
preserve remains of two forms of the early Celtic speech of
Gaul. These forms are said to show clear resemblances to
the Irish, and fewer resemblances to the Welsh.[2]

Almost all these inscriptions are votive or dedicatory—
commemorating, that is, the dedication of some altar,
drinking utensil, amulet, or other object, to some deity.
They are for the most part written in Roman characters,
but include two in Greek characters, and one, found in
Italy, in two languages, Gaulish and Latin—the Gaulish
being written in Etruscan characters, in many points re-
sembling those of the much earlier " Eugubian Tables,"[3]

---

[1] This is the opinion given in a private communication by the late
Dr. Rowland Williams, who is known to have bestowed much attention
upon this question.

[2] For a full account of these interesting memorials, see Pictet's *Essai
sur quelques Inscriptions en Langue Gauloise*, 1859 ; Roget de Belloquet's
Ethnogénie Gauloise, 1858; also a paper by Mr. D. W. Nash, F.S.A., in
the *Transactions of the Royal Society of Literature*, vol. viii., 1865.

[3] See Sir W. Betham's *Etruria Celtica*, p. 88, &c.

and in less degree prefiguring the much later so-called "Bardic Aphabet" of Wales.[1]

Although written in the Roman character, the inscriptions are insufficient to prove that the Gaulish tribes had not an alphabet of their own prior to their subjugation by Rome. That the Druids knew the art of writing when Cæsar came in contact with them is testified by himself, but he also states that they wrote in Greek characters, which they may have found more useful than their own.

Nor can we say that these inscriptions supply clear indications as to the localities respectively occupied by the Cymric and Gaelic tribes. They are nearly all found in the regions termed by the Classic writers *Gallia Celtica*—the part of Gaul south of the rivers Seine (*Sequana*) and Marne (*Matrona*), and said by Cæsar to be inhabited by Celtic Gauls, while the country north of those rivers was peopled by the "Belgæ." If M. Amedée Thierry's opinion (developed in his *Histoire des Gaulois*) be correct, namely, that the Celts of *Gallia Celtica* were originally of the Gaelic or Irish type, afterwards intermixed with an intrusive Cymric element, while the "Belgæ" of *Gallia Belgica* (of whom Cæsar was informed that they were mostly of German origin) were of the pure *Cymric* type, the conjecture that the Celtic words found in the inscriptions resemble Gadhelic or Irish more nearly than Cymric will acquire increased plausibility.

But when we remember that no less a man than Zeuss, in spite of these Gaulish inscriptions, has held that the language of Gaul was of one single type—the Cymric, and also that Leo, an almost equally able Celtic *savan*, held that the language of *Gallia Belgica* was Gadhelic, and that of Gallia Celtica, Cymric—the direct contradictory of Thierry's theory,

---

[1] For an account, more amusing than reliable, of this Alphabet, see *Coelbren y Beirdd*, pp. 6, 7, 15, 20—25 ; *Iolo MSS.* pp. 424, 617—623.

and nearly as much at variance with that of Zeuss, it is seen how much has yet to be discovered before we can speak with determinate confidence on the subject.

It must be confessed that the materials supplied by the Gaulish inscriptions are very scanty, and that the interpretations as yet given them are imperfect, and by no means adequate as data for conclusions. They may safely be taken as handing down remains of a tongue clearly Celtic, but showing inflexions which it would be hazardous to say are identical with any now found in Irish, or dissimilar to any at one time found in Cymric.[1]

3. The *Celts* of Britain and of Gaul generally. In Britain and in Gaul the Celtic race was broken up into a great variety of tribe distinctions. In Gaul they are said to have constituted sixty-four states or bodies politic (civitates[2]); and Cæsar mentions four "kings" among the

---

[1] One word, supposed to be Celtic, is very prominent in these inscriptions, and is understood to be the verb of the sentence in each case, expressing the act of dedication. This word is IEVRV, and has given rise to much discussion and conjecture, since in none of the modern Celtic dialects is there found a term corresponding with it in form and meaning. It is just possible that this is an archaic Celtic word cognate with the Greek ἱερεύς, priest, and ἱερεύω, to dedicate; or, since the Greek alphabet was known to the Druids, and the Greek language itself may have been known, this word, and others (including many of the vocables common to Welsh and classic Greek) may have been borrowed by them from the learned tongue, as many Latin words, as proved by these inscriptions, were borrowed.

Upon the whole it seems highly probable—and these Gaulish inscriptions add to the weight of probability—that the *Galli* of Cæsar were in the same line of Celtic descent with the Irish, and that the name is preserved to this day in Gadhel and Gael, and commemorated also in the Triad *Galedin*, *Celyddon*, and *Gwyddyl*, as well as in *Caledon*ia, Γαλαται, Κελται, and Celtæ. It is also nearly certain that these Galli or Gaels were the first to colonize Britain, and probable that they were the first to colonize Gaul, and that in both cases they were closely followed by a people of the same original stock and using a similar language, called Cymry, Cimbri, and in earlier times Κιμμεριοι, Cimmerii.

[2] Tacitus, *Annales*, iii. 44.

Britons of Kent alone in league with Cassibelaunus against the Romans.[1]

Whatever length of time may have elapsed since the British Celts had left the parent stem, it is clear that intercourse and recognition of kinship had continued. Cæsar's reason for invading Britain—that "in all his wars with the Gauls" the Britons had rendered them assistance, is proof of this. Their communications with each other were frequent and rapid. Cæsar no sooner purposes to invade, than his purpose is known to the islanders through "merchants" passing to and fro.[2] The warmest national sympathy was exhibited when danger threatened, although probably—as the manner of the race has always been—they allowed no delay in fighting each other, when no foreign foe threw down the gauntlet.

The relationship of the islanders to the tribes of the Continent is clearly stated by Cæsar, although his words, "pars interior ab iis incolitur, quos natos in insula ipsa memoria proditum dicunt," seem to intimate an interior population in Britain of singular antiquity and origin. In the names which all these people continue to give each other we recognize the accents of ancient consanguinity. The French, descendants in the main of the ancient Galli, call the Welsh Gallois; the Welsh call the Irish Gwyddyl; the Highlanders call both themselves and the Irish Gaël—distinguishing themselves as "Gael Albinnich" from the Irish "Gael Erinnich."

As to *language*, Tacitus has left a most significant statement: their speech was nearly alike—"Eorum sermo haud multum diversus."[3] As to *religion*, the same Druidic

---

[1] *De Bell. Gall.*, v. 18.

[2] *De Bell. Gall.* iv. 18. And yet the Emperor Napoleon thinks " the Britons had no shipping in the time of Cæsar."—*Hist. of Julius Cæsar*, vol. ii. p. 184.

[3] *Vita Agric.* xi.

cultus prevailed in Gaul and Britain, only the latter seems
to have been considered its chief seat. The same kind
of houses were built. The social and political institutions
of both had much in common; in their manners and
customs, modes of dress and life, as well as in personal
appearance and temperament, they manifested all the
characteristics of one and the same people.

As to the inhabitants of that part of Gaul, called in
earlier times Armorica, and now Brittany, or *Bretagne*,
evidence, both of history and of language, is superabundant
to prove their close relationship with the Cymric Celts of
Britain. The language of both people, in spite of a separation of more than a thousand years, and the natural
changes in inflection, through loss or addition of words,
through the influence of Latin and French on the Armorican, of Latin, English, and Norman-French on the Welsh,
are still so nearly alike as to merit no stronger separating
name than that of "dialects" of the same speech. History
relates the conquest of Armorica by the Britons, and the
settlement at different times of vast hosts of them, now by
force, now by permission, in that land, mixing anew the
blood of ancient kindred, and swelling into a more copious
body the vocables of long-separated branches of the one
ancient speech. Hence the correctness of the statement
made by M. Emile Souvestre: "Le bas Breton actuel
n'est donc pas un reste de Gaulois, mais de langue
Britannique."[1] It is beyond doubt that, while the language of ancient Amorica, along with that of Gaul generally,
not omitting Belgica, belonged to the generic Celtic, that
same language, through more modern vicissitudes, may
now be termed Birtannic-Celtic, rather than Gallic-Celtic.

4. The Celts of Ireland and Caledonia. In the absence
of historic record, we are justified in presuming, on grounds

[1] *Les Derniers Bretons*, i. 144.

of antecedent probability, that Ireland would receive its
first inhabitants from Wales or Scotland. Wonderful
explorers were those ancient Celts! Probably they soon
pushed their way through thicket and swamp to the Highlands of Scotland, and finding there an end to their
territory, they then from the highest eminences looked out
westward, and descried the misty coast of the Green Isle.
The early separation of these pioneers of the Gallic race
through their crossing to Ireland, whether from Scotland
or Wales, is quite sufficient to account for the marked
difference now existing between the Gaelic or Irish language
and the Welsh.

The first tribes to arrive in Britain would probably be
the first settlers in Scotland and Ireland. Pressed towards
the interior by subsequent arrivals, nomadic hordes but
slightly attached to any particular spot, they would readily
move forward to new pasturages, rather than long contend
for the old. The Gaelic or Gadhelic people, therefore, may
be presumed to have had the advantage of priority of
occupation. But the ground, of course, is one of presumption—not one of historic statement, much less of induction
from a large array of facts.

The Gaelic language undoubtedly differs very widely
from the *Cymraeg*. So does the Irish. These two, the Irish
and Gaelic, are so nearly alike, that for the general purposes of philology, they may be considered as one, and in
this light we treat them, here and in the chapter on philology. Adelung, and with him Schloezer, followed our great
Cambrian philologist and antiquarian, Edward Lhwyd, in
directing special attention to the divergence of these two
dialects of the Celtic language from the Welsh. Modern
philology has pursued the inquiry to further results, and
has established beyond question not only the fact that
Welsh, Gaelic, Irish, Cornish, Armoric, and Manx are

cognate languages, or rather *dialects* of the same mother language, but also, that these six are to be divided into two groups of three each, according to their nearness of approximation to each other :—

1. Gaelic Branch
- Erse, in Ireland.
- Gaelic, in the Highlands of Scotland.
- Manx, in the Isle of Man.

2. Cymric Branch
- Welsh, in Wales.
- Armorican, in Brittany.
- Cornish, extinct.[1]

An unwritten language, having no guarantee for the permanence of its forms, but the organs of hearing and speech, commences the process of becoming two languages the moment those who speak it separate into two communities occupying different territories. The number of communities formed determines the number of new languages, or dialects, to be developed. All things being equal, divergence will increase according to time given. These positions are allowed to be indisputable. If, therefore, the Irish, Gaelic, and Manx have diverged from the Welsh more than the Armorican and Cornish have done, this is proof only of longer separation. The insular position of the Gaels of Ireland would almost completely cut them off from their brethren in Britain, and thus facilitate the growth of dissimilarity in the cognate languages, or dialects. The Armoricans, though in like manner separated by the sea, are proved by history and tradition to have, through many hundred years, maintained intercourse with their British kindred, and to have at times received large accessions of population from them. The effect of territorial separation would by this means be greatly

[1] The *Lexicon Cornu-Brittanicum*, by the Rev. R. Williams, M.A., of Rhydycroesau, is the best contribution yet made to Cornish philology, and demonstrates the propriety of this mode of grouping the Celtic tongues.

neutralised, and the substance and forms of the two dialects be kept more nearly alike. As to the Cornish, this was lopped off from the Cymric stock in comparatively recent times, and its divergence therefore is not great. If we take Wales itself as an example, we shall find that the provincial estrangement, through the wars of the Middle-ages between the North and the South, caused a divergence so great in the language of the two sections, that a man of Anglesey is scarcely understood in Glamorgan. The same thing is seen if we compare the speech of Yorkshire with that of Kent.

The greater similarity of modern Irish to modern Gaelic than of either to modern Welsh [1] may be seen at a glance by comparing one sentence of the Lord's prayer in each :

English : Give us this day our daily bread.
{ *Irish*   : Ar narán laéathamhail tabhair dhuinn a riu.
{ *Gaelic* : Tabhair dhuin an diugh ar n'aran laitheil.
Welsh : Dyro i ni heddyw ein bara beunyddiol.

The Armoric bears decided similarity to the Welsh.

Armoric: Ro deomp bep deiz hor bara pemdeziec.
Welsh : Rho i ni bob dydd ein bara beunyddiol.

Again :—

Armoric : Merc'hed Jerusalem, na oucilit ked warnoun me, *mes* goueilit warnoc'h hoc'h-unan, &c.
Welsh : Merched Jerusalem, na wylwch o'm plegid I, ond wylwch o'ch plegid eich hunain, &c.

One sentence to show how much the Armoric has been corrupted by French.

---

[1] But how much more similar to each other were all these Celtic dialects a thousand or fifteen hundred years ago it is needless to remark. The old Cornish vocabulary of the thirteenth century, in the British Museum (*Cotton. Bibl. Vespas.* A. 14) will show the student who is familiar with the Welsh of the twelfth century how much nearer these two languages were then to each other, than the *Cornish Remains of the Fifteenth Century*, recently published under the able editorship of Mr. Norris, are to the Welsh of the present time.

Armoric: *Mes* araog an holl draouze hei a lakaio o daouarn warnoc'h hag o *persecuto*, o *livra* ac'hanoch d'ar sinagogou, hag o lakaad ac'hanoc'h er *prizoniou*, hag e veot caset dirag *rouaned* ha *gouarnerien*, *&c.*

The Cornish language comes nearer to the Welsh than does the Armoric. Words italicised are corruptions.[1]

Cornish.	*Welsh.*
Pan welas na ylly *delyffrè*.	Pan welodd na allai draddodi.
Nyns us pons war dhour Cedron.	Nid oes pont ar ddwr Cedron.
Yma gena un bê da, gorra hag eys kemyskys.	Y mae genyf un baich da, gwair ac yd cymysg.
Mesk ow pobel ny vynnaf na fella agas godhaf.	Ymysg fy mhobl ni fynaf yn bellach eich goddef.
Dour ha lêr, ha tan, ha gwyns, haul ha lour, ha *steyr* kyffris, . . . anken y a wodhevys.	Dwr a llawr (daear), a thân, a gwynt, haul a lloer, a ser yn gyfryw, ing a oddefasant.
Godheveuch omma lavur, ha gollyouch genef.	Goddefwch yma lafur, a gwyliwch genyf.
Pan y'th welaf, bôs hep hyreth my ny allaf.	Pan y'th welaf, bod heb hiraeth mi ni allaf.
Yn levyr yma scrifys, dre cledhe nep a vewo, ef a vyru yn sur dredho.	Yn y llyfr y mae yn 'scrifenedig, y neb a fo fyw drwy y cleddyf, ef yn siwr a fydd farw drwyddo.
Mi a credy yn Dew an Tas Olgallusek, Gwrêar an nef ha'n 'oar.	Mi a gredaf yn Nuw Dâd Hollalluog, Creawdwr nef a daear.
Ny a whyth yn dhy *vody sperys*, may hylly bewé.	Ni a chwythwn yn dy gorph ysbryd, mal y gelli fyw.
Govyn orto mar a'm bydh *oyl* a *vercy* yn dywedh.	Gofyn wrtho (iddo) pa un i mi fydd olew trugaredd yn y diwedd.

From the foregoing examples it is evident, that all these six divisions of Celts are nearly related to each other, and that nearest to the Cymry come, first the Cornish, and next the Armoricans. The Gaels, or Gaedhils of Ireland, have departed further from the Cymric type, in language, if not also in blood.

The *Picts* and *Scots* have usually been associated with

---

[1] Confer Williams's *Lexicon Cornu-Britann.* On the analogy of the different Celtic tongues, see at length Zeuss's *Gramm. Celtica*, 2nd Ed., *passim*; on the conjugation of the verb, especially, pp. 425—606.

E

Caledonia. These names are recent in origin, being used
only by later Roman writers.[1] *Bede* (sixth cent.) calls
Caledonia " provincia Pictorum ; " and it would seem that
in his time the name Picts, or Pehts, had nearly superseded
the older term Caledonii—derived from the Cymric *Celyddon*,
and this related to the generic *Galatæ*, *Celtæ*, *Galli*.

That the Picts were a branch of the *Cymry*, and the
Scots immigrants from Ireland,[2] where the name *Scoti*
originated, is to be considered as certain. The name
" Picts " is of doubtful origin ;[3] but that the people who had
probably pushed their way from the Cumbrian kingdom
into the hilly regions of South Caledonia were Cymry in
language is evidenced by the local names they impressed
on that region, and also by the names of some of their later
kings found in a MS. in the Colbertine library. We find
the words *ben* and *pen* used to designate mountains and
eminences, as *Ben*-Nevis, *Ben*-Lomond ; and *Pen*-val is
said by Bede to have been the Pictish name for a place at
the " termination of the wall" of Antoninus. Now *Ban*
and *Pen* are also Cymric words of like meaning, as seen in

[1] Neither Cæsar nor Tacitus has any mention of Picts. Nor has
Ptolemy or Dion Cassius. Eumenius's Oration to Constantius Chlorus,
A.D. 296 : " Solis. . . . Pictis modo et Hibernis adsueti hostibus," first
brings forward their name in British history. They are alluded to
repeatedly by Amm. Marcellinus. All details respecting the " Pictish
question " are contained in Pinkerton, Chalmers, Ritson, Prichard,
Grant, and Betham.

[2] Bede, *Eccles. Hist. b. 1. c. 1.*

[3] As the valley of the Loire (*Liger*) has strong claims as the former
home of the *Lloegrians*, and probably also of the Brython, the name
Picts leads us to favour the idea that these people last came from a part
of the same region (now Poitou), where a tribe called *Pictones* are said
to have dwelt. The only objection to this view is the statement of the
Triad—that the Picts (Gwyddyl Fichti) came to Alban by the sea of
Llychlyn (North Sea) ; but they might well have come to Britain by that
Sea, and yet have previously dwelt in South-Western France, as well as
have Scandinavia for their more ancient seat.

*Bang*or, *Ban*au (pl.), as B. Brycheiniog (the Brecknockshire Beacons), *Pen*cader, *Pen*maenmawr. The Pictish name *Pen-val* is pure Cymric in both its parts; *pen*, top, head, extremity, and *gwal* (constr. state, *wal*) giving the signification "wall's-head," or termination—the same as that of the Gaelic rendering of Pen-val, *Cenail*, (*Cean*, head, and *fhail*, of the wall) the modern Kinneil.

Bryneich, the orignal of the Latin Bernicia, is probably a Pictish name. The Welsh etymology of the word is from *bryn*, a hill. In Fife are the *Ochil* Hills (Welsh, *uchel*, high). *Cairn*gorm has many correspondences in Wales, as *Carn*edd Llywelyn, *Carn*edd Dafydd, *Carn*edd y Filiast, Tref*garn*, &c.

The register of Pictish kings from the fifth century downwards contained in the Colbertine MS. gives several names which are Cymric : TARAN (Welsh, *taran*, thunder); UVAN —a slight modification of the Welsh *Icvan, Ivan* or *Owen*; TALORG—Welsh, *tal*, high, as *talcen*,[1] high part of the head, "forehead"; *Tal*iesin; local names, *Tal*garth, *Tal*og; WRGWST — Welsh, *Gwrgwst*; DRUST — Welsh, *Trwst*; DROSTAN—Welsh, *Trwstan*, &c.[2]

The word *Aber*, applied in Wales to a confluence of waters, whether of inland streams or of rivers and the sea, was used in Caledonia in a similar way. Many places once called *abers* in Scotland have been changed into Gaelic *Invers* (*inbhir*). No *aber* exists in Ireland. And it may be remarked that the word *aber* is used in modern Cymric not only as an historic local name but also as a word for haven, creek of the sea, &c., as *aber Milford*. The Triads say : " In Britain are three chief rivers, Thames, Severn and Humber,

---

[1] The *cen* in this word is the Ir. and Gael. *cean*, head. Lewis Glyn Cothi (circà 1450) uses *tàl* for "head": "A dawn Duw'n flodau'n ei dàl." *Works*, p. 110. Now obsolete.

[2] See Garnett's *Essays*, p. 196, et seq.

and one hundred and forty three chief *abers*." Many of the
rivers in Scotland and Wales almost exactly agree in name:
The Tweed, Towy; Tay, Tâv; Dee, Dee; Clyde, Clwyd;
Nith, Nêdd; Avon, Avon; Ayr, Aeron; Esk, Wysg;
Teviot, Teivi, &c.

The ancient topographical names of Caledonia, the
country of the Picts, even of its northern parts, more
nearly correspond with those of Wales than do those of
Ireland, the early home of the Scots. Greater nearness of
kinship is thus indicated. At the same time, the evidence
of language, local names, traditions, history, combine to
prove that all these countries were inhabited by people
descending from the same great Celtic family, which may
all be classed together as Ancient Britons.

Now in conjecturing the causes of divergence of these
Celtic languages no difficulty need be encountered. The
process of change is obvious. *Time* and *territorial separation*, as already shown, are elements amongst these causes.
Another and main source of dissimilarity is the condition
under which all unwritten language is propagated.
Writing, and especially printing, powerfully aid in fixing
and perpetuating the standard of a language. But in the
absence of all such mechanical means, and when the eye
had no agency in fixing the form of words and phrases, but
all was transmitted phonetically, departure from the
standard, if "standard" could be said to exist, would be
facile and rapid. Variation imperceptibly introduced would
form a "dialect." A dialect would soon grow into what
would be termed a "language." Let an educated Englishman from Suffolk or Essex enter any village smithy near
"Ratchdaw" (Rochdale) or "Owdum" (Oldham), and he
will hear a language he would by no amount of persuasion
believe to be English. Let him employ an exact phonetic
shorthand writer, and have the sounds which are uttered in

his hearing faithfully represented on paper, and he will still
be nearly as sceptical. "Fattle be i'th the foyar" has the
looks of an outlandish tongue, but divested of contrac-
tions and Lancashire articulation, assumes the homely garb
of "the fat will be in the fire." So of "Si geet oop bi
shrike o dee, on seet eawt, on went ogreath tilly welly
coomb within a moile oth teawn, when o tit wur stonning
ot on ealheawse dur":—So I got up by break of day, and
set out, and went right on until I well nigh came within a
mile of the town, when a mare was standing at an alehouse
door. "Im wur off neaw in eer eh wur":—I am worse off
now than ever I was.[1]

Let only the peasantry of such a district as this emigrate
into a distant region, after the manner of the nomades of
ancient times, and soon their language will be as different
from that of Kent as Breton is now from Cymric, or Erse
from either of these.

5. The Lloegrians and Brython. The Lloegrians, from
whom is derived the modern Welsh name for England—
(*Lloegr*), a branch of the "Nation of the Cymry," came
from South-Western France, the valley and region of the
river *Liger*, modern Loire, and settled in the south and
east of Britain. The Brython probably came from the
same part of France, held the same relation to the "Nation
of the Cymry," and settled in the North of England. These,
in all probability, have their name still preserved in the
common designation "Bretons." But more of the
Lloegrians and Brython in the next sub-section, where we
give the evidence of the Welsh *Triads*.[2]

---

[1] See, *Works of Tim Bobbin.* Ed. 1862. Pp. 41. 83.

[2] The Welsh *Triads*, or *Trioedd Ynys Prydain*. are given in full in the
Myvyrian Archaiology of Wales. Vols. ii and iii.

(d.) The Welsh Triads on the early Settlers in Britain, and the identity of their origin.

Whatever value may attach to the *Triads* as historic records, they are at least in many respects documents of great interest, and may be received even by the most hypercritical Wolfian as corroboratory of other evidence. They are echoes and exponents to us of what the long lost records of Welsh history contained, and of the voice of ancient tradition.

The *Triads* are clear and positive in according the first colonization of Britain to the Cymry (Cimbri). *Triad* First says :—" Three names have been given to the Isle of Britain from the beginning. Before it was inhabited it was called Clâs Merddin, and afterwards Fêl Ynys. When it was put under government by Prydain, son of Aedd the Great, it was called Inis Prydain (the Isle of Prydain), and there was no tribute paid to any but to the race of the Cymry, because they first possessed it, and before them no men dwelt in it, nor anything else except bears, wolves, beavers, and the oxen with the high prominence. "

The fourth *Triad* contains the following :—" The three national pillars of the Isle of Britain :—First, Hu Gadarn (Hu the Mighty) who originally conducted the nation of the Cymry into the Isle of Britain. They came from the summer country which is called Deffrobani [where Constantinople now stands], and it was over the hazy sea [the German Ocean] that they came to the Isle of Britain and to Llydaw [Armorica, Bretagne] where they continued, &c."

The fifth *Triad* says : " The three honourable (*addwyn*) tribes of the isle of Britain : The first was the nation of the Cymry that came with Hu the Mighty into the isle of Britain, &c. The second was the tribe of the *Llocgrwys*, [Loegrians, *Ligurians ?*] that came from the land of Gwasgwyn [Gascony ?] *being descended from the chief nation of the Cymry.* The third were the *Brython*, who came from the land of Armorica, *having their descent from the primitive stock of the Cymry;* and they are called three tribes of peace, because they came by consent of each other in peace and quietness." [1]

Now these Three *Triads* are categorical on the following heads :—

1. That the first inhabitants of Britain were the Cymry.

2. That the region whence they came was the "summer country," and that their path was across the German Ocean.

3. That the same people settled also in Armorica.

4. That besides and after the Cymry, two other tribes, the Lloegrwys from Gwasgwyn, and the Brython from Armorica, came over.

No attempt at chronology is here made, but an order of succession is plainly indicated. All the tribes are of one blood. The later comers settle, as if for consolidation, with the consent and friendship of the first possessors—the Cymry. Note also that the regions whence they came are those frequently mentioned by Roman historians as parts inhabited by the Celtæ. In all this there is no tone of hypothesis, no hesitation in statement, no clashing with the utterances of authentic history. Avoiding, therefore, the scepticism which is as hostile to the investigation of historic truth as the weakest credulity, we receive the *Triad* account as substantially worthy of reliance.

Next comes a *Triad* which puts a little change upon the scene. The Cymry and their kinsmen the Lloegrwys and Brython were not to have it all their own way in the "isle of honey." Still, as yet, there are no hostile arrivals, but certain "refuge seeking" people from the far north, and from across the water. "The three refuge-seeking tribes

[1] *Myv. Arch. of Wales.* ii. 57.

who came in peace, by consent of the nation of the Cymry, without weapon or attack : The first was the people of Celyddon in the north ; the second was the Gwyddelian tribe who dwell in Alban [the Highlands of Scotland] ; the third were the men of Galedin [Holland ?], who came in naked vessels to the Isle of Wight when their country was inundated, and where they had land assigned them by the nation of the Cymry ; they had no right of possession in the isle of Britain beyond the land and protection accorded to them under limits, and it was stipulated that the rights of the primitive Cymry should not be theirs until the end of the ninth generation." [1]

No intimation is given that these arrivals were of another race. They came as brethren seeking shelter when in distress, and were allowed, upon definite conditions, to settle down as part of the family of states. Who can doubt, therefore, that the regions of Caledonia (Celyddon), and Alban (the Highlands), were in these early times peopled by tribes the consanguinity of which with the Cymry was well known ? And who can fail to perceive that the names "Celyddon" and "Galedin" are cognate with Galatæ, Celtæ, and Galli ? As yet, then, we see that, according to the *Triads*, Britain, north and south, was inhabited by one single race.

But now times of trial are coming. The seventh *Triad* relates that the ancestral estate is invaded by strangers. "The three invading tribes that came unto the isle of Britain, and never departed therefrom : [2] the first were the Coraniaid, who came from the country of Pwyl [Poland ? more probably some region of northern Germany] ; the second, the Gwyddyl Ffichti [Gaelic Picts], who came to

---

[1] *Myv. Arch. of Wales.* ii. 57.

[2] In allusion to the Romans, &c., who, when the *Triad* was written, had taken their departure.

Alban by the sea of Llychlyn ; [1] third, the Saeson (Saxons). The Coranians are situated about the river Humber, and the shores of the German Ocean ; and the Gwyddyl Ffichti are in Alban, on the shore of the sea of Denmark. The Coranians and the Saxons united, brought the Lloegrians into confederacy with them by violence and oppression, and afterwards took the crown of monarchy from the nation of the Cymry. Of the Lloegrians who did not become Saxons there only remain those who inhabit Cornwall and the Commot of Carnoban in Deira and Bernicia."[2]

The following remarks we subjoin :

1. The events shadowed forth in these later *Triads* occurred after the departure of the Romans, and in Saxon times.

2. Some, even of these "invading" tribes, are kinsmen to the Cymry. The "Gwyddyls"[3] are the people mentioned in a preceding *Triad*, as one of the peaceful refuge-seeking tribes, and come from the same region of "Alban." This reflection upon their character as intruders, therefore, must have reference to their first appearance from "the sea of Llychlyn," or to a change in their disposition and conduct in Saxon times, and after a long residence in the country.

3. The "Coranians" who came from the country of Pwyl, supposed by some, as Edward Lhwyd, to mean Poland, are a people unknown in history. From the position of their settlement about the Humber, it is probable that their preceding home was North Germany or Denmark. The

---

[1] *Llychlyn* may be translated "the lake of pools," and would, therefore, be applicable to the inland waters of Denmark, opposite to which, in Alban, the *Triad* immediately afterwards locates them.

[2] *Myv. Arch. of Wales.* ii. p. 58.

[3] *Gwyddel* is probably the Cymric depravation of the name Gadhel = Celt, borne by the more Westerly tribes.

Triad contains no intimation that the Coranians were of
an alien race. They took possession by force, and afterwards conspired with the Saxons; and this rendered them
obnoxious. Had they been of an alien race, this would
probably, under the circumstances, have been mentioned
to their further discredit.

4. The "Lloegrians," who also conspired with the Saxons,
are said in the seventh *Triad* to be from Gwasgwyn, and
were, therefore, if this region is in the south-west of France,
of remoter connection, although of the same stock, with the
nation of the Cymry, and hence more liable to be won over
into confederacy with the "invaders." But if the *Triad*
is correct in making the people of Cornwall a remnant of
them, they must have been nearly related to the Cymry, as
the Cornish language sufficiently implies.

The "Saxons" are the only intruders, hitherto enumerated, certainly known to have been of Teutonic race
and to have made good their stay in Britain. All others
are either expressly claimed by the *Triads* as relations to
the "nation of the Cymry," or are presumably such.
Lloegrians, Brython, the people of Celyddon, the *Gwyddelian*
tribe of Alban, the men of *Galedin,* are all relations and
friends. The *Coranians,* though an invading tribe, are not
said to be of alien race. The *Gwyddyl Ffichti,* another
invading tribe, are certainly kinsmen. Saxons alone, therefore, known by positive declarations of history to be
strangers in blood, are in this *Triad* declared to be alien
invaders of the country.

We have accomplished this portion of our task. The
substantial unity of race of the early inhabitants of Britain
has been shown. These multifarious tribes, all of one
kindred, though arrived from different countries, across
different seas, at different periods of time, we embrace
under the one general designation ANCIENT BRITONS.

Having done this much, we next proceed to give an estimate of their general condition, social and intellectual, with the view of establishing *à priori* the presumption, that such a people would not be bodily dislodged, much less utterly extirpated, but would continue on the soil, and enter into the new nationality established by their conquerors.

SECTION II.

An estimate of the Social Condition and Civilization of the Britons at the time of the Roman Conquest.

The early Greek and Roman historians — the only sources we are disposed here to rely upon—give but few and fragmentary accounts of the Ancient Britons ; and of these accounts we propose noticing only such as tend to show that the aborigines were by no means the low type of barbarians which ill-informed writers have too commonly represented them to be. They were as the poet, speaking from a Roman point of view, describes them :

" Penitus toto divisos orbe Britannos ;" [1]

but their life had still a connection with the greater life which pulsated on the continent. They were of the race which had captured Ancient Rome, had been led by Brennus, had foiled Mallius and Caepio. They had divers means of intercourse with distant peoples, and had received into their bosom and retained many of the attributes of the old Eastern civilization.

(1.) *Early Notices.*

What is said by Herodotus and Aristotle is of no weight. Festus Avienus, a writer of the fourth century, in a geo- — graphical poem, furnishes a very interesting piece of

---

[1] Virgil *Eclog.* I.

information, of the correctness of which we have no reason
to doubt. Avienus, be it observed, wrote in the fourth
century; but his statements on the matter in hand relate
to a time 700 years earlier. He says that in the fourth
century before Christ, Himilco, the Carthaginian, penetrated
beyond the Pillars of Hercules, and surveyed the coast of
Britain. Pliny, referring to the same voyage, assigns it to
the time when Hanno explored the Western Coast of Africa,
and when Carthage was at the height of its glory—
"Carthaginis potentia florente."

Now according to Himilco, what, at that early time, was
the character of the Britons? They were not the contemptible barbarians, the painted savages, depicted by
some of our "historians." They were "a numerous and
powerful race, endowed with spirit, very dexterous, all busy
with the cares of trade."[1]

Midway between Himilco and the Christian era, Polybius
simply indicates the importance of Britain by remarking,
that "many had already treated of the Britannic isles and
the working of tin."[2] Diodorus Siculus, a contemporary
of Cæsar, says that the Britons in their wars, "used
chariots, as the ancient Greek heroes are reported to have
done in the Trojan war; were simple in their manners, and
far removed from the cunning and wickedness of men of
the present day . . . that the island was thickly inhabited
—εἶναι δὲ καὶ πολυάνθρωπον τὴν νῆσον—that those of Cornwall
were particularly fond of strangers and civilized in their
manners—φιλόξενοι τε διαφερόντως εἰσὶ καὶ διὰ τὴν των ξένων εμπόρων
ἐπιμιξίαν ἐξημερωμένοι τας ἀγωγας—&c.[3]

---

[1] *Ora Maritima.* Ed. 1791.
        ". . . . . Multa vis hic gentis est,
        Superbus animus, efficax sollertia,
        Negotiandi cura jugis omnibus."
                                Vv. 98—100.
[2] Polyb. *Hist.* iii. 57.   [3] *Diod. Sic.* v. 21, 22.

Strabo, the geographer, describes the inhabitants in a still more picturesque way: They were "clad in black cloaks (μελάγχλαινοι), with tunics (χιτῶνας) which reached to the feet, and girt about the breasts (ἐζωσμενοι); walking with staves in their hands (μετα ράβδων περιπατοῦντες), and bearded like goats; subsisting by their cattle, and leading for the most part a wandering (νομαδικῶς) life."[1] Strabo was no poet, but rather a matter-of-fact geographer, and yet this description gives the picture of a people far advanced in culture, and enjoying almost ideal happiness.

(2). *Cæsar and Tacitus.*

Cæsar, in his account of Britain, speaks with the ill-concealed bias of a not very successful invader, and betrays on occasions very imperfect knowledge of his subject. He never saw far into the interior, for the very reason that the inhabitants were not the helpless barbarians he at times describes them, and of the Cymry especially he had no knowledge whatever. Be it observed that what is implied in some of Cæsar's statements, and clearly expressed in others, takes off completely the edge of his most damaging descriptions. For example: Britain, he tells us, was well peopled, full of houses built after the manner of the Gauls; brass and gold money was used, and iron rings of a certain weight (in barter).[2] The men of Kent were the most civilized, differing but little from the Gauls. The greater part of those in the interior tilled not their land, but lived on flesh and milk, and were clad in skins—precisely the mode

---

[1] *Geogr.* lib. iii. 5. It is generally allowed that Strabo by his καττιτέριδες, and Herodotus by his κασσιτέριδες, referred to the British Isles.

[2] *De Bell. Gall.* v. 10. On the "ring money" of the Celts, Comp.— Sir W. Betham's paper read before the Royal Irish Acad., Dublin, 1836. On the text of Cæsar, respecting the coin of the Britons, see further under (d) in this Section.

of life, by the way, followed by the " more civilized " Gauls.
Then comes the libel about a community of wives, which
hostile critics have made ready use of, but which no fair
and competent historian of our day for a moment believes.[1]
The position of woman and the respect paid to wedlock
generally among the Ancient Britons sufficiently neutralize
this unsupported assertion of Cæsar. Individual cases
might occur, but the *custom* could not prevail.

But in addition to being workers in tin, coiners of money,
smelters of iron, they were, even according to Cæsar himself, possessed of great skill and courage in battle, were
competent to manœuvre with cavalry, and constructed a
species of chariot-machines which did terrible execution
among the Roman legions. " It evidently appeared," he
somewhat unguardedly adds, " that our heavy-armed
legions were no match for such an enemy."[2]

Tacitus seems to have had his doubts whether the first
inhabitants of Britain had been " born of the soil" —*indigenæ*—or were adventitious settlers.[3] This he considers
a question lost in the mist of antiquity— an indirect testimony of value, it may be remarked, to the remote origin of
the Britons, and their long occupancy, even then, of the
island. He considers them generally similar to the Gauls
—which they might well be since they were a kindred
people ; but he ascribes to them the superiority in energy
and courage—qualities which the Gauls, after once possessing, had, through the loss of liberty, lost.[4] So independent,

---

[1] *De Bell. Gall.* v. 14. " Uxores habent deni duodenique inter se
communes, et maxime fratres cum fratribus, parentesque cum liberis ;
sed, si qui sunt ex his nati, eorum habentur liberi, quo primum virgo
quæque deducta est."

[2] *Ibid.* v, 16.   [3] *Vita. Agric.* xi.

[4] It is difficult to know on what ground, in the face of Tacitus's
testimony, Makintosh could describe the Britons as generally inferior
to the Gauls. *Hist. of Engl.* i. 14.

fierce and obstinate were the Britons, that had there only
existed among them union and concert, they might have
baffled the Roman power to the last ; but wanting mutual
confidence and coherence, when attacked by the foe, they
fought separately, and were thus subdued.[1]

Tacitus confesses that though in the time of Agricola (circ.
A.D. 80) the Britons were conquered, they were not even then
disheartened ; they were reduced to obedience but not to
bondage. He adds that even Julius Cæsar, the first of the
Romans who had set foot in Britain at the head of an
army, could only be said by a successful battle to have
made himself master of the sea-shore. Having failed to
conquer the island, he only, as a discoverer, made it known
to others who came after him. Rome could not boast of a
conquest.[2] How much is here implied !

(3.) *Organisation and Government.*

It has been pronounced useless to inquire what form of
government prevailed among a people so low in culture.
This is taking for granted the thing to be proved. They
were low enough in culture, doubtless, when judged by the
standard of to-day ; but it has not been proved that they
were so low in culture that organization, government,
salutary customs, and a strict moral code, did not exist
among them.

We have the authority of Cæsar, amongst others, for
saying that the Britons' form of Government was monar-
chical. They had as many as four kings in Kent alone.[3]
The power of the king was tempered by an element of
popular right exercised in public assembly, and by the
influence of the Druidic priesthood. This indicates

---

[1] *Vit. Agric.* xii.   [2] *Ibid.* xiii.
[3] *De Bell. Gall.* v. 22.

organization, subordination of states, checks and counter-checks—the results of experience and wisdom. That the states were small is no argument against the fact of government. The kings of the Britons were not tyrants, military adventurers, hap-hazard products of revolution, but, in the main, hereditary sovereigns, governing by force of public law.

The influence of the Druids in the conduct of public affairs, whatever may be thought in our day of their superstitions, argues the subjection of the popular mind to the governance of religious ideas ; and if we are to judge of the quality of the Druidic teaching from the ethical maxims of the *Triads*, the guidance received from this quarter could scarcely be otherwise than salutary.

(4.) *The Arts of Civilized Life.*

The above remarks naturally suggest the inquiry, how far those arts and usages which we generally associate with the term *civilization*, and are considered to rescue a people from a state of barbarism, had a place among the Ancient Britons. If our expectations be moderate, as they ought to be, we shall not be disappointed. The Britons, in Cæsar's time, had some knowledge of the arts of life. They were not barbarians. Were they semi-barbarians ?

Skill in warlike tactics and in the construction of war implements is not, we admit, the best exhibition of know-ledge ; but it yet remains *skill*, and is evidence of culture of a certain sort, however ill applied—otherwise what becomes of our boastful modern civilization one of whose main and most costly developments is concerned in it ? This culture to a considerable extent the Britons had, and Cæsar was bitterly convinced of the fact.

What was better, they were industrious, devoted to "trade." A tribe, however obscure, was never yet touched with the *negotiandi cura* ascribed to the Britons, but that it entered thereby the school of civilization. Four hundred years before Christ, or thereabouts, the Britons were found by Himilco to be adepts in the matter. They were "fond of strangers"—a sign that they were either in a helplessly early state of national childhood, or advanced beyond that condition of barbarian life where strangers are deemed as enemies. In Cæsar's time, they were workers in metals; coiners of a kind of money; builders of houses like those of Gaul; lived in entrenched towns and villages, and worshipped in colossal, though rude and mysterious, temples, which time itself seems incapable of demolishing. Cæsar testifies—not surely with the object of exalting his own skill in taking it—that the capital of Cassivellaunus (Caswallon) was admirably defended—*egregie munitum*.[1] The Britons' skill in fortification is evidenced by the remains of their great works which continue to this day, *ex. gr.* the *dun* or *dinas* called the *Catterduns* in Scotland, *Chun Castle* and *Caer-bran* in Cornwall, the camp on the Malvern Hills, *Caer Caradoc* in Shropshire, *Tynwald* in the Isle of Man.[2]

But a word further on the account given by Cæsar concerning the kind of money used by the Ancient Britons. The text which reads, "brass money and iron rings," &c., is allowed to be corrupt. Mr. Hawkins, having examined and collated all the MSS. of Cæsar within his reach in England and on the Continent, states that *they all* give the reading thus : "Utuntur aut aere aut nummo aureo, aut annulis ferreis at certum pondus examinatis pro nummo." "They (the Britons) use either brass or gold coin, or iron rings, suited to a certain weight, for money." This is a

[1] *De Bell. Gall.* v. 21.
[2] Confer *Monumenta Antiqua.* vol. i. p. 27 ; Meyrick's *Origin. Inhab.*, p. 7 ; *Camden,* Gough's Ed., i. 700.

most important correction, and gives fair ground for the belief that brass and gold coins were in use among the Britons before Cæsar's arrival.

The compiler of the important work issued by the Master of the Rolls, says, with respect to this question, " The existence of a large number of coins found in various parts of the island (the types and fabric of some of which are unlike any which have been discovered in other countries, and have all the appearance of being some centuries older than Julius Cæsar's first expedition into Britain) appears greatly to support the opinion that the Britons were acquainted with and practised the art of coining previously to that event. . . If the Britons refused to take foreign money (as Solinus states) . . . and coins considerably older than Julius Cæsar's invasion are found in the island, the money so found must have been coined in the national mints of this country. . . . . The reign of Cunobelin may be considered as the time when British coins reached their highest perfection."[1] Nine of the coins of Tasciovanus, supposed to be the father of Cunobeline (Cynfelin), and fifty-three of the coins of the latter, some of them showing delicate workmanship, are figured in *Plate I*. Most of them are to be seen in the British Museum. The most important work by far which has yet appeared on the ancient British coinage is that of Mr. Evans, where the Britons' knowledge of the art of coining is clearly proved. A large number of the British coins are illustrated and described in this work, and it is shown that the Monumenta Catalogue is very incomplete.[2]

---

[1] *Monumenta Historica Britannica; or, Materials for the History of England from the Earliest Period.* Published by command of Her Majesty. London, 1848. P. cli. See also *the Coins of the Romans relating to Britain,* by J. G. Akerman, London, 1836, and Birch's *Dissert. on Coins of Cunobeline. (Numis. Soc.)*

[2] The *Coins of the Ancient Britons,* by J. Evans, F.R.S., F.S.A., &c.

That the arts of life had been considerably developed among the Ancient Britons has been very unexpectedly illustrated within recent years by the opening of barrow-tombs. Proofs of skill in the manipulation of pottery are found in drinking cups, incense dishes, cinerary urns, of graceful forms, found in these sacred receptacles. Gold ear-rings, ornaments of amber set in gold, beads of curious construction have been discovered.[1] The bossed shields, the flat circular shields with metal coatings in the Goodrich Court Collection,[2] and the celebrated golden breast-plate, embossed with beautiful figuring, discovered near Mold,[3] all testify to superior knowledge in the metallic arts.

We thus go to the tombs of the dead to read the history and know the habits and acquirements of the living. The depositions here made are those of impartial witnesses, whom no prejudice can bias, no sophistry baffle. The great fortresses in which they dwelt, many of their majestic temples, like their weapons of war and tools of handicraft, have passed into oblivion; but the repositories of their ashes and calcined bones have been proof against the decay of time, and preserved for us more of the history—the history of the internal life—of the people than of their mortal remains. We might distrust or lightly hold the glowing portraiture of the British bard, or the wondrous later legend of the romancer, and repose but qualified faith in the Greek or Roman annalist; but the characters written

---

[1] Comp. Hoare's *Ancient Wiltshire, passim*.

[2] See *Archæologia*, vol. xxiii. p. 95.

[3] This interesting relic is at the British Museum. That the Britons were highly skilled in the designing and casting of bronze spear-heads is proved by the contents of various collections of antiquities. In the small temporary Museum of the Cambrian Archæological Association at Knighton, 1873, a few British bronzes of this class, newly discovered in excavations, were exhibited, which gave evidence of remarkable taste in design and manufacture.

on the walls of the solemn mausoleum are faithful, and when read amid its deep and monitory silence, sink with conviction into the mind.

It is of interest to notice the "imports" and "exports," such as they were, of the Ancient Britons. "Painted savages"—the reader of school histories will say—"what could they know of transactions only befitting Liverpool or London?" But let us see. The plain Britons, it may be granted, had no deep knowledge of trade-lists and prices current; but neither had we ourselves five hundred years ago. At that time Liverpool consisted of a few fishermen's huts, and London itself was a small collection of straggling wooden tenements. If we are to believe Strabo, these people carried on a good trade with the Romans[1]—sending their produce to the continent, and receiving back such articles as they needed. Of course he speaks of their commerce at a period anterior to the Roman Conquest, and when, therefore, their ideas of trade and of luxury, and skill in working in metals and pottery had not been heightened by contact with this new instructor. Strabo enumerates among the goods exported from Britain, gold, iron, silver, corn, cattle, skins, fleeces, dogs; and among the imports, ivory, bridles, gold chains, cups of amber, drinking-glasses, &c.—all articles suitable to a people whose ideas were somewhat advanced beyond the brass buttons and glass beads so much in demand among savage tribes.

The personal ornaments of Britons of the better class were tasteful and costly. The Gauls are said to have been fond of dress (φιλοκοσμον)[2], and to wear gold collars around their necks and arms.[3] The Gauls were now not savages, and their ornaments were not mere flaring tinsel. Now the

---

[1] *Geog.* lib. iii. 197, 239; lib. iv. 278.   [2] *Ibid.* iv. 197.
[3] *Livy*, vii. 10.

custom observed by the "civilized Gauls" was precisely
the custom which prevailed in Britain—in the kingdom of
Cumbria, and doubtless in Wales, even down to Saxon
times.[1] Merddin Wyllt, in his poem, the *Avallenau* (circ. A.D.
580), says, "In the battle of Arderydd I wore the golden
torques ;" and Llywarch Hen, the prince bard, bewailing the
desolation of family and country (circ. A.D. 620), says :—

> " Four and twenty sons I have had,
> Wearing the golden wreath, leaders of armies."[2]

Dion Cassius informs us that five hundred years before
this time, Boadicea wore such a collar of gold. The poet
Aneurin in his *Gododin*, describes the march of three
hundred and sixty-three warriors thus decorated into
the battle of Cattraeth.

Golden torques were given at a later time as prizes of
skill and valour; and the phrase, *dwyn y dorch*, "to win the
torque," is to this day to be heard in Wales for winning
any prize, although the rings themselves have long ago
disappeared, and the historic allusion is not comprehended.

(5.) *Intellectual Culture.*

A still better proof of "civilization" is furnished by intellectual development and culture. Trade in degree argues
culture ; certain luxuries and refinements of life argue the
same; but there are positive exhibitions of it which are still
more conclusive. The Druidical system was one of

---

[1] The Welsh "golden torques" found at Harlech in 1692 are described and illustrated in *Camden*. See Gough's Ed.

[2] " Pedwar meib ar ugaint a'm bu,
    Eurdorchawg, tywysawg llu."

The date of the above poems, of course, is questioned, but this is a
point not requiring discussion here. The custom is known to be ancient,
and is conceded. And it may be observed, in passing, that no competent
adverse criticism of the age of the Welsh Poems has yet appeared.

elaborate regulation, of stringent discipline. It is impossible to read Cæsar's account of the Druids of Gaul, without allowing that it presents an order of teachers—waiving all consideration of their religious doctrines and rites—whose sphere of thought was comprehensive and lofty, and whose method was adapted to stimulate and enrich the intellect.[1] But Cæsar also states that Britain, and not Gaul, was the proper and high seat of Druidism, and that those who wished to be perfect in the system, travelled to Britain for instruction.[2] An eminent modern historian says that the Druidic superstition took refuge in Britain in preference to Gaul, in order to find a more congenial home amongst the " blindest votaries," and to "fly from the scrutiny of civilized and inquiring men." It is rather strange that " the civilized and inquiring men " of Gaul should send their sons to be educated amongst the blindest votaries, and it is to be remembered that the country of these civilized and inquiring men was itself a Druidic country. Cæsar, who is acknowledged to be the best authority on this matter—*summus auctorum divus Julius*, as Tacitus calls him—puts probably the true construction upon the circumstance. The Gauls who wished to be perfect in the system of Druidism—the only system of Celtic intellectual culture then in vogue—went to Britain for instruction. Now, the people who thus supplied the best teaching, may fairly be considered as being themselves the most cultivated.[3]

[1] *De Bell. Gall.* lib. vi. 13. Comp. *Strabo*, lib. iv. 4. Pomp. Mela *De Lit. Orb.* iii. 2. *Diod. Sic.* lib. v., Strabo and Pomp. Mela apparently only copy Cæsar.

[2] *De Bell. Gall.* lib. vi. 13.

[3] Pliny says of the Druidic teaching :—" But why should I commemorate these things respecting an art which has passed over the sea and reached the bounds of nature ? Britain, even at this time, celebrates it with so many wonderful ceremonies that she seems to have taught it to the Persians." Book xxx.

It would be instructive to inquire into the intellectual and moral aspects of Druidism, as a great national force and stimulant—force and stimulant, we mean, of a mental and contemplative kind, quite consistent with, if not indeed conducive to, inefficiency in warlike conflict when opposed to odds such as the Romans presented. Into this question at length we cannot enter. But certain principles implied in Cæsar's description may be briefly noticed as we pass. Young men, we are told, were kept under the care of the Druids, sometimes as long as twenty years. So great was the care taken in instruction—so great the work to be done. Instruction was imparted orally, and all had to be committed to memory. This indicates, not merely initiation into an esoteric system of doctrine, kept *unwritten*[1] the better to protect it from vulgar gaze—but also great speciality and minuteness of indoctrination.

A method so purely mnemonic, would, as a matter of course, employ artificial means, such as rhythmical formulæ, both to facilitate attainment and retention. Now there are signs of the descent of such a system in the early poetry as well as prose of the Britons. Probably alliteration in poetry, and the *Triad* form in prose, are nothing less than the remains of the Druidic mnemonic system. The Icelandic poets used alliteration early, as shown by Percy; it is found among the Finns and among the Tamul tribes of India; early Latin Church hymns display it; and the Anglo-Saxon English practised it in the middle ages, as seen in Caedmon and Piers Plowman: but nowhere did it exist so early, nowhere has it obtained so rank a growth,

---

[1] That a certain class of knowledge was kept unwritten argues the existence of writing for general purposes. That the art was known to the Britons is beyond doubt. Cæsar says (*De Bell. Gall.* iv. 13) that the Druids of Gaul practised writing, using Greek characters (Græcis utantur literis). But if in Gaul, *a fortiori*, they did so in Britain, the chief seat of their authority and learning.

as in Wales; and nowhere else has it continued to the present time in all its extremest grotesqueness.

Piers Plowman's Vision was written so late as the 14th century, and is about the best specimen in early English of a poem composed on the alliterative principle, displaying also an imperfect terminal rhyme; but how undeveloped its alliteration and its rhyme, when compared with those of the much earlier Welsh!

> " In a *s*omer *s*eason | when hot was the *s*onne
> I *s*hope me into *s*hroubs | as I a *s*hepe were,
> In *h*abit as an *h*armet | un*h*oly of werkes
> *W*ent *w*ide in this *w*orld | *w*onders to heare."

This is *Piers Plowman.* But seven hundred years before this was written (allowing the earlier age ascribed to the Welsh poems to be correct), we find in Aneurin, along with *terminal rhyme*, such complex alliteration throughout the verse as this:

> " *C*aeawe *c*ynnyviat *c*yvlat erwyt
> *R*huthyr eryr yn y *l*yr pan *l*ythiwyt
>   *   *   *   *   *
> Hyder gymm*ell* ar *v*reith*ell* *v*anawyt
> *N*y *n*odi *n*ag *y*sg*e*th *n*ag *y*sgwyt."

The poet Golyddan, assigned to the 6th century, and writing a language so primitive as to be as completely unintelligible to a Welshman of to-day as to an Englishman, writes thus:

> " *D*ysgogan awen *d*ygobryssyn
> *M*archann*edd* a *m*eu*edd* a *h*edd genhyn
> A phenn*aeth* ehel*aeth* a ffr*aeth* unbyn
> A gwedy dy*h*edd an*h*edd ym*h*ob *m*ehyn
> *G*wyr *g*wych yn tryd*ar* casn*ar* dengyn
> *E*sg*ud* yngnof*ud* ryh*yd* diffyn ·
> *G*waethl *g*wyr hyt *g*aer *W*air *g*wasgarawdd Ellmyn
> *G*wnahawn *g*orfoledd *g*wedy *g*wehyn," &c.

Perhaps the prettiest specimen of alliteration in this early age is in another part of the same poem:

"*Cyneircheid, cyneilweid,* unrhaith *cwynyn*!
Un *gor,* un *gyngor,* un *cisor yut.*"

Let them (the Cymry) be summoned, called together, rise unanimous!
They have one heart, one judgment, one common cause.

In the 12th century Cynddelw makes a further advance :

"DRAGON o *dwyr*ag DRAIG o *dwy*rain
Draig WEN *ollewin well* y dichwain
O*ed* CLEUdae*r oed* CLAC*r* CLEdyf uch gwain
A *lli*non yg gnif a *lla*fnae *lla*in
*Lla*fn yn LLAW a *lla*w yn LLAD pennain
*Lla*w ar LLAfn ar *lla*fn ar LLU nordmain
Ac *cry*foed *trwm* rag *trem*yd angen," &c.

All this at last culminated in the *Pedwar Mesur ar Hugain* (the Four-and-Twenty Metres—most appropri-ately called *Caethion*—"bondage metres") of the 14th century, which are still in force among the "poets" of Wales, and despite their prettinesses and the consonantal jingle which delights the bards, operate so disastrously upon the genius of the country.[1]

This has been the case with respect to alliteration. If we enquire into the use of terminal *rhyme* by the early Welsh poets, the result will be similar. Archbishop

---

[1] Of this one specimen will suffice—an "Englyn" by the late Mr. Davies, called *Bardd Nantglyn*—one of the most accomplished and "legitimate" of Welsh poets. The subject is the balloon. A translation, not our own, but taken from *Ceinion Awen y Cymmry,* is added, from which an idea may be formed of the "regular" poetry of the Principality. The numbers and letters mark corresponding consonants.

"Awy*ren,* BELe*n,* glud BALI—DRWY CIIw*a*
  1 2 3 1 2 3 a b c
DERCII *h*ynt hyd wybreni ;
a b c
*N*wyf *weib long,* ban *nawf, heb li,*
1 2 3 4 1 2 3 4
A *llaw dyn* yn *llyw dani.*"
1 2 3 1 2 3

Trans.—"That air-filled body, the *Balloon,* a silken vehicle, by a blast,
  View soaring on its course through ethereal regions :
  As a ship of lively range, aloft it swims, without a flood,
  Having for a guide the hand of man beneath."

Trench acknowledges that the Welsh used final rhyme as early as the 6th century.[1] The Latins, as early as Ennius, Virgil, and Ovid, display an occasional terminal rhyme, perhaps accidental, as in Virgil :

> Necnon Tarquinium ejectum Porsena jubebat
> Accipere, ingentique urbem obsidione premebat.

And in Horace :

> Multa recedentes adimunt. Ne fortè seniles
> Mandentur juveni partes, pueroque viriles.

But rhyme came into prominence in the Latin language at a much later period, and as a substitute for the old metres which in the Greek and Roman poets depended on *quantity*. Durandus[2] has shown that its use as an aid to memory was early taken advantage of in the calendar and offices of the Church. Early in the 12th century, in the Latin hymns of Adam St. Victor, Abelard—natives, by the way, of *Brittany*—St. Bernard of Clairvaux, Bernard of Clugny, &c., terminal rhyme became an essential element. But it has been shown above how, many centuries before this, the Cymric poets had used it, and Guest[3] has come to the conclusion that in all probability the Latins received rhyme from the Celtic race. The truth seems to be that it grew up simultaneously among different peoples, but that its quickest growth was amongst the Celts, and especially the Cymry of Wales.

That the *Triad* is a relic of the Druidic system is, to say the least, probable. It bears the guise of antiquity, and its form is well adapted for the memory. Its quality of threefoldness, expressed in its name, may intimate a Platonic or a Christian origin. The language, however,

---

[1] *Sacred Latin Poetry*, p. 39.   [2] *Rationale Divin. Off.*, i. 8.
[3] *Hist. of English Rhythms.*

in which the Triads have come down to us, has received a
modern complexion from recent copyists.

Now we think that none will deny, after examination,
that these interesting remains contain a fund of human
wisdom quite extraordinary for the early times when they
are supposed to have originated. They display a style of
thought at once analytic, acute, speculative, discursive,
practically ethical, sympathetic towards man, reverent
towards the Deity. Their psychology and morals savour
more of the Pythagorean and Platonic than of the Aris-
totelic. They deal familiarly with the loftiest forms of
thought without losing sight of daily human concerns.
Not unfrequently on the principle that

" .   .   . . Brevity is the soul of wit,
    And tediousness the limbs and outward flourishes."

they exhibit wonderful terseness and concentration of idea
and expression. They also show by frequent peculiarities
of opinion and phraseology acquaintance with the Greek
writers, and occasionally with the Roman. That some of
them should be embodiments of Biblical truths—which is
the fact—is natural. Whatever relation they bore to the
Druidical institution, in passing down the stream of ages
they have become somewhat tinged with the systems of
thought they encountered on the way. They have been
shaped, in a measure, to meet the temper of times and
faiths, and thus have exchanged the theology of Druidism
for that of Christianity.

Be this as it may, we take the *Triads* as a fair index to
the type of mind dominant among the *Cymry* in ancient
times, and especially in the Early Middle Ages, and to the
social and moral condition of those subject to the principles
they enshrine. Thought stands at the head of all affairs,
and a people into whose minds great and pure thoughts
have been ingrained, cannot be a weak and contemptible

people. Low as the condition of the multitude may be, if in the governing few there is intelligence, the whole community will be under guidance to high ends, and will more or less receive the inspiration of wisdom.

" Rex noster animus est,"

is the universal confession of mankind, and in so far as history affords any utterance in the matter, its one testimony is, that the Druids were not merely severe disciplinarians, but that their superior knowledge and high character warranted the exercise of authority, and that this authority on the whole was wielded for the individual and public weal.

If the reader is inclined to take the Welsh *Triads* now existing as remote reflections of the Druidic teaching, well and good. If he is not, he will at least take them as faithful exponents of the condition of intellectual culture among the Welsh people at an early time in the middle ages—for *this* they are allowed by all competent judges to be. This is all we claim for them.

Let the following serve as examples of the *Triads*:—

By three things shall a person be quickly known: by what he likes, by what he dislikes, and by such as like or dislike him.

The three characteristics of godliness: to do justice, to love mercy, and to behave humbly.

Three things which cannot be brought under discipline of strict law and order: love, genius, and necessity.

Three things that are honourable in a man: to have courage in adversity, to observe moderation in prosperity, and piously to conduct himself in both.

The three points in goodness: wisdom, fortitude, and love; and where those three are not found together, good qualities cannot be expected.

Three things that discover a man's disposition and principles: his eye, his speech, and his actions.

With three things a man ought to purpose all good actions and knowledge: with all love, with all understanding, and with all ability.

Three things that, from being rightly understood, will cause peace and tranquillity: the course of nature, the claims of justice, and the voice of truth.

There are three actions which are divine: to succour the poor and feeble, to benefit an enemy, and courageously to suffer in the cause of right.

The three efficiencies of all things from the beginning: necessity, choice, and chance; and from one or other of these doth come and is done everything.

The three necessities of the Being of God: essence. life, and motion; and from these are all substance, life, and motion, by inchoation, *i.e.*, from God and his essence are all things whatsoever.

The three priorities of being—which are the three necessities of Deity: power, knowledge, love; and from the union of these three are force and existence.

The three foundations of wisdom: youth to learn, memory to retain what is learned, understanding to put it rightly in practice.

Now it is by no means necessary to argue that the whole mass of the early Britons were familiar with sentiments like these, in order to entitle them to exemption from the charge of being "barbarians." In what nation, in what age have the masses been so happily conditioned? Were they so in Greece when Plato taught, when Praxiteles all but made the marble breathe? Were they so in Rome when her legions ruled the world? Were they so in England when our Miltons and our Addisons wrote? Are they so in England *now?*

It is to be remembered that the wisdom of the *Triads*, be its value what it may, was not, in later ages at least, esoteric. Its depositaries were the bards. The bards were popular teachers through minstrelsy, song, and recitation. The retainers of every lord and prince of the land were pupils of the castle bard and genealogist, and the wisdom he happened to possess was freely imparted to them all. We are now referring to times less remote than the Roman Conquest; but there is reason to suspect that in very ancient times, before the Roman ever trod on our soil, the Cymry, as indeed many other ancient nations, had their popular bardic and minstrel institution.

Having thus in some measure stretched forward our view
of British civilization and intelligence beyond the Roman
period, let us now for a moment recur to the earlier epoch,
and here first direct attention to a class of influencies connected essentially with Druidic teaching not yet touched
upon: we mean the *religious*. Of course, many of the
theological dogmas of the Druids were erroneous—many
of their rites, although their grossness and cruelty have
been sadly exaggerated, would be in our day revolting. At
the same time they taught elevating doctrines, stimulated
the moral nature to heroic efforts after virtue, fixed the
imaginative Celtic mind on things enduring and spiritual.
Cæsar shows that they taught the immortality of the soul.
Amm. Marcellinus tells us that they believed the human
spirit was to exist in another world. Diogenes Laertius
comprises their religious doctrines under three precepts :
to worship the gods, to do no evil, and to act with courage.
There is no reason for doubting that their doctrine concerning the Deity was monotheistic—identical, in fact,
with the doctrine of Plato. Such teaching must have
exerted a mighty influence on the popular mind. Lucan,
in his *Pharsalia*, thus acknowledges the fact :

> " And you, O Druids, free from noise and arms,
> Renewed your barbarous rites and fearful charms.
> What gods, what powers in happy mansions dwell,
> Or only you, or all but you, can tell.
> To secret shades and unfrequented groves
> From world and cares your peaceful tribe removes,
> You teach that souls, eased of their mortal load,
> Nor with grim Pluto make their dark abode,
> Nor wander in pale troops along the silent flood,
> But on new regions cast, resume their reign,
> Content to govern earthly frames again.
> Thus death is nothing but the middle line,
> Betwixt what lives, will come, and what has been.
> Happy the people by your charms possessed !
> Nor fate, nor fears disturb their peaceful breast ;

On certain dangers unconcerned they run,
And meet with pleasure what they would not shun ;
Defy death's slighted power, and bravely scorn
To spare a life that will so soon return."

Let the ennobling influences of the Druidic *Religion* be
added to the facts and considerations already enumerated.
Do not all these together amount to more then we claim
for them? Do they not present the Ancient Britons as a
people free, industrious, ingenious, spirited, with superior
knowledge of the arts, working in metals, commercially
enterprising, ready to welcome strangers, holding intimate
communication with the continent, subsisting in small
kingdoms, each under its hereditary sovereign, proving their
respect for woman by entitling her to the throne, and so far
advanced in intellectual, religious, and general culture, that
the Gauls sent their sons to Britain for the most advanced
education, especially in that higher department of wisdom
officially presided over by the Druids? These, and many
other equally notable features in their character and condition, we learn, not from the pens of their own historians,
much less from the fervid imagination of their poets, but
from Greek and Roman annalists whose words on all other
matters are received with respect. We therefore conclude
that in the Ancient Britons are found a people greatly
removed from barbarism, and that for hundreds of years
before Cæsar's arrival they had been marked by the same
characteristics. To represent them as our popular and
unenquiring historical writers have usually done is to belie
history, travesty facts, and do a manifest and gratuitous
injustice to a brave people.

Is it not, therefore, fair to argue, *à priori*, that such a
people, if conquered, would be conquered only in one sense
—as Rome was conquered by the Goths, and France by the
Franks—by being deprived of territory and Government?

Failing of victory in the field, they would still conquer for themselves, as the Gauls did in France, a position in the new community which arose upon the ruins of their own political and social existence. To destroy them bodily were impossible. Their expatriation we know was not contemplated by the Romans, who only wanted rule and tribute. We argue that it was not done or attempted by their Anglican and Saxon conquerors. To commit suicide they never attempted, but quite the reverse! A love of life, individual and national, was their passion. And if ever people clung with almost præternatural strenuousness to their native soil, language, customs, name, and all that human independence would call its own—that people were the Ancient Britons, more especially in the Cymric section of them. To suppose that such a race should vanish, because their *political* existence ceased, were to judge in contravention of all the evidence, as well as of common sense. The erection of the empire of Charlemagne extinguished not the Gallic blood of France. The British rule in India will not extirpate the Hindoo race. Nay, the Anglo-Saxons themselves were not all put to the sword, or driven into the sea by the Danes, or subsequently by the Normans, though completely conquered by both. Why, therefore, arbitrarily stipulate that events must happen differently in the case of the Ancient Britons?

Our next step will be to furnish a bird's-eye view of the various conquests of Britain, presenting as distinctly as possible in brief space the contrasted strength of invaders and invaded, and carefully distinguishing between the founding of new *governments* and the destruction or replacement of *peoples*.

PART II.

The Invasions of Britain.

PART II.

——◆——

THE INVASIONS OF BRITAIN:
THE ELEMENTS OF ADMIXTURE ACCUMULATING— ADMIXTURE COMMENCING.

——◆——

BRITAIN, which through various fortunes has at last fought her way to inviolable liberty and peace, and become the asylum of the oppressed of all lands, was herself for a thousand years the prey and sport of strangers. She excited the cupidity, now of imperial Rome, now of the lawless rovers of the German and Scandinavian Seas, now of the warlike and more chivalrous Normans of France. How in those rude twilight ages the mysterious virtues of this *Fêl Ynys*, this "eye of the world," this "masterpiece of nature" became so widely known, it is hard to say; but, in the absence of any but the most imperfect means of locomotion by land or water, the fame of this *Ultima Thule* seems to have reached, before the Christian Era, almost all the tribes and nations of Europe, and many of them elected to quit their fatherlands to seek a better inheritance on her shores. Then, as now, her climate, as Tacitus describes it, was marred by frequent rains, and an overcast sky—(cœlum crebris imbribus ac

nebulis fœdum), her shores were rugged, her seas stormy.
Nothing signified.   Many an adventurous land and sea
captain, with or without the rights ascribed to Brutus by
our imaginative Geoffrey, heard a Diana, as clearly as Brutus
heard her, say :—

> ". . . . there lies beyond the Gallic bounds
> An island, which the western sea surrounds,
> By giants once possessed ; now few remain
> To bar thy entrance or obstruct thy reign.
> To reach that happy shore thy sails employ," &c.

And so it came to pass that century after century, wave
after wave of incursion beat, like the billows of her seas, on
her devoted strands.   Whether we listen to the plain statements or the implications of classic history, or to the glowing
utterances of myth and fable—they all alike echo the
splashing of oars and the clash of weapons of invading
hosts, or, on occasions, the friendly greeting of flocking
cognate tribes.   They come, and crowd from the four
quarters of the heavens—from the mysterious Deffrobani,
the summer country, from sunny Gascony, from "Pwyl,"
from the marshes of the Lower Rhine, from Armorica,
Northern and Eastern Gaul, from rugged and inhospitable
Scandinavia—nay, the isle of Britain even excites the
ambition of great Rome herself, and she empties her coffers,
pours forth the blood of her best legions, consumes the life
of her most renowned commanders, and wearies the hearts
of many of her emperors through the space of 400 years in
her stubborn resolve to subdue and possess it !

CHAPTER I.

THE ROMAN INVASION.

THE struggle at Rome to establish the first Triumvirate of Cæsar, Pompey, and Crassus, was no sooner over than the ambitious Cæsar set out for the conquest of Britain. In B.C. 55, he finds Rome torn by faction, and hastening towards decay; and he wisely seeks relief in an active campaign, and food for ambition in conquest. Rome, if rendering herself inglorious by dishonouring her own laws, and exhibiting in caricature her own institutions, must be made renowned abroad by deeds of arms ; and if bent on suicide, she must find a saviour as well as master in the mightiest of her sons.

In all his wars with the Gauls the Britons had sent aid to his opponents.[1] He resolves to punish their audacity, and at the same time win laurels by their subjugation. Late in the season, in B.C. 55, he prepares to embark for Britain, apparently believing that for the conquest of such a people, the small portion remaining of that year would suffice. From the coast of Gaul, somewhere between Calais and Boulogne, across the narrowest part of the channel, he views the cliffs—the towering white chalk-cliffs—of the coveted island, glistening in the sun, and prepares for

[1] *De Bell. Gall.* lib. iv. 20.

embarking his legions. The little port of *Itium*[1] is the place where the great Roman, chafing at the insolence of the Britons, collects his fleet of eighty ships—collects his heavy-armed legions. The eighty ships are filled with two legions, numbering about 12,000 infantry. The cavalry embark from another point, and in other boats. The great flock of triremes, with regular stroke of oars, makes across the channel, watched by the Gauls from behind, watched also by the wary Britons. After a little beating about for a convenient creek, they halt, and prepare to land. The Britons are prepared to meet them. A hard struggle ensues, without decisive victory. The Roman soldiers are shy of fighting in the water, while the eager Britons advance to attack them breast high in the sea. At last the natives fall back, and the Romans land, and wait for their cavalry. A truce is formed; the Britons, who well knew of Cæsar's doings in Gaul, and the great power he had behind him, conditionally submit. Again a little fighting with a foraging party, and again a truce and submission; and then Cæsar, having accomplished nothing proportionate to the extent of his preparations, at once decides on quitting the island. News of this success reaches Rome, and the Senate order rejoicings for *twenty days*—a proof either that Rome must be in sad want of something to rejoice at, or that the triumph as yet obtained in Britain had been most grossly exaggerated.

Cæsar clearly felt that he had begun a work of greater difficulty than he had anticipated. Having received hostages from the Britons, he returns to Gaul to quell a rising

---

[1] " Itium, which the divine Cæsar (Καῖσαρ ὁ θεὸς) used as his naval station, when about to pass over to Britain." Strabo, *Geogr.* B. iv. 278. The late Emperor Napoleon maintains that the port of Itium was Boulogne and not Witsand, as generally supposed. He is most likely right. *Life of Julius Cæsar*, vol. ii. 201.

insurrection among the Morini. He remains in Gaul over winter, and meditates a grand scheme of conquest in Britain in the spring. He makes diligent preparations—builds transport ships, collects troops, amasses material of war The spring approaches, and nothing is left unaccomplished to secure complete success for this second expedition.

Having returned from a journey to Italy, he finds himself in the spring of B.C. 56 in possession of nearly 700 ships, all built on purpose for the invasion of Britain. Did great Rome, and "divus Cæsar," make these mighty preparations in order to invade a handful of feeble, painted barbarians? At the same port of *Itium* (probably Boulogne) he puts on board his 700 transports an army of 30,000 infantry, besides a complement of cavalry, and, after a delay of some weeks through adverse winds, weighs anchor and reaches Sandwich haven in Kent,[1] about the spot of the first landing. Greater preparations on the part of Cæsar have been met by greater on the part of the Britons. They have learned wisdom, and now encounter these teeming legions, not with the piece-meal forces of individual tribes, or a small federation of tribes in the one district of Kent, but with an "allied army," combining the military strength of several powerful states, or so-called "kingdoms." These, probably, comprehended our modern Kent, Middlesex, Essex, part of Suffolk, Berks, &c. Cassivelaunus (Caswallon) is the brave chieftain to whom they entrust the command. Dreadful encounters follow. "The enemy's horse," says Cæsar, "supported by their chariots, vigorously charged our cavalry." Though gaining advantages, the Romans found it costly work. "It evidently appeared," he adds, "that our heavy-armed legions were by no means a fit match for

---

[1] Different opinions have prevailed respecting the point of debarkation, some identifying it with Sandwich, some with Walmer. The Emperor Napoleon decides in favour of Deal. *Life of Julius Cæsar*, vol. ii. 208.

such an enemy, nor could even the cavalry engage without great danger," because of the quick evolutions and peculiar tactics of the Britons. The bloody work, however, goes on; and at last the capital of Cassivelaunus, which Cæsar declares was admirably fortified (egregie munitum), is stormed and taken; the tribes in active hostility are subdued, promise tribute, deliver hostages, but retain their usages, laws, and government, their kings henceforth ruling by nominal authority from Cæsar; and so, before the end of the summer of that same year the conqueror returns to Gaul, *leaving no troops in Britain.* Cæsar is destined never more to set foot on British soil; and the Britons, once he has departed, are virtually as free and independent as before. Such, and only such, was the conquest of Britain by Cæsar, as shall be further shown in a future page.

The great commander has now other work to attend to. His stormy rivalship with Pompey taxes all his energies. He succeeds; wins his way to the Dictatorship, obtains the great victory of Pharsalia, struggles up the steps of power till he is deemed and proclaimed "divine," and, ten years after defeating the heroic Caswallon, falls in the Senate House by the daggers of Brutus and Cassius! This was the end of him who had boastingly exclaimed, " I, by whom you have subdued the Gauls and conquered the *Britons*," &c.[1]—an exclamation which, though claiming more than was due, implies volumes of eulogy on the power and valour of our ancestors!

For a hundred years after the death of Cæsar, Rome had no leisure to molest the Britons. Augustus and Tiberius gave them rest. The islanders profited from the peace, and grew in wealth and culture. The Brigantes in the North (Yorkshire, &c.), and the Silures of South Wales and Herefordshire, under Caractacus, became powerful states.

[1] *Dion. Cass.* xli. 34.

The successor of Caswallon, Cunobeline, (*Cynfelin*), ruled in South Britain over a prosperous people. In his time, the Britons were not low in civilization. We have already shown that they executed a regular coinage, and that long before Cæsar's time they had both brass and gold coin in circulation.[1]

Claudius was the first Roman *Emperor* whose ambition reached so far as Britain. A year after he made Herod Agrippa King of Judæa and Samaria, A.D. 43, he sent his General, Aulus Plautius, with a great force to Britain. The Trinobantes of Essex and Suffolk, were now, as before, the chief to bear the brunt of the attack. Vespasian, afterwards Emperor, and his son Titus, were amongst the officers in command. Claudius himself came over. The submission of the Britons was speedily won. Claudius obtained the honour of a triumph, and received the surname *Britannicus*[2]—another indirect proof of the importance attached at Rome to the subjugation of the Britons.

As yet, the sea coast of the south, and the country a little way into the interior alone had been brought under tribute. *Caractacus*, king of the Silures,[3] and the Britons of the mid-country, and of north, east, and west, had not been affected.

Ostorius came next. He lost no time, but immediately pushed on towards Shropshire and Lancashire, and was brought to a stand by Caractacus. This puissant prince, after the noblest efforts on record for the defence and

---

[1] *De Bell. Gall.* v. 12. See pp. 65, 66.

[2] *Dion. Cass.* lx. 23.

[3] Caractacus is said by Dion Cassius, who wrote two centuries after his time, to be the son of Cunobeline, already mentioned; but the testimony of the *Triads*, which have the advantage of native tradition, if not of written record, as a basis, is clear that he was the son of Brân the blessed, son of Llyr.

honour of his country, was destined to defeat at the hands of Ostorius, and to betrayal at the hands of Queen Cartismandua,[1] (a " Roman Matron," as Richard of Cirencester calls her—who had married Venutius ruler of the Brigantes) with whom he had sought shelter. But his defeat was not an easy or sudden thing. For nine whole years had this heroic man kept the field against the power of Rome, fighting meantime many battles, and inflicting terrible losses on the imperial army. When led a captive to Rome, his arrival created one of the most exciting and impressive spectacles history has depicted. " Curiosity was eager," says Tacitus, " to behold the heroic chieftain who for such a length of time made head against a great and powerful empire. Even at Rome, the name of Caractacus was in high celebrity."[2] What Briton can read the speech put into the foiled warrior's mouth by Tacitus without emotion ? "If to the nobility of my birth, and the splendour of exalted station, I had united the virtues of moderation [careful direction] Rome had beheld me, not in captivity, but a royal visitor and a friend. The alliance of a prince descended from an illustrious line of ancestors, a prince whose sway extended over many regions, would not have been unworthy of your choice. A reverse of fortune is now the lot of Caractacus. The event to you is glorious,—to me humiliating. . . . The ambition of Rome aspires to universal conquest. I stood at bay for years : had I done otherwise, where on your part had been the glory of conquest, and where on mine the honour of a brave resistance ? I am now in your power ; if you are bent on vengeance, execute your purpose : the bloody scene will soon be over, and the name of Caractacus will sink into oblivion. Preserve my life, and I shall be to late posterity a monument of Roman clemency." Carac-

[1] *Aregwedd Foeddawg ?*   [2] *Annales*, xii. 36.

tacus won the favour of Claudius and was set at liberty; but whether he ever left Rome, or what became of him or his family, history, strange to say, does not relate.

> ". . . . Nimius vobis [Cimbrica] propago
> Visa potens, superi, propria hæc si dona fuissent ! "

Britain, as far as Yorkshire and Wales, was under Ostorius made tributary to Rome. After Ostorius, a long line of generals, including several of the emperors in person, commanded the invading forces. A. Didius Gallus, *Suetonius*, who conquered Mona (Anglesea), slaughtered the Druids,[1] and quelled the rising under Boadicea,[2] when 80,000 men are said to have fallen—Cerealis, Frontinus, and *Agricola*, a wise and brave governor, invader of the Caledonians, and the fortunate father-in-law of Tacitus, whose pen has made his name illustrious for all coming ages.[3] In this last commander's time the rampart from the Forth to the Clyde was erected as a barrier to check the unsubduable Caledonians, and the subjugation of Britain may be said to have been in a sense completed. In A.D. 121, Hadrian, the "travelling emperor," paid a visit to Britain, and "Hadrian's Wall," more southerly than that of Agricola, was built from the Tyne to the Solway. Then came Marcellus, Albinus, and the Emperor Severus, who in A.D. 209, constructed the famous wall of solid masonry from Tynemouth in the East to Bowness in the West, and two years afterwards died at York. Next came *Constantius*, said to have married the British princess Helena,[4] who died also at York, and *Constantine* the Great (Cystenyn Fawr) his son, who for thirty years promoted

---

[1] Tacitus, *Annal.* xii. 30.   [2] *Ibid.* 31 *et seq.*

[3] In his *Vita Agricolæ.*

[4] Geoffrey of Monm. *Hist.* v.; Richard of Cirenc. ii. 1, 24.   This story must be allowed to be " doubtful."

peace and prosperity among the Britons, and died A.D. 137.
Then follow Constans and Theodosius; and lastly, Maximus (who in Welsh history is called *Macsen Wledig*), following whose fortunes many thousand British youths are
said by Nennius to have left for Gaul, and eventually settled in Armorica.[1] In a subsequent section on the extent
and power of the British population under the Romans,
the operations of some of these great commanders will be
treated of at some length.

Overwhelming troubles were now gathering in store for
the Roman Empire. The storm in which she foundered
and sunk soon broke in fury upon her. In A.D. 395 the
empire is parted between the sons Theodosius the Great.
The Huns devastate the eastern provinces. The Goths,
under Alaric, invade Italy, and in A.D. 410 sack and burn
the Eternal City. Two years later the Roman legions are
recalled from Britain, and the Britons are left their own
masters and their own protectors.

The withdrawal of the Roman army from this island
took place just 465 years after the first landing of Julius
Cæsar. This, then, was the extreme period of the Roman
occupation of Britain. But from *Cæsar* to *Agricola* was 135
years, and this length of time elapsed before the Roman
arms became victorious over the southern, central, and
western parts of the island, and succeeded in hemming in
the Caledonians to the mountains of the north. From
Agricola to Maximus was 330 years, and this long period
it took, first to establish a kind of general government of
the island, and then to convince the Romans that the occupation was more costly than pleasant or profitable. Both

---

[1] Nennius, *Hist.* 23. This whole story is very doubtful. Lobineau,
in his *Histoire de Brétagne*, totally rejects it, as inconsistent with the
fact that Maximus's expedition landed on the Rhine, and not in
Armorica.

these facts are of material importance in their bearing on our argument, and to them, in the proper place, we must recur.

During this long period of Roman conflict and ascendancy, a stupendous change had been effected in Britain. The Roman civilization had been completely introduced; the condition of the Britons—barring the loss of independence and freedom for which nothing could compensate—had doubtless been greatly improved. Military roads had been constructed from end to end of the country, and vast works of public utility and ornament had been completed. The bridges, gardens, baths, and villas of Rome had been reproduced in Britain, and all the pomp and luxury of the Imperial Court made familiar to our forefathers. The complete and rigid municipal government of the Roman cities, and the Roman laws generally, tempered by the chastening spirit of Christianity, had prevailed for nearly 300 years.[1] In fact, Britain had lavished upon her all the care and attention which the chiefest of Roman *Provinciæ* enjoyed. In the words of one of our ablest historians: "The country was replete with the monuments of Roman magnificence. Malmesbury appeals to those stately ruins (which still remained in his time—twelfth century) as testimonies of the favour which Britain had enjoyed: the towers, the temples, the theatres, and the baths . . . . excited the wonder and admiration of the chronicler and the traveller."[2] Malmesbury says, "That Britain was held in high estimation by that people (the Romans) may be collected from their history, and be seen also in the ruins of their ancient build-

---

[1] For the laws which were in force in Britain, see Heineccii *Hist. Jur. Rom.* i. 379. The Theodosian Code did not embrace the whole Roman law. As to the Justinian Code, or *Corpus Juris*, this, of course, was not yet compiled.

[2] Palgrave, *Engl. Comm.* vol. i. 323. See also Girald. Cambr. *Itin. Cambr.* lib. i. 5.

ings. Even their emperors, sovereigns of almost all the world, eagerly embraced opportunities of sailing hither, and of spending their days here."[1] Tacitus tells[2] us that Agricola "encouraged the natives to build temples, courts of justice, and commodious dwelling-houses. . . . . The Roman apparel was seen without prejudice, and the toga became a fashionable part of dress. . . . . Baths, porticoes, and elegant banquets grew into vogue," &c.

This impressive display of power and refinement would of itself be a valuable teacher to the youth of Britain. Prompted by natural disposition, and encouraged by their governors, they would soon lay aside the simple attire of their ancestors and don the Roman toga, intermix with the lessons of the Druids the study of Cicero, Livy, and Horace, and receive in silent admiration the impress of grace and beauty produced by the sculptured marble ornamenting every temple pediment, every porch, and every garden.

But all was not magnificence, solidity, and peace. To counterbalance these advantages, a heavy sorrow weighed on the heart of the British race. The image of their lost independence ever stood before their eyes. Oppression sat as ruler. The Roman procurator, as a rule, in those degenerate times, was an extortioner; and this operated as chief cause in the insurrection under Boadicea, and in many other breaches of the public peace. The British youth were, according to Roman custom in a conquered country, drafted into the imperial legions and sent off on foreign service. An army of some 50,000 men was maintained by a grinding taxation in order to keep in subjection the very people taxed.[3] The native population, deprived of all power, restrained from the exercise of self-

<hr>

[1] *Gesta Regum Anglor.* i. 1.   [2] *Vit. Agric.* 21.
[3] See Horsley's *Brit. Romana*, B. i. and ii.

government, although improved by contact with refinement
and knowledge, sank into a condition of inaction and
dependence. Though externally cultured, and surrounded by
all the tokens of taste and magnificence, they were internally
debased; and in the very presence of power and learning
were deprived of the native force and genius which in former
times they had displayed. However ridiculous the exaggerations ascribed to Gildas, and credited with eagerness
by historians,—but as will hereafter be shown, credited
without sufficient reflection—concerning their helplessness
in the face of their old northern assailants, their kindred
the " Picts and Scots," it cannot be denied that on the
departure of their Roman protectors, they exhibited much
of the weakness and disorder to be expected from a race
which had been under tutelage, and trained to obey rather
than command. And what a demonstration is here supplied
of the compatibility under despotic governments of the
highest culture and splendour in the governing with advancing sickliness and decrepitude in the governed!

We must not pass from this part of our subject without
noticing the grandest event of all in this eventful period
in British history—the *introduction of Christianity*. During
these 465 years of Roman occupation what a change had
this great moral power effected in the British heart and
life! The people had lost their liberty, but had gained at
the same time those great moral truths which gave liberty
to the spirit while the person was a bondsman—truths
which were destined as ages advanced to make Britain the
ruling power on earth—the home of liberty and the refuge
of the oppressed of all lands.

This was a stirring time, not in Britain alone. The
wonderful spirit of migration and conquest which had
possessed the northern barbarians, led to a remodelling of
most of the communities of Europe. The Christian Church

had become a great power. Her influence and life had permeated the Roman Empire, and many of the emperors had professed the faith of Christ. This was the time when Augustine and Jerome, Eusebius and Socrates (the historian), Chrysostom, Cyril, and Theodoret, flourished. The sun of Athanasius, Basil, the two Gregorys, had scarcely set. The spirit of Denial had also confronted the Faith. The mental struggles and bold theories of Arius, of the Welshman Morgan (Pelagius), and of Celestius, belong to this age. It may be doubted whether the stir of thought, the battle of truth and error, in our day of boasted mental activity, are greater and more earnest.

CHAPTER II.

THE ANGLO-SAXON INVASION.

NO sooner has one affliction taken its departure, than another, and a heavier one, sets in. The occasion is known to all. The Picts and Scots of Caledonia, old enemies of both Romans and Britons, though of the same Celtic stock with the latter, rush over the wall of Severus, and devastate the land. They have learned that Rome has withdrawn her army, that the Britons are torn asunder by faction on questions of rank and precedence in the establishment of a new Government, and, taking advantage of the opportunity, threaten suddenly to overwhelm the country. The Britons, though numerous, and determined enough to maintain their ground, having an imperfect organization, and having recently been deprived of their military leaders, find themselves unequal to the emergency.

They appeal to Rome for assistance, and Rome—to her credit—came to the rescue. Although herself in greatest straits, and having hardly a man to spare, once and again she despatched a force to Britain, and assisted to clear the country of the foe. This is an account received, not on the authority of Gildas, which to all intents is untrustworthy, but on that of Nennius and Bede as well.[1] But it is to be feared that in some of their statements the latter had copied Gildas.

[1] *Nennius*, 30. Bede, *Hist. Eccles.* I. 12.

But Rome at last grew tired of rendering assistance, and, in fact, grew unequal to it. Gallio Ravennas, it is said, was the last Roman general who trod on British ground. He chastised the Picts and Scots, repaired the wall of Severus, gave directions for its future defence, and, after exhorting the Britons to be brave and hopeful, took his departure for good in A.D. 427, just fifteen years after the withdrawal of the Roman army and occupation.

Would that some one had written a book—that some quiet Nennius, or Robert of Gloucester, had chronicled the events of that dreadful interval—of all intervals in the life of the British people in historic times the most fascinating in its mystery! An impenetrable veil hangs over it; and yet its great eventfulness cannot be doubted. Nennius tells us that after the termination of the Roman power the Britons were in a state of alarm forty years.[1] Some sort of government had been set up when the Romans left in A.D. 412. Probably several small kingdoms had been formed, and a confederacy attempted. But bitter disputes intervened on the question especially of the Pendragon-ship. A time of anguish and perplexity, of great fears and great hopes, was this first age of recovering but totter-ing independence. What wonder if the longing spirit of a people wildly imaginative and fervently patriotic, after centuries of cruel subjection, should now, at the first dawn of a new era of liberty, conceive wild dreams of Messiah deliverers in heroes of præternatural power and genius, and should see omens and miraculous prodigies? King *Arthur*, and his knights of the Round Table, whether fabulous or veritably historical—a question we need not strive to settle here—were characters which had their origin in this age. The terrible struggles which took place in the sixty years following the recal of the Roman legions between

---

[1] *Hist. of the Britons*, 31.

Britons and Britons, between Britons and the men of
Caledonia, and between Britons and Saxons, have never
been recorded, and shall never more be heard of. But
that was a gloomy, eventful, sanguinary time, which doubtless called for, and we would fain believe witnessed, the
rise of a man of the genius and prowess ascribed to Arthur,
the renowned son of the Pendragon of Britain. The life
of Arthur, it is true, has been charged with an abundance
of mythological fiction ; so also has the life of Charlemagne
and of Rollo ; but neither Arthur, Charlemagne, nor Rollo
can be changed into a myth on this account.[1]

Vortigern (Gwrtheyrn) had, it seems, become king of *South-
west* Britain during this period of trouble. To him, and to
the Britons for ages, as well as to the Romans, the so-
called "Saxons"—a branch, not unmixed, of the great
Teutonic family which had spread itself along the shores
of the Baltic, and between Holstein and the Rhine,[2] had
not been unknown. They had frequently paid threatening
visits to the British shores, and, as explained elsewhere,

---

[1] For the fabulous history of Arthur, the fertile seed of the Romance
literature of all Europe in the middle ages, see *Geoffrey of Monmouth*,
B. ix. For a defence of Arthur's really historic character, see Turner's
Anglo-Saxons, vol. i, p. 268 *et seq*. Every critic will allow that Geoffrey
is highly legendary, but nothing but the dilettanteism of criticism
would therefore consider as legendary the whole story of King Arthur.
True, neither Bede, Florence of Worcester, nor the *Saxon Chronicle*
mentions him. But the *Annales Cambriæ* (*sub ann*. 516, 537), the *Liber
Landavensis*, Nennius (*Hist. Brit*. 62), Henry of Huntingdon (*sub ann*.
527), and the British *Bruts* and *Triads*, are express and circumstantial
witnesses in his favour. That the supposititious Gildas makes no mention of the British hero is quite in keeping with the overflowing spite
and prejudice which the *De Excidio Britanniæ* everywhere shows towards
the Britons ; and as to Bede, his notices of this period in Wales are
extremely meagre. Although his history is specifically ecclesiastical,
he never names David of Menevia (St. David) and Dubricius, contemporaries of Arthur, nor the Sees of Llandaff and Caerleon.

[2] Bede, *Eccles. Hist*. i. 15; Ptolemy, *Geogr*. ii. 2; *Sax. Chron*. ann. 449.

had probably formed extensive settlements. They had obtained unenviable notoriety for their roving and plundering habits, and their terror had fallen on all the shores of the German sea.

It would seem that about the year A.D. 449, Vortigern, who was in some sort an usurper and rival for the chief rulership with other native princes, thought he might strengthen his claim to the chief Sovereignty, or Pendragonship, and put a stop to the ravages of the Caledonians, by forming an alliance with some of these freebooters. Hengist and Horsa (whom we take as historical and not mythic personages) and their followers, were therefore invited to his assistance. This is the Saxon account. Nennius's representation is that the Saxons first came in as it were by accident. "In the meantime three vessels, exiled from Germany, arrived in Britain, commanded by Hengist and Horsa, sons of Wihtgils. Vortigern received them as friends," &c.[1] Their coming over— whether by accident, invitation, or plundering design— was the entrance of the wedge which, by and by, wrenched the greater part of the island from the dominion of the Britons.

Britain presented an appearance of fertility and beauty which the men of the North Sea did not find in their native regions. Once they had found a firm footing, therefore, pretexts were easy for the prolongation of their stay. They had come over, let us suppose, as the Britons' protectors ; but *Quis custodiet ipsos custodes ?* The end was open hostility, a declared intention on the part of the strangers to enjoy a home in Britain. The scorn of the old Cymry at this proposal may be imagined. They, the original, only rightful possessors, now to be quietly deposed! Not so! But the wary north-men, to strengthen their case, invited horde

[1] *Hist. Brit.* 31.

after horde of their lean and needy countrymen to join them. Their enterprise became every day more hopeful, and therefore, after their code of morals, juster. More and more adventurers arrived. They came "like swarms of bees," says an old chronicler. Repulsed at one point, they only seemed to gain renewal of strength at another ; the more they were vanquished, the more they replenished themselves with new supplies from Germany.[1] News flew from the Rhine to the Elbe and thence far into Denmark, that Britain, the fairest of islands, was becoming a prey to the first comers, and the passion for settlement on her shores became so strong that, according to Bede, the regions about the Baltic and the south of Holstein—regions, however, which cannot be supposed to have ever sustained a large population—were left well-nigh depopulated. After inviting them as friends, for 150 years it became the employment of the Britons to contest the possession of their country with them as invaders, and after fighting, to grant them room. Not inapt to the circumstances are the lines of Horace :—

> " Cervus equum pugnâ melior communibus herbis
> Pellebat, donec minor in certamine longo
> Imploravit opes hominis, frenumque recepit :
> Sed, postquam victor violens discessit ab hoste
> Non equitem dorso, non frenum depulit ore."[2]

It will be sufficient for our purpose to enumerate in the briefest form the successive arrivals of the Angle and Saxon Bands, and their settlements in different provinces of Britain. The Anglo-Saxon conquest, like the Roman, was effected by slow degrees and at terrible cost to both parties. The *slowness* of the conquest is a feature which has a most material bearing upon our argument, and to this the especial attention of the reader is invited. There

---

[1] Nennius, *Hist. Brit.* 65.   [2] *Epist.* i. 10. *vv.* 34—38.

must have been specific reasons for that slowness; and those reasons all tell, *à priori*, in favour of the conclusion, at which, step by step, we arrive.

The Anglo-Saxon Arrivals.

1. A.D. 449, and just 22 years after the departure of the Romans, Hengist and Horsa, by invitation of Vortigern, arrive, and after 20 *years of conflict*, succeed in founding the small Saxon kingdom of Kent in A.D. 473.[1] These were *Jutes*, and the Saxon Chronicle says their conflicts were with the *Welsh*, (*with Walas*), meaning, probably, "the strange people."

2. A.D. 477. The *Frisians*, or Old Saxons, make an incursion under Ella their chief, "in three ships," (*mid thry scipum*),[2] and *in* 20 *years*, or thereabouts, establish the kingdom of the South Saxons, or Sussex; that is about the year 496. They, also, fight with the *Walas*.

3. A.D. 495. Cerdic, with his son Cynric, comes to Britain "in five ships," (*mid fif scipum*), "and the same day," says the chronicler, "fought with the Welsh," (*gefuhtun with Walas*);[3] and in A.D. 519, find themselves in possession of the kingdom of the West Saxons or Wessex. This was after 24 *years of fighting*. These were Saxons.

4. A.D. 530. Ercenwine, or Aescwin, with his *Saxon* followers, arrives, and after *about* 12 *years' contest*, succeeds in forming the kingdom of the East Saxons or Essex, comprehending modern Essex, Middlesex, and part of Herts, &c. "It is doubtful," says Sir F. Palgrave, "whether this kingdom ever enjoyed independence." It became subject to Mercia in the seventh century, and was merged in Wessex in 823.

---

[1] Bede, *Eccles. Hist.* i. 15; *Sax. Chron.* ann. 449—473.
[2] *Sax Chron.* ann. 477.   [3] *Ibid.* ann. 495.

5. In A.D. 540, the *Angles*, under Uffa their chief, established themselves in "East Anglia," which included Norfolk and Suffolk.

6. In A.D. 547, Ida, with a tribe of *Angles*, established a footing in the North of England between the Tweed and the Forth, and formed the kingdom of North-Humber-land,[1]—the most important of all the original Anglo-Saxon settlements.

7. About A.D. 585, was established the kingdom of Mercia, it is said by Crida, whose followers were *Angles*.

This was the last of those successive incursions which may with some latitude of expression be termed "Saxon invasions," and this last took place just 136 years after the first intrusion under Hengist and Horsa. What an amount of conflict and carnage is here implied! And what evidence is furnished of the power and persistency of the Ancient Britons. To this aspect of the question we shall very especially and repeatedly have to recur.

It will be useful here to mark the topography of the various settlements. "Winning their way by slow and painful efforts," observes Gibbon, "they advanced from the North, from the East, and from the South, till their victorious banners were united in the centre of the island." This conclusion of their labours, however, thus rather rhetorically, and in few words set forth, was not accomplished without some 300 years of contest: for the Saxon power was triumphant in England only with Egbert of Wessex, whose reign ended in A.D. 836. The efforts were truly "slow," and equally "painful!"

The first invasion made the Jutes in *twenty* years masters of the whole of Kent. The second in another *twenty* covered Sussex and Surrey—(South Saxons, and South-

---

[1] *Sax. Chron.* ann. 547; Ethelwerd's *Chron. ibid.*; Nennius, *Hist.* 61.

rica, or kingdom). The third, under Cerdic, included
Hants, Wilts, Somerset, Dorset, Gloucestershire, Oxfordshire, Berks, and Bucks. This was a work of *twenty-four*
years. The fourth embraced Essex, Middlesex, and part
of Herts; and was the work of about *twelve* years. The
fifth included Norfolk, Suffolk, Cambridgeshire, and part
of Lincolnshire and Northamptonshire. The sixth, and
most important of all, made the Angles masters, we do not
know in how long or short a time, of part of the South of
Scotland, Northumberland, Durham, Westmoreland, Cumberland, Lancashire, Cheshire, Yorkshire, &c. The seventh
set up Mercia, the particulars of whose establishment are
rather obscure: but that it embraced Chester, Derby, Not-
tingham, Lincoln (or part of it), Shropshire, Staffordshire,
Leicestershire, Rutland, Northampton, Huntingdon, Hereford, Worcester, Warwick, is known.

The question will perhaps be asked: If so, where were
now the *Britons?* Another question were exactly appropriate: Where were *not* the Britons? To suppose that
from all England, thus at last covered with nominal Saxon
governments, the Britons had been *expelled*, is to involve
the task of answering the question, *Whither ?* Wales had
its own people, as Offa of Mercia painfully knew, and could
at best but offer asylum to a limited number of fugitives,
persistent patriots, who refused on any terms submission to
Anglo-Saxon rule. The body of the people must have
remained where they were, as far as the unsettled times
would allow, compounding with necessity, taking the conquerors as their masters, but still in many instances enjoying their own national customs, laws, and language, until
by degrees, through intermarriage, the experience and
exhibition of kindly offices, and the healing influence
of time, they and their subduers became one people. But
the illustration and proof of this will be the business

of the next part of our work. We now only indicate materials.

We have thus had just a glance at the people, who, by bold adventure and steady pertinacity, obtained the mastery in government over the aboriginal British race, and gave England her name and institutions. The name *England* is derived from the *Angli* of Northumberland, and they succeeded in thus perpetuating their name in the country, not because the state they had founded was the most important of the Heptarchy, but probably in part because in their northern home they were the parent stock, and partly, and even chiefly, for a very different reason. It was the Church, in point of fact, that attached the name of the Angli to this land. It is at once a baptismal designation, and a memento of affliction and misfortune. All know the story about the British youth exposed for sale in the Roman Forum, and Pope Gregory's exclamation, "non Angli sed Angeli," and the consequent mission of Augustine to the Anglo-Saxons (A.D. 597.)[1] Ethelbert, King of *Kent*, whose Teuton subjects were not Angles, but *Jutes*, was by Gregory styled "Rex Anglorum." It would appear that the inhabitants of Britain were henceforth in all ecclesiastical documents styled *Angli*, and in process of time the country was by a statute of Egbert called *Engla-lond*—whence our modern *England*.

While Britain was thus the theatre of conflict between the *Wealas* and their Angle and Saxon troublers, what great events have we seen transpiring elsewhere? The whole of Europe and a great part of Asia has been in a

---

[1] It seems almost unaccountable that the Britons had made no efforts up to this time to convert the Anglo-Saxons. The force of Christian charity seems to have been overcome by national antipathy. Gildas is not far from faithfully reflecting the British feeling when he styles the Saxons, " *nefandi nominis Saxoni, Deo hominibusque invisi.*"

state of ferment. The Goths have taken and consumed
Rome. The Western Empire has been extinguished. The
renown of Clovis, Theodoric, Alaric, Belisarius, has been
established. Mohammed has founded a new religion and
a new epoch; and Abu-beker, Omar, and Ali have had
their names emblazoned as champions of the faith.
Charlemagne has created a magnificent empire. Boethius
has thought. Justinian has compiled the civil code.
Aneurin, Taliesin, Merlin, and Llywarch the Aged, in the
language of the Cymry, have courted the muse; and
Columba and Winifred (Boniface) have gone forth in the
spirit of true apostles to publish the Gospel in heathen
lands. Truly, an eventful time.

CHAPTER III.

The Danish Invasion.

The Britons are no sooner overpowered and swallowed up by the Anglo-Saxons, than the Anglo-Saxons are invaded by predatory bands from the same country, and almost the very regions whence they themselves had come. Denmark (*Dane-mark :* the line or boundary of the Dane) once more pours forth its fierce warriors and intrepid sea-captains on the shores of Britain, and the Saxons of the South and Angles of the North, when just beginning to settle their mutual differences, and sit down quietly in the seat of empire, are called out to measure swords with new claimants, who insolently propose to share the plunder, or, as an alternative, take the whole of it.

As early as A.D. 787, nearly fifty years before Saxon power had been consolidated in Egbert of Wessex, the Danes begin to make their appearance in British waters. In Egbert's time they greatly increase in boldness, in strength, in mischief; and in spite of this king's success in fortifying the Anglo-Saxon cause by the concentration of power in Wessex, the Danes, inch by inch, win their ground, until at last, in about 150 years after Egbert had reached his zenith, they succeed in placing a warrior of their own race—Canute—on the throne of *all England !*

The overthrow of Saxon power by the Danes, therefore, was, by a great deal, more speedy than the overthrow of

Ancient British power by the Saxons! This may appear
very marvellous at first sight ; but there is really no mystery
in the matter. We have been accustomed to under-rate
the number, power, and civilization of the Britons, and
hence find ourselves incapable on any rational grounds of
accounting for the length of the contest they maintained.
We cling fondly to a theory we have *created* independently
of facts, and are then brought to a pause by facts which
totally belie it. We have been willing to forget that the
Britons succeeded in maintaining their long and weary
contest despite the circumstance that at the outset they had
been caught under the disadvantage of mutual jealousies
and divisions—as they had indeed been caught before by
the Romans. If we take these two circumstances into
account, viz., the Britons' weakness, through division
among themselves, when first attacked by the Saxons, and
the fact that notwithstanding this, they contrived to keep
the foe at bay for 150 years, we *must*, on all grounds of
truth and fairness, give them credit for a good share of
political vitality, as well as martial power. No historian
denies that the Anglo-Saxons, when the Danes disputed
with them the empire of England, were powerful, numerous,
and, thanks to the tutoring they had received from the
subdued Britons, somewhat civilized. But, we repeat it,
Anglo-Saxon power was broken by the Dane in less time
than British power was broken by the Anglo-Saxon. It
has been said that the Dane had one great advantage on
his side as compared with the Saxon, namely, that while
the latter had to fight with a nation which came forth as
one man to oppose him, the former found frequent help
from the oppressed and smarting Britons, who preferred a
change of masters to a continuance of the hardships they
were enduring. But the former part of this representation
is as contrary to fact as the latter part is in harmony with

the same. The Anglo-Saxons had *not* to encounter a united British people; whole tribes, the *Lloegrians* and *Brython*, went bodily over to them, and we contend that, whenever they conquered a district, they incorporated the natives, and made them fight their battles.

Glance now at the progress of the "Danish-men." Brithric married in A.D. 787, Eadburga, daughter of Offa of Mercia, and "in his days first came three ships of Northmen out of Haerethaland (Denmark). These were the first ships of Danish men which sought the land of the English nation." [1] "First" indeed perhaps to seek the land, but by no means the first to seek plunder. Nor are they the last. More come in their wake, and more again. Like the Saxons before them, they soon "swarm like bees." The wild rovers of the Baltic, the fierce banditti of the Norwegian and Danish mountains, embark in their "cheols" and make for the coveted isle, safe of winning something, safe of losing nothing. They increase in number. In A.D. 840, they came in *thirty-five ships*.[2] In A.D. 851 came *three hundred and fifty ships* to the mouth of the Thames, and the crews landed and took Canterbury and London by storm; but "King Ethelwulf, with his son Ethelbald, with the army of the West Saxons, fought against them at Ockley, and there made the greatest slaughter among the *heathen* army" [we Saxons are Christians by this time!] "that we have heard reported to the present day, and there got the victory." [3]

But the "heathen men" were not to be cowed by a single victory. They meant to find a home, and in choosing one, were not inferior in taste, perseverance, or daring, to the Saxons. In A.D. 853 there was more hard fighting "in

[1] *Sax. Chron.* ann. 787.   [2] *Sax. Chron.* ann. 840.
[3] *Ibid.* ann. 851.

Thanet;" and two years later it is significantly recorded: "This year the heathen men for the first time remained over winter in Sheppey."[1] Ten years further on, "the heathen army" again "sat down in Thanet," "and the men of Kent promised them *money* for peace"![2] The heathen men were clearly improving their fortunes.

Ethelred, brother of the great King Alfred that was coming, now ascended the throne of Wessex—now the leading kingdom of the so-called Heptarchy—and in the year succeeding his accession (A.D. 866) an army of north-men, numbering 20,000 men, landed in East Anglia, under the command of Inguar and Ubbo, sons of Ragnar Lodbrog, and at York the day declared in favour of the invaders.[3] A second fearful encounter ended in the same way. The Saxons lose heart: many fly, but a few, true and brave, resolve to make another attempt, and conquer or die. The latter they are destined to do. Through a whole day they continue immovable against a numerous host; but the "heathen men" feigning a retreat, the patriots fall into the trap, are surrounded, and cut down almost to a man. The victors spread havoc far and wide. No lives are spared. Town after town, fastness after fastness, fall into their hands. The kingdom of the East Angles, as well as Northumbria, becomes subject to the Danes.

The army of locusts moves on—eating up every green thing. In A.D. 871, "the Pagan army of hateful memory," as Asser calls it, invades the kingdom of Wessex; but at Reading meets with a severe check. "The Christians gained the victory."[4] And again at or near Ashdun or Ashdown, when young Alfred first encountered them, "the Pagans, not able to bear the attacks of the Christians, and

---

[1] *Ibid.* ann. 855.   [2] *Ibid.* ann. 865.
[3] Asser, *Life of Alfred*, ann. 867; *Sax. Chron.* same year.
[4] *Life of Alfred*, ann. 871; *Sax. Chron. ibid.*

having lost the greater part of their army, took to a disgraceful flight."[1] Their bodies covered the plain of Ashdown. In this one year eight battles were fought, and before its end peace was concluded: but, by the terms of this peace, the Danes were allowed to remain in the country —though still a hostile force under arms. Two years after this "peace," the Danes took possession of the kingdom of Mercia—the last founded state of the Heptarchy—and the year following reconquered the Northumbrian kingdom, and ravaged the British kingdom of Strathclyde.[2]

Thus, while Rollo the Dane was invading France, and forming a part of Neustria into *Normandie*, his countrymen were spreading desolation over Britain, and both alike were preparing new forces which by-and-bye were to meet in deadly combat on the field of Hastings, and inaugurate a new dynasty and a new nobility for England!

The Danes swept over the country in all directions, now obtaining advantages, now encountering reverses; but wherever they went their presence was like the blast of the lightning. At last King Alfred rose to be the hero of the Saxon race. He made prodigious exertions by sea and land to meet the emergency. He collected supplies, built a navy, organized troops, fought battles, and displayed unparalleled personal bravery and endurance. In a time of extraordinary stress and agony, when his own subjects, instead of bravely aiding his efforts were indifferent and mutinous, and Saxon liberty and Christianity itself in Britain seemed to be lost, Alfred, in bitterness of spirit, retired into the woods of Somersetshire—probably to tear himself away from the strife of parties and unavailing care of the world for a season, and in the enjoyment of internal peace to hold calm communion with

[1] *Sax. Chron.* ann. 871.
[2] Asser, *Life of Alfr.* ann. 875; *Sax. Chron.* same year.

Heaven. Here after a while, accompanied by a few of his faithful followers, and an ever-increasing crowd of fugitives, he led the life of an unknown guerilla chief. But in the spring of the year 878, he came forth from his retreat, and was at once surrounded by great hosts of the "men of Somersetshire and the men of Wiltshire"— almost all of the Ancient British race—who had looked upon their king as dead. "They were joyful at his presence," and the recalcitrant Saxons of all Wessex now eagerly followed him to meet the enemy. Near Westbury, probably on the eminence of Eddington Hill, a great battle was fought, which ended in a complete victory for Alfred.[1] Gudrun, king of the Danes, now sued for peace, and promised to receive baptism as a bond of friendship.

The great army of the "heathen men," however, was soon again in action. Baptism and oaths were forgotten, pillage and bloodshed were resumed. After ravaging great part of the country, they crossed the Channel into France; they returned again to England in A.D. 893, having apparently never disbanded, landing at Tynemouth in 250 ships. Accumulating trials now drew the divided Saxon states more closely together. The old dominions of Kent and Sussex sought union under Alfred, whose name and character, notwithstanding the stringency of his rule, seemed to charm away hostility, and Wessex now embraced the whole of Anglo-Saxon England. The Danes had thus succeeded in for ever obliterating the ancient divisions of the Heptarchy. In A.D. 901, however, after many years of various toil, in war, in government, in study, the good and great Alfred died, "six days before the mass of All Saints." He "was king over the whole English nation, except that part which was under the dominion of the Danes; and he held the kingdom one year-and-a-half less

---

[1] *Sax. Chron.* ann. 878.

than thirty years."[1] The death day of this brave and pious king was a dark day for the land!

For thirty years after the death of Alfred England continued to be a battle-field. The sword during this weary time did not rest in its scabbard, nor the blood of Saxon and Dane cease to flow. But the balance of advantage was in favour of the Dane. The English had now been reduced to the miserable necessity of systematically purchasing peace for *money*—so exhausted were they of soldiers and so broken in heart. At first £10,000 was given, then £48,000. The Danes for a little while retired, but soon got a pretext for returning. They continually increased their price. They next extorted £160,000, and a fixed *annual* tribute of £48,000. Thus was the country, already exhausted of men, completely drained of its money. Rage and impotency now entered into alliance, and the *massacre* of the Danes was resolved upon. Many thousands of their warriors unquestionably perished by this dreadful deed; but so far from crushing, it only exasperated that people, both in England and abroad, to more terrible deeds of vengeance—"outrages even beyond the usual tenor of the Danish cruelty." The end was not far. Sweyn, King of Denmark, in the year 1013, was placed on the English throne. Canute the Great, his son, became king of all England in A.D. 1017.

Now what very forcibly strikes the thoughtful reader is the fact that these usurpations were effected by a compara tively small number of strangers. The Danes, it is true, came over in vastly greater numbers than the Saxons and Angles had done; but the Danes that came over in ships —though these ships were numbered by the hundred at a time—were but a handful compared with the people, now

---

[1] *Sax. Chron.* ann. 901.

grown numerous on the soil, whom they contrived to sub-jugate. They were in fact an organized horde of adven-turers, who, by overmatching the military force of the Anglo-Saxons, usurped dominion over the land. The Danish conquest was a parallel with the Saxon, effected by a few against a numerous and more cultured people; but students of English history have not always kept in mind that it was effected in less time and with greater ease.

Long and desolating wars, such as those of the Danish period, are doubtless very destructive of population. But as both sides would suffer about equally, the proportion at the end, as between Saxon and Dane, would be about the same as at the beginning. But since these were both alike of *Teutonic race*, if their united number at the end was much larger than the Anglo-Saxon population itself (with its ancient British element omitted) was at the beginning, this excess must in fairness be allowed as a gain of *Teutonic* over *Celtic* blood through the Danish conquest. That there was a gain we admit; but the gain was small.

Both the Danish and Anglo-Saxon *régimes* were purely *military* creations. The superiority which prevailed was simply superiority of fighting force. It had no relation to preponderance of *population*. The British element of population was by far the more copious in Saxon times. The British, with its admixture of Anglo-Saxon, was in-conceivably the greater in Danish times. The change was a change of *ruling men*—of legal, political, and ecclesi-astical arrangement and policy. How does this tell upon the question in hand?

CHAPTER IV.

The Norman Invasion.

It has already been mentioned that the Normans, the
next invaders of England, were of kindred blood with the
Danes, as both were with the Angles, Jutes, Frisians, and
Saxons, who had now lost the ascendancy in Britain.

Rollo, a freebooter, the ancestor of William the Conqueror, had fought for himself a settlement in Neustria
in or about the years 898—911.[1] A hundred and fifty
years after, that is, in the year 1066, his descendant William
obtains the title " Conquæstor," and sits on the throne of
England. This great event of the Conquest was preceded
by no long-continued struggle. The fighting was, appro-
priately, between Northmen and Northmen; the prize
to be won was the throne of a country to which neither had
any right beyond that which the sharpest and longest
sword confers.

A time of fearful retribution now comes upon the English
race. Already crushed to the very dust by the strong arm
of the Dane, they are destined to still deeper humiliation
from the heel of the contemptuous Norman. In their fall
before the Dane, they had the consolation of seeing the
victor adopt their language; but now their language is
cast aside, as fit only to be articulated by " ceorls " and
mean persons. Normans become the great, the " high

[1] Thierry, Conquête d'Angleterre, liv. ii.

men," and the Saxons are deemed " low men," as Robert
of Gloucester hath it in his Chronicle :—

> " The Folc of Normandie
> Among us woneth yet, and schulleth ever wo :
> Of the Normannes beth thys *hey men*, that beth of thys lond,
> And the *lowe men* of Saxons."

Ethelred, the Saxon King, while less than a match for
the Danes, who, under Sweyn, made their triumphant progress through the land, had rashly engaged in hostilities
against Richard II., Duke of Normandy, but this dispute
being arranged, had, with better policy, sought the hand of
Emma, the Duke's sister, in marriage; and thus, in A.D.
1002, the Northmen of England, and the Northmen of
France became re-united, and the foundation was laid,
which, sixty years afterwards, supported the claims of William of Normandy to the throne of England. Ethelred,
by and by deserted by his subjects—who, by force or choice,
became obedient to Danish rule—fled with his family to
Normandy, and Sweyn first, and then Canute, obtained
the title of King of all England.

Canute, who, on the death of Ethelred the Saxon, had
married his widow, Emma, of Normandy—so easily did
ladies of that rank and time transfer their affections!—
died in the year 1035, leaving a son by Emma, called
Hardicanute. Harold, an illegitimate son, first became
king for four years, and then Hardicanute for two ; after
him, his half-brother, Edward the " Confessor," son 'of
Ethelred the Saxon, and the last of his race on the English
throne. Edward invited many Normans to England, and
gave them offices, emoluments, dignities. Being himself
the son of a Norman princess, and having spent the whole
of his early life in Normandy, he was more a Norman than
an English King ; and the fact was not unfelt by his
subjects. The preference he ostentatiously gave to Norman

favourites, and to the Norman - French language and manners, expedited the progress of their disaffection, and prepared the way for the great events that were approaching.[1]

When William came over on a visit of ceremony to the Court of Edward—not without secret ambitious purpose— he found his countrymen teeming in every department of the public service. Normans commanded the fleet at Dover, Norman soldiers commanded the forts at Canterbury, Norman captains and Bishops came to salute him.[2] "Edward's favourites came to pay their respects to the chief of their native country, and thronged round their natural lord." William appeared in England more a King than Edward himself. William, with eagle-eye, saw his advantage, and no longer despaired of one day being King of England: "but he said not a word."[3]

When Edward died, William averred that the King had by will made him his successor; and Harold, the illustrious son of the noble Earl Godwin, chief of the Saxon party in England, had been induced by William during his visit in France to swear a dreadful oath over relics of saints, that he would promote his claims. The nation, however, thinking they had had enough of the Normans, crowned Harold King. William, when he heard the news, was deeply agitated. He immediately began preparations for invading England, and conquering its crown by main force. What to him was the will of the people? Such was the prologue to the drama about to be acted.

Unfortunately for Harold, his eldest brother Tostig,

---

[1] Guilielm. Malmesb. De Gesta Reg. lib. ii.; Thierry, Conquête d'Angl. liv. ii.

[2] Roger de Hoveden, Annales.

[3] Ingulf of Croyland, Hist. i. 65. "De successioni autem regni, spes adhuc aut mentio nulla facta inter eos fuit."

this juncture, with an army of Norwegians and Flemings, set up in opposition to him in the North—probably not without collusion with William the Norman. Many battles were fought between the two brothers. The Danish portion of the population, especially in Mercia, gave Harold little support. Northumbria was kept from joining the enemy only by strong Saxon garrisons. Harold's strength was thus wearing away, and William looked on, "biding his time." At last he saw that the moment to act had come. A great fleet of 400 ships, and more than 1,000 transport boats, containing, as is commonly reported, an army of 60,000 men,[1] crossed the Channel, and disembarked at Pevensey, near Hastings, on the 28th September, 1066, only two days after Tostig's defeat by Harold at Stamford Bridge. Harold hastened to the South. On the evening of the 13th October, the Norman army and the army of the King of England encamped, confronting each other.

The morning of the 14th October dawned, and William, mounted on a Spanish charger, harangued his soldiers. The terrible man said : " Remember to fight well and put all to death ; for if we conquer we shall be all rich. What I gain, you will gain ; if I conquer, you will conquer ; if I take their land, you shall have it," &c.[2] The conflict was stubborn and bloody in the extreme. The Normans were repeatedly repulsed. Once they fled in a panic, when the false alarm was given that Duke William himself was slain. At last, however, the tide of battle turned against the English. King Harold and his two brothers fell ; the English army was routed ; the Normans won the victory

---

[1] This number, however, is considered by many historians exaggerated, and 25,000 to be more like the truth. See Macintosh's *Hist. of England,* vol. i. p. 97, and Sismondi, *Histoire des Francais,* iv. 353.

[2] Thierry, *Conquête d'Angl.* liv. iii.; *Roman de Rou,* ii. 187, *et seq.;* *Chron. de Normand. Rec. Hist. de la France,* xiii. 232.

of Hastings, and, without further controversy, the crown of
England was placed on the head of William Conquæstor.
This, in brief, was the *Norman Conquest*.[1]

Now, what is most pertinent here to remark as touching
our proper subject is this : The Normans who conquered
England in 1066 were William of Normandy and his 60,000
more or less fighting men. A host of these was left dead
on the field of Hastings. The Norman accession to the
population of England, therefore, even if all these warriors
had been of Norman blood, was not relatively large. If
we allow again that already, through the favour of Ethelred,
of Emma of Normandy, and of Edward the Confessor,
many thousand Normans had found home and fortune in
the land, and also that after the accession of William
thousands more would flock to sun themselves in the
light he had created; still the number, compared with the
whole people of England, was not large. The power of
the Normans, even far more conspicuously than that of the
Danes, was not the power of *numbers*, but of individual
will and heroism on the part of William and his followers
on the field of Hastings.

But this number, whether great or small, is, by authority
of history, to be materially reduced when calculated for
the purposes of an ethnological inquiry. The fact is, that
a very considerable proportion of William's army was
made up of genuine *Breton* soldiers. Many of his most
renowned captains, who became historic names among the
" Norman " aristocracy of England, were of pure *Celtic*
blood—cousins of the people of Wales.[2] Each of these

---

[1] See Dugdale, *Monast. Anglic.* vol. i. 312; *Chron. de Normand.* xiii.
235, 236, &c. ; *Guil. Pictav.* p. 202 ; Math. Westmonast. *Flor. Hist.* p.
223; Guil. Malmesb. *Hist.* p. 102; Math. Paris, i. 2.

[2] Comp. Thierry, *Norm. Conq.* i. 161-4; Palgrave, *Normandy and
England*, iii. 446; Turner, *Hist. Angl. Sax.* ii. 335.

brought his company of retainers, also of Celtic blood, and the whole together would constitute no slight portion of the traditional 60,000 "Norman" warriors of the 14th October, 1066. This subject shall receive careful analysis in its proper place, when we come to discuss the ethnological influence of the Norman Conquest. Meantime, it is just possible that not a few of the foremost among the English Aristocracy who are proud of tracing their descent from a "Norman Origin" must be allowed to be, in fact, neither English nor Norman, but authentic CELTS from *Brittany*, *Poitou*, *Anjou*, *Normandie*, and, through previous emigration, from Wales itself.

Then it must be remembered that as the old *Neustrians*, over whom Rollo had established sovereignty, were in the main descendants of the ancient Gauls, it follows that the mass of William's common soldiery, though Norman in name, were of *Celtic* race. But of this hereafter.

PART III.

The Argument for Admixture of Race.

PART III.

—•—

The Argument for Admixture of Race.

The Question, To what Extent is the English Nation of Celtic Origin? *Discussed*.

——◆——

CHAPTER I.

The Historical Argument.

SECTION I.

The Compound "British" People.

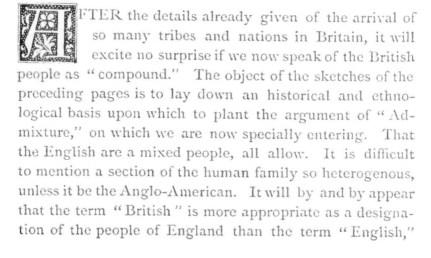

FTER the details already given of the arrival of so many tribes and nations in Britain, it will excite no surprise if we now speak of the British people as "compound." The object of the sketches of the preceding pages is to lay down an historical and ethnological basis upon which to plant the argument of "Admixture," on which we are now specially entering. That the English are a mixed people, all allow. It is difficult to mention a section of the human family so heterogenous, unless it be the Anglo-American. It will by and by appear that the term "British" is more appropriate as a designation of the people of England than the term "English,"

and that "Anglo-Saxon" is sanctioned by nothing but an unhistorical usage.

The *Celtic* race—itself a compound of multitudinous elements—forms the first stratum. Next over that are placed the Romans. Then come Saxons, Jutes, Angles, Danes, Normans, Flemings, in quick and crowding succession, including fractions of numerous less important communities, but nearly all more or less connected by a link of *Teutonic* kinship.

We have already recognized the fact that at a period of great remoteness these two generic stocks, the Celtic and Teutonic, would, if traced backwards, meet in one. That period lay in pre-historic times; but the lines drawn by history, although they disappear from our view, are converging lines, and must as unavoidably meet in a point as the rays of a candle, or the channels of an arterial system. The languages of all these people also display such congruities as justify their classification (along with many others) under one common name as "Indo-European." Very remote, doubtless, was the time when these languages all sprung from one dialect—itself again a variety of a still remoter speech. Less remote by many ages was the point of divergence of Saxons and Danes, Iberic Celtæ, and Cymry; and still more recent—so recent as to have left unobliterated the genealogies of particular households— the separation of the two Norse lines of Danes in England, and Normans in France. Not much further removed was the point of departure of the Celts of Armorica who came over in William's army, and the Celts of the West of England and of Wales, who met them on the field of Hastings.

But, however remote or approximate the points of *departure* of these fractions of the human race, their con-

vergence and amalgamation in Britain has been the work
of a few hundred years. The whole operation took place
between the fifth and eleventh centuries. The cementing
has been perfect—the elements of the mosaic work, except
in fine shadings, are now happily undistinguishable. Some
preponderating race may have gained in strength; the
features of another, weaker and less numerous, may have
paled and disappeared. But each has been influenced by
all the rest. The foundations of the great nation—the
most painstaking, the noblest in valour, charity, religion
on earth—to which, indeed, our patriotism, perhaps insular
in its excess, is apt to grudge no eulogy—has been laid in
concrete. Its greatness and solidity are partly attributable
to the smallness and variety of its component parts : for it
has actualized what was symbolized in the Roman *fasces*—
it has united in one the forces of many.

But while we as a people are thus furnished with a
ground of boasting, we are by the same circumstance also
somewhat humbled. We have little claim, as "English," to
a long and remote ancestry. Our *pedigree* is ridiculously
short; and the parties concerned in "founding the family"
are not all of the sort to be proud of. At the door of the
Herald's College what are we compared with Jews, Chinese,
and Indians? We must find a ground of boasting, if
boast we will, in the fact that we are *novi homines*, or to
speak in a figure, that we are the harmony arising from
the junction of all sounds—the pencil of light produced by
combination of all the rays. The " Ancient Britons" have
receded into the shade; the Saxons find their name a
dispute among schools of antiquarians and philologists :
the Danes and Normans are only spoken of as a
foreign people who once held temporary and usurping
rule; and the resultant community which in its com-

prehensive bosom holds them all in one is called the
English Nation—

"Sic rerum summa novatur
Semper, et inter se mortales mutua vivunt.
Augescunt aliæ gentes, aliæ minuuntur,
Inque brevi spatio mutantur sæcla animantum ;
Et quasi cursores, vitaï lampada tradunt."—*Lucretius.*

Again, it will not appear strange that this compound
race is denominated the *British* people.

It is of no use pleading that we are called *British* because
we are inhabitants of *Brit*ain. People are not called after
countries, but countries after people. The French are not
called so from France, nor the Welsh from Wales, nor
Scots from Scotland.

The truth, which lives in the inner sanctuary of history
will in one way or other assert itself, and it is the business
of science to give it expression. Names, as memorials
of the past, are true witnesses, because imposed in the past,
for simple purposes, and with no view to meet and
humour the conveniences or prejudices of the present.
The Ancient Britons, whether or not they are allowed
to have formed the staple of the people of England during
the first 700 years of our era, are commemorated in a
singular way in one of the most familiar designations of
our nation—*The British.* This fact contains, at the very
least, a suggestion. The *Angli*, the most influential tribe
of the Jute-Anglo-Saxon invaders, are the tribe whom history has continued to honour beyond their Germanic
brethren by crystallizing their name in that of *England*,
and of the *English.*[1] The Jutes, who with Hengist founded
the state of Kent, have now no memorial in our topographical nomenclature, the Ancient British name of *Kent*
having to this day asserted its place, and effaced all traces

---

[1] Comp. Dr. Bosworth, *Compend. Grammar of Anglo-Saxon*, p. ix.

of the conqueror's presence. The Frisians, who, under the command of Ella, set up the South Saxon kingdom, are allowed a faint inscription on their tomb in the name of *Sussex*. The extensive and powerful kingdom of Wessex—Cerdic's great achievement—is well-nigh forgotten, having no modern name to commemorate its glory—its very capital, *Win*chester, having throughout, and down to the present day retained its Ancient British name.[1] The East Saxons still live to memory in the county name, Essex. The Ancient Britons and the Angles alone are privileged to furnish titles, the one to the whole *British* people, and the other to the whole territory of *England*.

This may be but the straw on the stream; but the philosophic historian may see in it much of meaning. It may be argued that the Angli only by accident gave their name to England. Had their youths not appeared as slaves in the Roman market-place, Gregory had never sent his missionaries to convert the Anglo-Saxons, nor entitled their king " Rex Anglorum"; nor would the Church ever after in her documents have maintained these designations, and thus led to their unconscious adoption in after ages by Briton, Saxon, Dane, and Norman. The people, it may be urged, are called " British," and the island " Britain," from the ancient name *Britannia*, and that name is derived nobody knows whence—perhaps from *brith*, because the natives painted their bodies in various colours,[2] or from *Prydain*, son of Aedd the Great,[3] or from some other thing or person. This is the old " Dryasdust" method—very learned, doubtless, but leaving nothing proved. The fact

---

[1] Welsh, *Caer Went*: the Latin modified this into *Venta* Belgarum, thence Sax. *Win*-ton-ceaster, *Win*chester. The root is *gwyn*, white, fair. The *Veneti* of Brittany, the *Veneti* of Italy, *Venetia*, or Venice at the mouth of the Po, *Venedotia*, *Gwynedd*, *Gwent*, in Wales, are all of identical derivation.

[2] So Camden thinks.   [3] So the Welsh *Triad* says.

remains unaltered : the people found here by the Romans were then called *Britanni*—whether that name was given them by themselves, or by the Phœnicians or Greeks, may be uncertain—and the people found here to-day, notwithstanding all admixtures, are called the *British* people, and have a pride in styling themselves "true Britons." Our Queen is called her *Britannic* Majesty. The Englishman who is proud of his descent from pirates, may associate the title of the Sovereign with the territory, forgetting that this, as a new application of an old name, will not really serve his purpose. This name, *British*, *Britannic*, is old, has been adopted by consent, without the force of authority—even in spite of the political and ecclesiastical prestige of the names Angli and England—adopted from instinctive perception of its suitableness as the description of a people whose infancy was purely " Briton," and whose manhood has reached its proportions through the vigorous blood and healthful constitution which that infancy imparted, together with the new blood, wholesome nourishment, and severe gymnastics, of subsequent times.

SECTION II.

The extent to which Britain was populated at the time of the Roman invasion.

How large was the population at the outset, when foreign materials began to pour in ? If small, then the accessions in Roman and subsequent times, though not in themselves great, would relatively be so. If *large*, and this can be made to appear, then we have already one of the bases of our argument laid.

Again, it must be remembered, there is a possibility that in Roman times the Celtic population of Britain, large though it might be at first, was by the invaders materially reduced. This might be accomplished by expatriation of the natives, or by such measures of severity as would cause them to waste away. What are the facts which bear upon this phase of the question?

We propose in this section to show : 1. That at the time when Julius Cæsar arrived, Britain was generally populated. 2. That the expulsion or destruction of the native population was not a part of Roman policy.

1. Britain at the coming of the Romans was generally populated.

This position would admit of strong *à priori* proof, supposing that positive statements in its favour were wanting. But let us look at the facts.

More than three hundred years prior to Cæsar's invasion, this island was the home of a people who, according to Herodotus, exported metals to the East; and who were described by Himilco the Carthaginian navigator as a "*numerous* race, endowed with spirit, with no little expertness, all busy with the cares of trade." This shadows forth to us something like a settled state of society. This people, even then, were not mere wandering hordes, existing only here and there on fertile spots, and gaining a precarious subsistence from the chase, or from their flocks. A taste for trade, and arrangements whereby commerce with distant nations can be carried on, are conditions befitting a population numerous enough and settled enough to be under government. If the tribes of Britain, in the time of Herodotus and Himilco, were numerous and settled, is it too much to conjecture that in 300 years more they must have greatly advanced, both in number and capacity, especially since, by trading, they were brought into contact with the most enlightened people of Asia, or perhaps of the world—the Phœnicians?

K

But we are not left to conjecture. Allowing the 300 years to be out of the calculation, we have later specific descriptions of the state of the Britons which leave no room for uncertainty. An eye-witness—a man whose habits, professional duty, and interest alike combined to make him a careful observer, and whose prejudices as an enemy were not likely to impart a favourable glow to his picture, has sent down to us certain interesting particulars on this point. True, Cæsar with his own eyes saw but little of the island, or of its people. He never set his foot in the Midland parts ; never saw the *Cymry* of the West and of Wales. But Cæsar saw much, and made careful inquiries from others respecting the extent to which the island was peopled. His first duty as general would lead to this. He ascertained the names, localities, and importance of the various tribes, far into the interior ; and the kind of rough census he thus gathered is the best that has come down to our time. It is impossible to take exception to that census.

Cæsar tells us that when he arrived (B.C. 55), Britain *was very largely peopled.* "The population is infinite, and the houses very numerous, built after the manner of the Gauls ; the quantity of cattle is considerable. The provinces remote from the sea produce tin, and those on the coast iron.[1] The inhabitants of Cantium (Kent), which lies wholly on the sea coast, are the most civilized of all the Britons, and differ but little in their manners from the Gauls. . . . . . The greater part of those within the country never sow their lands, but live on flesh and milk."[2]

[1] *De Bell. Gall.* v. 12.   Strabo says (*Geogr.* iv. 197), that the houses of the Gauls were generally circular, boarded, and covered with straw. Diodorus Siculus also informs us that the cottages of the Britons were constructed of wood and covered with straw. Can anything much better be said of the greater number of the houses of our English peasantry of the present day ?

[2] *De Bell. Gall.* v. 14.

Note that Cæsar's account of the population as being very great, even "infinite," and the buildings or houses "very numerous," is not from the legitimate construction of his language to be limited to that part called Cantium, where the people were most like those of Gaul, but is applied generally to the island. Much of the information he thus embodies in his history he had received from others; but as a keen observer and cautious general, assiduous in the employment of spies and in collecting particulars from all available quarters respecting the countries he sought to subdue, he must be taken as an adequate authority for the external aspect of the island, though not for all its institutions and customs. The designation, position, resources, and warlike reputation of tribes, would be amongst the easiest points to be ascertained, while upon habits of domestic life, and rites of religion, he might occasionally fall into grave error. It is true he may have been tempted to represent the population as large, in order to add importance to the difficulties he had to meet, and the measure of success he had obtained; but upon this point we have no evidence, and mere surmise is no argument.

Of the southern tribes with whom Cæsar came in contact, the Cantii, who were by him distinguished as the most civilized, were not those who offered the strongest impediment to his progress. Did he call them more civilized because they more tamely submitted; or did they so submit because they were less powerful than the tribes of the interior? These latter, whatever their mode of life, were at least the most difficult to overcome, even after Kent had been secured as a base of operations. The Cantii, like the Gauls, soon came to terms, and gave hostages during his first visit. Penetrating a little further inland on his second visit, he found no such ready compliance. The Trinobantes

(Ptolemy's Τριυοάντες) in Essex, the Cenimagni or Iceni of
Norfolk and Suffolk, the Segontiaci of Berks and Hants,
the Ancalites of Wilts and Berks, the Bibroci, the Cassi,
and others, were stubborn, unmanageable tribes. Whatever people were the subjects of the brave Cassibelaunus
(Caswallon)—and it is difficult to determine their identity—
they were beyond doubt a spirited and powerful community.
Cæsar ought to have immortalized their *name*, if only for
the reason that they gave the Roman legions the best
opportunity of showing their power in battle. The bravery
and resolution of these people—supposed to be the Cassi,
and the Catyeuchlani (Ptol. Κατυέυχλανοι) inhabiting parts of
Herts, Bucks, Beds, and Northamptonshire—together with
the power gained by confederation, unity of action, and
command in the person of Cassibelaunus, proved a worthy
match to the forces which Cæsar brought over on his second
expedition.

There are, in fact, good reasons for believing that the
Roman general found the Britons so numerous, brave, and
powerful, while the hope of booty which their patriarchal
mode of life afforded in case of conquest was so slight, that
he was glad to leave the island with a show of triumph,
rather than risk more prolonged and unprofitable fighting.
The Romans, therefore, soon withdrew, and offered the
Britons no further molestation until the reign of Claudius,
more than ninety years after the invasion by Cæsar.

Strabo, who flourished soon after Cæsar, in his work on
Geography, speaking of Britain, says that a great part of
the island had become well known to the Romans through
the collectors of *revenue*. This is an important indirect
testimony respecting population.

That the Britons had generally submitted to the Romans
before Cæsar's departure, may be admitted. At the same
time we may mark what submission in that case signified.

It signified simply that the chief states professed friendship, gave hostages, and promised to pay tribute. Technically, they were *tributarii*, who continued to live under their own laws and government, and not *vectigales*, who were subject to more severe exactions. No change had taken place in the government of the kingdoms or states; but a new class of officers were appointed as representatives of the Roman power, whose duty it was to proceed through the country under the protection of the native rulers, to receive the tribute. If the greater part of the island had become known to the Romans through these representatives of the Procurator, it must have been capable of *yielding taxes*—for on this ground alone would they make their visitations. If capable of yielding taxes, then there was a population, and not merely a population, but one that was taxable—in other words, a population possessed of goods, engaged in trade, and under distinct and fixed government. We may notice, in passing, a remark of Strabo's which shows the slightness of the hold established by Cæsar on the Britons. After saying that "divine Cæsar returned, having effected nothing of consequence, nor proceeded far into the country," he observes concerning the temper of the Britons, "they bear *moderate* taxes," and adds, that these were laid on "imports and exports from Celtica." The words which follow, are significant as not obscurely intimating the mildness of the Roman rule, and the careful abstinence from force and provocation observed in the raising of taxes; "it would require at least one legion and some cavalry to enforce *tribute* φόρος, (*tributum*), and some danger would be incurred if force were employed."[1] The revenue raised, then, was not the *tributum* proper, but simply an impost on trade, and this was raised under the sanctions of a treaty, and without the use of force.

[1] Strabo, *Geogr.* lib. iv. 278.

Britain, in the time of Cæsar and Strabo, therefore, was, from their showing, a place of large and widely distributed population, whose power required that Rome should handle it with discretion.

2. The expulsion or destruction of the natives was no part of the Roman policy. Neither in Cæsar's time, nor at any subsequent stage, was there any attempt at expatriation or extirpation, To attempt the former were in direct contravention of the invariable policy of Rome. To attempt the latter would be absurd ; for the island was large, and the natives myriads in number, while the invaders were few, and their presence often elsewhere demanded by public troubles.

The policy of the Romans was, to subjugate in order to *use*. Hence, they sought to encourage, rather than retard, growth of population. Their keen insight had penetrated into that principle of political economy now universally recognised—that public prosperity and increase of population go together. Dead men pay no taxes. Broad acres, if not tilled, produce no corn. The extirpation or exile of the natives would leave the fields uncultivated and the flocks dispersed ; and such fields and flocks would pay no imposts.

Cæsar manifested every desire to cultivate the friendship and alliance of the Britons, if they only consented to recognise the supremacy of Rome. He protected Mandubratius, King of the Trinobantes, and established his authority as that of an ally of the Romans against surrounding, and, as yet, unsubdued states.[1] In this, he observed the policy of his countrymen. Not only the people, but their institutions, their religion, their language, were, as far as practicable, always held in respect ; and

[1] *De Bell. Gal.* v. 20.

thus the prosperity which lay at the basis of revenue, and the goodwill which was the best guarantee against revolt, were promoted. As remarked by Niebuhr, the power of Rome over her "colonies" was in theory, and generally in fact, "the supremacy of the *parental* state, to which the colonies, like sons in a family, even after they had grown to maturity, continued unalterably subject." As to the *provinciæ*, restraint here was still more mild. But in the crude state of things in Britain, as left by Cæsar, there was neither the shadow of a *colonia* nor *provincia*, but simply the general recognition by the natives of Roman supremacy, the delivering of hostages as guarantees of fidelity to treaties, and the payment of certain imposts in aid of the public revenue.

The wisdom displayed by the Romans in the government of conquered provinces, has never been surpassed. In science, in the industrial arts, in the conception of liberty and the practice of morals, the Romans have doubtless been left behind by ourselves and other nations; but in dexterous use of force in the acquisition of empire, and in the adaptation and administration of *government*, it may be doubted whether they have been outshone by any. As their own poet has said :—

> " Excudent alii spirantia mollius æra,
> Credo equidem ; vivos ducent de marmore vultus ;
> Orabunt causas melius ; cœlique meatus
> Describent radio, et surgentia sidera dicent :
> Tu regere imperio populos, Romane, memento ;
> Hæ tibi erunt artes ; pacisque imponere morem,
> Parcere subjectis, et debellare superbos." [1]

Æneid, vi. 847.

[1] " Let others better mould the running mass
Of metals, and inform the breathing brass ;
And soften into flesh a marble face :
Plead better at the bar, describe the skies,
And when the stars descend and when they rise.

Other ancient nations often pursued the blind policy of exterminating or reducing to slavery the conquered. The Romans no sooner completed a conquest than they sought to pacify, often to initiate into the rights and immunities of citizenship. This policy may have originally arisen, as M. Guizot conjectures, from the situation of most of the neighbouring tribes on which Rome first made war.[1] They were dwellers in towns. *Caere*, which gave refuge to the Vestal Virgins when the Celts of Gaul took Rome (B.C. 390), was the first town which preserved its laws and magistrates, and was honoured with the privileges of citizenship.[2] Others soon followed; and the precedents worked so well that a rule of policy was the result.

The Romans, however much they may have striven after political solidarity, seem never to have conceived the idea of an Italian Nationality. From the beginning to the very end they viewed the empire, the republic, or kingdom, whichever it happened for the moment to be, more in the light of an agglomeration of states, than of a huge and homogeneous unity. Hence it was that they never used their power to crush and efface the institutions of conquered tribes, and reduce the whole to one level of uniformity. Liberty, independence, and territory were alone sacrificed by submission to Rome; life, religion, language, all the rights which the laws conferred, and the unfailing favour and protection of Rome were guaranteed.

> But, Rome, 'tis *thine* alone with awful sway,
> To rule mankind, and make the world obey:
> To tame the proud, the fettered slave to free;
> These are imperial arts, and worthy thee."

[1] *Ess. sur l'Histoire de France ; prem. Ess.* p. 5.

[2] *Livy*, v. 40. It is obvious to remark how similar the name of this old Etruscan city is to the Cymric *Caer*, and the pronunciation by the Roman would be identical with that of the Cymro.

Perhaps it was in imitation of this Roman principle of confederation that the Britons, after the withdrawal of their masters, established the sovereignty of the *Pendragon*, and that the Saxons afterwards had their *Bretwalda*, by virtue of which Wessex had a sort of supremacy over the other states.

Upon these considerations there can be no hesitation in concluding that the British population not only was not diminished, but was vastly increased during the occupancy commenced by Cæsar.

SECTION III.

Extent and Power of the British Population during Subsequent Stages of the Roman Occupation.

We shall apply two tests: *first*, the elements of power implied in the prolonged resistance offered by the natives to the completion of the conquest: *secondly*, the statistical details left by ancient authors touching the distribution of the population.

1. The prolonged resistance offered by the Britons to the Roman conquest.

The history of the Roman progress and occupation divides itself by the nature of the events into three portions: 1. The commencement made by Cæsar; 2. The period of strenuous action from Claudius to Severus; 3. The time of comparative repose from Severus to the abandonment of the province. On the first we have already sufficiently touched. The details of the second are of great significancy to our argument.

(a.) From Claudius to Severus—A.D. 43—211.

To stand against great Rome for a single day was no mean adventure. That colossal power under the emperors was the parallel of one of the great military states of modern Europe. If the conquest of India took England a hundred years to accomplish, it were a sufficient proof either of the weakness of England, or of the power of India. If we grant that England was strong, it follows that India, so long able to resist it, must have been strong also. But it took Rome a *hundred and thirty years* of very determined effort, with only occasional intervals of repose—intervals quite as useful to the aggressors as to the invaded—to subdue the Britons as far as the wall of Severus. This it took them without counting the work of Cæsar, and the long interval of inactivity which followed his departure. The subjugation of Britain was not an approximate consummation until Agricola's labours were completed. The tremendous sacrifices it cost Rome to bring about this consummation will be learnt by those who will read the eloquent pages of Tacitus. It were idle to say that she was not in earnest, and strained not every nerve. Rome never did things by halves. Granted that times of corruption had set in, that the emperors vied with each other in disgracing the old Roman character, corrupting the citizens, and squandering the public treasury—it is still true that the power and resources of the empire during the first 150 years of supremacy in Britain were enormous, and capable of instantly crushing a weak and barbarian state. And yet the Britons supplied the Roman legions, the chiefest of the Roman generals, several of the Roman emperors in person, with more than sufficient work to complete their conquest in 150 years; and rendered it an irksome and all but impossible task to keep them in subjection for 300 years more.

The patience, energies, and resources, of the Romans were confessedly worn out when their occupation was brought to a close in A.D. 412. This event was not altogether occasioned by British obduracy, for under Roman tutelage the Britons had at length lost their elasticity; but it was mainly caused by the unparalleled corruptions which had crept into the administration, the general degeneracy of the Roman people, insurrection and usurpation, and the concurrent irruptions of the northern barbarians.

For eighty or ninety years after Cæsar, Roman ascendancy in Britain was a thing in name only. Neither Augustus (B.C. 31) nor Tiberius (A.D. 14) undertook the responsibility of an expedition. Both were content with receiving such tribute as could be obtained, leaving the greater part permanently unpaid. The Britons had leisure to cultivate their lands, and study from a distance the laws and government of Rome. Their efforts were probably seconded by the Roman officials and merchants settled among them. Their towns grew in importance. London became a city. The coinage of money improved.[1] Many Britons travelled abroad, especially to Rome, the fame of whose magnificence had a peculiar fascination to all subject to her sway. But the sense of security and growing power which they now began to entertain, rendered the people by degrees more tardy in the payment of tribute—a badge of subjection which no people ever more impatiently bore than the Britons. This contumacy, and the pressing need of the imperial treasury, at last spurred the Emperor Claudius to action, and in A.D.

---

[1] We have already shown that the Britons coined money previous to the Roman invasion. See *ante*, pp. 65, 66.

43 he sent an army to check the rising spirit of the islanders.

Aulus Plautius Silvanus, a man of prætorian rank, and soldier of high reputation, was the general chosen, and four complete legions, or some 25,000 men, with auxiliaries, probably equal in number, were placed at his command. As Rome had a footing in the island, landing was effected without opposition. Fighting soon commenced, with results favourable to the imperial troops, but bearing evidence also of skill and stubbornness on the part of the Britons—commanded in one of two battles by Caractacus, and in another by his brother Togodumnus. The Trinobantes of Essex, whose capital is believed to have been Colchester (Camalodunum), were foremost in this revolt. The Emperor Claudius himself came over to superintend the campaign. The legions, it seems, were from the beginning little pleased with the duty of fighting the sturdy islanders, and it was found expedient to animate their courage and fortify their constancy by the emperor's presence in the camp. The Britons, after hard and bloody conflicts, were overcome, and Claudius, returning in triumph to Rome, received from the Senate the surname *Britannicus*, in token of his great achievement in Britain.[1] Surely, in the opinion of the Romans, Claudius had subdued no contemptible foe.

But Caractacus, who from the first arrival of Plautius held the chief command, had not yet surrendered. He collected in a short space of time so great an army that for five more years he maintained the defensive, fighting between *thirty* and *forty* battles, and causing the Romans infinite damage both of life and supplies. The Roman commander was hardly a match for him in strategy, and greatly his inferior in energy.

While Plautius was thus employed in the mid-parts of

[1] Dion Cass. *Hist.* lx. 2, 3.

the island, Vespasian was active to the south of the Thames, and is said to have fought not less than thirty battles. Was all this activity, with all these legions, in different parts of the island at the same time, under different generals, merely to chastise a few painted savages? The language of Tacitus is that "Vespasian here laid the foundation of his great distinction, that several states were conquered, kings were led into captivity, and the fates beheld Vespasian giving an earnest of his future glory."[1]

Plautius was succeeded in A.D. 50 by the great general Publius *Ostorius* Scapula, who at once gave presage of the distinction he was to win in Britain, by marching forthwith, although in the middle of winter, to confront the insurgent troops. The Romans had by this time, after seven years of fighting, won their way as far as the rivers Severn and Avon,[2] on which streams Ostorius established powerful military camps, or stations, to restrain incursions from the West and North. The Southern and South-Eastern parts of the island, comprehending some sixteen of our modern counties, were now subjugated anew, with the exception only of the country of the powerful Iceni— the people of Norfolk and Suffolk, and parts surrounding. These had not yet been attacked, and had not sent in their submission. They now rose in great fury against Ostorius; but after a most obstinate and heroic resistance,[3] were at length totally defeated.

Ostorius now advanced more boldly towards the North, leaving the Southern districts under the guard of strong garrisons. He found that the Britons were spread over

---

[1] *Vita Agric.* xiii.

[2] Camden is of opinion that the reading *Antona* (the river Avon), in *Tacitus*, is an error, and that *Aufona* (the Nen), would be the correct reading.

[3] Tacitus, *Annal.* xii. 31, 32.

the parts now included in Cheshire and Lancashire; but the population here was sparse, and offered no resistance. It was otherwise when he went further on to the territory of the Brigantes (Yorkshire). These made a determined stand, and had to be reduced by hard and costly fighting. No sooner was this accomplished than the Silures of South Wales, Herefordshire, and Monmouth, the fiercest and most persistent enemies of the Romans, were in a state of revolt under the leadership of the redoubtable Caractacus. But after repeated encounters, wherein neither party gained decisive advantage, they at last came to a stand and challenged battle on the intrenched eminence, it is believed, of Caer-Caradoc, in Shropshire—a few miles north of Knighton.[1] It was to be a decisive and sanguinary battle. Tacitus tells us that Caractacus harangued his brave warriors in these memorable words: "This day must decide the fate of Britain. The era of liberty or eternal bondage begins from this hour! Remember your brave ancestors who drove the great Cæsar himself from these shores, and preserved their freedom, their property, and the persons and honour of their wives and children."[2] The Britons were ardent for the fray. The Romans moving onwards for the attack, forded a stream and then approached a strongly entrenched position which seemed to defy further progress. Ostorius was dubious of the result. The skill and science displayed in the construction of the work surprised him, and the intrepid bearing of the prodigious multitude of warriors for a time seemed to awe

---

[1] The evidence, on the whole, is, as Camden concluded, in favour of the hill still called "Caer-Caradoc:" but Coxwall Knoll is thought by some to come nearer to the description of the place given by Tacitus. The chief objection lying against Caer-Caradoc is the absence of a river in its near neighbourhood. But Tacitus uses very general terms, and was not himself an eye-witness of the scene.

[2] Annal. xii. 34.

him. The signal for attack, however, after some hesitation was given. For a time the tide of battle was clearly in favour of the Britons: but when the helmeted legionaries pressed on to close combat, the patriots gave way, and fled to regain the crest of the hill. The day was lost to the Silures. Caractacus escaped, but his wife and daughter and brother were taken prisoners. The brave commander made his way to his stepmother, Cartismandua, queen of the Yorkshire Brigantes, who lent him but a treacherous shelter, for she heartlessly betrayed him into the hands of the Romans. He was sent in chains to Rome, where his presence created the greatest excitement and curiosity, as described in a previous section.

But though their great leader was lost, the spirit of the Silures was not yet broken. In a short time they rallied their forces, fell upon the Roman camp, and broke it to pieces, killing the prefect, eight centurions, with the flower of the troops, and routing a foraging party sent to the relief of the camp. By energetic and rapid movements, they foiled the attempt to erect a line of fortresses across their territory, and made prisoners of two whole cohorts of auxiliaries.[1] Ostorius, worn by harassment and excessive fatigue, found relief in death; and it was the boast of the implacable Silures, that they had compassed his destruction, if not by the sword, at least by the toil and vexation they had occasioned him. It is material to observe that it was more than *twenty years* after the death of Ostorius before this intrepid people, in the time of Julius Frontinus's command, became subject to the power of the Romans. We think such facts tell a good deal for the number and strength of the British population of these parts.

It would seem as if the power of the Romans had been paralysed by these fierce and sanguinary campaigns. For

[1] *Annal.* xii. 38.

a season, little or nothing was done to extend or consolidate conquest. An army of 40,000 had not done much under Cæsar. Aulus Plautius, with 50,000, had done still less—for he, and his next in command, Vespasian, afterwards Emperor, had only succeeded with this enormous force in reducing the parts south of the Thames, with a small strip of territory to the north of that river; and even this acquisition was so insecure, that, immediately on the recall of Plautius, it was retaken by the Britons. Ostorius, as we have seen, though on the whole a victor, was made thoroughly sensible that he was waging war with a race difficult to subdue. The number of his army is unknown to us; it was, doubtless, very large—proportioned to his eagerness for conquest, to the danger, and the difficulty. But it could hardly be said to have accomplished its prescribed work: it left the Silures active and defiant in the field.

The next governor of Britain was the celebrated general Paulinus *Suetonius*, who continued his command from A.D. 59 to 61. Suetonius, ardently ambitious, was bent upon making his career in Britain brilliant. He had the ill-fortune to undertake two enterprises, which, while felt to be essential to the establishment of Roman ascendency, raised to the highest pitch the indignation and enmity of the natives, while they also tarnished his own fame. He undertook the cruel task of exterminating the Druids in the Isle of Mona (Anglesey),[1] and to suppress the rising under Boadicea with a coarseness of violence befitting a meaner man.[2]

To show the massiveness of the population, and the strength of the Anti-Roman party, where the Roman cause might be fairly expected to be strongest, Tacitus informs us, that at Londinum (London), which, though it

---

[1] Tacitus, *Annal.* xiv. 29, 30.   [2] *Ibid.* 31, *et seq.*

had no name in Cæsar's time, had now grown into a
"great mart of trade and commerce" (copia negotiatorum
et commeatum maxime celebre); and that at Verulamium
(St. Alban's), the insurgent Britons massacred 70,000
allies of Rome.[1] Camalodunum (Colchester), which had
long been garrisoned with Roman soldiers, was desolated,
and the garrison put to the sword. The ninth legion on
its way to their relief was fallen upon and nearly annihilated.[2] At calamities so great, prodigies were not absent.
The statue of Victory (simulacrum Victoriæ) at Camalodunum, says Tacitus, with a tone of sadness, "fell from
its base, without apparent cause, as if it yielded to the
enemy." "The sea assumed a blood-red colour."

Suetonius was now on his way to encounter Boadicea,
who, at the head of a vast multitude, was ravaging a part
of the country which acknowledged Roman rule. A dreadful battle was fought, which ended in the defeat and dispersion of the native army. The intrepid Queen, as all know,
rather than fall into the hands of the enemy, terminated
her own life by poison.[3]

To obtain this signal victory, Suetonius, be it observed,
had to make extraordinary exertions. None of the steps he
took indicate an opinion on his part that he was dealing with
an impotent foe. If a woman was the leader of the native
battalions, it only proved the heroic character she possessed,
and the respect the Britons paid to her sex. Though the
army under Boadicea was gathered from a portion only of
the British States, the Romans were evidently alarmed by
the attitude they presented. So imminent was the peril
from which the Roman cause was by this victory rescued,
that the imperial Government, when the crisis was passed,
began to devise means for conciliating so stubborn and
untameable an enemy, and sent instructions to the officials

---

[1] Tacitus, *Annal.* xiv. 33.   [2] *Ibid.* 32.   [3] *Ibid.* 34—37.

to deal more leniently and justly by the Britons. The underlings of the Procurator—the tax-gatherers—had been the great oppressors, whose extortions the pillaged natives had risen in fury to avenge. The Romans perceived that destroying the tax-payers would in no wise increase the revenue, and felt also that the Britons were too strong to be trodden in the dust after the manner of slaves. Seutonius received a reinforcement of some thousands of men from Germany to make sure against another insurrection, and gradually, under careful management, the excitement subsided, and peace was restored.

Suetonius was soon afterwards recalled. A period of inactivity ensued; the Romans received the tribute-money, and were satisfied. No efforts to extend dominion in the island were for a while attempted.

It was some fifteen years after Seutonius's departure when Julius *Frontinus*, A.D. 78, felt it necessary to commence measures against the Silures. This people had maintained an attitude of opposition to Rome for a period of thirty-five years—ever since their territory had been first attacked by Claudius; but now, more than twenty years after their great Prince, Caractacus, had been led in chains to Rome, when by many their separate existence is supposed to have ceased, a great campaign is inaugurated against them, and their final suppression is decreed. Listen to Tacitus. " The *ablest* officers were sent to reduce the island; powerful armies were set in motion;" with the Brigantes " various battles were fought, with alternate success and great effusion of blood; the fame of Cerealis," who conducted these operations, " grew to so great a height that the ablest successor might despair of equalling it," and " yet, under that disadvantage, Julius Frontinus undertook the command," and proceeded to the task of subduing " the powerful and warlike Silures" (validamque

et pugnacem Silurum gentem), "winning fame and glory
by the success of so great an enterprise." Evidently,
therefore, these parts of the country were largely peopled,
and by a race of no mean capacity in war.

The next governor of Britain (A.D. 78) was C. Julius
Agricola, whose government and military exploits in this
country have been better illustrated through the graphic
writings of his son-in-law Tacitus, than those of any other
general. Agricola had to begin his command by repeating what Suetonius thought he had finally accomplished—
the conquest of the Isle of Mona. This completed, he
immediately gave proof of the wisdom and moderation of
his nature by trying what effect a kindly treatment and
education might have. He interested himself in the
prosperity of the natives, encouraged industry and trade,
promoted the formation of schools for the young, and
testified, on witnessing the progress of the British youth
in learning, that they were possessed of natural genius
superior to that of the youth of Gaul (et ingenia Britannorum studiis Gallorum anteferre.)[1] While doing the work
of conciliation by tolerance and friendship, however, he
was assiduous in using every available means of extending
conquest. In three years after his arrival, he had succeeded in pushing his way far north, making himself
master, probably, of the whole of Lancashire, as yet thinly
populated, Westmoreland, and Cumberland. About this
time he created the great rampart, called after his name,
from the Tyne to the Solway, as a barrier against the
Caledonians.

In his next campaign, if we judge from Tacitus's narrative, he occupied himself in securing what he had gained,
and made no new acquisition of territory. The country
now called the Lowlands of Scotland, extending from the

[1] Tacitus, *Vita Agric.* xxi.

Tyne to the Frith of Forth, or from the wall of Agricola to the line along which the wall of Antoninus was subsequently erected, still remained to win. But was this space at that early time settled by a fixed population ? If we are to judge from the dearly bought experience of Agricola and his soldiers, and of others after them, this region, as well as the great mountainous district stretching far on to the extreme north of Caledonia, even at that time swarmed with an energetic and warlike people.

The next two years, A.D. 81, 82, were therefore devoted to the Lowlands or Southern parts of Scotland. Many battles were fought. In the second year Agricola boldly penetrated into the North-East of Caledonia. Fearing "some general confederacy of the nations beyond the Frith of Forth" (Bodotriam), says Tacitus, "he ordered his fleet to cross the Forth," and explore the coast. "The fleet, now acting for the first time in concert with the land forces, proceeded in sight of the army, forming a magnificent spectacle, and it frequently happened that in the same camp were seen the infantry and cavalry intermixed with the marines, all indulging their joy, full of their adventures, and entertaining each other with their respective tales of the mountains and the sea." [1]

In the Caledonians, whom Agricola now met in conflict, he found a people fierce and unbending as the Silures had proved themselves to Ostorius. They not only fought the legions in front, but by rapid manœuvres and stratagems, often gained unexpected advantage. They slipped behind the army, cutting down the rear, and destroying the forts just erected for permanent garrisons. They attacked in the night the ninth legion, which was strongly entrenched, committing such havoc as nearly to annihilate it. More fighting, however, by and by, resulted in their dispersion.

[1] Tacitus, *Vita Agric.* xxv.

Next year, A.D. 84, occurred the great battle of the Grampian Hills, when Agricola completely defeated the Caledonians. In this battle the native commanders marshalled a host of 30,000 warriors. They used war-chariots with scythes in their axles as the South Britons did, and displayed other signs of acquaintance with the art of war which surprised the Romans. It is to be noted that this great force was raised exclusively in the districts of North Caledonia—for the Trinobantes, the Silures, the Brigantes, and other "great nations" of the south and midland parts were not now in a state of revolt—and these districts were populous enough to yield such an army just 138 years after the first invasion of Britain by Cæsar, when, if we believe the representations of some "historians," the interior of Britain contained hardly any inhabitants, and such as were found were naked, shrinking savages! They are so figured in some School Histories, with lank limbs, horrid faces, and flying plumes, like the veriest cannibals of the jungle.

The description of the battle of the Grampian Hills is one of the finest passages in the writings of Tacitus. It shows, as in a dissolving scene, the impetuous attack of the patriots, the firmness of the massed Roman legions, the frightful slaughter on either side, the confusion and distraction of the natives when overpowered, and the heart-rending spectacle presented by the field when the terrible work had done.[1] There are signs still remaining of the campaigns of Agricola, to the North of the Forth, in the Roman forts at Coupar Angus, Invergowrie, Keithock,— and other places.

Agricola, after extending the Roman possessions far into Scotland, and placing them under such good government that for more than thirty years the island enjoyed uninterrupted tranquillity and prosperity, was recalled to Rome.

[1] Tacitus, *Vita. Agric.* xxxv—xxxviii.

Domitian could not endure the growing popularity and success of so good a man ; both Agricola and Roman interests, as well as the people of Britain, must suffer, rather than allow the name of a general to outshine that of an emperor and a tyrant.

Domitian was assassinated, A.D. 96. Both Nerva and Trajan, who next enjoyed the purple, gave the Britons quiet. As usual, when the legions were reposing, the Britons unloosed their shackles, practically enjoying independence. We are told by Appian that the Roman government in his time (circ. A.D. 140) did not take the oversight of much more than half the island, and that it managed this half at a loss ;[1] and we imagine the case was pretty much the same during a large portion of the occupation.

In the reign of *Hadrian*, about A.D. 120, the North Britons once more mustered to arms. The whole of the country north of the rampart of Agricola was at once lost to Roman rule. Hadrian was wisely content with the country south of this line.

Antoninus Pius, A.D. 138, resolved to reconquer the lost territory ; and later still, in 207, *Severus* made a most costly and hazardous campaign to the heart of the Highlands, penetrating even far beyond the limits reached by Agricola. The perils and hardships were so great that 50,000 men are said to have perished in this expedition. But in the end Severus hemmed in the Caledonians within the rampart of Agricola, and built a solid wall on the same line as a permanent frontier, confessing by the act a consciousness that to maintain dominion further north was impossible.

This wall of Severus was certainly a wonder of that age, and may be compared with the greatest public works of even modern nations. The stupendousness of the under-

---

[1] Appiani Alexandr. *Roman Hist.* pref. v. and lib. iv. 5.

taking is an index to the power of the people it was intended to restrain, and to the value placed on the possessions it was intended to shelter. This wall, unlike the rampart of Agricola, which was of earth, with castles at certain distances, was a huge barrier of solid masonry, 8 feet thick and 12 feet high, with lofty battlements on the side facing the north. It had 81 castles and 330 turrets, distributed at certain intervals along its whole length. Its extreme length was 74 miles! So firm and durable was the construction that large portions of it remain to this day.[1]

Severus died at York in A.D. 211, while on his way to punish the Caledonians for a new display of their irrepressible courage. Caracalla, his son, made peace with them, and soon after left the island. Then supervened a period of seventy years of quiet, during which the lowlands between the wall of Severus and the Friths of Clyde and Forth were settled and cultivated. The people of the Midland and Southern parts of Britain, also, were placed by Caracalla in possession of citizen privileges; the municipal laws of the Empire were introduced, and the liberty of the subject was placed under the responsible

[1] In addition to the wall, a ditch, 15 feet deep, was sunk on the northern side. On the southern side a military road ran the whole length, connecting station with station. The following rough sketch will give an idea of the wall and ditch in section.

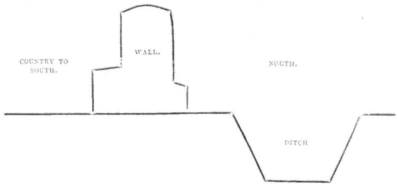

COUNTRY TO SOUTH.   WALL.   NORTH.   DITCH

guardianship of the magistrate. The country south of the
wall of Severus was very generally, in most parts well,
populated ; large and flourishing towns grew up, many of
them Roman municipia and military stations, connected
together by high military roads, passing from end to end
of the island. Trade, commerce, and agriculture prospered. The military stations and the towns had their
clusters of Roman people—the officials of the government
and their families, with such merchants and other seekers
after wealth as the fame of the province had attracted from
Italy and Gaul. By this time the centres of Roman
residence in Britain, such as York, Verulam, Caerleon,
Richborough, would begin to emulate in the sumptuousness
of their dwellings and the beauty of their gardens and
terraces, the costly villas of Rome and Baiæ. But the
country around, stretching from station to station and from
sea to sea, while conscious of the presence of a foreign
governing power, and confessing to the influence of these
centres of life, was of a primitive complexion, and its population—what from time immemorial it had been—*purely
British.* The only change felt was a change from freedom
and independence, when they called Britain and all that it
contained their own, into a condition of subjection to a
foreign and iron yoke. The wars had doubtless swept away
large numbers of the males of the country, both British
and Roman, and many of the British youth had been
drafted off for foreign military service, but this diminution
would be small, relatively to the whole mass, and would be
speedily replaced by the growth of a young population.

(b.) *Retention of the Conquest; Troubles, and Preparations for
Departure.* A.D. 211—412.

The events of the next reigns were not of special importance to our subject. Up to the year 284, when Diocletian

ascended the throne, quietude prevailed. When he divided the Empire between himself and Maximian as joint Emperors, or "Augusti," Galerius and Constantius being rulers of secondary grade, or "Cæsars," the portion assigned to Constantius included the province of Britain.

Constantius found the island in an unsettled state. Carausius, a naval commander, on account of great bravery and skill in his profession, had been entrusted with the task of punishing the Saxon pirates, who in vast numbers began about this time to ravage the coast of Britain. Carausius succeeded in his enterprise ; but having thereby obtained influence and wealth, he was suspected at Rome of harbouring traitorous intentions, and it was resolved to get rid of him by violent means. Understanding this, he took a bold step. Having acquired power, he resolved to use it, and is said to have got himself proclaimed by the army in Britain Emperor!

Britain had thus become a young Empire, under a usurper of daring and resources. Constantius was making preparations to assert his right over the island, when Carausius was assassinated by a chief officer, Allectus, said to be a Briton, who in turn himself, for about three years, assumed the title of Emperor, but was defeated and slain by an officer of Constantius. Both Allectus and Carausius had employed the Frankish and Saxon pirates as auxiliaries against the Romans — one proof among others that the expedition under Hengist and Horsa was not the first from that quarter to set foot in Britain.

Constantius now came into full power. Geoffrey of Monmouth, in his beautiful romance, informs us that he married a British lady, the princess Helena, daughter of King *Coel*, who became mother of Constantine the Great.[1] She it was who became so famous in the history of the

---

[1] Geoff. of Mon. *Brit. Hist.* vi. ; *Rich. of Cirenc.* ii. 33.

Church, as the discoverer of the Holy Cross.[1] Let these stories be taken for what they are worth.

Constantine, who was destined to become first imperial patron of Christianity, arbiter of orthodoxy at the Council of Nice, and the object of Eusebius's unmeasured laudation, was thus, if this story of his parentage be true, and we know of no reliable contradiction to it, a half-blood Briton. He began his reign over Britain A.D. 306, and continued till 337, part only of which time he spent in the island. The Britons during these thirty years had a season of peace and growth.

About this time, the "Picts and Scots" began, under that name (instead of Caledonii) to make devastating incursions from the North. They crossed the wall of Severus, committing depredations on life and property far into the lowlands. Great hosts of "Scots" came over from *Ireland*, their original home, and managed to settle in the southern parts of *Scotland*.[2]

From this time forward till the year 412, when the Romans quitted Britain, the occupation of the island was as irksome to them as to the Britons. The empire was agitated by civil wars or by the inroads of the northern barbarians, and internal corruption festered in every limb of the body politic, threatening speedy dissolution. For about a hundred years Britain was left to the care of officials, who won from lax supervision their own aggrandisement. The extortions of the procurators and their underlings became a matter of universal complaint. Indeed, at a period much earlier than this, Seneca (the moralist), who had lent the Britons money to the extent of £322,000, to

---

[1] Eusebius, *Vita. Const.* iii. 46, 47; *Zosim.* ii. 8; *Sozom.* ii. 1; *Theod.* i. 18.

[2] Nennius, *Hist. Brit.* 13; *Rich. of Cirenc.* i. 8, 9; Bede, *Eccles. Hist.* i. 1, 12, &c.

meet exactions which he himself had promoted, by a harsh
and sudden demand for payment contributed to the revolt
under Boadicea.[1] Their next troubles arose from the
inroads of the Scandinavian, Frankish, and Saxon freebooters on the one hand, and the Picts and Scots on the
other—enemies with which the Roman forces in the island
were hardly equal to cope. The retention of the province
became a difficulty. The usurper Constantine, under
Honorius, proclaimed emperor by the troops in Britain,
took the last remnant of the army away from the island, in
order to make himself master of Gaul. Rome, by treachery
in her own camp, had become totally unable to defend
herself against the hungry enemies who besieged her on
all sides. She left the Britons, therefore, to enjoy freedom
if they could, or to be subject to the next powerful foe that
cared to invade them.

(c.) *Recapitulation.*

From the above sketch we see that the struggle with
Rome continued from the landing of Cæsar in B.C. 55, to
the erection of the wall of Severus, A.D. 209, or for a period
of 264 years. This period equals the time from the
accession of Elizabeth to the present year of Queen Victoria.
The brave Britons, though sadly disjointed, seldom, if
ever, united as a whole—fought, revolted, and fought
again, against the most powerful empire of the world, for
as many years as it has taken the English nation to
conquer almost all its liberties, and develop almost all its
resources. To meet the trained legions which Cæsar
brought against them, they supplied numbers, courage,

---

[1] Xiphilinus, *Epit. Dion Cass.* lib. lxii. 1—4. This enormous amount—
a thousand myriads of money (χιλίας μυριάδας)—is said by the historians
to have been "lent" the Britons "against their will!"

and patriotism, but unequal science and inferior armour.
Still, Cæsar's invasion was, as Tacitus, their own historian,
has declared,[1] a failure. The only wisdom displayed by
Caligula was associated with the most puerile freak
recorded in history. After preparing a large army to
complete the conquest Cæsar had commenced, instead of
proceeding to encounter the Britons, he commanded the
troops to feign a charge upon the *ocean*, load themselves
with *shells* as plunder, and return to Rome to enjoy the
glory of a "triumph!"

It took Aulus Plautius *seven years* to subdue the country
south of the Thames. Ostorius met in the Silures as
stubborn and invincible a foe as Cyrus met in Greece; and
when Caractacus was eventually led captive to Rome,
Claudius treated him with the respect due to an equal in
rank—mindful "how much the dignity of the vanquished
enhances the glory of the conqueror." The victory over
Caractacus " was mentioned in the Senate with the highest
applause as an event no way inferior to what had been
witnessed in ancient times, when Publius Scipio brought
Syphax in chains to Rome, or when Lucius Paulus led
Perses in captivity."[2] Ostorius died, baffled and disheartened; and his successors were for years obliged to
act on the defensive. Suetonius, stern and resolute, came
with a military force proportioned to meet a strong and
capable enemy, and that enemy, although unsuccessful in
the engagements which followed, proved how willing they
were to fight, and how prolific their resources in men, by
leaving, it is said, 80,000 warriors dead on the field. This

---

[1] Igitur primus omnium Romanorum divus Julius cum exercitu
Britanniam ingressus, quanquam prospera pugna terruerit incolas ac
littore potitus sit, potest videri ostendisse posteris, non tradidisse.
Vita Agric. xiii. See also *Annales*, 34.

[2] Tacitus, *Annal.* xii. 37, 38.

is Tacitus's statement, and not that of a Welsh "bard."
That it was no easy victory, and gained over no contemptible antagonist, is proved by the words of the
historian : "The glory won on that day was equal to that
of the most renowned victories of the Ancient Romans."[1]
The glory of the "victory" could only be measured by the
strength of the vanquished. To conquer a horde of savages,
would entitle no imperial army to glory.

Frontinus and Cerealis occupied seven years in subduing
the Silures and Brigantes. Agricola consumed eight
campaigns in carrying the Roman arms through the north-
western parts between Siluria and Caledonia. Severus, as
we have seen, had hard work with the Caledonians ; lost in
one campaign 50,000 men ; and at last confessed both the
invincibleness of the enemy in its own territory, and the
resolution of his government to preserve the province of
Britain, by erecting a colossal wall 74 miles long as a
barrier against incursion.

In a word, the conquest of Britain and its retention
were among the costliest labours of Roman ambition in
the West. The subjugation of Gaul was easy in comparison—it was done "without much trouble to the
conquerors" and occupied not a tithe of the time.[2] The
wars in Egypt, in Parthia, in Pannonia, and the successive
contests with the great Mithridates, were of much less
consequence, if expenditure of time, life, and treasure is
the criterion of importance.

And what does all this imply ? What does it imply
especially with respect to the condition and power of that
"barbarian" people who sustained so long these repeated
shocks from a giant aggressor? Let these questions be
fairly answered. Of the resources and resolution of Rome

---

[1] *Annal.* xiv. 37.
[2] Ammian. Marcell. *Hist. Rom.* xv. 12.

we need not speak. These resources were to the fullest
extent brought to bear; the resolution is legible in every
appointment of a general, in every plan of a campaign, in
every vote of the Senate. Let it be rembered, too, that
the Britons stood alone in the conflict. We hear of no
allied hosts from Gaul repaying assistance formerly
rendered by the Britons. Gaul was now herself a vanquished
friend. Few or no foreign mercenaries were employed,
for though the Saxon pirates hung upon the shores, the
idea of conciliating them by subsidies or employment had
not yet entered the minds of the Britons. They were only
employed in counter movements by the Romans themselves,
as in the case of Carausius. Worse than all, the Britons
neutralized their aggregate strength by mutual jealousies.
Mutual distrust, the evil genius of all clannish confederacies,
whether Celtic or Teutonic, distracted their counsels in
this time of peril, and compassed their destruction. "A
confederation of two or more States, to repel the common
danger," says Tacitus, "is seldom known. They fight in
sections, and the nation is subdued."[1] But broken though
they were into factions so suicidal, they managed to bring
into the field forces capable of meeting Roman troops
numbering thirty, forty, fifty thousand men at a time. The
importance attached to Britain by the aggressors is in
keeping with the populousness and resources here implied.
Picked troops were selected for her conquest; the most
celebrated generals were put in command; the Emperors
themselves in several instances, as Claudius, Hadrian,
Severus, Constantine, took up their abode in the island,
and superintended operations. So great an influence did
successful commanders in Britain obtain throughout the
Empire that they not unfrequently aspired to the imperial

---

[1] *Vita Agric.* xii.

throne.[1] To conquer the Britons was from the first deemed the apex of renown. Hence Cæsar's defiant exclamation : "To what purpose have I so long possessed the pro-consular power, if I am to be enslaved to any of you, or vanquished by any of you here in Italy, close to Rome—I, by whom you have subdued the Gauls and conquered the Britons?"[2] " Here within these walls he (Cæsar) perished," says Dion Cassius, " by conspiracy, who had led an army even into Britain in security."[3] "To be trodden under foot by an Egyptian woman (said Augustus) would be unworthy of us—we who have vanquished the Gauls, and passed over to Britain."[4] The quality of the men employed and the eclàt connected with their operations at head-quarters, are measures of the estimate formed by the Romans of the quality and power of the people they were in the process of subjugating. The number and equipment of their armies and the time it took them to accomplish the work of conquest offer testimony to the same effect. It were to prove ourselves either incapable of appreciating evidence, or capable of ignoring or distorting it, to deny in the face of these indubitable facts, that Britain in the time of the Romans, was inhabited by a numerous, brave, and powerful race.

(d) *The Conquests of the Christian Church in Roman Britain.*

Amid all the confusion and bloodshed of the period from Claudius to Constantine, the Christian Church had not been idle or unsuccessful. Tertullian, about the end of the second century, boasts that the Gospel had subdued the

---

[1] On this account the island was called by Porphyry, one fertile in usurpers—*insula tyrannorum fertilis.*

[2] Dion. Cass. *Hist. Roman.* lib. xli. 34.

[3] *Ibid.* xliv. 49.   [4] *Ibid.* l. 24.

tribes of Britain, *who were yet unconquered by the Romans*.[1]
Origen (circ. A.D. 236), says that the Divine goodness of
our God and Saviour is equally diffused among the *Britons*,
the Africans, &c.[2] British Christians were numerous at
the time of the Diocletian persecution, and some of them
became martyrs to the faith. " The Britons, Alban, Aaron,
and Julius, with a great number of men and women, were
condemned to a happy death." [3] Wales had the honour of
contributing her martyrs, for though Alban was a citizen
of Verulam, and has his name commemorated in the Abbey
and town of St. Alban's, it appears that Aaron and Julius
were citizens of the great Roman station and *Colonia, Isca
Secunda*, or Caerleon on Usk,[4] called also "urbs legionum."
Constantius put an end to this persecution; and as a
consequence, " the faithful Christians who had been hiding
in woods, deserts, and caves, reappeared, rebuilt the
churches which had been levelled with the ground,
founded, erected, and finished the temples of the holy
martyrs, and, as it were, displayed their conquering
ensigns everywhere. . . . . . This peace continued in
Britain till the time of the Arian madness."[5]

In a few years Constantine convoked the Council of
Arles, and there we find three British bishops, one British
presbyter, and one deacon.[6] There were Britons present,
it is thought, at the Council of Nice, A.D. 325. Pelagius,
the man who startled Christendom in the 4th century with

<hr>

[1] *Adv. Judæos*, p. 189, Ed. 1664. " Britannorum inaccessa Romanis
loca, Christo vero subdita."

[2] *Homil. in Lucam.*

[3] *Richard of Cirenc.* ii. 1, 31. See also Bede, *Eccles. Hist.* I. 7.

[4] Bede, *Eccles. Hist.* B. i. 7. " Passi sunt ea tempestate Aaron et
Julius *legionum urbis cives.*" See Geoffr. Mon. *Hist.* ix. 12.; Gildas
Hist. 10.

[5] Bede, *Eccles. Hist.* B. i. 8.

[6] See Spelman, tom. i. ; *Concil. Galliæ*, p. 9. Paris ed. 1629.

the boldness of his speculations, was a highly cultivated Briton, and a person of undoubted virtue. He erred in a too eager attempt to reconcile human responsibility with Divine grace, whereby he is judged to have lessened unduly the sphere of the Divine agency. But his countrymen—then, as now, apt for theological subtleties—in great numbers approved his speculations. Bede relates that the British bishops sent to Gaul for the assistance of logicians to confront the innovator, and adds that those who had embraced the false doctrines were confuted and put to shame, both by argument and *miracles*.[1] It appears from Matthew Paris, that the conference took place at St. Albans.[2] It must not be confounded with the battle of *Maes-Garmon*, near Mold (as if "Garmon" meant *Germanus*, one of the Gallic debaters), or with the preaching of St. David, placed by tradition at Llanddewi-Brefi, in South Wales.

2. Statistical details left by ancient authors, touching the distribution of the British population in Roman times.

We have already, in Section 2, briefly inquired into the extent of the British population before and at the time of the invasion by Cæsar ; and, in the last section, offered details of conflicts which imply a greatly augmented population in later times of the Roman supremacy. We now propose to furnish certain statistical information respecting the position and importance of towns and cities existing in the same period, and to draw such inferences respecting *population* as they may warrant.

The simple fact, that the Roman armies met such opposition as to make the subjugation of the island the work of *two hundred and sixty-four years* (B.C. 55—A.D. 209)

---

[1] *Eccles. Hist.* b. i. 20. Matt. Par. *Flor. Hist.* Ann. 446.

[2] Stillingfleet, *Origin. Brit.* ; Hughes' *Hora Britann.* p. 154 ; Usseri, *Eccles. Brit.* cap. xi.

—that is, from Cæsar's first expedition to the conclusion of the contests with the Caledonians, under Severus—argues, beyond contradiction, the existence of a powerful aboriginal race. It is morally certain that since Cæsar's time the population had greatly increased; and that the different communities, or kingdoms, into which it was divided, had gone on advancing in civilization; so that, when Ptolemy, the geographer, wrote his work in Alexandria, great towns had sprung into existence, surrounded in each case by a widely-spread rural population, fostered not merely by the policy, but by the humanity of the Romans, as well as by the growing intelligence of the Britons, and the divers new quickening influences which wrought upon them.

It is fortunate that we have at hand, written by men in no sense biassed, and at a time when the objects described were in existence, such statistical accounts as render it unnecessary to base our arguments on doubtful facts or conjectures. Though we have no census of the people, no tables of property assessments, to guide us to an estimate of the wealth of the land, still we have factors which are of almost equal value, when the object is not to arrive at specific enumeration, but at a general estimate of the populousness of the island. The following are sources for the kind of information we wish here to supply :—Cæsar's Account of the Tribes of Britain ; Ptolemy of Alexandria's *Geography ;*[1] The *Itinerary* of Antoninus ;[2] The *Notitia Imperii ;*[3] and Richard of Cirencester's *State of Britain.*

Britain, according to Cæsar and Ptolemy, contained a

---

[1] *Cl.. Ptolemæi Geographia.* Ed. Lugd. Batav. 1618. Analysis of, in *Monumenta Hist. Britannica.* Pp. x.—xvi.

[2] *Itinerarium Antonini Augusti.* Excerpt. in *Mon. Hist. Brit.* p. xx. et seq.

[3] *Notitia utriusque Imperii.* Excerpt. in *Ibid.*

large accumulation of confederacies of tribes, sometimes called "nations," but which can only be viewed as clans or princedoms with separate governments under hereditary chiefs, and speaking dialects of one common speech. Ptolemy's account was written in the first part of the second century, and is supposed to relate to the state of the island about, if not before, the time of Cæsar. These two authors, therefore, may be taken as contemporary in the effect of their descriptions. The *Itinerary* of Antoninus was a work drawn up for the public service, of uncertain date, and contains a survey of all the roads of the empire, including the roads and towns of Britain within the Roman occupation, as they stood when the Roman sovereignty had been established. The *Notitia Imperii* contains a detailed account of all the civil and military establishments of the empire, including those of Britain. These establishments were peculiarly *Roman*, but we argue that to whatever extent they prevailed, to that extent must have existed also a body of Britons to be governed and taxed.

There is also a work ascribed to Richard of Cirencester, which gives a geographical and political account of Britain. The genuineness of this work is called in question by some, though maintained by many others. Professor Bertram professed to have discovered it in a MS. at Copenhagen in 1757. Opinion seems now to run in favour of the idea that it is nothing more than the composition of a clever and unscrupulous scholar of modern times, and that the author was none else than Professor Bertram himself. This controversy cannot materially affect the use here made of it. Even if a work of imagination, its geographical descriptions and historical statements may yet be in harmony with truth. Whether written at an earlier or a later period, many of its positions are borne out by ancient

authors, and few of them are impeached by modern investigations.

(*a*.)   *The tribes of Britain mentioned by Cæsar.*

We have to premise that as Cæsar saw but a small
portion of the island, his information must be expected to
be only partial, given, though probably not inaccurately,
in great part at second hand.

Tribes.	*Supposed to inhabit :*
The Cantii	Kent.
The Trinobantes	Essex.
Cenimagni (Iceni of Tacitus ?)	Norfolk, Suffolk, and Cambridge.
Segontiaci	Parts of Hants and Berks.
Ancalites	Parts of Berks and Wilts.
Bibroci	Part of Berks and adjacent counties.
Cassii	Part of Berks (?).

Cæsar had more or less visited all these tribes, and had
engaged most of them in war. Whether the names he
gives be always correct, it is impossible to say. Perhaps
some of them went by different names, or adopted, or were
called by, other names afterwards, but it is to be noted
that Ptolemy covers the regions above enumerated with
tribes bearing for the most part other names.

(*b*.) *Tribes of Britain enumerated by Ptolemy, with the districts they
inhabited.*

Tribes.		*Occupying :*
1 Brigantes	Βριγαντες	Durham, Yorkshire, Cumberland, Westmoreland, and Lancashire.
2 Parisi	Παρισοι	The south-east of Yorkshire.
3 The Ordovices	Ορδουικες	North Wales.
4 The Cornavii	Κορναβιοι	Cheshire, Salop, Stafford, and Worcester.
5 The Coritavi	Κοριταυοι	Derby, Nottingham, Lincoln, Leicester, Rutland, and part of Northampton.

Tribes		Occupying:
6 The Catyeuchlani	Κατυευχλαυοι	Bucks, Beds, Herts, Hunts, &c.
7 The Simeni (Iceni ?)	Σιμενοι	Norfolk, Suffolk, and Cambridge.
8 The Trinobantes	Τριυόαντες	Essex.
9 The Demetæ	Δημῆται	South Wales : Carmarthen, Cardigan, Pembroke.
10 The Silures	Σίλυρες	South Wales : Brecknock, Glamorgan, Monmouth, Hereford, Radnor.
11 The Dobuni	Λοβοῦνοι	Gloucestershire, Oxfordshire.
12 The Atrebatii	Ατρεβάτιοι	Berkshire (?).
13 The Cantii	Κάντιοι	Kent and parts of Surrey, &c.
14 The Regni	'Ρῆγνοι	Surrey, Sussex, and part of Hants.
15 The Belgæ	Βέλγαι	Parts of Somerset, Wilts, and Hants.
16 The Durotriges	Λουροτριγες	Dorsetshire.
17 The Dumnonii	Λουμνόνιοι	Devon, Cornwall, and part of Somerset.

These, according to Ptolemy, were all the tribes in Britain *south* of the wall of Severus, *i.e.*, in that part of the island constituting the Roman province proper, and now denominated *England and Wales*, as distinguished from Scotland. All these tribes were found in these parts in Ptolemy's time, or in the first part of the second century, and probably much earlier.

As to the people dwelling further north, Ptolemy gives some *eighteen* tribes ; but their names and situations need not here be quoted. It is sufficient to say that they were the Caledonians, rendered for ever celebrated by the writings of Tacitus.

(*c.*) *Tribes mentioned by Richard of Cirencester, which are not included in Ptolemy's account.*

The Segontiaci.
The Ancalites.
The Bibroci.
The Cassii.
} As in Cæsar's enumeration.

And also :

The Hedui	In Somersetshire.
The Cimbri	In Devonshire.
The Volantii and Sistuntii	In Lancashire.
The Rhemi	In Surrey and Sussex.

These lists of obsolete names would in themselves be scarcely worth recording in these pages, were it not for the truth they *imply*, beyond what they distinctly express. Nothing is said of the *number* of each separate clan. We are given the bare fact of the subsistence, at the time referred to, of so many more or less organised communities. But this fact of existence is pregnant with meaning. Nothing less is involved in it than that the whole surface of Britain was settled upon by distinct and independent sovereignties. The population, described by Cæsar as dense—" hominum est infinita multitudo, creberrimaque ædificia "[1]—may then, or subsequently, in remoter districts, have been sparse, and there might be wide tracts still monopolised by primeval forests and morasses ; but the country was recognised in all its regions as belonging to known bodies of men bearing common names, united together by common bonds, claiming possessions in land, and capable of enforcing their rights.

This is simple fact, and in its barest form is of no small import to our argument. There are implications in it of greater significance than anything shown on the surface. Of necessity, these communities, before they could for a single day subsist as independent States, must be in command of a great variety of resources. Each State, however small, must have possessed all the attributes of a kingdom, with modes of administering laws, levying taxes for the public expense, organizing armies for offence

[1] *De Bell. Gall.* v. 12.

and defence. Judged by modern notions of a "kingdom," of course these little sovereignties must appear very insignificant ; but for the times, and relatively to their neighbours, they bore quite a different character. At all events each community must have possessed all the essential attributes of a "State"— the augmentation or diminution of the bulk surrounding those attributes, or vitalized by them, would not essentially affect the issue.

It is probable that a community of feeling existed among all these States arising from neighbourhood or affinity, or both. Not that they displayed any excess of virtue in the direction of peace amongst themselves. Their normal state was probably one of bickering. Even in times of national peril, agreeing upon terms of joint action was to them a difficulty. As in similar stages of society elsewhere, if not eminently as a Celtic attribute, a personal sense of importance and strong individuality ruled, and led to the disastrous issue marked by Tacitus—they fought separately as tribes, "and the nation was subdued."

Still we have on record that they formed confederacies. This was shown on the second invasion by Cæsar, and frequently afterwards. The great tribe or nation of the Brigantes often sent troops to assist the southern parts in checking the advance of the Romans ; and even between the clans of the extreme North and the tribes of the South there existed a friendly intercourse. Distance, in those times, would seriously bar association ; but as intelligence of events is prized, so its mysteriously rapid communication prevails among less civilized tribes. Horse and foot messengers are preternaturally fleet among "barbarians." There is reason to believe that the Caledonian clans, not only knew of all events happening in the South as the Romans gained ground northwards, but that they acted from impulse of sympathy, and sent their contingents to assist in repelling the foreigners. If we take the speech of Galgacus, the general opposed to Agricola at the battle of the Grampian Hills, as his own, and not the invention of Tacitus, he was well acquainted with the Roman progress through South Britain, and looked upon the subjugation of that part as a misfortune befalling kindred of his own. "In the battles which have been hitherto fought with alternate success, our countrymen might well repose some hopes in us; they might consider us as their last resource; they knew us to be the noblest sons of Britain, placed in the remotest recesses of the land, in the very sanctuary of liberty .... let us dare like men .... the Trinobantes[1] [the people of Essex] who had only a woman [Boadicea] to lead them on, were able to carry fire and sword through a whole colony, and shall not we, &c. .... In their own ranks we shall find a number of generous warriors ready to assist our cause. The *Britons* know that for our common liberties we draw the avenging sword," &c.[2] In these passages we hear the tone of national sympathy. Identity of race and identity of interest between the mountaineers of the North, and the dwellers five or six hundred miles to the South, are clearly indicated.

If, again, we limit our attention to individual tribes, we shall see that some of them, even when standing alone, were not so ill matched against the armies of Rome. It is sufficient to mention the names of the *Trinobantes, Silures,* and *Brigantes,* to justify this remark. These may be allowed to have been the most powerful in the island; but others were found whose resources and valour were by no means contemptible, as the Cantii, the Iceni, the Catyeuch-lani, the Ordovices, the Dimetæ.

---

[1] The correction of the text from "Brigantes" to "Trinobantes" is allowed by all to be good.

[2] Tacitus, *Vita Agric.* 30—32.

Now the fact that there existed south of the wall of
Severus some *twenty* different States, or tribes, some of them
displaying great resources; and that north of that wall,
according to Ptolemy's enumeration, there existed some
seventeen or eighteen other tribes, of whose temper we may
judge from what we know of the "Caledonii"; and that all
these were contemporaneous and existing in the early part
of the Roman occupation, is sufficient for our purpose
in this place.

The strenuous opposition offered to the Romans for a
period of 264 years, and this generally diffused and energetic population, explain each other. The former without
the latter were impossible. The latter makes the former
antecedently probable.

In this generally diffused population—diffused, yet com-
pacted into independent sovereignties, we find not only the
reason for Rome's long labours, but for the still longer
conflicts of the Anglo-Saxons. Here, moreover, we find
the most indubitable proof of the preponderance of the
Celtic element in the compound people of Britain in the
early centuries of our era. Not only were these tribes
Celts, but they were powerful and numerous. Not only
were they numerous when the Romans began their subjugation, or in the earlier time when Ptolemy wrote, but it
is fair to conclude that during the Roman occupation they
became greatly more numerous. Rome not only settled
over them a regular guardianship, but *cultivated* them, as
a garden is cultivated, with a view to the fiscal produce
they bore. The next part of our statistics will bear upon
this aspect of the question.

(d.) The Roman Settlements, Municipia, Coloniæ, &c., as evidence of Population.

Great towns in Britain were things of Roman creation. The chief towns established were *Municipia* and *Coloniæ.* The former were free towns of the highest order, whose inhabitants enjoyed, by imperial authority, all the rights and liberties belonging to citizens of Rome itself.[1] The *Coloniæ*[2] were also privileged towns or settlements, intended by their constitution and government to be miniature representations of the parent State, as Gellius calls them— " Ex civitate quasi propagatæ, populi Romani quasi effigies parvæ simulacraque." Our information concerning the *Coloniæ* in Britain is limited, and, therefore, even were it essential to our purpose to determine to which grade of *Coloniæ* these towns belonged—for there were several kinds of *Coloniæ* as well as *Municipia*—we are not in a position to do so.

All these great settlements were centres of military power, of trade, fiscal administration, and social intercourse, In some respects they formed parallels to what we find under British rule in India, where the English residents are grouped together under the protection of the military, and where the army is made subservient in the administration of law and the collection of revenue. In these towns would appear all the indications of Roman pomp and wealth, the refinements of cultivated life, the luxury, dissipation, intrigue, which Rome herself, and the great Italian cities displayed.   It may be presumed that the

[1] Comp. Rosini, *Antiq. Rom.* x. c. 23.

[2] Savigny, *Ueber das " Jus Italicum "*, *Zeitschrift*, vol. v. ; Niebuhr, *Rom. Hist.* ; Madvig, *De Jure et Cond. Coloniarum Pop. Rom.*; Zumpt, *Ueber den Unterschied der Benennungen,* " *Municipium,*" Colonia, &c. ; also the Articles " *Civitas,*" " *Latinitas,*" " *Colonia,*" in Smith's *Dict. of Gr. and Rom. Antiq.*

majority of Roman immigrants and their descendants would be congregated in these chief towns.

Now, while keeping in mind the purport of these settlements—the *government* and *taxing* of the native population surrounding them—let us inquire into their number and locality. The number of their inhabitants we cannot ascertain—for no census has come down to us—but the names and position of the towns are fortunately within our reach. Our chief authorities are the *Notitia Imperii*, Ptolemy, and Richard of Cirencester. The *Itinerary* of Antoninus serves to point out the military roads, and the stations which divided them.

"Among the Britons were formerly," says Richard (or, as some think, the scholar who chose to wear the mask of Richard, and who has given a description of Ancient Britain, which at least cannot be invalidated), "*ninety-two* cities, of which *thirty-three* were more celebrated and conspicuous—two *Municipal*, Verulamium [near St. Alban's], and Eboracum," [York, the residence of the Roman Emperors when in Britain.][1] In reply to an objection supposed to be submitted : "Where are the vestiges of those cities and names you commemorate? There are none;" he very pertinently replies : "This question may be answered by another. Where are now the Assyrians, Parthians, Sarmatians, Celtiberians?"[2]

Richard proceeds to describe with much minuteness the remaining great cities. We give also the Greek names from

---

[1] The 88th *Triad* runs thus : "The three principal cities of the Isle of Britain : Caer-Llion upon Wysg in Cymru, Caer Llundain in Lloegr, and Caer Evrawc in Deivr and Bryneich." Caer-Llion, as the seat of King Arthur, obtains from the Triadist pre-eminence even superior to the two Municipia, London and York. It would seem that when the *Triad* was written, Verulamium had fallen into obscurity, and London had taken its crown.

[2] *Anc. State of Brit.* i. 7.

Ptolemy. Richard often gives two Latin names, adding the more recent to the older.

These nine were Roman *Coloniæ*.

1	Londinium, *Augusta*,	Modern	London	Δονδίνιον.
2	Camalodunum	„	Colchester	Καμουλοδύνον.
	Geminæ Martiæ			
3	Rhutupis	„	Richborough, Kent	'Ρουτούπιαι.
4	Thermæ, *Aquæ Solis*	„	Bath	'Ύδατα Θερμα.
5	Isca, *Secunda*[1] (Silurum)	„	Caerleon on Usk	
6	Deva, *Getica*	„	Chester	Δηουνα.
7	Glevum, *Claudia*	„	Gloucester	
8	Lindum	„	Lincoln	Λινδον.
9	Camboricum	„	Cambridge	

Of the above, only two have become insignificant—3 and 5.

Ten were under the " Latian Law " :[2]

1	Durnomagus	Castor-on-Neve, or Water Newton[3]	
2	Caturracton	Now Catterick, Yorkshire	Κατουρρακτονιον.
3	Coccium	Now Ribchester, Lancashire	
4	Lugubolia	„ Carlisle	
5	Pteroton	„ Burghead, Scotland	Πτερωτον στρατοπεδον.
6	Victoria	„ Dealgrin, Ross, Scotland	Ουικτορια.
7	Theodosia	„ Dumbarton, Scotland	
8	Corinium	„ Cirencester	Κορινιον.
9	Sorbiodunum	„ Old Sarum	
10	Cambodunum	„ Slack, Yorkshire	Καμουνλοδουνον.

[1] Strangely enough this town, so celebrated in Roman times, is not mentioned by Ptolemy. When he wrote it had not risen into notice. The only Silurian city he gives is Βούλλαιον (Builth.)

[2] Cities *latio jure donatæ* were inferior in privileges to the *Coloniæ*: but they had rights corresponding to those granted to the ancient inhabitants of Latium. They were allowed their own local laws and were exempt from the jurisdiction of the Roman prætors. See Rosini, *Antiq. Rom.* x.; and **Art.** *Latinitas*, in Smith's *Dict. of Gr. and Rom. Antiq.*

[3] The modern name, *Water*-Newton hands down, translated, the ancient Celtic element, *Durnomagus* ; Welsh, *dwr*, water, so common in Celtic local names. See Part III. chap. ii. § 3 ; 1 (*b*).

Twelve were "Stipendiariæ";[1]

1	Venta Silurum	Now Caer Gwent, Mon.	
2	Venta Belgarum	,, Winchester	Ουεντα.
3	Venta Icenorum	,, Caistor, or Norwich	Ουεντα.
4	Segontium	,. Caer Seiont, Carnarvon	
5	Maridunum	,, Carmarthen	
6	Ragæ	,, Leicester	Ραγε.
7	Cantiopolis	,, Canterbury	Δαρουενον.
8	Durinum	,, Dorchester[2]	
9	Isca	,, Exeter	Ισκα.
10	Bremenium	., Ribchester, Northumberland	Βρεμενιον.
11	Vindoaum	Near Andover (Egbury Camp, probably)	
12	Durobrivæ	Now Rochester	

The above lists, along with the two *Municipia*, Verulam and York, embraced, according to Richard's enumeration, the *thirty-three* "more celebrated and conspicuous" cities of the Romans in Britain. "Let no one," he, however, adds, "lightly imagine that the Romans had not many others besides those above mentioned. I have only commemorated the *more celebrated*." Of the "ninety-two," he leaves fifty-nine unmentioned, as being less noted, and probably less populous places.

Of the size and population of these more "celebrated" towns we have no information, and of course must not judge of their celebrity from the examples of great towns of modern times. The importance of a Roman city would often depend on the strength of its fortress, or on the family or official dignity of the *comes*, *dux*, or *propractor*, as the case

---

[1] The "Stipendiary" citizens were those who were subject to a fixed money tribute, called "Stipendium," in contradistinction to the "vectigales," who paid a certain portion, as a tenth or twentieth part of the produce of their lands, &c.

[2] Welsh, *dwr*, water. *Dorchester* is on the river Froom. Names of towns having this element in them, almost without exception, are of Celtic origin. Of *dwr*, in Rochester, the *r* alone remains.

might be, who formed the centre of its society, and guided its affairs.

The subsidence of many of these once wealthy and splendid cities into obscurity, so that in some instances not even a trace of them is easily discoverable—such as *Sorbiodunum* (Old Sarum), *Segontium* (Caer Seiont), and even the great Municipium *Verulamium*, itself—not only shows how evanescent are the noblest creations of man, but also how varying at different epochs are the conditions under which local prosperity is guaranteed. These great cities, sinking through sheer inanition, have wasted away and totally disappeared, while the population of Britain in the gross has immensely advanced. But the conditions of urban prosperity in Britain have totally altered since those cities grew into note. Great military roads and stations no longer nourish *nuclei* of population into growth and wealth. Cities are born and nurtured in our times from causes different and superior—the demands of the arts of peace, of trade and commerce, of health and taste.

But now let us observe the *position* and *distribution* of the above principal Roman cities. We think we may find here an interesting clue to the distribution, density, and wealth of the aboriginal inhabitants. These cities we consider as watch-towers to survey the surrounding population, and as granaries to be filled from the produce of their toil. If this view of the history and political life of the period is correct, then we may expect that wherever the Romans were well established—carried on a prosperous trade—had to keep in check a numerous subject race—and were surrounded with ample means of revenue—there *coloniæ*, military stations, and other Roman centres of population would most abound. Let us now test the theory by the facts as borne out by the preceding tables.

One only of the *coloniæ* is found in Britannia Secunda,

Roman Cities of Britain

1. Isca (*Exeter*).
2. Durinum *Dorch.*
3. Sorbiodunum (*Old Sarum*).
4. Venta Belgarum (*Winchester*).
5. Vindonum.
6. Durobrivae.
7. Cantiopolis.
8. Rhutupis.
9. Londinium.
10. VERULAMIUM.
11. Camalodunum.
12. Thermae.
13. Corinium.
14. Glevum.
15. Venta Silurum.
16. Isca Silurum.
17. Maridunum.
18. Camboricum.
19. Duromagus.
20. Ragae.
21. Venta Iceni.
22. Lindum.
23. Deva.

24. Segontium.
25. Cambodunum.
26. Coccium.
27. ERORACUM.
28. Caturracton.

or Wales. This is *Isca*, or Caerleon on Usk, the reputed seat of Caractacus when leader of the Silures, and in post-Roman times, of *Arthur* and his fabled Knights of the Round Table. Three other but inferior cities are located in Wales, Maridunum (Carmarthen), Segontium (Caerseiont) near Carnarvon in the North, and Venta Silurum (Caerwent, or Caergwent), on the eastern limit of Wales towards the South—thus relatively to each other occupying a triangular position, and well distributed. These are of the inferior order of *stipendiariæ*. In Richard's enumeration, Scotland was supplied with three : Theodosia (Dumbarton), Pteroton (Burghead), and Victoria (Dealgrin) ; and all these belonged to the third order, or cities of the " Latian Law."

Now as to the freest and most privileged cities : Shall we find these situated where wealth most abounded, where population was thickest, and where considerations of public safety, as against the incursions of the Frankish and Saxon plunderers, would advise protection ? We think we shall. Let reference be made to the outline map the other side. These cities cluster about the Thames, especially in Kent, more than in any other part of the island. Here we find London, Canterbury, Rochester, Richborough, Colchester, St. Alban's, and Cambridge. They also abound in the tract of country between the Isle of Wight and Gloucester ; here are Dorchester, Exeter, Old Sarum, Winchester, the town Vindonum, near Andover—of which there remains no trace—Bath, Cirencester, Gloucester, Caerwent, and Caerleon. These are suited by position not only to fleece an abounding population, but also to check the Britons of Cornwall, Devon, and Wales. But for the whole of the Midland counties in Richard's list, Leicester stands alone ; and the town Venta Icenorum, near Norwich, Castor and Lincoln are the only other stations he gives for the whole of the Eastern counties as being " celebrated " cities.

Thus *eighteen* of the thirty-three important towns enumerated by our author were south of a line drawn east and
west from Cambridge to Carmarthen ; while only *ten* were
located in the whole remaining territory, from that line to
another, drawn from Tynemouth to Carlisle, or the line of
the wall of Severus—a district thrice as large.

Something is doubtless to be learned from the superior
celebrity of these thirty-three cities—although we must
carefully keep in mind, in forming judgment respecting the
number of the native population, and the Roman residents
respectively, that these were less than half the actual
number of towns which Richard says existed. These were
so distinguished above the rest, as to deserve, in his
opinion, special mention. The remaining fifty-nine, whose
names he omits, were of less importance. Since he gave
his list from a document drawn up, as he says, by " a
Roman general," corrected by comparison with " Ptolemy
and others," we may take its contents as substantially
reliable ; and shall probably not be far from the truth, if
we take the greater celebrity of these thirty-three cities, as
arising from their military and commercial importance.

But we should fall far short of an adequate idea of the
state of things in Roman Britain, if we took these as the
only cities worthy of mention. Richard's may have been
cities all celebrated at the *same time*—the time of the
particular " Roman general" referred to—and " celebrated," by reason of attributes, mainly, which would strike
a *general* as of prime value, such as their strategical
advantages, their strength as fortresses, their capacity as
castra or camps, and their situation amid a region affording
abundant supplies ; or they may have won celebrity at
different times in the course of the Roman occupation
before the document was compiled. But, that other great
cities existed, which at one time or other of the Roman

dominion, equalled the chief of these thirty-three of Richard's in fame and wealth, cannot for a moment be questioned. We have marked the positions of seventy or eighty of these on the map by a circlet. The names of all of them are well known, and the positions they occupy show that no part of the island was destitute of some great centre of Roman life and influence. The following are among the better known :—

1. In Britannia Prima,[1] or South Britain.

Dubris (Dover).	Ad Aquas (Wells).
Clausentum (Hants).	Tamesis (Wallingford).
Avalonia (Glastonbury).	Reguum (Chichester).
Ischalis (Ilchester).	Calleva Atrebatum[2] (Silchester).
Maldunum (Malmesbury).	Uxella (Bridgewater).
Anderida (Pevensey).	Abone (Bitton).
Bibracte (Wickham).	Noviomagus (Holwood Hill).
Tamara (Tamerton).	

2. In Britannia Secunda (Wales).

Menapia (St. David's).	Branogena (Worcester).
Nidum (Neath).	Luentium (Llanddewy).
Bannium (Old Brecon)	Conovium (Conway).
Gobannium (Abergavenny).	Bullæum (Builth).
Ad Vigesimum (Ambleston).	Mediolanum (? Clawdd Coch).

[1] It hardly needs mentioning that the island was divided by the Romans into five parts, exclusive of Caledonia, as shown in map :—1. *Britannia Prima*, in the south ; 2. *Britannia Secunda*, or Wales ; 3. *Flavia Cæsariensis*, midland ; 4. *Maxima Cæsariensis*, further north, far as the Tyne ; *Valentia*, thence to Firth of Forth and Clyde.

[2] See a graphic description of the present state of the site of this famous Roman city in C. Knight's *Old England*. "We look round and we ask the busy thatchers of the ricks where are the old walls ? for we can see nothing but extensive cornfields bounded by a somewhat higher bank than ordinary—that bank luxuriant with oak, and ash, and springing underwood. . . . It is a tribute to the greatness of the place, that to whomsoever we spoke of these walls and the area within the walls, they called it *the city*. Here was a city, of one church and one farmhouse," &c.

N

Bovium (Cowbridge).   Varæ (near Bodffari).
Ariconium (Weston).   Bravinium (Leintwardine).
Leucarum (Loughor).   Rutunium (Rowton).
Burrium (Usk).   Bovium (Bangor Iscoed).
Magnæ (Kenchester).   Uriconium (Wroxeter).

3. *Flavia Cæsariensis.* (*Midland and Eastern parts.*)

Trajectus (Aust).   Cambretonium (Tuddenham).
Durolitum (near Romford).   Utocetum (Uttoxeter).
Magiovinium (Fenny Stratford).   Crococalana (Brough).
Brinavæ (Chipping Norton).   Mancunium (Manchester).
Villa Faustini (Bury St. Edmunds).   Sulloniacæ (Brockley).
Venonæ (Claycester).   Forum Dianæ (Dunstable).
Mediolanum (Chesterton).   Lactodorum (Towcester).
Causennæ (Ancaster).   Durolipons (Godmanchester).
Condate (Congleton).   Iciani (Ickboro).
Durocina (Dorchester).   Derventio (Lit. Chester).
Cæsaromagus (Chelmsford).   Branodunum (Brancaster).
Ælia Castra (Alcester).   Segelocum (Littleborough).
Tripontium (near Lilbury).   Ad Banum (Doncaster).
&c., &c.

We must cease this kind of enumeration. Suffice it to say, that many more cities of note at one time or other during the Roman occupation, lie further north in the two provinces of Maxima Cæsariensis and Valentia. The names above given (which are all represented on the map by the circular marks) show how thickly strewn were the Roman settlements.

Our argument from all this is brief, and has already been stated. These settlements would have no meaning without a native population around each to govern and tax. The Romans never attempted settling in this island with the view of expelling the natives, and colonizing it with their own countrymen. Their *Coloniæ* here were what Cicero calls the old Italian Coloniæ, "propugnacula imperii," defences or bulwarks of the empire, like Cremona or Placentia. They were specifically what we have described them—*military* and *trade* settlements, chiefly the former. When the soldier could no longer be spared here, the body of the Roman population left with him,—a sufficient indication of the relation of the one to the other. The greater number of chief cities being in the south, near the Thames, and the coast of Gaul, indicates a thicker native population, and more solid settlement of the invader. From one end of the map to the other, whenever we notice the Roman city, there is the Roman military road, the favourable military post, the well-watered and productive country —and, doubtless, *there* was found, at the time the spot was fixed upon, a surrounding native industrious peasantry, an agricultural and mercantile class, whose field labours and trade would prove remunerative to the tax-gatherer. The very considerable number of these centres of military, fiscal, and municipal administrations, must be considered as conclusive proof of a generally diffused and numerous British population.

3. The addition to the population through the accession of Roman residents.

However general the answer which must necessarily be given, we cannot avoid, in the conduct of this argument, asking the question : What was the comparative strength of the British and Roman races during the supremacy of the latter in the island? If the influx of Romans was so large and permanent as to cast into the shade the aboriginal inhabitants, then the influence of ancient British blood in the future compound population must be correspondingly reduced. It would seem that, relatively, the Romans permanently residing in Britain were very few ; and we shall by and by have to show that out of these few only a fraction remained when the imperial army was ordered to depart.

N 2

(*a.*) The first and largest accession of Roman blood was
in the army. This portion, however, had little chance of
settlement on the soil. They gradually disappeared
through casualities of war, natural mortality, or removal
to foreign stations, and seldom had opportunity of con-
tracting home attachments in this land. It is also to be
remembered that the legions, though called "Roman,"
were, in fact, recruited from all nations subject to Rome,
and that those which fought in Britain were in great part
recruited from Gaul. Their children, therefore, if they
married British wives, as they were at liberty to do, and in
all likelihood occasionally did, would only contribute to
swell the *Celtic* population. That Germans, as Leo thinks,[1]
were numerous in these legions; nay, indeed, that men
from all lands acknowledging Roman sway, were found in
them, is all but certain, as we shall by and by have
occasion again to indicate. But the point to be here noted
is, that the army, however itself compounded, was not an
appreciable ingredient in the sum total of the inhabitants.

(*b.*) The next element of Roman population were the
numerous civil functionaries, and their families, who, along
with the military officers, and their families, would form
the society of every *Colonia*, and other chief town.

Rome, and all her provinces, were eaten up by these
people. Under the governor of the island, as we learn
from the *Notitia Imperii*, were placed five assistant
governors for the five provinces already enumerated.
These were, two *Consulares*, or men of consular rank,
for the two provinces of the North, Valentia and
Max. Cæsariensis, and three *Præsides*, or presidents for
the three more southern provinces. Then there were other
three great officials, whose functions were more general;

---

[1] *Vorlesungen über die Gesch. des Deutschen Volkes und Reiches*, vol. i.
268.

one called *Comes litoris Saxonici* (Count of the Saxon
shore), to watch over the piratical depredations of the
Saxons on the Southern and South-Eastern coast; another,
called *Comes Britanniarum*, and a third the *Dux Britanniarum*, whose duties related to the military operations and
great strategic posts of the island.

Under these chiefs, the subordinate functionaries, military, civil, and ecclesiastical, would be counted by thousands.
Then would come their families and dependents, numbering
many more thousands, and forming in every Municipium,
Colonia, and other city, a compact Roman residentiary
body.

(*c.*) The merchants, tradesmen, artists, &c., formed
another very considerable ingredient in the Roman
population proper.

(*d.*) But we may note that all these people were confined
to the cities and towns we have been enumerating; and
that in these same towns was resident a large population
purely British. If the whole population in the Roman
cities had been Roman, it were a serious item in the whole.
But probably in these very towns the great majority of
the inhabitants were of the original race of the country.
These cities, in most cases, had once been British cities,
and the men and women who once ruled, as well as those
who served there, had now been made servants to the new
possessors, until such time as, one after another, they
might again win their rights of citizenship. The great
body of the servile class were, doubtless, Britons—the
"hewers of wood and drawers of water" were not brought
from Italy while so many were to be found among the
conquered people. The masters were now Romans, the
servants Britons. But all Britons were not servile. Britons
would be at liberty to improve their ruined fortunes as
they listed. As tradesmen, dealers, merchants, mechanics,

agriculturists, gardeners, &c., they enjoyed freedom of action. Submission to the laws was all that was exacted.

We have given, we think, as ample a view of the Roman element in the population as the truth requires; and yet feel warranted in concluding that this element, compared with the whole population throughout the country, was but a small—an almost inappreciable fraction.

4. The Roman residents withdrew, *en masse*, from Britain when the military occupation terminated.

The fact thus stated, if true, is a very surprising one. The Romans had been masters in Britain for more than *four hundred years*. They had been engaged in all the enterprises in which a conquering people delight in a newly-acquired land. They had made colossal fortunes; had been born and educated here for eight or ten generations running in the same families; their sires and grandsires for as many generations were buried here; cities, large and splendid—temples, classic and colossal—villas and baths, rivalling those of Baiæ and Pompeii—fortresses, roads, bridges, amphitheatres, which would command the admiration of ages, had been reared by them all over the island; and the images and altars of their gods consecrated a thousand spots from South to North; and yet, no sooner does the army vanish, than the Roman people quit the island, leaving all these splendid and precious memorials of their wealth, genius, and piety to be the property of the liberated Britons! It is an astounding fact.

The Romans must have had hard times of it in Britain, and the times must have been growing worse, to lead to such an issue. It was so. After much and long prosperity, adversity asserted her right, and bore down upon them with unsparing severity. Civil commotions increased. Property became insecure. Military adventurers snatched the sceptre of authority from the hand of the ruler. The army became divided and fought against itself. Rome torn up by faction, weakened by corruption, harassed by external foes, became incapable of protecting her distant though favourite province. The spirit of the Britons re-gained its elasticity, and seized on the heritage of its late rulers. The Romans saw no prospect of quiet, and so, compounding with necessity, they went to try their fortunes elsewhere.

The Saxon Chronicler informs us that, A.D. 418, " the Romans collected all their treasures that were left in Britain, and some they hid in the earth so that no one has since been able to find them, and some they carried with them into Gaul." [1]

The *Triad* relates that " the third invading tribe which came to the Isle of Britain, *and departed from it,* were the Cæsarians, who through violence continued in this island upwards of four hundred years, until they went back into the country of Rhufain (Rome)" . . . " and there remained of these only women and young children under the age of nine years, *who became a part of the Cymry.*" [2]

Scarcely is anything of the kind known elsewhere in history ; and yet we can hardly disbelieve the representa-tion. We may have a difficulty in accounting for it, but the fact cannot be cavilled at. It is clear that, while successive Emperors had squandered untold wealth in Britain, as if they would compensate for the decay which

---

[1] *Sax. Chron.* ann. 418. This was the year of the *first* great departure ; the entire clearance took longer time. On one or two occasions, too, they returned to assist the Britons ; hence the year 426 is often given for the final evacuation.

[2] *Myv. Archæology of Wales.* ii. 58.

was wasting Rome by adorning this remote limit of the Empire with

"High towers, fair temples, goodly theatres,
Strong walls, rich porches, princely palaces,
Large streets, brave houses, sacred sepulchres,
Sure gates, sweet gardens, stately galleries
Wrought with fair pillars and fine imageries,"

the Roman people did not find in this country a congenial home. The splendour was the creation of the authorities. The British population were kept under guard of the military. The Roman traders, capitalists, functionaries, &c., were here to push their fortunes, like the English now in India under protection of force. The machinery was lubricated by the legions. When these became demoralised and faltered in their allegiance, setting up emperors of their own, until at last they were led to Gaul by their last chosen, Constantine, "the tyrant," and the island was left exposed, confusion at once ensued, and no time was lost when the legitimate Emperor, Honorius, became impotent to succour, in deciding upon quitting the island for ever. The guilty feeling of usurpers, no longer capable of holding their ground, possessed the whole body. Such only as were on intimate terms with the Britons, with young children and women, from whom nothing was to be feared, continued to live in Britain. However distinct the Roman people had kept themselves, in the mass, from the natives, it is impossible but that in 400 years a home feeling would grow up, alliances take place, friendships be formed, and interests established which would cause many a Roman to feel among the Britons and be treated by them as one of themselves. But these would be few compared with the whole. The truth remains that the Roman race quitted the land, and left the ancient possessors, who were spread, as we have shown, over its old surface, in quiet enjoyment of all it contained.

At the departure of the Romans, therefore, the Ancient Britons were a numerous, and comparatively unmixed people. Our conclusion on the former is categorical, and certain; on the latter, it is subject to qualification, as we now proceed to explain.

SECTION IV.

Admixture of Race during the Roman Occupation.

THE Roman law contained no prohibition against inter-marriage. If any impediment arose, it would be from the repugnance of the natives. But in all nations there are persons little governed by national sentiment, ready to adapt themselves to circumstances, and preferring personal intercourse and advantage to abstract ideas. Residence in the same neighbourhood through life would make friends of Roman and British families. In 400 years antipathy would stand little chance of retaining its vigour among the peasantry, and persons of equal rank in towns. Neighbourly feeling, cherished by deeds of common politeness, and of kindness in seasons of need, would overlay opposite senti-ments, and friendships and matrimonial alliances would occur. Whether it be a fact or not that Constantius him-self set the example by marrying a British princess (Helena), the circumstance that the statement was made in early times, and credited, shows that the event was not im-probable—that, in other words, the relations of conquerors and conquered were not such that persons of the highest rank might not intermarry with the natives.

The soldiery who came without wives would, in many cases, marry native women. Where the soldiers were

Celts from Gaul, or elsewhere, as already intimated, the
junction would produce no intermixture of *race ;* but we
must remember that the Roman army was a conglomeration
of fragments from almost every nation in the then known
world. The cases of inter-marriage between soldiers and
British women might, therefore, include curious examples.
We need only consult the *Notitia Imperii,* and the
inscriptions discovered on tombs, altars, &c., to see that
the legions were composed of Spaniards, Thracians,
Dacians, Cilicians, Sarmatians, Dalmatians, Tungrians,
Germans, Moors, and even Indians. Did some of all these
marry British wives? When we remember how in succeeding generations the characteristics of ancestry reappear,
as evidenced by the natural history of man, how can we
wonder at the variety of cranial development, physiognomy,
complexion, temperament, displayed in the streets of every
village and town of England and Wales!

The "women and young children" are allowed by the
Triad to have become "a part of the *Cymry.*" They
merged into the mass, adopted the speech and manners of
the Britons, and were soon in their descendants not dis-
tinguishable from them.

Let it be kept in mind that long before the departure of
the Romans, Christianity had been embraced by a large
proportion of both peoples. Constantine the Great had
become a zealous patron of the Church, and the Britons in
large numbers received the faith. The wall of separation
as between Christian and "heathen" having thus been
broken down, and a new ground of sympathy and confidence, more sacred than any other, found, intermarriage
would more freely take place.

Rome profited from such alliances, and gave them every
encouragement. Amity and goodwill sprang from them.
Every family tie was a tie between the people and their

masters, made oppression less galling, and conquest more secure.

The etymology of proper names, though a dangerous guide, is not altogether to be discredited. In times long subsequent to the evacuation of Britain there were numerous personal designations current in the island which indicated Roman origin.

The corruption of the British language by the introduction of Latin vocables, made greater progress both in Roman and post-Roman times than is usually acknowledged. In the estimation of some of our "Welsh literati" it were a proof of traitorous intentions towards the *Cymraeg* to say that its vocabulary is intermixed with Roman words; but the fact is beyond question, as our chapter on Philology, and Appendix A., will show. At the same time it cannot be too frequently insisted upon, that intermixture of languages is not a certain index to a *proportion* of race intermixture. In the chapter referred to, we have endeavoured to distinguish between the two, and to show how the former is an evidence of the latter as fact, and in what respect it may be considered evidence as to its measure.

The introduction of Latin into the Cymraeg might be the fruit of respect for the speech of the ruling class; and might still more arise from the respect entertained by the better instructed—the clergy—for the Latin, as the depository of ancient learning. That the Britons had to some extent cultivated the Latin is certain. The indications of history are few, but we have shown that Agricola used special efforts to induce them so to do. The works of Taliesin (say 6th cent.) give evidence of his acquaintance with the classic writers, both of Greece and of Rome, and Cymricised Latin words are often met with in his verses. Also in Aneurin's *Gododin* (6th cent.) vv. 231,239, we meet with many corruptions, ex. gr. *fossawt*, for fosse, a ditch

(Lat. fossa), *Calan Jonawr*, the first of January, v. 268, (Lat. kalendæ) ; Llywarch Hen (6th cent.) has *gwydr* (Lat. vitrum), &c. Latin words became further naturalized in the speech of the Cymry in the middle ages ; thus, at the very opening of the laws of Hywel Dda[1] we meet with the word *emendaäsant*, "improved" (Lat. emendo); and in the elegy of Meilyr on *Gruffydd ap Cynan* (12th cent.) we meet with the epithet, "*rex* radau," King of gifts or graces. How the terminology and technical phrases of superior languages, or the languages of superior nations, are adopted as in some sort signs of presumable culture by the uneducated, we need not say : the Welsh of the present day afford ample and humiliating illustrations.

We have few means of knowing how far the culture of Latin proceeded among the Britons during the stay of the Romans. Mr. Wright is assuredly wrong in the opinion that Latin had become the fixed and only language of Britain, and was the speech in general use on the arrival of the Saxons. Not only is there no evidence that the Romans, here or elsewhere, made a point of imposing their language ; but the traditions, early literature, and subsequent vigour of the Cymric tongue, conclusively prove that the language had remained as fixed as the people.

We have said, that Agricola set on foot measures for teaching Latin to the Britons. But how did he proceed ? He wisely began with the sons of the chief people— "principium filios," expecting that the example of the high would be followed by those below. All this would tend to prove that up to Agricola's time, when Rome had already been master some hundred and thirty years, the Britons had made no acquaintance with the Latin tongue. As yet the children of even princes and the nobility had not been

---

[1] See Wotton's *Leges Walliæ*.

taught it.   But soon the administration of the laws came
to be in Latin.   Latin was the language of official life.   In
two or three hundred years, it would infallibly make progress, especially among the instructed classes, and would
become the chief, if not only, language spoken in the
Municipia, *Coloniæ*, and Roman towns generally ; and
would thus become a powerful instrument in the fusion of
the two peoples.

The languages would doubtless, as languages of daily
intercourse, mutually borrow.   The process for both would
be facilitated by the numerous Celtic vocables already
existing in the classic Latin, and belonging to its primitive
and most venerated materials—memorials of some ancient
common origin between it and the Cymraeg—and by the
similarity of articulation of the two tongues.   As an
example of a common inheritance, the Welsh word *taran*,
thunder, may be cited.   Ennius, in earlier Latin, says,
" Jupiter tarans," while Virgil has, " Jupiter tonans."

These philological indications, added to other reasons
already mentioned, for left to be understood, justify the
presumption that amalgamation took place between
Romans and Britons, but how far this fusion proceeded
we cannot of course determine.   Taking what has already
been shown—the relative smallness of the Roman residentiary population—as our guide, it seems reasonable to
conclude, even after making the amplest allowances, that
its progress was not great.   When the Romans withdrew,
the population of Britain was substantially Celtic, as they
found it.   Neither the occasional immigrants from North
Germany, nor the influx from Italy during the imperial
rule, produced any such change in the inhabitants as to
render it inappropriate still to call them *the Ancient
Britons*.

SECTION V.

The influence of the Roman Conquest upon the Celtic character of Western Britain.

THAT the eastern side of our island retains hardly any traces of the Celtic aborigines, and that the western has become their favourite, though not their only home, cannot admit of debate. Had the Romans any hand in determining this state of things? Or were the determining causes at work in times anterior to the Roman Conquest, and have they continued so in later times?

The great line of march for the Roman troops was from South to North through Leicester, York, and Newcastle. On this line the great military stations are found. To the east of this line, from time immemorial, the piratical rovers of the German Sea would have some influence, and here and there effect settlements. Here probably settled the "Coritani." We read of no great Celtic power at any time inhabiting these regions; under the behests of nature, they had been left in a state of comparative wildness, abounding in forests, moorlands, and swamps. Up to comparatively recent times, indeed, the "Fen Country" was but a thinly peopled, unwholesome, sadly uncultivated tract. The Celt had no love for it. But if we look to the Western side, along the entire length of the island, the *Cymry* are found predominant—in Cornwall, in Wales, in Cumberland, and Strathclyde far into Scotland.

Now it appears by no means certain that the Romans had any hand in causing this distribution of the Cymry. The unhistoric representation about the Romans, and after them the Saxons, "driving the Ancient Britons into the mountains of Wales," is utterly groundless. A preference for the West would arise from the nature of things, unless the aborigines were a people without either imagination or reason. The cold morasses, stagnant lakes, and tangled forests of what are now called Cambridgeshire, Norfolk, and Lincolnshire, were not likely to be more inviting than the crystal streams, sheltered vales, and towering hills of the West. Once discovered, the western side of Britain, in the most primitive times, and to the most untutored tribes, would be more covetable than the eastern.

Previous to Roman times also, as afterwards, the German Sea marauders were the plague of the Britons. To avoid their presence, and to keep their flocks and property out of their reach, the inhabitants would naturally incline to the interior, except where their strength was adequate to check their unwelcome visitors. The power of the Iceni and Trinobantes in Essex, Norfolk, Suffolk, &c., was not sufficient to prevent them from committing depredations, and even forming settlements, on their shores ; nor was the power of the Romans altogether sufficient for the purpose. It is, therefore, conceivable that their visits would cause the aborigines in their earlier stages of possession to feel no strong attachment to those parts even if the landscape had been pleasing, and the soil fertile.

The condition of things when the Romans began their conquests, was therefore something like the following : The southern and western parts were well peopled. As far as the mountains of Caledonia, the different tribes of Britons, all speaking the same tongue, were found in more or less teeming multitudes. In the central parts of the island also they abounded in almost equal numbers, as evidenced by the vast forces they brought into the field to stem the progress of the Romans. But in proportion as Rome established her power, in that proportion did a select few, the more brave and defiant, seeing resistance was useless,

quit their native locality, and seek shelter among the
unconquered tribes of the West, in Wales, Devon, Cumberland, and the region still further north.   Thus an intense
hereditary spirit of nationality was concentrated in *Wales*
which never ceased to fulminate its most terrible thunder-
bolts against all aggressors on the sacred soil of Britain,
and has not even allowed its powerful vocabulary to fall
into complete desuetude even in these latter days.
Although all real reason for its use has long ago vanished,
the phantoms of the past appear, now and then, sufficiently
real to call forth a malediction.

It is just possible that to pirate freebooters of North
Germany allusion is made in the Welsh *Triads*, where
amongst the "three invading tribes which came into
the Isle of Britain, and never departed from it," are
mentioned, "the Coranians, who came from the country
of Pwyl," and settled about the river Humber and the
shores of the German Ocean.[1]   This may refer to a period
anterior to the Hengist incursion, or subsequent to it, and
the intruders may have been of Germanic or of mixed
origin.   We cannot rely upon such general statements,
made without date or definite order of succession ; but they
may legitimately be received as suggestive, and corroboratory of other proofs, in building up a structure of argument.
We, therefore, accept this *Triad* as indicating one of the
causes which in early times induced a brave remnant of
the Cymry to move by degrees towards the opposite
western coast—probably in that particular case, more
towards Lancashire and Cumberland than towards Wales.

There was a poetic fitness in this migration of the
ancient possessors into the more hoary regions (if geology
will pardon a figure) of the island.   And the step might

---

[1] *Myv. Arch. of Wales.* vol. ii. 59.

well have been suggested by a prophetic foresight also.
The western side is the region of primary formations,
which not only determine the picturesqueness of the surface,
but the underground wealth. Nearly all the mineral
treasures of Britain are carefully laid up on the Western
side—the region whither their good genius conveyed so
many of the staunchest of the Ancient Britons. But war,
oppression, and sentiment prevented the Cymry from
finding the concealed riches. Is it, therefore, that the
slow and searching Englishman—the compound of Saxon
and Celt—must follow them to the West, to aid in the
discovery and converting to use of treasures which so long
had lain under their feet? The Celt, though not wanting
in constructive power, has not for many ages in the British
Isles turned it to the highest account. Poetic, airy and
sentimental, his aptitude is small for burrowing the earth.
He is naturally at home when ranging the breezy hills, or
the fairy intellectual dream-land. But when he with his
quick perception and prompt action is joined to the
profound, persistent Teuton, then comes forth the inventive
discoverer of worlds above and worlds beneath—the man
who can extract gold from the quartz rock, and dig coal
and iron from the bowels of the hills.

We do not think that Roman influences contributed in
very large degree to the movement of the aboriginal race
westwards. They led to the overlaying of the features of
Celtic nationality in the South, and all other parts except
the West and extreme North ; but this was done by displacement, not of the race, but of the language, and other
elements of national character. That the race had not been
displaced, but remained in vast numbers on the soil, was
demonstrated on the departure of the Romans. The British
kingdom of Lloegria was immediately set up, with London
as its capital. The Saxons had to fight the old Britons

O

twenty years for possession of Kent; and afterwards for every inch they gained from Kent to the Highlands.

Nothing can be more conclusive as proof that the Romans had never dislodged the Britons from the soil of England than the universal movement alluded to, for the reconstruction of the native States. Once the land was free from the repressive power of strangers, the original race resumed its old position; and we need no better evidence that the government of Rome had never obliterated the distinctions of rank and family recognised among the Britons, than the fact that when this resumption of power was set on foot, the genealogies of the princes were known, and the rightful claimants to power identified. A dispute arose respecting right of precedence to the supreme office of *Pendragon* (an office similar to the Saxon "Bretwalda"), but the princely families and their order of descent were all known, and, doubtless, the ancient laws and usages were in safe keeping against the moment of political resurrection, when the barriers of oppression were removed from the national tomb.

What had been the precise condition of the princely and noble families of the Britons during this time of suppressed political existence, it is now impossible to relate. How far did they consent to accept military employment abroad: how far were they domiciled and pensioned from the public Treasury; were their sons and daughters married into wealthy Roman families; were they encouraged to tread the path to a convenient oblivion through extravagance, dissipation, and shame; or did tyranny crush them all, wherever it could, with impartial and implacable vengeance? The last supposition is totally inadmissible, being so obviously in conflict with the known temper and custom, as well as interest of the Roman people. Some consideration was extended to rank and station, and the gentle and helpless, overtaken by misfortune through no fault of their own, but through the ambition of imperial Rome, were dealt with as humanely as the necessary assertion of power would permit. Moreover, the hope of redemption ever sustained the British heart, and in the later ages, as signs increased of the coming downfall of the Empire, that hope grew brighter and more buoyant. A Census, though perhaps unwritten, was carefully kept of the survivors of distinguished families—for the Celts through all times have been warmly loyal to their chiefs—and when the moment came round, the names, with their genealogies were proclaimed.

SECTION VI.

The Numerical and Material Strength of the Britons at the Anglo-Saxon Invasion.

We have been anxious to present as faithful a picture as possible of the Ancient Britons, their number and distribution throughout the island, under the Romans ; for here lies the basis of the whole argument. This being done, and the interval between the liberation of the Britons from Roman rule and exposure to Anglo-Saxon attack being so short, part of the proof implied in the wording of this section is already furnished. If the Britons were spread over the island, and in powerful bodies, under the Romans, and at the time of cession of Roman rule, nothing short of a miracle could prevent their being so when the incursions of the Picts, Scots, and North Germans, took place. Such as the Romans left them, such the Anglo-Saxons found them. This is true, notwithstanding the emigrations to Brittany, and the hosts which are said to have followed the fortunes of Maximus and Constantine the usurper to Gaul.

But we must, in the briefest form, give a few details respecting this critical period in the condition of the Ancient Britons.

1. The effect of the Roman dominion on the spirit and capacity of the nation.

It has been shown that it was in harmony with the policy of the Romans to encourage the increase and prosperity of subject races. But it was neither their policy nor their practice to develop the British *mind*, to encourage habits of self-reliance, or the exercise of self-government. They consistently promoted such development as tended to the increase of revenue, without impeding the action of a rigid military rule. The increase of population, the improvement of agriculture, commerce, mining, were encouraged, since men for the army and taxes for the treasury were thereby furnished.

But, side by side with this tilling, planting, and irrigating, there was at work a method of exhaustion. The British youths were drafted into the legions, and many sent on foreign service, it being the custom of the Romans to gain new provinces by the aid of troops drawn from the old— a custom, by the way, superior in its wisdom to that pursued by the British in India until the late disastrous mutiny.

Offices of trust and emolument, calling into play talent and acquirement, were, as a matter of course, bestowed on Roman candidates. A chief qualification for these posts was indubitable loyalty. In the army, Britons might be promoted, but with discretion, and exclusion from chief command. When a common soldier lik Constantine "the tyrant," could rise to be *imperator*, nothing could prevent, here and there, a Briton from obtaining subordinate command. Allectus, who rose against and destroyed Carausius,

and assumed the imperial title he had usurped, is said to
have been a Briton. But, as a rule, with numerous exceptions in favour of the unquestionably loyal, the natives
were not promoted in the army.

When, therefore, the Roman Government was withdrawn,
the Britons were found in a condition of prostration little
adapted for the management of affairs. Bede, with a tone
of deeper colouring than the truth demanded, tells us that
"the South of Britain," destitute of armed soldiers, of
martial stores, of all its active youth, which had been led
away never to return, was wholly exposed to rapine, as
being totally ignorant of the use of weapons.[1] The
untrustworthy Gildas has already painted the same picture,
but follows his bent by dashing in darker lines.[2] Things
were bad enough, though not quite so bad as this. Among
the chief causes of the weakness and bewilderment of the
Britons may be counted the following :—

(1.) The moral impotence incident to dependence on the
guidance and authority of others through 460 years.

(2.) Exhaustion of property by confiscation and taxation.

(3.) The necessity of creating a new army, settling
property in land, establishing a fiscal system, &c.

(4.) Divided counsels — the marked misfortune of the
Celtic race.

2. The recovery of the ancient spirit and rule.

Rome in recalling her army 'if, in the confusion which
accompanied the usurpation by Constantine, and the removal of all the troops under his command to Gaul, such
an act as "recalling her army" can be ascribed
to Rome, left in Britain certain officials with nominal

---

[1] *Eccles. Hist.* i. 12. See also *Sax. Chron.* ann. 443.

[2] De *Excid. Brit.* 14. 15. It is well known that Bede's account is only
a copy, with alterations, of that of Gildas.

authority and bearing nominal command, but of their
functions very little can now be known. Whatever
they may have been, the natives, in the absence of the
army, were not likely long to respect them. The chiefs
of the different tribes overhauled their pedigrees and began
to advance their claims to rule the country. The record
of descent was always an important care with the Britons.
Their social and political organization was based upon
their elaborate genealogies. Never was there a people
more aristocratic and oligarchial. Referring to their
descendants of the thirteenth century, Giraldus says : "The
Welsh esteem noble birth and generous descent above
all things, and are therefore more desirous of marriage
alliance with high-born than rich families. Even the common people retain their genealogy, and are not only able at
once to recount their grandfathers and great grandfathers,
but even refer back to the sixth or seventh generation, or
even beyond."[1] Every district belonged to a particular
family connection or clan, which had grown up around
some chieftain (called *Pen-teulu*—caput familiæ),[2] and no
person not by birth related within the *ninth* degree to such
pen-teulu could possess land or hold rank in that district.
His pedigree, therefore, was the Briton's title to dignity and
property. The princes and great men—precisely after the
analogy of all early Oriental nations—kept their bards or
genealogists as a necessary family institution, filling the
functions of general annalists, musicians, and moralists.

The Isle of Britain was soon astir with the work of
repairing the ancient desolations. Not only tribe governments or kingdoms, North, South, East, and West were
established, but an effort was also made, amid much distraction and division of counsels, to cement a bond of union

---

[1] *Cambriæ Descript.* i. 17.   [2] *Laws of Hywel Dda*, iii. 1.

between the different kingdoms by a confederacy and the appointment of a supreme prince called *Pendragon*. This may have been an arrangement known among the Britons in ante-Roman times. Something of the kind existed among the Gauls. Or it may have been in imitation of the practice of the Romans, who looked upon the Empire, not as a *unity* so much as an aggregation of unities, with Rome as supreme and directing centre. The seat of the *Pendragon* was established in London—the chief city, by this time, of the *Lloegrian* Britons.

It was in this very effort at a wise arrangement for defence, that the Britons managed to discover a bone of contention and occasion of their own defeat. Every prince of course would like to be *Pendragon*. The Lloegrians were the tribe whose capital had been fixed upon, at least · by themselves, as the seat of the *Pendragon*. But the *Cymry* claimed to be the first colonists of Britain—the hosts and patrons of all subsequently arrived tribes—and nothing appeared to them so just and natural as that their ruling prince should be *Pendragon*. The enemy was already knocking at the gate, but the wranglers could hear nothing but the din of their own contentions. Reason reeled, and the appeal was made to arms. The people, who were already too feeble to repel an invader, increased their impotency by shedding each other's blood. In this war of rival claimants, *Vortigern*, the Lloegrian, was loudest, most daring, and successful in demanding the Pendragonship.

It must be confessed that the endeavour to establish a native government after the ideal conceived was a failure. All that can be scored to the credit of the Britons during this painful interval is a spirit of thorough-going, heroic patriotism. The sorts of government that were established under Vortigern, Ambrosius, Uthyr Pendragon (said to be

father of Arthur), granting for a moment that the accounts
we have received are worthy of credit, were not adequate
to self-protection, and were hardly anything better than
fortuitous experiments of rivals for supremacy.   It is impossible to determine at this distance of time how far
Roman intrigue was concerned in frustrating a restored
British monarchy; and how far credit is due to the representations of Geoffrey respecting *Ambrosius* as claimant
with Roman proclivities against his brother *Vortigern* as
the national champion.   There may be truth underlying
the representation.   All we certainly know is that the
national spirit was now thoroughly roused.   Not in Wales,
but all over England, the Britons were politically active.
The old chroniclers shadow forth to us in that dim age
weighty transactions, powerful and violent rivalries,
audacious courage.   But the scene is one of power mingled
with weakness — private passion and intrigue warring
against reason and the common weal—usurpation, insu-
bordination, interminable disorder.   No picture more
affecting could well be offered to the study of the historian
than a noble, heroic people, long-oppressed, but just let
free, holding in a trembling hand the cup of their destiny,
and in the mad eagerness after a drop of its contents,
dashing it all to the ground !

There now occurred a strange coincidence in the fortunes
of Rome, the mistress of the world, and of Britain, her
late province—both became the prey of " Northern barbarians."

3. The Britons, at the coming of the Anglo-Saxons,
widespread and numerous.

It has been already said, that such as the Romans left
the Britons, such the Anglo-Saxons found them.   It is
beyond dispute that their number had vastly increased, in

spite of all diminishing influences, during the Roman occupation, and that, in all conceivable respects, the practice of self-government excepted, they had become a greatly superior people to what they were at the commencement. They were better educated, better trained to arms, better practised in all the arts of life: in a word, they had received all the advantages of the Roman civilization, and were, therefore, in point of general culture, pretty much on a par with the Romans themselves.

We may take it as proof of the teeming numbers of the Britons rather than of their desire to abandon their native country that so many scores of thousands of them are said to have emigrated about this time to *Armorica*. Maximus is related to have led as many as 60,000 British youths to Gaul.[1] Usher calculates that the number would be more like 30,000 soldiers, with some 100,000 peasants to form the settlement.[2] On this subject of Maximus's expedition to Brittany, there remains a good deal of obscurity. Lobineau, the historian of Brittany, disbelieves it. But nothing can discredit the fact so universally admitted that vast numbers of the Britons did settle in Brittany. Breton tradition to this day bears it out; local names and language are strongly in its favour. Our next section will show that the country was populous enough to spare these hosts, military and otherwise, and yet remain well inhabited.

4. The resistance offered to the Jutes, Saxons, and Angles, an evidence of the numerical and material strength of the Britons.

It took these invading tribes, usually called "Anglo-Saxons," a *hundred and fifty years* to establish themselves

---

[1] Richard of Cirenc. *Anc. State of Brit.* ii. 2, 35; *Nennius*, sect. 27.

[2] Usseri, *Antiq. Brit. Eccles*, pp. 107, 108.

on British soil.   The value of resistance is to be calculated according to the force resisted.

The Anglo-Saxon invasions, and the wars which succeeded them, continued as we have shown from A.D. 449 to A.D. 828, when Egbert, of Wessex, received the dignity of Bretwalda.   This length of conflict tells an instructive as well as a ghastly tale.   We do not disguise the fact, that much of the obstruction to Saxon progress in the later ages of the Conquest, proceeded from the Saxons themselves—one Saxon state waging war with another—but throughout this long and most dreary period, the Britons never ceased to be conspicuous in the field, mostly as the only opponents.

When Vortigern invited Hengist and Horsa and their companions to aid against the Picts and Scots, and probably also against a party amongst the Britons who sympathized still with Roman supremacy, the martial tone and equipment of the Britons must be confessed to have been inferior.   But they had men among them who knew the Roman art of war.   They had workers in iron and brass, who had been taught to fabricate the Roman arms.   Romans of rank, and most likely officers of the army, were still in their midst, though not perhaps earnest helpers in the defence of the island.   In Cæsar's time the Britons had no better weapons than the Germans ; they had no steel, though probably they had bronze blades ; but after long schooling under the most martial nation of the earth, they could no longer be in so ignorant a condition.   Their misfortune was, that they were poor—"without martial stores," as Bede expresses it—and that the means and men they commanded were divided under leaders of different opinions and sympathies.

Vortigern was a party leader, and many of the people of the land refused to enlist under his banners.   The Welsh *Triads* inform us that the Cymry were opposed to

the invitation sent to the Saxons. But Vortigern per-
severed; and on this account, the invitation having turned
out disastrously to the whole British race—he is always
spoken of in the *Triads* with unsparing bitterness and
contempt.[1] This dissension greatly reduced the force first
confronted with the invaders. The party of Ambrosius
was numerous, and they were opposed to all Vortigern's
acts. The Cymry were also numerous, probably much
more so than the Lloegrians and the Ambrosian party
together. Until, therefore, the danger of losing their
country stared them in the face, and their own annihilation
was threatened, they kept apart and neutralized each
other's effective action. The invaders had comparatively
easy work of it. So it was that Hengist managed at
length to settle his handful of followers in Kent, and found
there a kingdom. Even under the circumstances, however,
it cost him *twenty years* of conflict to do the work.

This first troop of Jutish Saxons was by no means
numerous, although they proved of great service at the
first to Vortigern in repelling the Scottish Celts. But their
number when they turned traitors, and forced a permanent
settlement in the country, rapidly increased. An old
Chronicler says, referring, it may be, to the whole of the
Anglo-Saxon invaders, that a "large multitude" joined
them from every province in Germany.[2] Geoffrey, with
his usual magniloquence, assures us that Hengist raised in
Germany an army of no less than 300,000 men, and fitting
out a fleet, returned with them into Britain.[3] The exaggeration is palpable. Nennius says, "at that time the Saxons

---

[1] Comp. *Triads, passim.*   [2] Ethelward's *Chron.* B. i.

[3] *Brit. Hist.* vi. 15. There is obviously here an enormous exaggeration.
To convey such a multitude it would require a fleet of 1,500 vessels,
giving 200 men to each : or even 7,000 vessels of the capacity of those
used by Cæsar in conveying his 30,000 men across. He used 700 ships.

greatly increased in Britain, both in strength and numbers."[1] We are told by Bede that their first victories over the Picts being known in Germany, " as also the fertility of the country, and the cowardice of the Britons, a more considerable fleet was sent over, bringing a still greater number of men, who being added to the former, made up an invincible army."[2] When Bede speaks of " cowardice," it is well to remember that he was himself a rather prejudiced German, and withal a borrower from the pages of Gildas—into whose trustworthiness it will be our duty by and by to examine. If the history of the Britons from beginning to end proves anything, it proves that in the virtue of courage they are beyond impeachment, except that not unfrequently its superfluity overbalanced their caution and discretion.

With all their reinforcements the invaders made but slow progress. With all the weakness which division created among the Britons, they still fought heroically. Vortigern being for the present, as represented by Geoffrey, in disgrace and deposed, owing to his marriage with Rhonwen, daughter of Hengist,[3] and, as was suspected, his secret plotting in favour of the Saxons, his eldest son Vortimer, in Welsh history called Gwrthefyr, took the command, and, according to Nennius, four times valorously encountered the enemy.[4] He drove them back to the isle of Thanet, thrice shut them up there, besetting them on the western side. In one MS. of Nennius it is stated that the Saxons took to their ships,

---

[1] *Hist. Brit.* 50.

[2] *Eccles. Hist.* i. 15; *Sax. Chron.* ann. 449; *Nennius*, 43.

[3] Geoff. of Mon. *Brit. Hist.* vi. 12. " It was through the devil entering into his heart that he who was a Christian should fall in love with a pagan."

[4] *Hist. Brit.* 43, 44.

and departed for five years ; and in the work bearing the name of Gildas, these most cruel robbers (crudelissimi praedones) as they are called, finding an opportunity, returned to their own country (recessissent in domum).[1] This, however, could only be for a season, and in order to obtain temporary repose and replenish their wasted forces. For twenty years had they to fight their way into possession of the first corner of the country—the very corner which Cæsar had also first coveted. They fought and failed, and fought again, however, until the object they desired was gained. "They fought at Ægelsthrep, and there Horsa was slain." They fought next year at Crecanford (Crayford), and there Hengist and Acsa, his son, "slew four troops of Britons with the edge of the sword." Next year there was a great conflict at the same place, when Hengist "slew four thousand men."[2] A few years later we hear of battles at Wippids-fleet, at Cymenes-ora, on the banks of the river Maercredsburn, at Andreds-cester—places difficult now to identify—but of the last it is said that Ella "slew all that dwelt therein, so that not a single Briton was there left." In 495, Cerdic, with his son Cenric, and "five ships," arrived, and the Britons, who by this time had allowed Hengist to settle down in Kent, and Ella in Sussex, contested several battle-fields in the South-West about Hampshire, disputing the ground inch by inch for a period of four-and-twenty years. Cerdic, however, had not come over to be beaten. In the year 519 he gained a decisive victory at Cerdicsford, "and from that day forth the royal offspring of the West Saxons reigned." But setting up a kingdom in other people's territory is one thing, to enjoy security and rest is quite another. Again and again the Britons return to the charge

---

[1] De Excid. Brit. 25.   Sax Chron. ann. 455—457.

and not till a new invasion on another part of the coast
demands their presence and prowess, is Cerdic allowed
leisure to fit on his crown. "It was not until fourscore-
years after the disembarkation," observes Mackintosh,
"that Cerdic, at the head of the West Saxons, made a
lasting impression on the Western Britons in a series of
battles where he was probably resisted by the valiant
Arthur." [1]

Already on the coast of Essex, Ercenwine, with a horde
of pirates, challenges the Britons to hold their own ; and
no sooner is this challenge accepted, than another is hurled
at them on the neighbouring coast of Norfolk and Suffolk
by Uffa and his Angles. Difficulties thicken, but the
islanders are not yet disheartened.

These invaders in turn, or simultaneously, having been
encountered, a still more powerful force from the same
inexhaustible region invades the North. In the year 547,
Ida and his Angles establish themselves between the Tweed
and the Forth. The Britons of these parts have hastily to
collect an army, and take the field. The regions now
covered by the counties of Northumberland, Cumberland,
Westmoreland, and the South of Scotland, become the
scenes of many sanguinary conflicts. This was about the
time when Aneurin and Llywarch Hên sang their verses,
and this was the country which a section of the nation
of the Cymry, called "Cumbrians," then called their
own. At this period was contested the disastrous battle
of *Cattracth*, wherein Aneurin fought, and which forms
the subject of his poem, the *Gododin*.[2] This battle
deprived the Cymry of their rule in those parts. Multi-

---

[1] *Hist. of England*, i. 31.

[2] The *Gododin* seems to be named after the tribe of the region, whose
name the Romans varied into "Ottadini."

tudes submitted to the victors. Aneurin and Llywarch Hên, of Argoed,

> " Arcades ambo,
> Et cantare pares,"

lost their country and their state, and retired, with their spirit of poetry and liberty unshackled, into the secure asylum of the mountains of Wales.

These sore conflicts in the North took place about a hundred years after the first settlement of Saxon tribes in the South. This interval was a time of gloom and horror to the Britons. It determined the question whether Britain was to be the prey of strangers. It relegated to the care of barbarism the whole of Roman civilization left in the country. Taken at a disadvantage, torn by faction, attacked in all directions, and with a fierceness almost unparalleled, by Picts and Scots, Jutes, Saxons, and Angles, who, acting as if by concert, seemed resolved upon compassing their total ruin, it had been no cause for wonder if they had succumbed to so hard a fate, and their name had been blotted out of the records of succeeding ages. But they managed to hold up their head, and to perpetuate their race and name. Whole bodies of them, it is true, entered into "confederacy" with the Saxons. The entire kingdom of Lloegria did this. The tribe of the *Brython* did this. They "became Saxons," as the *Triad* expresses it, thus diminishing the influence and power of their own brethren, and swelling the ranks, and augmenting the power and territory of the invaders. But the "true Britons," (as they might well call themselves) never wavered, never flinched. Where they could they kept possession of the walled towns, and strong castles and camps, left so thickly strewn over the island by the Romans; and, where obliged to quit these, they converted hills and forests into new fortresses, and carried on for ages a guerilla warfare in the very heart of the Saxon States.

After the Anglian conquest of the North and the setting up of the Kingdom of Northumbria, British resistance took the form, chiefly, of occasional devastating incursions, and insurrections. These were not movements originating merely in the West. They occurred as the work of a people still existing in the heart of England. The insurgents are often termed "Welsh" (*Wealhas*), but not because they came from *Wales*, but because this was the name the Anglo-Saxons gave to a people not belonging to their own race. We find that though the Kingdom of Wessex had been in a manner founded since A.D. 495 or thereabouts, Cerdic and his successors had frequent occasion to meet the Britons in the field long years after that time. In A.D. 552, the very year Ethelbert, first Christian king of Saxon race, was born, they fought a severe battle at Searo-byrig (Old Sarum, in Hampshire); the following year at Berin-byrig (Banbury, in Oxfordshire); in 571 at a place in Bedfordshire; six years later in Gloucestershire, and seven years later still at Fethan-lea, a place identified by some with Frethern.[1]

Mighty conflicts and innumerable skirmishes of which no record has reached us must have taken place between the Cymry and Midland Anglo-Saxons, for the Kingdom of Mercia was only founded in A.D. 586—a *hundred and thirty-seven years* after the Hengist incursion—and its position would necessitate manifold quarrels with the Britons of Wales and neighbouring regions, many of whose possessions it swallowed up.

After this we come to a period of greater repose to the Britons. The Anglo-Saxons, before they had settled all their differences with the original inhabitants, began in earnest to

---

[1] *Sax. Chron.* ann. 495—584.

·quarrel amongst themselves. A long series of desolating wars occurred between Wessex, Mercia, and the Northern Kingdom, which continued to rage with greater or less fury until the time of Egbert, when the whole were united under one general government. For 200 years or more we hear little of contests between the Anglo-Saxons and the Britons, beyond occasional raids and outbreaks.

What has now been adduced is sufficient to show that a powerful opposition was offered to the Anglo-Saxons, and continued for some hundreds of years, by a fraction only of the Ancient Britons. If they had been all united, and presented a combined and well-compacted front to the foe, it is clear enough he could never have made good his footing in the land. Celtic disunion alone made possible Anglo-Saxon triumph, and was the "good-and-evil" agent in originating the majestic creation of the modern English nation. If, with their numbers reduced by this cause, they still accomplished what history, impartially read, gives them credit for, they must have been a people not only of undaunted courage, but of great resources. They at last set a limit to Anglo-Saxon progress. The wave of conquest met with an unyielding barrier. A people so ambitious of territory as the Anglo-Saxons were only by the sheerest inability to advance prevented from incorporating the whole of Wales, Strathclyde, and West Wales, or Cornwall, into their own proper dominion. It is quite conceivable that but for the mutual jealousies of the Anglo-Saxon kingdoms, this work might, in course of time, have been accomplished. Northumbria would long have anticipated the conquest of Strathclyde by Kenneth III. of Scotland (A.D. 973) if Mercia had not been treading on her heels; and Mercia would in

P

time have incorporated Wales had not Wessex been
so powerful as her rival. The different States of the
Heptarchy, or Octarchy, and especially the three just
named, had, by the tenth century, in spite of the
destruction of life by almost incessant wars, greatly multiplied in population, having received, *en masse*, the Lloegrians, Brython, and probably the Coranians, into their
body at an early stage of the Conquest, as well as myriads
of Britons of the Cymric and other stocks in subsequent
times ; they had continued advancing in numbers for three
or four hundred years, and had spread themselves as
naturalized possessors, of a mixed race, over the greater
part of the island, excepting the countries mentioned on
the Western side. Here, still, a brave people guarded their
" Thermopylæ," hurling grim defiance at the invaders'
advance, and here the so-called Anglo-Saxons ceased
advancing.

SECTION VII.

*The Extent to which the Britons and Anglo-Saxons became
incorporated into One People.*

The preceding pages have made the conclusion certain
that amalgamation between the two races took place. We
have now to make manifest the *extent* of that amalgamation.

It is generally allowed, even by " Anglo-Saxon " enthusiasts, that the English have not derived an immaculate
descent from the North Sea freebooters. But in the conception of most people, the amount of Celtic blood intermixed
is very small. " When the Saxons arrived, the Ancient
Britons were all slain, or driven into the mountains of
Wales." This is the strain of the " school histories of
England," and from these, repeating the same note, most

people take their impressions, and nurse their prejudices, and it will take a long time before the thorough-going, unscientific Englishman brooks the idea that he is anything less than a Saxon. Somehow this piece of adventurous imagination has been taken as a postulate in English history. Even some writers of attainment, and learned college lecturers, still slide into so fallacious a mode of representation—a mode, it need hardly be said, unworthy of an age of historic research and boasted scientific progress. If the history of England, and of British Ethnology, when read rightly, and only with a view to truth, teaches anything, it teaches that the English people have to a far wider extent had their origin in an amalgamation with the aborigines of this island, than we have been accustomed in our easy, unenquiring way, to believe. The question however, we may note by the way, is not one relating solely to the Anglo-Saxons and the Ancient Britons, for a great variety of elements have been introduced into the population of Britain, as we have already in the course of our discussions explained. But the two largest contributories to the stream of English blood are the Celtic and the Germanic, or, limiting terms more strictly, the *Cymric* and *Anglo-Saxon*. Our present section has to treat upon this specific part of the general subject. In showing how far the aboriginal and Anglo-Saxon races coalesced upon the subjugation of the former, we begin by proving the vast preponderance in number of the former at the outset of the struggle, and that the latter suffered as great a diminution by the casualties of war as their competitors, so that their relative strength continued the same; and then offer a variety of arguments in support of the position that the soil of Central Britain was never deserted by the first possessors, but gradually became the common inheritance of a complex but united race.

1. Gildas Examined.

Before proceeding further, it is necessary to search into the foundations of the popular belief respecting the state of the Britons at the crisis of the Anglo-Saxon invasion, and their complete expulsion by that invasion from the soil of England. That belief is to the effect that the Britons, after the departure of the Romans, were in a completely prostrate condition, were incapable of offering resistance to Picts, Scots, or Saxons, and were ruthlessly mown down by the sword without deliverance, a small "remnant" only barely escaping, like sheep from the jaws of devouring wolves, into the mountains of the West, or as miserable fugitives across sea to Brittany. This belief, instilled to this day alike into the child's mind in the nursery, and the student's in the lecture-room, is, in all probability, as palpable a superstition, as devoid of foundation, as gratuitous, and as impossible of rational credence, as any wild and idle romance ever imposed upon unsuspecting childhood.

The story upon which this notion is founded is graphic and compact as any in Homer, and, of course, highly flattering to our Saxon pride, and it is only a pity it is not true. But how did it originate, and who is responsible for its first propagation? Has it any countenance in any authentic ancient historian, or in any induction which may be arrived at from contemporary circumstances and facts? We answer the former question by saying, the story is authenticated solely by the monk Gildas—himself scarcely authenticated; he is alone responsible for it: and the latter, by saying, it receives no credence whatever from any independent and credible historian, or from the candid examination of any known contemporary facts. That a belief based on so uncertain a foundation should be found as part of the faith of modern Englishmen, only shows how fondly mankind cling to established ideas, and by what subtle and easy processes groundless ideas sometimes become established.

Let us quote Gildas's story, and then examine its trust-worthiness. In a work called after his name, and entitled *De Excidio Britanniæ*, he gives the saddest picture imaginable of the condition of the Britons after the with-drawal of the Romans, and finishes off the last and darkest shades with two strokes of his brush representing the afflictions wrought by the Picts and Scots, and the Saxons. The Britons, now a "wretched remnant," pressed by the Picts and Scots, send a letter to Aëtius, a powerful Roman citizen, as follows:—"To Aëtius, now consul for the third time: The groans of the Britons. The barbarians drive us to the sea; the sea throws us back on the barbarians: thus two modes of death await us—we are either slain or drowned." [1] This is a picture of helplessness scarcely surpassed. The Romans not responding in this last extremity, the Britons take counsel what to do. But they go from bad to worse. "Then all the councillors, together with that proud tyrant Gurthrigern (Vortigern), the British king, were so blinded, that, as a protection to their country, they sealed its doom by inviting in among them (like wolves into the sheep-fold) the fierce and impious Saxons, a race hateful both to God and men, to repel the invasions of the Northern nations. Nothing was ever so pernicious to our country. . . . A multitude of whelps came forth from the lair of the barbaric lioness. They first landed on the Eastern side of the island. . . and there fixed their sharp talons. . . . Their mother-land, finding her first brood thus successful, sends forth a larger company of her wolfish offspring, which, sailing over, join themselves to their bastard comrades." [2]

[1] *De Excidio Britanniæ*, 20. [2] *Ibid*. 23.

" Some, therefore, of the miserable remnant being taken
in the mountains, were murdered in great numbers ; others,
constrained by famine, came and yielded themselves to be
slaves for ever to their foes, running the risk of being
instantly slain, which truly was the greatest favour that
could be offered them ; some others passed beyond the seas
with loud lamentations instead of the voice of exhortation :
' Thou hast given us as sheep to be slaughtered, and among
the Gentiles hast thou dispersed us.'   Others committing
the safeguard of their lives, which were in continual
jeopardy, to the mountains, precipices, thickly-wooded
forests, and to the rocks of the seas (albeit with trembling
hearts) remained still in their country." [1]

This is the story upon which the popular belief has been
built.   We are not unmindful that Venerable Bede and
Nennius give the same general account as that given by
Gildas; but as these authors flourished the former more than
a century, the latter about three centuries, later than Gildas,
and drew their materials from his pages, their accounts can
offer no corroboration to his, and are worthy of no consideration, if his can be shown to be unreliable.   Besides,
if any narrators subsequent to Gildas had pretended to
draw from original British sources, the testimony left by
Gildas would go to confute them, for he expressly states
that he himself was unable to draw from such sources,
there being none such in existence—but drew from foreign
accounts (*transmarina relatione*).   Those, therefore, who
accord to Gildas's account the character of credibility, must,
in so far as the state of the Britons at the Saxon conquest,
and the achievement of that conquest are concerned, take
Gildas as their *sole* authority.

Our attention, must, therefore, centre upon Gildas ; and
the value of the doctrine that the Britons were a craven

[1] *De Excid. Brit.* 25.

crowd, incapable of resistance, instantly scattered, driven into the sea, and into the mountains, must be measured by the value of his testimony.

Let us inquire, then, briefly, into the history of Gildas, and without fatiguing the reader with minutiæ, scrutinize with some degree of care the value of his narration.

As to who Gildas was, and when he flourished, we cannot do better than quote the words of Mr. Hardy, in his preface to the great work already frequently cited in our pages.[1] "Gildas (or Gildus, as the name is given by Beda and Alcuin) claims, on account of his antiquity, the earliest place in this collection. His life has been twice written at different times; the first is attributed to St. Gildas de Ruys in Brittany, in the 11th century, and the second to Caradoc of Llancarvan, who flourished in the 12th century."

It will appear, therefore, that these biographies were written, one five hundred, the other six hundred years after Gildas's age. Not only from this fact, but especially from the subsequent words of Mr. Hardy, their accounts must be held totally devoid of value. "As both these authors have confounded the actions of two persons at least of the name of Gildas, it will be advisable in this sketch of his life to rely on the few and obscure notices relating to himself, which are to be discovered in his work." Nothing of value is known of the author, therefore, except what is said of him in the work. But what is the value of this? It must be conceded, of course, that the work called by Gildas's name, was written by some one; but it is an immense demand upon our credulity to require the belief that the known work is correct in all that it says of the otherwise unknown author.

But what is the work's account of its author? Let Mr. Hardy again speak. "It appears from these notices, that

[1] *Monumenta Historica Britannica.* See pp. 59, 60.

Gildas was born in Britain, in the year of the siege of Mount Badon;[1] that he exercised some sort of ecclesiastical function; . . . . . that he crossed the sea, and that, at the earnest request of his friends, after ten years' entreaty, he composed his epistle. Various dates have been assigned to the siege of Mount Badon, but according to the *Annales Cambriæ*, apparently the best of all existing authorities, it took place in A.D. 516. In that year, therefore, let us say Gildas was born. It appears to have been generally allowed, from a passage in the work,[2] that he wrote his epistle in Armorica. We are to conclude that he went abroad at least as early as A.D. 550. If he took ten years to consider and mature his history, it would bring the period of its composition to A.D. 560." [3]

Such then is the man. His life has been written by two different biographers, but both lived more than 500 years after his time, and both have confounded together the lives of two different individuals of the same name. If they have ascribed to A, the acts of B, and *vice versâ*, it is quite conceivable that they should ascribe the acts of both to a person perfectly supposititious. These biographers being unworthy of any but the most sparing credit, we are thrown back for all that we know of Gildas upon a few obscure allusions contained in a work ascribed to himself. Gildas may have been an authentic person. But the evidence is, to say the least, defective, and it is just possible that Gildas is simply an assumed name attached by an unknown writer to a work which for the most part was a work of imagination. The name seems to have been common, for there are at least two or three persons called Gildas, contemporaries, mentioned —Gildas Sapiens (our supposed author), Gildas Cambrius,.

---

[1] *De Excid. Brit.* 26.   [2] *Ibid.*

[3] *Monumenta Hist. Brit.* p. 60.

and Gildas Quartus, and it is to be noted that the work of Nennius, the *Historia Britonum*, was for many ages ascribed to a Gildas.

On the whole there is reason for the language used by Mr. Stephenson in his preface to the original Latin edition recently published by the English Historical Society : "We are unable to speak with certainty as to his (Gildas's) parentage, his country, or even his name, the period when he lived, or the works of which he was the author."

But, allowing for the moment that Gildas was an authentic person, and the author of the *Excidium Britanniæ*, how far is his book an adequate authority for the belief founded upon its representations ?

Mr. Hardy says: "The Epistle of Gildas contains but very few incidents of historical interest, and those are involved in a multitude of words. The account which he gives of his materials in chap. 2 prepares his readers to expect a very meagre narrative, and such is precisely the character of the work. In the earlier portion, he exhibits but an indistinct acquaintance with the events which took place towards the conclusion of the Roman domination in Britain and during the following century ; his narrative is general, confused, and declamatory, and except in very few instances, it cannot be traced to any known source. It is remarkable that when he comes to his own times, he is, if possible, more obscure and his facts less copious. As to his authorities, Gildas says that he wrote more from *foreign relation* than from *written evidences pertaining to his own country*.[1] And the vague and meagre manner in which

---

[1] Quantum tamen potuero, non tam ex scripturis patriæ scriptorumve monumentis, quippe quæ, *vel si qua fuerint*, aut ignibus hostium exusta, aut civium exsilii classe longius deportata non compareant, quam *transmarina relatione*, quæ crebris irrupta intercapedinibus non satis claret.

the Roman transactions in the island are hinted at, rather than described, perfectly coincides with his own acknowledgment. For the second period [the period which specially concerns our subject] his veracity must rest entirely on his own authority, as none of the contemporaneous Greek or Roman writers afford it any support, *but the contrary;* his statement relative to the abandonment of the island by the Romans from the Empire of Maximus, and the subsequent erection of the Roman walls, are wholly irreconcilable with their testimony. From the early part of the 5th century, however, when the Greek and Roman writers cease to notice the affairs of Britain, his narrative, on whatever authority it may have been founded, has been adopted without question by Beda and succeeding authors, and accepted, notwithstanding its barrenness of facts and pompous obscurity, by all but general consent, as the basis of early English history." [1]

It should excite no wonder then that Gibbon should characterize Gildas and his History in the following words: "A monk, who, in the profound ignorance of human life, has presumed to exercise the office of historian, strangely disfigures the state of Britain at the time of its separation from the Roman Empire. Gildas describes in florid language the improvements of agriculture, the foreign trade which flowed with every tide into the Thames and Severn, the solid and lofty construction of public and private edifices. He accuses the sinful luxury of the British people—of a people, according to the same writer, ignorant of the most simple arts, and incapable, without the aid of the Romans, of providing walls of stone, or weapons of iron, for defence of their native land."

Now it is a canon in historical criticism that an author is worthy of credence in proportion as he draws from

[1] *Monum. Hist. Brit.* p. 61.

authentic sources, or was himself an eye-witness of the events recorded; is supported by other independent testimony; and is free from bias and prejudice. On all these points Gildas falls short. He himself confesses that as to sources he was in command of " no documents of the country " where the events took place, but depended on reports which reached him beyond sea (transmarina relatione). He does not even hint that any stray documents which had escaped the fire of the barbarians and safely crossed the seas, had fallen into his hands. So far from this he even implies a doubt as to whether any such ever existed—" if there ever were any of them " (si qua fuerint).[1] It was certainly to his credit that he delayed ten years, as he informs us, committing his story to writing, and only did so at last at the pressing entreaty of his friends; but it is just as likely that his reluctance arose from conscious untrustworthiness as from modesty or the purpose of further elaboration.

Gildas's Blunder, or Fraud, detected.

From the facts now about to be narrated, it will appear extremely probable, nay, even morally certain, that the description given by the author of the *De Excidio Britanniæ* of the impotence and distress of the Britons, did not in strictness apply to the insular Britons at all. It will appear that the celebrated letter to Aëtius, Consul for the third time, entitled, " The Groans of the Britons: The Barbarians drive us to the Sea,"[2] &c. (see p. 213), of which

---

[1] *De Excid. Brit.* 2.

[2] Repellunt nos barbari ad mare, repellit nos mare ad barbaros: inter haec óriuntur duo genera funerum, aut jugulamur aut mergimur.—*De Excid.* 17.

so much has been made, in all probability never proceeded from the Britons. It may be said that the very form of this letter, so rhetorical, sententious, and antithetic, casts doubt upon its authenticity. No people under pressing misfortune would write to the Roman Governor in such pedantic language; and that the pretended historian had never come upon such a British document in written form is conclusively proved by himself, when he confesses that he drew not his narrative from documents of his own country, there being none such existing, but from "foreign relation." He was writing at a distance of more than a hundred years after the supposed events; he was writing without the authority of a single document belonging to Britain; in no other independent author do we find a syllable respecting a letter, message, or deputation from the insular Britons to Aëtius, deploring their helplessness, and miserably craving succour. Is it possible that this author, for some reason unknown, charged to the brim with the bitterest hostility towards the Britons, has caught at any rumour floating in Brittany, where he was writing, or has fallen in with some general record of some message or embassy to Aëtius, proceeding, not from the Britons, but from the Bretons, and that in his eagerness at detraction, or in his blundering haste, he has applied the whole to the former? Can it be that upon such a blunder, or such a piece of historic fraud, believed in for 1200 years, has been founded the doctrine taught by almost general consent in our modern histories, and in our schools and families, concerning the utter ruin and extirpation of the Ancient Britons!

Let us examine some well-authenticated facts touching a message to Aëtius. We all know that St. Germanus, Bishop of Auxerre, paid two visits to Britain in the defence of the Catholic doctrine against Arianism, and that the

latter of these visits was in A.D. 447. During the first
visit, about fifteen years before, when he was accompanied
by Lupus, Bishop of Troyes, occurred the alleged "Alle-
luiatic Victory," when the enemy was convinced " both by
preaching and by miracle." The second visit was short,
the heretics were confuted and silenced in a public discussion. Germanus now, having settled the Britons in the
faith, returned to Gaul. It is important to remember that
this was in the year 447, and also that this was the very
year in which Aëtius was "Consul for the third time."

Zeuss, in his learned work on the Germans,[1] has a passage respecting this return of St. Germanus into Gaul,
with a reference to Constantius's life of Germanus, which
suggests more than it expresses. He says : " Presbyter
Constantius relates that as Bishop Germanus was returning
from Britain, where at the time the Saxons had made a
descent, his intercession was besought by envoys from the
Armoricans, against whom, on account of their defection,
Aëtius [then Controller of the Empire—rempublicam
gubernabat] had let loose the King of the Alans that he
might chastise them. They [the Armoricans] are not as
yet called Britons, but soon they are often so called." [2]

---

[1] *Die Deutschen und die Nachbarstämme.* München, 1837.

[2] " Als Bischof Germanus, erzählt Presbyter Constantius, aus Bri-
tannien, wo damals die Sachsen eingefallen waren, zurückkehrte, baten
ihm Gesandte der Armoricker um seine Verwendung, den Aëtius hatte
wegen ihres Abfalls den Alanen König zu ihrer Züchtigung gegen sie
losgelassen. Britannen sind noch nicht genannt ; bald wird ihrer
öfter gedacht." *Die Deutsch. und die Nachbarstämme,* p. 576.

With reference to the point that the Armoricans were at an early period
—earlier than Gildas—called *Britanni,* he says (p. 194): "The Franks
called the warlike people inhabiting the North-Western part of Gaul
Bretton : the Latin writers since the 5th century called them *Britanni* and
Brittones, and their country *Britannia Cismarina."* Die Franken (nannten)
das Kampflustige Volk in der Nordwestecke von Gallien Bretton : die
Lateinischen Schriftsteller schon seit dem 5 Jahrhundert Brittanni,

It does not appear that the facts here referred to as re-related by Presbyter Constantius in his life of St. Germanus —a work of considerable interest and of authority, written by a contemporary of the bishop [1]—suggested anything to the mind of Zeuss beyond their own bare contents. To Dr. R. G. Latham, however, reading the passage in Zeuss, the coincidence of date and of an appeal to Aëtius appeared very striking.[2]

Brittones, ihr Land Britannia Cismarina (Bretagne). Lappenberg places as early as the usurpation of Maximus in Britain (A.D. 383) the settlement of a Roman military colony, consisting of British warriors, in Armorica, which has given name as well as a distinct character and history to Bretagne.—(Gibbon, vol. iv. p. 391, note.) In Sidonius Apollinaris (A.D. 468), iii. 9, pp. 73-74; Jornandes (A.D. 550), c. 45, p. 678; and in Gregory of Tours (A.D. 570), we have accounts of another early military settlement of Britons in Armorica, or on its confines on the River Loire. "The feeble Emperor, Anthemius," says Gibbon, " could only procure for their (the Gauls) defence the service of 12,000 British auxiliaries. Riothamus, one of the independent kings or chieftains of the island (' Britonum rex '—Jornandes) was persuaded to transport his troops ('oceano a navibus egressus'—Jornandes) to the Continent of Gaul ; he sailed up the Loire, and established his quarters in Berry, where the people complained of these oppressive allies, till they were destroyed or dispersed by the arms of the Visigoths."—Milman and Smith's Ed. iv. 288.

[1] *Acta Sanctorum*, vii. 216. (The Bollandists.) Constantius's words are: "Vix domum de transmarina expeditione remeaverat, et jam legatio Armoricani tractûs fatigationem beati Antistitis ambiebat. Offensus enim superbâ insolentiâ regionis vir magnificus Aëtius, qui tum rempublicam gubernabat, Eochari, ferocissimo Alanorum regi, loca illa inclinanda pro rebellionis praesumptione permiserat, quae ille aviditate barbaricae cupiditatis inhiaverat. . . . Medioque inter-prete primum precem supplicem fundit. . . . Ad stationis quietem rex exercitusque se recipit; pacis securitatem fidelissimam pollicetur, eâ conditione, ut venia, quam ipse praestiterat, ab imperatore vel ab Aëtio peteretur. Interea per intercessionem et meritum sacerdotis rex com-pressus est, exercitus revocatus, provinciae a vastationibus absolutae."

[2] Dr. Latham immediately communicated his impressions to the author, who, he knew, was revising this work for a new edition, counselling further enquiry. We believe the question had never before been raised.

Bishop Germanus proceeded on his journey to Ravenna, where, having succeeded in his good offices on behalf of the Armoricans by obtaining peace for them from the Emperor (Valentinian III.) and Aëtius, soon after, in July, 448, he died.

Now the coincidences to be accounted for are these : Gildas, writing a century after the event, says that the Britons sent a "letter" to Aëtius beseeching his protection; Constantius, living at the time, says that the Armoricans (early called "Brettons") obtained the good offices of St. Germanus on their behalf with Aëtius : the supposed letter of the Britons was sent in the year when Aëtius was third time Consul, which we know was A.D. 446-7 ; the well-authenticated mission of St. Germanus on behalf of the Armorican Brettons was in the same identical year ; both appeals were against " barbarians," the barbarians in the case of Brittany being the Alani, led on by their King Eochar—in the case of Britain, the Picts and Scots.

It is, of course, not absolutely impossible that events so nearly coinciding should have taken place in the case of two peoples at the same time. If we had in Gildas the authority of a contemporary writer, with the names of persons and details of circumstances given, as we have in Presbyter Constantius, it might be difficult to choose between the two, as we might be compelled to admit the equal reliableness of both ; but Gildas lived ages after the pretended " letter to Aëtius " was written, and confesses that for his statement he had no documents of the country (Britain) to consult, but relied simply upon a report which reached him across sea (transmarina relatione). The narrative given by Constantius has come down in its integrity to our day : no allusion to the letter to Aëtius containing the "groans of the Britons" is found in any writer except Gildas, and the personality of Gildas, with the trustworthiness of the author of the *De Excidio Britanniæ*, whether we call him

Gildas or by some other name, are so problematical as to constitute no foundation for our faith.

The evidence is circumstantial and moral, and in the trial of all questions, whether historical or criminal, no evidence is so reliable. This case must be decided by the balance of *probability*. It is improbable that all the co-incidences above mentioned should have taken place, and we think it is impossible for any enlightened and honest judgment to resist the conclusion that the writer called Gildas has in this matter applied to the Britons of Britain what properly belonged to the "Brittones" of "Britannia Cismarina,"—so-called before his age, and deriving their name from blood-relationship with the insular Britons.

It may be added that Gildas drew from no authentic sources except when treating of times earlier than the period of which we are now inquiring—the early Saxon period—and even when treating of those earlier times, he comes into helpless collision with trustworthy historians, such as Cæsar and Tacitus, on points involving the credit of the Britons—points which those historians were under no temptation to distort to the advantage of the islanders. But neither was he himself an eye-witness of the struggle he portrays. In fact, he wrote—or, more strictly speaking, the book was written—a hundred years after the main events we are now concerned with had transpired.

One question remains to ask : Was Gildas an unbiassed witness ? It is impossible to read his pages and note his pervading tone of depreciation towards the Britons, and of eulogy and flattery towards the Romans, without feeling that he was not. He never lets slip an opportunity of heaping on his countrymen epithets of disparagement and reproach, and he seems willing to include the Saxons, Picts, and Scots, in the same category. The Britons are cowards, poltroons, hares and chickens, neither brave in war nor faithful in times of peace ; the Saxons, dogs, wolves, a race hateful to God and men ; the Picts and Scots, brutes, inspired with avidity for blood, and " all more eager to shroud their villanous faces in bushy hair than cover their bodies with decent clothing." But the Romans are lions and eagles, generous and noble friends, mighty in war, magnanimous in victory.

The one-sidedness and disingenuousness of Gildas are of themselves sufficient to vitiate and condemn his work as a history. No special pleading can be history. Palpable exaggeration, strained and bitter invective, unreasoning and blundering partiality—main characteristics of Gildas's production—would disentitle any pretended annalist to credit.

An example or two of Gildas's partiality and exaggeration will suffice.

His picture of Britain as a Roman province belies all history and all probability. "The Romans having slain many [Britons], and retained others as slaves, that the land might not be entirely reduced to desolation, left the island, destitute as it was of wine and oil, and returned to Italy, leaving behind them taskmasters to scourge the shoulders of the natives, to reduce their necks to the yoke, to chastise the crafty race, not with warlike weapons, but with rods." And yet we know that Britain was a favourite province, and a favourite abode of many emperors, a rich mine of wealth to numerous procurators, and a field of renown and glory to many of Rome's leading generals.

On the return of the Romans to aid against the Picts and Scots, he uses the following pompous style of description :—"Upon this the Romans, moved with compassion . . . . send forward, like eagles in their flight, their unexpected bands of cavalry by land, and mariners by sea, and planting their terrible swords on the shoulders of their enemies, they mow them down like leaves which fall at the

Q

destined period, and as a mountain torrent swelled with numerous streams, and bursting its banks with roaring noise, with foaming crest, and yeasty wave rising to the stars. . . . ."[1] But the sentence, like most, indeed, of this turgid author's, is too long to be fully quoted. Of the Britons, on the other hand, he says :—To oppose the Picts and Scots, " there was placed on the heights a garrison equally slow to fight, and ill adapted to run away, a useless and panic-stricken company, who slumbered away days and nights on their unprofitable watch. Meanwhile the hooked weapons of their enemies were not idle, and our wretched countrymen were dragged from the wall and dashed against the ground. But why should I say more ? They left their cities, abandoned the protection of the wall," &c. " The enemy butchered our countrymen like sheep, so that their habitations were like those of savage beasts, for they turned their arms upon each other,"[2] &c.

He calls Boadicea " that deceitful lioness," although history has clothed her with all the attributes of true nobility and heroism. After the revolt which she headed, when the Romans sent their legions in vast force to avenge it as already described in our pages, he asserts that the Britons had no marshalled army, no preparations for resistance, but " made their backs shields against their vanquishers, presented their necks to their swords, and stretched out their hands to be bound like women, so that it became a proverb far and wide that the Britons are neither brave in war nor faithful in time of peace."[3] A representation more mendacious was never put on record.

He charges his countrymen with being an indolent and cowardly race, totally subjugated and dispersed by the Saxons from the outset, although he knew, or ought to have known, that in his own time—a century or more after their

---

[1] *De Excid. Brit.* 17.　　[2] *Ibid.* 19.　　[3] *d.* 6.

asserted total overthrow—they were still in possession of half the island, and stubbornly maintaining, though with waning fortunes, the fight against the invader !

It is time to have done with Gildas. It is clear, that, allowing he was a real person, and wrote his history at the time commonly supposed, his statements in all matters pertaining to the Britons, are wholly unworthy of credence.

He pursues them with an animosity that is never satiated, and belies all authentic history in branding them with the character of timidity, cowardice, and tame submissiveness, when their country was being torn from them by strangers.

It is impossible to dignify such a chronicler by the name of historian, and it is utterly impossible to receive his statements as anything else than the splenetic exaggerations of an ill-informed, and prejudiced monk. Gildas is therefore not mentioned by Lappenberg as an authority for early English history.

And yet upon the representations of this writer has been based the faith of Englishmen concerning their own purely Teutonic descent. From him alone has proceeded the doctrine that the Britons were exterminated, or driven clean off from English soil, into " the sea," or into " the mountains of Wales." There exists no other authority whatever for such notions. We are compelled in deference to truth to reject the authority of Gildas, and pronounce the notions based upon it as visionary and historically " superstitious."

Having so far cleared the way, we now proceed to consider more in detail the strength of the British population after the departure of the Romans.

2. The Aboriginal Britons surpassed in number their Anglo-Saxon invaders.

In almost all invasions, the aggressors are few compared with the inhabitants. It was so in the Roman invasion of Britain. It was still more so in the Norman. At the time when the Saxons and Angles first made a regular attack on the island, the inhabitants—already numerous even in Roman times, as proved by the large towns, and military and fiscal stations existing all over the country, and in our pages enumerated—with the increase which had since the departure of the Romans taken place, were a powerful and widely distributed race. In the North, in the South, in Wales, the population was not sparse. In all these parts considerable states flourished. What, therefore, compared with this wide-spread and multitudinous people, for the proper government and taxation of which the Romans had at least above a hundred towns, cities, and strongholds, could the invaders, coming over in their small *cheols*, miscalled " ships,"—three "ships"—five " ships," at a time,[1] amount to ? What could they amount to, making every reasonable allowance for the thinly inhabited regions of the East, and for the hosts which had emigrated to Gaul and Armorica ? The number given by Geoffrey of Monmouth (300,000) as having come over to support Hengist is perfectly imaginary. It is not to be supposed that the Saxon " ships" were to be compared in capacity to the Roman triremes, and yet Cæsar had to build, as he himself declares, 700 transports to convey an army of 30,000 across the Channel, with baggage and all appurtenances. Supposing that the Saxon keels were actually equal to the Roman in capacity—it would take a fleet of some *seven thousand* such " ships" to bring an army so enormous as that mentioned by the imaginative and romantic Geoffrey!

---

[1] Some ingenious writers have recently discovered that " three " and "five" are not to be understood literally, as giving the bare number of ships, but figuratively, meaning three or five squadrons ! We do not find the *Saxon Chronicle*, and other such works, so very imaginative as all this would imply.

The creation of a fleet a tenth of the size is inconceivable under the circumstances.

We readily admit, for the clear voice of the old chroniclers bears it out—that immense numbers of soldiers, pirates, miscellaneous adventurers, came over with, and after, the different Saxon and Anglian Chiefs. This concession is simply a relation of the truth. We have even given prominence to this fact in preceding pages, as the means of exhibiting in stronger relief the power whereby the Britons for so long a time maintained the contest. But the invading body, though large when considered absolutely, and in the mass, was small when held in comparison with the teeming thousands which inhabited the many score cities and wide plains of Britain. The success of the Anglo-Saxons, like that of the Romans before them, and that of the Normans against the English afterwards, was not the success of *numbers*, but of a military and brute force, superior in concert, fiercer in resolve, more practised in arms than that which it had to confront.

The people who fought the Romans for so many long years, not without some success, and who were afterwards for centuries nurtured, protected, cultivated by them ; a people numerous enough to yield by taxation a revenue sufficient to maintain the military and civil service of Rome in the island, and yield a surplus sufficient to enrich emperors, procurators, governors, and their underlings for three or four centuries, however they may have passed their lives in the forced indignity of subjection, cannot for a moment be compared with any multitudes of adventurers crossing the German Sea in open boats. If the objection, already so often answered, be still repeated : " The Anglo-Saxons must have been as numerous as the Britons, because they conquered them;" we can only meet it by saying :—The Normans under William must have been, by parity of rea-

soning, as numerous as the people of England, and the
Northmen led by Rollo must have been as numerous as the
inhabitants of Neustria—an hypothesis so absurd as to
need no exposure.

3. The Britons did not suffer, relatively, a diminution of
number from war.

The point is not whether they were not diminished, but
whether they were more diminished in proportion than
their opponents.   Granted, modes of warfare in those barbarous times were destructive enough of human life.   But
if well-forged and sharpened weapons counted for anything
in the trial of battle, one would suppose that here the
Britons would have a marked advantage.   They had been
taught the forging of blades and spear points, and the
forming of shields and helmets, by the Romans, as well as
all the tactics of attack and defence.   However furious,
therefore, the onsets of the terrible warriors of the North,
there is no reason for concluding that the brave and better-
trained Britons, with the advantage of a better panoply,
would leave more men *hors de combat* than their enemies.
The fierce and less regular movements of the latter, on the
contrary, would frequently expose them to more serious
losses.

The most stubborn and devastating conflicts took place,
no doubt, at the first stages of the invasions, and victory
at that time would be followed by unsparing severity, on
whichever side it turned.   Whole towns and villages would
be depopulated, and misery and desolation spread far and
wide.   On the other hand, it is to be borne in mind that in
those more primitive times, when men were less hampered
with property, and less attached to locality, the inhabitants
of whole towns and districts would readily retire before an
approaching foe, and find easy shelter in the forests and

woodlands which everywhere abounded, and in the absence of regular garrisons, soon again return to their homes. The Anglo-Saxons, although they never seem to have repaired, would, doubtless, at first, eagerly use the great lines of military roads constructed with so much labour by the Romans, conducting their attacks mainly along these lines, while the wide districts lying between, being less easily approached, would be left comparatively unharmed, and become places of rendezvous and shelter for the inhabitants.

It may be asked how, if not by the sword, were the Britons so sadly decimated? The question assumes what we deny to be the fact. The Britons were not so sadly decimated. If so, it may again be asked, how, to all appearance, did they diminish so rapidly in number, that very speedily all over England we find none but Anglo-Saxons? This question again assumes too much, although in perfect keeping with popular opinion. It so happens that the Britons did not " so rapidly diminish in number," even " to all *appearance*," and that we do not " very speedily find none but Anglo-Saxons all over England." Our imaginary questioner has been, to all appearance, reading his " School History," which often helps him to find Teutons where he ought to have discovered true Celts, and Anglo-Saxons where he ought to have found Britons. It is true that in process of time the Celtic language disappears from the Anglo-Saxon parts, and that gradually the population throughout the greater portion of the Heptarchy, or Octarchy, or Hexarchy, as we may choose to call the Saxon States—for it is uncertain whether seven or eight States, properly independent, ever contemporaneously existed—assumes the appearance of a homogeneous race; but this was a result which was very slow in taking shape. It was, for example, far from complete in the time of *Athelstan*; for then communities of *Cymry*, using their own language, and observing their own usages, were in integral existence in the heart of Wessex itself. This was *five hundred years* after the arrival of Hengist. In the reign of Egbert, the counties of Dorset, Somerset, Wilts, as well as Devon, were all considered as belonging to the *Weal-cynnc*,[1] (the dominion or kingdom of the Welsh) a sufficient proof of the nationality of the inhabitants. This was nearly *four hundred years* after the settlement of Hengist. Of course this designation, *Weal-cynnc*, could only mean at that time that the inhabitants were the *Wealas* —"the foreigners"—as the Anglo-Saxons, with admirable audacity, termed the people, who for a thousand years had their home in the country—the *government* under which they lived was nominally that of Egbert, who was styled not merely King of Wessex, but King of England.

The Anglo-Saxons might well multiply with rapidity when whole tribes or states of the Britons entered into "confederacy" with them and "became Saxons," as the *Triad* indignantly expresses it. Lloegrians, Brython, and probably many others, did this; and the Britons would of course in appearance diminish in proportion under such a process. But this is a different question, and when thus settled, only tells in favour of the general position we adopt. If the Lloegrians, and their companions in ready submission, had their *blood* changed into other than Celtic blood by the method whereby they "became Saxons," well and good. Change of government—mere recognition of a new dynasty—is all that is required, in that case, to convert a Jew into a Gentile. The Mauritanians and Celtiberians, the Syrians and the dwellers on the Ganges, by submission to the

---

[1] *Will of King Alfred*, pp. 14, 15. Ed. Pickering, 1828. Reprinted from the Oxford ed. of 1788.

prophet of Mecca, all became genuine Arabs according to
that theory. But of the general fusion of the Celts of
Britain and the Anglo-Saxons we have to treat in our
next section. Our subject here is the diminution of the
Britons, not through cession and absorption, but through
the casualties of war.

Making every reasonable allowance for the reductions
made in the British inhabitants, on the one hand by political arrangement, and on the other by sheer destruction
in the field, they were still a numerous and active race two
hundred years after the founding of the first Saxon Kingdom. Throughout the country, even in the central parts,
as at Bedford, Banbury, Petherton, Bath, we find so late
as A.D. 552, 584, 658, &c., mighty battles fought by the
Britons proper of those districts, who rose to avenge the
oppressive exactions of their conquerors.[1] If these had
been the incursions of marauding hordes from Wales or
Cumbria, penetrating for the moment far into the enemy's
country, and retreating with their booty, their presence were
of no value to our argument. But they were nothing of
the kind. They were spontaneous movements of the
dwellers in those regions. What other commotions went
on throughout the country from similar causes we do not
know, or have no space to relate. But it is certain that
the Britons were a powerful part of the people of England
in these times, either in the form of communities still
wearing the badges of their nationality in language, laws,
and customs; or as more complying subjects of the
different Saxon states. Then it is to be remembered that
during all this time "West Wales," or Cornwall and
Devon, great part of Somerset, Wilts, Gloucestershire,
Worcestershire, Herefordshire, Shropshire, Cheshire, Lancashire, Yorkshire, Westmoreland, Cumberland, and the

---

[1] *Sax. Chron.* under those dates.

South of Scotland, as well as the whole of Wales—the *patria intacta* of the Cymry—were in the possession of those Britons who had hitherto kept themselves wholly unmixed with the Teutons. In all this there is nothing which sounds like a diminution of the British race through war.

If, therefore, the Britons were reduced in number, relatively to the Anglo-Saxons, it was the effect not of casualties of war but of absorption into the new nationality now in process of formation. At the coming of the Saxons, as we have shown, the Britons greatly surpassed them in multitude, and it necessarily follows, granting to each side nearly equal losses through fighting, that the great majority of the subjects of the so-called Anglo-Saxon Heptarchy were not Saxon, or any species of Germans, but Britons, and, through marriage of Saxon men with British women, half-blood Britons. Whole tribes or kingdoms of Britons had at an early stage sent in their submission. Necessity, convenience, family ties, interest, led thousands more to remain where they were, and prepare for peaceful union with the iron Northmen. As the German warriors cannot be supposed to have brought many women over, a mixed breed would speedily multiply through their taking British wives. The Cymry alone, and only the more enthusiastic and unyielding of these, retired to seek shelter with their brethren in Wales. This section of the Ancient Britons from the outset protested against all dealings with the Germans; they never ceased to criminate and denounce Vortigern for his first alliance with them; and to the last they consistently maintained an attitude of protest and defiance.[1] The remaining Britons in process

---

[1] Thus the bard Golyddan (7th century) exclaims :
   "O, Son of Mary, whose word is sacred! woe's the time that we sprang not forth
   To resist the dominion of the Saxons—that we cherished them !
   Far be the cowards of Vortigern of Gwynedd ! "
Arymes Prydain Fawr. (See *Myv. Arch. of Wales*, i. p. 156.)

of time "became Saxons;" and so it was that the Ancient Britons diminished in number, and the Saxons "mightily multiplied."

But we must now, with the greatest care and minuteness, search out what evidence is available upon this vital point in our argument.

4. On the Extent to which the Britons remained on the Conquered Territory and amalgamated with their Anglo-Saxon Conquerors.

The tenor of the conclusion we shall arrive at on this point the reader has already gathered from the preceding discussion. The facts there cited and the reasoning founded upon them, left us no alternative but to conclude, even long before the whole of the case was gone into, that the claims put in for the Britons were good. The additional evidence to be now presented will conduct us to the same verdict, but, if possible, with an emphasis of conviction many times multiplied. We shall distribute the results of our researches under three chronological divisions, thus : (*a*.) from the first Saxon invasion to the founding of Mercia. (*b*.) From the founding of Mercia to the union under Egbert of Wessex. (*c*.) From Egbert's time forward.

(a.) The first Saxon Invasion to the Founding of the Kingdom of Mercia in A.D. 586.

There can be little question but that myriads of the Britons, as soon as the territory on which they were settled was taken possession of by the invaders, and some form of government was established, made their submission, and transferred their allegiance. It is so in almost every instance of conquest known in history. The masses are not swayed so much by sentiments of nationality as by attachment to their native soil, their homes, familiar scenes, and the property, be it ever so little, which they, like greater folk, delight to call their own.   Hence the case and apparent indifference with which they consent to a change of masters.   Promises of protection under better laws and lighter taxes, of kind masters and cheaper fare, are usually abundant on such occasions, and these are the things which in the main carry influence with the impassive multitude of every country.   The Alsatians, since the recent conquest of their district by Germany, have shown a persistent loyalty to France which is strangely exceptional.

It is very true that times have been when the British princes had enormous influence over their followers.   They could, by appeals to their passions and patriotism, rouse them to a frantic pitch of excitement, and bid them follow through any perils, and at any sacrifice.   But the age which succeeded the withdrawal of the Romans was not the time for such enthusiasm.   The Britons were fatigued and exhausted.   Though they made extraordinary efforts, their movements were like those of a person toiling under bodily pain and weariness.   Such was their condition when they found their country attacked at all points by a new and ruthless enemy, that they would hail peace and quietness almost at any price.   None but those who were inspired by the loftiest sentiments of patriotism, and the most powerful impulses of valour, could take the lead at such a time as this, and impart to the sluggishness of their wearied countrymen the resolve still to fight and conquer, or die.

The Lloegrians, with Vortigern as their king and London as their capital, at first maintained a hot contest with the invaders.   But it seems that their courage at last flagged ; they sued for peace ; enticed by the Coranians, they entered into confederacy with the aggressor, and " became Saxons."   The Lloegrians were a people of the same stock

with the Cymry, had arrived in the island at a time
subsequent to the Cymry, and by their consent ; and from
their Southern position, we may fairly judge that theirs
was a third wave of immigration, following that of the
Brython, also sprung from " the same primitive race with
the Cymry," who had been pushed forward to the region
above the river Humber.[1]　These are said by the *Triad* to
have come from Armorica.　They also, since they are never
said to have united themselves with the Cymry during the
Saxon troubles, in all probability by degrees became, like
the Lloegrians and Coranians, united to the Anglo Saxons.
It is worthy of remark that Taliesin, in his poem, *Gwawd
Lludd Mawr*, specifies three nations besides the Cymry
and Saxons as inhabiting Britain in his time (6th Cent.)
These he denominates by the very intelligible names *Eingyl,
Gwyddyl, and Prydyn*—Angles, Gwyddelians (or Gaels), and
Britons, or *Brython*.[2]　All these, excepting only the Cymry,
seem to be in his time associated with the Saxons.　Possibly by the *Gwyddyl* he meant the borderers on Caledonia
who had been absorbed into the kingdom of Northumbria
along with *Deivr* and *Bryneich*.　But be this as it may, the
intimation concerning the *Prydyn*, the point which here
concerns us, is important.

These two communities, or nations of Celts, the Lloegrians
and the Brython, along with the inhabitants of *Deivr* and
Bryneich (Deira and Bernicia) also confessedly Celts, and
by the Angles incorporated into the kingdom of *North-
humbra-land*, would take at once the greater part of the
Ancient Britons residing in the part of the island now

---

[1] In the name *Humber* we have several of the radical elements of
Cimbri, Cumbri, Cymry.　The hard initial consonant has been changed
into an aspirate in *Humber*, probably in compounding *North-Humbra-
land*.

[2] See the poem *Gwawd Lludd Mawr*, in the *Myv. Arch. of Wales*, vol. i.

denominated "England" out of the pale of the British race, and so far swell the proportions of the Anglo-Saxon population. Is it too much to say, that this incorporation alone would be so considerable as to more than double the number of the unmixed Anglo-Saxon population ? We think not.

It will not be amiss to refer for a moment to the intimations given in the *Saxon Chronicle*—next to the *Annales Cambriae*, the most reliable of all the Ancient Annals of Britain, and valuable in the present instance, and throughout this Essay, as being free from all favourable bias towards the Britons—as to the localities where the Cymry were found, and found active in battling for their rights, at comparatively late periods of the Saxon contests. In A.D. 571, it is recorded in the *Chronicle* that Cuthulf fought against the Britons, or Welsh, (*Bretwealas*) at Bedcanford, (Bedford), and took *four towns*—Lygeanbirg (Lenburg), Aegeles-birg (Aylesbury, Bucks), Baenesington (Benson), and Egonesham (Eynsham). Then after six years, A.D. 577, Cuthwine and Ceawlin fought against the Britons (*Brettas*), and slew three kings, and took three cities, Gloucester, Cirencester, and Bath. Again, in A.D. 584, Ceawlin is said to have taken "*many towns*, and spoils innumerable."[1]

Now several of the towns here mentioned were cities of importance under the Romans;[2] and if now, after a *hundred and fifty years* of opposition to Saxon supremacy, the Britons still kept them in their own possession, the fact is significant. At the date last mentioned, the invaders had not succeeded

---

[1] Florence of Worcester says, "Much booty and many vills." Flor. is a mere copyist from the *Sax. Chron.* and Bede.

[2] Gloucester and Bath were both *Coloniæ*; and Cirencester, a privileged town under the *Latii Jus*, was a most important military post, having no less than six military roads meeting in it as a centre.

in founding Mercia, but they had in a manner established
their rule in the other six states, Northumbria, the last,
having now existed some forty years. When Mercia was
set up, it completely extinguished the hopes of the Britons
beyond the Severn, and doubtless converted the mass of
the inhabitants from the Severn to the Wash, and northwards as far as the borders of Lancashire and Yorkshire,
into tolerable " Saxons."

The simple fact that at the late period mentioned the
Britons were in possession of the chief strongholds of
Gloucestershire and Somerset, and in the very centre of
England held Bedford, and four neighbouring towns— how
many others we do not know, but four they held and lost—
and that besides these, Ceawlin took from them " many
towns, and spoils innumerable," is decisive evidence which
cannot be set aside, that they were strong and numerous in
the land, and gives fair ground for the presumption that
they had never yet been effectually disturbed in their possessions in these places since the time of the Romans. We
shall by and by see that these were not the only places far
in the interior of England which were at that period in the
hands of the Britons. These were but a few of the many
which they held. Others they continued in undisturbed
possession of, even for hundreds of years after the last of
the above dates ; but these they lost, with many others only
obscurely hinted at in history, when the seventh kingdom
of the Saxons, Mercia, was established.

Now, what became of the subjects of the " three kings,"
and the inhabitants of the seven towns, and " many towns,"
and of the districts surrounding them, when their conquest
was effected ? Were all these people slain ? Did the conquerors so blindly mar their own fortunes as to clear the
fields of their cultivators, the towns of their merchants and
traders, the workshops of their mechanics, &c., possessing

themselves merely of the empty shells of walled towns, and of desolated acres, which could neither pay tribute nor pro-vision an army ?   We may be sure that our Saxon ancestors had more wit than this.   Once they overpowered the war-rior part of the population, their policy was to obtain the submission and friendship of the rest, and as speedily as possible gain strength and profit from multiplied subjects and extended empire.   The Britons, on their part, had the example of their brethren before them in yielding submis-sion when hopelessly overcome.   All around them they found their own kith and kin in the condition of a subject race.   In short, necessity left them but one alternative—either accept the new rule or perish.

It was by the conversion of the former inhabitants into subjects that the Saxons could by any possibility make the territories they won into " kingdoms."   They had no means of planting such a large tract as Mercia with new settlers, when, after years of ruinous conflicts, they succeeded in becoming its nominal masters.   They wanted to be " kings of men," and the men must be found, for the most part, in the Britons they had conquered.   Without this, the Saxon states could not, by any method conceivable to us, become the populous communities they appear to have been in the time of Egbert and Alfred.   " Some writers have asserted," says Edmund Burke, " that except those that took refuge in the mountains of Wales and in Cornwall, or fled into Armorica, the British race was in a manner destroyed. What is extraordinary, we find England in a very tolerable state of population in less than two centuries after the first invasion of the Saxons.   It is hard to imagine either the transplantation, or the increase, of that single people, to have been in so short a time sufficient for the settlement of so great an extent of country."

The Saxon and Angle conquerors did not, any more than

the Romans, carry on a war of extermination. Their object was to obtain settlements, wealth, and rule. They had sagacity enough to see that a large population is a source of wealth and the only means of replenishing an army. The conversion of the Britons who, by their superior civilization and their bravery in war, gave promise of good materials for the erection of new states, into friends and obedient subjects instead of having them as formidable opponents, was an object worthy of the ambition of the noblest of the Saxon chieftains. The Britons were the depositaries of all the culture which the Romans had been able, by more than four hundred years of example and instruction, to leave behind them, while the Anglo-Saxons were rude and completely illiterate. If by brute force they could subjugate the Britons, the fame of ruling where great Rome had ruled, and the advantage of inheriting all the treasures of refinement and learning which Rome had bestowed upon this its valued province, would be theirs. Thus interest, generous ambition, and sentiments of humanity, combined in sparing the lives of the natives wherever submission could be obtained.

(b.) From the Founding of Mercia to the Union under Egbert of Wessex
A.D. 586—828.

Our information consists frequently of mere scraps, mere intimations, sometimes of mere implications. The old chroniclers merely wrote *lists* : they seldom reflected—never philosophized on the facts they chronicled. But the bare isolated, unaccounted-for *facts* are now to us very precious, and at times disclose a whole world of truth respecting the political and social condition of England in early ages. Thanks, therefore, to the chroniclers.

It is seldom that we meet with such a burst of eloquent

description as is contained in the following short passage of Bede's, and yet the words are more valuable to us by what they imply than by what they state. "At this time (A.D. 603), Ethelfrid, a most worthy king, and ambitious of glory, governed the kingdom of the Northumbrians, and *ravaged the Britons more than all the great men of the English*, insomuch that he might be compared to Saul, once king of the Israelites, excepting only this, that he was ignorant of the true religion: for he conquered more territories from the Britons, *either making them tributary*, or driving the inhabitants clean out, and planting English in their places, than any other king or tribune."[1]

If the redoubtable Ethelfrid gave the inhabitants the option of becoming tributary subjects, we may safely gather that the other Saxon chieftains would do the same, and most of them even more. The tenor of the passage shows that making the Britons "tributary," allowing them to live on the land, and enjoy their own customs, was as much aimed at by this notorious ravager, as their expulsion. He was satisfied to establish his own supremacy, making their princes *reguli* under him, and receiving tribute in acknowledgment of subjection from the whole people. This being the policy of him, whom Bede afterwards describes as one "ravaging like a wolf," the presumption is legitimate, that the Saxon conquest, as a whole, was characterized by milder measures.

Moving a few years further on, we meet with the Britons maintaining their rights by wage of battle in the centre of *Oxfordshire*. "Afterwards Cynegils received the kingdom of the West Angles, and, in conjunction with Cuichelm, he fought against the Britons at a place called Beaudune, and slew more than 2,040 of them."[2] There is no shadow of

---

[1] *Eccles. Hist.* i. 34. This is the Ethelfrid who is said to have slaughtered the monks of Bangor.

[2] Ethelwerd's *Chron.* ch. vi. *Sax. Chron.* ann. 614.

intimation that these Britons, whose army was so numerous that they left 2,040 dead on the field, were intruders. They were the inhabitants of the parts. This battle was fought *a hundred and sixty-five years* after the settlement of Hengist in Kent, when Wessex was a great power, and Mercia had been established some eight-and-twenty years.

If we come down a little further, to the year 658, in the interior of the South-Western parts, a conflict is seen raging between the Saxon King Kenwalh, and the Britons, " and he drove them as far as Pedrida " (Petherton).[1] The host was not driven farther into its own territory than Petherton, in Somerset.

It is very curious and significant that we now find a Briton by name on the throne of Wessex ! All know how in the North the great Welsh Prince Cadwalla, or Cadwallader, in 634 defeated Edwin of Northumbria at Hadfield. In 685 a king of the same British name rules in Wessex. He was probably a person of mixed extraction, but his name suggests a British relationship.

We have repeatedly noted the fact, that to a late period great parts of Somerset, Wilts, Dorset, &c., were inhabited by the Britons. We see above, that they were fighting in the heart of Somerset, in the middle of the 7th century. There will be, again, occasion to show that they were in these same parts at least two hundred years later than this date. The inference is fair that they had continued there throughout the interval, even occasionally putting a prince of there own race on the West-Saxon throne, and unless their expulsion was effected at some point subsequent to the latest period named, we must conclude that they were never expelled at all, but gradually merged into the English population of Wessex. History does not inform us of any extensive migration from these regions into Wales, or any

[1] *Sax. Chron.* ann. 658: Ethelwerd's *Chron.* ch. vii.

other quarter. The conclusion is fair, that since extermination was not the policy of the Anglo-Saxons, the natives never did migrate, but amalgamated with the ruling race.

Egbert, who mounted the throne of Wessex, in A. D. 800, found the Britons numerous and troublesome throughout his kingdom. Their discontent, and frequent insurrections in territory claimed by Wessex, had been the plague of his predecessors. Fifty years before his accession, Cuthred had to make war upon them. After him, Cynewulf " fought very many battles" with them. Payment of tribute seems always distasteful to our Britons. They are in their own country, and " before them there were none here except bears, and wolves, and the oxen with the high backs ;" why, therefore, should they pay tribute to strangers ? This was their favourite, conclusive argument, and this spurred them to incessant mutiny. Egbert made up his mind that there should be an end put to this grumbling, and Wessex should have peace from Winchester to the Land's End. After settling himself upon his throne, therefore he gathered, in the year 813, a mighty host, and set to work against West Wales (*Weste Walas*). He " harried the land" from east to west, *i.e.*, from the settled parts of Wessex as far as he could towards Cornwall. But he failed in obtaining recognition of his authority beyond that celebrated border stream, the river *Tamar*, a stream as often made sacred by the tincture of Saxon and British blood in about equal proportions (for hereabouts both parties fought till they could fight no longer) as any in the island of Britain. The British princes paid formal court to the *Bretwalda*—the great, widely reigning King,[1] and promised some amount

---

[1] Mr. Kemble totally rejects the idea that the *Bretwalda* was a " king of kings," or lord-paramount over the other sovereigns of the Heptarchy. The fanciful derivation, Bret-wealda, " wielder of the Britons," he also rejects. His more rational etymology is, *bryten*, wide, and *wealda*, a — ruler : a great, far-reaching king or governor. *Hist. of Angl.-Sax.*

of tribute, and there ended the matter for a time. "All these details of indecision and repeated struggles," says Palgrave, "attest the important fact, which would otherwise be concealed, of the strength and compactness, of the British population. Had they not been nearly equal to the English, such a stubborn resistance could never have been maintained."[1] Precisely so.

Now, it may be asked, how proving the persistence and continuous power of the native race contributes to a proof of their *amalgamation* with the conquerors. The question is natural and to the point ; and we answer it by saying, in the first place, that the longer we can show the Britons to have endured, the higher is the probability that they were never as a race exterminated ; and secondly, if we can show that so late, say, as the eighth, or ninth, or tenth century, their number was still great, their language, and some of their institutions, still tolerated, even in the midst of some of the Saxon kingdoms, the presumption is made very strong that their ultimate disappearance was not through extinction but through incorporation ; at least the burden of proof is justly thrown upon those who maintain the contrary. If at the present day there existed in the midst of England the remains of an ancient people who continually harassed our rulers as the Fenians of Ireland are doing, and with far greater effect, would not the phenomenon be evidence of a state of things such as we are contending for ? Or, if districts or towns were now existing in Warwickshire or Bedfordshire, inhabited by representatives of former possessors of all the surrounding territory, would that not be sufficient proof for most reasonable persons that expulsion or extermination had not been the law of the strongest ? Again, if wholesale abandonment of the conquered territory had been resorted to by the Britons, should

[1] *English Commonwealth*, vol. i. p. 409.

we not have some account of it in reliable authors? From the eighth century forward to the Conquest we hear not a syllable of any migration of the Britons to other lands, any more than of measures adopted for their destruction. If they ceased to exist as " Britons," therefore, it was because they changed their form, and existed thenceforth as " Saxons."

Of the manner in which the fallen race was sometimes disposed of we have a curious and instructive instance about the end of the seventh century. Egfrid, king of Northumbria, makes a grant of the district of Cartmel, "*with the Britons thereupon*, to the See of Lindisfarne." [1] Cartmel is in Furness, Lancashire. The inhabitants of Lancashire at the date of this summary and pious transaction (A.D. 685) seem therefore to have been Britons, and it moreover appears that when an Anglo-Saxon King obtained the power of absolute disposal of the whole body of the inhabitants of a district, he exercised that power, not by their extermination, not by their consignment to perpetual and degrading servitude, but by bestowing them as a holy gift upon Mother Church, thus handing them over to the best protection then existing, and conferring upon them what doubtless in that age would be deemed the greatest honour a subject race could receive.

Of the number and position of the aborigines in *Lancashire* about this period very little is known; nearly as much obscurity hangs over this great region as over the Eastern shores. So quiet, and perhaps so thinly peopled was it, that a few scattered notices of the slightest description are all that is vouchsafed to it for five or six hundred years after the Roman occupation of it ceased. The above account of the donation of the Britons of Cartmel is by

---

[1] See Camden, *Britannia*, Ed. Gough, iii. 380; Palgrave, *Engl. Commonw.* i. 436; *Proofs and Illustr.* cccxi.

far the most important of all the pieces of information received. The *Saxon Chronicle* just makes a passing allusion in the year 923 : "King Edward went with his forces to Thelwall (Cheshire), and commanded the town to be built, and occupied, and manned; and commanded another force, also of Mercians, the while that he sat there, to *take possession of Manchester*, in Northumbria, and repair and man it." Manchester was nominally in Northumbria ; but it was in a state of ruin without garrison. The fortress had probably been left to crumble ever since the Romans occupied it.

Thus was a district, one day destined to be the centre of the manufacturing and commercial world—the most densely peopled, most industrious, wealthiest of all parts of industrious England, allowed to rest as a land of solitudes and silence. The Britons scattered over it were few, and the soil unproductive ; so that the conquerors of Northumbria, though claiming jurisdiction over it, allowed the inhabitants to go and come pretty much as they listed. No one dreamed of the exhaustless treasures which lay under its moorlands. No one saw through the mists of the future the gathering of the peoples of all lands to partake of, and multiply its wealth. For eight or nine centuries it was the most neglected by our chroniclers of all the counties of England. We think it may be inferred from this that Lancashire, and parts adjoining, were left in the quiet possession of the Ancient Britons, and that, therefore, until the late influx under the guidance of manufacturing enterprise, the mass of the inhabitant was of that race.

The notice we shall give of the North Britons lying beyond to the furthest extremities of Strathclyde, will more naturally fall under the next period.

Of the condition of the native populations of the Eastern

parts during this period, nothing whatever is known. If
we could venture to base a conclusion upon mere probability, it would be that the Ancient Britons there were
few in number, and less unmixed in blood than in other
parts of England.

The kind of conquest effected by Egbert over the Celts
of the West of England, and of Wales, in no respect
involved the removal of the people from the soil. All he
aimed at was to extort from their princes a recognition of
his supremacy, they continuing to rule as before, but under
him as feudatories. It was this kind of conversion which
in time made the Britons English. But it was a long
process. The wars he waged were many, and extended
over a long series of years. Egbert's authority was at last
acknowledged by the princes of West Wales (Cornwall),
and North Wales (Wales), a few years before his death.[1]
The great combination of Danes and Britons defeated at
the battle of Hengistes-dûn was the last attempt to cast off
his authority.[2] But this work was to be done over again,
as we shall see, by Athelstan. The Britons had not
diminished in number, had not left the land, had not relinquished their ancient language and usages, had not been
deprived of the government of their own princes, notwithstanding all the show of supremacy which Egbert had
established.

In fact, to suppose that the conquests of Egbert involved
the removal of the British race from Wessex, carries with
it the absurdity of supposing that the rule he established
over Wales (called by William of Malmesbury " North
Wales ") involved their removal from Wales; and that his
making the Saxon-Anglian kingdoms of Mercia and
Northumbria tributary (A.D. 827), involved the banishment

---

[1] *William of Malmesbury*, ii. 1, 6.
[2] Lappenberg, *Hist. of Eng. under Ang.-Sax. Kings*, vol. ii. p. 5.

of his own race from those regions. The Britons, when overcome, were made tributary ; the Saxons, when overcome, were made tributary; the one, like the other, remained undisturbed on their territories, and equally contributed to build up the slowly-growing body of the great English nation.

Egbert was the man who first worked out the idea of a fusion of the different kingdoms into one. He it was who capped the whole with the name "*England*"—(A.-Sax. Engla-land). At a great Witenagemot, at Winchester, was this matter, by statute, accomplished. "Egbertus rex totius Britanniæ, in parliamento apud Wintoniam, mutavit nomen regni de consensu populi sui, et jussit illud de cætero vocari Angliam."[1] The collective name—the name of the island—had always been in Latin, *Britannia*.[2] The Romans had sectionized it as already shown into five portions under names *Brit. Prima, B. Secunda* (Wales), *Flavia Cæsariensis, Maxima Cæsariensis* and *Valentia*. Then came the different designations of the Anglo-Saxon kingdoms, and the names the new conquerors gave the countries of the Britons— *Wealas*, &c. The *people* of the Teutonic states were most likely called *Angles*, and *Englischmen*—the name " Anglo-Saxon " having not yet come into vogue.[3] Egbert now wished to remove all the old nomenclature, banish all division, and call the country, whether inhabited by Saxons, Angles, or Wealas—*England*. The Church first gave

---

[1] *Monast. Anglican.* vol. vi. p. 608. " England " is simply a *modern* English corruption of Egbert's vernacular Engla-land, literally *Anglorum terra*, taken from the master people.

[2] There are occasional instances in the Chroniclers where Wales is called by the name *Britannia* ; *ex gr.* Asser, *Life of Alfr. ann.* 853.

[3] *Inæ Leges*, xxiv. The name " Saxons " has always been the favourite one with the Britons ; and it has usually carried with it a measure of reproach, like " Sassenach " with the Irish ; but this feeling is now, happily, nearly extinguished in Wales.

prominence to the name of the Angli, and the usage thus
established was consolidated in the Saxon speech, and the
name applied to the country.

(c.) *From the death of Egbert to the Conquest, and forwards.*

Nothing occurred between the death of Egbert and the
accession of Alfred to disturb the Britons, for other cares
than their suppression or extermination pressed hard on
the rulers of Wessex.   The visits of the Danes became so
frequent and desolating that self-preservation rather than
conquest became the first idea of the English.   The Britons,
partly aided by the Danes, became bolder, threw off the
restraints put upon them by Egbert, and revived their
national character in parts where it had suffered partial
obscuration.   The policy of Alfred was to conciliate and
unite ; and he experienced the benefit of such a policy in
finding the *Britons* of Somerset, &c., when he emerged
from his temporary retirement, flocking by tens of thousands [1] under his standard, to fight the Danes and scatter
them, on Eddington Hill.

The populations named were " true Britons "—Britons
in blood as well as in spirit.   They were recognised as
such in the language of the time.   In the age of Alfred we
all know that those regions now distributed under the
county names of *Dorset, Wilts, Somerset, Devon,* were denominated in the Anglo-Saxon language, *Weat-cynne*—the
territory or dominion of the " strangers," or Britons—a
designation which clearly shows that though the supreme
authority might by arrangement under stress of conquest,

---

[1] " All the men of Somerset and the men of Wiltshire, and that portion of the men of Hampshire which was on this side of the sea [*i.e.* not
in the Isle of Wight], and they were joyful at his presence." *Sax Chron.*
ann. 878.   See also *Will of King Alfred*, pp. 16, 17.

be in the hands of the Wessex King—"rex totius Britanniæ"—the Britons occupied the soil and maintained virtual rule. From before the Romans they were there.
Every hill and stream throughout the region was named
in their language. There, owners by original settlement,
occupiers during Roman supremacy, owners again by
Roman cession, from age to age they had remained, and
there, under the guise of doers of homage, in the persons
of their hereditary princes, to the "great king" of the
West Saxons, they still continued. Why should they quit
the soil of their fathers if under form of feudatorial subjection they were invited to remain?[1] True, this kind of
arrangement for a proud and warlike race was hard to
bear, and the most restive and daring spirits to the end
rebelled and died, or retired to plot and create insurrection;
but the great majority would settle down to pursue immediate interests, reconciling themselves to an inevitable fate.

Even as late as the reign of Athelstan, who died A.D. 940,
or within a hundred and twenty-six years of the Norman
conquest, Exeter, the ancient capital of the Damnonii (the
people of *Dyvn-naint*) was governed by a compromise
between the two races.[2] The city was divided into two parts
—the British part and the English part, and each had equal
power in the government of the place. It was not till this
period that this power of the Ancient Britons, in their distinct, unmixed character, was disturbed in Exeter. Till
now, *by law*, their ancient authority was recognised by their
conquerors as co-equal with their own. A change now
took place. "Fiercely attacking them," says William of
Malmesbury, he [Athelstan] obliged them to retreat from
Exeter, *which till that time they had inhabited with equal
privileges with* the Angles."[3] After all that had been

(¹) Comp. Kemble, *Saxons in England*. pp. 20, 21.
(²) See Will. Malmesb. *Hist. of Kings of Engl.* ii. 3. ³ *Ibid.* ii. 6.

accomplished by Egbert more than a century before, and
fixing the Tamar, fifty miles further westward, as the im-
passable boundary, here are the Britons, under the ægis of
Wessex law, maintaining intact their own nationality at
Exeter, and only forfeiting their rights by the irrepressible
passion of their race for uncontrolled liberty. From the
Tamar to the extremity of Cornwall (the *corn*, or horn of
the *Wealas*, or Welsh) they still were, in effect, rulers.
Athelstan did not here much trespass upon their right.

But more than this is borne out by history. It shows us
that the Britons of these parts continued to enjoy their
pristine privileges when Wessex itself had fallen, and the
rule of the Saxon race in England had been extinguished.
The Norman conquest upset the dominion of the Anglo-
Saxons for ever, and for a time paralysed the English
speech, but on Cornwall the Conquest had but slight effect
—on the Celtic *speech* of Cornwall, none at all, for that
speech continued to live on, until, by natural death through
absorption of the people into the English pale, it recently
passed away.[1]

Domesday Book, that black and dismal record of acreage,
tenements, and tax-paying human chattels, might be
expected to afford valuable information in Celtic *names* of
occupiers. But in this we are disappointed. Such was the
rage of royal cupidity after houses, acres, " sac and soc,"
that Domesday hardly ever takes time to afford us the
slightest glimpse at the social condition, the nationality,
or the speech of the inhabitants. It seems on purpose to
ignore whatever did not "pay taxes to the king." Its whole
strength is employed either in gloating over the taxable,
or in bemoaning the ruin which the war of conquest had
brought upon the taxable. Things were so and so, " tem-
pore Regis Edwardi," acres yielding so much to the king,

[1] See Camden's *Britann.* Gough's ed. vol. I. 15.

tenements yielding so much to the king, castles yielding so
much to the king; but now, alas! they are all "vastata,"
and yield neither sac nor soc. Of Exeter it is said : " In
this city forty-eight houses have been destroyed since the
King's arrival in England."[1] The compilers, in the hurry
of completing inventories of all the properties in England,
never trouble themselves with the insertion of *British*
names of the chief men of the *Weal-cynne* and Cornwall—a
circumstance which has emboldened some writers to assert
that none such existed—that the British race, in fact, had
been utterly obliterated.

Now such a conclusion could only be arrived at from
sheer ignorance of the history of the time, or from stubborn
adherence to a preconceived theory in the face of facts. A
good body of evidence exists, partly detailed already in
these pages, that in a large portion of the West of England
in William the Conqueror's time, no language but the Welsh
or Ancient British, commonly called *Cornish*, prevailed.
The inference is inevitable that many of the Thanes and
heads of townships enumerated in Domesday were of British
blood and British speech. But it is quite conceivable that
they had assumed Saxon names, and had learned the Saxon
speech in addition to their vernacular ; or, perhaps, had
Saxon names given them, in addition to the British, for
convenience of record and other reasons.[2]

Evidence is not wanting that, although the people of
Devon after Athelstan's time were not under rulers of their
own, they had still conceded them a certain amount of self-
government by British law and custom. They possessed
some semblance of state machinery, co-ordinate with the
English government, though, of course, in reality not of

---

[1] " In hac civitate sunt vastatæ 48 domus, postquam rex venit in
Angliam."

[2] See Palgrave *Eng. Commonw.* 1. 240. *Proofs and Illustr.* ccxl. iii.

equal weight. They retained, for example, the power of
treating with the King of Wessex respecting their peculiar
rights, almost as if they still continued a separate independent kingdom. They held courts of their own, administering their own laws, in their *own language*. Compacts
were formed between them and the English. The Witan
of Wessex recognised the authority of the *Racd-boran* of
the British as equal with its own. Each guarded the immunities of its own subjects, and when disputes arose, they
met on equal terms, through representatives of equal number from each to discuss and arrange.[1] This, be it remembered, was the state of things just on the eve of the extinction
of the Anglo-Saxon power through the Conquest.[2] We
are thus brought to the first half of the 11th cent. *Seven
hundred years*, therefore, after the landing of Hengist and
Horsa, the Britons are proved to form a recognised, but
separate, portion of the Kingdom of Wessex.

About this time was concluded a compact between the
"lawmen" of the two parties, whose record ends thus:
"This is seo geraednisse the Angel-cynnes Witan and
Wealh theode Raedboran betwox Deunsetan gesatten";
rendered thus, in Lambard and Wilkins; "Hoc est
consilium quod Angliæ nationis sapientes, et Walliæ
consiliarii, inter Monticolas constituerunt." Palgrave remarks : " By reading Devnsetan instead of Deunsetan,
all difficulties [in making out the meaning of the statement]
disappear, and we find that it is a treaty between the
British and English inhabitants of *Devon*, and which
establishes the very important fact that the Britons still
existed as a people unmingled with their conquerors."[3]

---

[1] These representatives were *twelve* in number from each side ; an
early form, doubtless, of our modern "jury."

[2] Palgrave, *Eng. Commonw.* vol. i. 240. *Proofs and Illustr.* ccxliii.
ccxliv.

[3] *Eng. Commonw.* vol. i. 240. *Proofs and Illustr.* ccxliv.

The race were recognised as a distinct people, but the tenor of this compact fully implies that at the time when it was formed, viz., some fifteen years before the Conquest, they were in Devon and Cornwall, subject to the dominion of the crown of Wessex. They were bound to render tribute. It is probable that they still enjoyed many of their old customs; but they were expected to obey the ordinances of King Edgar in the same manner as the English themselves; and this they would find the less difficulty in doing since many of their own ancient laws had been incorporated in those of Wessex. "All these facts," observes Palgrave, "will afford much matter for reflection, and convince us of the great difficulty of penetrating into the real history of nations. Read the *Chroniclers*, and it will appear as if the Britons had been entirely overwhelmed by the influx of the Teutonic population; and it is only by painful and minute inquiry that we ascertain the existence of the subjugated races concealed amidst the invaders."

On the whole, with regard to the Britons of "West Wales," it may be concluded that at the time of the Norman Conquest the river Exe rather than the Tamar was their boundary. From the latter stream, and probably from a point more western, they gradually shaded off, as one travelled eastward, until they assumed in Devonshire, Dorset, and West Somerset, the character of *Englisc-men*. To the West of the Tamar they were as demonstrably Celtic as the people of Wales are to-day; and to the East of the Exe, in the whole of Devon, Dorset, Wilts, and Somerset they were as *really* Celtic in race, however disguised as Saxons by the adoption of the Saxon language and manners, as are the inhabitants of modern Cornwall, or the "French" of the Côtes du Nord, or Ille et Vilaine.

We have now to cast a glance towards the North. All

admit that as you travel northward in a straight line from Gloucester to Manchester and Carlisle you pass through a country which was substantially Celtic in the sixth and seventh centuries. To the east of this line the Britons who were willing to pay tribute had gradually " become Saxons." The further west you went from the same, the more purely Celtic did you find the inhabitants. To show that the bulk of the inhabitants of the Lowlands of Scotland, and of the North of England from the Scottish border to the Mersey, is Celtic, we need only refer to the ancient kingdoms of *Strathclyde* and *Cumbria*, and the comparatively recent date of their extinction. This recent date is a very material as well as interesting point. We are not left to plead for the Celtic character of these wide tracts of country—forming, along with Wales and the West of England, fully *one-fourth* of Roman Britain—at some dim legendary period of the far past ; evidence is not wanting which points to comparatively recent times ; and to these times alone need reference here be made. If these states existed, whether as tributary or otherwise, until within a comparatively modern period, and their inhabitants were then Celtic, then the point is settled that the bulk of the people of those regions are in blood Celtic still (with greater or less admixture of Danish and Anglo-Saxon), unless there be some ground for believing that since that comparatively modern period the original dwellers were bodily expelled, or spontaneously quitted the land. But neither of these suppositions is entertained by any one.

Northumbria obtained nominal supremacy over Bernicia *(Bryneich)*, as well as Deira *(Deivyr)*. But that supremacy must have been of a very short-lived, or of a very superficial character—most probably both. *Strathclyde* embraced the greater part of Bernicia. It reached from the Clyde to the Solway, and west and east from the Irish Sea to the Lothians. The kingdom of *Cumbria* continued southward from the Solway to the Mersey, including, on the west, Cumberland, Westmoreland, and Lancashire, and stretching considerably to the east into Yorkshire. In this great region of Strathclyde (*Ystrad-Clwyd*) and *Cumbria*, was the chief seat of Ancient British power and culture for many centuries.

Asser tells us that the "army of the pagans" (the Danes) in the year 875, reduced all Northumberland, and ravaged the Picts and *Strath-Clydensians*.[1] Whatever may have been the meaning of the supremacy once obtained by the Angles over Bernicia, its consequence was not the extinction of the kingdom of Strathclyde. At *Alclwyd* Dumbarton)[2] was the chief seat of the Britons continued until the Danes over-ran the country. But even then, that ancient kingdom was not extinguished; for it was in existence under a recognised sovereign of its own, in the year 924, when it is said by the Chronicler, that *the king of the Strathclyde Britons* and all the Strathclyde Britons (*Strac-lacd Wealas*), or Welsh, chose King Edward (the elder, son of Alfred), for father and for lord."[3] If it should be said that this only means that he became master of those regions, that there was actually no "kingdom" and no "king" in existence—it may be replied that not only would this be in contradiction of the plain statement of a

---

[1] *Life of Alfred*, ann. 875.

[2] *Alclwyd* is a purely Celtic word: W. *allt*, a hill or eminence, and *clwyd*, the name of the river; the hill or fortress on the Clwyd. "Dumbarton" is a curious instance of the tautology as well as historical growth of local names. The first syllable is the Celtic *dun* or *din*, a hill or fortress; the second is the A.-Sax. *burh* or *byrig*, a translation of the Celtic *dun*; the third is the A.-Sax. *tun*, a "town," or enclosure, but slightly differing in meaning from *burh*.

[3] *Sax. Chron.* ann. 924.

recognised authority, but it would involve the absurd conclusion that there was no " king of the Scots," and no
" dwellers in Northumbria," in those days; for all these,
and others, are said in the same passage to have chosen
Edward, " for father and for lord."

To the same effect is the testimony of William of
Malmesbury, who says, that Edward brought under all the
Britons who were called Wallenses; " Brittones omnes,
quos nos Wallenses dicimus, bellis profligatos, suæ ditioni
subegit."[1]   And Ethelred, in proof of Edward's goodness
and influence, tells us that he induced "the Scots, the
Cumbri, the Wallenses, &c., to choose him, not so much as
lord and king, as father."[2]   This certainly looks as if they
were still in existence as distinct states.

The affection which prompted this choice of Edward
seems, however, to have been but a very slight and momen-
tary passion, for before Athelstan's reign, we see them
again turning recalcitrant towards the English. Athelstan's
forces, commanded by himself and his brother Edmund,
regained their allegiance, without their affection, by the
memorable victory of Brunanburh, gained over the combined armies of the Scots, Strathclydians, Cumbrians, and
Danes.

> " These mighty smiths of war
>   O'ercame the Welsh (Wealas) :
>   Most valiant earls were they,
>   And gained the land."[3]

Owen (Eugenius) was the name of the prince of Strathclyde
in this great contest.

A few years after this the brave Cumbrians furbished

---

[1] Lib. ii. c. 5.

[2] " Eum, non tam in dominum et regem, quam in patrem, cum omni
devotione eligerunt." Ethelr. Rievall. de Geneal. Regum, p. 356.

[3] Sax. Chron. ann. 937.

their swords anew, and took the field in concert with the
Danes. This time Owen's son Donald (*Dyfnwal*) was their
leader; and once more were they destined to be subdued
by Edmund,[1] brother of Athelstan. Edmund, now himself
king, hands over his authority over Cumbria to Malcolm I.,
king of Scotland, on condition that he should assist the
English by sea against all comers.[2] In this compact
it was arranged that Cumbria should be governed
not by the Scottish king, but by his son and successor (*Tanaist*).[3] In the time of Canute, Duncan was
the ruler of Cumbria. The Danes' authority was
resisted by the Cumbrians, but they were quelled.
Duncan ascended the Scottish throne A.D. 1033, and his
son, Malcolm III., according to the arrangement just noted,
became the regulus of Cumbria. Some twenty years only
before the Norman Conquest, Cumbria was, by Edward the
Confessor, vested in the Scottish king.

It was at this late date that all their territories, with
their numerous inhabitants, were thus cut off from the
stock of more southern Celts, and made to appear as if
they belonged to a more northern race. The "Picts and
Scots" are now seen melting into the one name, "Scots,"
and the country to the north of the wall of Severus is
henceforth called "Scotland."

But although a united "Scottish" government is thus

---

[1] *Sax. Chron.* ann. 945. To this same contest probably reference is
made in the *Brut*: "*Ystrat Clut adiffeithwyt y gan y Saeson.*" Strathclyde was devastated by the Saxons. *Brut y Tywysogion*, ann. 944.

[2] *Sax. Chron.* ann. 945. Owing to this arrangement, Dyfnwal (Donald,
Dunwallon) is deposed, and is said by some authorities to have gone to
Rome. "*Ac ydaeth Dwnwallawn brenhin Ystrad Clut y Rufein.*" And
Dunwallon, King of Strathclyde, went to Rome. *Brut y Tywysogion*,
ann. 974.

[3] W. *tan*, under, below; *cistedd*, to sit: one who occupies the next
seat of authority.

established, the older designations of the people are not
all at once forgotten. In the old " *Brut* of the Princes " it
is recorded that " Malcolm, son of Dwnchath, king of the
Picts and Albanians, and Edward, his son, were killed by
the French." [1] This was Malcolm III. (Canmore), called
king of " Scotland " in the public records. The people,
both " Picts " and " Albanians," were still the same—all
the difference effected was a difference of government.
The stone was only put in a new setting.

We find passing references to the old race of Strathclyde,
under the name " Picts," at a still later period than the
above. John of Hexham, and Henry of Huntingdon, both
mention them. They fought against Stephen in the battle
of Clitheroe, and in the battle of " the Standard," in the
year 1138.[2] The fight at Clitheroe was contested on the
Scottish side by " Scots and Picts " against the English.[3]
" The Scots, therefore, and the Picts, scarcely held on from
the beginning to the third hour of the conflict," &c.[4]

From these historical notices it is evident that Strathclyde maintained its independence, or at least its form as a
government either independent or tributary, much longer
than the more southern Cumbria. This country of the
Ancient Brigantes suffered more, perhaps, than any other
district long maintaining Celtic rule, from attacks both
from cognate and from alien despoilers. It was frequently
set upon by the Strathclydians. Northumbrian Angles
were continually ravaging it. It was seldom free from
Danish incursions. The Anglo-Saxons from the South,

---

[1] *Brut y Tywysogion*, pp. 55, 57.

[2] *Sax. Chron.* ann. 1138.

[3] " Hoc bellum factum est apud Clithero inter Anglos, Pictos, et
Scotos," &c. *Johann. Hagust.* p. 260.

[4] *Ibid.* p. 261. " Scoti itaque et Picti vix a prima hora initi conflictus
usque ad tertiam perstiterunt."

the Scots from the North, in later ages, made it their prey. So reduced at last was Cumbria, that when William the Norman came to take his inventory in Domesday, he "found it not in his heart" to exhaust it further, but remitted all its taxes. The population had evidently become thin and impoverished—for nothing else could have mollified the heart of William—and it took long ages to repair the desolations which had been wrought. Great numbers of the Cumbri had retired into Wales after the disastrous battle of *Cattracth*. Their places had been partly filled by Pictish incursions from Strathclyde, and by Danish settlers who had arrived by the Irish sea, and the traces of these are discoverable in the local names of Cumberland and Westmoreland to this day.[1]

At the same time we are far from admitting that any such displacement of the Ancient British element had taken place as rendered the ancestry of the present inhabitants less Celtic than Teuton. Far otherwise; sparse as the population might be, the bulk of it was Celtic. The traditions, superstitions, dialectic peculiarities of the country prove this; as do also the general character, temperament and complexion of the people.

From this survey of the extreme North of England on the Western side, including the Lowlands of Scotland, there need be no hesitation felt in asserting that the Ancient British population were never dislodged from their native soil. Where the Angles, Saxons, Danes, and Normans found them, there they left them. Partial dislodgment, doubtless, took place, as will always occur amid great

[1] The mountains bear names imposed by the various races mentioned, as: Scaw *Fell* (Dan.); Bow *Fell* (Dan.); High *Pike* (Celt.); Black Co*mb* (Celt.); Saddle-back (Sax.); *Dent* Hill (Celt.). So of rivers: Derwent (Celt.); Esk (Celt.); Sark (Dan.); *Cambeck* (Celto-Sax.—W. *Cam*, crooked; Sax. *beck*, a brook); Duddon (Celt.); Croglin (Celt.); Nent (Celt). Few streams bear other than Celtic names.

commotions and conflicts of nations; but no such dislodgment is witnessed to by history, and no such wholesale
immigration of foreign races, as would entitle the historian
of this day to conclude that the race-character of the inhabitants had been changed.

If we retrace our steps southward, we shall everywhere
find on the line of our present survey, traces of the Ancient
British population at recent dates.

In the latter half of the eighth century, Shrewsbury, then
called *Pengwern*, was the capital of the Kings of Powis :
and Offa gave proof to succeeding ages how great was the
difficulty of confining the Cymry of North Wales within
limits by the construction of his stupendous " dyke." [1]
That great earthwork, *Clawdd Offa*, measuring a hundred
miles long from the mouth of the Dee to the Bristol Channel, is an abiding memorial of the terrible power of the
Britons, and the unfailing resolution of the brave old Mercian king. In those rude times rude strength was occasionally manifested on a magnificent scale ; and this is an
instance of it. The modern soldier would pronounce the
building of a huge rampart a hundred miles long, from sea
to sea, a clumsy and unmilitary method of checking an
invader ; but we must bear in mind that Offa had the example of the Romans before him, and that they had been
able, with all their strategy, to discover no better method
of hemming in the uncontrollable Caledonians than building great earthworks and walls across the country. Neither
Offa nor the Romans had heard of the grandest erection
of the kind (in existence probably even then) the wall of
China ! The plan was adopted in Britain as an exceptional
expedient to meet an exceptional case of peril.

As to Herefordshire, not only is the staple of its popula-

[1] See Lappenberg, *Anglo-Saxon Kings*, vol. i. 231.

tion known to be purely Celtic, but it continued to a very late period to associate itself with the *Cymry* of Wales in uncompromising opposition to the Saxon kings. In the twelfth century (temp. Henry II.) Hereford city was considered as "in Wales," although it had been the chief city of Mercia in the reign of Offa. Part of the county was assigned to the Welsh by Offa's dyke; and it continued as one of the regions of the "Marches"[1]—indeed, *the* region, *par excellence*, of the "Marches," for it gave the name of "Earl of March" to Mortimer[2]—to be the general boundary-land" between the English and the Welsh, allowed as such to belong partly to both—for many ages after the kingdom of Mercia had been swallowed up in the general dominions of the English kings. All this implies an intimacy and sympathy between the *Cymry* and the inhabitants of these parts which could arise from no other cause than identity of race.

But it is needless to multiply facts to prove a point so generally admitted. Not only will no one who has pondered the early ethnography of England, deny that the people of Herefordshire were genuine Celts, but he will freely grant that the inhabitants of Worcestershire and Gloucestershire also were almost entirely of the same race. He finds no account of extensive displacement. He hears nothing of a Saxon population transported from other regions, and located in these. The country is found always peopled, apparently by the same race, whether the name it bears is *Maxima Cæsariensis*, imposed by the Romans, *Myrenarice*, or Mercia, in Anglo-Saxon times, or the more familiar

---

[1] Anglo-Sax. *Meare*, a mark; hence a boundary-line, border, separating different kingdoms. The kingdom of *Mercia* itself had its name from its being the *meare* or boundary region between the Britons of Wales and the East Angles.

[2] His chief residence was Wigmore Castle, in Herefordshire.

county designations of the present day. Different kings
of different races rule, different laws and different languages
prevail ; but the *people* are immortal, conveying down from
age to age the blood of the same British race (with more or
less Teutonic admixtures), and continuing still, in their
physiological characteristics, manners and customs, superstitions, dialects, to form a *Myrcna-rice*, a border kingdom,
between the purer Celts of Wales and the Celto-Saxons of
England further East.

Of *Monmouthshire* we need not speak. It was certainly
from no considerations of race that this county, so late as
the eighth Henry, was numbered with the counties of
England. To this day a very large proportion of its
inhabitants even retain the Welsh language ; and the
whole, with the exception, of course, of the immigrant
element which the rapidly-developed trade and manufactures of the county have attracted—are of Celtic blood.

We have now completed the survey we intended
making. We have seen in the early stages of the
Saxon conquest, whole populations, tribes, or kingdoms,
in the South, and in the Central, and North-Eastern parts
—Lloegrians, Brython, the men of Galedin, the Gwyddelians, and the Coranians—pass away, and melt almost
simultaneously into the mass of the Anglo-Saxon people.
In the South-West the great kingdom of Wessex has by
degrees stretched forth its long arms, and gathered into its
embrace the Britons of the South coast counties of Hants
and Dorset, along with those further North in Somerset
and Wilts, casting its spell with more or less power over
the dwellers in Devon, and far into Cornwall. The primary
Celtic colours have slowly mingled with the complementary
Teutonic hues, forming at last a settled mid colour, but
fringing off at all the extreme points in the bright

unequivocal " red-dragon " Celtic. In the extreme North, Strathclyde and Cumbria, large and powerful Celtic king-doms, covering nearly, if not fully, one-fourth of the surface of Roman Britain, eventually disappear, drawn into the all-absorbing Maelstrom of a now English-speaking race. The same sort of change is seen progressing in the intervening space along the border lands of the " Marches " —Cheshire, Shropshire, Herefordshire, Monmouthshire, Gloucestershire, and Worcestershire. Thus, in the course of 600 or 700 years, more than half the face of our island (omitting Wales and Scotland) is plainly seen with the " naked eye" of history, without telescopic or micro-scopic aid of conjecture, assumption, or myth, to pass by slow but appreciable gradations from a Celtic into the out-ward seeming of a Teutonic territory. In a word, nothing more, nothing less, can be said of the teeming multitudes of Ancient Britons once inhabiting the parts referred to, than was intimated by the 9th *Triad* of the Lloegrians— viz., that they " became Saxons ;" and nothing more can be said of the agency of the Germanic and Scandinavian race in bringing this to pass than what is ascribed by the *Chronicle* to the Normans, in a particular case—viz., that they reduced all, small and great, *to be Saxons*.[1]

What *proportion* of Ancient British blood is indicated by this picture as having passed into the ancestry of the present English, we shall not seek precisely to determine. It, however, immeasurably surpasses in copiousness any-thing that has ever yet been acknowledged by our histo-rians. Of the immense preponderance of the Britons over

---

[1] *Brut y Tywysogion.* Rolls office ed. by Rev. J. Williams, Ab Ithel, p. 63. This was, however, a very superficial mode of making Celts into " Saxons." It is applied to the conquest of the Isle of Anglesea, whose inhabitants have never displayed many signs of being " Saxons."

their Saxon and Angle conquerors during the first stages of the Conquest, few sane persons can have a doubt. That they did not continue to maintain this preponderance, has never yet been proved. That they gradually dwindled away in the character and outward expression of Britons, over the greater part of the island, is clear; and the causes and manner of the change have just been explained. But that this kind of change is tantamount to extinction of *race* elements, no person of ordinary capacity will pretend to believe. If that were true, the English-speaking subjects of the English crown in Scotland and Ireland would no longer be Celtic in blood, but Saxon. The radical unsoundness of the idea is seen from its liableness to be so easily reduced *ad absurdum*.

But the Jutes, Saxons, and Angles, of earlier or later immigrations, are not to be considered as the only factors along with the Ancient Britons in determining the ethnological character of the English people. The Danes and Normans are also to be taken into the account.

SECTION VIII.

Influence of the Danish and Norman Invasions on the Ethnological Character of the English People.

In speaking of the English or Anglo-Saxon nation from this time forward, it must not be forgotten that they were no longer a Teutonic, but a mixed race. When the Danish and Norman conquests were effected, the process of amalgamation with the ancient Britons had far advanced, although still, especially in the time of the former, far from being completed.

1. The Danish invasion in its influence on the distribution and admixture of race.

The distribution or location of races in the British Isles had been pretty well completed before the settlement of the Danish rule. For many ages prior to this, and even prior to the Saxon and Anglian Kingdoms themselves, the country had been afflicted by Danish invasions on a larger or smaller scale ; and Danish settlements in great number had been effected on our coasts. But neither the earlier nor the later Danish incursions materially affected the boundaries of the Cymry of Wales and Cornwall ; although in Cumbria and Strathclyde they may have had some effect. The Norman conquest having occurred still later, not only effected much less by way of race intermixture than the Danish, but in the way of race distribution produced hardly any change. All that these conquests can be held to have done, therefore, in this relation, is the effacing still further the already obscured signs of Celtic nationality on the western border of England, the displacement of a portion of the Britons of Cumbria, and the confining of the uncompromising *Cymry* more strictly within the limits of Wales, and " West Wales," or Cornwall. During neither of these conquests were large masses of Britons, except those who came with the conquerors, brought into a state of fusion with the English ; nor were any portions of Wales proper annexed to the English sovereignty.

What the Saxon *Chronicler* relates of the work of Edmund in ravaging Strathclyde in A.D. 945, and granting it to Malcolm, King of the Scots, on condition of his becoming a fellow-worker with him, " by sea and by land," we have already shown. Malcolm, was, of course, to become a fellow-worker " by sea," emphatically for the purpose of checking the Danes.

The Danes, pressing especially on the Eastern coast, by degrees became masters of Northumbria, Mercia, and East Anglia. We have shown that they indeed swarmed in prodigious numbers on all parts of the coast of Britain, coming at one time in "three hundred ships," and numbering at another time as many as 30,000 men. Alfred, with all his extraordinary exertions, was completely unable to expel them from the Southern parts of the island. He therefore adopted the wise policy of paving the way, since they were known to be essentially of the same race with the Anglo-Saxons, for their gradual fusion with the inhabitants. He accordingly arranged for their peaceful settlement in the country, ceded to them, under conditions, the Kingdom of East Anglia, and laboured to the extent of his power to promote a good understanding between them and their Anglo-Saxon opponents. By this time they had obtained power over nearly *two-thirds* of the territories of the Heptarchy. This they had accomplished through a series of conflicts as bloody and disastrous as any which the history of this much-enduring land has ever chronicled.

It has been stated by some writers (incorrectly, we venture to think), that the Danes about the time when their horrid massacre was planned by Ethelred, A.D. 1002, numbered nearly *one-third* of the inhabitants of England. One-sixth would probably be nearer the truth, and even that proportion was diminished by the atrocious deed referred to. It was, however, more than restored soon afterwards by the avenging invasions of Sweyn, Thurchil, Knut (Canute), and other great commanders, with their teeming hosts. Under Canute, who in A.D. 1017 became sole monarch of England, perhaps the Danish element may, without exaggeration, be said to have constituted nearly one-fifth of the population—the Anglo-Saxons,

including the Saxonized Britons, furnishing the remaining
four-fifths. The Danish element held the highest place in
East Anglia, and the Eastern side of the island throughout,
to the extreme of Northumbria.

The British kingdom of Cumberland was inundated in
the latter part of the tenth century by the *Norwegians*, who
found their way thither by the Irish Sea—a sea well known
to the Northmen from times much earlier; for it was the
route they pursued on their way to France. The kingdom
of *Strathclyde* having by this time been annexed to the
dominions of the Scottish king, it is probable that the incursions of these new Norwegian hordes affected chiefly
Southern and South-Western *Cumbria*, still inhabited by
the comparatively unmixed Welsh-speaking Celts ;[1] and
that numbers of these were forced to flee the country, and
seek a home among their brethren in Wales. The Norwegian immigration was so large that it gave a Scandinavian tinge to the region now included in the counties of
Cumberland and Westmoreland, visible, as we have shown,
to this day in the local names of the district; and contributed to hasten the entire extinction of the Cymraeg of
the region.[2]

We must guard, however, against the supposition that
the displacement of the original population was on any
large scale. The Celts and Saxons, and even Danes
throughout Northumbria, had doubtless largely intermixed
before the arrival of these new comers, giving room for
the probable conjecture that those alone would be compelled to evacuate the country whose attachment to the

---

[1] The language of Cumbria is proved to be identical with the Welsh
by the literary remains of the Cumbrian bards, *Aneurin* and *Llywarch
Hen*, and by dialectic words and local names.

[2] See Ferguson's *Northmen in Cumb. and Westm.*; and Worsaae's
Danes and Norwegians in England, *passim*.

ancient speech and usages was too stubborn to bend, and who, therefore, scorning to coalesce with the hated North-men, retired into Wales.

Whatever may be the truth as to the Scandinavian ad-mixture in Cumbria, it is on all hands admitted that the North of England was more affected by it than the South. But, of course, no amount of intermixture with Danes or Norwegians could affect the *race* quality of the Anglo-Saxons, supposing for the moment that the Anglo-Saxons existed now in their unmixed integrity in the land, for we all know that Danes, Norwegians, Angles, and Saxons, were of the same Teutonic race. Under the actual circum-stances, the people of England at the time being a *com-pound* of Celts and Teutons, the effect of receiving into their body a quantum of Danes and Norwegians would simply be the increasing of the proportion of Teutonic as compared with Celtic blood in the mass. It cannot be denied that the Danish invasion and conquest did operate in this manner. The Norman conquest, as will by-and-by be shown, contrary to the traditional faith prevailing, had hardly a preponderating effect in favour of Teutonism.

When endeavouring to gauge the influence of the Danes on English ethnology two related but antithetic ideas occur to the inquirer. The rule of the Danes in England was brief; but the era of Danish incursions was long. They held sovereignty in this country only for some *eight and twenty years*—A.D. 1013—1041, i.e., from the accession of Sweyn to the death of Hardicanute. But ever since the year 787, when they first made serious attempts upon the country, they never ceased to pour in accessions, more or less numerous, to the Teutonic population. Dr. Donaldson is therefore probably in error when denying that the Danish and Norman "settlements produced any con-siderable effect on the ethnical characteristics of the country." [1] In the sense of adding a new element of race, they, it is true, effected nothing; but in the sense of altering the relative proportions between the Celtic and Teutonic elements they did something, and that something was in augmentation of the Teutonic, and the production of the Dane rather than the Norman.

2. The effect of the Norman Conquest on the ethnical character of the English people.[2]

Though we are accustomed to look upon the Normans as a new people, distinct from the Saxons and the Danes, it must be now kept in mind that they were so in reality, as far as they were Normans, only as arriving in Britain at a later time and from a different direction, and swayed by opposite interests. As the Danes were brethren—though not loving—to the Saxons, Jutes, and Angles, so were the old pure Normans brethren, or rather sons—though neither loving nor filial—to the Danes. The Northmen, or Danes, who had for ages been the plague of Britons and Anglo-Saxons, and bore rule in the country when William demanded the crown, were the same people, ethnically, who had in the early part of the 10th century entered France under Rollo, and converted Neustria into *Normandie*. Rollo had recognised the Danes in England as brethren in race before his descent upon France, for we remember that he had come over to assist Guthrum the Dane in conquering East Anglia. Having, years after this, succeeded in establishing himself and a horde of followers, in Neustria, to which he gave the name *Normandie*, because he had converted it into an abode of the " men

[1] *On English Ethnography*, *Camb. Essays*, 1856. *P.* 53.

[2] Portions of this section are reproduced from a paper read by the author before the British Association at Brighton, 1872, and before the Ethnological Society of London.

of the North," he began to create a race which, under
the name Normans, were in reality not so. He at once
adopted the language of the conquered territory, and
proceeded to knead into one the Celtic inhabitants
and the colonists he had introduced. The work of
amalgamation proceeded; Rollo extended and consolidated his sway; the Normans became quite as much
Celts as the Celts became Normans; the population grew;
a feeling of kindred also prevailed between the old inhabitants of Normandy and those of Brittany—for originally
they were the same Celtic race—in great measure, indeed,
actual contributions to that race, as shall again be shown,
from the insular Britons; and after some 150 years of
advancement in the arts of civilization under French
culture, these Celto-Normans come over under William to
achieve the Conquest of England.

If this representation is a correct one, it will follow that
the "Normans" who conquered England were only in a
very qualified sense descendants of the old Scandinavians.
This representation we claim as substantially correct. It
is supported by history, and contradicted by neither history
nor fable. It is contradicted only by the "School
Histories of England," and popular ignorance.

Even if it were true—which it is not—that the followers
of William the Conqueror were in the main, or entirely,
pure Normans, the ethnological revolution they would
effect in England would still be very insignificant. In
their application to the Norman conquest, under *this* view
of it, the words of Dr. Donaldson are true : " The Scandinavian settlers were rather chieftains and soldiers des-
potically established in certain districts, than bodies of
emigrants who affected the whole texture of the population." As already observed, the Danes through a long
series of years had been pouring in their hordes, and

fighting for themselves settlements in different parts of the island; but the "Normans" under William came as a body of "chieftains and soldiers," and accomplished their great exploit all at once through sheer superiority in one battle-field. The battle of Hastings, the first they fought, was also the last before their supremacy was a *fait accompli*, for what fighting followed was only in settlement and defence of that supremacy, against the contumacy of different sections of the country. The whole of the fighting from first to last was done in *four* years. By 1071 the whole of England, from Cornwall to the Tweed, and from the Eastern borders of Wales to the German Sea, was the prize —the blood-stained prize—of the Northmen's valour ! The wars with the Welsh only serve to prove the vitality—the unextinguishable spirit—which animated that people. No change was produced in their location—none to speak of in their ethnical character.

We have said that William's followers were not pure Northmen ; and also that even if they *had* been such, they had only produced a faint change in the ethnical character of the English people, by reason of their comparative fewness. We have already intimated that the people of Normandy, from systematic amalgamation of the natives with the conquerors, were a highly mixed race. That the race inhabiting the old district of Neustria were in the main Celts, we need not stay long to prove, for few will deny it ; that the amalgamation took place is the unambiguous testimony of history, and its truth is, at least, corroborated by the significant fact that the language of the natives became the sole language of the compound people. We have throughout rejected the doctrine that the adoption of a language is proof of preponderance of number on the side of those whose vernacular it was ; and we reject it here. But be the

T

number of the natives of Neustria great or small, it is clear that they were all taken, as they were found on the land, as subjects of the conquerors, and that in course of time a complete fusion took place between the two peoples.

But we must here more closely enquire into the race elements of the regions whence the so-called "Norman" conquerors of England were derived.

To determine this matter we must cast a glance at those regions as they were settled before the North-men had a place as a ruling community in France—and then at the nature of the Norman conquest of Rouen and the surrounding country, the nucleus of *Normandy*, estimating, as far as we can, the amount of *northern blood* introduced into the region afterwards so called. It will soon appear that the *name* was no faithful exponent of the race, any more than the name of France is of the nationality of that country. This region was a part of that territory which, as Cæsar tells us, was inhabited by the *Galli* —a people usually considered more purely Celtic than the Belgæ of the North-east, more Celtic, therefore, than the Cymri and Britons, and divided by a still wider line from the Aquitani or Iberi of the south-west. It was possessed of a large number of towns and a considerable population, divided into several tribes or clans. On the breaking up of the Roman Empire in the fifth century, Clovis, or Chlodwig (A.D. 486), the head of a Teutonic tribe, and of the family of Merowig, which occupied a tract of country between the Rhine and the Somme, pushing his way westward, became master of the *Galli* as far as the eastern limits of Armorica. It would seem from the best authorities that the conquest effected by Clovis and the hordes which followed him under the name of "Frank-manni," or "freemen," was comparatively without bloodshed. They met with strenuous opposition in the eastern parts, the territory of the Belgæ; but on reaching Rheims, Clovis became a Christian, and of the orthodox Roman Church ; and henceforward his progress, as argued by Thierry, was a matter of diplomatic arrangement through the bishops, the customary mediators between the Roman Emperor and the provincials. From the Somme to the borders of Brittany the Franks were admitted as masters almost without opposition ; in fact the people who had been ruled by the Romans wanted masters. The change was simply a change of rulers, with the addition of some Germanic rules respecting the relation of classes and the occupation of land. The masters were alone Frank-manni, all others being in a state of more or less subjection or bondage. The title "Franks" was thus for a long time applied as a social rather than an ethnological designation, until at last it lost its specific meaning, and settled down as a national and geographical term. The new sovereignty thus set up by the Frank-manni extended from Antwerp to Rennes, and from Calais to Nevers.

What is worthy of especial notice in this new occupation is the fact that it reduced but by a very small number the native Gallic population, and added but a very small proportion of Frankish immigrants. The district occupied was large : the Merovingian tribe, though terrible in warlike power, was small. The parts subsequently embraced under the name Normandy were the most distant westward, and the last and easiest brought under rule, so that here the disturbance was smallest and the influx of alien blood least. M. Guizot notifies a striking difference between the Neustrian Franks and their brethren of the *Oster-rike*, or Austrasian kingdom on the Rhine, in that the latter were far more dense and compact than the former. The Neustrian Franks had, indeed, taken possession of so wide a territory that they were obliged to spread themselves sparsely over the underlying native race.

This was the first Frankish conquest of the region. In about 300 years another followed. This was brought about by that more concentrated and more intensely Germanic family of Franks which held the Austrasian kingdom. In the 8th century, when the earlier Franks and the natives had well-nigh forgotten their separate origin and were nearly fused into one people, Pepin and his son Charlemagne overran the whole country, and established a new Frankish dynasty—the Carlovingian. The change now introduced, though not accompanied by greater violence, was far more radical and disturbing than the former. A large proportion of strangers was thrust in, the old social system was more disintegrated. But the language, religion, and manners which Rome had given Gaul were not dislodged. And as Charlemagne aspired to create an empire even transcending in glory the Roman, he pursued a policy similar to that of the Romans in his humane treatment of the subjugated. In fact the new order of things was greatly in favour of the natives. Of the conquest by Pepin, M. Guizot says: "Never was a revolution accomplished more easily and noiselessly. Pepin possessed the power; the fact was converted into right; neither resistance nor protest of sufficient weight to leave a trace in history was offered. Everything seemed to remain the same; nothing was changed except a title. Yet it is certain that a grand event had happened—that the change marked the end of a particular social state and the beginning of another, a veritable epoch in the history of civilization in France."

In this second Frankish conquest, therefore, as in the first, no attempt was made to dislodge the inhabitants. The high places of society were occupied by the ruling

Franks; but the next lower strata, and especially the multitude below, continued what they had always been— substantially Gallic or Celtic.

We may mention, in passing, that after the death of Charlemagne and the dismemberment of his empire, during a period of anarchy and confusion scarcely equalled in the history of civilized nations, and mainly through the power of feudalism, several dukedoms or countships were set up, which virtually were independent sovereignties, although doing nominal homage to the King of what was now called France. Brittany had always preserved a kind of independent existence; but now arose, one after another, the countships or dukedoms of Anjou, Poitou, Maine, Guienne, Burgundy, Champagne, Provence, &c., to define and synchronize which has always proved an impossible task to French historians. This was in fact the period when feudalism grew into full stature, and spread with mysterious rapidity over all Europe. With several of these sovereignties William the Bastard had intimate relations, of which he availed himself to the full in raising his army of invasion.

It was at this time of confusion, when the kingdom of France proper was in its weakness, and every feudal lord was carving out a petty kingdom for himself, that the Norman Rollo, with a troop of followers, made a descent upon Neustria. It will be well at once to mark and estimate the volume of race-intrusion. Rollo was the captain of a robber-band. He had been banished for a misadventure from the Danish Court, and set out to mend or make his fortune by such means as might be effectual. He led no army. He carried, as was the fashion in those days, a troop of desperate freebooters, in small boats capable of skimming shallow rivers, and even of being dragged up the banks, to pass bridges and obstructions.

His men were picked, daring, and strong of limb. He chanced to fall on the coast of Neustria, probably not without knowledge of the fertility of the land and the sweetness of the climate, and went up, plundering his way, until he approached Rouen. There was no army in existence to meet them. Charles the Simple could scarcely protect his own capital of Paris. Accustomed as that coast had been to devastation from Danish adventurers (for Rollo was by no means the first, though he was the most terrible visitor of his kind), there was no concert or organization for defence, each feudal lord being satisfied if by thickness of wall and depth of moat he could keep scatheless his own castle, and pass on the unwelcome strangers to his next neighbour. The common people, carrying their whole world on their backs, made the forest and the crags their safe retreat. Rollo's fleet of boats had nearly reached Rouen when the inhabitants heard of them. The city was filled with consternation. Rouen had many stalwart men, probably far outnumbering the Norman plunderers ; but they were not fighting men in the feudal sense of the term ; and it would take many men of strong make, unaccustomed to arms, to meet the giant Rollo himself. There was no attempt at defence. The archbishop, taking the customary lead, went forth to meet the pirates and to arrange terms. Rollo and his followers were admitted through the gates as conquerors. The Normans went round to view the city ; and finding it a strong and gainly place, chose it as their home and centre for further operations.

This is the representation given of the matter by Depping, in his *Expéditions Maritimes des Normans,* by Wace in his *Roman de Rou,* and, following them, by Thierry.

Having now secured a footing, the chief recruited his

small fighting force from the citizens of Rouen and the district around. The great town of Bayeux (the seat of the old Baiocasses), and Evreux (of the old Eburovices), and others were soon captured. No time was lost in forming matrimonial connexions. Rollo took to wife the daughter of the Count of Bayeux, and by adopting a method of ruling at once strong and mild, demanding nothing but feudal subjection and tribute, became popular with the natives. As a stroke of policy, he professed himself a Christian; he made peace, after successful conflict, with the King of France, and married his daughter, having put away his former wife on the singular ground that he was now a Christian man. The land of Normandy was granted him in fief, and was duly parcelled out among his followers. The Northmen now freely intermarried with the natives, and, strange, to say, in two generations, as Sismondi has shown, had generally laid aside their Northern speech, and adopted the Romance language.

Now, in pondering these events, one cannot fail of feeling surprise at the fact that a body so small could conquer and possess a region so large and populous, the fief of an established and civilized kingdom, and studded on all sides with baronial castles and intrenched cities. The exact number of the immigrants cannot be ascertained, nor the populousness of the towns and districts they subdued; but from the tenor of the whole account it is perfectly clear that the conquerors were but a mere handful as compared with the natives. To remove our surprise, however, we have only to remember the maxims and practices of the time. Feudalism, now dominant, had its stringent and omnipotent laws. The bearing of arms was an honour conferred only on the few. Men-at-arms were gentlemen. The commonest grade of people, from whom the soldiery in our days of standing armies are drawn, were not *men*:

and " chattels " could not be supposed capable of bearing
arms. The fiefholder, or lord, had a claim for military
and any other kind of service from his retainers; and the
king, as suzerain of the lord, had a claim on him. But
the lord, as already observed, was often in practice the
master of his own territory, and the protectors of that
territory were his own men-at-arms. To bring the army
of the king to his assistance might be a work of long
negotiation and doubtful result. When, therefore, an
enemy stronger than the local guardians attacked a territory, the day was his own. This was precisely how it was
that Rollo, prompt in action, fell in purpose, with few
companions, but companions of the right mettle, surprised
Rouen, and obtained ascendancy over the populous city
and districts surrounding it. In those days the prowess
and bodily strength of one man not unfrequently scattered
a multitude, and turned the tide of battle when the foe had
well-nigh seized on victory. The Homeric mode of warfare had almost been reproduced. Whoever has read
" Ivanhoe " will scarcely forget the graphic picture of
feudalism and its practice of arms there given, or the prodigious valour and exploits of such knights as Ivanhoe,
Brian de Bois-Guilbert, and the Black Knight.

Now, when a district had been won by the sudden
descent of such a small body of men as Rollo and his companions, and the conquest extended by the aid of the
subjugated, it were absurd to suppose that the race-elements
of the country were greatly affected. The land was still
tilled, the vines tended, the cattle herded, by the same race
which had done so before. The conquerors would soon
stamp their own name on the country, and even on its inhabitants ; but the real change would only be a change of
name and of name-givers. The conquerors might begin
at once to enter into marriage alliances with the natives,

and might abandon their own speech, adopting that of the
land they had won ; but this would only give advantage
to the native race.

This was precisely the case in Western Neustria, afterwards called Normandy. The disturbance of the native
race by the Norman was even less than that caused by the
Frankish conquest. The land was not more the same land
than the people who dwelt upon it were the same people
as they had been for ages ; that is, they were substantially
Gallic.

And if this was the case in Normandy, *a fortiori* it was
the case in the regions lying eastward and southward of
that territory, while Brittany, to the west, was in a more
marked degree than any held by a native race—a race,
according to the best authorities, not omitting scientific
searchers of the present day, more Cymric than the Belgæ,
and nearly related to the so-called Celts of Britain, through
various accessions between the 4th and 7th centuries from
the Cymri of Wales. The wide and fertile regions on both
sides of the river Loire, where afterwards we find the
duchies of Maine, Anjou, Poitou, Touraine, the seats of
the ancient Arvii, Pictones, Turones, Ligures, and on the
east as far as the Somme, and even the Scheldt and the
Meuse, the land of the ancient Belgæ, were all marked by
an immense preponderance of the native race, the intrusive
Franks having only given it the faintest tinge of Germanic
blood. All the great writers and almost all the scientific
explorers of France agree that the modern French are
what in popular phrase we designate them, a "Gallic"
people—considerably Aquitanian or Iberian, dark-haired
and swarthy, to the south and south-west, but prevailingly
Gallic in the much more extensive central and northern
part, Cymric or Belgic in the east, and emphatically
Cymric in the extreme north-west. We should not omit

to mention that M. Broca, the celebrated ethnologist of
Paris, has recently confirmed this view—the view also of
M. W. F. Edwards and the two Thierrys—by minute and
carefully conducted calculations. He has found, taking
the measurements of the military conscription as his
basis, that a line drawn diagonally across France
from near Coutances in La Manche to Lyons, and
another parallel to it from a little west of the mouth of the
Somme to Geneva, cut off to the north-west the shortest in
stature, whom he classes as purest Celtic, and to the north-
east the tallest, that is, the people of Belgic race, corresponding with the *Gallia Belgica* of Cæsar, leaving in the
intervening space a people of medium height, representing,
as M. Broca thinks, the ancient Galli proper. He holds
the Bretons to be the most unmixed Celts of all the inhabitants of France, and considers them the key to the ethnology
of that country : "la clef de l'ethnologie de la France est
en Bretagne."

We have said so much on this point of the substantially
Gallic and, so-named, Celtic character of these regions
with a distinct purpose ; for we now desire to point out
that from all these parts in greater degree from some, in
less from others, were drawn the forces which William the
Conqueror used in his descent on Britain. It is clear that
this·is the most satisfactory way to estimate critically, in
the absence of definite statistics, the ethnological influence
which the Conquest exerted on our population. The *degree*
of that influence must more appear from other considerations again to be mentioned.

What, then, was the field whence William gleaned his
army ? Normandy, of course, was the first and principal
part of it. A line drawn from Abbeville through Mantes
and Alençon to Granville, in the Contentin, will nearly
describe the inland limits of this country. It generally

PARTS WHICH SUPPLIED THE NORMAN ARMY.

corresponded with the modern departments of La Manche, Calvados, Orne, Eure, and Seine-Inférieure. Having first, with due forethought, got permission of the Pope to enter and plunder England, and establish there the tax-office of Peter's-pence, his next step was to call a council of his barons and most intimate friends. They agreed to his proposals. In ordinary cases this alone would be required; but the enterprise was of a nature so grave that, according to the *Chronique de Normandie*, the barons advised that the *people* of Normandy should be consulted. This was a departure from the rules of chivalry and feudal policy of great import for us to note; for it led to the result that William's host was not a feudal agglomeration of fief-holders and their men-at-arms simply, but an armed multitude, under recognized chiefs, gathered from *all* ranks of the people far and near. William called a popular assembly, and requested a free expression of their views. Opinions differed; for he had now consulted men many of whom prospered by peaceful pursuits—merchants, tradesmen, agriculturists. But the hero's tact and resolution at last prevailed, and all Normandy began to pour in its contingents.

His next step, very significant to our argument, was to make proclamation through all the surrounding states, wherever any kind of influence could avail him, inviting indiscriminately all who had in them a love of adventure, all who needed a better fortune, all who could bring sword and lance, to come to the conquest and partition of England. From William of Malmesbury, Guilielmus Gemeticensis, and Ordericus Vitalis, we learn that the call was promptly answered from all quarters.[1] Brittany, to whose ducal house William was nearly related, was first and most liberal in response.

---

[1] Will. of Malmesb., b. iii; Ord. Vital. *Hist. Eccles.* p. 494.

Two of the duke's sons, Alain Fergant and Brian, and the lords of many castles and important fiefs, such as Rouel de Gaël, Robert de Vitry, Bertrand de Dinan, were among the Breton volunteers. The young Count Alain alone, according to Hume, was followed by no less than 5,000 men. Others flocked in from Maine and Anjou, from Poitou and Flanders, Burgundy and Aquitaine, and from the very borders of the Rhine and Italy. Most who came from these distant parts were hungry adventurers and military vagabonds, whose trade it was to follow the standards of any chief who would pay or promise pillage, and who scarcely had a right to anticipate the day when noble families in England would proudly trace their lineage to them as "Normans who came in with the Conqueror!" All who came to swell the ranks were welcomed with eagerness. Broad manors, castles, titles, pillage, were freely promised. The terms had a charm that operated mightily. Some joined on regular pay, some on the simple condition of licence to plunder, some on the promise of a Saxon heiress in marriage.[1] All were satisfied with promises, and all were ardent for the fray. Proud and poor Norman barons, Breton, Flemish, Anjevin counts had already marked for themselves those Saxon estates which suited their cupidity. Outlaws and thieves, humble villeins and serfs of Gallic and Frankish blood saw a chance of "founding a family." Power of muscle was now a precious possession; for he who did most execution on Saxon flesh would most win the Conqueror's favour. The spirit of the terrible man's harangue before the battle was already interpreted before the Channel was crossed:—
" Remember to fight well and put all to death; for if we conquer we shall be all rich. What I gain you will gain: if I take their land, you shall have it."

[1] *Chron. de Normandie*, p. 227.

Thus the Conqueror's great army was gathered and made ready for embarkation. It crossed the Channel and won the battle of Hastings, and by this one blow secured for Duke William the throne of England, and for every man who did his work well a substantial recompense.

But we must more particularly examine the non-"Norman" part of William's invading army. It is a fact —and a most interesting fact in the treatment of our present subject—that a very large proportion of William's followers, as already intimated, were genuine *Bretons*, and that not a few were *Britons*.

We advance, therefore, a *second* step. Already it has appeared that the soldiers raised by the Conqueror in his own duchy of Normandy, must in great measure have been of Celtic origin : we now have to show that in addition to these, he had in his train auxiliary forces which had no taint of Norman blood at all, but pure unequivocal Celts, close relations of the *Cymry* of Wales and Cornwall ! Some of his chief captains were princes and lords of Brittany, and among these were men who became possessors of some of the chief baronial estates, and founders of some of the chief "Norman" families of England !

Of course, this statement will be received with a measure of incredulity. Many who have only read the "history of England," in their school books have never become aware of the fact. The Norman conquerors were *Normans* representing all the puissance and chivalry of France, and, beyond dispute, of the high breed of the sea-kings and terrible warriors—the Vikings and Thunderers of the North. This is their faith. But its basis is very sandy, and when that is washed away, it will be easy to see that the Norman conquest, if it added a good deal of Teutonic, added also a good deal of Celtic blood to the already mixed blood of England. Alas, then, in many cases, for the pride of pure Norman descent!

The Normans, having conquered and established themselves as rulers over the Celts of the region which they called Normandie, naturally excited the jealousy and hostility of the Celts of Brittany; but still, amid frequent conflicts and constant rivalry, the rulers by degrees contracted alliances by marriage, and it came to pass that William the Conqueror himself, when a child, was entrusted to the care of his father's cousin, Alain, the ruler of Brittany, as guardian. If the ruling families were thus related, the populations were much more so. Originally identical in race, they had for many centuries freely settled in each other's territories, and largely contracted alliances by marriage. It was not therefore strange, if Breton soldiers came to fight side by side with Normans in William's invading army.

We have shown that when William's resolve was fixed, he immediately invited all the assistance he could command. His proclamation, dispersed through Brittany and other neighbouring countries, such as *Poitou* and *Anjou*— offering good pay and the pillage of England—attracted immediate attention, and brought multitudes to his standard. William was complaisant and full of promises; his liberality by anticipation made many friends; old feuds and sores between him and the Bretons were healed, and many of them came forward well armed for the conflict.

Eudes, whose father, Conan, William was suspected to have got poisoned, was now Count or regulus of Brittany under Norman influence. It has been already mentioned that his two princely sons, *Alain* and *Brian*, were among the first to arrive, with their train of followers, numbered by thousands—strong Breton "men at arms" ready for the fray.[1] These two young leaders were called by their knightly followers "*Mac-Tierns*"—sons of the ruler (W. *teyrn*, chief, king), and both were destined, but Alain more especially, to obtain the highest prominence in the "Norman" baronage of England. The chief command of the second division of William's army on the field of Hastings was entrusted to Alain.

Other Breton knights of renown, each leading his company of warriors, were, *Rivallon* de Gael, otherwise called Raoul de Gael, and Raulf de Gael, lord of the castle and city of Dôl; *Bertrand de Dinand*,[2] and *Robert de Vitry*, the last two somewhat mixed in blood and bearing French names, but recognised as Breton chiefs, and, like the others, accompanied by a "numerous train of followers," all of the Breton race. The captains of companies from Anjou and Poitou are not so plainly named; but the fact is stated that many came from these Celtic[3] states, and joined the forces of the Conquest.

Alain Fergant, the son of Eudes of Brittany, already named, with his 5,000 followers did noble service at the battle of Hastings, and is commemorated by the old rhyming chroniclers thus :—

---

[1] Lobineau, *Hist. de Bretagne*, i. 98. Alain attained to the highest celebrity in England. Brian also proved a distinguished warrior. Three years after the battle of Hastings we find him leading Norman troops to a decisive victory in Devon, on the river "Tavy," now Taw, where nearly 2,000 men on the Saxon side fell. *Sax. Chron.* ann. 1068.

[2] The pretty little town of *Dinan*, once a powerful fortress, bears to this day a purely Celtic name. The older form of it, with the terminating *d*, *Dinand*, suggests the derivation *dyfn-nant*, its situation being on the brink of a deep ravine. The simplest derivation, however, is *din-nant*, the hill, or fortress on the valley. Dinan is a good specimen of an old Breton town.

[3] These were, probably, notwithstanding the Frankish conquests, as prevailingly Celtic as was Brittany itself apart from the accessions it received from the Cymry.

> " Li quiens Alain de Bretaigne
> Bien i ferit od sa cumpaigne ;
> Cil i ferit cume baron,
> Mult le firent bien Breton."—*Geoff. Gaimar*.[1]

> " Alain Fergant, quens de Bretaigne,
> De Bretons mene grant cumpaigne ;
> C'est une gent fière et grifaigne,
> Ki volentiers prent e gaaingne.
>
> .   .   .   .   .
>
> " Bien se cumbat Alain Ferganz,
> Chevalier fu proz e vaillanz ;
> Li Bretonz vaid od sei menant,
> Des Engleiz fait damage grant."—*Benoit de St. Maure*.[2]

The Breton warrior did not lose his reward. A vast region of country north of York fell to his share ; and here on a steep hill overlooking the river Swale he built the great castle which he called *Riche-mont* (high or wealthy hill), now Richmond in Yorkshire.[3]

Riwallon de Gael became Lord of Norfolk, and built for his residence the great fortress of Norwich Castle ; but he was by and by found plotting against his master, and was obliged to retrace his steps to his native castle of Dôl.

The first Lord of *Coningsby* is by an old ballad thus traced to Brittany :—

> " *William de Coningsby*,
> Came out of Britany
> With his wife *Tiffany*,
> And his maide *Maufas*,
> And his dogge *Hardigras*." [4]

---

[1] See *Monumenta Hist. Brit.* vol. i. p. 828. "Alan, son of the Duke of Brittany, supposed by some to have been the original stock of the royal house of *Stuart*, followed his standard." Mackintosh, *Hist. of Eng.* i. 96. For the credit of the Breton prince, it is to be hoped he had no such posterity !

[2] Chroniques de Norm. i. 496.

[3] " Et nominavit dictum castrum Richemont, suo idiomate Gallico, quod sonant Latini divitem montem." Dugdale, *Monast.* i. 877.

[4] Hearne, *Præf.* ad Joh. de Fordun, *Scoti-Chron.* p. 170.

It may be possible, though difficult, to assign to all the Celtic knights in William's army their true localities in Brittany and the border lands between that state and Normandy. Concerning many of them the matter is clear enough, for the towns and castles which were called after them remain, and bear their ancient names, under slight disguise, to this day. We have selected from the old lists of William's companions, still extant, those names which are plainly Celtic, whether of Breton, Anjevin, or other origin. Several of the strongholds they inhabited, it will be observed, are in the "Contentin"[1] —the intervening promontory between Brittany and North Normandy, having *Cherbourg*,[2] the great naval arsenal of France, at its extremity; but as all this district was intensely Celtic before the conquest of Gaul by the Franks, and was not much altered in its ethnical character by that event; and was moreover the part of Normandy least affected by the Norman immigration, it seems likely enough that at the time of William's expedition, people of Celtic derivation were mainly its inhabitants, and it is morally certain that those lords of castles and manors which bore Celtic names were themselves of Celtic descent. The following particulars, though highly interesting to the Celtic student, are not brought forward here as of unqualified importance, though still of some significance in our discussion. Unless we had the actual pedigree of each family before us, we cannot be absolutely certain that all knights bearing Celtic names, and holding castles

---

[1] This local name, "Contentin," is a curious corruption of the name of Constantius Chlorus, who honoured the town of Constantia (now *Coutances*), with a designation following his own name.

[2] Cherbourg is a bilingual name. Its first part is the Celtic *caer*, a city. or fortress; its second, a Saxon translation of the first, *burh*, or *burg*. Its name, when Richard III. made a grant of it to King Robert's daughter, was *Car*-us-bure.

U

bearing identical names with their own—for lord
and manor had one appellation—were of pure Celtic
descent; nor is there guarantee that every designation
apparently Celtic is actually and undoubtedly such. The
following few taken from a large number found in the Roll
of Battle Abbey,[1] are most probably all Celtic—as much
so as Dynevor, Powis, or Penmon in Wales. They are
nearly all situated in the Contentin.

Bertrand de *Dinand* . . in Brittany. (Dinan, from *din*-as, or *din-*
nant.)
De *Briquebec*, Contentin, (*brig*, top, summit, similar to *din*, *dun*, or
tor. See further on, on *Local Names*.
From this knight descend, by the female
line, the Earls of Huntly and Dudley.

---

[1] Battle Abbey and Monastery, whose ruins are now inconsiderable,
were built by William the Conqueror, on the slightly swelling ground
about seven miles from Hastings, where the chief brunt of the battle
which secured for him the crown of England fell. The plan of the
church was so laid that the altar stood on the spot where the English
standard was taken, and where King Harold is said to have fallen. The
real site of the altar and choir was discovered only a few years ago,
when excavations were being made which brought to light the pave-
ment and crypt foundations of the " Lady Chapel." These interesting
remains, parts most likely of Duke William's original work, having lain
for centuries under the debris of the great Abbey, are now open to the
view of visitors. The "Roll of Battle Abbey," is of uncertain origin,
but was drawn up by reason of a command left by William, that the
names of his companions in arms in the conquest of England should be
carefully recorded and hung up as a memorial in the building which was
itself a greater memorial of his vast achievement. Various copies of this
Roll extant, show that it varied at different times, owing, it is suspected, to
the willingness of the monks in charge to humour the vanity of families
in subsequent ages, who were anxious to have their ancestors' names
among the heroes of Hastings.

The great entrance gateway and most of the other buildings, whose
remains are visible, are of a later age than that of the conquest. Some
assign them to the time of Edward III., and the gateway is held by
many to be of the Tudor period.

De *Morville*, Contentin,		(Celt. *môr*, sea. Fr. *ville*, town : a town near the sea.)
De *Tourville*,	,,	(Celt. *twr*, *tor*, high place or fortress, as Tor-point, Tor-bay, Twr-gwyn, Hey Tor.)
De *Barnville*.	,,	(Celt. *barn*, judgment, award. So named as the castle or place where matters were decided. A court.)
De *Bolville*,	,,	(Celt. *bol*, a round body, a hill or swelling in the surface of the earth, &c.)
De *Cambernon*,	,,	Camber, Cimber, Cymro, are all of one derivation. This name afterwards changed into Chambernoun. The first of the name in England settled at Madbury, Devon.
De *Trely*,	,,	(Celt. *tre*, an abode, settlement.) More than one baron of this name was settled in England. Present descendants not known.
De *Carences*	,,	(Celt. *caer*, a city, or fortress.) The *Carbonels* were owners of this castle, and came over with William, but probably afterwards returned.
De *Mordrac*	,,	(Celt. *môr*, sea.) One of this house, Henry Mordrac, was Archbp. of York.
Carrog	,,	From the Castle of Carrog (*Caerog*) came the Maresmenes. *Palgrave.*
De *Tregoz*	,,	(Celt. *tre*, an abode, settlement.) The lord of Tregoz appears as chief figure in all lists of the Conqueror's companions. There is a place called " Lidiatt Tregoz" in Wiltshire.
De *Graigues*	,,	(Celt. *craig*, rock.) The Mordrac family held this castle. Fr. orthography, though not pronunciation, is faithful to the true etymology of this name.
De *Canisy*	,,	(Celt. *can*, *cain*, white, fair.) Hubert de Canisy was a prominent man in the conquest army.

The above, along with many others, such as *Breery* (*brig*), *Canville* (*can cain*), *Garnotote* (*carn*, *cairn*, a heap), *Brasville* (*brás*, large, great), were all in the same district, a district which, from its position as a promontory, was likely to maintain its ancient characteristics of race comparatively unchanged. Some of the above names were known in pre-Roman times,—and, thanks to the wonderfully enduring nature of personal and local designations, are known to the present day; and it is not too much to presume that those warriors who bore them in the 11th century, were direct descendants of the race which had handed them down from early ages.

From a multitude of names given in the old chroniclers —names which no Celtic scholar would be surprised to find in a list of Welsh or Cumbrian magnates—we have selected the following—all of whom are given as fighting under William's standard:—

Bolbeke . . (*bol*, and *bychan*, small).	*Fynkensy* . (*pen*, head, end; *can*, or *cain*, fair, white).
Cantemor . (*cant*, hundred, a district; *mawr*, large.)	St. *Môr* . . (*môr*, sea; or *mawr*, great.)
Caroun . . (*caer*, and perhaps *Iwan* or *Owen*).	*Talbot* . . . (*tal*, high, head, and *bod*, habitation).
Coudre . . (*coed*, wood, and *tre*).	*Tornay* . . (*twr*, *tor*).
Gomer . . . (*Cymber*, *Cymro*).	*Tracy* . . . (*tre*).
Nerville . . (*ner*, lord).	*Tragod* . . (*tre*, and *coed*, wood).
Penbri. . . (*pen*, head, and *bre*, a hill; comp. Penberi & Penbre in Wales).	*Turbeville* (*twr*, *tor*).
	Turbemer (*twr*, *tor*).

—*Brompton's Chron.*

(Rer. Anglican. Scriptor. Ed. Selden, i. 963.)

Breton . . . (Same derivation as Britain and Briton).	*Kyriel* . . (*caer*).
Corby . . . (*caer*; or *cor*, a circle, and perh. the Norse *by*).	*Morley* . . (*môr*, and *llc*, place; a situation near the sea).
Doreny . . (*dwr*, water, river).	*Morteigne* (*môr*, *tain*, a plain).
Duraunt . (*dwr*, water).	*Mortivans* (*môr*).
Glauncourt (*glân*, margin; *côr*, circle).	*Ry* . . . (*rhi*, chief, leader).
	Rysers . . (*rhi*, or *Rys*, prop. n.).
Howel . . . (Cymric proper name).	*Tally* . . . (*tal*, high, tall; *llc*, place).
Kymarays (*Cymro*, Cimbri).	*Thorny* . . (*twr* or *tor*).

Tourys	. (*twr*, *tôr*; or *dwr*,	*Tregylly* . (*tre*, *gelli*, grove)
	water, and perh.	*Trivet* . . (*tre*, *tref*).
	Ry or *Rys*.)	*Turley* . . (*twr*, *tor*, and *lle*, place;
Tregos	. (*tre*).	or perh. *dwr*, water).

—From *Leland*.

(Collectan. de reb. Brit. Ed. Hearne i. 206.)

Now from these dry details of names, with their probable derivations, what is there to gather that will be of use in our argument? Two things, certainly :—

First : That the addition made by the Norman Conquest to the population of England was not a clear *Teutonic* addition. And this will apply with as much force to the chivalrous and aristocratic class as to any other.

Secondly :° That, taking into account the Celtic basis of the " Norman " population itself, and the large number of *Breton*, Anjevin, and Poitevin, warriors, that swelled the ranks of the invading army, a very material proportion of the addition made to the population of England through the conquest was beyond all question *Celtic*.

It can scarcely perhaps be said that a moiety of William's knightly companions in arms were of Celtic race,—probably, of this class, the majority was in favour of Norse blood ; but it would require a good amount of presumption to assert that the majority of the supposed 60,000 men who fought, and won a kingdom on the field of Hastings, belonged to the Teutonic race. It only seems a marvel that such a thing should ever have been believed.

Now then comes the consideration of *quantity*. To what degree did the army of the Conquest add to the non-Germanic element in Britain? Confining our attention to the army and its crowds of ministering attendants, the answer of course would be that the degree would depend on the number of the invaders. This is not the whole of what must be considered ; but it is the first part of it.

It has been said by Mackintosh and other historians who

have somewhat critically scanned the accounts of this descent, and especially the capabilities of William's transport vessels, without calling in question the number of vessels given, that the multitude which formed the Conqueror's army could not be fairly taken as exceeding 25,000 men. Four hundred knights or captains are mentioned by name in the Roll of Battle Abbey; and it is said by men who have understanding in these matters that the custom of the time would assign to that number of knights such a proportion of cavalry and infantry as would give a total in round numbers of about 25,000; but it is obvious that this would mean 25,000 soldiers. The traditional total is 60,000. Who first sent the ball rolling by mentioning this number none can tell. Considering the way things of the kind are magnified by the popular wonder-loving and imaginative faculty, it is satisfactory to find the army which at a stroke brought England to the feet of the Norman, estimated with so much moderation. We are willing that the traditional number should stand, especially as the concession will only operate favourably to our argument. The more you augment the common soldiery, the more you will augment the non-Norman element.

Now, even if we allowed that all the 60,000 men had been veritable Norsemen, the augmentation of Scandinavian blood in Britain would not be relatively very large, despite the fact that the total population of England at the time was probably under three millions. But the considerations already advanced will not allow the supposition. Perhaps not more than half the knights commanding companies were Normans—we mean in the qualified sense in which William himself, whose maternal ancestors in more than one instance were of the earlier inhabitants of the country, was a Norman. We have seen that a number of the chief knights were Bretons, followed by their Breton soldiery. Many were Poitevins, many Anjevins, &c. The names of a large proportion of them are palpably Celtic or Gallic, with Norman-French accretions, as De *Mor*ville, De *Tour*ville, De *Tre*by, De *Tregoz*, De *Carroy*, De *Bras*ville, *Pen*bri, *Tal*bot, *Morley*, &c.

If a large proportion of the lieutenants were thus Celtic or Gallo-Frankish (though it is admited that their being called after Celtic local names is not conclusive evidence that in every instance they were of Celtic or pre-Norman race), what must we not believe as to the nationality of the common soldiery and camp-followers? Each knight had brought as many retainers, dependents, villeins, and serfs as he could persuade to follow him. The nationality of these is clear. Their class was that which conquest and feudal law had made either servile or holders of humble fiefs. Into this class few of the Norman fraternity had been suffered to descend. If race-characteristics can be supposed to be so persistent as many hold, without renewal from the original stock, in that multitude there were some with features as Roman as any that had landed on the same strand with Cæsar, and some with the German red hair and round head which followed Merowig and Chlodowig from the Rhine country, and not a few from the lustrous-eyed and black-haired Iberians of old Aquitania. But it is impossible to doubt that the great majority were authentic Gauls and Celts.

If this representation be correct, then the effect of the Norman conquest, so far, on the ethnology of Britain must have been greatly gainful to what was already in the main a non-Teutonic or Old British, that is, a Gallo-Celtic population.

But there are two or three slightly qualifying facts to be mentioned. The conquering army was not the only channel guiding Norman blood into Britain at this period. Before the conquest, and after the conquest, hosts of Normans, perhaps as pure in extraction as any, had settled here. All know that in the time of Edward the Confessor, whose mother was a Norman, and who had spent so large a portion of his life in the Court of Rouen that he was said to be more French than English when he was placed on the throne, great numbers of his relatives and friends had been brought over, or had brought themselves over, and had been placed in high positions, and made the owners of large estates. Malmesbury, with his usual moderation, only says, "The King had sent for several Normans who had formerly ministered to his wants when in exile." So far had this work of favouritism gone on, however, that the greatest discontent and apprehension had been excited among the English party, and a strong feud already existed, which required but little to kindle it into open war. The Norman party was, indeed, small, but it was also influential. Bishops in those days were potent in state matters; and Edward had seated Norman prelates at Canterbury, Rochester, and London. About the King's person, in high offices of state, in chief posts of command, were found Normans. When William the Bastard, therefore, a few years before the Conquest, came over on a visit to his royal relative, he found himself surrounded by such troops of his own countrymen that he felt nearly as much in Normandy as if he had not crossed the Channel. It is surmised that this was the time when the idea of becoming ruler of England first took shape in his mind. It is true that as yet the addition to the Norse blood of England, apart from the Danish importation, was but small, being confined to chief families and their domestics and dependents; but such as it was it must be taken into account.

A much larger influx occurred after the Conquest. The barriers had now been thrown down, and all had a right of entry. The cowards who could not fight, the soft and luxurious, the idle loungers and waiters on the tide-strand of fortune could now come. The land of the kingdom, all the patronage of the kingdom, had been seized by the Conqueror, and was held in his single hand ; and on whom he pleased he bestowed favour. His terrible besom swept away all Saxon influence, and left the ground clear for his own partisans. Under William and under his immediate successors, thousands of Normans came over who had no hand in the Conquest as such, except as they contributed to fortify the position. But in such a body of emigrants purity of Norman descent would rarely be found ; nor, probably, was it in any case demanded. All who came with Norman sympathies, Franco-Norman speech, and, haply, Norman names, were " Normans," were registered as such in the Saxon mind, and for ever after in English history.

This then is the conclusion we arrive at from this necessarily general review of the subject in all its parts. The people who came in with William the Conqueror, though called " Normans," were Norman in blood in a lesser, Cymric and Gallo-Frankish in a far greater, degree ; and making every allowance for those of purely Norman extraction, who before and after the Conquest settled permanently in the country (for many after a time returned), the preponderance lies greatly in favour of those racial characteristics which were ascendant in Britain after the Saxon conquest, and had been scarcely balanced by the Teutonic after the incursions of the Danes.

This is about all the gain to our argument which accrues at present from this branch of our inquiry. The positive advantage it proffers is not strictly within the range of

our subject matter, being in favour of the Celtic *genus*,
rather than of the "Ancient British" *species*. Most
undoubtedly it gives quite a new aspect to the change
effected by the conquest in the ethnology of Britain, for it
gives a presumption in favour of the hypothesis that this
change was in the direction of Celticizing rather than of
Teutonizing the English nation.

But although it has been admitted that the Celtic
addition thus made to the English, was not an addition
directly derived from the Britons, and therefore cannot be
fully appropriated in furtherance of our specific position, still,
indirectly, much of that addition may be shown to have
actually come from that quarter. Great multitudes of the
Cymry of Britain, as we have shown, had emigrated to
Brittany within the five or six hundred years preceding
the conquest; and their descendants who joined William's
army, and merged into the English people on their settlement here, may not unfairly be claimed as additions from
the Ancient British stock. It is more than probable that
the feeling which excited the Bretons to join an expedition
intended to humble the Saxons, was a desire to avenge
the wrongs which had been heaped on their ancestors, and
which had forced so many of them to quit their native land
to seek a shelter among their brethren in Brittany, or, as
it was then generally called, Armorica.

Intimate intercourse had always subsisted between the
Cymry and the Armoricans. They felt themselves to be
but one people; and the immigrant Cymry were received
and allowed to settle in Armorica just as the Armoricans,
under the name Brython, had been allowed to settle in
Britain ages before. We have frequent intimations of this
intercourse through the space of at least 700 years, and
reaching to within a short distance of Rollo's conquest of
Normandy.

Whatever may be thought of Conan Meiriadog's expedition under Maximus (in A.D. 383), as to its details, there can be no reasonable doubt but that in that age hosts of the Cymry did go over to Armorica. The Breton historian, Lobineau, rejects the story of Conan's settlement in Brittany under Maximus, on the ground that Maximus's fleet landed near the Rhine, and not on the Armorican coast. This, however, does not make it impossible that Conan and his followers should, and that under Maximus's auspices, reach, and settle in, Brittany.

M. Lobineau, who has most laboriously investigated the history of his native country, is of opinion that large settlements of Cymry were effected on the coasts of Armorica. They called the parts where they settled *Llydaw*, a word meaning "the sea-coasts," and identical in sense with Armorica.[1] They established themselves at Dôl, St. Malo, St. Brieuc, Treguier, St. Pol de Leon, Quimper, Vannes, &c.; and spread gradually from those centres into the country around, and the interior. They reached Rennes and Nantes.[2] The names of Devonshire and Cornwall, which they imposed on the districts of their adoption, are evidence that a large portion of the colonists were from those counties in Britain.[3]

It is impossible to read the local names which still survive in Brittany, some of them slightly disguised by French orthography and additions, without feeling that the people who imposed them not only used the language of the Cymry, but also were guided by the same ideas in the designation of places of abode, positions of defence, sanctuaries for Christian worship, as the Cymry. Take the

---

[1] Lobineau, *Histoire de Bretagne*, pp. 5, 6.

[2] *Ibid*, p. 6.

[3] *Histoire de Bretagne*. See also Sharon Turner's *Hist. of the Anglo-Saxons*, vol. ii. p. 183.

following as a few specimens: *Dól* (situated in a vale),
Dinan, *Plancoet*, *Lanvollon*, *Lannion*, *Perrhos* (pen); *Lan-
meur* (*mór*—it is on the sea); *Taule* (*doleu*, on the marshes,
near the sea); *Morlaix* (*mór*, and *llc*, a place on the sea;
or *mór* and *clais*, a ditch, ravine, a narrow sea entrance);
Landivisio; *Lanilis*; *Lysnevin*; *Hywel-goet*; *Carhaix*;
Penmarch (a headland); *Concarneau*; *Pontaven* (avon);
Pontivy; *Landevan*; *Hennebon* (hên-bont); *Vannes*; *Maur*;
Nantes; *Carnac*; *Morbihan*; *Caen* (in Normandy); *Lam-
bader*; *Roscoff*; *Creisker*; *Abervrach*; *Tregastel*, &c.

These were, beyond doubt, abodes and sacred spots of
the old Cymry. Then the villages and homesteads, the
brooks, ravines, hills, crags of Brittany, bearing Cymric
names, are beyond number, and attest most distinctly the
identity of the people with those of Wales.

In the sixth century it is said that *Caradog Vreichvras* (of
the strong arm), king of Cornwall, a friend of Arthur, and
one of the Knights of his Round Table, emigrated to
Armorica with a large company of his subjects.[1] This
account, it must be allowed, savours somewhat of the
legendary.

Alain of Vannes having (in the ninth century) got rid of
his rival, Judichael of Rennes, became sole king of Brittany, and completely overpowered the Normans. He died
in 907, and his son-in-law, Mathnedoi, unable to cope with
the Normans, fled to England, and placed himself and his
family under the protection of Athelstan. He does not
seem to have ever returned to his home; but his son *Alan*,
when he had grown to manhood, collected forces, landed
on the coast of Brittany, surprised Dól, St. Brieux, &c.,
and regained the throne of his ancestors.[2] This event took
place within an age or two of the Norman Conquest; and

---

[1] Sharon Turner, *Hist. of Anglo-Saxons*, vol. ii. 189.
[2] *Ibid. p.* 190.

it is impossible to doubt that Alan had been assisted in this expedition by the Cymry, many of whose children, or children's children, might enrol themselves among the hosts which came over with William.

Another instance is given, at an earlier period than this, of intercourse between Brittany and the Cymry. Another Alain was in the year 682 King of Brittany. The royal race of the Welsh having become extinct through the death of Cadwalader the Blessed, at Rome, "Ivor, son of Alan, King of Armorica, reigned, not as a king, but as a chief or prince. And he exercised government over the Britons for forty-eight years, and then died. And Rodri Moelwynog reigned after him." [1]

All these and numberless other facts, some of which have already been specified (see p. 221, *note*), show clearly that the people of Armorica and the Cymry were on terms of closest intimacy, and mutually recognised each other as one race or nation. The narrowness of the intervening channel admitted of frequent interchange of visits, and the many wars in which both were engaged gave constant opportunity for mutual assistance.

When William, therefore, invited the warriors of Brittany to join his standards, can it be doubted that thousands, allured by promises of lands and castles in the country of their forefathers, now in possession of a tottering race of usurpers—for in their estimation the Saxons were nothing else than usurpers, and that they were in a tottering condition after the wars with the Danes and the feeble reign of Edward the Confessor, no one could doubt—would eagerly respond. Hence it was that Alain Fergant, the chief prince of Brittany, and Brian his brother, and such heroic men as Raulf de Gael of Dôl, Bertram of Dinan, &c., with their numerous troops of horsemen, were the first to proffer aid. The martial spirit and the hope of plunder,

[1] *Brut y Tywysogion, in Monumenta Hist. Brit. vol. i. p. 847.*

once aroused, would quickly win their way among the excitable Bretons, and all over the land the great Duke's call to arms would not resound uselessly. The feeling of friendship and relationship towards the Britons, of grudge and vengeance towards the Saxons who had caused the exile of their forefathers, and of eagerness for gain as well as for wild adventure, combined to draw the sons of Brittany to the field of Hastings.

The popular poetry of the Bretons is not without some allusions to the time. In Villemarqué's collection is a song bewailing the loss at sea of one of the young Breton heroes, which begins thus :—

"Between the parish of Pouldregat and that of Plouare,[1]
Young gentlemen were levying an army,
To go to war under the Son of the Duchess,
Who has *collected many people from every corner of Brittany* :

" To go to war, over sea, in the land of the Saxon.
I have a son, Silvestik, whom they expect ;
I have a son, an only son, my Silvestik,
Who departs with the army in the train of the knights.

" One night on my bed I was sleepless,
I heard the maids of Kerlaz singing the song of my son," &c.

---

[1] As the original supplies a good illustration of the similarity of the language to the Welsh, we give the opening portion of it :—

"Etri parrez Pouldrégat ha parrez Plouaré,
Ez-euz tudjentil iaouank o sével eunn armé
Evit monet d'ar brezel dindan mab ann Dukés
Deuz dastumet kalz a dud euz a beb korn a Vreiz ;

"Evit monet d'ar brezel dreest ar mor, da Vro-zoz.
Me meuz ma mab Silvestik ez-int ous hé c'hortoz.
Me meuz ma mab Silvestik ha né meuz ne met-hen,
A ia da heul ar stróllad, ha gand ar varc'héien.

" Eunn noz é oann em gwélé, ne oann ket kousket mad,
Me glévé merc'hed Kerlaz a gane son ma mab," &c.

Barzaz-Breiz, publié par M. de la Villemarqué, vol. i. 104. Paris 1839. Other publications of the Vicomte H. H. de la Villemarqué, illustrating the literature of Brittany, &c., are—*Poèmes des Bardes Bretons du VIe. Siecle.* Paris 1850 ; *La Legende Celtique, en Irelande, en Cambriae, at en Bretagne,* St. Brieuc, 1859.

The "son of the duchess" is understood to be the *Alain Fergant* already mentioned, son of the count or duke of Brittany, here called son of the "duchess" in honour of his mother. It is worthy of special notice that this old song—and popular songs and ballads are generally good reflections of the truth—shows that many people from all parts of Brittany were collected for the war.

Facts might be indefinitely multiplied to the same effect, but these must now suffice. They establish the probability, and indeed the certainty, that great numbers of Bretons were ranked among the forces of the Conqueror. They prove beyond this that among the Bretons of those times were large numbers of the Cymry of Britain, exiles from their country by reason of the Saxon conquests ; and as such men would be the first, whether in their own persons or in the persons of their descendants, to embark in a war upon the English, it were perversity and wanton abuse of history to doubt that a good proportion of the "Norman" settlers were genuine children of the Ancient Britons. We have thus, therefore, advanced another step, and proved, Thirdly : That a non-Teutonic element was added to the English population through the Norman Conquest which was not merely Celtic, but in substance, though not in exact form, Ancient British.

The conclusion we draw from the whole of this section, therefore, is ; that while the Danish Conquest considerably augmented the Teutonic blood of England, the Norman Conquest had the opposite effect.

SECTION IX.

The History of the Political and Social Relations of the People as indicative of the presence of the Ancient British Race, and of its Condition, in the Settled Anglo-Saxon Kingdoms.

This is a tempting, though a difficult, subject, and its suitable treatment would require far wider limits than can be here assigned to it. Through the few openings we propose making in the veil which conceals the humble and subject class from view, while warriors and princes monopolize the open field of public attention, sufficient will be seen to form in the thoughtful reader's mind a strong abutment to the structure of argument we have been endeavouring to erect.

As far as seeing the actual condition of *society* in the mid-age of Anglo-Saxon power is concerned, the historian is as yet at a point of view far down the slope towards the dark, mist-covered valley, at the bottom of which, until recently, he had always dwelt. The laborious investigations of Palgrave, Strutt, Sharon Turner, Kemble, Wright, Thorpe, and others in England, and of Lappenberg, Thierry, Sismondi, Pauli, Schmid, &c., on the Continent, have thrown no little light upon the subject; and probably much yet remains to be thrown, and that after a while the hill summit will be reached, and a clear view obtained of things still concealed.

Do we already know sufficient to warrant the conclusion that political and social arrangements existed among the Anglo-Saxons which indicate the presence in their midst of an Ancient British element of population? It signifies nothing here whether that element belonged to the free or to the servile class; the question is—Was it there or was

it not ? There seems to be more than mere intimations—
something amounting to proof is, we believe, discoverable.
Part of the matter bearing on this subject belongs to the
chapter on Laws; here, therefore, the exhibition of even
the little that is known must be partial.

1. The Constitution of Society among the Anglo-Saxons.

The entire people of England in Edward the Confessor's
time—Britons, Saxons, and Danes together—are to be
probably estimated at not more than *two and a half millions*
—or about twice the present population of Wales. This
estimate, which is the largest allowed by the researches
of the most competent historians, suggests a thousand
thoughts respecting the woeful waste of life in Britain since
the time when the Romans governed a population requiring
a hundred military strongholds to keep it in check, and
effectually tax it !

This population of two millions and a half was divided
by the same kind of demarcations of "parishes,"
"hundreds," and "shires," that we have at present;[1] and
it is not at all improbable that the parishes and villages of
England in those times numbered more than *one-half* what
they do to-day. The estimate is a moderate one, that in
Edward's time England had 10,000 parishes. Our vastly
increased population has not so much increased or altered
the divisions of the territory, as created larger towns, and
a more thickly-spread village and rural population.
Domesday Book gives a gross population of only about
300,000 ; but this great instrument was drawn up, not as
a census of the whole people, but for revenue purposes ;

[1] This refers, of course, to the part of Britain known as " England."
County divisions in Wales were first instituted by Edward I., and completed by Henry VIII., when the district of the "marches" was
divided into the " shires " of Denbigh, Montgomery, Radnor, Breck-
nock, Glamorgan, and Monmouth.

and enumerates, therefore, only such persons as had property profitable for the king. Hence, it takes cognisance, *ex. gr.*, of only 42 persons as inhabitants of Dover, and only 10 for *Bristol*.

The whole country was divided into townships, or districts surrounding the *tuns*, or enclosed settlements of the lords ; and into *cantreds (cant, tref*, hundred abodes) or " hundreds,' a division copied absolutely from the Britons. Each *tun* had its own goverment—its own fiscal officer, acting under the lord of the land, but chosen by the tenants (tenentes), who was called *tun-gerefa*, town-reeve. He received tolls and dues for the lord, who was the proprietor of the *tun*, and these dues were of the nature of rents,[1] Each township had its own police. When a crime was committed, the "hue and cry" was raised, and the whole township was responsible for the arrest of the guilty man. The government was thus distributed over the country, each township and shire governing itself. The king was the main centre in which all the parts and authorities met and cohered.

The people were divided into two great classes—the *eorls* and the *ceorls*, or the " Twelf-haendmen" and the " Twihaendmen "—persons possessing a dozen, or only two, hands, *i.e.*, having so much legitimate power and value in the community. There was also, after the time of Alfred, but not before, a class of inferior *eorls* called *sithcundmen*, or " Six-haendmen," whose value was midway between the *eorls* and *ceorls*, because of their limited possessions.

The *theowes*, or servi, were not considered a part of the people at all ; they were chattels, and counted with the cattle. They were reduced to this degraded condition as persons taken in war, as criminals, or as the descendants

[1] Palgrave *Engl. Commonw.* i. 82.

of such.   The idea that the *theowes* were all "Ancient
Britons," is entertained by no competent historian.[1]

The *ceorls* formed the great majority of the inhabitants.
They included all classes or degrees, from the humblest
"legal" subject to the merchant and tradesman, corresponding, in fact, to the whole of the "middle" and
"industrious" classes of modern times. Every lay person
who was neither *eorl* nor *theowe*, was a *ceorl*. The clergy
were a distinct class, but being in those days the best
educated men, and having by the Church cast around them
a character of sanctity, were ranked with *eorls*, and were
of more *value* than they ; for the compurgatory oath of an
eorl was only equal to that of six ceorls (or twelve hands
against two), while the priest's was equal to that of 120
ceorls, a deacon's to sixty, and a monk's (neither priest nor
deacon) to thirty. Bishops having much to do with law-
making, it was ordained that a bishop's word, like the
king's, was conclusive without oath. Every priest, even
the lowest, ranked as a thane—a "mass-thane," or religious
man of rank. Truly the Anglo-Saxons were very pious
after a sort! Yes; but the fact of the matter is, they
yielded rank to the man who had real *power*, of whatever
kind, in the community.

It does not appear that the servile class, the *theowes*, numbered high. *Domesday* notices only between 20,000 and 30,000
—less than one-tenth part of the men of property, leaving
out of account the general body of the ceorls. They were not
hopelessly shut up to perpetual bondage. They were not
prevented from acquiring property, and not unfrequently
purchased their own freedom. Masters often manumitted
their slaves, or by will decreed their future freedom. If
therefore, it could be made out—which it cannot—that the
class of the *servi* was made up of the descendants of the

[1] See Lappenberg, *Angl. Sax. Kings*, ii. 320.

subjugated Britons, no proof whatever would be thereby supplied that descendants of the Britons were not to be found in the classes of freemen, and even Thanes.

The ceorl class included a most singular subdivision. These were persons who were perpetually attached to the land on which they were born, and although "legal" and "free," passed with the land when it was sold, and were under obligation to render service to their new, as they had been to their old master. They were cultivators of the soil, dwellers in villages—corresponding, therefore, to the *villani* of the Romans, and in some respects, to the *villeins* of feudal times. Tacitus describes a class of this sort as existing among the ancient Germans; and the laws of Howel the Good show that such existed among the Britons ; probably, indeed, all the nations of Europe possessed an arrangement somewhat similar.

Now, it has been argued by some historians—very learnedly by Palgrave—that this class of the ceorls was in great measure made up of the subjugated British race. The nature of their relations to the classes below and above, gives an air of probability to the theory. The *villani* were not slaves, but at the same time they were not wholly free. They were not allowed to leave the soil on which they were born ; and had no political power whatever—a condition likely enough to be decreed for the subject race. Whether all classes of ceorls were thus politically powerless, may be doubted. The *bordarii*, the *sockmanni*, the *liberi homines*, were all ceorls, but of a higher order—the first holding cottages (*bord*); the second and third holding land ; and as it should seem, not tied perpetually to the place of their birth.[1] The "liberi homines" were of the highest rank of ceorls, and held their land by military tenure.

[1] See Sir H. Ellis's *Introduction to Domesday*.

That the *Britons*, to whatever class they were doomed in special instances, were on the whole treated with some consideration, we have every reason to believe. As a race, they were not merely allowed to continue on the conquered territory, but, as already shown, were tempted to do so by various advantages. An extraordinary fact, surely, in a conquered country, conquered too, after unexampled sacrifices—was the continued residence of the subjugated in towns of their own, and under laws and magistrates of their own, within the bounds too of the victors' jurisdiction ; as was the case with the *Wealas* of Wessex (as at Exeter), until the time of Athelstan's extension of the West Saxon dominions westward.

Though the pride of the conquering Teuton denominated the fallen nation *Wealas*, and Wyliscmen, or strangers, it went not so far as to deprive them of all liberty. In the rank of *servi*, they were put only as Saxons, Angles, or Danes themselves were put, *i.e.*, they were subjected to bondage when taken as prisoners of war, or when convicted of crime of a certain degree of enormity. They generally belonged rather to the different classes of *ceorls*. Their princes were allowed in some qualified form to maintain their status, though, of course, deprived of all power ; and their best families were only prevented by want of means from occupying the rank of Thanes. It is true, most of the land of England had been divided among the successful warriors—the king taking a goodly portion himself ; but we have no authority for supposing that *all* the land had been taken from the Britons. It was not the practice of the northern nations to rob the conquered of all their territory. The Burgundians in Gaul, the Visigoths in Spain, pursued the policy of taking only a portion of the land, charging the portion still held by the natives with tribute for the king.[1] But Saxon supremacy had been most dearly bought in Britain—the brave Cymry having defended their own with a persistent resolution which found no parallel in Gaul, Spain, or Italy, and it is therefore just possible that more of their land had been taken than was usual in cases of the kind.

That there were *Wealas*, or *Wyliscmen*, who were possessors of land, and had their appropriate *wer-gild*, or personal value,[2] just in the same manner with the ruling race, is shown beyond all doubt by the laws of King Ina, compiled at the close of the 7th century.[3] These laws prove that there were *Wealas* who were free (for they had their *wergild*), but who possessed no land; and also *Wealas* who were proprietors, of various degrees, and subject to divers charges. If the free *Wealh* possessed no land, his *wergild* was seventy shillings;[4] but if, in addition to paying *gafol*, or rent to the king,[5] he also held a "hide" of land (variously estimated at from 40 to 100 modern acres) then his *wergild* was a hundred and twenty shillings.[6]

---

[1] See Allen's *Rise and Growth of the Royal Prerogative in Engl.* p. 138, &c.

[2] From A. Sax. *wer*, man, and *gild*, money. The *wer-gild* was a fine which a person was obliged to pay for homicide, &c., and varied in amount according to the rank of the slain. A person's status in society, therefore, was expressed by his *wer-gild*. Slaves had no *wer-gild*. See Bosworth's *Angl.-Sax. Dict.* sub verb. *Wer*.

[3] *Inæ Leges*, 23, 33, &c. Comp. Dr. Rein. Schmid's *Die Gesetze der Angelsachsen*, esp. on *Ine's Gesetze*. Dr. Schmid's work contains also the *Laws* of Alfred, of Edward, of Ethelbert, and of Athelstan.

[4] No Saxon shilling coin has been discovered, but its value is computed at about fourteen pence of our money.

[5] From Cymric *gafael*, to hold, a "hold," signifying in this case, by payment of toll, that the king had a claim on the man. The legal term *gavel-kind* is from this same word, and represents a purely ancient British custom.

[6] *Laws of Ina*, xxxii.

Now it would be impossible to find more conclusive evidence than is here supplied in support of the positions:—

(1.) That the Ancient Britons were properly incorporated into the body of the Saxon population of Wessex.

(2.) That they were so incorporated, not as servile, but as free men.

(3. That they were granted the dignity of a graduated personal value according to the property they held.

(4.) That they were holders of land.[1]

It also seems clear that the Britons, like the Saxons themselves, were free to ascend in the social scale, according to their loyalty, talent, industry, and increase of means. We have already explained the rank of the " Sithcundmen " or " Six-haendmen," as the medium class of aristocracy. Now it was provided that the Wyliscman who should be in possession of *five* " hides " of land should enjoy the rank which was held by the six-haendman, or Thane.[2] This was the qualification also for the Saxon's advance to the position of Thane, or titled noble. The Saxon ceorl could rise to this elevation, provided the five hides of land had been in his family for *three* generations ; that is to say : A ceorl became possessor of five hides, his son succeeded to the estate, this son's son did the same, and this last man's son was entitled to the rank of Thane, by authority of Wessex law. The Briton and the Saxon were thus treated alike.

It is worthy of remark, however, that the very laws which thus secured to the Britons similar privileges to those of the ruling race, distinguished their nationality from that of the Saxons. They are marked as *Wealas.* A difficulty was evidently experienced in bringing about a

---

[1] See Lappenberg *Hist. of Anglo-Sax. Kings*, vol. ii. 320, and Schmid's *Die Gesetze der Angelsachsen*, passim.

[2] *Laws of Ina*, xxiv.

thorough amalgamation, and toning down the meeting
waves of colour, so as to present the appearance of a uniform
hue.   It cannot be doubted, the *Wyliscman* was then, as
now, a stubborn subject, proud of his ancestry, boastful of
his "antiquity," contemptuous of late-born authority
obtained by brutish force, and by no means anxious to
coalesce with the Saxon.   The Saxon on his side, felt himself every inch the superior.   Had he not beaten the
Wyliscman in open fair fight, and taken his land by right
of his broad *scax*, which was his only law and title of
acquisition, and gave his nation its name?[1]   Thus, for
ages, a line of demarcation was maintained,—old memories
lingering like embers, rekindled by every casual whiff of
wind, the old Cymric language cherished with a brave,
nervous, unreasoning earnestness, which demanded public
recognition in the statutes of the realm.   This was perfectly
natural—the precise result to be anticipated from the known
temper of the Britons, and indicative too of generous and
discreet policy on the part of the Saxon Kings.   Let
it not be said that generosity was out of the question
with a people like the Saxons.   The lion is at times
innocent, both in look and purpose, although when
occasion suits, he can shake the hills with his roar, and
make a fearful spring on his prey.   The Anglo-Saxons,
though unpoetical as the plains of the Elbe, were a
thoughtful purposing race, grim and iron-handed in
execution, and withal capable of a sense of sweet
satisfaction, when the prize of valour was won.   They
were not an irreligious people,[2] and though *Thor* put

---

[1] The derivation of Saxon from *scax*, a sword, is familiar, and from
its appropriateness naturally thought correct. They were a nation of
"swordsmen."

[2] It requires some qualification in speaking of the religiousness of the
old Germans. Here, as everywhere else, since their doings on the

no veto on the "plan" which they uncompromisingly pursued :—

"That he should take who had the power,"

Odhinn counselled discretion ; and there was an *Alfadur* (Father of all), higher than either Odhinn or Thor, who embraced the *Wyliscmen* like the *Englen* and the *Seaxan* as his children ; and a *Valhalla* above, which was more likely to be reached, if heroic fighting and victory were followed by heroic magnanimity.

2. Britons in a state of bondage.

Domesday Book gives some grounds for believing that in the latter age of the Anglo-Saxon power a large proportion of the *Theowes* were Ancient British prisoners of war. We have to remember that the statistics of Domesday refer to things as they were immediately after the Norman Conquest. Now it is well known that the contest between the English and the Britons had of late ages been mainly confined to the border parts, between the territories of the Heptarchy and the country still held by the *Cymry*. If prisoners of war, therefore, were often consigned to bondage, we should naturally expect to find the *Theowe* class numerous in the regions referred to, especially since the struggle in more recent times was conducted with greater bitterness, if possible, than had marked it at any former stage.

British stage have come to view, they have not been indifferent to the "useful." Cæsar says of them: "The Germans acknowledge no gods except those that are objects of sight, and by whose means they *plainly benefited*." (Quos cernunt, et quorum aperte opibus juvantur.) *De. Bell. Gall.* vi. 21. Is this Germanic temper, with its subsequent alliance with Celtic idealism and warmth, at bottom of the fact that tendencies to superstition in England are ever put under check of rationalism, and that on the other hand a too intellectual scepticism is still tempered by an emotional piety and faith ?

Now the facts presented in Domesday very remarkably tally with this antecedent probability. The *Theowes* enumerated are found to be in the parts last yielded up by the Britons. In Gloucestershire, for every *three* freemen there was *one* bondman. In Cornwall and Devon they were in the proportion of *five* freemen and *one* bondman. Staffordshire presented the same proportion. Unfortunately, this great survey omitted the counties of *Cumberland*, *Westmoreland*, *Northumberland*, *Durham*, and part of *Lancashire*, so that we have no means of judging of the condition of things in the parts embraced by the Celtic kingdom of *Cumbria*. The further we remove from Wales, the fewer slaves we find enumerated. Almost everywhere, eastwards however, the proportion of slave to free is found to be about *one* in *ten*; that is, the reader will remember, one in ten of the people registered in Domesday; for Domesday took no notice of the great majority of the *ceorls*, who were possessed of no property. But there is a notable exception in the case of *East Anglia*, where the proportion of slave to free is only one in *twenty*; and a still more notable exception in the case of the Eastern part of *Mercia*, embracing the counties of Lincoln, Huntingdon, and Rutland, and of the county of *York*, where not a single slave is noticed! In Nottinghamshire the servile class was very small, amounting to one only in 215 persons registered. On the other hand, in these parts the section of ceorls attached to the soil—the *villani*—appear to be very numerous, giving rise to the suspicion that here the *theowes* had been permitted, in course of time to work themselves up to the condition of the lowest type of *ceorls*, thus securing, at least, recognition by the law as human beings, and parts of the nation, although their actual comforts might not be at all thereby augmented.[1]

[1] See Lappenberg, *Angl.-Sax. Kings*, ii. 321.

From this necessarily hasty survey of the condition of society under the Anglo-Saxon dominion, we rest in the following conclusions :—

(*a.*) That the community embraced a goodly proportion of the Ancient British race.

(*b.*) The Britons were not *as such* incorporated into the servile class.

(*c.*) They were granted the dignity of a graduated personal value according to the property they possessed.

(*d.*) They were holders of land.

(*e.*) They were permitted, like the Anglo-Saxons themselves, to rise from one class of society to the other, even to the rank of *thanes*, and probably of *eorls*.

(*f.*) They, like the Anglo-Saxons, when taken as prisoners of war, &c., were liable to the degradation of bondage.[1]

The political and social arrangements of our ancestors viewed from a modern stand-point have their cheerful as well as their gloomy aspect. It cannot be denied that the maxims that ruled in the days we have now been reviewing, were the dicta of power rather than justice—the voice of the lord rather than of the aggregate wisdom of the many. By law, human beings were adjudged to be mere chattels, not to be counted with men, bought and sold with the acres on which they were reared—as if men were, not only according to the ancient fancy, αὐτόχθονες, born of the soil, but still continued a veritable part of its substance—and had a value, recognised by society, affixed to their persons and life, not as being in themselves of intrinsic worth, but of worth only in proportion as wealth, and the wealth of land, was associated with them. By the accident of

---

[1] Hallam is of opinion that a large proportion of the serf population consisted of Britons. *Middle Ages*, ii. 386, 387.

birth or fortune, the issue of a single combat, or a battle, men were made irresponsible masters of the happiness and lives of many equal to themselves by nature, and possibly greatly superior in the higher qualities of humanity. The high were subject to the low—the refined and princely hurled down to the footstool of the accidentally powerful. And yet, in so far as society was at all settled, there was a strong law of justice recognised. The time was one of mingled darkness and light, when the severities brought into vogue by ages of conquest and bloodshed and unrestrained passion were being gradually tempered by equity, and institutions which are now the pride of England were being painfully planned and reared out of ill-shapen materials, conveyed, many of them, from distant lands. Even then, struggling against the stern and brutal usages current, an instinctive sense of right made itself heard in Saxon society, and the very slave was encouraged, by obedience to the hard behests of law, to hope for manumission and honour. By lawlessness nothing was to be hoped for—the strong arm ruled and would avenge the infringed law, be it the best or the worst—but by patient endurance, and heroic confronting of adverse fortune, much might be hoped for, and obtained. Out of this hard nurture in adversity have come forth the solid and resolute qualities which distinguish the British race—a race which still, and more than ever, honours and maintains the supremacy of law, and also more than ever studies to moderate the rigour of justice and smooth the path of misfortune.

CHAPTER II.

THE EVIDENCE OF PHILOLOGY.

" Willst du die Menschheit . . . kennen lernen, so studire die
Menschensprachen, und diese werden dir von manchem Kunde geben,
was in keinem Geschichts-buche steht."—Dr. F. A. POTT.

IT is to be noted, *in limine*, that we do not propose in
this chapter to show the relations of the English language
to all the Indo-European tongues. Such a field of inquiry
would involve a hundred points irrelevant to the subject of
this work. Our task is to show how far the Ancient
Britons have entered into the body of the people now
called English. By making it manifest that the *language*
of the Ancient Britons has permeated the speech now
spoken by the English people, we shall furnish a presump-
tive proof that the *blood* of the former has to a greater or
smaller extent tinged the blood of the latter.

This, then, being our question, we have no business to
wander away into the wide domains of comparative philology. We need not touch upon the affinity of English
to Sanscrit, or of Cymric to Sanscrit, for no one dreams
that Sanscrit has ever been in use on British soil. Nor
must we be tempted into the enticing exercise of descanting
on the relation of Cymric to Greek; for besides the fact
that Greek was never, as a spoken language, a medium
whereby Celtic words, whether in Cymric or other form,
passed into English in Britain, we are far from believing

in any closer relationship between Cymric and Greek than that of two languages proved by comparative philology to belong to one class or family of languages called Indo-European or Aryan, and to have taken their departure from the parent stock and from each other at a point less remote than the departure of the Cymric and Sanscrit, or Cymric and Gothic, from each other.

How far has the Celtic speech influenced the English, and how far does this render probable the coalition of the Celtic race in Britain with the so-called Anglo-Saxon? This is now our question.

The witnessing of philology on this point, is, it is believed, distinct and categorical. That Celts and Teutons lived long together, as one people, and on British ground, would be declared loudly and clearly by the English language itself even if history were silent. Much of the record once existing has doubtless been effaced ; but much still remains which is perfectly legible and gives a connected and unambiguous sense.

The antipathy of race, the soreness produced by defeat, the revulsion accompanying a sense of wrong, would continue to be felt only by those British tribes which kept separate from the Anglo-Saxon settlements, maintaining an attitude more or less defiant. Those who had submitted, continuing in their native districts, content to work their way upwards from the condition of the " ceorl " to that of the freed-man, would by degrees forget the old hatred, and would maintain friendly intercourse with the conquering race. Continuing themselves to speak their native language, their children would gain some knowledge of the Saxon also, and their children's children still more. By degrees the difference of race, commemorated by a diversity of speech, would, by the adoption of the Saxon and by frequent intermarriage, be obliterated. During this state of transition, not the Saxon only but the British tongue as well, would receive a tinge of foreign materials. The Saxon, as being the less cultivated tongue, would be most liable to innovation, supposing that the social condition of the contiguous or intermixed races were equal. New ideas, tendered by the Romano-British civilization for reception, would require terms which neither Jute, Saxon, nor Angle possessed ; for ideas, and the words which are their signs, always go and come in company. The Latin language, even if the Britons generally spoke it—of which we possess no sort of evidence—was as strange to the Teutonic conquerors as the British itself. No means, therefore, remained to secure free intercourse but the vernacular of the conquered, until the conquered could be persuaded to adopt the Saxon speech. These remarks present the general social condition under which a transfusion of British Celtic materials into the Anglo-Saxon language would of necessity take place. But as we have proceeded on the assumption that the vernacular of Britain at the time was the Ancient British, this question must receive some further notice.

SECTION I.

Early Stages of Relation between the Anglo-Saxon and British Celtic.

1. Language of Britain at the Saxon Invasion.

Of considerable significance is the question, What was the language spoken by the Britons when the Angles and Saxons came over? If it was not in the main the Ancient British, then the idea that the Saxon tongue became charged with Celtic in the early times of the Conquest, and through intercourse with the Britons, must be futile. It has been strongly maintained by some that the Ancient British tongue, during the Roman occupation, had been superseded by the Latin. To this, with due deference to Mr. Wright and other equally accomplished men, we must without hesitation demur. No adequate evidence to support such an hypothesis exists.

It was the practice of the Romans to leave the people they conquered unmolested in the use of their own language. Agricola, after Roman power had lodged itself in this island for the space of a hundred years, only seems to have thought of inducing the sons of the chiefs (principum filios) to learn the Latin tongue. Prichard is doubtless right in saying that "in Britain the native idiom was nowhere superseded by the Roman, though the island was held in subjection upwards of three centuries." It is true that Gallia when subdued readily adopted the Roman speech and abandoned the Celtic. So did Hispania. So did Dacia. But the analogy of these countries is not necessarily followed elsewhere. It was no part of Roman policy to urge it. Besides, the continuous life of the Celtic speech in Britain to this day invalidates the theory. After the long train of conquests—Roman, Anglo-Saxon, Danish, and Norman, and their united dominion of 1800 years, the language spoken on British soil before Cæsar set foot on it is still the vernacular, for weal or woe, of a million and more of its people, and until very recently was the vernacular of many more. Cumberland and Westmoreland, Devon and Cornwall, the greater part of Scotland, and all Wales, along with considerable tracts adjoining, were British in speech long after the Romans retired from the country. Who will say that the central and southern parts were not likewise British?

But if the analogy of other countries is of essential import, let it be allowed. The Romans conquered Greece as well as Britain. Was Greece made Roman in speech? They conquered Northern Africa. Did Africa yield up its vernacular in exchange for the Latin? They conquered Thrace and the two Mœsias, inferior and superior. Did these become Latin? In all these, as in Britain, the Roman provincial government was established, and Latin doubtless was used as the official speech. But the people of these countries did not therefore speak Latin. Greece retained its grand old language; and after many more conquests and revolutions—even after subjection to the Moslem, has retained it to this day. Africa cannot be shown to have done otherwise. Servia and Bulgaria are witnesses that Mœsia did not become Roman in language, and Roumelia bears similar testimony respecting Thrace. If these countries yielded not their vernaculars as did Gallia and Hispania, why should it be contended, in the face of the still surviving *Cymraeg* and the only recently extinct Cornish, that Britain did so?

The exigency of argument has led some writers, in spite of evidence freely allowed in similar cases, to question the antiquity and genuineness of the poems of Taliesin, Aneurin, Myrddin, and Llywarch Hên; but if these are allowed to be productions intended to be understood by the Britons of the 6th and 7th centuries of our era, they furnish sufficient evidence that the *Cymraeg* was at that time a language widely prevalent, not in Wales merely, but also in the north-western parts of Britain. Taliesin only was resident in Wales, the others belonged to Cumbria. Did these bards sing in Celtic to a people, who, a century or two before, knew only Latin?

But history has a still distincter voice in the matter. Venerable Bede has left on record that in his time (8th cent.) the Island of Britain, "following the number of books in which the Divine Law was written," was inhabi-

ted by " five nations—the English, Britons, Scots, Picts,
and Latins, each in its own peculiar dialect, cultivating
the sublime study of Divine Truth." [1]   This was in Bede's
own time *(in præsenti)*, and the languages he enumerates
here were book-languages, and not living tongues representing so many nations—for the "Latins," as a people,
had long ago left the island. But in another passage he
speaks more distinctly—not of languages, including the
Latin as the ecclesiastical and book language, but of
peoples, speaking different languages ; and it is to be
noted that he is now discoursing of an age considerably
nearer Roman times than his own, and when the Latin,
if ever it had attained to universal prevalence, might be
expected still to be generally prevalent. All the nations
and provinces of Britain, he says, in the reign of Oswald
(circ. A.D. 635), a hundred years before the writer's time,
were " divided into four languages *(quatuor linguas)*, those
of the Britons, Picts, Scots, and English." [2]   The Latin is
not a spoken tongue, then, in the reign of Oswald.   The
Britons, in the 7th century are denoted a separate people
through the use of a separate speech.   Had they managed
to regain a knowledge of their ancient tongue between the
departure of the Romans (A.D. 426), and the reign of
Oswald (begun A.D. 634) ? On the contrary, it is clear
they had never lost it.

That the English language began its course in Britain
in the form of an uncultured Gothic vernacular cut up into
divers dialects, coming into contact with a literary and
ecclesiastical language, the most polished then in use, the
Latin—and with a nearly universally diffused British
tongue, enriched with all the treasures of Roman knowledge, and largely charged with the Latin, as our first
Appendix will suggest, need hardly be more than simply

---

[1] *Eccls. Hist.* B. i. c. 1.   [2] *Ibid.* B. iii. c. 7.

stated. How it has received a tinge from the former,
every tyro knows: how far it became charged with the
elements of the latter, it now becomes our duty to investigate. The English language, like the people who speak
it, has become a great reservoir to receive the contents of
many fountains. As Professor Max Müller says : " There
is, perhaps, no language so full of words evidently derived
from the most distant sources. Every country of the globe
seems to have brought some of its verbal manufactures to
the intellectual market of England." [1]

2. The Anglo-Saxon replaces the Celtic in the Anglo-
Saxon States : An Objection, based on this fact, considered.

Against the doctrine that the Britons equalled in number, if they did not vastly out-number, the Saxons at the
commencement of the Saxon dominion, it is objected : If
so, why was not the British language, in preference to the
Anglo-Saxon, adopted as the language of the new kingdoms ? It will be readily seen that the argumentation here
attempted is inconsequential.

Doubtless the British, in point of copiousness and polish,
was the superior language of the two. The Britons were
also, at first, as every reader of history will allow, infinitely
more numerous than the troops of invaders who came in
small open boats to subdue them, and who succeeded,
there is reason to fear, by treachery as much as by resolution and force. But it remains a matter of fact that the
Anglo-Saxon language became, from the outset, the language of the new settlements. Is this fact calculated to
excite wonder ? The objection assumes that it is so
calculated. Have the conquering few always or generally

[1] *Lectures on Science of Language.* Lond. 1861.

adopted the speech of the conquered many ?   History says
not so.

It has been said that the British was the superior language ; and it is clear that political wisdom would have
counselled its adoption. Close and prolonged intercourse
with the civilization of the Romans, and the elevating
power of Christianity, had produced a mighty change in
the British mind. The British tongue had correspondingly
expanded. The rude Saxon must, by its side, have appeared meagre and uncouth. But the rude Saxon suited
the Saxon mind, as it then was ; and as to its meagreness,
it contained the vocabulary which corresponded with the
Saxon's wants—it had terms for fish, flesh, and fowl—for
boat, spade, and fire, and, pre-eminently, for the indispensable sword (seax), whose importance was so great in the
Saxon economy, that it is said to have baptized the whole
people after its own suggestive name. Then it may well
be supposed that our piratical visitors had no greater
respect for a cultured and enriched language than they
had for the Roman villas, temples, and bridges they found
in the land, and which, in their fondness for their *seaxes*,
they allowed for ever to crumble and perish, if, indeed, they
did not deliberately destroy them, as an offence to their
taste.[1]

On account of its superiority, doubtless, it was that the

---

[1] Comp. Hartshorne's *Salopia Antiqua*, p. 263, &c. The Romans were
celebrated for their bridge-building. How their chief religious officer
came to be called *pontifex*, the bridge builder, it may not be so easy to
conceive, but the title sufficiently indicates the importance and even
sacredness they attached to the erection of bridges. See Rev. I. Taylor's
Words and Places, p. 266. It is strange that with models before their
eyes, and notwithstanding the great convenience of bridges for military
transit, the Anglo-Saxons should have totally neglected the repairs or
re-erection of the Roman bridges of Britain. Their neglect of villas
and temples, less *useful* though more magnificent, is more easily understood.

Latin became the language of Gaul, and that the Romanized Gauls afterwards succeeded in imparting it to their Frankish and other Teutonic conquerors. It was for a similar reason that the Neustrians of the regions afterwards called Normandy, taught it in the form of French to their Norman masters, and that these same Normans at a still later period forced it for a time upon the Saxons and Danes of England.

The Danes, moreover, as conquerors, had received the speech of the Saxons they had subdued and decimated, and received it chiefly because of its superiority and wide diffusion. It is true the Anglo-Saxon was nearly the same with the Danish, but it had, since its naturalization in Britain, become subject to the influences of a higher civilization, receiving new elements from the British, as the British had received from the Latin, and thus obtained the precedence due to merit. The Saxon of the subject paralysed the Danish of the ruler. As with other cases already enumerated,[1] similar mastery in similar circumstances was not obtained by the Ancient British.

It is quite explainable that the ruder speech of a conquering horde should displace the language of a fallen race, however cultivated. Indeed, *primâ facie*, this is the result to be anticipated. But still more likely is it, when the conquerors are confederated tribes of boundless energy, bringing along with them customs and institutions to which they are devotedly attached, including a system of religion based on a venerable mythology, which maintains its authority with an iron grasp, and which they are bent upon transplanting into their new dominions. We know that the Arabian language was thus promulgated along with the faith of the Prophet of Mecca through many lands, whose inhabitants were more civilized than the Mussulmans. The Norman-French paralysed the English,

[1] See p. 356.

while the Danish completely failed to secure a footing, although introduced by teeming multitudes, and given a theatre of action in different centres north as well as south. The Norman-French, introduced by a few, not only ruled supreme as the Court and official language, but its adoption by the aristocracy, and all the world of fashion, was complete. Hence its power to inoculate the speech of the nation. When its time of subsidence came round, therefore, it was found that an immense number of its vocables had found a lodgment in the body of the Saxon language (precisely in the same manner as the English is infusing its elements into the Welsh, and the French into the Breton, of our time), and, what is still more astonishing, that it had induced the Saxon to abandon the greater part of its old noun and verb inflexions—cases of nouns, persons of verbs, plurals especially—a sacrifice which was doubtless conceded by way of imitating the royal and fashionable speech.

History, in short, affords abundant examples of this kind. The explanation is to be sought in other and deeper causes than mere preponderance of number. The conquered may be few, and their language may be adopted by their subjugators, or the conquerors be few, and yet dictate their tongue to the conquered. Mere numbers tell infallibly neither way.[1]

Nor does the simple superiority of a language, whether consisting in the perfection of its grammatical arrangement, or in the amplitude of its vocabulary, guarantee its adoption.

---

[1] Here the author of an able little brochure, *The British People*, is probably in error when he says, "The Romanic and Celtic elements in our language fairly represent the Celtic elements in the *population* of the three kingdoms," p. 60. At the same time, he may not have intended to convey the idea that the Celtic elements in the language represented the *measure* of the Celtic elements in the population.

In the particular case of the Celtic in England, it failed
to stand its ground against the Anglo-Saxon owing to such
causes as the following :

a. Want of concerted action amongst the British tribes.
They fought and were conquered in detail. They themselves, and their language, therefore, failed to inspire the
respect which otherwise would have been conceded.

b. The different British tribes, although speaking substantially the same language, yet spoke it in different
dialects—a circumstance which weakened the effect of their
speech upon their conquerors.

c. The Saxons, Jutes, and Angles, all spoke the same
language, and hence the general diffusion of their speech,
despite their frequent quarrels amongst themselves. It is
true that dialectic peculiarities existed, although not to a
wide extent—except in the case of immigrants who seem
to have arrived from other quarters than Holstein and
Jutland.[1]

d. By means of prior settlement of Saxons in the East
and South of Britain, their language had already in a
measure become naturalized. That such settlements had
taken place, without conflict, in the course of ages, is more
than probable. We are informed that even a century before
the time when Hengist and Horsa arrived, Saxons had
taken London, and slaughtered the count of the "*Sax n*
shore." Why should there be a shore called *Litus Saxonici. m*
at all in Britain except as the result of Saxon descent and
Saxon settlement? The story of the Saxon conquest of
Britain, in fact, does not begin with the subjugation of

---

[1] It is more than probable that even in these early times the Saxons
were not left to share the island with the Jutes, Angles, and Frisians
alone, but that even Franks and Longobards, Norwegians and Danes,
claimed some portion of the general spoil. See Procopius, *De Bell.
Goth.* iv. 20, 93 ; Palgrave, *Engl. Commonwealth*, i. 2.

Kent. Both the shores of Gaul and Britain were infested with sea-rovers and plunderers at the very time when Roman legions professed to maintain the efficiency of the imperial sway, and it was for the purpose of checking these disturbers, as already shown, that Carausius the usurper received his command. Names of places on the coast, from Norfolk to Sussex, and opposite, from Dunkirk to the Somme, to this day testify to the early settlement of Teutons in those parts.[1]

e. The elementary political and municipal principles, and the religious mythology they brought with them and so tenaciously held, could hardly be translated into the language of the Britons.

f. The implacable hostility which the leading British tribes—the Cymri and the Cumbrians—manifested towards the conquerors, of itself prevented the diffusion of the vernacular amongst them. Neither would the Britons promote it, nor the Saxons receive it if offered. So virulent was this hatred, that the Christian Britons would not even proffer the truths of Christianity to their heathen masters. They were not the men, therefore, to offer their language, which they considered, next to their religion, the most sacred of all their possessions.

g. The book-learning of the Britons—the language of which would most readily be embraced by the conquerors, after they had learnt letters—was in all probability in Latin. The old Celtic speech being the every day language of the common people, the Saxon mind would be naturally prejudiced against it as such.

3. The comparative freedom from Celtic of the earliest Anglo-Saxon literature, considered and accounted for.

---

[1] See Grimm, *Geschichte der Deutschen Sprache*, p. 626. St. John, *Four Conquests of Engl.* i. p. 44.

Charged to repletion as our present English is with
Latin and French, Cymraeg and Irish, which, in combination, certainly more than equal the whole bulk of the
Anglo-Saxon portion,[1] it is remarkable how free from these
foreign elements it presented itself in the first stages of its
Britannic history. The Anglo-Saxon of the times of
Cædmon and *Alfred* is hardly at all impregnated with
Latin, except in the terminology belonging to ecclesiastical affairs. *Biscop* (episcopus), *munuc* (monachus), *pall*
(pallium), *psalter* psalterium', *sanct* (sanctus', *macsse* (missa',
prædician (prædicare), *pistel* epistola', are among the terms
already borrowed from the Church Latin.[2]

Nor do we find any but the sparsest signs of Celtic.
The "miraculous hymn" of *Cædmon*, the first Anglo-Saxon
writer whose productions are extant, is free from foreign
intrusions :

Nu we sceolun herigean	Now we shall praise
Heofon-rices weard	The Guardian of Heaven.
Metodes mihte	The Creator's might,
And his modgethanc,	And his mood-thought (counsel',
Weorc wuldor-fæder ;	The Glory-father of works ;
Swa He wundra gehwaes.	How He of all wonders,
E'ce drihten,	Eternal Lord,
Ord onstealde, &c.	Formed the beginning, &c.

Here and throughout the poem are no traces of Latin or
Celtic. And though this precious relic exists in divers
dialects of the Anglo-Saxon, such as the West Saxon and
the Northumbrian, in none of them do we find foreign
elements.[3]

Nor is the case different, if we move on to the time of
Bede, Alfred, and Ælfric. The dying words of Bede,

---

[1] De Thommerel, in his *Recherches*, after laborious computations. fixes
the proportion at 13,330 Anglo-Saxon, against 29,335 other words.

[2] Comp. Guest's *English Rhythms*, b. iii. c. 3.

[3] See Latham's *English Language*, c. iv. 61.

uttered in Anglo-Saxon, the versions executed by the hand of King Alfred, the colloquy and vocabularies composed by Ælfric, all evidence the scrupulous care with which the well of Anglo-Saxon "undefiled" was guarded. The following specimen from Ælfric's *Colloquium ad Pueros* (10th cent.), may serve as an illustration :—

We cildra biddath the eala lareow, thaet thu taece us sprecan [rihte], fortham ungelaerede we syndon and gewaemmodlice we spreccath.

We children request thee, master, that thou teach us to speak correctly, because we are ignorant and speak badly.

Hwaet wille ge spreccan ?

What do you wish to speak about ?

Hwaet rece we hwaet we sprecan buton hit riht spraec sy, and behefe naes idel othe fracod.

What care we what we speak of except it be proper and useful, not idle and bad.

Wille [ge beon] beswungen on leornange ?

Do you like to be flogged while learning ?

Leofre ys us beon beswungen for lare thaenne hit ne cunnan ac we witan the bilewitne wesan and nellan onbelæden swincgla us buton thu bi to-genydd fram us, &c.

We prefer being corrected that we may learn rather than not learn, but we know thou art good-natured and unwilling to give us the rod unless we force thee to it, &c.

So again of Ælfric's *Vocabularies* (10th cent.) These consist of Latin words explained in Anglo-Saxon, as the means of teaching Latin to the English youth. It is true that, professing to give Anglo-Saxon equivalents, it was right to use Anglo-Saxon terms, pure and simple, even though the daily speech of the people were far from pure. The author would only use barbarous vocables as a matter of necessity. This is our explanation of the comparative Anglo-Saxon purity of these vocabularies. They were intended, not to reflect and perpetuate the barbarisms of the popular tongue, but to correct them. That, under

---

[1] See *Vol. of Vocabularies*, ed. by T. Wright, M.A., F.S.A. Privately printed for Jos. Mayer, Esq., F.S.A., &c. 1857. Pp. 1, 2.

these circumstances, they contain some few Celtic terms, not derived from Latin, as shown below, is proof of the naturalization, even at that time, of Celtic ingredients in the daily-life language of the Anglo-Saxons.

We give an extract from Ælfric (10th cent.), showing a slight admixture of Latin and Celtic, mainly in names of agricultural implements, with modern English added.

Latin.	A.-Saxon.
Vomer	: Scear, a ploughshare.
Aratrum	: Sulh, plough.
Aratio	: Eriung, ploughing.
Buris	: Sulh-beam, plough-handle.
Stercoratio	: Dingiung, stinking.
Fimus	: Dinig, dung.
Dentale	: Cipp, harrow.
Stiba	: Sulh-handla, plough-handle.
Occatio	: Egegung, harrowing.
Rastrum	: Raca, a rake.
Traha	: Cithe, a drag.
Runcatio	: Weodung, a weeding.
Tragum	: Draege, a drag-net.
Aculeus	: Sticel, a goad.
Veractum	: Leneglen-erthe, spring.
Sulcus	: Furh, furrow.
Circus	: Withthe, a band.
Funiculus	: Rap, a cord.
Proscissio	: Land-brace, breaking the ground.
Ovile	: Sceapa-hus, sheep-house.
Bucetum	: Hrythra-fald, cow-fold.
Falcastrum	: Sithe, a scythe.
Serula	: Saga, a saw.

Latin.	A.-Saxon.
Vitularium	: Cealfa - hus, calf-house.
Bobellum, (old form of bovillum)	: Falt, a fold for cattle.
Subula	: Ael, an awl.
Scops	: Bisme, a besom.
Caule	: Sceapa-LOCU (Lat. locus), sheepfold.
Equiale	: Hors-ern, place for horses.
Vanga	: Spada, a spade.
Conjuncta	: Fortogen, gathered.
Sarculus	: Screadung-isen, tearing iron.
Terebrum	: Navegar, a borer.
Pastinatum, (in Classic Latin, land prepared for planting)	: PLANT-sticca (Lat planta), a planting stick.
Fossorium (p.-Classic)	Costere, vel delf-isen, vel spada, vel pal, a spade.[1]

[1] The modern Welsh for spade is pal. If the word is not Celtic, we have here an instance of an old Saxon term being preserved in the British tongue while it has no memorial in the English. So also W. rhaith, judgment, A.-Sax. racd ; caib, a hoe, A.-Sax. cipp.

Latin.	A.-Saxon.
Plaustrum :	*Waen*, a waggon.
Rota	: *Hweol*, a wheel.
Bovile sta-	
bulum	: *Scepen-steal*, vel *fald*,
	sheepfold.

Latin.	A.-Saxon.
Ligo	: *Becca*, a stake.
Cantus	: *Felge*, a felly.
Radii	: *Spacan*, spokes.
Sarcina	: *Berthen*, a load.
	&c., &c.

We have also such ecclesiastical terms as the following :—

Latin.	A.-Sax.
Encenia	: Niwe - *circ* - halgung
	[from Gr. κυριακον]
Anastasis	: *Digel*nyssum, resur-
	rection.[1]
Capitulum :	*Cappa* (W. *cap*) a cap
(in sense of	
head cover-	
ing).	

Latin.	A.-Sax.
Fibula	: Oferfeng, vel *dalc*, a
	Clasp.[2]
Sculptura	: *Graeft*, a Carving.
	(W. *cerfio*, to carve.
	crafu, to scrape.)
	See Append. B. sub.
	verb. *crafu*.

The Saxon instrument for writing was called *graef*. The relation of this and *graeft*, sculpture, to Gr. γραφω "to write," and Welsh *crafu*, to scrape, scratch, and *ys-grifio*, to write, is obvious. But the Anglo-Saxon may have had the word previous to the time of making its habitat in Britain. *Rebellio* is rendered by wither-*cwyda*, a compound term, part of which, the prep. *wither*, against, is proper Teutonic, and the latter part proper Celtic. W. *codi*, to rise, has as one of its forms, *cwyd*. The meaning, thus, would be, to rise against, to rebel. If from A.-Sax. *cwide*,

[1] " Digelnyssum " is clearly a hybrid word, having no proper derivation from A.-Sax., except in the *nys*, parent of Engl. " ness," marking quality, as in dark*ness*. The terminal *um* is Lat. The A.-Sax. has *digel*, but in the sense of " a secret," and having a meaning, therefore, quite the opposite of *anastasis* (αναστασις)—rising to view, a resurrection. The *digel* of the A.-Sax. is most probably borrowed from the Celtic. The Welsh has two words, *digel*, meaning open, obvious, unconcealed, from *di*, priv. and *celu*, to conceal ; and the opposite *dygel*, hid, concealed, from *dy*, intens. and *celu*. The A.-Sax. *digel* seems to be borrowed from the latter ; it has no cognate or analogue in A.-Sax.

[2] W. *dal*. to hold ; this fibula being a dress fastener, as well as ornament. A.-Sax. *dalc* has no cognates in that language.

speech, this again is identical with the Celtic : W. *gweyd*, to speak, *chwedl*, report, and the less satisfactory meaning of *resistance in speech* would be derived.

The above will suffice to indicate how the Anglo-Saxon of Ælfric was not free from some little admixture of Celtic, as well as Latin. The next step from the 10th and 11th centuries would bring us to the " Semi-Saxon " age, but to the peculiarities of that age we shall have occasion more specially to refer under another section.

Suffice it further to remark, that the Anglo-Saxon language in the specimens we have received of it from the time of *Caedmon* to that of *Ælfric*—brief specimens it is true, but which, if longer, would not greatly vary the result —show a comparatively pure, yet not an entirely pure speech ; and that the reason of that comparative purity is that the specimens are reflections of the literary and not of the popular tongue.

SECTION II.

Celtic Elements in the English Language.

The revived interest now displayed in the study of Celtic literature, including the Celtic languages, assists to rescue the subject in hand from the grasp of national prejudice, and transfer it to the care of science. We shall be led to confess, by degrees, the confused character of the conceptions we had entertained even of our own ancestry, and that the analysis of our own English language—not altogether a language " undefiled "—in the light of an improved Celtic scholarship, had been one means of correcting our notions.

To the Germans, as is usual in all matters of minute, painstaking scholarship, we are mainly indebted for the

results already attained in Celtic studies. The extraordinary zeal and talent displayed in the study of the
Celtic languages by a prince of the Imperial Family of
France, Prince Lucien Buonaparte, are well known to all,
and have greatly aided in giving tone and impulse to the
study. The names of Chevalier Nigra, in Italy, with
Adolphe Pictet, in Switzerland, De Belloguet, Monin,
Renan, &c., in France, must not be omitted. German
scholars have, after a fashion of their own, by laborious
analysis and synthesis, determined the relation of the
Celtic languages to the whole family of Indo-European
tongues; and also, in a more limited field, applied the
results of their labours to the elucidation of English
Ethnology and English History. Adelung and Vater in
their remarkable work,[1] had years ago supplied voluminous
materials; Arndt, in his *Ursprung und Verwandschaft der
Europäischen Sprachen*; Diez, in his *Lexicon Etymologicon,
und Grammatik*; Holtzmann, in his *Kelten und Germanen*:
Leo, in his various learned productions;[2] Meyer, in his
Importance of the Study of the Celtic languages; Diefenbach,
in his *Celtica*; J. C. Zeuss, in his *Grammatica Celtica*; and
Ebel in his *Celtic Studies*, and in his additions to Zeuss's
Gram. Cell., are amongst our chief assistants. We must
not forget also the labours of Pott, Grimm, and Bopp, in
Comparative Grammar and General Philology. In our
our own country the study has been cultivated by Edward
Davies, Lhwyd, Whitaker, Prichard, Archdeacon Williams,
Halliwell, Latham, Garnett, Guest, Norris, Stokes, and

---

[1] *Mithridates, oder Allegemeine Sprachen-Kunde*. Four vols. Berlin,
1806—1817.

[2] *Vorlesungen über die Geschichte des Deutschen Volkes und Reiches*.
Halle, 1854—1861. *Feriengeschriften, vermischte Abhandlungen zur
Geschichte der Deutschen und Keltischen*. Halle, 1847—1852. *Rectitu-
dines Singularum Personarum*. Halle, 1842. A work on Saxon local
nomenclature.

others, with considerable success. We have now so far advanced that we cannot recede. New light will still pour in upon English ethnology and history from the searching converging lens of philology.

It comports with the nature and design of the present work to direct attention more to vocabulary than to grammar. The Science of Comparative Philology is of necessity based upon an analysis of Grammar, inflections and phonetic laws, but the object we have, in view in this chapter requires not a discussion of the principles of this Science. No one now denies that the Celtic is a sister tongue to the Teutonic. To enter upon a comparison of Celtic and English inflection and syntax were to begin a task too long; for, to say nothing of the complexity of the subject, from the multiplicity of Teutonic and Romance diversities represented in our present English, the changes which have occurred in the inflection and construction of the Celtic dialects themselves, as witnessed by their written literature, would deprive us of any reliable stand- ard by which to test examples.[1] If, for instance, it were desired to compare the syntax or the accidence of Welsh with those of English, in order to show that the latter had become partaker of the features of the former, the question at once offers itself: What Welsh should be the standard—that of Taliesin, of Cynd- delw 12th cent.', or that of the present age? The truth is that the Cymraeg of to-day is as different from the Cymraeg of Aneurin's *Gododin* (say 6th cent.), or even of the laws of *Hywel Dda* (10th cent.; but the *language* in which they now appear is believed to be that of the 12th cent., as modern English is from the Gothic of Ulphilas—

---

[1] Compare, for instance, the grammar of modern Welsh and modern Irish. When the two are compared in their earlier forms, as in Zeuss's *Gram. Celtica*, they exhibit a nearer approach.

as different, not in lexical substance merely, but also, and chiefly, in grammatical forms and combinations.[1]

It were easy to fill too much space with examples; let one or two suffice. Aneurin's *Gododin* opens thus :—

> " Gredyf gwr oed gwas,
> Gwrhyt am dias."
>
> Of manly mind was the youth,
> Heroic mid din of battle.

How many of these terms and inflexions are familiar to the modern Welshman of good education ? Not more than two of the terms, *gwr*, man, and *gwas*, a youth, and even the latter of these has come generally in modern Welsh to mean not " youth," but " servant." The inflexions are all obsolete.

The first line in the sixth stanza of the same poem will show how words still in use are differently inflected and governed.

> " Gwyr a aeth Ododin, chwerthin Ognaw."
> The heroes marched to Gododin, and Gognaw laughed.

The line in modern Welsh would be : " Y" (art.) gwyr aeth*ant* (3rd pers. pl. past) *i* (prep.) Ododin, chwerthin*ai* (3rd pers. sing. past) Gognaw." This may be taken not only as an illustration of the fact that Welsh, like English, abounds more than in earlier times in the use of the article, prepositions, and other particles; but that, also, unlike the English, it has increased its conjugating forms.

Llywarch Hên's expression, in his *Geraint ab Erbin*,

> " Ac elorawr mwy no maint,"
> And biers beyond number.

---

[1] The hopelessness of the attempt of some Celtic critics to prove that the language of Taliesin and Aneurin is as late as the 12th or 14th century, is at once seen by its comparison with the language of the *laws* of Hywel Dda. The latter language, allowed to belong substantially to the 12th century, is much more similar to modern Welsh than the former—a fact sufficiently conclusive against this hypothesis.

though all the vocables are more or less familiar to the Cymro of the present time, is still as an expression completely unintelligible to him, and that by reason of the disguise thrown over the words by an inflexion no longer known, and by the use of a word in a sense no longer attached to it. *Elorawr* here is the pl. of *clor*, a bier, but the plural termination *awr* is now obsolete, the plural of *clor* being *clorau; no*, than, has long given place to *na*. *Maint* is now used for magnitude or quantity, rather than for number.

In prose the change is equally great. It is not less marked in the vowels, and mutations of initial consonants, than in numbers and cases of nouns, tenses of verbs, and connecting particles. The truth is that the modern Cymric has felt the influence of surrounding tongues, has assimilated its grammar and syntax to theirs, while occasionally imparting to them, in return, some of its own peculiarities. The same thing holds true of modern Irish. The grammarians of this language find its forms so changed and corrupted that to rectify them properly they are obliged to have recourse to the most ancient MSS.

But it is clear that if any Celtic grammatical forms are to be employed in proof of Celtic influence of this kind penetrating the English, the forms must not be those of Modern but those of Ancient Celtic; and then, of course, the signs of the influence must be sought for, not in the present English, but in the language at some very distant point in its history—in Semi-Saxon, if not rather in the Anglo-Saxon itself. The signs of interchange must in all reason be inquired after under the period when the languages were most brought in contact, and were most liable to modification. Conditions having changed, Cymric cannot be supposed to have lent its characteristics to the English in recent ages.

Some writers[1] have attempted a comparison of the Cymric and Greek languages, with the view of proving the oft-debated point that the former is a *near* relation of the latter. But the theory can hardly, by any amount of linguistic lore, be established, if the comparison instituted is between the grammar forms of modern Welsh and those of ancient Greek. The principle would hold equally good if the comparison were made with modern English. At the same time it cannot be doubted that a remote relationship does exist between the Celtic and Greek, as well as Latin. They are members of a family, the Celtic having probably broken off from the parent stem, as Prof. Schleicher thinks, at an earlier period than either Greek or Latin. It must not be taken for granted that the mutations and inflexions of any language, Welsh included, are the same in all ages of its history; to secure this permanence the language must become "dead," and be embalmed or fossilized in written form. The grammatical features of Modern are very different, as already shown, from those of Ancient Cymric.

If M. Halbertsma had known that the sound *th* was present in Cymric of all ages (as far as the language can be traced), he would have refrained from putting the query, whether "the English *alone* could boast of having preserved the true sound of the old *dzh* (th) which has disappeared from the whole Continent of Europe, so as not to leave the means of forming a faint idea of the sound of this consonant without the aid of English?"[2] The Welsh

---

[1] The exaggerations of Pughe and others in finding coincidences between Welsh and Greek are well known. Many of the coincidences pointed out are nothing but words borrowed by Welsh from the Greek —some of them through the Latin—as, *eigion*, ocean, ὠκεανὸς; *dagr*, a tear, δάκρυ; *pesgu*, to feed, βόσκω, Lat. pasco.

[2] Comp. Dr. Bosworth's *Origin of the Engl. Germ., &c., Langs.*, p. 37.

has this sound in both its forces, as in Engl. *the*, and *th*ought.   But this can hardly be said to be proof of a peculiar connection between Welsh and Greek, although the latter has the sound *th*, represented by the character θ, because the same sound was possessed by the old Gothic and Anglo-Saxon, although it has now disappeared, as M. Halbertsma lamented, " from the whole Continent of Europe." But there are signs, it must be confessed, that the sound *th*, both soft and hard, was much less frequent in ancient than it is in modern Cymric.

When we pass from the evanescent grammatical features of a language to its lexical materials, the ground seems to become solid.   *Words*, in their substance, though it may be not in their inflectional modes, are permanent. Of the language of to-day they are as genuine parts as they were of the same a thousand years ago, and passing under various modifications into its divided dialects, and by degrees into separate languages, still continue unequivocal mementoes of a past connection and relationship of these languages amongst themselves.   They are like stones which, once dug from a particular rock and wrought into a particular temple, have passed in the course of successive ages into edifices of different styles and purposes—triumphal arches, amphitheatres, monasteries, churches, fortifications, asylums—and at each exchange of locality and service have passed under the mason's chisel into a new form, but throughout have retained, in what remains of them, their original body, stratification, and quality, and may be compared by the geologist with rocks of the same stratum from any part of the globe.

Proceed we now to the question of the chapter—the Celtic lexical elements of the English language.   The following positions are indisputable.

Z 2

First.—The English language now contains a large infusion of words introduced from the Celtic tongues.

Secondly.—The English language once contained multitudes of Celtic words which it has not retained.

Thirdly.—The Celtic words it now contains have not all been assimilated in Britain, and from the Celtic tongues in Britain. Many came along with the Anglo-Saxon from the Continent; and many, incorporated in Britain, were so incorporated from the Latin, or some other tongue than the British, whether of the Cymric or Gaelic branch. Norman-French, Dutch, Danish, German, have been filters through which Celtic has distilled into the English, and multitudes of the Celtic ingredients it now contains had belonged to the Anglo-Saxon in common with many of the Indo-European family of languages long before Britain had become the theatre of its development. Why these materials should be called " Celtic " we shall endeavour to explain under our second head.

Now, the question to be determined by this Essay being, How far the present English nation can be shown to have been compounded of Teutonic and *Ancient British* materials, from the evidence, among other things, of its *speech*, our philological argument must be shaped and limited so as to include the following topics :—1. The Celtic elements which the English language has derived directly from the Celtic tongues, and subsequent to the Saxon Conquest. 2. Celtic elements in the English language derived by that language from the Latin. 3. Celtic elements in the English language derived by that language from the Teutonic tongues, and from the Norman-French.

Neither of the last two can be taken as evidencing admixture of race, as between Anglo-Saxons and Britons, but as simply contributing to the general philological question concerned. Their importance in this last respect claims for them admission into the present discussion; and they are, therefore, introduced. Our analysis of Celtic-English shall be conducted in the order above indicated.

1. Celtic elements in the English language derived directly from the Celtic tongues, and subsequent to the Anglo-Saxon conquest.

This section itself opens before us a very wide field of treatment. It is clear that our witnesses must be summoned not only from the modern English dictionary, but from the vocabularies of the language in any age since the Saxon conquest, and from that living English which floats on the popular tongue unconfined as yet to any lexicon. If the Celtic in Britain, whether Cymric or Gaelic, ever infused its vocables into the Anglo-Saxon speech, even though every tittle of such infusion had disappeared from the standard tongue prior to the age of Chaucer, but still can be traced as a fact once existing, we gain force to our argument from the fact—for we have evidence of such prolonged intercourse of the two peoples, and of such junction and fusion of race as we are in search of. Again, if the living *dialects* of our English are found to contain numerous elements which are undeniably Celtic, though never dignified with a place in the lexicon, we have as expressive and faithful indices to the past intercourse of the two peoples as any Norman-French or Danish terms now recognised as classic can be to the junction of Normans and Danes with the population of England.

We, therefore, summon these solemn witnesses from the dead past, and these fugitive tell-tales from the obscure nooks and corners of our present England, to unfold to us the details of a transaction which no written history so clearly, impartially, and incontestably attests.

It is impossible now to say what multitudes of terms from the speech of the vanquished and incorporated Britons became familiar as " household words ". to the English of the Heptarchy. Doubtless, they were far more numerous, in proportion to the extent of the language, in early times than at present. That in process of ages they have disappeared, leaving, however, thousands of their kindred behind, only shows that they were subject to the same law which has swept from the Saxon so many of its own vocables. Hosts of these, as we all know, no longer appear in the English dictionary. Let a few instances in proof be given, under the first letter of the alphabet only :—

Abie, " to pay for."	Alegge, " to confute."
Abraid, " to open."	Alond, " on the land."
Agrise, " terrify."	Anethered, " conquered."
Afterwending, " following."	An, " grant," " allow."
Agrill, " annoy."	Amanse, " curse."
Awhene, " vex."	Aschend, " injured."
Aken, " reconnoitre."	Aschreynt, " deceived."
Allyng, " entirely."	Atbroid, " seduced."
Arm, " poor."	Awend, " go."

These were once standard words in the English, but are now not to be heard. Any reader of *Havelock the Dane*, *King Alysaunder*, the *Owl and Nightingale*, *the Ormulum*, or the *Life of Beket*, may multiply instances without difficulty.[1]

And not only have many hundred miscellaneous words disappeared, but many others, which, from their antithetic or other peculiar character, might naturally be expected to have been retained. The English was once enriched, not

---

[1] Confer also, *A Dictionary of Oldest Words in the Engl. Language*, by H. Coleridge. Lond. 1863.

only with the former, but also with the latter words of the
following couples :—

{ Neither	{ Inmost	{ Income
{ Nother	{ Outmost	{ Outgo
{ Highest	{ Overcome	{ Heretofore
{ Nythemest	{ Overgo	{ Thereafterward
{ Thither	{ Therein	{ Somewhere
{ Therehence	{ Thereout	{ Somewanne, &c.

So great, indeed, has been the process, if not of degradation, at least of deprivation, that it may be safely affirmed
that about *one-seventh* of the vocabulary of the 13th century
has entirely disappeared. To render a reason for the
abandonment of materials so useful, and belonging so
essentially to the language, may not be easy. The disturbance which ensued on the introduction of the Norman-
French had doubtless much to do with it, and, at a much
later period, the passion which grew up for the "enrichment"
of the language by the use of words of classical derivation,
were among the causes in operation.

We shall see also in the course of our discussion that not
only Teutonic, but Celtic materials, once forming part of
the English tongue, have dropped out of their places in
the progress of ages. And in this there is nothing strange
or improbable. If the materials of the English itself have
been disintegrated, Celtic materials, subject to the same
influences, would become subject also to the same fate.

Out of the whole body of Celtic materials now in the
English language, only a small portion, as already intimated, can be fairly claimed as a direct witness to *amalgamation of race*. To determine that portion, and to bring it
down to the smallest proportions necessary to constitute a
genuine factor in the argument, certain *criteria* must be
adopted, and when adopted rigorously applied. We must
separate and classify under their proper heads all words

which, while containing Celtic roots, are presumably or demonstrably not of *British* origin, *i.e.*, have not been incorporated *since the Saxon tongue became a denizen in Britain;* and also such as have within that very period been incorated, but *not from the speech of the Ancient Britons.* It is essential to the integrity of our argument that this distinction should be made, for we are arguing for race-amalgamation on British soil, and no amount of speech admixture, through the coalescence of the Celts and Teutons on the Continent, in ages antecedent, can here be of any avail.

The magic skill of etymologists is proverbial, and all dealing with the results of their manipulations requires the utmost care. The transformations of words, moreover, in passing from language to language, from land to land, and from age to age, the disguise they assume through transposition, elimination, agglutination of parts, and their occasional perverse change of meaning, make the labour of the most sober and skilful student by no means easy of accomplishment, or certain in result. The same word, at different periods of its history, and in the same language, assumes forms so different as to be scarcely recognisable. To give one or two familiar instances : our indefinite article, " a " was once "*ane*;" the personal pronoun, "I" was at different times *Yk*, *Ik*, *Iche*, and also *Ich*; "always" was once *algates*; "hateful," *ateliche*; "lord," *hlaford*; "lady," *hlæfdige*; "solemnly," *solempenly*. Even the same word, in the same language, and *at the same time*, occasionally appears under very diverse shapes. The whimsical transpositions of the Welsh *'nawr* into *'rwan*, and the squeezing into both these forms of the phrase, *yr awr hon*, "this hour," will be a well-known instance to the Cymro. Again, it is not an uncommon thing to see a word retaining its form more tenaciously in a foreign language than in its own. Thus the Anglo-Saxon *pic* is better preserved both as to sound and orthography in the Welsh *pyg* than in the English "pitch" ; *naeddre* is better represented by the Welsh *neidr* than by the English "adder," and *raca* by W. *raca* than by the English "rake." Words of this sort, especially such as have relation to agriculture and domestic life, are very numerous, and a most interesting list might be collected. Such words being found in large number in the *Welsh* and *Cornish* are extremely suggestive as to the commingled state of the Saxons and *Cymry*, both adhering to their own languages and usages, in ages earlier than the formation of our present English.

And again, instances not a few occur where English words which still exist, but with a modified meaning, continue to retain in the Cymric the genuine sense and character which belonged to them in their old English home. Shakespeare uses "brave," not in the sense of "courageous," but "fine,"—brave words, brave clothes, &c. The Welsh say *tywydd braf*, fine weather, *dillad braf*, fine clothes. In the English version, Moses is styled "a proper child," *i.e.*, comely, fair ; and in North Wales this very word " proper " is commonly used for beautiful, decent—*dynes bropor*, a beautiful woman, *gwisg bropor*, a decent dress, &c.

Not only so, but, curiously enough, the Cymric and other Celtic tongues may be shown to contain many Teutonic vocables, in all likelihood borrowed through intercourse and intermixture in Britain, of which there are now no traces in the English. They are flies in amber, with the difference that they are still alive and doing service. Caught, like stars falling from one region, and saved from destruction, they are sent rolling in other circuits—on the tongues and in the literature of another race. The Anglo-Saxon *egida, egithe*, a rake or harrow, is preserved in W.

oged, harrow; A.-Sax. *pal*, in Ælfric's vocabulary given as the equivalent of Lat. fossorium (post-class.), a digger's instrument, and synonymous with *delf-iscn* "a delving iron," is not found in the English language, but is safely handed down in the Welsh *pál*, a spade. This question, however, has another side : it is possible to argue that both these, and a hundred other words similarly preserved in the Celtic tongues (see p. 369, note 1), were not borrowed at all from the Teutonic, but are Celtic words which the Anglo-Saxon itself for a time borrowed and then relinquished. Words perhaps, like men, have a congeniality for their old homes, and after long and distant wandering, return thither, for final rest. So it is that old Saxon words are now creeping back to our English, and putting to shame the Anglicised Latin, weak and affected, as well as alien.

Caution is sometimes required lest words of similar *meaning*, having also an approximately similar *form*, should be supposed to have an identical ultimate derivation. *Arsmetric* and *arithmetic* are of identical meaning, and are as much alike in form as thousands of words derived from the same roots, and yet the former is from *ars* and *metrica*, the latter from ἀριθμός, words of totally different signification. The classical scholar will be intimate with many such instances.

But although etymology is beset with difficulties, it is not, therefore, to be depreciated. In our present inquiry its services are invaluable. Many thousand words exist in the English language whose pedigree is as clearly ascertainable at least as that of any Norman baron, and many hundred words concerning whose Celtic origin no well-informed philologist can for a moment hesitate. But there are some of these, about the *time* of whose assimilation there is much room for debate. Independently of earlier Latin, and more recently added Teutonisms, a few, if not several hundred words now enrich our language (without counting Norman-French and classical novelties), concerning which no competent Celtic and Anglo-Saxon scholar would hesitate to say that they formed no part of the speech which Hengist, Horsa, Ella, or Cerdic brought over from the Continent.

Now to distinguish these latter elements from the former is a task of prime importance to our discussion, and a task which has never hitherto, to our knowledge, been attempted. Speaking of things, Plato, in his Cratylus, says that they possess φωνή, σχῆμα, and χρῶμα, sound, form, and colour. In like manner it may be said of words that they have sound, form, and meaning; and the nearness to each other of words in these three respects, to whatever languages they may belong in our day, must determine the measure of their consanguinity. At the risk of greatly reducing what might with much reason be construed into Celtic material in the speech of Englishmen, we have adopted the following *criteria*:—

(*a.*) That a word be ascribed to that language as its *nearest* source in which it is found, as to root and meaning, most accurately and fully represented. Thus, " person " comes from Lat. *persona;* W. *carchar,* from Lat. *carcer*;[1] " malady," from French, *maladie.*

(*b.*) That a word found to prevail in two different families of languages, such as the Teutonic and Celtic, be assigned to the one or the other, according as it is found in its authentic root to permeate most numerously the dialects or tongues of that family. An English word found in Irish and Welsh, or Welsh and Cornish, or Welsh and Armoric, or in any greater number of these tongues, and found else-

---

[1] This, notwithstanding the fact that Lat. *carcer* itself is of etymons essentially Celtic (*car*), or belonging to a primitive language, from which archaic Latin and Celtic have sprung in common.

where only in Dutch or Anglo-Norman, or German, or in more than one of them, but displaying a fainter affinity, is classified as a Celtic word, and with that branch of Celtic with which it most harmonizes.

(*c.*) When a word is equally represented in two languages, or in two families of languages, it is assigned to a particular source according to preponderance of probability derived from historical, or other considerations. On this principle, " hour," W. *awr*, Fr. *heure*, Lat. *hora*, is considered as immediately borrowed from the French, itself already borrowed. " Goose," W. *gwydd*, Ir. *geadh*, Corn. *godh*, Germ. *gans*, Anglo-Saxon *gos*, is classed as Teutonic.

The Celtic elements, determined according to these *criteria* to belong to the English language, and to have coalesced with it subsequent to the Saxon Conquest, so-called, are distributed as follows :—

(1.) Celtic words in the English Dictionary.
(2.) Celtic words in the living *dialects* of England.
(3.) Celtic words once found in the written English, but now discontinued.

(1.) *Celtic words in the modern English Dictionary.*

[Other derivations are capable of being assigned to several words in the following table. In such cases the question to be settled is: Out of two or more possible sources, which is the probably *immediate* source whence it was borrowed by the English ?

The Celtic languages are represented thus : Welsh, *W.*, Irish, *Ir.*, Cornish, *Corn.*, Armoric, *Arm.*, Manx, *M.* Gaelic and Irish being so similar, are classed together under Ir. The Teutonic tongues are marked thus : Anglo-Saxon, *A.S.*, German, *G.*, Danish, *Dan.*, Dutch, *D.*]

English.	*Celtic.*	*Teutonic or other Cognates.*
Aeric	: W. *eryr ;* Corn. *er ;* Arm. *erer ;* Ir. *iolar ;* M. *urley,* eagle.	Gothic, *aro.* The word has no relation to Lat. *aer,* Gr. *anp.*
Babe	: W. *ab,* son ; *baban,* babe ; Corn. *baban* and *mab.*	G. *bube.*
Backgammon	: W. *bach,* small, and *cammon,* combat.	
Bait	: W. *bwyd,* food ; *abwyd,* bait ; Corn. *buit ;* Ir. *biadh ;* Arm. *boued.*	A.S. *batan,* to bait ; Gr. βιότος.
Bank	: W. *ban, banc ;* Ir. *beann ;* Corn. *ban* and *banean ;* Arm. *bancq.*	A.S. *banc ;* Fr. *banc ;* Gr. βουνός.
Bar	: W. *bar ;* Ir. *barra,* v.; Corn. *bara,* v.; Arm. *barren,* v.; M. *barrey,* v.	
Bacon	: W. *bacwn ;* Ir. *bogun.*	G. *bache,* " wild sow."
Balderdash	: W. *baldorddi,* to babble ; *baldorddus,* babbling.	
Banner	: W. *baner* (fr. *ban,* high, &c.); Corn. *baner ;* Arm. *bannier.*	G. *fahne ;* Fr. *banniere ;* A.S. *fana,* standard.
Barb	: W. *barf ;* Ir. *bearbh ;* Corn. *barf ;* Arm. *barf.*	Lat. *barba.*
Bard	: W. *bardd ;* Ir. *bard ;* Corn. *bardh ;* Arm. *barz.*	Lat. *bardus ;* Gr. βάρδος.
Barley	: W. *barlys ;* Corn. *barlys.*	A.S. *bere ;* Lat. *far.*
Barrel	: W. *baril ;* Arm. *baraz ;* Gael. *baraille.*	Fr. *baril.*
Base	: W. *bas ;* Corn. *bas ;* Arm. *baz.*	Fr. *bas.*
Basin	: W. *bas,* shallow, *basn ;* Ir. *baisin ;* Arm. *basdhin.*	Fr. *bassin.*
Basket	: W. *basged ;* Ir. *basgaid ;* Corn. *based ;* M. *baskaid.*	
	Corn, *bas,* shallow ; Arm. *bas ;* shallow.	Fr. *bas,* low (from Celtic).
Bastard	: W. *bastardd, tarddu,* to spring ; Ir. *basdard ;* Corn. *bastardh ;* Arm. *bastard.*	D. *bastaard ;* Fr. *b.itard.*
Beagle	: W. *bach,* little, or W. *bugail-gi,* shepherd's dog.	No Teutonic cognate.
Belly	: W. *bol ;* Ir. *bolg ;* Corn. *bol.*	Lat. *bulga ;* Gr. βολγός.
Big	: W. *baich,* a burden ; *beichiog,* with child.	

English.	Celtic.	Teutonic or other Cognates.
Bo! excl.	: W. *bw!* Exclamation to excite fear.	
Bodkin	: W. *bidogyn*, a dagger; Ir. *bidcog*.	
Boil (s.)	: W. *bol* round body, Ir. *buile*, Arm. *buil* ; Corn. *bol*.	A.S. *belge*, belly ; Fr. *bouiller*, to boil.
Bother	: W. *byddaru*, to deafen.	No Teutonic cognate.
Bothy (a hut)	: W. *bwth*, a hut, *bendy*, an out-house ; Ir. *both* ; Corn. *bouti*.	Sansc. *váti*.
Bowel	: W. *bol*. (*ib*.) Ir. *bolg* ; Corn. *bol*.	Gr. μολγòς, βολγòς.
Bowl	: W. *bol*. ,. ,, ,,	,, ,,
Boy	: W. *bach*, little, *bachgen*, boy, youth ; Ir. *beag* ; Corn. *bechan* : Arm. *bigan*, *bian*, little, *buguel*, a child.	Pers. *bach*, child.
Brae	: W. *bré*, mount, hill ; Ir. bri, ib. ; Corn. *bré*. *Bray*, as name of place, freq. in Cornwall. *Carn Brea*, (Corn.) *Penbré*, (Wales) hills.	Sansc. *vára*.
Brace (arch.)	: W. *braich*, arm ; Ir. *brach* ; Corn. *brech* ; Arm. *brech*.	Lat. *brachium*, Fr. *bras*. Gr. βραχίων.
Brag	: W. *brag*, a shooting forth, malt ; *bragio*, to boast.	
Brent	: W. *bryn* ; Corn. *bryn, bre*, hill.	
Brigand	: W. *brig*, hill, summit ; *brigant*, highlander, pl. *brigantwys*, Brigantes.	Fr. *brigand* (from W. or older Celtic.)
Brisk	: W. *brys*, haste, *brysg*, quick.	
Browse	: W. *brwys*, buds; *pori*, to browse ; Arm. *brouz*.	Fr. *brouter;* Gr. βιβρώσκω, fut. βρώσομαι.
Bulk	: W. *bwlg* ; Ir. *balc*.	
Bump	: W. *bwmp, pwmpian*.	
Bunch	: W. *pwng, pwng o fiodau*, b. of flowers.	Dan. *bunke*.
Cb	: W. *cab, caban*, a hut ; Ir. *caban*.	
Cabin	: W. *caban* ; Ir. *caban*.	
Cantred	: W. *cantref—cant*, a hundred, and *tref*, abode.	Lat. *centum*.

English.	Celtic.	Teutonic or other Cognates.
Cairn	: W. *carn;* Ir. *carn;* Corn. *carn;* Arm. *carn;* M. *carn.*	
Carol	: W. *carol;* Corn. *carol;* Arm. *caroll.*	
Carse (a fen)	: W. *cors,* a bog, fen ; Corn. *cors :* Arm. *cors.*	
Cart	: W. *cario,* to carry, *cart;* Ir. *cairt;* Corn. *carios;* Arm. *carr;* M. *cayr.*	Lat. *carrus;* Sansc. *car.*
Cast (in play)	: W. *cast,* a trick; Corn. *cast.* Arm. *cacz.*	Dan. *cast,* a guess.
Cell	: W. *cell,* closet, *celu,* to hide; W. and Corn. *celli,* a grove.	Lat. *cella.*
Clack	: W. *clec, clecian, cloch,* bell; Ir. *clogaim :* Corn. *cloch,* bell; Ir. *clog,* ib ; M. *clagg.*	G. *glocke,* bell.
Clean	: W. *glan,* clean, pure; Ir. *glan;* Corn. *glan :* Arm. *glan.*	No Teutonic cognate.
Clamp	: W. *clwm,* a tie, *clwmi,* to tie.	G. *klammer ;* D. *klamp.*
Clock	: W. *cloch,* bell; Ir. *clog ;* Corn. *cloch,* &c.	G. *glocke ;* A.S. *glucca,* or *glugga.*
Club	: W. *clob, clwb, cloppa.*	G. *kloppel ;* D. *klubbe.*
⎯ Cock-boat	: W. *cwch,* a boat ; Corn. *coc ;* Ir. *cuach.*	
Coot (fowl)	: W. *cwtiar,* from *cwta,* short ; *cwtiar,* short-tailed hen.	
Cope	: W. *coppa, côb ;* Corn. *cop.*	A.S. *caeppe, cop,* head, L.
Corner	: W. *corn, cornel;* Ir. *cearn ;* Corn. *cornel ;* Arm. *corn.*	Lat. *cappa.*
Coracle	: W. *corwg, corwgl.*	
Could	: W. *gallu,* power, also *gallud :* Corn. *gallos, gally ;* Arm. *gallout.*	Lat. *valeo ;* Sans. *gall.*
Crag	: W. *craig ;* Ir. *craig :* Corn. *carrag.*	
Creak	: W. *cryg, crecian, ysgrech :* Corn. *cri,* noise ; Arm. *cri.*	A.S. *ccarcian :* Sansc. *kär,* to resound.
Cricket	: W. *cricell, crician,* v.	” ” ”
Cringe	: W. *crycha, crino,* bend, wither, *crynu,* shake ; Corn. *crenne,* tremble.	G. *krischen.*

English.	Celtic.	Teutonic or other Cognates.
Crockery	: W. *crochan*, hollow vessel, pot, *cragen*, shell; Corn. *crogen*, shell.	A.S. *crocca*.
Cromlech	: W. *cromlech—crom*, bending, *llech*, flat stone; Corn. *crom*, bent; Ir. *crom*.	
Crone	: W. *crino*, wither; Ir. *criona*, old.	Gr. γερων, old.
Crook	: W.*crwc*, s. *crwca*, a.; Ir. *cruca*.	
Croom (a crooked fork, provincial)	: W. *crwm*, a bending, *crymu*, to bend; Ir. *crom*; Corn. *crom*.	G. *krumb*; Dan. *krum*.
Crouch	: W. *crychu*, v. neut, to bend, wrinkle. This is possibly the root both of "cringe" and "crouch," perhaps also of "crook," but it is more probably itself derived fr. *crwc*, with the *w* modified into *y* in the verb.	
Crowd	: W. *crwth*, mus. instr.; Ir. *cruith* : Corn. *crowd*.	Lat. *chrotta Britanna*, in Venant. Fortun.
Cudgel	: W. *cogail*, distaff; Corn. *cigel*.	
Cut	: W. *cwta*, a. short, *cwtäu*, shorten; Corn. *cot*; Ir. *cutach*. No trace of this word in any of the Gothic languages.	Lat. *curtus* seems to be of cognate origin.
Cuttle (fish)	: W. *cuddio*, to hide, *cuddigl*, retreat; Corn. *cudhe*, to hide; Arm. *cuza*. Eng. "hide" is of same origin as *cuddio*, the A.S. *hydan* substituting initial *h* for the Celtic *c* or *k*.	Sansc. *kud*.
Dad	: W. *tad*; Ir. *taid*; Corn. *tad*.	
Dainty	: W. *dant*, tooth, *dantaith*, feast; Corn. *dans*, tooth; Ir. *dead*; Arm. *dant*.	Lat. *dens*, tooth; Gr. όδούς-οντος; Ion. όδων; Goth. *tunthus*.
Dale	: W. *dôl*; Ir. *dail*; Corn. *dol*; Arm. *dôl*. This word is	G. *thal*; D. *dol*; Rus. *dol*.

English.	Celtic.	Teutonic or other Cognates.

	found in names of places situate in valleys all over Wales, Cornwall, and Brittany; Dolbadarn, Dolau, Dolywhiddens, Dolgoath, Dol, &c.	
Dally	: W. *dal*, *dala*, to hold; Ir. *dail*, delay; Arm. *dalea*, to stop, delay; Corn. *dalhen*, holding.	
Darn	: W. *darn*, a piece; Corn. *darn*, Arm. *darn*.	Fr. *darne*, slice; Sansc. *darana*.
Dastard	. W. *bastardd* (?) mean, of low birth. If this with change of *b* inc. into *d* is not the origin of this word, it seems impossible to discover one. The *idea* associated with "*d*astard," to some extent, though by no means wholly, enters into the word "*b*astard." Both are ignoble.	[No trace of this word in any of the other Aryan languages.]
Denizen	: W. *dinas*, city; Corn. *dinas*, from *din*, a place of strength; *dinesydd* in W. is a citizen: term. *zen* as in citizen.	[Good authorities give old Fr. *deinsein* as origin, but the word is more likely a corruption of Cymric.]
Dicker (ten, as, a "dicker" of gloves)	: W. *deg*, ten, Corn. *deg*.	Gr. δέκα, Lat. *decem*.
Dock	: W. *tocio*, to shorten, clip.	
Doll	: W. *dull*, form, *delw*, image; Ir. *dealbh*; Corn. *del*, semblance, form	G. εἴδωλον.
Druid	: W. *derwydd*, fr. *derw*, oak; Ir. *darach* oak; Corn. *derow*, do. Though *derwydd* is a satisfactory derivation of "Druid," it is not so clear that *derw*, oak, is the root	Gr. δρῦς, oak.

A A

English.	Celtic.	Teutonic or other Cognates.
	of *derwydd*, the *ydd* taken as a termination, and giving the idea of a person having to do with the oak, as *mesurydd*, a measurer, *melinydd*, "a miller." A Druid was not so much concerned with the oak itself as with religion, knowledge, and science, under the shadow of the oak grove. True, he esteemed the fruit or seed of the oak sacred. Still this analysis of the word *derw-ydd* is more probable than Dr. W. O. Pughe's, *derw-gwydd*, "oak-knowledge."	
Flabby	: W. *llib*, *llipa*, *gwlyb*, flaccid, soft, moist.	
Flag(stone)	: W. *llech;* Ir. *liach*.	
Flasket	: W. *fflasg*, *flasged*, a basket made of straw or wicker.	Mid-age Latin, *flaskettus*, from the Welsh.
Flimsy	: W. *llymsi*, spiritless, flimsy.	
Flippant	: W. *llipan*, a glib chatterer.	
Fool	: W. *ffol*, *ffwl;* Corn. *fol*, Arm. *foll*.	Fr. *folle*, *fou*.
Frith	: W. *ffridd;* Gael. *frith*, a forest, park. A.-Sax., in name, *Fyrhthe*. Leo acknowledges the word to be Celtic.	["Frith," an arm of the sea, Lat. *fretum*, has no relation to this word.]
Fudge	: W. *ffug*, deception, a feigning; Corn. *fugio;* Ir. *bog*. "Fudge" is a made-up story, pretence, "stuff."	Lat. has *fucus*, a dye, for false appearance.
Funnel	: W. *ffynel*, air-hole, chimney.	
Gale	: Ir. *gal*, gale, blast of wind; W. *awel*, breeze; Corn. *awel;* Arm. *awel*.	Gr. ἄελλα, Lat. *aeolus*.
Gown	W. *gwn;* Corn. *gun;* Ir. *gunna;* M. *goon*.	Low Lat. *gunna;* Late Gr. γοῦνα.
Gable	: W. *gafael*, a hold. The gable	

English.	Celtic.	Teutonic or other Cognates.
	gives timbers a hold, support. Ir. *gabhaidh;* Corn. *gaval.*	
Gag	: W. *cêg,* throat, *cêgio,* to choke.	No Teutonic cognate.
Gavelkind	: W. *gafael,* a hold, to hold. See *index* " gavelkind."	
Grouse	: W. *iar,* or *giar,* a hen, and *rhos,* moor—a " moor-hen." This is the common name of the bird in many parts of Wales.	No Teutonic cognate.
Grudge	: W. *grwgnach.*	Lat. *rugio,* Gr. γρύξω.
Guess	: W. *ceisio,* seek, inquire; Ir. *geasam.*	D. *gissen.*
Guiniad (a fish)	: W. *gwyn,* white—the colour of the fish.	
Gull (bird)	: W. *gwylan ;* Corn. *gullan.*	
Gun	: W. *gwn;* Corn. *gun,* a scabbard.	
Gyve	: W. *gefyn,* fetter, *gafael,* hold ; Ir. *geibheal :* Corn. *gavel.*	
Haft	: W. *gafael,* a hold ; Corn. *gavel.*	
Hag	: W. *hagr,* ugly; Corn. *hager ;* Arm. *haer.*	G. *hager.*
Haggard	: ,, ,, ,,	
Happy	: W. *hap,* chance, luck (?)	
Harlot	: W. *herlawd* [very doubtful etymology]; Corn. *harlot,* a vile man, rogue, villain. Is *herlawd* itself a Cymric or Celtic word at all ? It is given here in deference to the opinion of others. " Harlot " may have had its origin in A.S. *ceorl,* G. *kerl,* a rustic, a slave, a " fellow," and in course of time, a coarse saucy person. The term. *ot* is not to mark the fem., as Charles, Charlotte, since in Chaucer " harlot " is used for profligate	[The classic tongues contain nothing cognate with this word; *ceorl, kerl,* are the nearest approach to it in the Teutonic.]

English.	*Celtic.*	*Teutonic or other Cognates.*
	persons of either sex, whence, perhaps, the Cornish *harlot. Herlod*, boy, stripling,; *herlodes*, damsel, are mod. W. without bad meaning attached.	
Hiccup	: W. *hic*, a hitch, a snap. The latter part of the word is perhaps a modification of "cough."	
Hitch	: W. *hic;* Corn. *hig*, a hook; Arm. *hygen.*	
Hoax	: W. *hocced*, deceit, cheating.	
Hog	: W. *hwch*, a sow; Corn. *hoch*, pig, hog; Arm. *houch, hoch*, a pig.	Gr. *ŭs*; Lat. *sus;* G. *sau*, a sow.
Hoot	: W. *udo*, howl, *hwtio*, hoot.	
Howl	: W. *wylo*, weep, cry; Ir. *guil;* Corn. *gwelvan.*	G. *heulen;* Gr. κλαίω; Lat. *fleo.*
Hurry	: W. *gyru*, drive.	Lat. *curro.*
Husk	: W. *gwisg*, covering; Corn. *gwesc*, husk.	
Hush	: W. *ust!*	
Kindle	: W. *cynneu :* Corn. *cunys*, fuel; Arm. *cened ;* Ir. *connadh.*	Lat. *ac-cendo, candeo.*
Label	: W. *llab*, strip, *llabed.*	
Lad	: W. *llawd*, boy, *lodes*, girl; Ir. *ath.*	
Lagging	: W. *llac*, loose, remiss; Ir. *lag;* Corn. *lac*, M. *lhag.*	Lat. *laxus.*
Lath	: W. *llath*, rod, yard, measure. Though found in Germ. *latte* and Fr. *latté* and perh. cognate to Lat. *latus*, the terminal sound *th*, which it assumes in none of these langg., seems to suggest its immediate appropriation from the Welsh.	Lat. *latus ?* G. *latte ;* Fr. *latté.*
League	: W. *llech*, a slab, a stone; Ir. *leac;* Arm. *leach ;* M. *leac.* A "league" was a measure of	Fr. *lieue*, fr. low Latin *leuca*, adopted in Gaul, "Quum et Latini

English.	*Celtic.*	*Teutonic or other Cognates.*
	distance marked by a stone standing on end.	mille passus vocent, et Galli *leucas.*" *Hieron.*
Loafer	: W. *lloffa,* to glean; *lloffwr,* a gleaner. A loafer is one who hangs about, picking up a precarious living.	[Certainly not from G. *laufen,* to run; running being far from the habit of such a person.]
Lubber	: W. *llabi, llabwst.*	
Lurk	: W. *llercian,* to loiter, lurk; Corn. *lerch,* a footstep, a trace; Ir. *lorg :* Arm. *lerch.* Because a person who lurks makes marks by which he is traced?	
Maggot	: W. *magu,* to breed, nourish; Corn. *maga,* to feed; Arm. *maga,* ib.	
Marl	: W. *marl,* rich clay; Ir. *marla.*	G. *mergel.*
Mead	: W. *medd;* Ir. *meadh ;* Corn. *medh;* Arm. *mez.*	Gr. *μέθυ*; Sans. *madhu;* Lith. *medus,* honey.
Mew	: W. *miwian* as a cat; a word invented to imitate the cry of the animal.	G. *miauen.*
Morrow	: W. *bore,* morning; *y foru,* to-morrow; Corn. *bore :* Arm. *beuré.* The former meaning of "morrow" was "morning," thence the morning to come — both which meanings are still retained in German. The W. has two cognate terms to express the distinctions, *bore* and *foru.* The change from W. *bore* to morrow, reducing the *b* into *m,* is less than the change of Germ. *morgen* into morrow, eliminating both the *g* and the *n.*	G. *morgen ;* Gr. *πρωΐ*; Sansc. *prac,* fr. *pur,* to advance. The A. S. has *morn* and *morgen.*
Moult	: W. *moel,* bare, *moeli,* to make bald; Corn. *moel,* bare; Arm. *moel ;* Ir. *maol.*	

English.	Celtic.	Teutonic or other Cognates.
Muggy	: W. *mwg*, smoke; Ir. *muig*; Corn. *moc*.	A.S. *smocca*, smoke.
Mustard	: W. *mwstardd*, *mws*, a strong scent, and *tarddu*, to spring.	Fr. *moutarde* (Gallic).
Niggard	: W. *nig*, *nigio*, to narrow.	G. *knicker*, Dan. *gniker*.
Nod, v.	: W. *nódi*, to mark; *am-naid-io*, to give a sign; Corn. *nod*, mark, token, Ir. *nod*.	Lat. *nota*, *nuto*.
Odd	: W.*od*, singular, notable; *odid*, rarity.	
Pall	: W. *pallu*, to fail, weaken; applied like the English word to failure of appetite.	
Pantile	: W. *pen*, top. A tile for the top of a house, a "roofing tile," which formerly was written *pen*-tile.	
Park	: W.*parc;* Corn.*parc;* Ir.*pairc*, Arm. *parc;* M. *pairk*. In this case, as the word *park* is not in the A.-Saxon, the Celtic is chosen as the source whence the word has passed not only into English, but also into French.	Fr. *parc;* G. *park* (Gallic).
Paw	: W. *pawen;* Corn. *paw;* Arm. *pâô*.	G. *fuss;* Gr. πούς; L. *pes*.
Penguin (bird)	: W. *pengwyn* (white-head), a descriptive name.	
Perk	: W. *perc*, smart.	
Pill	: W. *pél*, a ball; Corn. *pél;* Arm. *pellen*.	Lat. *pila*, *pillula*, dim.
Plait	: W. *plethu*, to weave, plait; Corn. *pleth*, a plait, wreath; Ir. *filleadh*.	Dan. *fletter;* Fr. *plisser*.
Poke	: W.*pwg*,what swells or pushes; Corn. *poc*, a push; *pock*, a shove, is still used in the Cornish dialect.	
Poll (head)	: W. *pel*, ball; Corn. *pel;* Arm. *pellen*.	G. *ball*.
Posset	: W. *posel*, *possed*, curdled milk.	

English.	Celtic.	Teutonic or other Cognates.
Quay	: W. *cac*, an inclosure; Ir. *ceigh*; Arm, *kae*; Corn. *cc*.	No Teutonic cognate, except D. *kaai*.
Queen	: *Vide* Appendix B, " Queen."	
—Quip	: W. *chwib*, *chwip*, a quick turn ; *gwibio*, to wander.	
Quibble	: W. id. To argue evasively and triflingly, ever starting and turning from the point in hand as may suit, would combine in W. both *chwipio* and *gwibio*—both perhaps in reality one word.	No Teutonic cognate.
Quirk	: W. *chwyrn*, rapid; also whirl.	
Rule	: W. *rcol ;* Corn. *rowlia ;* Arm. *rcolia.*	A.S. *rcgol ;* G. *rcgcl ;* Lat. *rcgula ;* Fr. *rcglc.*
Sad	: W. *sad*. firm, sober, thoughtful; applied in Eng. because of the quiet thoughtfulness of sorrow.	
Sallow	: W. *sal*, ill, *salw*, mean ; *salw'i olwg*, dejected and sallow in appearance.	
Scare	: W. *yscar*, to separate; Corn. *cscar*, enemy	
Screech	: W. *ysgrechain ;* Ir. *screachaim ;*	G. *schreien.*
Scrip	: W. *yscrepan*, *crop;* so "crop" of a fowl, which is a purely Celtic term, though found in A.S. Germ. and D. The idea is that of a place to hold, a cavity.	A.S. *crop ;* G. *kropf.*
Sham	: W. *siom*, a disappointment.	
Shriek	: W. *ysgrechain*, Ir. *screachaim.* " Shriek " and " screech " are the same in derivation, varied in orthography as if to meet a slightly different shade of meaning.	G. *schreien.*
Slab	; W. *llab*, *yslab*, a thin strip.	Lat. *lam-ina.*
Spigot	: W. *pig*, *yspigod*, a point, spigot; Corn. *pigol*, a pick.	A.S. *piic*, a little needle or pin ; G. *pickc*, a pick-axe.

English.	Celtic.	Teutonic or other Cognates.
Spike	: W. do. a point, a nail.	
Squeeze	: W. *gwasgu;* Corn. *gwyscel,* Arm. *gwasca;* Ir. *faisg.*	
Squeak	: W. *gwychian.*	
Stain	: W. *taenu,* to spread, *ystaen,* a covering spread over the surface, whether to colour or protect.	Lat. *stannum,* an alloy; Gr. τείνω, to extend.
Tall	: W. *tàl,* Corn. *tal;* *Tal Carn,* the high rock in St. Allen.	
Task	: W. *tasg,* Ir. *tasg.* Possibly the first use of the Eng. "task" was to mark a quantity to be learned, under instruction, then to be done under direction. If so, *dysgu,* to teach (the word also means to "learn," like *lernen,* in Germ.) may have been its origin.	Gr. διδάσκω, Lat. *disco,* are not the immediate source; Fr. *tache.*
Through	: W. *trwy;* Ir. *tre;* Corn. *tre,* over.	A.S. *thurh;* G. *durch.* Archaic Celtic root.
Torch	: W. *torch,* a ring, wreath; probably applied to the flaming substance on account of circling motion of flame. (*Vide* Append. B. "torch.")	Lat. *torqueo;* Fr. *torche,* It. *torcia;* Span. *antorcha.*
Torque	: W. *torch, id.; tor* is common in Celtic to express roundness, protuberance, &c. *Torrog,* as adj. expresses the quality of fulness; a bulging form. W. *torchog* is circling, coiling, as *y sarph dorchog*—the coiling serpent. W. *troi,* to turn, twist. W. Corn. Arm. *tro,* a turn, circuit. (*Vide* Append. B. "torch.")	Lat. *torqueo.*
Tudor, (adj. as	: W. *Tudyr,* the name of Owen Tudor, of Wales, who mar-	

English.	Celtic.	Teutonic or other Cognates.
"Tudor style.")	ried Catherine of France, widow of Henry V., and from whom descended the "Tudor" Royal Family of England.	Possibly from Theodore, Gr. Θεοδῶρος
Twaddle	: W. *chwedl*, gossip, a story, *chwedlena*, to prattle, talk.	
Wail	: W. *wylo*, to cry, weep; Corn. *wole* and *ole*; Ir. and Gael. *guil*; Manx *gul*. This word appears in Semi - Saxon period, *ex. gr.* in Alysaunder, but the A.-Sax shows no trace of it, unless by a violent interpretation it be referred to *wael*, slaughter, death, and *waelhlem*, "a slaughter, or war cry."	It. *guaiolare*; Lat. *fleo*; Gr. κλαίω.
Whim	: W. *chwim*, a brisk motion, a turn.	
Whole	: W. *holl*, *oll*, altogether, the whole. It is barely represented in A.-S., but found in Semi-Sax. *ex. gr.* Robert of Gloucester, 377. The aspirate *wh* was more probably inherited from the Celtic than from Gr. Ir. *huile* and *oll*; Corn. *oll*, Arm. *holl* and *oll*.	Gr. ὅλος; A.S. *al*; G. *all*. A.-Sax. *al*, and Germ. *all*, are related.

The above list could not perhaps be greatly augmented —it is just possible it ought to be, by one or two words, curtailed. It is much shorter than the extravagant expectations of some Celtic enthusiasts would dictate, and too ample to be received without demur by others. The Englishman who believes himself to be a pure Teuton, would rather it were not proved to him that he is every day talking so much Celtic. It is perplexing, however, to see in such a work as Marsh's *English Language*[1] the following, and other equally unlikely words, derived from the Celtic—mostly from the Welsh:—barrow, broider, clout, kiln, tenter, fleam, flaw, frieze, griddle, gruel, wall, wicket, flannel, housing, locker, flummery, mesh, pail, pitcher, pottage, ridge, drill, solder, size, tackle, tassel, —clearly none of them of Celtic, but nearly all of well-known Teutonic origin.

Let it be noted that the affinity with Brito-Celtic claimed above is not that of mere general *relationship* and *similarity* existing between two branch languages of the old Aryan stock; but the affinity of distinct and immediate descent. The language now called English, it is believed, possessed them not in its earlier forms. It borrowed them bodily from that Celtic speech it encountered in Britain, just as it has borrowed hundreds of others from the Latin. If it did not so borrow them, by all means let it be shown.

The Welsh, of all the Celtic dialects, as might be expected from the greater intercourse of the Cymry, has yielded the largest number of derivatives, and its forms are the forms most closely imitated. The above list is the result of much sifting, and repeated examination of each separate term, and is presented with some degree of confidence in the Brito-Celtic character of nearly the whole, with slight reservation respecting a few, among which may be mentioned: "basin," which some may prefer deducing from Fr. *bassin* ; "cope," of whose Teutonic kinship there exist some suspicious indications; "harlot," apparently disclaimed by all languages, except the Cornish ; "denizen," which some derive from old Fr. *donaizon*, or *deinzein*.

---

[1] Ed. Dr. Smith, 1862, p. 45.

In this list we have included all those Celtic vocables
in our present standard English we wish to rely upon as
directly evidencing in favour of our argument. They are not
given, be it again remarked, as the whole of the Celtic now
found in modern English, but as the approximate whole
of the Celtic which coalesced with the English in Britain,
and has survived. As will be seen hereafter, the English
contains not a little Celtic which it has received through
Latin, possibly in Britain, possibly elsewhere, but this is
not taken as evidence of race-intercourse and admixture.
The words in our list, at least, have remained to this day ;
how many more survive, in situations less prominent—in
the dialects of the widely separated provinces of England,
and in the obsolete vocabulary of ancient records only now
beginning to see the light—we shall by and by have opportunity briefly to discuss.

It is pertinent here to observe, and the philosophic historian would deem it a point of no slight significance
—that the above list is in some degree an index to the
social condition, as well as to the mental idiosyncracies,
of the people it commemorates. Here are few terms used
in law, art, science, or government. The Britons who
amalgamated with their conquerors had been taken out of
these spheres of thought and action. Their power to
impregnate the intrusive speech would be the power of
humble daily intercourse, while engaged in domestic, agricultural, or military toil. The superior civilization they
had inherited, their nobler faith and carefully digested
laws, would doubtless at first have forced upon their
Anglo-Saxon masters a vast number of technical terms
and formulæ, names of objects and places, of customs,
festivals and offices ; but these were speedily got rid of
when a Saxon priesthood grew up with sufficient learning
to adapt their own strong and rugged speech to the new

inheritance of ideas on which they had entered. We have already seen how Celtic terms were carefully excluded from the earlier written Anglo-Saxon. The Vocabularies of Archbishop Ælfric, and the Anglo-Saxon Vocabularies of the 11th century, furnish evidence of this; and the literary history of King Alfred—notwithstanding that this noblest of all rulers was much under the influence of a Celtic scholar, the Welshman Asser—conclusively shows that he bent all his energies to constitute his own much-beloved Anglo-Saxon the vehicle of all the ideas of his time.

But, while, under royal authority, the revived Anglo-Saxon scholarship of that age rejected the "barbarisms" which had crept in, the same barbarisms continued to hold their own in the language of daily life—in the market-place, in the corn-field, in the smithy; and by and by, like a deeper current concealed for a time from view, burst again to the surface. Accordingly in the written literature of the "Semi-Saxon" period, two centuries after Alfred, we meet with a large number of purely Celtic words. To these we shall in due time return.

The train of our argument leads us in the next place to glance at the Celtic materials found in the living *dialects* of the English language.

(2.) *Celtic Words in the living Dialects of England.*

In the "nooks and corners" and over the wide plains of our country are tens of thousands of people whose scanty vocabulary contains hundreds of vocables which the columns of no standard dictionary have ever contained, and amongst these are numerous remains, pure and genuine as chips of diamonds, of the Ancient British tongue. Admirable is the unconscious fidelity of these sons of toil in handing down from father to son these precious memorials of the past![1]

To what extent the Celtic of the dialects can be claimed as *British* contributions—*i.e.*, contributions made since the Anglo-Saxon conquest—is hard to determine. Some can be traced through the Latin to the misty pre-historic times when from some sources now untraceable Celtic drops were distilled into all the Indo-European tongues—some through the Anglo-Saxon—some through German. But many others find no reflections in these languages. A multitude confess, by orthography and significance, to relationship with the *Cymraeg*. This, as might be expected, is notably the case in Lancashire, Cumberland, Westmoreland, Yorkshire, Shropshire, Wilts, and—what was formerly termed —"West Wales"—Devon and Cornwall.

The Celtic local or geographical names, as we shall by and by have occasion to show, still in great numbers remain, clinging with far greater tenacity to the soil than do the strongest fortresses or the most renowned cities. But with a fixedness which is still more wonderful, because under conditions apparently less allied to permanency, pure Celtic idioms and vocables manage from age to age to survive, defying the purism of lexicographers, defying the withering breath of time, hiding themselves for safe shelter amid the obscurities of peasant life, and with in-

---

[1] Abundant materials in proof may be found in the following, among many other contributions of laborious collectors:—*Tim Bobbin ; The Lancashire Witches;* Carr's *Craven Dialect ; The Dialect of Leeds and its Neighbourhood;* Halliwell's *Dict. of Archaic and Provincial Words;* Grose's *Glossary of Provincial Words ; The Cornish Provincial Dialect ;* Dickinson's *Words and Phrases of Cumberland;* Barnes' *Hwomely Rhymes in the Dorset Dialect;* Baker's *Northamptonshire Words and Phrases ;* Evans's *Leicestershire Words, Phrases, and Proverbs ;* Cooper's *Glossary of the Provincialisms of Sussex;* Akerman's *Provincial Words, &c., of Wiltshire;* Clark's *John Noakes and Mary Styles, in the Essex Dialect.*

genuity like that of instinct, disguising themselves in such voluminous drapery of Saxon grammatical forms, as demand all the skill and patience of the philologist to unloose.

Great has been the industry of collectors of dialectic words and phrases! But great also has been their neglect of etymology. They have collected *words*, apparently without a thought of the world of ethnological interest belonging to them. Even so useful a work as Halliwell's *Dictionary of Archaic and Provincial Words* loses half its value to the thorough student through this omission—an omission, by so zealous a labourer in early English, scarcely to be accounted for.[1]

To give a collection of all Celtic dialectic words discoverable, were to compose a dictionary. We must select a corner of the wide field, and give the result of our gleaning as a specimen of the whole. Let us turn to Lancashire, and touch also upon a side of Cumberland. In Lancashire, almost all the words are found to assimilate to the *Welsh* dialect of Celtic.

Celtic in the Dialect of Lancashire..

Awf, a horrid person	W. *wffl*, interj. shame! fie!
Bam, mocking tale, gibe	Armoric, *bamein*, to deceive.
Bitter-bump, the bittern	W. *bwmp-y-gors*, "the bwmp of the moor," the bittern; first word expresses the bittern's hollow cry.

---

[1] An occasional etymological note, however, is given by Mr. Halliwell. The following account of the first use of a purely Celtic word is scarcely reliable:—"The word *pen* was first introduced into Cornwall, where the Phœnicians had a colony who worked the tin mines. Hence we have many names in Cornwall which begin with *pen*." (*Dict. of Arch. and Provin. Words*, sub verb. *Pen*.) Many names beginning with *pen* exist in Wales and Brittany. Did the "Phœnicians" also import these? And what special qualification had the Phœnicians for introducing the word *pen*, a word which essentially belonged to the speech of the people who inhabited Cornwall, probably, long before the Phœnicians saw it?

Bodikin, a bodkin — W. *bidog*, dirk, bayonet.

Boggart, an apparition — W. *bwgan*, hobgoblin.

Braggot, spiced ale — W. *bragod*, spiced ale.

Brawse, brambles, furze — W. *brwyn*, rushes.

Bree, to fear a person — W. *braw*, fear, terror.

Byes, cattle — W. *buwch*, cow; Arm. *bu*; Ir. *bo*; Corn. *buch*, cow.

Cam, to make crooked }
Cammed, crooked   } — W. *cam*, crooked; *camu*, to make crooked.

Costril, a small barrel — W. *costrel*, a bottle, jar.

Craddy, *Craddins* — "to lead craddies" is to perform some bold, adventurous trick or feat — W. *gwrhydri*, heroic action.

Crom, to stuff — W. *cromil*, the crop of a fowl.

Crony, a companion, intimate — W. *carenydd*, kindred; *car*, friend.

Durn, the fastening by which gates are held — W. *dwrn*, a hand clenched, a fist, a handle.

Foomart, wild cat — W. *ffwlbert*, the polecat.

Frump, to sulk, mock — W. *ffromi*, to be angry, in a pet.

Gar, force — W. *gyru*, to drive, urge, force.

Ginnil, a narrow passage — W. *cynnil*, sparing, saving, close.

Gorbelly, large bellied — W. *gor*, extreme.

Greece, a slight ascent — W. *gris*, a stair, step (this from Lat. *gradus*).

Gealo, *healo*, modest, shy — W. *gwylaidd*, modest, diffident.

Harr, to snarl like a dog — W. *her*, challenge.

Hitter, keen, daring — W. *hyder*, confidence.

Huff, *huft*, to treat scornfully — W. *wft*, for shame, fie.

Jim, *jimp*, neat, spruce — W. *gwymp*, smart, fair.

Keather, cradle — W. *cader*, cradle.

Keen, to burn — W. *cyneu*, to kindle.

Knep, to bite readily — W. *cnoi*, to bite, masticate.

Knowe, a rise, a brow — W. *cwnni*, to rise; *cwnwg*, *cnwc*, summit, mound.

Lake, to idle, play truant — W. *llechu*, to hide, skulk.

Lither, to thicken broth — W. *llith*, mash; Gael. *leite*, gruel.

Lobb, a heavy, clumsy fellow — W. *llob*, a blockhead.

Luver, open chimney — W. *llufer*, chimney.[1]

Mulloch, dirt, rubbish — W. *malwch*, chaff, sweepings.

---

[1] Whence the name of the "Louvre," Paris, from its chimney.

Oandurth, afternoon

W. *anterth*, morning. Can *o* in "oandurth" be the Celtic prep. *o*, "from"—"separate, or proceeding from the morning"?

Peigh, to cough

W. *peswch*, to cough; *pych*, id.

Pilder, to wither

W. *pallder*, a failure, abortiveness.

Pinc, a finch

W. *pinc*, a finch; given to the bird from the cry he utters. Germ. *finke*, whence Engl. "finch."

Reeak, rick, shriek, scold

W. *crech, ysgrech*, shriek.

Rhiggot, a gutter

W. *rhig*, a groove.

Scrannil, a lean, bony person

W. *asgyrnog*, bony, lean.

Seely, weak in body

W. *sal*, ill, frail; *salw*, id.

Shurn, dung

W. *sarn*, stable litter.

Scut, the tail of a hare

W. *cwt*, tail.

Threave, a crowd

W. *torf*, crowd, multitude (*turba*.)

Ted, to spread abroad as hay

W. *teddu*, to spread out.

Tin, to shut to the door

{ W. *tynu*, to draw.

Tinned, shut

{ W. *tyn*, drawn close, tight.

Toyne, shut }
Toynt, shut }

W. the same

Trest, a strong bench

W. *trawst*, a beam.

Turnil, an oval tub

W. *twnel*, a tub or vat.

Wear, to lay out money

W. *gwario*, to spend, disburse.

Wherr, very sour

W. *chweru*, bitter, sharp to taste.

Witherin, large, powerful

W. *uthr*, terrible, awful.

Wy-kawve, a she-calf

W. *hi*, she.

Wyzles, stalks of potato

W. *gwydd*, small trees, brushwood.

Yeandurth, before noon

W. *anterth*, morning.

This list might be largely augmented. All doubtful words, and words not properly "dialectic," have been rejected. Some, hitherto approved by respectable authorities have been winnowed out, as not being clearly Celtic, or not properly belonging to the "unwritten" language. Dade (used in Lancashire for holding a child by the arm to teach him to walk), garth, lurch, natter, sow (for head), can hardly be derived, as Mr. Davies thinks,[1] from W. *dodi, garddd, llerchio, naddu, siol;* nor can fag-end, fog,

[1] See *Transactions of Philolog. Soc.* 1855, p. 210.

garth, lurch (which is nothing but lurk), hap, muggy, pelt, pick 'to dart), reawt (which is only a form of pronouncing "road"), spree, tackle, treddles, whop, be considered as words belonging to the Lancashire, nor, some of them, indeed, to any "dialect," and we are inclined to believe that of the above, only lurch (from *llerchu*, to skulk), pelt (from *pél*, a ball), pick (from *pig*, a point, dart), muggy (from *mûg*, smoke), can be safely traced to Celtic.

In Lancashire, it is seen, almost all the Celtic words are from the Cymric. In Cumberland they seem to have descended in about equal degree from the Gaelic, or Erse.

Celtic in the Dialect of Cumberland.

Beel, to bellow	Ir. *beul*, the mouth (bawl).
Boggle, to be brought to a stand, a ghost	W. *bwg*, hobgoblin; *bwgwl*, threat.
Cammed, crooked.	W. *cam*, crooked; Corn. Ir. Arm. id.
Corp, a dead body	W. *corph*, body, dead body. Lat.
Gope, to talk foolishly	Ir. *gob*, the mouth (gabble).
Gowl, to weep or cry	Ir. *guil*, to weep; W. *wylo*, to weep.
Lam, to beat	Ir. *lamh*, the hand; W. *llaw*, id.
Marrow, equal	Ir. *mar*, like to; W. *par*, pair. Lat.
Rag, to abuse, scold	Ir. *rag*, abuse; *bally-rag*, town or street abuse; W. *regu*, curse.
Sad, heavy, thick	W. *sad*, firm, sober.

That Cumberland should present remains of the Gaelic as well as of the Cymric Celtic is perfectly natural, and accordant with history. The Scots bordering on the Ancient Cumbrian kingdom were from Ireland, and would contribute both to the population and speech of Cumbria from the North, while the Cymri did the same from the South. The two streams of men and languages in time met and coalesced, and we have proof of their admixture in the dialect of the present day. That the language of the Cumbrian Kingdom in the 6th century, however, was substantially the same as that of Wales, is proved by the

remains of *Aneurin*, and *Llywarch Hen*, both Cumbrian
bards. The people of Cumbria, also, in their times of
misfortune, invariably fled to Wales as their natural and
ever available refuge.

The above samples of dialects must suffice. Similar
contributions might be drawn from half-a-dozen other
districts, all equally pregnant with the same kind of
evidence. Those of Essex, Norfolk, Lincolnshire, East
Yorkshire, are less charged with Celtic, a fact antecedently
probable from the testimony of history concerning settlements in those parts. The whole district of " West Wales,"
and of the Marches of Wessex and Mercia, on the other
hand, are rich in Celtic.

What, now, is the value of these dialectic facts? Do
they not intimate very plainly that a subjugated race
could never have so instilled its vocabulary into that of its
conquerors as to form a vital portion of it after the lapse
of many hundred years, unless the two peoples had long
lived in intimate intercourse for a great length of time?
Large bodies of Britons must have remained on the soil
in the various capacities of small holders by permission,
as ceorls, or servitors, tillers of the fields, and handicrafts-
men. They must by degrees have merged into the
dominant race, and with them, their language, in its
attained portions, into the language of that race. No
other hypothesis can explain a phenomenon so authentic
and significant. Such a phenomenon never occurred in
the history of mankind without antecedents such as are
here presumed, and in our historical chapter conclusively
proved.[1] The Celtic words we now find in the standard
English and its dialects form a vital portion of the
people's speech. They entwine themselves around the

---

[1] See, especially, Sections vii. and ix. (pp. 210 and 304), *ante.*

most cherished customs, and are the familiars of the most
sacred associations. They bear the air of belonging as
much to the soil as the peasantry which loves to articulate
them, or the oak of the forest. Surely they are not there
as sole memorials of their first owners. They are but
audible and visible companions of the now undistinguishable British blood which throbs in the veins of those who
have them on their tongues! To assume that the words
of an ancient language have continued to be spoken,
while the nation to which they belonged had been wholly
expelled or extirpated, is to assume a marvel greatly
more unaccountable than the amalgamation for which we
argue.

The comparative fewness of the Celtic vocables surviving argues nothing as to the *proportion* of Ancient
Britons which had merged into the mass of Anglo-Saxon
society. Twenty to one might be Celtic among the
people, as in the case of Gaul under the Romans, while
the language became all but completely new; or, on the
other hand, the conquerors might adopt wholesale the
speech of the discomfited race, as the Danes did in
England, and the Franks in Gaul. When conquerors are
eager to establish their own language, as was the case
with the Anglo-Saxons, whatever the proportion of the
conquered incorporated, their language is as a *whole* under
ban, and can gain admission into the authorized speech
only by subtle methods, and small unguarded entrances.

From the day the Anglo-Saxons became virtually
masters, everything favoured the process whereby the tide
of the new speech overwhelmed the old. From that time
till now the precious words which, notwithstanding all
difficulties, lodged themselves in the ruling speech, have
been gradually disappearing; and yet there are many
hundreds, perhaps thousands, still in being, and likely to

continue. What, then, must have been their number at first? And what must have been the number of the people who, under the circumstances, could have secured entrance for so many!

The fact, however, must be kept in mind that the subjugation of the Britons was far from being a prompt achievement. They and their language lived concurrently with the Anglo-Saxons in parts of England for many ages after the Saxon and Anglian kingdoms were first established. The Ancient British speech was under ban only in those parts where Saxon power was completely dominant, and through the space of two centuries those parts over wide England were few. It was by slow degrees that the Britons were brought under, silenced, and incorporated, and this circumstance favoured both admixture of race and admixture of language.[1]

(3.) *Celtic words once found in the written English, but now wholly discontinued.*

Some short time ago the writer made a pilgrimage to the site of the once celebrated city of Caerlleon (*Isca Silurum*) the reputed seat of King Arthur and the Round Table. There, in addition to a few faint indications in the external aspect of the place of its former renown and magnificence—fragments of Roman pottery, portions of the city wall, the "mound" of the castle, the circular hollow where the Roman amphitheatre stood—he found in the small museum of the local Antiquarian Society a number of disentombed British and Roman remains of some interest—a partial resurrection of the great past of Britain after many centuries of oblivion. It occurred to him that, in like manner, the old British words found in the early literature of Saxon England, long entombed and

[1] See pp. 235—366.

forgotten, but now gradually being brought to light, and curiously examined, are exponents to us of a former state of things.

Notice has already been taken of the comparative freedom from Celtic terms of the earliest Anglo-Saxon— literature (*temp.* Cædmon, Bede, Alfred, Ælfric), and the reason of that freedom was conjectured. Two hundred years later, the Anglo-Saxon tongue put on a very different appearance. It became marred, or beautified—as opinion may incline to pronounce—with a multitude of foreign terms—Celtic, which had long floated in the vulgar speech, and Norman-French, which had come across the Channel and conquered the Court and the *élite* of the English nation. The language had now reached the stage which we are accustomed to designate "semi-Saxon." The new importations were more Norman-French than Gallo-Celtic. These had affected the contents and forms of the English language even more materially than the men who had brought them had affected the race-character of the English nation. But Celtic elements from other quarters had also come in.

We have now to give specimens of these, that is, in so far as they have disappeared from the modern English dictionary. Dragged into light from rare and ancient MSS. in the Museums and Public Libraries of the kingdom, though few, they are still as authentic and vital as the wheat grains preserved in the folds of an Egyptian mummy, and tell as true a tale of forgotten ages.

The following list, again, is only given as containing specimens. Of the Celtic contents of the English in the semi-Saxon period, a much larger number has been collected than our space will admit. Mr. Coleridge's little Dictionary,[1] which has been carefully consulted and found

---

[1] *Dict. of Oldest Words in Engl. Lang.*, Lond. 1863.

of service, strange to say, hardly marks a dozen words through its whole length as having their origin in the Celtic tongues. But this absence of breadth and minuteness of scholarship marks many other recent works on Early English.

(*a.*) *Celtic words, from different English Authors, now obsolete.*[1]

Old English (*now obs.*)	Celtic Origin.
Aeele, to seal, hide (Lat. *celo*)	W. *cell*, a hiding place; *celu*, to hide; Corn. *celes*.
Acore, grieve, make sorry	W. *cur*, anxiety, pain.
Acoryc, chastened, punished	W. id.
Arvel, a funeral, funeral cake	W. *arwyl*, funeral solemnity.
Asele, seal—(same as *acele*)	W. *celu*, to hide.
Atprenche, to deceive	W. *prancio*, to play tricks.
Avoth, take in, hear	W. *yfed*, drink, imbibe.
Awene, prompt to think	W. *awen*, the poetic muse, genius.
Bali, belly	W. *bol*, belly; Corn. *bol*, id.
Bast, of illegitimate birth	W. *bas*, low, mean; Arm. *baz*, id.
Bay, in the sense of "to bait"	W. *bwyd*, food.
Bemothered, confused (cogn. with *mither*) ; contr. "bothered"	W. *byddar*, deaf; *byddaru*, deafen.
Bick, fight	W. *bicra*, to quarrel, fight, fr. *pigo ;* Corn. *piga ;* Arm. *pica*, id.
Blin, tired, fatigued	W. *blino*, to tire.
Bolken, to belch	W. *bol*, belly.
Bollen, swollen	W. The same.

---

[1] Our sources, with one or two exceptions, have been the following: *Havelok the Dane*, Ed. by Sir F. Madden, for the Roxburgh Club; *The Owl and Nightingale*, Ed. by Mr. Wright, for the Percy Society; *Specimens of Lyric Poetry*, temp. Edw. I., by Mr. Wright; *King Alysaunder*, in Weber's Metrical Romances, Ed. by Mr. H. Coleridge; The *Land of Cokaygne*, in Hickes's *Thesaurus*, vol. i.; The *Life of St. Margaret*, ib.; *Layamon's Brut*, Ed. by Sir F. Madden, 1847; *The Ormulum*, Ed. by Mr. White, three vols., 1847; *A Moral Ode*, Hickes's *Thesaurus*, vol. i.; *Life of Thomas Beket*, Ed. by Mr. Black, for the Percy Society; *Robert of Gloucester's Chronicle*, Ed. by Hearne, 1810 ; *Fragments in Harleian MSS.*, Brit. Mus., Nos. 913 and 2277; *Vocabularies*, Ed. by Mr. Wright for Jos. Mayer, Esq., 1857.

Old English (now obs.)	*Celtic Origin.*
Braid, treacherous (rel. to A.-Sax. *þræt*, craft)	W. *brad*, treachery; Corn. *þrat*, a cunning trick.
Bulies, bellows	W. *bol*, belly.
Capull-hyde, horse-hide	W. *ceffyl*, a horse.
Carke, to pine away	W. *cur*, anxiety, pain, *curio*, to pine away.
Crouthe, fiddle	W. *crwth*, fiddle; Corn. *crowd*.
Dizele, secret, concealed	W. *dygel*, concealed, *dy*, intens. *celu*, conceal.
Earth-grine, earthquake	W. *dacar-gryn*, earthquake; *crynu*, to tremble.
Ferth, road (A.-Sax. *ford*, a shallow in a stream)	W. *ffordd*, road; Corn. *fordh*. (*Ferth*, for "road," is Celtic *usage*, whatever the ult. derivation).
Frith, a wood, copse	W. *ffridd*, forest, wood.
Fyke, to deceive, flatter (fudge)	W. *ffugio*, to dissemble; Corn. *fugio*; Ir. *bog*.
Gaff, an iron hook	W. *gafael*, hold (Fr. *gaffe*).
Gris, a step, a stair	W. *gris*, a step (Lat. *gressus*).
Gain, elegant (gainly)	W. *cain*, bright, fair; *can*, white; Corn. *can*; Ir. *can*; Arm. *can*.
Gruche, to murmur, grumble (probably early form of "grudge")	W. *grwgnach*, grumble.
Hattren, clothes	W. *di-hatryd*, to doff one's clothes; *di*, privative.
Kendel, a litter of cats	W. *cenedl*, progeny, family.
Ledron, thief, robber	W. *lleidr* (pl. *lladron*) thief; (Fr. *larron*; Lat. *latro*).
Ma, more	W. *mwy*, more.
Panne, head ⎱ *Poune*, ib. ⎰	W. *pen*, head; Corn. *pen*; Arm. *penn*.
Pretta, to deceive (A.-Sax. *þræt*, craft)	W. *praith*, an act, a trick; Corn. *þrat*, a cunning trick.
Pulk, a pool (A.-Sax. *pól*, a pool)	W. *pwll*, a pool; Corn. *pol*; Arm. *poul*; Ir. *poll*; Manx, *poyl*, a pool, a pit.
Rhoxle, grunt	W. *rhochi*, grunt.
Shruke, wither	W. *crychu*, wither, shrink.
Teh, ill-humour	W. *dig*, angry; *taiog*, rude; Gael. *taoig*, a passion.
Terry, to vex, incite	W. *taeru*, to contend, urge.

Old English (now obs.)	Celtic Origin.
Treye, sorrow (A.-Sax. vexation)	trega, W. traha, oppression.
Unplye, unfold (un, priv.)	W. plygu, fold, bend; Corn. plegye, plait.

A hundred years' advance brings us to the age of Chaucer—"the father of English poetry." After a hard heat of reading in the *Canterbury Tales*, one is startled by the reflection that Spenser has called him the "pure well of English *undefiled!*" If Norman-French can defile, surely Chaucer daubed the "English" sadly enough. But there must be some truth in Spenser's judgment, and we can therefore conclude that Chaucer, instead of running with the fashion of the day in making a display of Norman-French, moderated the mania, and aimed at restoring the Saxon to its proper place. But Chaucer moved among, and wrote for, persons of quality and rank ; he was therefore bound to some extent to honour the speech patronised by courtly people. That he was conscious of the corruption of the language and of the want of reformation he gives frequent proof. Of the want of uniformity in writing the English he complains in his *Troilus and Creseide* :—

> " And for there is so great diversite
> In English, and in writing of our tongue ;
> So pray I God that none mis-write thee,
> Ne thee mis-metre for defaut of tongue."

Amid the confusion, and the struggle, on the one hand to corrupt, and on the other to restore, the English, did any Celtic terms escape destruction in the age of Chaucer ? Very many. We have culled the following from the poet's pages[1] as amongst Celtic words then in the English language, but which are no longer there.

---

[1] *Chaucer's Works*, Bell's Ed. Eight vols. 1854.

(*b.*) Celtic Words in Chaucer, now obsolete.

Augrym : "augrym-stones" were counters or calculi for facilitating calculations — W. *awgrym*, a sign, hint. W. is derived from Lat. *augur*, but the form in Chaucer is a copy of the W.

Bollen, bulged — W. *bol*, belly.

Bragat, a drink made with honey — W. *bragod*, a sweet liquor ; *brag*, malt.

Brokking, throbbing, quivering — W. *brôch*, din, tumult ; *brochi*, bluster.

Capil, a horse (not fr. Fr. *cheval*) — W. *ceffyl*, a horse ; Ir. *capall*.

Carrik, a ship — W. *corwg*, a boat, a coracle.

Karole, to dance and sing — W. *caroli*, to sing ; *côr*, a choir.

Mase, a wild fancy, ecstasy — W. *mas*, ecstasy ; *maws*, delight.

Meth, a liquor made with honey — W. *medd*, mead, drink made with honey ; Gr. μέθυ.

Nyfle, a trifle, unsubstantial thing — W. *nyfel*, *niwl*, a mist, fog.

Ocy, the nightingale's note — W. *cos*, nightingale ; *cosi*, to sing like the nightingale.

Poupe, to make a noise with a horn — W. *pib*, a pipe ; *piban*, to sound the horn

Rees, an exploit, eager action — W. *rhys*, ardency ; *rhyswr*, combatant.

Rote, a musical instrument, to "sing by rote," to sing along with an instrument — W. *crwth*, a violin.

Scrivenlich, after the manner of a writer — W. '*scrifenu*, to write.

Strothir (prop. name), valley in North of England. — W. *ystrad*, a dale ; and *hir*, long.

None of these had reached the English through Latin or Norman-French. They were borrowed from the *Cymric* language, and though now lost to the English—with one or two exceptions with a change, as "mead" for *meth*— are to this day living portions of the language of Wales. But for Chaucer we might not have known that such fragments of the old Celtic speech had played on the lips of the courtiers of Edward III. The tongue of the educated Englishman nowhere articulates them in our day.

We have to remark in concluding these last sub-
sections :

1. That if these few old chroniclers and rhymers, whose
writings, along with Chaucer's, we have been putting
under contribution, have furnished so many Celtic
remains when the language they represent is the
language of the more cultured class, then the vernacular
of the common people of England at the time must be
presumed to have contained a much larger amount of
materials of like nature. The proportion of Celtic terms
to the total of the vocabulary of the peasant class, was,
therefore, very large. Of the 40,000 usable words in
our present English, an educated man is supposed to
have at command about 10,000, while a rustic rarely
learns beyond 400.[1] We conclude that the common
people of the semi-Saxon period, however great the
zeal of the higher classes to cultivate an Anglo-Norman
speech, had a vocabulary in very large proportion Celtic.

2. The critical student will also observe with regard to
the first list—the British-Celtic of the modern dictionary
—that a large proportion of the vocables therein contained
must have been assimilated *since* the semi-Saxon period
—otherwise the vocabulary of that period would have
contained them. Now the interval from the 14th to the 19th
century was not a time of much intercourse between the
English and the Welsh, or any others of the Celtic stock—
not of such intercourse, we mean, as would transfer many
Celtic terms into the English. The first portion of that
period was a time of utter alienation between Wales and
England. Whence, then, came those Celtic words, of
clearly British origin, added during that time ? There can
be no difficulty in answering the question. They came
from the lips of the common people of England! There

---

[1] Comp. Prof. Max. Müller's *Lect. on Science of Language*, p. 268.

they had continued to play ever since their first appropriation, and there they continue to this day. And the next
coming age, under the guidance of a taste for the simpler
archaic dialectic treasures of the language, Saxon or
otherwise, will admit many more such materials—not
indeed because they are Celtic, but because they belong
to the home and heart speech of the English people.
There are many, many hundreds of them in the various
counties of North, West, and South, waiting for admission;
and, fortunately, the Latinising rage of Johnson is not a
failing of the literary men of our times.

3. It is to be noted that the great majority of British-
Celtic words tabulated, whether of the standard English,
of the dialects, or of the obsolete printed vocabulary,
belong to the *Cymric* branch. This is of some moment
to the solidity of our argument. Facts here again
echo to antecedent probability. Probability, planting its
argument on the intimations of history, says : If there exist
Ancient British terms at all in the English language, they
must be Cymric more than Irish, and Irish more than
Armoric (an offshoot of Cymric for the most part), because
contact with the *Cymry* (including the Cumbrians and
" West Wallians ") was more close and frequent than with
the Gaels of Ireland and Scotland, and contact with these
was more frequent than with the Armoricans. The Lloegrians and the Brython were also of the same branch as
the *Cymry*. These were completely incorporated in early
times, and not improbably are partly represented by
the blood of the West of England, including Devon and
Cornwall. All the nation of the Cymry, except those who
fell in war, retired into Wales, or crossed over to Armorica,
were also by degrees incorporated ; their language therefore might well permeate in larger measure the Saxon
tongue than the other branch of Celtic. With this

reasoning, the phenomena of modern and old English completely agree.

4. Some acute Anti-Celtic reasoners have started the following objection :—"If things are so—if admixture of language is proof of admixture of race (which is granted), and if incorporation of the Ancient Britons has carried Celtic elements into the English language, then, by parity of reasoning, since the English and the Romans have, doubtless, in some measure merged into the nation of the Cymry, there ought to be a corresponding tincture of these languages in the Welsh of to-day." The argument is perfectly fair and logical; but its effect, though expected to be crushing, is perfectly innocuous. We accept it without qualification, with all its consequences. Unhappily, it assumes what is not the fact, viz., that "the Welsh of to-day" is an immaculate Celtic tongue.

The Welsh people have, unquestionably, received no small admixture of Roman and Saxon blood; and the simple answer to the above objection is, that the Welsh language has received a very considerable infusion of Latin and Anglo-Saxon words.[1] Nay, more; the Welsh people are not free from Scandinavian, Flemish, and Norman-French admixtures, as proved by history, physiology, and proper names; and the Welsh language is not free from a corresponding tincture of Danish, Flemish, and French.

[1] Even so early as the time of Aneurin (See *Gododin*, vv. 630, 268, 231, 743, 629, 191) the following Latin corruptions, among numerous others, occur: *ariant* (argentum); *calan* (kalendæ); *fossawd* (fossa) *periglawr*, the word for priest, one to stand between the soul and "danger" (from periculum); *gwydr* (vitrum); *plwm* (plumbum). We find in this early age traces even of Anglo-Saxon corruptions. The bard Meigant, *circ.* A.D. 620, uses the word *plwde* (see *Myv. Arch. of Wales*, i. 160) for a bloody field, or blood, which he could only obtain from A.-Sax. *blod*, blood, *blodig*, bloody; and Aneurin has the word *bludwe* (v. 142) for what appears to have been the battle-field. No Celtic dialect now contains this corruption.

The school of Dr. W. O. Pughe (who, in ignorance of the teaching of comparative philology, seemed to consider the Welsh a language *per se*, separate and distinct from all other languages, developing all its forms and compounds from its own exhaustless store of roots) cannot well brook the doctrine that the Welsh is largely Latinized and Anglicised. There is no word which their convenient etymological legerdemain will not at a touch resolve into Cymric "roots," however obviously Latin, Greek, or Saxon its origin. It is impossible to argue gravely with people who will, ex. gr. derive *eglwys*, W. for church (ἐκκλησία), from such Welsh "roots" as *eg*, "what opens," and *glwys*, "fair, beautiful"—"because the church opens its doors to the holy!" The science of philology is now fast dispelling such linguistic folly.[1] By a rigid analysis of the materials of separate languages, it discovers what elements are common to many, or to a few, and finds here the safe principle of classification and key of relationship. It proves beyond contradiction that there is no tongue on earth which is a language *per se*, distinct from all other tongues, and evolving all its forms from its own resources. Dr. W. O. Pughe, the learned author of the chief Welsh dictionary extant, seems to have proceeded on the quiet assumption that the Welsh was such a language, and his great work contains many hundreds of derivations from Welsh "roots" which are palpably fanciful and misleading.[2]

[1] Few scholars will question the correctness of Mr. Max Müller's statement that "large numbers of words have found their way from Latin," and even German, into the Celtic dialects, and "these have frequently been taken by Celtic enthusiasts for original words, from which German and Latin might, in their turn, be derived." *Lectures on the Science of Language*, First series, p. 200. Our note p. 380, but more at length, Appendix A, will supply proof of this.

[2] Mr. Geo, the publisher, of Denbigh, has in the press a new edition of Pughe, which it is hoped will be conducted under the guidance of competent scholarship, and be brought up to the present state of knowledge. 1873.

The long history of the corruption of the Cymric language needs not detailing in these pages. Its stages, of course, are Roman, Saxon, Danish, Norman, and English. The language has some few elements common to it with the Latin which can hardly be termed either corruptions or borrowings, since they seem to have been equally the property of each from a very early age, and to have been borrowed or derived by each from that primitive Aryan source which has tinged so many of the European languages, Classic, Teutonic, and Celtic alike. Hence also the Welsh, like the Irish, has many words kindred to A.-Saxon and German, as, fem. *gwen*, fair, white, beautiful ; Anglo-Saxon, *cwen*, woman, queen, whence Eng. queen : *côr*, a choir, Anglo-Saxon *chor*, a chorus ; Germ. *chor*, a chorus : W. *malu*, to grind, *melin*, a mill; Anglo-Saxon, *milu*, a mill : Germ. *mahlen*, to grind, *mühle*, a mill : W. *pobl*, people; Germ. *pobel:* W. *cloch*, a bell, Germ. *glocke*, a bell, Anglo-Saxon, *clucge*, a bell, &c., which elements appear to be as congenial and native to the Teutonic as to the Celtic—to the Celtic as the Teutonic. But since the Celtic is on the whole invested with more features of a venerable antiquity than the Teutonic, if advantage must in this matter be claimed by either, the Celtic must have it.

But multitudes of vocables are now found in the Welsh, and are in all dictionaries assumed to be properly Welsh words, which no modern philologist can fail to recognise as foreign. Most of them belong to the Latin, and to the classic period in Latin. Some are post-classic, and belong to ecclesiastical nomenclature. But many are Teuton, derived from the Anglo-Saxon of the Conquest, and many more are immediately derived from the English, inherited by that language from Latin, Greek, Saxon, or Norman-French. Not a few are words which have passed directly from the Norman-French, without apparent contact with the English. Such seem to be *anturio*, Fr. aventurer; *cessail*, Fr. goussel ; *crys*, Fr. creseau ; *dedwydd*, Fr. deduit ; *gwersyll*, Fr. guerre-sella ; *neges*, Fr. negoce, &c.

On account of the interest of this subject to philologists, we have taken some trouble to form a reliable list of words, usually considered Welsh, which are derived from the different sources above enumerated ; but to save space, the biographies of doubtful, or apparently doubtful words, tracing the various phonetic changes they have undergone, and which it would have been interesting to add, have been omitted. The immediate derivation, and, in some cases, a further or ultimate derivation is supplied.[1]

The materials of Appendix A. are quite sufficient for. the purpose in view. Every reasonable person will allow their force, as proving that the people and language of Wales are by no means free from foreign admixture. Having granted so much, we only expect equal candour and obedience to evidence on the other side.

5. But besides these obviously foreign accretions, the Cymric has a multitude of words which it possesses in common with many other Indo-European tongues, and which are as native to it as they are to any of the others, but which are frequently, by over-zealous classicists, considered as borrowings from Latin or Greek.[2] Such words, are *argraph*, imprint ; *aru*, to plough ; *caer*, a fortress, a city ; *genu*, to give birth to ; *côr*, a choir ; *llewyrch*, light ; *llyfr*, a book ; *mel*, honey ; *medd*, mead ; *swn*, a sound ; *taran*, thunder ; *torch*, a ring, wreath ; *torf*, a crowd ; *twr*, a tower, &c. In Appendix B. will be found a small collection, capable of extension, of words of this class, indicating materials inherited by the Welsh from that ancient fountain of Indo-European speech, whence the

[1] See Appendix A.   [2] See Appendix B.

Hellenic, the Romance, the Teutonic, as well as the Celtic tongues, have so largely flowed, and which is now usually denominated Aryan. Appendix A. will prove that the writer is free from Celtic fanaticism, while Appendix B. offers a few impartial gleanings, which, if virtually justifying the claims of Celtic, also illustrate the close relationship of the various tongues and races of Europe.

2. Celtic Elements in the English language derived immediately from the Latin.

We have now to pass on from the consideration of *British*-Celtic materials in English—on which chiefly, as the reader has been already warned, we rely for direct support to the argument—to a few specimens of words found in Celtic, but whose transmission into English has been through the Latin. This is done partly by way of digression, and in the interests of general philology.

Assuming for the moment that these elements are entitled to the designation "Celtic," it is obvious that their passage into English through the Latin, without any contact between Anglo-Saxons and Celts in the British Isles, would be very possible. The Latin had brought them down from the early ages of its own history, having first adopted them either by contact with the Ancient Celts, or from the common Aryan source, whence they passed also into Celtic, and, many of them, into Gothic tongues.

Of course it is competent to ask, wherefore, then, call them "Celtic" at all? We may with equal reason ask, why call them Latin? If on the ground of apparent natural affinity with the language in which they are found, their constant presence from early times in that language, and the absence of evidence of their ever having been borrowed from a contemporaneous tongue, words can be pronounced as belonging to the language of which they form a part, then these words can quite as properly be termed Celtic as Latin. But if to belong to a language words must be incapable of being traced to any other, then it will follow that no language has more than a very meagre vocabulary of its own. Let it be allowed that these words are also entitled to be considered Latin, since they cannot be proved to have been borrowed by Latin from Celtic; they are on the same ground, at least, entitled to the appellation, "Celtic," since it cannot be proved that Celtic borrowed them from Latin, or any other tongue known to history. They may be, and probably to a great extent are, common property derived from a common prehistoric source, although their passage into English is allowed to have been directly from the Latin, and their use here is mainly, if not exclusively, to establish a link of relationship between the Classic, Teutonic, and Celtic tongues, as members of the same family.

Words of this class are numerous. To be on the safe side, many which have an apparently good claim for reception have been omitted. To save space, only one Celtic cognate is in most cases given. W. *Welsh*; Ir. *Irish*; G. *Gaelic*; C. *Cornish*.

English.	Latin.	Celtic Cognate.
Acclaim	Clamo	W. *llefain*, to cry, shout; C. *lef*.
Act Action	} Ago, Actum	Ir. *aige*, to act; W. *egni*, energy.
Admire	Ad-miro	W. *mir*, fair.
Alien	Alienus	W. *ail*, another.
Amenity	A-moenitas	W. *mwyn*, kind, pleasant; G. *min*, tender.
Arduous	Arduus (high)	Ir. *ard*, high; C. id.
At	Ad	W. *at*, to.
Candid	Candidus	W. *can*, white; Ir., C. id.
Co-eval	Co-aevus	W. *oes*, age.
Conceal	Concelo	W. *celu*, to hide.

C C

English.	Latin.	Celtic Cognate.
Congeal	Congelo	W. *ceulo*, to curdle.
Corrode	Cor-rodo	W. *rhwdu*, to rust, eat away.
Council	Con-cilium (fr. root *cal*)	W. *galw*, to call.
Crisp	Crispo	W. *cras*, parched, dry.
Crust	Crusta	W. *cras*, dry.
Dean	Decanus	W. *deg*, ten; C. *dec*, id.
Decency	Deceo	W. *têg*, fair; C. *dek*, id.
Decimal	Decima	W. *deg*, ten; C. *dec*, id.
Define	De-finio	W. *min*, edge, limit.
Devour	De-voro	W. *pori*, to graze, eat.
Diminish	Di-minuo	W. *mân*, *main*, small.
Fable	Fabula	W. *ebu*, to say (?).
Incendiary	In and candeo (to shine)	W. *can*, white; Ir. id.
Lamina	Lamina	W. *llab*, *llafn*, a slab, a blade.
Lateral	Lateralis, latus	W. *lled*, breadth; Ir. *leid*; C. *ledan*, broad.
Latitude	Latitudo	W. Id.
Laud	Laus—dis	W. *clod*, praise; Ir. *cliu*, id.
Mamma	Mamma	W. *mam*, mother.
Minim Minor Minute	} Minus	W. *mân*, *main*, small.
Nebula	Nebula	W. *nifel*, *niwl*, mist; Ir., C. *nial*; G. *neal*, id.
Negation	Negatio, nego	W. *nage*, no, *nacáu*, refuse; C. and Arm. *nag*, no.
Noun	Nomen	W. *enw*, name.
Plausible	Plaudo, laus-dis	W. *clod*, praise; *bloeddio*, to cry, shout.
Plenary	Plenus	W. *llawn*, full: C. *lawn*, id.
Radius	Radius	W. *gwraidd*, root.
Radix	Radix	W. The same.
Reside	Sedeo	W. *sedd*, a seat; C. *sedhue*, a seat.
Scribe	Scribo	W. *ysgrifio*, *crafu*, to scrape.
Scripture	Scriptura	W. The same.
Seat	Sedeo	W. *sedd*, a seat.
Senior	Senis	W. *hên*, old; C. ib.; Ir. and G. *sean*, id.
Spike	Spica	W. *pig*, a point.
Spine	Spina	W. *pin*, stile, pen.

English.	Latin.	Celtic Cognate.
Terrene	Terra	W. *tir*, earth, land; G. and C. id.
Tribe	Tribus	W. *tref*, a dwelling; Ir. *treabh*; C. *trev*.
Trope	Tropus	W. *troi*, to turn; W., C., and Arm. *tro*, a turn.
Union	Unus	W. *un*, one; Ir. *aon*; C. *un*; Manx, *un*.
Unity	Unitas	W. The same.
Vacant	} Vaco, vacuus (root	W. *gwag*, open, empty; C. Arm.
Vacation	} *vag*)	id.
Venus	Venus	W. *gwen*, fair, white; used as epithet for woman, same as A.S. *cwen*, Engl. queen. *Vide* Append. B. "*gwyn*."

3. Celtic Elements in the English language, derived through the Teutonic tongues, or through Norman-French.

The Teutonic tongues, including Anglo-Saxon, Danish, German, and Dutch, are naturally entitled to be classed together as sources of modern English; and Norman-French, being mainly a mode of Latin, should, if it were convenient, be also in some manner classed along with that language, or stand by itself as a hybrid. But words derived from the N.-Fr. cannot be said to be a direct gift of the Latin. They are cut off from their primal source by the intervention of this new tongue. Convenience and simplicity of arrangement have decided in favour of the present grouping.

Some words in this table are of doubtful origin; but the contest is hot between Celt and Saxon for a right in them. For the most part we have given the benefit of the doubt to the latter. Who can decide with certainty as to the immediate quarter whence the English obtained the word *pilgrim?* We shall be told that it came from the L. *peregrinus*. Of course it did. But the question as it affects

the English language is not whence it came at the *first*,
but whence it came at the *last* step. From Fr. *pelerin?*
Germ. *pilger?* Corn. *pirgirin?* Ir. *pirgrin?* or W. *pererin?*
It is curious to note the metamorphoses of this word in the
different languages. The Germ. and the Fr. have agreed
to banish the *r* from the first syllable. The Engl. follows
in this, as well as in the introduction of the *l*. It seems
therefore to have borrowed the word from one of these
languages; but you have no sooner gone to rest upon this
conclusion than you observe that it has tacked to the word
an ending different from both. We cast into the scale the
agreement with the Germ. in the letter *g*, and give the
Teuton the victory. This is the kind of chase the etymologist has often to pursue. The word *parsley* is another
instance.[1] *Turnip* is quite as perplexing.[2]

It will be borne in mind that the same qualification
applies to this table as applied to the last—it is not relied
upon as evidence of admixture between the Ancient Britons
and the English. The Celtic roots which have reached the
English through the languages here given as *direct* sources
were probably the common property of the Celtic and
Teutonic languages, and of the original, for the most part,
of the N.-French *(Latin)* for ages far anterior to the
junction of Celts and Teutons on *British* ground. Let the

---

[1] Gr. πετροσέλινον, Lat. *petroselinon*, are plain; but the order of descent
in the following is not so easily ascertained:—A.-S. *peterselige*; Germ.
petersilïé; Dan. *petersille;* (now the *t* is dropped), Ir. *peirsill;* W. *persyll;*
Fr. *persil*. Which is the next of kin to the Engl. " parsley?"

[2] The Teutons and Celts alike have perceived some suitableness or
other in the letters *ump* or *omp*, with a variety of initiatory forces, for
expressing the idea of a full, rounded, or protuberant body; but the law
which determined the adoption of this or that leader, in the shape of a
first letter, may be too occult for even a clever etymologist to discover.
Trump has these relations: *lump, bump, hump, rump, clump, dump*, and
W. *clamp, swmp;* and across the Channel, Danish, German, and Swedish,
klump; and Dutch, *klomp*.

junction of Celts and Teutons on *British* ground. Let the table be valid for its own object only—viz., to show how far the English tongue is charged with Celtic elements, or, at any rate, elements which are as much Celtic as they are anything They may belong to a period of human speech far preceding any form which may be distinctively termed Gothic, Hellenic, or Celtic, and we might be pushed in the last resort to confess that they can only be classified in a general way as Indo-European, or Aryan, but they are found, apparently in their natural *habitat*, in modern Celtic, and offer no signs of foreign derivation or relation. They serve at the least, like the preceding table, to show the interrelationship of the languages concerned as members of one family.

It is especially to be noted that many of the Norman-French contributions were obtained by that language, not from Latin, but from the Ancient Gothic or the Celtic. They are marked (*).

The list given is by no means complete, and only one Celtic cognate is given with each word. [A. S. *Anglo-Saxon*, Dan. *Danish*, D. *Dutch*, G. *German*, Fr. *Norman-French*, W. *Welsh*, Ir. *Irish*, C. *Cornish*, A. *Armoric*.]

Celtic Elements in English borrowed from Teutonic or Norman-French.

English.	Teut. or N.Fr.	Celtic Cognate.
Abide	A.S. bidan	W. bod (be).
All	A.S. eal	W. oll.
Anomaly	Fr. anomalie	W. hafal.
	(ὰ ὁμαλός)	
Anvil	A.S. anfilt	Ir. inneon.
Ape	A.S. apa	W. epa.
Ball	Fr. balle ; G.	W. pel.
Barm	A.S. beorm	C. burm.
Baron	Fr. baron	Ir. fir (L. vir).
Be	A.S. beon	W. bod.
Beak	A.S. piic	W. pig.

English.	Teut. or N.Fr.	Celtic Cognate.
Beat	A.S. beatan	W. baeddu.
Bed	A.S. bed	W. bedd.
Beef	Fr. bœuf	W. buwch.
Beer*	Fr. biere	W. and A. bir.
Begin	A.S. beginnan	W. cyn.
Boat	A.S. bat	W. bâd.
Boss	Fr. bosse	W. bôth.
Bottle	Fr. bouteille	W. bôth.
Bride	A.S. bryd	Ir. brideog; W. priod.
Broth	A.S. broth	W. berwad (decoction).
Brother	A.S. brather	W. brawd. (?)
Bruit	Fr. bruit	W. brudio, brut.
Buck	A.S. buc	W. bwch; Ir. boc.
Cable*	Fr. cable	W. gafael.
Cat*	A.S. catt	W. câth.
Caress	Fr. caresser	W. câr.
Care	Goth. kar	W. cur.
Cargo	A.S. carc	W. cario.
	(Span. carga)	
Castle	A.S. castel	W. castell.
Cede	Fr. ceder	W. gado.
Chair	Fr. chaire	W. car.
Charity	Fr. charité	W. cariad.
Cheek	A.S. ceac	W. cêg.
Cherish	Fr. cherir	W. cir, câr.
Choir	A.S. chor	W. côr.
Clay	A.S. claeg	W. clai.
Clew	A.S. cleow	W. clob.
Close	Fr. clos	W. clyd.
Cloth	A.S. clath	W. id.
Cluck	G. glucken	W. cloch.
Cob	A.S. cop	W. cob.
Come	A.S. cuman	W. cam (step).
Con v.	A.S. connan	W. gwn (I know).
Cony*	Fr. conin	W. cwning.
Coquette*	Fr. coquet	W. coeg.
Cord	Fr. cord	W. corden.
Cot	A.S. cot	W. cwt, cyttiau, pl.
Crab	A.S. crabba	W. crâf-u.
Crack*	Fr. craquer	W. rhwyg.
Cramp	A.S. hramma	W. crym-mu.
Cranny*	Fr. cran	W. ran.

English.	Teut. or N.Fr.	Celtic Cognate.
Crave	A.S. cravian	W. cref-u.
Crump	A.S. crump	W. crwm.
Cry*	Fr. crier	W. cri.
Cup	A.S. cupp	W. cwpan.
Daub*	Fr. dauber	W. dwb-io.
Deal	A.S. daelan	W. di-doli.
Deep	A.S. deop	W. dwfn.
Demand	Fr. demander	W. mynu.
Deny	Fr. denier	W. na, nac.
Deploy	Fr. deployer	W. plygu.
Display	Fr. deployer	W. plygu.
Door	A.S. dur	W. dôr.
Double	Fr. double	W. dau-plyg.
Dower	Fr. douer	W. dodi.
Dragon	Fr. dragon	W. draig.
Earth	A.S. eorth	W. daear, âr.
Eat	A.S. eaten	W. bwydo.
Egg	A.S. aeg	W. wy.
Ell	A.S. elne	W. elin.
Employ	Fr. employer	W. plygu.
Etiquette*	Fr. etiquette	W. tòc, tocyn (a ticket).
Falcon	Fr. faucon	W. gwalch.
Fife	G. pfeife	W. pib.
Finch	A.S. finc	W. pinc.
Fine	Fr. fin	W. main.
Flap	A.S. laeppa	W. llab.
Flat	Fr. plat	W. lled, llydan.
Floor	A.S. flor	W. llawr.
Four	A.S. feower	W. pedwar.
Freeze	A.S. frysan	W. fferu.
Full	A.S. full	W. gwala.
Gallant*	Fr. gallant	W. gallu.
Garden	G. garten, A.S. geard	W. cae, caer.
Garter*	Fr. jarretierre	W. gâr (leg).
Glass	A.S. glaes	W. glas (green).
Glave*	Fr. glaive	W. llafn, glaif.
Glen	A.S. glen	W. glyn.
Glib	Dan. glib	W. llib, llipa.
Glow	A.S. glowan	W. gloyw.
Goad	A.S. gad	W. gwth.
Goose	A.S. gos	W. gwydd.

English.	Teut. or N.Fr.	Celtic Cognate.
Gormand*	Fr. gourmand	W. gor (extreme).
Grace	Fr. grace	W. râd.
Grave	A.S. grafan	W. crafn.
Gravel	Fr. gravelle	W. graian.
Ground	A.S. grund	W. graian.
Guard	Fr. guarder	W. caer.
Guise*	Fr. guise	W. gwedd; Arm. giz.
Herald*	Fr. heraut	W. hèr, herawd.
Hide	A.S. hydan	W. cuddio.
Hive	A.S. hyfe	W. cafn.
Horn	A.S. horn	W. corn.
Hour	Fr. heure	W. awr.
Iron	A.S. iren	W. hairan.
Kin	)	
Kind	} A.S. kyn.	W. cyn, cenedl.
Kindred	)	
King	A.S. cyng	W. cûn.
Know	A.S. cnawan	W. gwn (I know).
Lap	A.S. lappian	W. lleibio.
Large	Fr. large	W. llawer; Corn. lour.
Lath	Fr. latte	W. llath.
Lather	A.S. lethrian	W. llathru.
Lead	A.S. laedan	W. llywio.
Leap	A.S. pleafan	W. llwff.
Light	A.S. liht	W. lluch.
Linnet*	Fr. linot	W. llinos.
Lip	A.S. lippe	W. llafn.
Load	A.S. lade	W. llwyth.
Lock	A.S. loc	W. clicied.
Lump	G. klump	W. clamp.
Mail*	Fr. maille	W. magl (net).
Malady	Fr. maladie	W. mall-dod.
Marine	Fr. marine	W. môr.
Marshal	Fr. maréchal	W. march.
Meal	G. mehl	W. mâl-u.
Mean	A.S. maene	W. mân, main.
Meat	A.S. mete	W. maeth.
Mellow	A.S. melewe	W. mâl.
Mile	Fr. mille	W. mil.
Mill	A.S. miln	W. mâl, melin.
Mince	Fr. mince	W. mân.
Mind	Dan. minde	W. myn.

English.	Neut. or N.Fr.	Celtic Cognate.
Mine	Fr. mine	W. mwn.
Minion	Fr. mignon	W. mân.
Mock	Fr. moquer	W. moc-io.
Mole	Fr. mole	W. moel.
Money	Fr. monnaie	W. mwn.
Morning	A.S. morgen	W. bore.
Mound	A.S. munt	W. mynydd.
Mount-ain	A.S. id.	W. id.
Mule	A.S. mul	W. mul, mil.
Murder	A.S. morther	W. marw.
Musk	Fr. musk	W. mws, mwsg.
Mutton	Fr. mouton	W. mollt.
Neat (clean)	Fr. net	W. nith.
Neck	A.S. necca	W. c-nwc.
Nedder	A.S. nedder	W. neidyr.
Needle	A.S. naedl	W. nodwydd.
Nephew	Fr. neveu	W. nai.
Nest	A.S. nest	W. nyth.
New	A.S. neow	W. newydd.
Nip	D. knippen	W. cneifio.
No	A.S. ne	W. na.
Noon	A.S. non	W. nawn.
Nut	A.S. knut	W. cnau.
One	A.S. aen	W. un.
Onion	Fr. ognon	W. wynwyn, cenin (?)
Over	A.S. ober	W. ar.
Ox	A.S. oxa	W. ych.
Pea-s	A.S. pisa	W. pys.
Peak	⎫	
Pike	⎬ A.S. peac, piic	W. pig.
Pick	⎭	
Pear	A.S. pera	W. pèr.
Pellet and	⎱ Fr. pelote	W. pèl.
Bullet	⎰	
Pin	A.S. pinn	W. pin.
Pioneer	Fr. piochier (pioche, *pick*axe)	W. pigo.
Pipe	A.S. pipe	W. pib.
Pique	Fr. pique	W. pig.
Plague	G. plage	W. plâ.
Plant	Fr. plante	W. plent (ray).
Plate	G. platte	W. lled, llydan.

English.	Teut. or N.Fr.	Celtic Cognate.
Plight	A.S. plintan	W. plygu.
Pool	A.S. pol	W. pwll.
Pottage*	Fr. potage	W. potes.
Practice [1]	Fr. or Sp. (?)	W. praith.
Press	Fr. presser	W. brys.
Pretty	A.S. praete	W. pryd.
Pure	A.S. pur	W. pur.
Quern	A.S. cwyrn	W. chwyrn.
Queste	Fr. queste	W. cais, ccisio.
Quit	Fr. quitter	W. gadu.
Radish	A.S. raedic	W. rudd.
Rag	A.S. hracod	W. rhwyg.
Rake	A.S. racian	W. id.
Range	Fr. ranger	W. reng.
Rank	Fr. rang	W. id.
Raven	A.S. hraeven	W. brân.
Ray	Fr. raie	W. rhe, rhedeg.
Read	A.S. raed	W. raith, araeth (?)
Recoil	Fr. reculer	W. cilio.
Red	A.S. red	W. rhudd.
Rend	A.S. rendan	W. ran-u.
Rent	A.S. id.	W. id.
Rhyme	A.S. rim	W. rhif.
Rind	A.S. rind	W. croen.
Road	A.S. rod	W. rhawd, rhodio.
Roast	G. rösten	W. rhost; Ir., C., and Arm.
Rock (crag)	Fr. roche	W. craig.
Root	Dan. rod	W. gw-raidd.
Rose	Fr. rose	W. rhos-yn, rhudd.
Rot	A.S. rotian	W. rhydd.
Rough	A.S. hreog	W. garw, crych.
Round	G. Rund	W. crwn.
Route* same as "road"	Fr. route	W. rhawd.
Row	A.S. rawa	W. rhes.
Royal	Fr. royale	W. rhi.
Rowel	Fr. Rouelle	W. rhod.

---

[1] The word "practice" has the corresponding Celtic root, *praith*, act, practice; but its direct descent is uncertain. Fr. *pratique* seems more probable than the Spanish *practica*. Ultimate derivation, πράσσω.

English.	Teut. or N.Fr.	Celtic Cognate.
Rub	G. reiben	W. crafu.
Ruddy	A.S. rude	W. rhudd.
Rune		
Runic	} A.S. run	W. rin, cyfrin.
Rush	A.S. reosan	W. brys
Rust	A.S. rust	W. rhwd.
Sack	A.S. saec	W. sach.
Saddle	A. S. sadel	W. sedd.
Sail	A.S. segel	W. hwyl.
Salt	A.S. salt	W. haien.
Scrape	A.S. screpan	W. crafu.
Search˚	F. chercher	W. cyrch.
Seed	A.S. saed	W. hâd.
Senate		
Senior	} Fr. senat (Lat.)	W. hên (old).
Serene	Fr. serein	W. sir-oil.
Shear		
Share	} A.S. scearan.	W. esgar.
Shell	A.S. scel	W. celu, cêll.
Shield	A.S. scyld.	W. cel.
Similar	Fr. similaire	W. mal, hafal.
Sit	A.S. sitan	W. sedd (t add. in eistedd).
Six	A.S. six	W. chwech.
Slough	A.S. slog	Ir. lough, loch.
Smoke	A.S. smoca	W. mwg.
Solder˚	Fr. souder	W. sawd, sodi.
Sound	A.S. son	W. sain, swn.
Sour	A.S. sur	W. sur.
Spur	A.S. spur	W. yspardyn.
Target	Fr. targe: A.S. id.	W. taraw.
Tarry		
Tardy	} Fr. tardif	W. tario.
Tear, v.	A.S. taeran	W. tòri.
Tear	A.S. tear	W. dagr.
Ten	A.S. tyn	W. deg.
Tenant	Fr. tenant	W. tynu.
Tend	Fr. tendre	W. id.
Tent	Fr. tente	W. id.
Thatch	A.S. thac	W. tô.
Thaw	A.S. thawen	W. toddi.
Thick	A.S. thic	W. tew.
Thin	A.S. thinn	W. teneu (?)

English.	Teut. or N.Fr.	Celtic Cognate.
Thorpe	A.S. thorpe	W. tref.
Thou	A.S. thu	W. ti.
Three	A.S. thri	W. tri.
Through	A.S. thurh; G. durch	W. trwy.
Thurs-day	A.S. Thors-daeg	W. taran (thunder).
Ticket*	Fr. etiquette	W. toc-yn.
Tin	A.S. tin	W. taenu.
Tinder	A.S. tendan	W. tân, tanio.
To	A.S. to	W. tua.
Tomb	Fr. tombe	W. tomen.
Torture	Fr. torture (L.)	W. torchi.
Tuft	Fr. touffe	W. twf.
Tumble	A.S. tumbian	W. twmp, a hillock.
Tun	A.S. tuna	W. tynnell, Celtic *tyn*, close, tight, straitened. A.S. *ton*, a town, seems to be from same archaic root, carrying the idea of an enclosure, a confined, protected place.
Turn	A.S. tyrna, turnan	W. *twr*, or *tor*, a rounded eminence, a projection, W. *troi*, to turn, W.C. and Arm. *tro*, a turn.
Vain	Fr. vain (the (Lat. vanus is a contr. for vacanus, fr. root VAG.)	W. *gwag*, empty; Corn. Ar. id., Ir. *guag*.
Vassal	Fr. vassal	W. *gwas*, a young man, a servant; Corn. *gwas*, a young person, a mean person, a fellow.
Waggon	Germ. wagen; A.S. waegn	W. *gwâg*, open, empty. From same archaic root (VAG) are Lat. vagina, vaco, vanus (for vacanus), &c.; and prob. also A.S. *weg*, Germ. *weg*, a way, an *open* passage through a forest or country.

English.	Teut. or N.Fr.	Celtic Cognate.
Wain	Id.	W. id.
Wan	A.S. wan	W. *gwyn*, white, pale.
Whine	A.S. cwanian	W. *cwyn*, complaint; Gael, *caoin*.

Concluding Remarks on the English Language.

Omitting from the account the materials derived by English from the Latin, Teutonic, and Norman-French, and confining our attention to the Tables preceding, we see a state of things which the enthusiastic stickler for the "Anglo-Saxon" character of the English will not love to contemplate. Fortunately the language is its own witness. A simple examination of its contents, in the light of modern learning, shows that it enshrines numerous portions of an ancient tongue nearly identical with modern Welsh. Others, not so numerous, might be traced to the Erse. History proves that for centuries the Anglo-Saxons fought, formed treaties, intermarried with the Cymric race, and nothing is therefore more natural than that certain portions of the speech of the latter should have been learnt and adopted by them. They received from these people the usages of civilised warfare bequeathed by the Romans—received from them the knowledge of letters—found among them the splendid architecture and sculpture which the wealth and genius of Rome had lavished on this land—learned from them how to make roads, build dwellings and bridges (though their learning in these respects produced for ages but little fruit, till the fields, cook their food, and decently dress their persons. They even themselves passed through intermixture out of the properly Anglo-Saxon into the Cambro-Saxon phase, constituting in fact a new race. What prohibition of fate could prevent them from learning and adopting terms by which new ideas imported were marked, as well as receive new ideas and race characteristics? Our tabulated witnesses will help to show that no such prohibition had issued. Cause and effect worked then as now, and the natural result was that the language of the new race, like the race itself, and the range of its conceptions, received a new character.

Like the nation the English language is one of the most elaborate of mixtures. So rapid has been its growth and change of aspect, that like the grown man, it would hardly recognise itself in the likeness of what it was at different stages of its progress. What would Macaulay's English say of Wycliffe's, or Wycliffe's of Ælfric's? King Alfred, King Henry VII., and our lamented Prince Consort wrote and spoke a very different tongue. With the growth of the people and of knowledge, with every addition of race or tribe—it has continued to widen and lengthen its dimensions, little heeding whether the accretions came from the alien Celtic, Greek, Latin, or Romance, or the nearer akin Dutch, Danish, or German,[1] so that whatever came was worth the having. Its acquisitiveness continues as keen as ever. All still comes well that meets the ever pressing demand, and contributes to the force and fulness of a language destined to be the most widely spoken, the most comprehensive, the most learned of all the tongues of earth—the language destined, according to Jacob Grimm, to be "the language of the universe." It has cast away, from time to time, myriads of useless and,

[1] So great has been the accumulation of foreign materials that not more than one-third of the modern *English Dictionary* is purely Teutonic in origin. And yet the power of custom induces many not illiterate men to talk of the English as a Teutonic tongue. See Prof. Max Müller's *Lectures on the Science of Language*, p. 76, and De Thommerel's *Recherches sur la Fusion*, &c., *passim*.

indeed, some useful vocables, and to this day, growing in stability and greed of acquisition, like the most diligent of misers, gathers from every available quarter every term which the progress of science renders necessary, and which the hand of philology can glean from the universal field of language. How long its progress onwards and upwards will continue, who can tell? It is likely enough that many of its present materials will again vanish, and many foreign take their place, and that the English of to-day, despite the permanency given by the press and by scholarship, will be nearly as strange to the people of 500 years to come as Chaucer's is to us. Thus the words of Horace will once more be realised :—

" Mortalia facta peribunt :
Nedum sermonum stet honos et gratia vivax.
Multa renascentur, quæ jam cecidere ; cadentque,
Quæ nunc sunt in honore vocabula, *si volet usus ;*
Quem penes arbitrium est, et jus, et norma loquendi."

CHAPTER III.

" In the earliest period, when our documentary history first throws light upon the subject, there are still found names unintelligible to the Teutonic scholar, not to be translated or explained by anything in the Teutonic languages ; nay, only to be understood by reference to Cimric or Pictish roots, and thus tending to suggest a far more general mixture of blood among the early conquerors than has generally been admitted to have existed."—J. M. KEMBLE.

SECTION I.

The Enduring Nature of Local Names.

NONE of the traces of human doings on earth are more durable, and few are more instructive, than the names borne by the chief features of a country—its mountains, rivers, valleys, creeks, &c.—next to which for tenaciousness of life may be classed the names of early settlements, towns, castles.

To the painstaking modern philologist and ethnologist, toiling to trace the footprints of the primeval inhabitants, catch the echoes of their language, and learn their pursuits, these local names are as serviceable as the fossil shells and bones of past geological periods are to the geologist or palæontologist when judging of the relation of species now existing to those which unmeasured ages ago waded through the marshes, rushed through the forests, or flew through the air of our planet. The *forms* of these local names, indeed, are not so proof against alteration as are those of the fossils fortified in their stronghold of adamant. Local names lie, as it were, on the surface, subject to attrition from successive waves of languages and peoples passing over them. One nation comes, another follows, and another, and another,—and the names imposed by the first, when not reduced to fixed form in writing, are taken up by each of its successors subject to its own means and methods of representing sounds, and to the caprice or occasion of the moment in adding or eliminating parts. Even the same people will, not unfrequently, mar and disfigure, through misconception or carelessness, the names bestowed by its ancestors, and etymologically significant in its own language. If Agmondesham has been metamorphosed by the English into Amersham, Wightgarabyrig into Carisbrook, Scrobbesbyrig into the euphonious Salopia, or Badecanwylla into Bakewell, and this in recent centuries, what may we not expect from untutored nations among whom writing was unknown, and from a long series of changes of occupation ?

And yet, notwithstanding all this, local names are a record almost indestructible—*monumentum acre perennius.* They survive the lapse of millenniums of years, and, like the statue of Memnon, the Sphynx, or the Pyramids, look calmly down on the stream of coming and vanishing nations continually passing by, without themselves seeming to partake in the universal change. They are more station- ary than even hills and mountains. The language they once belonged to, may be, has altogether, except the parts contained in themselves, vanished from the earth; the busy multitudes who articulated its sounds have all been long forgotten, and no other memorial of their existence remains, but there, faithful to the trust reposed in them, like sentries at their posts, after thousands of years of service, stand

D D

those significant and well-chosen epithets, proffering to the modern student a clue at once to the speech and race, the migrations and era, of those who placed them there. From breezy mountain tops, from streams and fountains, from haunted ruins of once majestic temples and more majestic cities—the spirit of a forgotten race speaks to men of the present time, and tells them who, and what sort of people, first called those mountains, rivers, cities their own, and gave them names corresponding to their nature, as Adam is said to have done to the creatures of a new creation.

A nation may disappear, and its place be repeatedly taken by others, different in language, religion, and race, yet its local names survive throughout. There are local names still known in Britain which were given by heathen Romans, heathen Saxons and Angles, nay, even anterior to all these—by heathen Cimbri and Gaels. There are names now in Palestine, and they are of world-wide fame, which were given by the Canaanitish tribes before the Hebrews had become a nation — as Baal-Hazor, Baal-Tamar, Kirjath-Arba, Kirjath-Sepher, Luz, &c.,[1] and by the Hebrews a thousand years before the Moslems who now rule there had received their faith—as Bethel, Beersheba—and neither change of race, faith, or time, has much altered them. Egypt in its inhabitants is Turkish to-day, but its great cities, temples, river, are not named by Turks. The Northern States of America are inhabited by an English-speaking people, mainly English in blood, religion, and customs ; but how many of their local names are memorials of a vanished Indian race! Alleghany, Mississippi, Wabash, Shenandoah, Potomac, Niagara, Massachusetts, Rappahannoc, Chicago—their very sound is barbarian !

---

[1] See Stanley's *Lectures on the Jewish Church*, p. 275.

SECTION II.

The various Uses of Local Names.

We derive from local names a four-fold service—*philological, geographical, ethnological,* and *historical.* Local names are shrines preserving precious relics of ancient tongues, not at all, or but imperfecly known, and aid us in tracing the nature and family relations of these tongues. They assist us in judging of the aspects of scenery, the fauna and flora of the country, the relations of land and water, courses of rivers, positions of shipping-places, and the changes which have taken place since the names were imposed. They give a clue to the migrations and inter-mixture of nations, the succession of their occupation of the same country, and their settlements.

No descriptive geography, except that of local names, is required to inform us that the district known as *Traethmawr* in North Wales (*traeth*, sea beach ; *mawr*, large, extensive) was once a sandy sea shore, though now a fertile agricul-tural tract of country—that the *Isle* of Thanet, now a part of the main land, was once an island—that Chertsey, Ber-mondsey, Chelsea, were once islands (A.-Sax. *ca, ey,* as Angles'*ey,* the Angles' island) or that the Cotswold hills Welsh, *coed,* wood, forest, and A.-Sax. *weald,* forest,—a one-word description in two languages) were at one time a forest, and successively named by two races of people. While the local names of this quarter of the globe remain there will be no lack of evidence that the face of Europe was once swept, or rather settled upon, by a race speaking a Celtic language.

Very various are the aspects under which names of places may be classified, according to the occasion which in each case determined their first use. They are epitaphs

or dirges, marking the graves of the fallen, or the site of
some terrible catastrophe—as *Waeddgrug*, in Flintshire
W. *gwaedd*, a cry, and *crug*, hoarse) the reputed locality of
a great slaughter of the Picts and Saxons by the Welsh ;[1]
Battle, in Sussex ; *Leckford* (Germ. *leiche*, a dead body), in
Kent; the villages *Slaughter* and *Leach*, in Gloucestershire ;[2]—votive offerings, as *Bethel ;*—altar inscriptions, as
Baalbec (Syr. the *bec*, or city of Baal) ; *Frathorpe* (Dan. the
thorp or village of the deity Frea) ; *Godstow ; Llanfair*
(Mary's holy place) :—geographical descriptions, as Ochill
Hills (*ochill* or *uchel*, high) ; *Eryri*, Snowdon (W. *eira*,
snow) ; *Dinmore* (W. *din*, fortress ; *mawr*, great) ; *Ebb-fleet*, a
port in the 12th century, though now half a mile inland ;—
fortress ensigns, as *Caer*fyrddin, Win*chester*, Edin*burgh*,
Wood*stock*:—homestead memorials, as Camberwell, Hamp-
stead, Trevychan, or Cheltenham :—mementos of great
achievements, as America, Columbia, Ware,[3]—tributes to
personal worth and public services, as Washington, Jeffer-
son, Pennsylvania.

Many places which are now of great importance, continue to be designated by names indicating a very humble
beginning. The French Emperor's chief residence is the
Tuileries,[4] or "tile-yard," the place, when Paris was as yet

---

[1] On the alleged "Alleluia victory," under Garmon, or Germanus,
see Rees's *Welsh Saints*, p. 121, and St. John's *Four Conquests of Engl.*
vol. i. p. 56.

[2] Camden's *Britannia*, by Gough, vol. ii. 131.

[3] Ware is said to bear the name of the " weir " which King Alfred's
genius constructed across the River Lea, whereby he cut off the retreat
of the Danish fleet. Camd. *Brit.*, vol. ii. p. 68 ; Turner's *Anglo-Saxons*,
vol. i. p. 398; Taylor's *Words and Places*, p. 321.

[4] No longer the residence of an Emperor, the empire being abolished
(1870), the Tuileries (along with many of the chief public buildings
of Paris) consumed by the madness of the Commune (1871), the
Emperor Napoleon III., deceased, a fugitive in England, Jan. 9, 1873.

small, where they manufactured building tiles. The *Vatican*, a word of potency throughout the Roman Catholic world, was the name borne by a small hill outside of ancient Rome. *Lambeth* is the "loam hithe," or landing-place once existing on that part of the Thames. The aristocratic residents of *Mayfair* rejoice in a designation which originated in a rustic annual "fair" held in that locality when all London was east of Temple Bar. *Covent Garden* was the garden of a convent, and the *Strand* was simply the river bank or "strand," along which people walked in going from London to Westminster.

SECTION III.

The Ethnological Value of the Celtic Local Names of England.

1. The Celtic local names of England as evidence of Celtic settlement.

As history is so distinct upon the settlement of the Celts in England, *i.e.*, generally over the whole face of Britain, the fact need not here be proved, but simply illustrated by reference to the names of places. The Ancient Britons, *Cymri* or *Gaels*, have left their marks, inscribed in their own proper tongue, all over the island from *London* to *Dover* in one direction, to *Gloucester, Manchester, York 'Evrog, Edinburgh* and *Aberdeen* in another. On the eastern side of the island, these marks are fewer than in other parts—a fact in harmony with the tenor of history—for at no period in the annals of Britain do we find those districts much frequented by the Celtic race.

It is remarkable that almost all the principal *rivers* of England bear Celtic names. The other great natural

features of the country—its mountains, hills, valleys,
brooks, creeks, downs, also abound in them. The sceptical
reader will want proof, and we proceed to give it. In
Scotland and Wales such names would, of course, be
expected to abound, and as their prevalence has no
bearing upon the question of race admixture in *England*,
they need not be here produced.

(*a.*) *Mountains and Hills* [1] (*omitting Scotland and Wales*).

Cymric words applied to elevations in the earth's surface,
are : *pen*, head, end, outstretching part ; *din*, a high place,
a place of defence ; *cefn*, a ridge, back ; *carn*, *carnedd*, a
heap, mound ; *craig*, a rock, a crag ; *ar*, *arran*, over, high ;
bryn, *bre*, hill ; *moel*, a bare eminence ; *twr*, similar in
signification to *din*, a high place of defence, natural and
artificial ; *ban*, peak, high land, beacon. Examples in
Wales : Penmynydd, Penrhyn, Penmaenmawr, Dinas,
Denbigh, Dinevawr, Cefn-pennar, Cefn-llys, Carnedd-
Llywelyn, Craigfargod, Penygraig, Twrcelyn, Arran-
Fowddwy, Arran-y-Gessel, Brynllys, Bryn-Croes, Penbré,
Bànnau Brycheiniog.[2]

---

[1] On Celtic local names of mountains, &c., comp. Diefenbach,
Celtica, i. pp. 104, 157, 170, &c. ; Adelung's *Mithridates*, ii. 54, 67, &c. ;
Zeuss, *Gram. Celt.* 2nd Ed., p. 66, et *passim*.

[2] In Welsh, *pen* and *bàn* are of like signification ; *pen*, however, is in
most use. The *bàn* of Wales is the *ben* of Scotland, as *Ben Lomond*,
Ben Nevis. The plural of *bàn*, *bànnau*, is seen in *Bànnau Brycheiniog*—
the Brecknockshire Beacons. Great stress, therefore, must not be laid
on the *pen* of Wales and the *ben* of Scotland as test words in proof of
a distinct and *prior* occupation of the country by the Gaelic branch of
the Celts.

Brandon Hill,	Ess.	London.	
Brandon Hill,	Dev.	Maldon,	Ess.
Brendon,	Dev.	Malpas (moel),	Derb.
Brent (bryn) Tor,	Dev.	Malvern,	Worc.
Bredwardine,	Heref.	Pembridge,	Heref.
Brinton,	Norf.	Pembury,	Kent.
Brinsop,	Heref.	Pencoed,	Heref.
Bryn-tor,[1]	Devon.	Pencomb,	Heref.
Chevin,	Shrop.	Pendennis (dinas)	Corn.
Cornwall,		Pendleton,	Lanc.
Cowden,	Kent.	Penhill,	Som.
Crick,	Derb.	Penketh,	Lanc.
Crick,	Northamp.	Pennard,	Som.
Cricklade,	Wilts.	Pennigant,	York.
Croken Tor,	Corn.	Penn Castle,	Salop.
Dennis (dinas)	Corn.	Penn,	Staff.
Doncaster,	York.	Pen,	Som.
Dundran,	Cumb.	Pen,	Bucks.
Dundry Hill,	Som.	Penrhyn,	Corn.
Dunmow,	Ess.	Penrith,	Cumb.
Dunnose,	I. of W.	Penshurst,	Suss.
Dunstable,	Bed.	Pentir,	Corn.
Fendraeth Hill,	Dur.	Pentridge,	Wilts.
Fur Tor,	Dev.	Penton,	Hants.
Hey Tor,	Dev.	Pentwyn,	Heref.
High Down,	Herts.	Penyard,	Heref
Kenchester (cefn),	Heref.	Penylan,	Heref.
Kensworth,	Herts.	Penzance,	Corn.
Keynton,	Shrop.	Tormarton,	Glouc.
Lexdon,	Ess.	&c., &c.	

As proofs of Celtic settlements in other countries of
Europe we have *pens*, *duns*, *thors*, and *bryns*, &c., as *Pen-*
march, *Pen*herf, Brittany ; *Pindus*, Greece ; *Taurus*, Asia ·
the Ap-*pen*-nines ; Campo*dunum*, now Kempten ; Taro-
dunum, now Dornstadt, in Germany ; *Thun*, Switzerland ;

[1] This is one of the numerous cases occurring where a name is
made up of two synonyms, sometimes of different, sometimes of allied
languages. Both here are Celtic ; so also Brandon, Pendennis, Penrhyn.
Brinton, Cotswold, Pembury, Penton, on the contrary, combine Celtic
and Anglo-Saxon.

Melo*dun*um (Melun); Lug*dun*um (Lyons), Vero*dun*um (Verdun), in France; Lug*dun*um (Leyden) in Holland; *Braun*berg, *Bren-den*-kopf, *Bran-den*-burg, in Germany; *Dindy*mus, in Phrygia: *Pen*telicus, in Greece; *Tyr*ol, &c.[1]

(*b.*) *Celtic Names of Rivers and Streams in Britain*[2] (*omitting Wales and Scotland*).

Almost all the chief rivers of England bear *Cymric* appellations. Cymric words applied to water, running water, rivers, brooks, are: *Aw*, *wy*, *dwr*, water; *lli*, *avon*, flowing water, collection of waters; *wysg*, water in rapid motion; *rhyd*, stream, also a ford across a stream; *clais*, an archaic word for brook; *nant*, a stream, or valley.

Examples in Wales: *Avon* and *dwr* are common nouns, applied, with some other qualifying term, in a multitude of cases. *Tav*, *Taw*, *Tawe*, *Towy*, *Teivi*, apparently compounds of *aw*, are familiar names, some of them being names of many streams. *Dwr*dwy, or *Dyf*rdwy, *Wysg*, *Rheid*iol, *Wy*, *Gwi-li*, *Llu-gwy*, E*dwy*, Dau*ddwr*.

Ad*ur*	Suss.	D*ee* (dwy)	Chesh.
A*une*	Dev.	D*er*went	Lanc.
A*uney*	Dev.	D*er*went	Yorks.
A*von*	Glouc.	D*er*went	Derb.
A*von*	Worc.	D*ovr*	Kent.
A*von*	Hants.	D*ore*	Heref.
A*xe*	Dev.	D*our*water	Yorks.
Cal*der*	Cumb.	D*urra*	Corn.
Cal*der*	Lanc.	D*ur*beck	Notts.
Cal*der*	York.	E*sk*	Dev.
D*a*rent	Kent.	E*x*	Dev.
D*art*	Dev.	I*nney*	Corn.
D*ar*wen	Lanc.	I*ce*	Cumb.

---

[1] Comp. Diefenbach, *Celtica*, ii. pt. i. p. 337, &c.

[2] Comp. Vilmar, *Ortsnamen in Kurhessen*, in the Hessian Zeitschrift des Vereins, for 1837, p. 255; Adelung, *Mithridates*, ii. 57; Pott, *Etym. Forschungen*, ii. p. 103.

Medway	Kent.	Thames (W. Tafwys).	
Nader	Wilts.	Thur	Norf.
Ouseburn (Wysg).		Washburn (Wysg).	
Rhea	Staff.	Wey	Dorset.
Rhey	Wilts.	Wey	Surrey.
Severn		Wye	Heref.
Stour	Ess., &c.	Wye	Hants.
Tees	Durham.	Wyre	Lanc.

&c., &c.

A multitude of our English rivers, again, have names, purely Celtic, expressing a certain quality, such as colour, smoothness, roughness, noisiness, slowness, briskness, &c. *Dulas* and *Dou-glas* both mean dark brook, from *du*, dark, and *clais*, old W. for brook, still used in South Wales, but still more in Ireland.

Aire	(W. *araf*, slow),	York.
Arav	(W. *araf*, slow),	
Arun	(W. *garw*, rough),	Suss.
Arrow	(W. *garw*, rough),	Heref.
Cam	(W. *cam*, crooked),	Glouc. Ess. &c.
Cam	Id.	Cambr.
Cambeck	Id.	Cumb.
Camil	Id.	Corn.
Creke	(W. *crech*, rugged),	Lanc.
Crouch	(W. *croch*, loud),	Ess.
Deben	(W. *dyfn*, deep),	Suff.
Dove	(W. *dof*, quiet, tame),	Derb.
Esk	(W. *gwisgi*, fem. *wisgi*, quick, brisk, gay),	Devon. Cumb. &c.
Gara	(W. *garw*, rough).	
Garrow	(W. *garw*, rough),	Heref.
Lavant	(W. *llefn*, smooth),	Sussex.
Leden	(W. *llydan*, broad),	Glouc.
Ledden	Id.	Heref.
Leven	(W. *llefn*, smooth),	Cumb. &c.
Morcambe Bay	(W. *mor*, sea; *cam*, crooked; a tortuous estuary),	
Rother	(W. *ruthro*, to rush),	Sussex.
Wear	(W. *gwyro*, to deviate, wander),	Dur.
Yar	(W. *garw*, rough),	Norf.
Yarrow	Id.	

It may be doubted whether the Lune, the Allan, the
Ellen, the Aln, and others of like elements, are not from
the W. *alon*, harmony, *alaw*, music; or from *alwyn*, white,
fair; or again from *clain*, fair, shining, splendid. Corn,
clyn; Ir. *aluin*. The names Ribble[1], Irwell, Ouse, Tyne,
are obscure. *Trent* is probably but a contracted form of
*Dar*ent, *Derw*ent, from *dwr*, and Ouse from *Wysg*.

In continental countries known to have been inhabited
by the Celtic race, we find numerous streams bearing
primitive names, identical in signification with those of
Welsh, Scotch, and English rivers. In *France: Avon*,
joining the Loire; *Avon*, joining the Seine; Cal*avon*,
Gar*umna*, Mat*rona*, *Dur*anius, *Dord*ogne, An*tura*, *Dru*-
entia, *Thurr*, *Dur*dan, *Dour*don, *Dour*on. In *Germany:*
The *Lahn*, Arg*ana*, Mer*ina*, O*der*, *Dur*bach, *Dür*renbach,
*Dürn*bach, *Dur*en, *Rhin*e, *Reg*en; and, perhaps, the
*Eis*ach, *Esch*az, *Eisch*bach, *Etsch*bach, *Esch*elbrunn, *Ags*-
bach, &c.[2] In *Spain*: The *Dour*o, *Tor*io, *Duer*na, *Dur*aton,
Avono. In *Hungary*: The *Thur*oig, *Waag*. In *Italy*:
The *Aufente*, *Avent*ia, *Savone*, *Avens*.

[1] On the name Ribble, the Rev. James North, M.A., of Liverpool,
after the appearance of our first edition furnished the following
annotation:—"The name by which Ptolemy designates it is *Belisama*,
compounded surely thus—*Bel*, the deity, and *Is*, water, and whence,
obiter, our *ice*, another English word in almost its original Celtic purity.
The ultimate syllable is plainly the Roman termination, and if the
penult follows the same course, it perhaps embodies the word
amnis. If not, what is it but the Celtic? Might we therefore say the
Chaldaic affix to Bel, whether denoting an attribute or an additional
name, which took the form of Ammon in Egypt and Palestine. The
direct translation of Bel-is into Latin was Rivus Beli; and what is
that but *Ribble*? Many of our Westmoreland names for things and
places would bear out your ideas forcibly." The " Bel" theory is doubtful.

[2] In fact, it is the testimony of Leo—and none is more competent
to pronounce an opinion—that almost every river name in North
Germany is of Celtic origin. See his *Vorlesungen über die Gesch. des.
Deutschen Volkes*, &c., i. p. 198.

(*c.*) *Celtic Names of Valleys, Dales, &c., in England (omitting Wales and Scotland.*)

Welsh words signifiying various kinds of surface depression are the following: *dôl*, a dale; *cwm*, a hollow, bottom, dingle; *nant*, a dingle, also a brook (Corn. *nans* ; Arm. *nant*) ; *cil*, a recess, corner (Corn. *cil*, a recess ; Ir. *kil*, *cul*, Arm. *k*. [1] Examples in Wales : *Dol*badarn, *Cwm*bran, *Nant*mel, *Nant*eos, *Cil*maenllwyd, *Cil*bebyll, *Dol*gelley.

Apple*dur-comb*	I. of W.	*Com*pton	Som.
But*combe*	Som.	Crow*combe*	Som.
Chala*combe*	Dev.	*Dal*ton	Lanc.
*Chum*leigh	Dev.	*Dol*ton	Dev.
Combe	Dev.	*Daw*lish	Dev.
Combe	Som.	*Daw*ley	Salop.
Combe	Oxf.	Fa*comb*	Hants.
Combe	Hants.	Gat*combe*	Glouc.
*Comb*ermere	Chesh.	Ilfra*combe*	Dev.
*Comb*erton	Worc.	*Kil*burn	Mid.
*Comb*eabbas	Som.	*Kil*danes	Lanc.
*Comb*elong	Oxf.	*Kil*dale	Yorks.
*Comb*efield	Worc.	*Kil*ham	Yorks.
Combe Florey	Som.	*Kil*peck	Heref.
*Comb*hay	Som.	*Kil*mersdon	Som.
*Comb*martin	Dev.	*Kil*sby	North.
*Comb*pyne	Dev.	*Kil*worth	Leic.
*Com*pton	Surr.	Para*combe*	Dev.

Cumberland abounds in *cums*, as noticed by one of its native rhymers—

> "There's *Cum*whitton, *Cum*whinton, *Cum*ranton,
> *Cum*rangon, *Cum*rew, and *Cum*catch ;
> And mony mair *Cums* i' the country,
> But nin wi' *Cum*divock can match."

---

[1] *Kil*, in Irish, has been extensively applied in the sense of an enclosure or retreat of a *sacred* nature (like *llan*, in Welsh); but this is a secondary use of the word—a specific and religious use. But the original idea is a narrowing, a dyke, a recess : and with this the Cymric *adj. cul*, narrow, agrees.

Wiltshire is equally rich, the name Combe, Coombs, in some of its forms, being frequently borne not only by places, but from them by families.

The word *nant* has been left by the ancient inhabitants in many a corner of England, but it survives chiefly in the parts nearer the borders of Wales, and in Cornwall.

*Nant*gissel	Corn.	*Nant*on	Worc.
*Nant*wich	Chesh.	Pen*nans*	Corn.
*Nant*on	Glouc.	Tre*nans*	Corn.
*Nant*head	Cumb.		

On the Continent are: *Nant*es, *Nant*ua, *Nant*cy, in France; and Val di *Nant*, *Nant* Dant, *Nant* Bourant, &c., in Switzerland. In the grandest depths of the Savoyard Alps, near Chamounix, several *Nants* still survive; as *Nant*-brun, *Nant* Bourout, Bon-*nant*, *Nant*-noir—in short, "nant" is a common name for mountain torrents in the Mont Blanc range—a fact very remarkable, as showing that these Celtic tribes had penetrated into these distant solitudes, not as fugitives seeking shelter, but as settled inhabitants—the name-givers of the regions, and that the names had become so ·current and settled under their influence that no power of new-comers and new languages has been able to dislodge them. They are enigmas to German and French writers who look not into a Celtic dictionary, and are derived by some of them from *natare*, to swim, "because of the water that is there."

(A.) Cities or Fortresses, Towns, Homesteads, &c., in England, bearing Celtic Names.

Cymric words in use are: *bod*, *tre*, *caer*, as *Bod*edern (Edern's abode), *Tre*madog (Madog's home), *Caer*narvon (the fortress in Arvon), &c. The prefix *tre* has been largely used in some counties in recent times, many scores of farmhouses in Pembrokeshire or Carmarthenshire alone being so designated. To the word *tre*, signifying abode or home, is generally added the name of the person who formed a settlement or built a house on the spot.[1] The prefix *caer*, a fortified place, almost invariably marks a work of defence of great antiquity—in the majority of cases coeval with Roman or even ante-Roman times.

The following are a few from among the multitude of names of this class found in England :—

*Bod*min	Corn.	*Ca*rgo	Cumb.
*Bod*iham	Suss.	*Ca*rham	North.
*Bod*enham	Heref.	*Ca*rhampton	Som.
*Bod*ney	Norf.	*Ca*rkin	Yorks.
*Bod*hel	Cumb.	*Ca*rperly	Yorks.
*Bod*hergest	Heref.	*Ca*rrocke	Cumb.
*Bod*ley	Berks.	*Ca*rlisle	Cumb.
*Bod*ley	Hants.	Daven*try*	North.
Brain*tree*	Ess.	*Tre*gonna	Corn.
*Caer*went	Mon.	*Tre*gony	Corn.
*Caer*leon	Mon.	*Tre*ligga	Corn.
*Car*den	Chesh.	*Tre*low	Corn.
*Car*thorpe	Yorks.	*Tre*neglos	Corn.
*Car*hallock	Corn.	*Tre*silian	Corn.
*Car*eby	Lin.	*Tre*thurgi	Corn.
*Car*colston	Nott.	*Tre*vissick	Corn.
*Car*brooke	Norf.	*Tre*vulga	Corn.
*Car*burton	Nott.	*Tre*wadlock	Corn.
*Car*deston	Salop.	*Tru*ron	Corn.
*Car*ey	North.		

Towns named from their situation on the waterside are numerous. The Celtic *dwr*, water, sometimes taking the form *dour* or *tur*, is often found in names of Continental towns as well as rivers. *Tours*, ancient *Tur*ones ; *Tour*nai, ancient *Tur*nacum ; *Dour*es, ancient *Dubr*is : several

---

[1] The terminating *try*, in Oswes*try*, is not, as some have supposed, the Welsh *tre*, but the English "tree," as applied to the Cross. The Welsh name is *Crôes*-Oswallt, Oswald's Cross—a translation of the old "Oswald's-tree."

ancient Bi*turi*ges in Gaul, indicating the meeting of *two* waters. Probably the incipient Bi (bis) was prefixed by the Romans to mark the confluence of two streams, both called *dwr* or *tur* by the natives. Instances in England are : *Dover*, ancient *Du*bris ; *Dor*king, *Dor*chester, *Dur*ley, a village in Hants ; *Dur*sley ; *Mor*combe, W. *mór*, sea, *combe*, a valley, or *cam*, crooked ; *We*ymouth, W. *wy*, water ; *Aber*ford, village in Yorkshire ; W. *aber*, a confluence, &c.

Less obvious Celtic derivations, but still genuine, are such as these : *Lin*coln, W. *llyn*, a pool, lake, and *coln*, Lat. *Colonia* ; in Ptolemy's Greek Λινδον, the *dun* or place of strength, or high place, on the *llyn*, or *lin*, pool—a name identical in etymology therefore with *London; Glou*cester, W. *gloyw*, fair, pure, bright, old W. name *Caerloyw; Man*chester (W. *man*, place, settlement) : *Tiver*ton (W. *dwr, dwfr*, water)—the town on the water—Tiverton being situated at the confluence of the rivers Exe and Loman ; *Dur*ham (Lat. Dunelm, W. *dwr*, and Norse *holm*, an island), Leland and others tell us, was originally a rock forming a river island—but how the *n* was introduced into the Latin Du*n*elm is not very clear ; *York* (W. *Evrawg*), old W. name *Caer-Evrawg*. The *Cots*wold Hills (W. *coed*, wood, and A.-Sax. *weald*, also wood), display the primitive Celtic and its Saxon translation in one word. *Cumber*land is the land of the *Cymri* or *Cumbri*. The people of "Devon" were by the Romans named *Damnonii*, in imitation of the Celtic *Dyfnaint* (W. *dyfn*, deep, and *naint*, pl. for valleys), the land of deep valleys or dingles. *Corn*wall, formerly written "Corn Wales" (W. *corn*, a horn, projection, and A.-Sax. *wealhas*, the Welsh), *i.e.*, strangers or foreigners— a name applied by the Teutonic race to all except themselves. *Wilt*shire—the shire of *Wilt*on—the town of *Wealhas* or Welsh, before their national characteristics of language, laws, and customs had died out in those parts.

Many of the Waltons were probably "Welsh towns," as
Nuces Gallicæ, walnuts, were "Welsh-nuts." (Germ.
Wälsche nuss, *i.e.*, foreign nut.) *Dorset*, the settlement of
the *Durotriges*, as they were called by the Romans (W. *dwr*
water, and *trigo* to dwell) dwellers near the water or sea ;
and so on in great numbers.

In short, to trace all the Celtic elements found in names
of places in England would occupy scores of pages. Let
the above suffice as a fraction of a body of evidence to the
ethnologist most interesting. Whithersoever the *Cymry*
have gone, whether into the body of a new race by junction with their conquerors, or to find shelter among their
already teeming brethren in Wales, the memorials of their
former residence in England remain unobliterated—well-
nigh unaltered—by change of language or lapse of time.
These names are not those of regions, kingdoms, or a
whole land, which might have caught hold of their objects
fortuitously, or might afford room for uncertainty as to
their real meaning and origin ; but they are the names of
hundreds and hundreds of the rivers, brooks, hills, vales,
hamlets and homesteads of England. They mark the
places of chief importance in early periods of society, and
in times when the inhabitants had to watch their foes from
their *dins*, and protect themselves from attack in their *caers*.
They lived in the sheltered dingles *nants*, pastured their
flocks in the fertile vales (*dôls*), marked their localities and
judged of distances by the highest surrounding hills or
mountains (*fens*, *craigs*, and *tors*), and drew their sub-
dividing lines along the course of the rivers and brooks
(*avons*, *dwrs*, *rhyds*, &c.) They gave all these names,
according to some specific feature in each, constituting its
differentia, and these names and objects have come down,
or rather have remained stationary, witnessing the lapse
of many ages, until we have made our appearance on the

scene to read their history, admire their appropriateness, and dream of the long past which their scanty light enables us faintly to discern. They speak to us in the language of the *Cymri*, and, amongst other things declare, in clear accents, that the *Cymri*, or *Cymry*, not only lived at the foot of those *pens* and *craigs*, on those *dóls*, and in those *caers*, but that when disturbed and dispossessed, they still continued so long and held such place of influence amongst their conquerors that the names of all the chief features of the country, although purely Cymric, became familiar to the Saxons, were adopted by them in detail, and became part and parcel of their own tongue.

2. The Celtic local names of England as furnishing evidence of admixture of race.

Is it not a fact virtually indisputable that the adoption by a new people of local names imposed by their predecessors involves *conditions* which unavoidably imply race-amalgamation? The case is precisely analogous to that of language. The language of an intrusive people cannot be penetrated and tinged, deeply and permanently, by that of the people subdued—as we have proved the English language to have been by the Ancient British— in the absence of that prolonged and familiar intercourse which could not fail of issuing in those social and domestic ties, that mutual good understanding and progressive assimilation which, by degrees, would obliterate all prominent distinctions of race. That the Anglo-Saxons should receive the geographical nomenclature of the Britons, if, as argued by some, the Britons had been swept from the land, must for ever remain inexplicable. The assumption of the displacement of the British race is so gratuitous that had it not somehow become the basis of an article of national faith, it could deserve no serious consideration. That it is entirely unauthorised by history, the reader, we would fain hope, is by this time fully persuaded. For any reliable and distinct statements which have reached us to the contrary, we are at perfect liberty to maintain that the Britons were no more displaced by the Saxons than were the Saxons afterwards by the Danes or Normans. They had not been driven out by the Romans ; they had formed the habit, so to speak, of clinging to their native soil under the rule of strangers ; the new rule of the Saxons found them a people partly predisposed, if an heroic effort for independence failed of success, to submit, and continue on the land which from time immemorial their fathers had called their own. Only the most stubbornly persistent patriots, too dazzled by the brilliant prospects of liberty to see the inevitable *fact* of their national overthrow, continued to struggle, receding further and further to the West with the setting sun of their hopes, and entrenching themselves at last in the natural fortresses of Cambria. Never did they cease, for seven hundred years, to do two things—fight the Saxon, and pronounce maledictions on those "recreant" brethren of theirs, who, by entering into "league and confederacy with the Saxons," took the "crown of monarchy from the nation of the Cymry."[1]

At the same time, though local names cannot fail to be of interest, furnishing, as they do, material proof in aid of our general argument, they must be allowed to have a limit in ethnological value, and that limit must be defined.

Topographical names, traceable to a certain language, are witnesses to the settlement in those localities of a people speaking that language, and that they were either the first or the most influential, or the longest dwellers there, so that the rivers, lakes, mountains, &c., ever after bore the designations they had impressed upon them.

[1] See *Triads, Myv. Arch. of Wales*, ii. 58.

But they do not absolutely prove the aboriginal character of their authors ; for in times when nomadic tribes moved freely from place to place, repeated occupation might occur before a settlement prolonged enough to tabulate the natural features of the country under fixed names was effected. Nor do they absolutely prove, of themselves, that the prolonged settlers who gave them, did not afterwards move off to foreign climes, and have a long series of successors to their ancient property before the properly historic age arrived, and that property was permanently appropriated. To make their evidence conclusive as to this matter, the witness of history must be introduced.

But granting all deductions and qualifications, topographical names have a substantial value in proof of race settlements and of national incorporation. Their very nature determines the race to which they originally belonged. Their transmission could only be effected by *intercourse*. In those days, when the Ancient British local names of England were transfused into the alien Anglo-Saxon speech, there existed no works on geography, no accurately drawn and coloured maps, no surveys with a well defined nomenclature, whereby, without *personal association* and *oral teaching*, the long imposed names of river, crag, and forest, fortress, road, and mountain, could be accurately learned. The Britons had no *Itinerary* describing their highways and military posts, no *Notitia Imperii*, naming every town and castle, river, marsh, and mountain in the land, by the reading of which on their casual discovery, and after the gigantic achievement of learning the unknown tongue in which they were written—a practical impossibility on the hypothesis that the whole race had suddenly and totally disappeared—the new comers might learn the names which had been in use. How, then, could the Anglo-Saxon come at a knowledge of the *avons*, the *pens*,

the *döls*, &c. ? How could he manage to make his own
language talk of the geographical divisions of the country
—the *cantreds* (W. *cant*, hundred, and *tref*, dwelling,
abode), the *commots* (W. *cwmmwd*, subdivision of a hundred`,
the *tres*, &c., &c. ? Imagination can only descry one way.
The Anglo-Saxon accomplished this difficult task in Celtic
nomenclature—so uncongenial to ages of war and semi-
barbarism—by the slow but certain method of *personal
intercourse* with the ancient inhabitants. The land, we
argue, was still in the main peopled by the old race—now,
indeed, in a subject state—tilling the fields, clearing the
forests, forging war implements, and fighting battles for
their masters, and by degrees winning freedom and citizenship by length of service and accumulated wealth. Many
portions of the country, many important towns in the heart
of what is now "Old England," were still entirely in the hands
of the Britons, who maintained their own usages, laws, and
language intact, acknowledging the Anglo-Saxons only as
nominal masters, and exercising over them the kind of
influence which the pupils of the Romans, unsuccessful
now in war, might be expected to use towards the untutored, but strenuous children of Schleswig and Holstein.
By degrees, the geography of the country would be
learned; the very dingles, rills, memorial stones, crom-
lechs, camps, castles, nay, the individual homesteads of
the different neighbourhoods, would become familiar by
their own proper Celtic names ; the native language would
die away into the aggressive Saxon, and the native population itself, forgetting old grudges, would form with the
ruling race an undistinguishable mass.

The three following positions are established by history
and the nature of the case.

1. Except where a developed literature exists, unless

there be a fusion of peoples, no fusion of their languages takes place.

2. Where no fusion of languages occurs, in the absence of writing, transmission of local names will be scanty.

3. Where the language of a conquering race is found to be extensively charged with the common vocables and local names of the conquered, prolonged social converse and commingling of blood are fairly deducible.

Let those who cannot deny the Celtic origin of thousands of the geographical names of England explain how these could have been adopted on any other hypothesis than that now maintained.

The aboriginal race of Britain, unfortunate in being commemorated by little of what may be termed authentic history, and in having this little discredited by its alliance with that mythic and traditional lore which at least represents the spirit rather than the form and reality of their existence, are still fortunate in having the evidence of their earliest possession of the soil, and of a language of a well-ascertained type, inscribed on the rocks and mountains, and over all the great natural features of the country, as with a pen of adamant, indelibly and for ever. Nations have existed which have passed away leaving no trace of long and eventful histories except a few scattered names of places, enshrining, as the amber does the fly, mementoes of their speech, and leaving to the research and learning of the ethnologist to conjecture to what stock and era they belonged; and here the poetry and romance of local names are perfect. The old Britons have not this poetic advantage; they have not entirely disappeared; and therefore, while their identity is better authenticated, the charm lent by mystery and distance is not cast around their story to the same extent.

Not only the *fact* of the occupation of Britain by various races is attested by local names, but the very *order* of occupation is clearly defined. No student of these interesting and instructive relics can doubt that the oldest of them belong to the Celts and the more recent to Danes, Normans, and English. The primeval footprints have been trodden upon by less ancient travellers, and the impressions made by these are again traversed, in some cases nearly effaced, by their pursuers. All the impressions bear a character, and are as incapable of being confounded with each other or referred to the same age or people as the legends of coins, the inscriptions of monuments, or the caligraphy of manuscripts of different eras and countries. The names which stretch back to the remotest historic, and doubtless to pre-historic times, and which have been articulated with more or less uniformity by the tongues of all the generations which have come and gone during the ages, as those of mountains, rivers, estuaries, unquestionably belong to the Celtic race. The great natural strongholds, which became in course of time cities, are either Celtic or Roman, or Roman and Celtic joined, as *London*, Chester, *Man*chester. Towns, again, which bear purely Saxon names are of more modern growth. The creeks, headlands, and maritime positions which have Norse appellations—the *wicks*, the *nesses*, and *holms*—are easily referred to the times of Scandinavian incursions. Norman local names are few, and younger than the Danish; while properly English names, though numerous, are demonstrably of very recent birth.

In some cases we find the history of a thousand years, with the order of occupation, and the nationality of the name-givers, compressed in the hieroglyphics of a single local name. DUM*bar*ton has the same idea of an entrenched place thrice repeated, covering, in due order of succession,

Celtic, Saxon, and later Saxon or English periods; PENT-
*low*hill, in Essex (Celt. *pen*, A.-Sax. *hlacw*, a heap, Engl.
hill), BRIN*don*hill, in Somerset, "hill" again thrice repeated in different succeeding tongues, cover pre-Roman,
Roman and Saxon, and post-Saxon ages. Moving
onwards and to shorter periods, we find in *Chester*ton the
Roman and Saxon ages combined; in *Sand*wich and *Fish*-
guard the Saxon and Danish; in Ash*by*-de-la-Zouch the
Danish and Norman-French; in Richmond (riche-mont)
and Montgomery, Norman-French itself; in Haverford,
Norman-French (*haver*[1], a port) and English. But in
*Dour*water (Yorkshire), the great gulf from Ancient British
to English times is completely bridged across, leaving
conjecture to say how the Celtic *dwr* (water), was allowed
so long to remain unwedded to a sympathetic synonym, and
the modern "water" came at last to see in it a thing of its
own flesh and blood.

It is much to be desired that the local names of Britain
afforded a sufficient light upon the supposed priority of the
Gaelic to the Cymric tribes as colonists. The test-words
wysg, *ben*, *inver*, *bally*, &c., hitherto so much relied upon
as evidence of prior occupation by the Gael of North
and East Scotland and Ireland, as well as parts of central
Britain, are quite unsatisfactory. These words may have been
present in ancient Cymric even if absent from modern Welsh,
for an enormous portion of the language has changed, and
the value of the theory now examined depends exclusively
on the supposition of a stability in human unwritten
speech through thousands of years which all experience
disproves. We rather rely on the probabilities of the case,

---

[1] Borrowed by French from Celtic, and identified with *aber* and *inver*.
The occurrence of this word in Normandy, as at *Havre* de Grace;
Avranches, &c., has already been noted. It is more frequently found
in Brittany, as *Aber*-vrach, &c.

as arising from ethnological and historic facts. It is more likely that the tribes which pushed their way farthest, and have in all historic times dwelt in the remotest quarters of North Britain and Ireland were the first to colonise these islands. New arrivals would be more likely to urge forward the earlier occupiers to fresh pasturage and settlements, than to outstrip them in the race; and that disembarkation from the Continent took place in all cases on the South Coast is morally certain. But if shades of distinction can be found in *aber* and *inver*, *pen* and *ben*, *tref* and *bally*, assigning the former to the Cymric, the latter to the Gaelic dialect, by all means let probability, having otherwise gained a footing, have its position thereby to some small extent strengthened. As *wysg*, however, and *gwisg* (see p. 38, note), are to this day present in Welsh, and *pen*, also present in it, is almost as near *ben* as it can well be without being identical, it is fair to surmise that *bally* and *inver* may have once been the common proper.y of Cymric and Gaelic—in fact that the former is only an euphonised form of *ban*, high, and *lle*, a place, all cities in early times being places of strength built generally on bold and high situations; and that *inver* and *aber* only represent the different ways in which the ancient scribes imitated the native pronunciation of the same thing, a confluence of waters—an hypothesis rendered highly probable by the occurrence of other variations of the terms on the Continent, as *Havre*-de-Grace, *Avr*-anches, already mentioned.

On the whole, therefore, although not assigning the first importance to local names as proofs of race-admixture, we are far from considering them as insignificant in their bearing on the argument. Where they fail to prove, they render probable; where they fail to render probable, they at least significantly suggest.

SECTION IV.

English Proper Names and Surnames.

We have seen it argued with great warmth, and equal ignorance, that since Englishmen are not called by Celtic names they have no participation in Celtic blood. A sufficient reply to this would be, that since Englishmen are not called after the names of their alleged forefathers, Hengist, Horsa, Cerdic, Ella, Ercenwine, Ida, and their distinguished pirate companions—therefore they have not descended from them, and since there remains no more probable ancestry, they have descended from none, but are veritably sons of the soil—*indigenæ aborigines;* or, if this be thought too absurd, then, as the Ancient Britons are declared by authentic history to be inhabitants of Great Britain before Hengist and Horsa's arrival, Englishmen must have descended from them.

But, in truth, strange as it may seem to some, the bearing of personsal proper names and surnames on the core of the subject is very slight. We introduce them here, rather with a view of demonstrating this fact, and thus of disencumbering the question of any adventitious matter, than of adding material force to the argument. At the same time we shall be treading on the heels of the subject, and shall occasionally really touch it, adding meantime a few points of specific interest to the historian and ethnologist.

1. Surnames a modern invention in England.

All names, philosophically considered, are simple signs to distinguish individuals. A person would naturally be described by some personal mark, ownership, or locality. The nations of antiquity usually gave a person one name—Abraham, Isaac, Jacob; Pericles, Themistocles,

Phidias ; Caradog, Taliesin, Gwyddno ; Edwin, Gurth, Harold, Rollo, &c. To define him more specifically, he was called the son of such a person, or (inhabitant understood) of such a place.

The Romans surpassed other early nations in the multiplication of names. Caius Julius Cæsar, Publius Cornelius Scipio, Cnæus Julius Agricola, Caius Cornelius Tacitus, Marcus Tullius Cicero, &c. The object was twofold—definition and dignity.

The Normans first established the practice of surnames in England, and probably first adopted it after their arrival here. Surnames—that is, names in addition to the single personal name, now called the "Christian" name, and descending in the same family from generation to generation—were not known among the Britons and Saxons. Even after the Norman Conquest, the practice was not introduced among the English population, so far as reliable records testify, for one or two hundred years.

In Domesday Book, the Norman families often bear names of addition, descending to their posterity. Darcy, Arundel, Devereux, Perci, Laci, are examples.

As late as the fifteenth century surnames were only of partial use in England. Thus in 1406, a person describes himself as Willielmus filius Adae Emmotson, who, in 1416, is Willielmus Emmotson—showing progress towards a settled surname. Another curious example ; a person described as Johannes filius Willielmi filii Johannis de Hunshelf, appears soon after as Johannes Wilson.[1]

The length of Welsh and Irish pedigrees is proverbial. In the later Middle Ages a man had one name, and was defined as the *Mac* or *Ap* (son) of another, he of another, and so on, in long series. In Wales, in the 15th and 16th centuries, the patronymic *ap* or *ab* is used not unfrequently

[1] Confer *Penny Cyclop.* vol. xvi. p. 71.

as many as six times, *cx. gr.* Gruffydd ap Will. ap Rob. ap Cadwal. ap Mered. ap Hug. ap Ievan. A document of the year 1460, relating to the Herbert family, is signed by two gentlemen styling themselves, " Ievan ap Rhydderch ap Ievan Lloyd, Esq.," and " Howell ap David ap Ievan ap Rhys, Gent.," followed by three others styling themselves " Bards." [1] But early British history shows the same usage as existing, though in more moderate form, among the ancient Cymry. Caractacus is often styled *Caradog ap Brân,* and his grandson was *Coel ap Cyllin.*

As specimens of the names prevailing among the better classes of Wales in the 13th and 14th centuries, we may quote from the lists still preserved in the *Bibliothèque Royale,* in Paris, of whole companies of Welsh soldiers who had fled their own country, and entered the service of the French King. The name *Gallois,* or *de Gallois,* is not uncommon in France, and is known to be borne by descendants of these Welsh refugees. The foremost of these was a young chieftain of the family of Prince Llewelyn, called by the French *Evain, or Yvain de Galles,* (Owain of Wales), an especial favourite at the French Court. He and *John Wyn,* or *Win, Robin ap Llwydin, Edward ap Owen,* and *Owen ap Griffith,* were all captains of troops of Welsh soldiers in the wars of France against England. Among the 100 Welshmen, more or less, following the fortunes of brave Owain, or *Yvain de Galles,* were men bearing the following names :

Hywel Ddu (standard bearer).	Llewelyn ap Jorwerth.
Morgan de² (ap) David.	Ieuan ap David Bâch.
Einion de (ap) Hywel.	Madog du ap Greffin.

---

[1] Fenton's *Pembrokeshire,* p. 47, App.

² The French substitutes the *de* for *ap* in some though not in all cases.

Gruffydd de (ap) Iorwrch.[1]	Iorwerth ap Grox ap David.
Ithel de (ap) Iorwerth.	Cadwaladr Hael.
Madog de (ap) Gruffydd.	Ieuan ap Gruffin ap Rait.
Hywel de (ap) Einion.	Robin Uchel.
Ioguen ap Morbran.	Gwilym Gwenarth.
Robin ap Bled.	Einion ap David *Sais*.
Gwilym Gôch.	Griffin ap Ieuan ap Roger.
Ieuan Gwilym ap Ogwen.	Hary Walice Mon.[2]

&c., &c.

Here, and in the other lists of followers of *John Win*,[3] *Robin ap Llwydin*, &c., such names as Ieuan, Hywel, Davydd, Gwilym, Robin, Gruffydd, abound. The same names occur often—a fact still observable in the onomatology of Wales. The few here pointed out are the chief names of the Welsh to this day, both Christian and surname: Jones, Davies, Williams, Roberts, Griffiths, Howells, are their Anglicised forms. *Ieuan* has propagated itself in a great variety of shapes, for from this one original appellative have descended the whole troop of John, Owen, Evan, Ievan, Jones, Ioan, and a few others.

2. The value of English surnames as proofs of inter-mixture.

It must be confessed that English surnames, being the creations mostly of the last 400 years, can be of no value as evidence of *early* intermixture between Celts and Saxons, though half the population were called Jones, Davies, Williams, or Roberts. They can only be proofs of *recent* intermixture. Multitudes of them are based on personal qualities, localities of birth, handicrafts, &c. (as were those of Wales, and as are those of Germany, and are often

---

[1] A mistake apparently for *Iorwerth*. Many of the names, as given by Thierry, are evidently incorrectly spelled.

[2] *Biblioth. Royale, Cabinet du Saint Esprit.*

[3] *Ibid. Titres Scellés de Clairamboult*, t. 114, fol. 8925.

found to be not only pertinent and expressive, but even beautiful—while a large proportion must be allowed to be grotesque, ludicrous, absurd, and not a few even indecent.

The *Christian* names of Modern England, so far from being either Celtic or Saxon in origin, strange to say, are in the major part derived from the Greek and Hebrew *Scriptures*. The influence of religion among Welsh and English has expelled most of the national names of both races, under the idea, perhaps, that they savoured of heathenism, substituting others consecrated by Old and New Testament associations. The names which are now in common use, and which cannot be cast aside without apparent singularity, are only some *fifty-three* in number! The following *twelve* are constantly occurring: John, William, Henry, George, James, Robert, Thomas, Francis, Charles, Edward, Richard, Samuel. Of these, *four* are Scripture names, *four* Norman, only *one* Saxon (Edward), three are from other sources. Not one is purely British. Of the 41 other names, composing the total 53, 28 are names of religion: so that out of the 53 current names which distinguish the many millions of our male population, 32, or *three-fifths* are *taken from the Scriptures!* If this were proof of piety, how pious were the people of England! Twenty-five of the 53 are of *Hebrew* origin, so that, if modern names were sufficient evidence of consanguinity, a moiety of us must stand confessed as of the seed of faithful Abraham!

3. The disuse, in modern times, of Celtic and Saxon names.

As far as personal nomenclature is concerned, modern Celts and Saxons alike have denied their progenitors, calling themselves, as seen above, after the names of strangers. Foreign languages, Hebrew, Greek, Latin,

have lent designations to *five* out of every *seven* of the
males of England and Wales!

The *Cymry* have dropped the renowned old names,

> Caradog, Caswallon, Einion, Arthur, Cadwgan,
> Ednyfed, Cynvelin, Aneurin, Cynddelw, Rhiwallon,
> Taliesin, Merddin, Madog, Goronwy, Edeyrn.

And the English have abandoned their equally noble,

> Winfrid, Thorold, Ida, Harold, Aldred, Ailwin,
> Egbert, Ella, Ethelbert, Ethelred, Kenelm, Oswald,
> Offa, Kenric, Ailred, Egfrid, Sigebert, Adda;

have never repeated even Hengist and Horsa, who at
least had the merits of adventurous pioneers and successful
colonists; and of the illustrious names of their ancestors
have honoured as they ought only Albert, Alfred, Edwin,
and Edward. The Queen of England has added new
lustre to the British *Arthur*, by giving it a place in the
royal circle, and it were well if so high an example were
followed in many directions, both as to Celtic and
Saxon names.

In the names of *females*, the departure from the custom
of our ancestors, both British and Anglo-Saxon, has been
equally marked. Among the female names of the Anglo-
Saxons were,

> Elfheld, Adeleve, Edburh, Algifa, Edgifa, Athelgifa,
> Winfreda, Ethelheld, Ethelfritha, Bertha, and Editha,

of which the last two only have been retained. In the Cot-
tonian MS. Tib. B. 5, the names of a whole Saxon family are
given thus:—"Dudda was a husbandman in Haethfelda :
and he had three daughters; one was called Deorwyn, the
other Deorswytha, and the third Golde. Wullaf, in Haethfelda, hath Deorwyn for his wife; and Aelfstan, at
Kengawyrth, hath Deorswytha, and Ealhstan, the brother

of Aelfstan married Golde."[1] We submit that we have here finer female names (all of which are also beautifully significant in Anglo-Saxon) than our modern Florence, Augusta, Georgiana, Frances, Blanche, Henrietta, Charlotte, Grace.

4. Recent Celtic Names.

If we look at the extent to which modern Celtic surnames prevalent in Wales, Scotland, and Ireland, have found their way into England, and take this as evidence of intermixture in *modern* times, we shall doubtless build on a good foundation. Only let this branch of evidence be understood as applied with this limitation. Names, usually considered Welsh, which have a large place in every English Directory of our day—the *London Post Office Directory* especially—are the following :—Jones, Williams, Hughes, Thomas, Griffiths, Owen, Parry, Bowen, Lloyd, Evans, Morgan, Jenkins, Lewis, Howell, Powell, Rees, and Davies. *Jones* in the London Directory fills about half the space occupied by the incomparable *Smith*. *Williams* fills lengthy columns ; also Griffiths, Thomas, Davies, Lloyd, &c., &c. The general conclusion to be drawn is, that the prospect of advancement in England has attracted large numbers from Wales within recent years. The process is still rapidly going forward : and it is observable that the Welshman, once he has acquired the manners, language, accent, of the Englishman, carries nothing in his complexion or physiognomy, and little now in his name, to distinguish him from the general type of Englishmen.

But large as has been the influx of Welsh names, that of Scotch and Irish has been far greater. If statistics of those who every year "cross the Tweed" and never return, and of those who come over from the Green Isle to make friends

---

[1] Comp. Turner's *Hist. of the Anglo-Saxons*, vol. iii. p. 9.

with " Sassenach " were carefully taken,[1] perhaps many
who believe to their great comfort in the Teutonic purity
of the English would feel a measure of dismay. Who
can number

The Camerons, Campbells, Craigs, Cunninghams,
The Dixons, Douglases, Duffs, Duncans,
The Grahams, Grants, Gordons, Guthries,
The Macdonalds, Macgregors, Macleans, MacLeods,
The Muirs, Munros, Murrays, Murdochs,
The Reids, Robertsons, Rosses, and Scotts :

And

The O'Briens, O'Neills, O'Connors, Murphys,
Dalys, Falloons, Donovans, Flannaghans, Mullonys,
Sullivans, Bradys, Donnels, and Patricks,

who contribute so much to the variety of our nomenclature
and to the balance and suppleness of our national mind?
What should we do without the prudent painstaking
Scotchman, quick in finding his opportunity, and never
remiss in its improvement? and what without the effer-
vescent hearty Irishman, who hews our wood and draws
our water, and withal substitutes elasticity for Teutonic
rigidness, and relieves with poetry, humour, and intellectual
vivacity our dull matter-of-fact uniformity—although in
his natural unmixed state, he often occasions a huge
amount of trouble? Welshman, Irishman, Scotchman,
German, Frenchman—all come with a welcome to our all-
absorbing nationality; weld them all into one mass, and
forth there comes a "good man and true," fit for any noble
deed of mind or hand that mortal can perform! As to the
political problem offered by the Irishman, it is feared that

---

[1] From the Census of 1861. (See *Papers*, &c., *in Brit. Mus.* vol. lii.,
part 1), we find that there were at that time *in London*,

12 Scotchmen for every 1000 people in Scotland.
15 Welsh   ,,   ,,   in Wales.
18 Irish   ,,   ,,   in Ireland.

the English legislature has scarcely yet apprehended rightly the temper and genius of his race. For ages, tyrannic force alone was used in their government. A philosophic study of the people, had our "legislators" been capable of it, would have shown that a frank and generous treatment, not unaccompanied by firmness, suited the case better than a suspicious hate-inspiring coercion. Irish disloyalty is the child of English love of force and hereditary routine, joined to foreign ecclesiastical inspiration. The former must cease, and the latter be blown out. That accomplished, the Irishman may become as loyal to the throne as he is brave in the field and eloquent in the forum. But always, as he merges into our population and "becomes a Saxon," he forms a valuable element in the peerless race of the English.

5. Teutonic Names of Persons and Places in Wales.

Names, in Wales, are suggestive of large intermixture. It is now no uncommon thing to meet with Welsh-speaking persons bearing such names as Wilson, Saunders, White, Smith, Hooper, Marychurch, Warlow, Cleaton, Gibson, Norton, Johnston, Chambers, Miils, &c.

In the parts of Pembrokeshire colonised by Flemings, temp. Henry I., and earlier by Danes and Normans, it may be expected that Teutonic names should abound; and such, to a great extent, is the case. A multitude of names suggestive of Anglo-Saxon, Flemish, and Danish origin are to be found. In these districts, the language spoken is a kind of English. The areas occupied by the Saxon tongue and by Saxon and Norse local and personal names, are about the same in extent, and nearly coincide.

About one-half of Pembrokeshire is occupied by a people of a mixed nationality speaking a modified English. Hence the name *Anglia Transwalliana* which Camden somewhat aptly applied to the district, and which has since become current as "Little England beyond Wales." The observant enquirer at once sees here the marks of an ethnological intrusion in the personal appearance and speech of the inhabitants, and the personal and local names he encounters. The account usually given of the Flemish immigration, and, as a supposed consequence of the type of language found in the hundreds of Roose and Castle-martin, although scarcely sufficient to explain all the features of the case, may be taken as correct as far as it goes. In the reigns of William Rufus and Henry I., we are told by William of Malmesbury, Giraldus de Barri (12th century), Hollinshed, and others, great numbers of Flemings were encouraged or allowed to settle in the North of England, the reason for such encouragement being that Matilda (Maud), wife of the Conqueror, and mother of Rufus and Henry, was daughter of Baldwin, Earl of Flanders, and that the immigrants had been driven in a state of destitution from their former homes by a great inundation of the sea. Having multiplied and become troublesome in the north, and the Normans, already settled in Pembrokeshire, being at the same time molested by the Welsh, whose lands they had taken, Henry hit upon the expedient both of relieving the northern districts of a nuisance and of protecting his kinsmen, the Normans in Wales, by transferring the Flemings bodily into Pem-brokeshire, giving them a portion of the lands taken from the Welsh for their support and the duty of "repressing the brutal temerity of the Welsh," as W. of Malmesbury expresses it, as a pastime and feudal obligation.

But it is to be noted that previous to the arrival of these particular Flemings in the North of England, a consider-able number of their countrymen had already come over in the miscellaneous multitude of the Conqueror's army.

William, we have already seen, had sent his enticing proclamation to Flanders among other neighbouring states,
inviting all who wished for conquest and booty in England
to rank themselves as brothers in robbery under his
standard; and Malmesbury informs us that in Rufus's
time such numbers of these people had come across the
Channel that they appeared burdensome to the kingdom.
The Flemings first settled in Rhôs, according to the
Annales Cambriae, in the year 1107, and according to *Brut
y Tywysogion* and Malmesbury, a year or two earlier. We
have also intimation in the *Brut* of another settlement in
the same parts in the year 1113; but this was probably
only one of the many small accessions which, at different
times before and after, were made to the general body.

The notices given are so meagre, after the manner of
the old chroniclers, that we can form but a dim conception
of the composition and organisation of the new settlers.
No hint is given as to their leaders, if they had any, of the
mode of their transit, of the specific spots where they found
shelter, or of the conflicts with the natives, whereby, with
the aid of the Anglo-Normans, they must by degrees have
fought for themselves a home. They were probably a
horde of humble, industrious people, having no persons of
exceptional influence to act as guides or leaders, obeying
the command of the king, as feudal discipline, joined to
necessity, had taught them to do, and placed in their new
homes under the military supervision of Norman officials.
As part of this arrangement, the Castle of Roch at one end
of their territory, and of Benton, on Milford Haven, at the
other, were well placed, and here we are told was stationed
Adam de Rupe (Adam of the Rock—*Roch* Castle being
perched on a solitary rock standing out of the plain) in
whose family was vested the hereditary office of *comes
littoris*, "Count of the Shore," holding the government of the

maritime district from Newgale Sands to the Milford Creek. Haverfordwest was the main centre for trade and defence of the Flemish territory. Giraldus, who flourished within fifty years of their settlement, and as a native of the parts, must have been well acquainted with their character and condition, describes them as a people brave and robust ; ever most hostile to the Welsh, well-versed in commerce and woollen manufacture ; anxious to seek gain by sea or land ; a hardy race, equally fitted for the plough or the sword. All this is likely enough to be true ; but they seem to have lost other qualities, which, if Giraldus is correct, made them a very extraordinary race. " These people," he says, " from the inspection of the right shoulder [bones] of rams, which have been stripped of their flesh, and not roasted, but boiled, can discover future events, or those which have passed and remained long unknown. They know, also, what is transpiring at a distant place by a wonderful art and prophetic kind of spirit." The " prophetic spirit " we fear has been lost, if ever possessed, but belief in fortune-telling and occult knowledge, though not peculiar to Pembrokeshire, is still exceptionally strong in these parts.

The facts above given are sufficient to account for the character of the *language* of the Pembrokeshire " Englishry." How the Flemings, who used in their original home a rather different speech, came to adopt English, is made clear only by their previous sojourn and settlement in the North and other parts of England. How they cast their English into a peculiar pattern, and made it a linsey-woolsey fabric of divers colours, will be at once understood from the mixture of Norman, English, Welsh, and Flemish, which constituted their society. For even Welsh would in time settle among them ; and that many English had been brought hither by the policy of Henry and his pre-

·decessors is not only probable, but almost demonstrated by the physical characteristics, the names, and the mixed language of the district.[1]

Pembrokeshire English has peculiar words, peculiar inflections, idioms, articulations. It has, in fact, no "words," but "*oo*rds;" is not pronounced but "pro-n*aaw*nced;" it often omits the auxiliary, saying, "I written," for "I have written;" the vowel *o* is frequently ill-used, "cold" being c*aau*ld, and "told," t*aau*ld; the terminal *ow* in "borrow" is sounded broad *à* (borr*a*); to "mow," is to "maaoo;" "going," is "gwain." The neuter gender is never recognised by the peasantry, but everything is either *he* or *she*, and the masculine objective is always *n;* "I told him," is "I taauld'n." "How" is universally used for "why." "How did you come" would here have no reference to the manner of coming, but solely to the reason for coming. For "I am not," "he is not," the common expression is "I arn't," "he arn't." A couple does not necessarily mean two of a kind, but most usually usurps the meaning of "a few." When a person does anything "leisurely," he does it "all by leshars;" one person throwing stones at another is said to "pile" him; "orra one" and "norra one" are used for "one" and "not one;" a cow addicted to pushing is said to "pilk;" a large piece of bread is a "culf;" a small loaf baked is a "cook," boiled it is a "trolly;" an article of good substance and bulk is said to have a good "sump" in it; one of stunted growth is "cranted;" one of weak condition of body is "hash;" one whose intellect is impaired is "dotty;" to be stern or brave is to be "dern;" an unworthy person is a "pelt;" to be showy is to be "filty," a woman over-dressed is "filty-fine;" oatmeal

---

[1] See the Author's *Annals and Antiquities of Wales*. London, 1872, vol. ii. 878; and *Cambr. Journal*, 1859.

gruel is "budram;" when a person talks incoherently it
is "a rammus;" to fallow the land is to "vedge" it; a
furrow is a "voor;" any small meadow is "burgage;" to
save water from running to waste is to "vang" it; to cover
a fire so as to keep it in over night is to "stum" it; to beg
is to "kedge," "soul," or "hoggle," and the second means
begging at "All Souls' time;" *man* is used very peculiarly
under the form "men," "no, my good fellow" is "no,
men;" "answer my lad," is "answer men;" a gap in the
hedge is a "slop." Traces of Welsh are found in "cowell,"
a kind of basket, W. *cawell*; "coppat," is the thatch on a
mow, or small stack of corn, W. *cap, coppa*; to "freeth,"
as in Devon, is to wattle, W. *ffridd*, a division, quick-set;
completely is "rottle," W. *trwyadl*, thorough; to pour is
to "hild," W. *hidlo*, to pass through a sieve; a great eater
is a "gorral," W. *gor*, much, extreme, and *bol*, belly.

The boundaries of the "Englishry" and "Welshery" in
this curiously mixed district are about the same to-day as
they were 650 years ago. An old antiquary of the county,
George Owen, about 260 years ago, writes;—"The shire is
well neere divided into two partes between the English
speeche and the Welshe, for the hundreds of Castle-Martin,
Rowse, and all Narberth, excepting the parishes of Llan-
ddewi and Lampeter, and all Dougleddy, excepting the
parishes of Llanvalteg, Langain, Landyssilio, Lanykeven,
and Crynow, doe speake the Englishe; and then the
hundreds of Kemes, Kilgerran, and Dewis-land speake all
the Welshe tongue; so that above seventy-four parishes
are inhabited by the Englishmen, and sixty-four parishes
more by the Welshe, and the rest, being about six, speak
both languages, beginning at Cronwere by Carmarthenshire, and so passeth up to Lanhaden, where both languages
are spoken, and from thence between Bletherston and
Lanykeven to New Mote, and soe between Castle-blythe

and Ambleston, and between Trefgarn and St. Dogwell's, and over the hills betweene Hay's Castle, and then turning down Newgall Moore, as the same river leadeth to the sea betweene Roche Castle and bridge, the southern part of which Lansker speaketh all English, and the norther side Welshe, well neere, as I sayde before, parting the shire in two equall halves betweene them." [1]

This description would probably apply with equal truth to the same district at any point of time between the 12th and 17th centuries, and illustrates in a remarkable manner the tendencies of language and race to maintain their limits, if not invaded by extraordinary forces. It would well apply, we believe, to the present state of things in the same parts, with one important qualification—viz., that the line of demarcation nowhere so distinctly and definitely separates the languages as it did when the description quoted was written. The reason of this is obvious. With the march of education, English slowly diffuses itself everywhere through the Welsh parts, not to the exclusion of the vernacular, but as a companion speech ; and on the other hand, the Welsh, drawn by trade and inclination, settle in no inconsiderable number among the once hated intruders. The hostility of the two races has nearly disappeared, leaving behind it only a faint residuum of dislike. Intermarriages take place. Long past is the time when the words of the antiquary already quoted were true, when the English "held themselves so close as to wonder at a Welshman coming among them, the one neighbour saying to the other, 'Look, there goeth a Welshman!'"

Names of places naturally follow race settlements. Names ending in *ton*, Teutonic for " abode," are almost as common

---

[1] *Cambr. Register*, ii. 78.

in Roose and Castle-martin as those ending in the synonymous Cymric *tre* are in Dewsland. But through all time
and circumstance, expulsion or absorption of race and hot
furnace of bloody conflict, not a few of the ancient Cymric
designations have survived almost unharmed and without
disfigurement even in the most Anglified parts. *Pembroke*, *Ten*by (*Din*), Narberth, and the various parish *Llans*
are conspicuous instances. With almost braver and more
strenuous affection, the obscure hamlets, farmsteads, rills,
and ridges cling to their early Cymric names,—Trefràn,
Camros, Talbeny, Coedganlas, Pennar, Pwll-y-crochan, as
well as Carew, Benton, and Begelly.

Saxon surnames in this country are numerous : such are
Starbuck, Taplin, Stokes, Sinnett, Barham, Tucker,
Scowcroft, Watt, Perrott, Nicholas, Scourfield, Mansel,
Parsell, Reynish, Brigstocke.

Norman-French names of persons and places are also met
with in goodly number—continuous memorials of those
Normans introduced by Henry I. and his predecessors.
Such names are Roche, Devereux, Bonville, Arnold,
Raymond. There are places called *Filbatch*, once owned
by William de Filbatch ; *Hascard*, owned by Richard de
Hascard ; *Dale*, given to de Vale ; *Picton Castle*, from which
was named William de Picton.

The question of local names brings into singular prominence the settlement in Pembrokeshire of another nationality—the *Danish*. In the 9th and 10th centuries, during
the long and severe struggle of this people to compass the
conquest of England, the creeks and islands along the
coast of Wales, and especially those of Pembrokeshire,
were much infested with these marauders. Such a harbour
as Milford Haven was not likely to escape the notice of
the Vikings. Hence the whole of that neighbourhood,
both on the margin and in the interior, shows signs of

their presence. They came hither chiefly in search of plunder. Their visits were sometimes hasty and brief, but at other times prolonged, and ending in permanent settlement. Where they impressed their mark so deeply as to leave a local name in their own language, it is presumable that the place had become their permanent home. The words *guard, garth*, a place enclosed, protected; *wick*, a creek; *thorp* or *drop*, a village; *by*, an abode; *holm*, an island; *stack, stakr*, a columnar rock, are all Norse, and are all, with several others of kindred origin, to be found in Pembrokeshire.

Fish*guard*.	*Wick* Haven.	Flat*holm*.
Good*wick*.	Ox*wich*.	Skok*holm*.
Has*guard*.	*Stack*pole Head.	Steep*holm*.
Gellys*wick*.	*Stack* Rocks.	Freys*trop*.
Wath*wick*.	Penyholt *Stack*.	Goul*trop*.
Little*wick*.	St. Bride's *Stack*.	Ten*by*.
Hel*wick*.	Burry *Holmes*.	Der*by*.
Mussel*wick*.	Grass-*holm*.	Col*by*.
Carn ar *wig*.		

Then there are such obviously Scandinavian names as Caldy, Skomer, Skerryback, islands; Studdolph, Hasguard, Haroldston, Hubbaston, Gomfreston, Herbrandston, homesteads; Strumble Head, Sker-las, &c.

As to *personal* names, Danish traces are discoverable in Colby, Skyrme, Buckley, Lort.

The same result would be obtained by a minute examination of *personal* names, and the *physical characteristics*, such as the complexion, hair-colour, and stature of the people; all would tend to show that the County of Pembroke has been largely visited by the North Sea Vikings, and that they have left here not only fragments of their language, but also a slight tinge of their blood. One other thing is evident, here as elsewhere in early British, and more recent

Saxon history, viz., that the lines of demarcation between
Briton and Saxon have been gradually wearing out (as is
always and unavoidably the case, when two types come in
contact), and that this process is brought to pass, to out-
ward appearance, by the merging of the Celt in the Teuton
rather than the reverse.

The Pembrokeshire people exhibit certain physical
aspects of a marked character which cannot well be traced
to a Norman or Danish origin ; and, on the other hand,
are scarcely to be considered Celtic.   The short and stout
build, the round and comely physiognomy, dark and curly
hair, and dark eyes, giving a type of countenance almost
Jewish, so often to be met here, powerfully suggest a foreign
origin.   How much of this is due to the cause suggested
by Tacitus (*Agric.* xi.) in his description of the *Silures*
(whose near neighbourhood may have led to admixture
with the more westerly Britons, when he ascribes their
dark complexion and curled locks to an Iberian source,
and how much to the Flemish intrusion, it is, of course,
impossible to tell ; but that a mixture of races has occurred
in these parts is as clear from the physical character of the
population as from their speech and local names.

CHAPTER IV.

EVIDENCE OF THE INFLUENCE OF THE ANCIENT BRITISH RACE UPON THE ANGLO-SAXONS, SUPPLIED BY THE DEVELOPMENT OF EARLY ENGLISH LAW.

COMMON sense and experience unite in telling us that if a conquering nation receive in whole or in part the laws of the conquered, the circumstance argues :—

First : The probable intellectual superiority, or superior civilization, of the subjugated race ; and

Secondly : That the conquest was not one of extermination, but of incorporation where the triumph was complete, of subjection to tribute where incomplete.

The phenomena of the Norman Conquest confirm this hypothesis ; but more especially in its second branch ; for it scarcely can be said that the Anglo-Saxons were, *intellectually*, in advance of the Normans. But William conquered England, not with the view of expelling the inhabitants, but with the view of making them his subjects ; and he ultimately found it desirable, nay indispensable, in order to make such a nation obedient to his rule, to respect its laws and institutions. He swore, after much manœuvring to avoid it, to " rule according to law,"—not the law of Normandy, not the more congenial one of his own overbearing will, but the law of Edward—the law of the English nation—that law which in its great formative elements had, long before William's era, swayed the British mind, and in substance continues to rule it still.

Now what is demonstrably true in the case of Normans and Anglo-Saxons, is constructively true, to say the least, in the case of Anglo-Saxons and Britons. If the Normans, having prosecuted a war of conquest and not of extermination, chose to appropriate the laws of the country, the probability is that the Angles and Saxons, if their object was to make a war of conquest and not of extermination, would in like manner respect the chief articles of public law with which the conquered were familiar. This is hypothesis : we want facts.

The question, therefore, is, *did* the Anglo-Saxons to any extent adopt the Ancient British laws? If they did, we hold it next to certain that they so did because of the reason involved in our hypothesis, and which has been seen to govern in the case of the Norman Conquest, viz., that the people whose laws they properly were, continued in great part to be subjects under rule.

Let us for a moment advert to the other reason which might be expected to obtain in the case of the Ancient Britons more than in that of the Anglo-Saxons, viz., their undoubtedly superior intellectual culture, and nearer approximation to a state of civilization.

A less civilized people is ever subject to the spell which the institutions of the more civilized are fitted to cast around them. We all know that the Britons of this island, after nearly five centuries of Roman government and culture, were a civilized people, and that the Angles, Jutes, and Saxons were not. Britain, at the arrival of these strong-armed, earnest-minded, needy aggressors, was such as the pride, favour, taste, and resources of Rome could have made her. She was deserted under stern decree of necessity) as a jewel is relinquished—as is a long-inhabited, sumptuously furnished mansion. The superb architecture, the refinement of manners, the well-adjusted machinery of

public law which Britain presented, could not be witnessed
by the rough but keen-eyed Teutons without winning for
the people of whose minds they were the exponents—though
they were a fallen people—a good measure of respect and
veneration.   Who does not remember the striking analogy
of the conquest of Greece by the old Romans?   If that
martial people in their earlier, less corrupted days, conquered Greece, the art, splendour, wisdom of Greece also
conquered them.   Jutes, Angles, and Saxons, like Normans
and Romans, were men—neither better nor worse than
men ; but it were to argue on the assumption that they
were something in stupidity and blindness which men
never yet have been, if it were contended that their admiration was not excited by the material magnificence, the
intellectual endowment, and social culture which they
encountered for the first time in this island.

   We must now recur to our question :—Did the Anglo-
Saxons to any extent adopt the Ancient British Laws?
We are not writing for the information of lawyers : they
all know that the question can only be answered in the
affirmative.   In truth, we are not writing for the purpose
of informing any intelligent person on this subject ; but
simply of recording an almost universally admitted truth.
The Anglo-Saxons certainly did, to some extent, embody
in their code, when they became ripe to construct one,
elements belonging distinctly to the Ancient British jurisprudence.   The quantum was perhaps small, but it was
there.

   The chief articles of public law, in those times, referred
to the relations of king and people, the tenure of land, the
class relations of the people among themselves, and the
administrative divisions and tribunals of the country, &c.
If in these, or some of these, we find exact correspondence
and agreement in the Ancient British and Anglo-Saxon

laws, our conclusion must be that the latter borrowed from the former—unless indeed it can be shown that both equally borrowed from a common source, as *ex gr.* the Theodosian Code.

Now on this point, Sir F. Palgrave—no mean authority —has written thus :—"Opposed as the native and the stranger were to each other, the main lines and land-marks of their jurisprudence were *identical*. They agreed in their usages respecting crimes and punishments ; they agreed in allowing the homicide to redeem his guilt by making compensation to the relatives of the slain ; they agreed in the use of trial by ordeal and by compurgation ; and these being the chief features of the law, and of its administration, the question whether such analogous cus-toms be of British, or of Saxon origin is little more than a mere verbal dispute," &c.[1]

Lest it should be thought that language to the same effect as the following, if it came from the present writer, would be that of a special-pleader for a foregone conclusion, we shall again quote Sir F. Palgrave in the judgment he pronounces upon the *quality* of the Ancient British legisla-tion. The readers of the "School Histories of England," will of course decline to understand such language. The Britons are known to have been "barbarians," and "there-fore," such sentiments must be absurd, &c.!

"The historical order prevailing in this code," [2] says

---

[1] *Rise and Progress of English Commonwealth*, vol. i. p. 38.

[2] The Code of Howel the Good (*Hywel Dda*), A.D. 906—948. This Code was a revision of the Laws of *Dyfnwal Moelmud*, which had long existed among the Britons, and of the tenor of which King Alfred had doubtless been carefully informed by his Welsh instructor, *Asser*. The Code of Hywel gives its own history thus :—" Howel the Good, son of Cadell, Prince of Cymru, summoned to him six men from every cantrev [hundred] in all Cymru. . . . And they examined the laws : such of them as might be too severe in punishment to mitigate, and such as

Palgrave, "shows that it was framed with considerable care, and the customs it comprehends bear the impress of great antiquity. . . . The character of the British legislation is enhanced by comparison with the laws which were put in practice amongst the other nations of the Middle Ages. The indignant pride of the Britons, who despised their implacable enemies, the Anglo-Saxons, as a race of rude barbarians, whose touch was impurity, will not be considered as any decisive test of superior civilization. But the Triads, and the laws of *Hoel Dda*, excel the Anglo-Saxon and other Teutonic customals in the same manner that the elegies of Llywarch Hên, and the odes of Taliesin, soar above the ballads of Edda. *Law had become a science amongst the Britons;* and its volumes exhibit the jurisprudence of a rude nation shaped and modelled by thinking men, and which had derived both stability and equity from the labours of its expounders." [1]

Great mystery hangs over the derivation of the greater part of the common law of England. We have no means of knowing how much of the customs, so-called, was included in the *Dom-boc* of King Alfred, who collected and digested the laws of the Heptarchy—for that precious book is lost. But we have laws of Edward the Confessor, of Alfred, of Athelstan, of Ethelbert, and of Ina.[2] The three celebrated codes in operation before Edward's time—the *Mercenlage*, the *West Saexenlage*, and the *Danelage*, doubtless contained a large portion of what is now

---

might be too lenient to render more rigorous. Some of the laws they suffered to remain unaltered; others they willed to amend; others they abrogated entirely; and they enacted some new laws." *Ancient Laws and Institutions of Wales.* Public Records Ed. B. iii. c. 1.

[1] *Rise and Progress of English Commonwealth*, vol. i. p. 37.

[2] See Dr. Reinhold Schmid's *Die Gesetze der Angelsachsen;* and *Ancient Laws and Institutes of England.* Public Records Ed., by Thorpe, 1840.

called the "un-written" law of England, and were probably brought together in a somewhat classified form in
the Confessor's Code, as intimated by Roger de Hoveden.[1]
Many of the rules, and very much of the terminology of
our jurisprudence, are derived from the Normans. Our
"common" law, however—termed "common" probably
from its being "common to all the realm[2]"—has no
special paternity. It is a collection brought in from all
quarters—extracted from the wisdom, consecrated by the
usage, and corrected by the experience of all ages, and of
all the nations now blended in one in the people of England. It may, therefore, contain an indefinite amount
originally derived from the Ancient Britons; and much of
that amount may have been previously derived by the
Britons from the Theodosian Code.

It is universally admitted that the law of *Gavel-kind*, in
Kent, and other parts—which ordains, among other things,
that the father's inheritance, including his lands, shall be
divided among all his sons equally—is borrowed from the
Ancient British law. This law was in force all over Wales
till the time of Henry VIII. Its designation is purely
Welsh; *gavel* meaning in that language, a "hold," a
"grasp," "*tenure*"; *kind* being probably the Anglo-Saxon
cind, "kindred," "relation," signifying a law which gave
to a man's family, or children, a hold or claim upon his
property. This is a better derivation than *gafael-ccnedl*,
which is rather uncouth and very improbable, *ccnedl* meaning "tribe" rather than children or family.

The Ancient British law of *vassalage* was in many points
an exact pattern of the Anglo-Saxon. The *villein* among
the Ancient Britons, however, was not so degraded a being

---

[1] *Annals*, vol. ii. On Henry. II.

[2] Stephen's *Blackstone*, vol. i. p. 45, 5th Ed.

as the *theowe*, but corresponded rather with the ceorl *(villanus)* among the Saxons. He was a "bondman," but he was still a man, not a mere thing, or animal. He held his *gavel* by prædial service rendered to the king, just as the Saxon ceorl held his "gafol-land." Work was to be done on the king's manor; a thirlage[1] rendered to the mill. The king's corn was to be reaped by the British vassal, and his hay to be mown : his hawks were to be kept, and his hounds fed.[2]   The rent paid in "kind," which was denominated the "farm"[3] among the Anglo-Saxons, is regulated in the same way, and described in nearly the same words in the laws of *Hywel Dda*, and in the Code of Ina.[4]

It has been already remarked that among the Anglo-Saxons the ceorl could rise to the rank of a *six-haend-man*, and be considered a person of gentle blood, if property to the amount of five hides of land had continued in his family for three generations ; and it has also been shown that the same privilege was granted to the *Wealas*, or Ancient Britons, settled among the Anglo-Saxons. Now there was a law precisely to this effect among the Britons themselves.   The laws of *Hywel Dda* enact that the descendants of a bondman shall become free in the fourth generation, if by grant from the king, he and the intervening descendants shall have held five acres of land[5]—

---

[1] A.-Saxon, *thrael*, a bond-servant ; hence English "thrall," and "thraldom."

[2] Some faint reflection of this is to be witnessed to this day, where the small farmer has to keep the squire's hound or spaniel.

[3] A.-Saxon *feormian*, to supply provisions, to entertain.

[4] See Wootton's *Leges Walliæ*, pp. 166—168, 175 ; *Laws of Ina*, lxxv. A more accurate and accessible work than Wotton's is the edition of the Welsh Laws of Hywel, issued by the Record Commissioners— *Ancient Laws and Institutions of Wales.*

[5] Wotton's *Leges Walliæ*, p. 154.

the acre of the Britons being about the same measurement as the Saxon "hide." This fact, says Sir F. Palgrave, "evinces a further conformity between the British and English laws."[1]

On the whole, it appears highly probable that the Saxon laws which Alfred found scattered among the three divisions of the country, the *Mercen-lage*, the *West-Saexen-lage*, and the *Dane-lage*, were largely derived from the codes existing among the Britons, and which themselves had been partly inherited from the Romans. Of the laws of Mercia this is especially probable, since a vast proportion of that recently-erected kingdom's subjects were Britons. Nor is there much reason to adopt a different opinion with respect to the laws of Wessex. The revisal of Alfred and the revisal of *Hywel Dda*, therefore, might be concerned with the very same ancient materials ; and it is not improbable that Hywel, who came last, might profit from the work of Alfred, as Alfred, through his Welsh counsellor Asser, was likely to have profited from the ancient laws of Wales beyond the border.

One thing is certain : the Britons, who had enjoyed such prolonged intimacy with the Roman mind and institutions, had an immense advantage, as compared with the Angles and Saxons, in the performance of any such task as the compilation of a code of laws. The Britons were at the outset in possession of this advantage. The Anglo-Saxons, at the outset, were a rude and illiterate people. For many ages their only work was fighting. Until they were Christianized they had but a poor pretence to civilization. As they had absorbed large numbers—even whole States—of the Britons into their dominions, it was but natural that they should avail themselves of the legal

[1] *Rise and Progress of English Commonwealth*, pp. 30, 31.

customs already prevailing among that people, and which were superior to anything which they could be supposed to have transported with them from the wild regions of the Baltic and the Elbe.

Appropriation has always been a law of action with the Anglo-Saxon race : appropriation of the *best*, come whence it may. This has been the rule followed with respect to territory, language, population, laws. Nothing comes ill that answers a good purpose ; nothing is rejected for its foreign origin, its novelty, its apparent want of artistic harmony with things already appropriated. Two questions alone are asked : Will the thing be useful ? and : Is it obtainable ? The next step is action and acquisition. Out of many sources of greatness, which the English nation may claim, this unfettered spirit of trading for material and institutional gain is one of the chief.

The corroboratory evidence furnished by these few particulars touching English law may be very small ; but, so long as it adds something to the balance of probability, we care not to claim for it any more important function.

CHAPTER V.

THE EVIDENCE SUPPLIED BY THE PHYSICAL, MENTAL, AND MORAL QUALITIES OF THE ENGLISH.

WE have hitherto been ranging distant fields of inquiry; —now, we return home, and sit down by the hearth. It is to be hoped that the handfuls of produce we have gathered from the far-distant Celtic and Teutonic times and regions, and the larger results of our gleaning in the broad and fertile fields of British History and Celtic Philology, have been found to furnish a somewhat substantial treasury of evidence in favour of the position we have adopted—viz., that a large proportion of the blood of England is truly Celtic blood. Our next contribution of evidence is to be drawn from the personal qualities of the living Englishman himself. We must try to understand this complex entity, the authentic Englishman; taking him first as a whole, in his synthetic unity, and then, dissolving the bonds of cohesion, reducing him to his original elementary race constituents.

What, then, is the "Englishman," and whence did he proceed? To define him, draw a line around him, marking off all projecting angles, all furtively receding niches, and all points, at which he is alone occupant, and where neither Cymro, Saxon, nor Norman, in any of his essential traits, has the least chance of standing-room, is, indeed, a task impossible to perform. But, as in a rainbow we can tell where the red and where the yellow is, though we fail to put our mathematical finger on the point where it ceases to be, so we may be able approximately to define and distinguish the Englishman. But, to define the Englishman is to define the English nation, and a definition of the English nation will bring it into comparison with the ancient Teuton and Celt, as well as with the modern Teuton and Celt, and empower us to judge whether it most resembles the one or the other, or partly resembles both.

Our present chapter embraces two distinct branches of science—one referring to characteristics belonging to physical organization, the other to mental characteristics, and we shall briefly survey them in this order.

SECTION I.

Physical Characteristics of the English People.

Amongst the English are to be found specimens of every description of physiognomy, complexion, temperament, and cranial formation discoverable among all the European and Asiatic varieties of the race. The ethnological student, walking along one of the great thoroughfares of London —that "Babel" which forms, not the point of dispersion, but the point of junction of all incongruities—with a slight effort at abstraction, forgetting for the moment that all the busy myriads that hurry to and fro are veritable English people, with, of course, not a few distinctly marked visitors from foreign lands—might fancy that he had unconsciously entered some great "exhibition," where every typical human *physique*, profile, cranium, complexion under the sun, had been brought together for the inspection of the curious.[1]

---

[1] London, as Dr. Donaldson has remarked (*Cambr. Est.* p. 72), is a good speculum in which to view the whole people of England, for its

Complexions dark and light—faces round, oval, triangular —profiles perpendicular, angular, slanting—eyes black, blue, grey, brown, oblique as Chinese, large and dazzling as Iberian—hair white as flax, black as jet, red as fire, brown as copper, strong as bristles, fine as silk, lank, straight, curly; the high Caucasian brow, the low, retiring, animal pate, hardly deserving the name of forehead; the broad, thick, pugnacious head and neck; the projecting chin and heavy jaws; lips as large as negroes', small and delicate as an Italian Madonna's; noses as straight as Apollo's—as crooked as a son of Abraham's.

But all this disjointed heterogeneous crowd—so infallibly suggesting the idea of Babel—if it but speak, articulates only one language, and in its movements displays the one leading characteristic of Englishmen, take them in London, Calcutta, or elsewhere—earnest pursuit of some gainful, probably honourable calling, and unflagging resolution to get on and prosper.

If our abstracted observer visit Liverpool, Manchester, Birmingham, Bristol, the result will be nearly the same. Not precisely the same; for in the North, and in the West, a larger proportion will be visible of forms distinctly and prominently Celtic. In the North, too, there will be frequent appearances of the light *Scandinavian* complexion —permanent witnesses of the settlement of the Danes in Northumbria and Caledonia. But with all this, there will

population is drawn from all parts of the island. Our *Population Abstracts* (*Census*, 1861), prove that nearly *one-half* the inhabitants of the two metropolitan counties, Middlesex and Surrey, are born beyond the limits of those counties, the numbers being—*Middlesex*, born in the county, 1,307,648, born elsewhere, 898,837; *Surrey*, born in the county, 434,317, born elsewhere, 396,776; but since the time when these figures were taken the proportion of extraneous births has largely increased. For London proper, the proportion of home-births is greater, being in 1861 as follows: born in London, 1,741,177; born elsewhere, 1,062,812.

be infinite variety everywhere. Dark, light, and many in-
termediate complexions—every conceivable form of limb,
profile, and skull.

This strange and perplexing variety suggests one of the
chief sources of the strength, genius, and glory of England.
To use a somewhat strong figure, the blended rays have
flashed forth in light. The daring, the perseverance,
patient application, ingenuity, force of muscle, clearness
and grasp of intellect, wealth of fancy, flight of imagination,
humour, wit, drollery, and warm sympathetic emotion and
benevolence, which have made the English nation the
wonder and the envy of the world, come from that unexampled blending of races which is reflected in that motley
crowd. But not these alone, alas! appear. There are also
signs not a few of all that is feeble, base, wicked, and
miserable !

If our observer proceed to a centre of population less
affected by extraneous influences, and, therefore, ap-
proximating more nearly to the staminal type of the
British people proper—say of the time of Alfred—when the
Britons and the Anglo-Saxons had become pretty well
kneaded into a consistent mass—*ex. gr.*, if he go to
Winchester, Oxford, Reading, or Leicester, he will still,
indeed, find variety, but not the same crowding abundance
of it. He will see the Celtic and Teutonic races in their
chief features, very plainly depicted ; but will find a nearer
approach to unity and homogeneity than he could hope for
in the Strand or Cheapside.

Our supposed ethnological student will perhaps wish a
subject of greater simplicity—a sharper division of the
Celtic from the Teutonic features ; in other words, he will
be ready to witness the process of *analysing* the complex
Englishman, and inspecting microscopically the elementary parts of him. He will be inclined to go to Wales to

see some portions, and to the most sequestered parts of
Norfolk, Lincoln, or perhaps Denmark, to see the others.
If he will permit a caution from those who have been
to those same parts, on the same errand before him,
he may be informed that the step would be comparatively useless and disappointing—that, in fact, the pure
breed of Celt is now rarely to be found, even in Wales,
Cornwall, or the Highlands, and the pure Teuton never in
the British islands, or anywhere else. He must be content
to listen to descriptions of ancient writers, and to the
results of modern scientific research. These, if carefully
attended to, will tell him a good deal more respecting the
origin and constituent parts of the present English people
than he can learn from any number of School or other
Histories of England, even though of the approved and
established authority of Hume or Goldsmith.

What, then, according to early writers, were the distinguishing physical characteristics of the Celts and
Teutons of past ages, and what are the conclusions of
science respecting them now?

Space will admit of the treatment of only two leading
and testing characteristics—*complexion* and the *form of the
cranium*.

1. Complexion, or Hair Colour.

What is the testimony of ancient writers respecting the
complexion of the Gauls and Ancient Britons, or *Celts*, on
the one hand, and Old Germans, or *Teutons*, on the other?
The answer to this will help us in the analytic part of our
inquiry. We shall afterwards arrive at the synthesis in
the modern Englishman, and shall be able to judge how
far he, in his complex personality, represents one or other,
or both of these. The popular belief is, as already often
intimated, that the Englishman is a descendant direct of

the Saxons and Angles of Schleswig and Holstein—a belief as groundless and fallacious as ever easy credulity entertained, and capable of being in some measure corrected by the discussion of our present subject.

Let us premise that it is more than probable that the Greeks and Romans,[1] to whose writers we are indebted for certain minute descriptions of the personal characteristics of the ancient Teutons and Celts, were themselves of a prevailingly *dark* complexion. This was especially the case with the Romans. From Homer we gather that golden locks were held in high esteem, at least by the poet himself, but whether they prevailed among Argives or Trojans is not hence deducible. The probability is that they were exceptional.[2] Hence, according to the usual rule of setting a high value on that which is rare, their writers took especial notice of the light or "yellow" hair

[1] Latham's *Var. of Mankind*, p. 542.

[2] Mr. Gladstone, *Studies on Homer*, v. 1, p. 552, says: "Now the result of all that we have drawn from Homer thus far would be to connect the Celts with the Pelasgi, with Media, and with the low Iranian countries; the 'Germans' with the Helli and with Persia. Observe, then, how the differences noted by Strabo between Celts and Germans correspond with the Homeric differences between Helli and Pelasgi. And, lastly, as to the auburn hair, which was with Homer in such esteem, Menelaus is ξανθός (*passim*); so is Meleager (Il. ii. 642); so is Rhadamanthus (Od. iv. 564); Agamede (Il. xi. 739); Ulysses (Od. xiii. 399, 431); lastly, Achilles (Il. i. 197). But never once, I think, does Homer bestow this epithet upon a Pelasgian name. None of the Trojan family, so renowned for beauty, are ξανθοί; none of the chiefs, not even Euphorbus, of whose flowing hair the poet has given us so beautiful, and even so impassioned, a description (Il. xvii. 51). Nothing Pelasgian, but Ceres (Il. v. 500), the καλλιπλόκαμος, is admitted to the honour of the epithet. It could hardly be denied to the goddess of the ruddy harvest,

'Excutit et flavas aurea terra comas.'—*Propertius*.

Now Tacitus, describing the Germani, gives them 'truces et Coerulei oculi, *rutilae comae*, magna corpora.' *Germ.* iv."

of the Germans, and of the less light hair of the Gauls and Britons, as a feature of comeliness. The authors of the *Crania Britannica*[1] say rightly : " The prevailing colour of hair among the Romans was that which is called black, yet it was not universally dark even, for blond or fair hair sometimes occurred, and perhaps, from being rare, was esteemed beautiful." To the same effect is the language of Dr. Arnold.[2] " The Greek and Roman writers invariably describe the Gauls as a tall and *light-haired* race, in comparison with their own countrymen; but it has been maintained that there must be some confusion in these descriptions between the Gauls and the Germans, inasmuch as the Keltic nations now existing are all dark-haired. *Compared with the Italians*, it would be certainly true that the Keltic nations were, generally speaking, light-haired and tall." Dr. Latham's opinion on the Roman complexion, guardedly expressed, is to the same effect. "At the same time the description of Tacitus[3] is no over-statement, since we must not only remember that he wrote as an Italian, accustomed to dark-skins and black hair," &c. So great, indeed, was their admiration of the German red tints, that the ladies of Rome, in their enthusiasm, hesitated not to have recourse to a colouring mixture in order to give their slighted raven locks the hues of aristocratic German yellow! The fever, swelling to the height of the silliest fashion, had gone all abroad, even in the ranks of professing Christian ladies, as far as Africa, and in that quarter called forth the following severe castigation from the faithful outspoken Tertullian : — I observe certain ladies who change the colour of their hair with the crocus (saffron). They are ashamed of their own nation, because they were not born Germans or Gauls;

---

[1] Davis and Thurnam's *Cran. Brit.* p. 24.
[2] *Hist. of Rome*, i. 530, 531.   [3] *Germania of Tacitus*, p. 31.

and thus change their country by their (coloured) hair!"[1]
We need not render the remainder of the invective;
the language used is strong. Possibly the ladies of
England, who are said to have a weakness now-a-days in
favour of yellow hair, might hear of it in church in the
nervous language of the African presbyter!

Owing to this widely prevalent custom of colouring
the hair in ancient times, it must be confessed that the
natural colour of a people cannot always be gathered with
certainty from the descriptions of historians. Nor have we
a more reliable guide in the works of the old painters.
These gave their figures, of whatever age or nation, the
complexion which was fashionable in their own day. There
can be little doubt but that the *Italians* and *Jews* have
always been, as they now are, prevailingly dark. The
painter, however, in his work, takes the liberty to follow
his own or his age's ideal of beauty. Hence, *ex. gr.* the
celebrated Italian *Botticelli* (A.D. 1473—1515) in his famous
works. *The Feast in the Forest, Summer, Spring, The Marriage Festival;* and Raphael, in his *Holy Family*, give the
hair of all the figures as truly *xanthous*.[2]

Still, while the historian often wrote according to the
artificial appearance, and the artist painted as his own
imagination, or the fashion in vogue, dictated, the historical
testimony left us is so abundant, varied, and apparently
prosaic and literal, that we cannot hesitate, upon the
whole, in receiving it as true to facts.

Our first authority is Tacitus. When Tacitus speaks of

---

[1] " Video quasdam et capillum croco vertere. Pudet eas etiam
nationis suæ, quod non Germanæ aut Gallæ procreatæ sint : ita patriam
capillo transferunt. Male ac pessime sibi auspicantur flammeo capite,
et decorum putant quod inquinant. Quis decor cum injuria ? Quae
cum inmunditiis pulchritudo ? Crocum capiti suo mulier Christiana
ingeret ut in aram ? " &c. *De Cultu*, ii. 6.

[2] See the paintings in the South Kensington Museum.

"Germans," let us bear in mind that he speaks of a people whose country comprehended all that wide region stretching from Bohemia to the Baltic northwards, and from Poland, westwards, to the Cimbric Chersonese, the cradle, therefore, of the Teutonic tribes who conquered Britain, and whose children the modern English are popularly supposed to be.

Now Tacitus tells us distinctly that the Germans were a *red* or *reddish* haired people ; and he goes so far as to say that they *all* bore this character—a comprehensiveness of statement which we may, at least, understand as signifying that the general run of Germans were red haired. His words are : " Unde habitus quoque corporum, quanquam in tanto hominum numero, idem *omnibus*, truces et cœrulei oculi, *rutilæ comæ*, magna corpora et tantum ad impetum valida." [1] " Hence (because they bore a distinct national character), although so numerous, they have the same personal appearance, and they have all fierce blue eyes, *red* (or yellow) *hair*, and large frames powerful for attack."

Juvenal was a poet, but poetic *allusion* is often the best history. Alluding to the same peculiarity of the German complexion, he says :—

> "Cærula quis stupuit Germani lumina, *flavam*
> Cæsariem," &c. ? [2]

Calpurnius Flaccus calls the Germans a people "*red* in their personal appearance" : *rutilæ* sunt Germanæ vultus, &c.[3] This, it is true, may be said to mean only ruddy, healthy, of fresh colour ; but, interpreted by the descriptions of other authors, it must be understood to mean more. And he is evidently referring to natural complexion, not to an artificially-produced appearance through painting ; for, he has just said that a peculiar aspect belongs by nature

---

[1] *Germania*, iv. Ed. Bekkeri, 1831.   [2] *Satir*. xiii. v. 162.
[3] *Declamat*. ii. Ed. Gronovii.

to every people (sua cuique genti etiam facies manet); and adds, that all are not tinged of like colour, but diversely, each according to its own peculiarities; (Non eodem omnes colore tinguntur. Diversa sunt mortalium genera; nemo tamen est suo generi dissimilis).

Strabo informs us that the Germans chiefly differed from the Celts (Κέλται, as he called the Gauls), by their greater stature and more xanthous hair. But of this again.

There can be no question, therefore, that in the opinion of both Greek and Roman writers, both poets and historians, the Germans of antiquity were a fair-complexioned, *blue-eyed, red, reddish*, or *yellow haired* people. Now Baron Bunsen had a little difficulty about this matter; and it so happens that his very difficulty turns eventually to the advantage of our argument. He informed Dr. Prichard that he had "often looked in vain among his Prussian countrymen for the auburn or golden locks, and the light cerulean eyes of the old Germans, and never verified the picture given by the ancients of his countrymen until he visited *Scandinavia ; there he found himself surrounded by the Germans of Tacitus.*"[1] Bunsen, probably enough, saw a smaller proportion of Prussians xanthous than corresponded with the strong description of Tacitus; but most observers in England know that the Germans who settle in this country are more frequently marked by fair, reddish, or dun-coloured hair, than are the English, and those of us who have spent any time in Germany, have seen that the same approximately xanthous complexion is there prevalent which is represented by the German residents of London or Manchester. The hair colour of the people alone tells you that you are out of England. The same dry, unclear complexion of skin—the same dun, third-part black, third-part red, third-part yellow, hair, is seen

---

[1] Prichard's *Natural Hist. of Man*, p. 197. Ed. 1843. Also *Phys. Hist. of Mankind*, iii. 192.

everywhere. The colour in the majority of instances is so peculiar that while you cannot describe it, you unfailingly recognise and classify it as "German :" it is a dingy tan produced nowhere but under the German sky—a kind of compromise or transition colour, which has departed from the regular red of Tacitus's German, and is now apparently on its way towards a higher "development" under the influence of an old Celtic and Sclavonic admixture.

But the fact that Bunsen found in the North of Europe, in Scandinavia, the country of the Danes and Normans (from whom William *Rufus* came), and the seat of the early Angles (for Denmark was in blood and genius truly Scandinavian)—the very characteristics described by Tacitus, is an interesting one. In those northern parts the early race has escaped the effects of admixture, has preserved its pristine features with greater completeness than was possible to the dwellers in less Northern and central Germany. The testimony of the acute and philosophic Bunsen is thus a strong support to that of Tacitus and other ancient historians, to the effect that the Ancient Germans were a *red* or *reddish* haired people.

But now comes the question : do the *English people* who are said to have descended from those Ancient Germans, display these same characteristics of race ? Are they prevailingly *blue-eyed* and *red*, or *yellow-haired?* Nothing of the sort. We have only to open our eyes to see the contrary. Some ladies by their skilful toilet-dyeing, testify to the contrary ! To become red or xanthous now-a-days requires some outlay of money—much of time and ingenuity. So rare is the genuine red, that it attracts attention, in a crowd, on the street. Dr. Prichard, who emphatically held that the modern English are darker than their supposed German ancestors, although he had his own way of accounting for the fact, was doubtless nearly right when he said that eight out of every ten of the inhabitants of England are dark-complexioned.[1] Either, therefore, the Ancient Germans are not correctly described by history, or the English are not descendants of the Ancient Germans. But, if history of the kind we have quoted is to be rejected, a new historic criticism and basis for a knowledge of the old world must be invented ; the utter uselessness of all existing records of the past must be demonstrated ; and history must be made to mean nothing more than the private reminiscences of each individual, as furnishing evidence to himself alone, of things which he himself has seen.

It is unquestionably our fortune, as English, to be so far from fair-haired, that we are at the nearest possible approach to what Prichard denominates the *Melanic* type of complexion. This has been made plain by experiment. In twenty large assemblages of English persons of both sexes, and all ages—and a person in childhood is known to be more fair-haired than he proves to be when adult— where 10,000 complexions have been marked for the purposes of this work, not one-fourth of the number were either red, reddish, or yellow-haired. The following tables contain an approximate exhibition of the general result :[2]

In London.

TOTAL OBSERVED.	BLACK AND BROWN.	LIGHT AUBURN.	FAIR.	RED.
6,000	4,500	1,000	350	150

North of England.

TOTAL.	BLACK AND DARK.	LIGHT AUBURN.	FAIR.	RED.
5,000	3,550	930	360	160

---

[1] *Phys. Hist. of Mankind*, iii. 19.

[2] The observations made for these tables were suggested by Prichard's *Physical History of Mankind*, iii. 119, &c.

This result is given as an approximation to actual fact. But the process is at the command of any one, and there is no need to depend on others' testimony. It is believed, however, that the effect of observation will in all cases generally harmonize with the above figures, with the allowance of a small margin of diversity for different parts of the kingdom, and the different conceptions observers may entertain of what is meant by red, fair, auburn, dark brown. Our tables show that the red and light colours prevail in the North of England, where the influence of the Scandinavian settlements in Caledonia and Northumbria have been felt, more than in London. It is highly probable that observations in the West of England, or in Wales, would give a larger proportion of *black* and " brown " than in London, the Celtic stock being in those parts less affected by admixture with the light Saxon.

Now, as race is proved by science and history to be, not absolutely unchangeable, but, on the whole, if kept free from admixture, permanent in its chief characteristics, it is incumbent on those who believe in the Anglo-Saxon derivation of the English people to explain, and account for this strange and wide departure in complexion from the original type. How have we English become a generally *dark-haired* race? Even granting that from difference of habit, town life, nature of employment, and food, some slight variation may have been caused in the complexion, as Dr. Prichard believes;[1] and that thus the Germans and the English alike have grown darker,

---

[1] *Natural History of Man*, p. 179. See also a Paper by Dr. J. Beddoe, *On the Permanence of Anthropological Types*, published in the Memoirs of the Anthropological Society of London. Vol. ii. p. 37. As far as town life is concerned, Dr. Beddoe is not of opinion that it has any influence in darkening the hair. In some cases, as in Somersetshire, he has found the natives of towns to be lighter than those of the surrounding country. P. 42. At the same time, his observations quite confirm the opinion "that the invading Teutons were fairer than the prior inhabitants " of the parts of Britain to which he refers.

much has yet to be explained in the wide divergence observed. Besides, on that theory, the people of Wales, as well as others, ought to be growing darker; dwellers in towns ought to be distinguished for their jet; and the negro race, from age to age ranging the open hills, desert, and jungle, ought to be found something else than black.

Recurring to our question we again ask: How have the English become a *dark-haired* race? Is there any way of solving the difficulty besides the too usual, but always unsatisfactory one of cutting the knot? What help does science proffer? We are a scientific people, or are in process of becoming such. We have a British Association for the advancement of Science. Can we advance the science of our own ethnological relations? The traditional ethnology which now rules, and which is ever iterating the dogma that the English are descended from the Germans, or, which, as intended, is the same thing, from the Anglo-Saxons, is in direct conflict with the findings of history, physiology, the natural history of man, and *ethnology*. Some of our men of science delicately and apologetically hint that perhaps the Ancient Britons have had some little hand in the matter of beclouding the bright gold of our Saxon complexion; and an occasional "historian" when he wants to account for so many slaves in Anglo-Saxon kingdoms is willing to venture a guess that they *might* be Britons. But on the whole we cling to our ancient faith, and allow science and history to go for nothing.

There is one hypothesis at hand to account for our complexional change—an hypothesis, too, which, if we mistake not, both history and physical science justify: The people of England have abandoned the "fierce blue eyes" and "red locks" of ancient times in favour of the hazel, brown, and black eyes, and the brown and black hair, through some decided modification of race relation. Has this modification been occasioned by contact with the Celtic aborigines of Britain? The affirmative of this seems to be the honest utterance of modern science.[1]

But are we sure that the Celts, and amongst them the Ancient Britons, were themselves of dark complexion? This we have hitherto of necessity assumed, and must now briefly prove.

The Welsh of to-day, though not free from admixture— with Flemings and Norsemen in Glamorgan and Pembroke, &c., with Iberians or Celtiberians—a modified form of their own stock—in the whole district embraced by ancient Siluria, and with English more or less all around the Principality, are on the whole the purest Celts we have in Briton (though by no means so unmixed as their cousins in Ireland), and are a prevailingly dark-haired people.[2] They were so in the middle ages; they were so in the times of the Romans.[3]

[1] The eminent Frenchman, M. Edwards, says that while the great linguist Mezzofanti, recognised in the *irregular pronunciation* of English the influence of the Welsh language, he, M. Edwards, saw in the complexion and *features* of the English people the images of the Ancient Britons. *Des Caract. Physiolog. des Races Humaines*, p. 102 et seq.

[2] The following incident came to our knowledge as this edition was passing through the press :—At a musical gathering of the Welsh in London, at Christmas, 1873, an English friend of the author was greatly struck with the almost universally dark complexion of the persons present, and casually mentioned the circumstance, being at the time unaware of the doctrine and argument of this work. Assemblies in Wales invariably produce the same impression.

[3] Tennyson confirms the opinion that the old Britons, as a rule, were dark. His works have done not a little to cast an air of unreality about the story of King Arthur, even those parts of it which are manifestly historical; but he has often managed by his allusions to give as correct representations as if he were writing history. Thus he makes Queen Bellicent, speaking of Arthur and his race, say :

> "Dark my mother was, in eyes and hair,
> And dark in hair and eyes am I, and dark
> Was Gorlois; yea, and dark was Uther, too,
> Well-nigh to blackness; but this king [Arthur] is fair
> Beyond the race of Britons and of men."—*Holy Grail*, p. 20.

No one can observe the names of persons scattered through the ancient records of Wales, the *Mabinogion*, the *Triads*, the *Boncdd y Saint* (genealogy of the saints), the *Bruts*, the *Laws*, &c.; and the names of families, chiefs, bards, &c.; without observing a phenomenon which the records of no other people perhaps so amply exhibit. We mean the frequent occurrence of names taken from the *colour of the hair.* It was a principle of name-giving with the Welsh to embody in the name (or surname, or nick-name) the personal quality most observable in the man, or the most marked circumstance connected with his history. The principle was one indeed followed by other nations, by the Teutonic nations, by the Romans. William I. was William the *Bastard;* William II., his son, was William *Rufus;* John was John *Lackland; Caligula* the emperor was known by this nickname (from *caligæ,* the foot-dress of the common soldiers) which he received when a boy, though his proper name was Caius Cæsar. The Welsh had a liking so deeply inwoven into their nature for marking personal peculiarities by names, that they have not to this day altogether abandoned it. In some districts it develops a vicious habit of using nicknames; but more generally it is a traditional semi-literary semi-heraldic custom, closely allied, however, in its seriousness to the serio-comic, and frequently in healthy keeping with the quiet humorousness of the race. Vortigern is doomed for ever to be known by the alliterative nickname, Gwrtheyrn *Gwrthcncn* (of per-verse lips), because he invited the Saxons (who indeed required no invitation) over to Britain, and put them in the way of winning the land. Warriors are often complimented for their strength, as Caradog *Vreich-vras* (of the large or strong arm); good princes for their moral qualities, as Ivor *Hael* (the generous), Hywel *Dda* (the good). Among the idiosyncracies registered, as we have said, the colour of hair is very frequently found.

The two colours most attended to are *black* and *red*, but with a considerable preponderance in favour of the former. Bards, when distinguished by their complexion, are almost always black or red, *du* or *coch*. Thus Gwilym *Ddu* (William the black); Llywelyn *Goch* (Llewelyn the red.) The softening of the initial consonant of the qualifying word is always observable—*d* into *dd*, or soft *lh*, and *c* into *g*, &c. Along with "black" and "red," we occasionally meet with "white" (*gwyn*), "grey" (*lhwyd*), but never, that we remember, with "yellow."

Among the "bards" registered in the *Myvyrian Archaiology of Wales* between A.D. 1280 and 1330, there are six bearing names of colour: four "blacks," one "red," and one "grey"—Gwilym *Ddu*, Llywelyn *Ddu*, Goronwy *Ddu*, Dafydd *Ddu* (black), Llewelyn *Goch* (red), and Iorwerth *Lhwyd* (grey).

In the registers of the Welsh men-at-arms who followed *Yvain de Galles* (Owen of Wales), *Jehan Wn* (John Wynn), and *Robin ab Lhwydin* (Robin the son of the little grey man), to France in the 14th century, we find several persons distinguished by the colour of their hair; but perhaps the soldier's partiality for the "red" led some to assume an epithet which their physical aspect but approximately justified—at all events, although this indicates but little, in these lists the reds are nearly as numerous as the blacks.

On the whole, general indications of this kind exist in sufficient number to show that the dark complexion was prevalent among the Welsh of the middle ages; and we all know that such is the case in our own day. If persons of royal rank, like Boadicea, or others of commanding position, who were not positively dark, or who fell in with the fashion of imitating the admired Germans by using saffron, are described in rhetorical phrase as "golden-haired," we know what value is to be attached to the description.

But now as to the complexion of the *Ancient Britons*. Of them, specifically, in this matter few notices remain, but there are a few, and these are suggestive, and as the Gauls and the Britons were identical in race, we can receive the description of one as applicable to all.

Tacitus,[1] speaking of the Caledonii, a people largely impregnated, be it remembered, with Scandinavian blood, says they had yellow hair *(rutilæ comæ)*; but as, with the eye of a keen observer, he sees in their complexions and stature signs of derivation from the Germans *(Germanicam originem)*, he probably was writing only of the seacoast settlers, who, at different times, had crossed over from North Germany and Scandinavia.

Of the *Silures* of South Wales, who, whether or not of Iberian race, were certainly more genuine Celts than the others—Tacitus, as already mentioned, says, that they had dark embrowned complexions *(colorati vultus)*, and that those nearest Gaul resembled the Galli. We must then ask, what as to complexion were the Galli?

With respect to the Gauls in the matter of complexion, it is a significant fact that in order to gain a high degree of xanthousness, they were obliged to have recourse to dyeing. Livy writes that they had, not *rutilæ comæ*, red hair, but *rutilatæ comæ*, "reddened hair." Most Continental scholars translate *rutilatæ* here in the light of the known custom among the Gauls, by the equivalents "reddened," or "made red": thus Heusinger has "geröthetes haar"; Schwartzkopf (1593), "rot gefärbt har"; and

---

[1] *Vita. Agric.* 11.

Guerni, "chevelure roussie." Somehow, the ancients had a liking for red hair. The Gauls possibly displayed this weakness under Germanic influence. A fashion fever had laid hold upon them. They had learned and had seen that the great and terrible nations of the Germans had by nature flashing blue eyes, and glowing red hair. How could they be equal to the Germans, and strike terror into their enemies by the fierceness of their looks, as well as participate in the admiration which all surrounding tribes felt for the Germans? The Germans were red by the gift of nature; they, to whom nature had been more niggard in this case, would make up the deficiency with *paint!* So they became a people possessing, not *rutilæ comæ*, red or ruddy hair, but *rutilatæ comæ*, hair made or *coloured red*. Would any people whose complexion and hair were by nature light and red, buy saffron to paint themselves so?[1]

We now recur to Strabo's words, already mentioned, where he said that the Gauls were not so red as the Germans, or, which is the same thing, that the Germans were redder than the Gauls. The Gauls' attempts at colouring were not quite successful; the disguise was too

---

[1] We have pleasure in giving here the opinion of a very acute ethnological observer, the late Rev. Dr. Rowland Williams, who, in a written note upon this passage—the original MS. having been submitted to his inspection before printing—says :—" I rather hold that Northmen, Germans, Gauls, were all light, or xanthous—the Northman lighter, Gaul yellower, German redder; but I still hold that the South of France with its Aquitanian, *i.e.* Iberian, blood, and with its warm, vinous climate, transformed the Gallic race, and we ascribe to the Celts, as Celtic, features which they only adopted from older or more southern races. Are not such characteristics generated *in situ*, and not merely inherited?" Many other valuable notes by the same hand were left on the MS., some of which have in substance been incorporated with the text.

transparent; they were still held to be a darker people
than the Germans.

But we have another piece of information by Strabo
which is very useful in this place. While the Gauls were
less xanthous than the Germans, he tells us that the
Britons were still less xanthous than the Gauls. " The
men are taller than the Celtæ (Gauls), *with hair less yellow*,
and looser built in their persons."[1]   The Britons were
therefore known to this acute and accurate writer to be
two degrees darker than the Germans; and Prichard has
been led by the circumstance to make this emphatic
observation : "The difference [between Britons and Gauls]
must have been strongly marked in order to have drawn
the attention of a writer who seldom takes notice of
physical characteristics. It appears, then, that the Britons
were a darker race than the Celts of the Continent."[2]
Prichard had thus advanced so far as to recognize and
declare the fact of the deeper tinge of the old Britons.
He had also, as we have seen, declared that the English,
unlike their reputed Germanic ancestors, are a race dark
in the proportion of *eighty per cent*. And yet he seems
never to have perceived how the old British hue could
have imparted itself to the modern English. This, however, was seen by later, and especially by Continental
naturalists—Pruner Bey, one of the best scientific writers
on the human hair, had, in 1864, come to this conclusion :
" Cross-breeds are recognisable by the fusion and juxta-
position of the characters inherent in the hair of their
parents. Whilst the red colour forms on the one hand,
as it were, a bond of union between the most disputed

---

[1] Οἱ δὲ ἄνδρες εὐμηκέστεροι τῶν Κελτῶν εἰσί, καὶ ἧσσον ξανθότριχες, χαυνότεροι δὲ τοῖς σώμασι. *Geogr.* lib. iv.   See also in *Monument. Hist. Brit.* vol. i. p. vi.

[2] *Phys. Hist. of Mankind*, iii. 192.

races, the *brown* colour may be considered as establishing
the transition between the light and the darkest shades."[1]
M. Pouchet adopted the same view, and published it in
his well-known work on the plurality of the human race.[2]

Suetonius says that Caligula compelled certain Gauls to
redden and let loose their hair, as well as learn the German
language, and assume barbarian names. "Coegitque non
tantum rutilare et submittere comam, sed et sermonem
Germanicam addiscere et nomina barbarica ferre."[3] This
were idle work, in the matter of *rutilare*, if their hair
was already red. At least these particular Gauls neither
had red hair by nature, nor had yet learned the art of
painting it.

Modern ethnology pronounces the Celts of the Silurian
branch "*black* in eyes and hair; complexion dark, with a
ruddy tinge."[4] "But," we may be told, "the Silurians
may have been Iberians." Yes, but the Siluro-Iberians
may also have been Celt-Iberians.

· Need more be said to prove that the Celts of Gaul and
Britain were darker than the Germans or Anglo-Saxons?

The conclusion we arrive at is, that the dark hair and
complexion of the modern English, amounting, at least, to
an average of *four-fifths*, or 80 per cent. of the population,
the proportion approved by Prichard, are owing in the
main to admixture on a large scale with the *Ancient
Britons*.

2. The form of the cranium.

It is not unusual to consider the stature, the physiognomy, the form of the hand and foot, as distinguishing
marks of race, but we omit these as too indeterminate.

The attention bestowed of late years upon the study of

[1] *Anthrop. Review*, Feb. 1864, pp. 23. 24.
[2] *Pluralité des Races Humaines.* Engl. Edit., p. 104.
[3] *Vita Calig.*, c. 47.   [4] Latham's *Varieties of Man*, p. 530.

the human skull, has been fruitful in most valuable results. A classification has been established which forms the basis of all approved comparison and reasoning on the subject. This classification is at least of some use in the present case, although it has by no means been satisfactorily shown that cranial measurements are of all the value which some have ascribed to them in this argument. As in phrenology, so here. The study of the cranium renders a safe foundation for certain general conclusions, though it fail in the minuter details.

It has been ascertained that a certain form of skull distinguishes each great variety of the race; that savage races have a form of head which separates them from the civilized; and that the most cultivated nations, by reason of their finer cranial development, are easily classified together. The influence of culture goes so far as to bring the skulls of different races into near approximation to each other, and it has been ascertained that the most advanced nations have a form of skull more approaching the *long oval* than the " square," or roundish, or short oval. " The most civilized races," says Prichard, "those who live by agriculture, and the arts of cultivated life, all the most intellectually improved nations of Europe and Asia, have a shape of the head which differs from both the forms above-mentioned" (the Australian and Mongolian). " The characteristic form of the skull among these nations may be termed oval or elliptical."[1]

Referring to the study of ancient skulls discoverable in pre-historic barrow-tombs in Denmark, Britain, and other parts, as means of judging of the primeval inhabitants, the same excellent writer says : " There seems to be good reason to believe that by a collection of skulls and skeletons from these different sets of barrows, an historical series

[1] *Natural History of Man*, p. 108.

may be established, each set displaying the remains of the races of people by whom they were erected."[1] The results of the Rev. Canon Greenwell's examinations of early British barrow-tombs on the Yorkshire Wolds have not yet been presented to us except in somewhat brief newspaper reports. They may be expected to throw much light upon the prevailing form of the Ancient British cranium, and to assist in testing the value of Dr. Thurnam's theory, which, as yet, is quite unsettled, and which affirms a coincidence almost too singular to be true, namely, that the skulls and the barrows in which they are found are of corresponding form—"long barrows, long skulls; round barrows, round or short skulls."[2]

Much of the work thus suggested by Prichard has now been performed both in Scandinavia and Britain, and the result, though not free from perplexities, yields on the whole a substantial aid to science. The most eminent Ethnologists, Palæontologists, and Anatomists, nearly coincide in the opinion that the typical *Celtic* and *Ancient British* skull is elongated—*long oval*; and that the typical *German* and Scandinavian skull, both ancient and modern, is not elongated, but rather spheroidal, or *short-oval*—"roundish," "broad and short," "square." This, however, is by no means the universal view. Dr. Barnard Davis, an eminent practical enquirer, has found among crania, considered ancient British, so many short and roundish, that he considered this the typical form. He says:—"We cannot assert that the Ancient Britons were brachycephalic, but only that they were brachycephalous. . . . . This was the prevailing type of their skull."— *Crania Britan.* p. 232.

The majority of writers competent to declare an opinion,

---

[1] *Natural History of Man*, p. 192.
[2] See *Journ. Anthrop. Society*, 1867, p. cxxiv.

however, are inclined to declare the British skull, and more generally the Celtic skull, oval and long, rather than brachycephalic. But to all rules there are exceptions: otherwise the science of probabilities would have no existence. It is not meant that among crania recognised as *Ancient British* or as "Celtic," there are none found which approach to the short oval, or rounded pyramidal form; or that among the latter, there are none of the long oval form. That were contrary to fact, and contrary to the known results which the freedom, exercised by nature, everywhere produces. All that is meant is, that careful induction on the whole sanctions the general principle that Ancient British and Celtic skulls are *long-oval* (dolichocephalous); and that Ancient German and Scandinavian skulls are short-oval or roundish (brachycephalous). We supply an illustration of both forms in Fig. i. and Fig. ii., following Lyell[1]; and also an European and Greek head (Nos. iii. and iv.) from Prichard[2], which are of the same class of form as the Celtic. The Greek profile and cranium, high and well rounded in forehead, of medium length, and good breadth, are usually considered the most regular and beautiful in form of all.

As to the form of head prevalent among the Greeks and Romans, ancient writers having left us no descriptions, we are obliged to rely upon the testimony of sepulchral remains, judging as well as we may, whether such and such remains are Greek, or Roman, according to the various accompanying signs. Pruner Bey considers that the Roman form is satisfactorily settled as oval or dolichocephalic, when viewed from above appearing arched and elongated, with a front almost upright. "La forme du crâne Romain est une des mieux arrêties. C'est ici le cas de dire: qui en a vu un, les a vu tous. Crane ovale,

---

[1] *Elements of Geology*, 1865.   [2] *Nat. Hist. of Man.*

ANCIENT GERMAN SKULL.

(Denmark)

FIG. I.

FIG. III.

EUROPEAN TYPICAL SKULL

ANCIENT "CELTIC" SKULL.

(Denmark)

FIG. II.

FIG. IV

GREEK SKULL.

dolichocéphale, orthognathe ; vu d'en haut, peu voûté et d'une forme carrée un peu allongée. Front presque droit, large et peu marqué."[1] His opinion of the Greek cranium was that its form, equally with the Roman, was oval, but differing more from the Roman in the length and height of the posterior part than in breadth. " Comparé au crâne Romain, le Grec, également de forme ovale, diffère par plus de longueur et de hauteur dans la partie postérieure et par moins de largeur."

The Danish and Scandinavian sepulchres yield two types of skull—the roundish and the oval, and there is room for a difference of opinion as to their comparative antiquity ; but there is no difference as to their classification. They are believed to belong to the successive periods of stone, bronze, and iron. " In the antecedent era of stone, the primitive population of the North are said to have buried their dead in sepulchral vaults, carefully constructed of large blocks of undressed stone.[2] From such burial places many sculls have been obtained by Scandinavian ethnologists which show that the ancient race had small heads, remarkably *rounded in every direction*, but with a facial angle tolerably large, and a well developed forehead."[3]

Some of these rounded skulls are found, according to Dr. Thurnam, one of the authors of the *Crania Britannica,* among the properly Celtic, oval skulls, in the ancient tombs of France[4] ; and these, with similar ones, found in Ireland and Scotland, according to the Swedish ethnologist, Retzius, are "so like those of the modern Lap-

[1] *Bulletins de la Soc. d'Anthrop. de Paris,* Jan., 1866.

[2] See, for a full account of these burial places, Worsaae's *Primeval Antiquities of Denmark,* pp. 76—115. London, 1849.

[3] Lyell, *Elements of Geology,* ed. 1865, p. 113.

[4] *Mem. Anthrop. Soc.,* i. 135.

landers, as to have suggested the idea, that the latter were the last survivors of the stone period in the North of Europe." [1]

Retzius, however, we must mention, gives it as his opinion, that the earliest barrow or stone immured skulls of Denmark, are *Celtic;* and these skulls are *oval.* He also calls the "long oval skull" of the modern French and English, "the real Celtic"; and the "shorter oval," with more protuberant sides, which he also observed in the same countries, he terms "Norman, and nearly related to the German." [2]

As is well-known by all versed in the subject, Continental anthropologists, almost without exception, agree that the typical Celtic skull is *long oval.* Retzius, of Stockholm, has been cited. For many years the leading French naturalists have been on the same side. De Belloguet, Pruner Bey, Broca, Edwards, may be mentioned. Von Baer, of St. Petersburg, is of the same opinion. The eminent American craniologist, Morton, firmly held, and illustrated with infinite labour, in the *Crania Americana,* the view that the Celts were dolichocephalous; and Dr. Daniel Wilson has powerfully advocated the same doctrine. In short, scarcely a distinguished name among craniologists, except Dr. Thurnam, holds to the contrary.

The two following positions with regard to the Teutonic skull seem to be pretty well established :

1. The typical German skull is the broad and short oval.

2. A decided resemblance exists between the old Anglo-

---

[1] *Ibid,* p. 113.

[2] *Ethnologische Schriften,* p. 64, "Ich fand die folgenden drei Formen in beiden Ländern gemeinschaftlich, aber in ungleichen Verhältnissen vorkommend: 1. Die runde Form, &c. 2. Eine lange, ovale Form, *die wahre Celtische.* 3. Eine kürzere ovale Form, mit gewölbteren Seiten, welche die *Normandische,* nahe verwandt mit der *Germanischen,* ist."

Saxon skulls found in the burial grounds of England, and the typical German skull.

We are now, then, in a position to state, without presuming too much, that modern science on the whole, is in favour of the conclusion, that Celtic sculls, including Ancient British, are of the *long oval* shape ; and that Teutonic skulls, including German and real Anglo-Saxon, are of the roundish, spheroidal, or *short oval*, shape.

But, then, what of the modern Celtic, and the modern English ? Our whole labour would be useless without a comparison of its results with the English cranium. Something, at least, although not all that we could wish, may be learnt from this comparison.

Now, it cannot well be questioned, that the prevalent form of head found in Wales, in Ireland, and in the Celto-English districts of Cumberland, Somerset, Devon, and Cornwall, is *long oval*, and that the prevalent form found throughout England generally, is *long oval* also. There seems to be no visible difference. In North Wales, in Anglesey more especially, there occur frequent instances of a high round head—the result, probably, of Danish admixture ; and in the South, in Pembrokeshire, colonised by Danes, Normans and Flemings, the same phenomenon is visible ; but taking Wales throughout, the prevailing head form is long oval.

That the general form of the skull in England is long oval need hardly be proved. On this point, in confirmation of our own experience, and of the prevalent opinion of English and French naturalists, we have the result of Retzius's enquiries into the subject. " During an excursion in Great Britain in 1855," he writes, " I was able to satisfy myself anew that the dolichocephalic form is predominant in England proper, in Wales, in Scotland, and in Ireland. Most of the dolichocephali of these countries

have the hair black, and are very similar to Celts."[1]
Retzius's judgment is justified by every one capable of
observing. Shorter in the main than the ancient *Celtic*,
and perhaps on an average very slightly shorter than the
modern Welsh, it is still far from being the "square,"
broad, or globular German or Scandinavian head.

How are we to explain this phenomenon? ⁂ How have
the descendants of the "square" headed, stern, pugnacious Saxons, become in the real, as they undoubtedly
always have been in the figurative sense of the word,
" long-headed"? We venture to answer, from the preceding findings of scientific and antiquarian research,
that they have become possessors of skulls of the *Celtic*
type *by extensive amalgamation with the Celtic race*. The
eminent writer, Dr. Daniel Wilson, as long ago as 1863,
embodied this idea in the following emphatic words :
"The insular Anglo-Saxon race in the Anglian and Saxon
districts " [as distinguished from Scotland] " deviates from
its Continental congeners, as I conceive, mainly by reason
of a large intermixture of Celtic blood traceable to the
inevitable intermarriage of invading colonists chiefly
male, with the British women. But if the Celtic head be
naturally a short one" [a notion he is combating], " the
tendency of such admixture of races should have been to
shorten the hybrid Anglo-Saxon skull, whereas it is essentially longer than the Continental Germanic type."[2] We
do not question but that this junction may to some extent
have taken place in the Cimbric Chersonese—probability
lies strong in favour of such a supposition, and that the
Celtic form as well as the Teutonic became subject through

[1] *Archives des Sciences Physiques*, &c. Geneva, 1860. See also Dr.
Wilson's Paper, *Anthrop. Rev. of London*, iii. 61.

[2] *Prehist. Annals of Scotland*, 2nd edition, 1863, i. 278. See also an
Article by the same Author in the *Canadian Journal*, Nov. 1864, reprinted in *Anthrop Rev.* of London, Feb. 1865.

this junction to modification, presenting thenceforth more freely the variety of "long" and "short" skulls, which Dr. Thurnam has found so puzzling, and which has given origin to his theory of a two-fold type of cranium representing two different waves and periods of early inhabitants—but the process must have mainly taken place on British ground.

On this whole question scientific research has yet much light to throw. Many patient inquirers must institute investigations, take measurements, and classify facts. It is a fertile and interesting field of study. At present, so far as enquiry has proceeded, the state of knowledge seems to be in favour of the view above enunciated. It is not advanced, however, as in itself conclusive; it is simply a contribution—a small weight thrown into the scale of our general argument.

SECTION II.

Mental and Moral Characteristics.

Here, again, we must necessarily limit our field of discussion, fixing only on some few leading features in the mental character of the English which suit our subject, and whose partial treatment will not distort, though it but imperfectly expound, the subject.

If, in finding the synthesis of the English character, we discover that it accords not with the old Teutonic character, we must search for the ground of the difference; and if that ground is revealed in the known characteristics of the Ancient Britons, we need not further pursue our search.

First, let us mark the broad mental and moral characteristics of the *generic* stocks—the *Celts* and the *Teutons*. No appreciable difficulty is encountered by philosophers in determining these two sets of general characteristics; they stand out in relief, inviting recognition; but as the inquiry approaches the specific branches which have shot out from the respective stocks, as for example, the Scotch on the one hand, and the Prussian on the other, divers difficulties, not easily got rid of, obstruct the way.

Dr. Kombst has given as fair and comprehensive a description of the Celtic and Teutonic idiosyncracies as any we know. The main points are the following :[1]—

Celtic Race.	*Teutonic Race.*
Quickness of perception; great powers of combination; application; *love of equality, of society, of amusement, of glory; want of caution and providence;* . . . . *national vanity;* fine blandishing manners; great external politeness, without internal sympathy; *irascible;* not forgetful of injuries; *little disposition for hard work; (abounding in wit, &c.)*	*Slowness,* but accuracy of perception; slowness, but *depth* and penetration of mind; not brilliant in wit like the Celts; distinguished for acuteness, fondness for independence more than rank; *provident, cautious,* reserved, hospitable : with aristocratic conservative tendencies; respect for women; *sincerity, adventurous,* &c.

This is the substance of Kombst's analysis, and it must be allowed to be on the whole faithful. In his full description, however, it is evident enough that he had the French before him as the type of the Celtic character; hence he has introduced some features which are by no means prominent in the Celtic populations of Britain, such as "great external politeness" "without internal sympathy," "love of glory," &c. It may also be fairly questioned whether he is right in including "application" as amongst the idiosyncracies of the Celtic race; this quality most certainly does belong to the Teutonic.

We want, however, to find out the *differentia* of the true

[1] See Berghaus's *Physical Atlas*, Johnstone's Ed. (Kombst's *Ethnographic Map* of Great Britain and Ireland).

Englishman as compared with the true Celt, and true Teuton. The Englishman is not a faithful copy of the genuine German of ancient times. He exhibits intellectual and ethical characteristics which did not prominently enter into the synthesis of the German character—we are not speaking of the *modern* German, for that would be beside the point and unquestionably unjust—such, for instance, as inventiveness, quickness, constructiveness, imaginativeness, tenderness, benevolence, liberality, individuality, and religious ideality. And as to the Celt, again, a great number of the weighty, solid, strong qualities of the English separate them widely from him.

The whole story of the Celt is, as an eminent writer has pictured it,[1] marked by not a little grandeur and mystery. He certainly has been a roving child of nature ; wild, impulsive, proud, irascible, uncalculating, feeble in purpose, unapt for government, ever attempting the sublimest, often the sublime and ridiculous in one—as *ex. gr.* now in Ireland—but ever accomplishing a failure. His deeds in past ages have been unique, heroic, terrible, and his miscarriages affecting. The Celts' progress through Asia and Europe, seen in the dim light of an imperfect history, and, therefore, probably partaking of the fascination and grandeur which mystery never fails to lend, deserves to be painted in hues befitting the trail of a comet. If you compare their march to that of a river, it is a succession of cataracts and foaming torrents. Everything seems to be abnormal and exceptional. Growth is not a steady development ; enterprise is not according to plan ; the most momentous predicaments are treated as unrealities ; means are not measured to ends ; the creations of fancy

[1] See *Cornhill Magazine*, March, April, May, 1866. These able articles by Mr. Matthew Arnold have since been published in volume form, entitled, *On the Study of Celtic Literature*.

are taken as facts. The Britons in all ages have been examples of all this. Vast numbers of the Irish of to-day are,
beyond all comparison, its most striking illustrators. Mr.
Matthew Arnold, with the insight of genius, has happily
hit upon the chief weakness of the Celt—his disbelief in
the authenticity of *fact*. The present disturbers of the
peace of Ireland persistently ignore the magnitude
of the power they wish to foil.[1] The true Celt idealizes
his own future according to an exuberant fancy, un-
governed by reflection, and proceeds to the enjoyment of that future like one whose path was clear,
and whose success was decreed by fate. Hence the grand
attempts often made—the occasional heroic achievements
—the frequent, even customary abortions. Physiology
and psychology tell us that the great characteristics of the
different branches of the Celtic race are brilliancy of conception, ardency of temperament, and uncontrollable desire for action. We all know how quick, fitful, whimsical,
and emotional they are,—how inapt for council, diplomacy,
organization, patient labour, and " biding of time."

The fancy and imagination of the Celt, as displayed in
Middle Age literature, have never yet been duly recognised.
Their manifestations were often grotesque, unconnected,
inharmonious, but most undoubtedly carried upon their
front the imprint of genuine poetry. Mental gifts and
habits, like physical characteristics, may re-appear after
long, partial, or total temporary obscuration. A nation's
life, like an individual's, may through violence or dis-
ordered function, be subject to suspension, and, after a
while, by degrees, again recover its former consciousness
and brightness. The seeds of poetic inspiration and genius
lodged in the Cymric mind, once under Roman culture,

---

[1] This was written at the height of the " Fenian " agitation in 1867.

were buried under heavy masses of rubbish during the
barbaric wars of the Saxon conquests. Little time was
then enjoyed for letters, and the stores of literary treasures
which had been accumulated were rudely swept to the
abyss. New generations with slighter culture grew up
and the intellect of the Cymry waned into a condition not
out of keeping with the sterner barbarism of their Anglo-
Saxon neighbours. The force which prevented the return
of deeper chaos and night, however weakened by corrupt
superstitions was Christianity. But though the depressing
influences were strong, the Cymric intellect was not wholly
stupefied; its schools of learning were the first in Britain
(see Appendix C), and to the *Cymry* of Wales, it is more
than probable, is due the honour of having imparted
to the thought and literature of Europe an impulse far
more powerful than was imparted in those times by any
other people. The mixed race peopling England were
slow in developing any kind of literature. The still comparatively unmixed Celts of Wales and Armorica were far
in advance of them, and by a happy combination of constructive power, love of the marvellous, and a fancy of
boundless range and fertility, succeeded in creating a type
of literature until then probably unknown in Europe.
The romance poetry, and prose which in the Middle Ages
swayed with such potency in Brittany, Provence, Italy,
Germany, and England, it is well-known had its origin
amongst the *Cymry*. Geoffrey of Monmouth is the real
parent of the whole brood. The adventures of Merlin,
King Arthur and his knights, Richard Cœur de Lion, and
a host of others, follow, and these culminate at last in the
Trouveres poems of France, the Italian epic romances,
and, with increasing extravagance of fancy, combined with
an ignorant superstition, in the saintly fables of the Church.
Among the Welsh *Mabinogion* are remains indicating a

fancy as playful, and a feeling as delicate and tender, as
are found in the productions of any age. How came this
to pass ? Can it be explained as being anything less than
the re-appearance of hereditary characteristics ? The
culture and genius which, dating from the pre-Roman
times, had received expansion from Roman enlightenment,
and asserted their presence from age to age, even under
the disadvantages of incessant political disaster, broke forth
at last from obscure situations, and spread a light and
a vivifying power over many lands, which the conquering
Teuton scarcely as yet knew how to appreciate.

Indeed the romance literature was of too airy a nature
to emanate from, or easily find entertainment by the truly
Teutonic mind—even allowing to that mind a larger share
of poetic susceptibility and inventiveness than is meted out
to it by the balances of severe pro-Celtic critics. But
in truth no such Teutonic mind has existed in Britain
since the first ages of the Saxon Conquest. Even the new
race of amalgamated Britons, Saxons, and Angles, called
English, was too matter-of-fact and sensuous, or too much
under the guidance of its ever present δαίμων _common-sense_,
to relish these imaginary creations about giants, elves, and
enchanters. These were the proper products of the Celtic
imagination, and found congenial reception among all the
nations of the continent, especially in Brittany, Normandy,
and Provence, where the Celtic race was in the ascendant.

Now, whatever the value of the romance literature considered in itself, it undoubtedly speaks much for the people
who gave it birth. We refuse credit to the pages of
Geoffrey as descriptions of authentic facts, simply because
they are not history, but fiction ; but estimated as fiction,
it is impossible not to accord to them admiration. The
question is not as to the absolute value, _per se_, of certain
productions concerning heroic or preternatural beings and

adventurers, but the mental force and fertility of invention they exhibit. In so far as the Middle Age romances display these, they display the genius and culture of the Celtic race of the times.

It is not of material import whether the cradle of that literature which produced the stories of Arthur, Merlin, Richard Cœur de Lion, Roland, Sir Ferumbras, and the hosts of others of similar vein, was Brittany or Wales, but probability decidedly inclines in favour of the latter. The natural course of propagation would be first to Brittany—with which the Welsh held constant intercourse—then to Normandy, then to the remoter provinces of France. The romances would receive from each country and language, as they advanced, some new conceptions, gradually assume new forms, and develop new characters, some of Southern and some of Northern paternity, and in course of time furnish reasonable grounds, in the absence of reliable accounts, for the conflict of opinion which has existed, some ascribing to them a Scandinavian, some an Italian, some a British origin.

Mr. Hallam—by no means predisposed to give the Celt undue credit for genius—is obliged, upon this question, to lean in his favour. Speaking of the origin of French literature, and having mentioned the versified lives of Saints by Thibault de Vernon (11th century), Taillefer, Philip de Than (*temp.* Henry I.), &c., he says: "but a more famous votary of the muse was Wace, a native of Jersey, who, about the beginning of Henry's II.'s reign, turned *Geoffrey of Monmouth's history* into French metre. Besides this poem, called *Le Brut d'Angleterre*, he composed a series of metrical histories, containing the transactions of the dukes of Normandy, from Rollo, their great progenitor—who gave name to the Roman de Rou—down to his own age. Other productions are ascribed to Wace, who was,

at least a prolific versifier, and if he seems to deserve no
higher title at present, has a claim to indulgence, and even
to esteem, as having far excelled his contemporaries,
without any superior advantages of knowledge. In emula-
tion, however, of his fame, several Norman writers addicted
themselves to composing chronicles, or devotional treatises,
in metre. If the poets of Normandy had never gone
beyond historical and religious subjects they would
probably have had less claim to our attention than their
brethren of Provence. But a different and far more
interesting species of composition began to be cultivated
in the latter part of the 12th century. Without entering
upon the controverted question as to the origin of romantic
fictions, referred by one party to the Scandinavians, by a
second to the Arabs, by others to the natives of Brittany,
it is manifest that the actual stories upon which one early
and numerous class of romances was founded are related
to the traditions of the last people. These are such as turn
upon the fable of Arthur ; for though we are not entitled
to deny the existence of such a personage, his story seems
chiefly the creation of Celtic vanity. Traditions current in
Brittany, though probably derived from *this island*, became
the basis of Geoffrey of Monmouth's Latin prose, which, as
has been seen, was transposed into French metre by Wace.
The vicinity of Normandy enabled its poets to enrich their
narrative with other Armorican fictions, all relating to the
heroes who had surrounded the table of the Son of Uther." [1]

Mr. Ellis is still more explicit. "Various theories have
been proposed for the purpose of explaining the origin
of romantic fiction, which has been successively ascribed to
the Scandinavians, to the Arabians, and to the Armoricans,
while some authors have supposed it to be of Provençal,
and others, of Norman invention. Bishop Percy, to whose

---

[1] *Europe in the Middle Ages*, chap. ix.

elegant taste we are indebted for the ' Reliques of Ancient English Poetry,' the most agreeable selection, perhaps, which exists in any language, has prefixed to his third volume a short, but masterly dissertation, in which he assigns to the Scalds the honour of having produced the earliest specimens in this mode of composition. He observes that these poets, the historians of the North, as the bards were of Gaul and Britain, continued for a time the faithful depositaries of their domestic annals ; but that, at a subsequent period, when history was consigned to plain prose, they gradually attempted to set off their recitals by such marvellous fictions as were calculated to captivate gross and ignorant minds. Thus began stories of adventures with giants, and dragons, and witches, and enchanters, and all the monstrous extravagances of wild imagination, unguided by judgment and uncorrected by art. He contends that the vital spirit of chivalry, its enthusiastic valour, its love of adventure, and its extravagant courtesy, are to be found in the Scaldic songs ; that these characteristic qualities existed in the manners of the northern nations long before the establishment of knighthood as a regular order ; that the superstitious opinions of these people respecting fairies and other preternatural beings, were extremely analogous to the later fictions of romance ; that the migration of a certain number of Scalds into France, as attendants on Rollo's army, is at least extremely probable ; and that, since the first mention of the stories of chivalry occurs in the song of a Norman minstrel [Taillefer] at the battle of Hastings, this filiation of romance is equally consonant to history and to probability.

"The only rational objection, perhaps, which can be adduced against this system is, that it is too exclusive. The history of Charlemagne, it is true, appears to have been very early in favour with the Normans, because the song of Rollo, certainly, and that of St. William very possibly, were anterior to the Conquest; and it is also likely that these and other fragments of traditional poetry may have contributed the principal materials of those longer works, which, at a much later period, formed the regular romances of Renaud of Montauban, Fierabras, Otual, Ferragus, and the other heroes of Charlemagne. But this does not account for the much more numerous and popular fictions concerning Arthur and his Knights, which occupy not only so many of the romances, but also of the lays and fabliaux of the twelfth and thirteenth centuries, and are evidently derived, as the learned editor very candidly acknowledges, from a different source. Besides, though the manners of chivalry, as exhibited in the Rolands and Olivers, are common to the Launcelots and Tristrams, nothing can be more opposite than the morals of the heroines; and the frailties of an Yseult, or a Guenever, afford a lamentable contrast to the severe chastity of a northern beauty. But surely, in surveying a system of fictions in which love and war are the chief agents, it is impossible to abstract our attention altogether from the delineations of female character.

"The third hypothesis which supposes Brittany to be the native country of romantic fiction, has been, with some modifications, adopted by Leyden in his very able introduction to the 'Complaynt of Scotland,' and has the advantage of being free from the objections which have been made to the preceding theories. Similarity of language proves the similar origin of the Armoricans and of the natives of this island; and the British historians, such as they are, affirm that a large colony of fugitives from Saxon tyranny took refuge in Brittany, and carried with them such of their archives as had escaped the fury of their conquerors. The Norman poets themselves frequently profess to have derived their stories from Breton originals ; and their positive testimony seems sufficient to prove that the memory of Arthur and his knights was preserved in Armorica no less than in Wales and in Cornwall. With respect to the tales of Charlemagne and his imaginary peers, unless we suppose them to have been imported by the Normans from Scandinavia, we must refer them to Brittany; because the Bretons were the first people of France with whom the Normans had friendly intercourse, their province having been attached as a sort of fief to Normandy at the first settlement of that duchy uuder Rollo. It is not improbable, as I have already mentioned, that a mutual exchange of traditions may have introduced Ogier, and other Danish heroes, to the Court of Charlemagne, and perhaps a similar commerce between the bards of Wales and Brittany may have given to Arthur his Sir Launcelot and other French worthies. The supposition that some traditional anecdotes concerning these two princes of romance were already current among the Normans, would explain the facility with which the very suspicious chronicles of Geoffrey and Turpin were received, and the numerous amplifications by which they were, after their translation into French, almost immediately embellished.

"The reader will perceive that the preceding systems are by no means incompatible, and that there is no absurdity in supposing that the scenes and characters of our romantic histories were very generally, though not exclusively, derived from the Bretons, or from the Welsh of this island ; that much of the colouring, and perhaps some particular adventures, may be of Scandinavian origin, and that occasional episodes, together with part of the machinery, may have been borrowed from the Arabians." [1]

[1] *Early English Romances.* Introduction, pp. 16-20.

The quantum of proof in favour of our general argument derivable from these considerations may be small, but to the extent of its measure is, practically, unassailable. The higher tone of mind in Britain, in the Middle Ages, was among the *Cymry*, as proved by its literary products. Brittany was in constant communication with Wales, receiving the impress of its culture, and assisting to hand over to the continent the productions of its intellect. If the semi-Teutonic mind of England and Normandy followed in the same wake and produced a romance literature of equal or superior merits when the example had been set by others, it may be worthy of commendation as an imitator and improver, but not of the crown of honour as originator. To the Celtic mind belongs this honour; and this mind was capable of the achievement by reason not merely of its rare characteristics of impulsiveness, sensibility, and brilliant fancy, but also of its antecedently inherited culture, which in its effects lay hid, like the latent force of a seed to be developed into vitality and visible form when the external conditions of germination favoured.

So far at present of the Celt. But now what of the Teuton—the old genuine German-Teuton, the ancestor, according to popular apprehension of the Anglo-Saxon, and through him, of the great English race. At what point of time can he have broken off from the vivacious imaginative Celt? By what strange differencing influences of climate, mode of life, intermixture with phlegmatic races, can he have been met since he quitted the paternal roof where the Celt and he were brothers? As long as history has known him, he has been a rather slow, deliberate, and cautious individual; and yet, though slow, a moving steady-going individual. You may, perhaps, expect nothing brilliant, tender, poetic, from the true, typical German;

but it will excite no surprise if he achieve something strangely great, in thinking or acting—for he is deliberate, clear-headed and strong! This in brief is the German-Teuton.

Now what shall we say of the Englishman? Is he a faithful reflection of either Celt or German-Teuton? Of the Celt, he certainly is not; most certainly not of the German-Teuton! Can it be said that he is a copy of both combined? Beyond question, think we, it can. His qualities are a selection from the best of both.

The English *must* be either Celtic, or Teutonic, or both. They have no choice of other derivation. But they are not Celtic: they present leading features diametrically opposed to the Celtic idiosyncrasy, and we find on examination that these features are German and Saxon! On the other hand, they are not German; for they present leading features which the slow deliberate old German never could have worn, and these features are *Celtic!*

The natural history of the English nation, we suspect, must turn out to be a description of the processes and stages whereby Celt and Saxon were welded into one, and came to exhibit the characteristics, in one personality, of two antecedent national factors. " School histories" will continue for many years to come to say: "When the Saxons came over, all the Britons retired into the mountains of Wales." " There were no Saxons in England after the battle of Hastings," may quite as truly be said. But " school histories" are not always the most critically accurate of informants; and it seems full time to put faith in better guides on the present subject. Whether our hypothesis be that there has been a large intermixture of Celtic with Anglo-Saxon blood in Britain, or the contrary, it is at least demonstrably certain that the present English people are the exact similitude of *the result which might be expected from such intermixture.* A people which is at once loftily ambitious and plodding; imaginative and practical; proud and patient; energetic and cautious; religious and "worldly;" fertile of philosophers and traders; of inventions and traditions; declares on every page of its autobiography as read in the deep imprint of its actual, and incomparably earnest life, that it is neither of Saxon nor of Celtic descent, but of *both*. And if not of both *equally—* then comes the question, on which side does the advantage lie.

It may be objected that our representation of the Celt is not correct; that, for example, the French have displayed great aptitude in diplomacy and government, although substantially a Celtic people. This is true. But the French people had the advantage of a Roman political education, of intellectual culture through the wholesale adoption of the Roman language, which latter the Celts of Britain and Ireland had not, and of a large Frankmannic infusion. Despite all this, and much besides, however, the French people display to this day the most essential characteristics, and amongst them, some of the weaker and more damaging characteristics of the Celtic race. Of these, we may mention a passion for excitement, political disquietude, frivolity, national vanity. The French want nothing for the accomplishment of the highest destiny, but a strong infusion of the Teutonic steadiness and gravity.

It may again be argued that our description of the Celt does not agree with the Scottish character, which is known by all to exhibit as much caution and steady plodding as that of the Englishman. We answer that our description of the Celt may be true, notwithstanding that it tallies not with Scottish idiosyncrasies. The Scotch are much less Celtic than the Welsh—infinitely less so than the Irish. The prevalence of brownish and yellow hair in Scotland is a living history of the Scandinavian descent of a large portion of the inhabitants. From the earliest periods, Danes, Norwegians, and Low Germans made settlements on the Caledonian coasts, especially north and east—as the local names of those parts, notably of the Shetlands and Orkneys, to this day testify; and all know that these islands, originally peopled by Celts, were in after times mainly peopled by Northmen, and long remained under Danish or Norwegian rule. The Danish conquest of England settled vast numbers of Northmen in the south of Scotland, and the Western coast was seldom free from the irruptions of Norwegian and Danish adventurers. All these sources of admixture have well-nigh obliterated the Celtic features of a large proportion of the Scottish people, and given them several of their most marked and valuable characteristics.

But to recur to our question: On which side does the advantage lie? In the constitution of the English people, does the Celtic or the Teuto-Germanic ingredient preponderate?

One man will say, the Germanic, because the language is chiefly Anglo-Saxon. But in the first place the English language is *not* chiefly Anglo-Saxon, and in the second place, even if it were so, the adoption of a language has no bearing on the question of *proportion* of race admixture. The language of Gaul became Roman, although few Romans merged into the population. The Norman conquerors of Neustria, on the other hand, adopted the French. In England the English people received the Norman.

Another will say the Germanic, because the government proves to be in the hand of the Saxon. But this again says nothing as to preponderance of race, and it moreover assumes a very important point—viz., that the people who now govern are proper Saxons. The Danes obtained the government : Were they therefore more numerous than the former inhabitants ? The Normans obtained the government. The Roman legions gained the government of all Gaul. The English now govern the millions of India.

A third—with a logic, by the way, more characteristic of the Celt than of the Saxon—will come forward and boldly declare the Germanic, because the whole character of the people of England is truly Anglo-Saxon—the mental genius of the nation is German from first to last. Now this is just what we have been showing that it is *not*. The character of the English is exceedingly far from being a copy of the Anglo-Saxon or Germanic ; and the *differentia* cannot be traced to the effects of external influences—not even to the powerful agencies of secular civilisation and religion.

Let the following summary of the leading psychological and ethical features of Celt, German,[1] and English be pondered. The characteristics given are universally allowed. Each student can judge for himself from which side—the Celtic or the Teutonic—the eclectic Englishman has borrowed most. Of course, it may be argued that the source of mental and moral characteristics is not *racial*, and to some extent this must be allowed to be true. But viewed in a broad light, the influence of race is seen to tell in no inconsiderable degree.

[1] The word "German" as used here cannot be taken as indicative of the people of modern Germany. It were incorrect to say that the Prussians, for example, are not an inventive people ; and to pretend to believe that the modern Germans are not possessed of a poetic imagination while they own the names of Goethe, Schiller, Lessing, Klopstock, Körner, Arndt, and Uhland, to say nothing of the un-paralleled imaginative creations in philosophy of the schools of Leibnitz, Kant, Fichte, Hegel, Schleiermacher, and Schelling, were a mark of either ignorance or disingenuousness. But the modern Germans can have no material share in the parentage of the English people.

Summary of Psychological Characteristics

Celtic.	English.	German or Saxon.
	Deliberativeness.	Slowness.
	Accuracy and thoroughness.	Accuracy.
	Directness.	Steady purpose.
Quickness and clearness of perception.	Clearness of perception.	
Powers of combination.	Powers of combination.	
Imagination.	Imagination.	
Wit, humour.	Wit, humour.	
	Providence.	Providence.
Individuality.	Independence.	
Loyalty to Princes.	Aristocratic tendencies.	Aristocratic tendencies.
	Adventure.	Adventure.
Love of society.	Sociability.	
Patriarchal or family government.	Sentiment of Home.	
Reverence.	Reverence.	
	Patient labour.	Patient labour.
	Silence and reserve.	Silence and reserve.
Generosity.	Generosity.	

The following are qualities which the English may be said to have inherited from Celt and Saxon alike.

Celtic.	English.	German or Saxon.
Quickness of perception.	Power of abstraction and generalization.	Depth of thought.
Hospitality.	Hospitality.	Hospitality.
Courage.	Courage.	Courage.
Individuality.	Self-assertion.	Sternness.

There are certain great features of the English people of which it is hard to say whence they have been derived. Are *truth*, *fidelity*, *sincerity*, characteristics of the Celt? Would the Cymry allow that these virtues belonged peculiarly to the kin of Hengist and Horsa? Public benevolence, or organised charity, seems almost to be an idiosyncrasy of the English.

Here ends our psychological discussion. It is simply suggestive—in no sense exhaustive. But it seems to prove that some of the noblest qualities, mental and moral, of Englishmen, are of *Celtic origin.*

In reviewing this whole subject of physical, mental, and moral characteristics, it appears that he must be a bold man, if a genuine Englishman, who will declare that he is more Teuton than Celtic, or more Celtic than Teuton ; and he must be a bolder man still who will assert that he is purely Celtic and not at all Teuton, or purely Teuton and not at all Celtic. The anthropology of the English nation we conclude is in favour of the position held in these pages —viz., that the English owe their origin largely to the Ancient British race. The evidence, in this branch of it, is deposed by a witness that cannot err. That witness is Nature, not History. Its evidence depends not on opinion, theory, illegible parchment, distorted party representation, vague tradition. It is read in the ineffaceable characters of living features of myriads of men, and beams forth perpetually in the intellectual and moral activities of the nation. The signs of descent supplied by the *physique* and mental manifestations of a people are more infallible in the estimation of science than even the most categorical declarations of individual historians. On the skin, in the eyes, on every fibre of hair, is written the pedigree of the man. It is useless for him to refer to mere personal names, family parchments, traditions of descent, &c., for though twenty generations ago he had William the Norman as his ancestor, the blood of the Norman has been intermixed many hundred times with many hundred times mingled blood of other races in the interval, and must by this time have become sadly diluted. To rely on the loose statements of popular historians in a matter of science were absurd. The deliverances of anthropology, anatomy, physiology, and psychology, as well as the patient findings of antiquarian research, as contributive aids to ethnology, are clear, positive, unhesitating. They prove that the English nation is a Mosaic work of divers and harmonious colours; but there are two colours which still predominate high above the rest—the light Teutonic, and the dark brown Celtic. The English *mind* is a compound of two classes of activities, each of essential moment in the creation of the highest order of thought—the energetic, warm, and ornamental Celtic, and the patient, profound, and stable Teutonic—

"Genus unde Latinum,
Albanique patres, atque alta mœnia Romæ."

RECAPITULATION.

It may not here be out of place to refresh the memory of the reader by bringing into a focus the chief lines of our argument, or rather of its results—necessarily omitting all details of facts and minute witnessings of history, science, and logic, which often carry with them the most convincing force.

The reader can mentally retrace from his present point of view (he will pardon us the natural vanity of believing that he has passed through all the tangled wilderness we have spread out for him), all the main paths he has traversed. The different inhabitants of Britain at the time of the Roman invasion, though divided into many tribes or states, are seen to be all of one race—"the Ancient Britons." Their number is great—spread out over all the land from Kent to the Highlands. They are far advanced in the arts of life, are fond of trade, work in metals, carry on commerce with distant countries, are terrible in battle, have a regular kingly government, coin silver money, &c. The Romans themselves have hard work to subdue them after a hundred and fifty years and more of fighting, and having at length accomplished this task, are obliged to garrison some hundred fortresses to maintain order and draw revenue.

The Romans after bestowing above 400 years of culture on Britain, resolve to leave it to the care of the natives, who at once set up rival governments in different parts of the country, and are caught in the confusion of reorganization by foes from without and from within, and are compelled while suicidally fighting with each other, to fight for home and life against a fierce and terribly needy foreign foe. They are found to be so numerous, brave, and powerful, that, though fated to compass their own ruin through perverse dissension and refusal to combine in time against the common enemy, they still manage by the isolated efforts of disjointed hosts, to dispute the ground for some hundred and fifty years, although in that time whole states, " becoming Saxons," had joined the aggressor, and turned their swords against their own countrymen.

No signs appear of an "exterminating" warfare being carried on by either Romans or Germans. The natives, if submissive, are everywhere allowed to remain in their native districts—their title to property and liberty being changed—by the Romans they are invited to the privileges of citizens of maternal Rome, and by the Germans they are pressed to " become Saxons." Whole tribes pass over accordingly, and hosts of the common people of other tribes follow. Those who wish to retain their language and customs are allowed to live in towns of their own, or to possess parts of towns, even within the bounds of the Anglo-Saxon kingdoms, and to live also under laws and magistrates of their own. Some 500 years after the first Saxon invasion, a great part of the South and West of England is called *Wealh-cynne*—the dominion of the Welsh, and the whole of Devon and Cornwall is still decidedly Celtic. In the North the kingdom of Strathclyde survives till within a few years of the Norman Conquest. At this time the inhabitants of Britain are mainly composed of the descendants of the Ancient Britons!

The Danes, if they add to the Teutonic population in their own persons, have previously greatly reduced it by their most sanguinary and desolating wars. The Normans bring over more Celts than Teutons.

K 2

The subject Britons are seen dwelling on the land under the protection of Saxon laws—holding land from the king—rising in the social scale from lowly to high conditions through possession of property—and having a personal *wergild* value, &c., just like the Anglo-Saxons themselves.

The English language, through the presence in the heart of the country of a population continuing to speak the Celtic tongue, becomes saturated with Celtic elements. Those elements are not such as were common to Anglo-Saxon and Celtic from times anterior to the Saxon Conquest—though many such exist—the result of pre-historic intercourse in the Cimbric Chersonese and North Germany—but actual introductions since the two races met on British ground.

The local names of England, imposed by the Ancient Britons, and adopted from them by the Anglo-Saxons—by their number and their prevalence in distant localities almost all over the island, are clear witnesses not only of *previous* occupation by the Britons, but of *conjoint* occupation for a great length of time—for by such conjoint occupation alone could a strange people speaking a strange tongue, and having no knowledge of writing, become familiar with the names whereby not only the great natural features of the country, such as the mountains, hills, rivers, vales, &c., but less prominent objects in sequestered situations, such as rivulets, dingles, knolls, homesteads, &c., had from time immemorial been known among the natives.

To the vast proportion of Britons thus seen to be mixed up with English society, and, under the ameliorating laws of the later Middle Ages, rising from a depressed to a free condition, and gradually forming an essential part of all ranks of the community, is added in later times, and especially in the present age, a constant stream of Celtic elements flowing in from Wales, Scotland, and Ireland, so that the name "Jones" is now more prevalent than either "Brown" or "Robinson," and is closely followed by the "Scotts" and the "Murphys," and only eclipsed by "Smith!" [1]

[1] The appearance of Mr. Smiles's book, *The Huguenots: their Settlements, Churches, and Industries in England and Ireland*, reminds us of an accession in modern times to the Celtic element of the population of England, seldom thought of, but of a peculiarly interesting and valuable kind. The French Protestants, who, between 1550 and 1700, but chiefly during the "wars of religion," and on the "revocation of the Edict of Nantes," took refuge in this country, were vast in numbers and of inestimable worth to the moral life and industry of England. For a hundred and fifty years the flow of Protestant refugees, the flower of the population of Flanders and the different provinces of France, was almost incessant. Not less than 400,000 emigrated at the revocation of the Edict of Nantes. In the first quarter of the seven-teenth century, London alone contained, among a population compara-tively small, not fewer than 10,000 foreigners, mainly *Huguenots*. They were also found in all the larger towns, in some, as Norwich, numbering several thousands. They were mostly of the merchant, manufacturing and artizan classes, and brought with them not only a peaceable, serious, religious spirit, but knowledge and skill in the industrial arts, especially in weaving, dyeing, tanning, and work in the precious metals. "Wherever they settled they acted as so many missionaries of skilled work, exhibiting the best examples of diligence, industry, and thrift, and teaching the English people in the most effective manner the beginning of those arts in which they have since acquired so much industry and wealth." They excelled as market gardeners, and the famous gardens of Wandsworth, Battersea, and Bermondsey, were amongst the results. Those who found refuge in England are estimated at *one hundred thousand persons*. They became leaders in the art and merchandise of the country. In paper-making they were supreme, and one of their descendants, Mr. Portal, is maker of our Bank-note paper of the present time. Many of their names became dis-tinguished in English history, literature, and science. Their hard application led to fortune and distinction, and some of our peerages are inherited by descendants of Huguenots, such as Radnor, Clancarty, De Blaquiere, Rendlesham, Taunton, Romilly; and their blood is mixed with that of Russell, Elliot, Temple (Palmerston), Cavendish, and Osborne. Speaking generally, the blood of the Huguenots was Celtic (Gaelic) blood, and was therefore a contribution to the Celtic element in the English nation.

If after this any doubt should exist as to whether the greater part of the actual population of England is a contribution from the Celtic race, nothing is wanted but simply to look the English in the face, scan their features, measure their skulls, watch the rapid, and profound operations of their *minds*, and the humane and pious actions of their lives. In all these things they are now what they never were in the persons of their partial ancestors before they trod on British ground, and had the good fortune of "taking in," in more senses than one, the simple " Wyliscman ! "

CONCLUSION.

WE have been engaged in slowly tracing the beginnings
and early developments of one of the most colossal
creations of time—the British nation! Were we to examine
the field of universal history, our survey would command
no other such ethnological marvel. In no epoch, in no
land has anything of the sort appeared. It would seem as
if the world, at the birth of the British people, had grown
consciously old and desolate, and that, like the fabled
Phœnix, it had undertaken, by a painful but sublime
process of fire, to renew itself; and the island of Britain
was selected as the theatre where the prodigy was to be
accomplished.

It took a long time to lay the foundations of this great
national superstructure. Some thousand years elapsed
before all the kinds of materials were brought together.
The Celtic tribes had inhabited the island probably for
many hundred years before the republic of Rome was
inaugurated; but, solitary and self-contained, they
possessed an insufficient amount of those elements of
expansion and development required for national
maturity. The Roman added a mighty impulse by
lodging in the mass the seeds of the old world's civilization.
Christianity added a still mightier and sublimer force.
The Saxons, Danes, and Normans, a rough and energetic race, poured in their successive contributions
of influence ; and by the union of all into one body,
and its tempering by long and painful discipline,

under the guidance of religion, commerce, science, and education, the result has come forth in the shape of this English nation, which is to-day not the envy, so much as the pattern and friend of all surrounding peoples, and promises to continue for many ages the exemplar and director, if not the virtual ruler of the civilized world.

We have on more than one occasion alluded to the secret of the greatness of the English race—namely: the complexity of its origin. It is inconceivable that any one of the races which have contributed towards the formation of this people could ever of itself have attained to this greatness—let the time given be however prolonged, and the circumstances however propitious. The best proof of this is the actual performances of unmixed races. The Saxon, wanting in vivacity, has here been supplemented by the excitable and imaginative Celt; and the Celt, fitful, incautious, irascible, believing in the unseen, often, while "building castles in the air," neglecting what lay in reality at his feet, has been brought under method and order by the infusion of the deliberate, "practical," and impassible qualities of the Teuton.

The English people by this admixture are possessed of all the attributes which are required for government—science, religion, the prosecution of trade, and the extension of empire. The love and practice of liberty—a liberty which prohibits lawlessness—exist nowhere, as the normal condition of the people, as they do in England. Religion goes forth to subdue the superstitions and idolatries of the world from no country as it does from Britain and the United States. The industrial arts, practical science, the enterprises of commerce, are by no other people pursued with such absorbing delight, and unfailing success.

If we look to the relative power, fame, and distinction of the British people—the wide reach of their dominion—

(though their home is but this small island of the West) the solidity and moral influence of their character, and the prodigious wealth of their resources, we naturally feel an inward exultation, which requires for its moderation the memory of other illustrious nations which from being high and commanding have long ago perished out of sight ; and are legitimately proud of belonging to a country which has been the cradle and the home of so mighty and peerless a race—a race which Milton has aptly described in his *Areopagitica* as " not slow and dull, but of a quick, ingenious, and piercing spirit, acute to invent, subtle and sinewy to discourse, not beneath the reach of any point the highest that human capacity can soar to," etc.

The doctrine of our essay being, that a good proportion, probably the larger part, of our nation is of Celtic blood, we are here supplied with a new ground of alliance and friendship with our distinguished neighbours of *France*, who are almost entirely Celtic in blood, although not in language. The policy of less enlightened times produced between us and that great nation sentiments of antipathy not in keeping either with our mutual interests, or ancient race relations. France has had her times of error and false ambition : she has had rulers and leaders whose trade was revolution, and whose instruments were rapine and blood. But she is now, we trust, taking the road of peace, and, under better counsel, aims at husbanding her great resources, becoming our rival, not in the barbaric pursuit of arms, but in the arts of industry, the creation of wealth, the culture of mind, and the guidance of nations.[1] The Celtic race in Britain should learn to look

[1] This was written in 1868, when the Second Empire had succeeded in producing at least the appearance of social repose, and laying the basis of commercial prosperity. But since that time another great change has come over France. A Republic has replaced the Empire.

with new interest on France in this her time of regeneration, and especially on that western corner of France, Brittany, where the old decaying language is lingering, an object of admiration to the antiquary and linguist, but a serious impediment to the people's progress, and where the Celt is seen in his integrity quite as much as in the mountains of Merionethshire, or the Vale of Teivy, while in the one like the other of these regions, he has enjoyed the advantage of a slight commingling with the Teuton, which he had lacked in the South and West of Ireland.

The student of history, and the ethnologist, are beginning to view with increasing interest that remnant of the old race and language of Britain still found in the Principality of Wales, and a feeling of reciprocation is growing in the Principality. These pages develop one chief reason of this. The fundamental rule of science, whether in history or elsewhere, is not what has been believed, but what is true. The inquiry into what is true, on the present subject, discovers a strong link of relationship between the *Cymry* and the English—a link of relationship, indeed, made doubly strong by the entrance on a scale of magnitude hitherto but slightly recognised, of Cymric blood into the people of England, and also, on a smaller scale, of English blood into the inhabitants of Wales. This being the case, let us ask what sentiments, on this ground of

The Franco-Prussian war, unhappily provoked by Napoleon, in a few months ended in the destruction of a great army, and the humiliation of France. But peaceful relations with Britain have not been disturbed; the self-renovating power of the country is again receiving a wonderful display; and soon France will be more powerful and prosperous than ever. It is only to be feared that the sore produced by defeat will go on festering, and that the spirit of revenge will, sooner or later, bring on another, and perhaps greater, calamity. The war demon is abroad, once more, among the nations, usurping for barbaric use the skill of art and the discoveries of science, and leading thoughtful men to enquire what is meant by our boasted modern civilization.

ethnological relationship alone, these two classes of the Queen's subjects ought to cherish towards each other? If considerations of race can be allowed to sway at all in the guidance of feeling between communities, they can be so allowed, and are trebly meritorious, when, as in the present case, the feeling generated is conducive to public order and the strength of the empire. We see no reason whatever for the cultivation of a narrow feeling of nationality on the part of the Welsh. Its root is ignorance, and its fruit disadvantage. Estrangement between two peoples under one rule helps only to starve the weaker. The Scotch have had sufficient perspicacity to recognise their own predicament, and profit from a rational course of conduct. Ethnologically, the pure Irish of the South and West do not occupy the same parallel. The Welsh of Wales—who, if our survey in the preceding pages be accurate, are now the most prominent and faithful representatives of the old *Cymry* who contributed the chief materials at least for the *foundation* of the English nation, and who, therefore, are entitled to see in that nation a near relation—are not so prompt in recognising their consanguinity, and claiming the advantages belonging to it as they ought to be.

Instead of seeking under the guidance of a few mistaken zealots to establish an exceptional state of things on their own behalf in Wales—a permanent wall of separation in language, and the revival of sore memories—they will do wisely to further the process of coalescence, and claim, not the title of ancient possessors merely of the soil of Britain, but, with a nobler and more profitable audacity, property in the greater part of the present *British people.* The foundation of this great national superstructure was verily laid by them : the ground colour in the texture belongs to them. If in suffering the lopping off of some branches of their national vine, they have only aided its propagation in more fruitful soil, why should they not rejoice ? If they have lost the greater part of their ancient territories—over which they generally managed so heartily to quarrel— they have the consolation of having, in that very process, contributed to constitute the nation which now owns and rules those territories; for without the Celtic ingredient the British race could not have had existence. *Language* is not a differencing attribute of nations. To consider language the main characteristic, and especially to deem all beyond the circle of its use as of another *race*, were wilfully to ignore the truth of fact, and adopt an absurd hypothesis. The French of to-day are not the less Celts because they happen to speak a modified Latin ; nor are the French-speaking Teutons of Canada the less Teutons for their French articulations ; nor, indeed, are the negroes of the United States the less negroes because they speak a kind of English. In like manner the blood of Anglo-Saxons, Danes, and Normans flowing in the veins of Scotch, Ulster Irish, and Welsh, is not the less Teutonic because it happens not to be accompanied in every case by the tones of the respective languages once belonging to it ; nor is the ancient Cymric blood now flowing in English veins the less Cymric although the persons owning it speak the English language. There is much more Cymric blood in England this day than in Wales, despite the fact that more Welsh is articulated in Cardiganshire than in all England together. Language is not by itself an index to race.

No valid reason exists, accordingly, why the Welsh should not feel that they and the English are ethnologically one people ; and it is better they should share in the honour and dignity, the intelligence and enterprise of England, than rest contented with the obscurity which blind adherence to antiquated customs, and to a speech

which can never become the vehicle of science or commerce, must entail upon them. The Welsh, like the
Scotch, should aspire to be in intelligence, enterprise,
culture, all that the English are, feeling that,

"Frei athmen ist das Leben nicht."

Merely to enjoy freedom is not to reach the highest ends
of national, any more than individual, life. Let the earnest
life of England—its strong steady aim at the high and
excellent, pulsate through all Wales, and the highest
models in thought, art, character, be emulated; let the
English language, which is destined soon to "make the
whole world kin," and which is the only medium for the
introduction into Wales of all the intellectual life and
civilization of England—without prejudice to the Welsh
as long as the popular instinct cleave to its use—be diffused
far and wide among the people. Let EDUCATION—the
most urgent need of Wales to-day—the best, the highest
education, be promoted both by the zeal of the people, and
by the just and paternal care and liberality of the Government—care and liberality which up to the present time
have been almost exclusively reserved for other parts, not
more loyal, not more needy, of the empire.[1] (See Append. C.)

---

[1] We believe that this would be a better course for Welshmen to
pursue than follow the counsels often given them at some of their
popular quasi-literary gatherings. Not a few people still survive who
foster a tendency to estrangement rather than coalescence between the
Welsh and the English, and generate a spirit which in essence is not
dissimilar to the Hibernic furor, though free from its disloyalty.
Efforts are made to maintain a clannish isolation, which, if left to the
arbitrament of the natural course of things, would soon cease to be.
The sensitiveness displayed under public criticism betrays a consciousness of weakness in the case, and that the critics are partly right. At
the same time these labours of a few to move back the dial of progress
in Wales, though it demonstrates the truth of Mr. Arnold's finding—
that the Celt is capable of resolutely disbelieving the reality of *fact*—

This subject should awaken certain wholesome reflections in that portion of the English mind which, through want of thought or want of information concerning its own ethnical antecedents, delights to consider itself *par excellence*, *Saxon*, as opposed to Ancient British—*Teutonic*, as opposed to Celtic. It is owing to this want of reflection that we so often hear of the wondrous achievements of the "Anglo-Saxon" in legislation, science, arms—of the sagacity, enterprise, practical aptitudes, &c., of the "Anglo-Saxon"—of the destiny of the world to become subject to the leadership and rule of the "Anglo-Saxon"—and divers other things of like nature.

A few years ago a journal called *The Anglo-Saxon*, destined not long to live, was brought into existence, charged with the duty of sounding abroad these sentiments, and doubtless had some share in establishing wrong notions in the public mind respecting the purely Anglo-Saxon descent of the English people and language. It was conceived and executed in the poetic and rhetorical style, much like orations at Welsh *Eisteddfods*, and, therefore, obtained no hold on the minds of scientific men. "The editors hoisted the standard of the race on the first day of the year one thousand eight hundred and forty-nine (p. 5), and an Anglo-Saxon messenger was forwarded by rail and steam to every corner of the globe recognised as an Anglo-Saxon settlement." Of course they were not oblivious of the saying of Gregory, *Non Angli sed Angeli*, when "the youthful Angli,[1]

are virtuous compared with the headlong folly, and blundering use of means to an end, displayed at present (1868) by " Fenian " disturbers of the peace in Ireland. The two things are similar only as mistaken race aspirations. The former co-exists with loyalty—the latter is conspiring and traitorous.

[1] Most probably British children sent as slaves to the Roman market by our Anglo-Saxon forefathers.

early leaflets of the mighty Anglo-Saxon branch, drew all the eyes of Rome to their angelic forms." The editors were not quite sure whether "the good old man, like the High Priest of old, spoke, not of himself, but by the spirit of prophecy; but whether inspired or not, the saying has not fallen to the ground. From that time forward the tree of the Anglo-Saxon race took root and flourished; for a thousand years the mighty trunk grew and shot upwards, rude and rugged perhaps in appearance, and then it spread forth its branches to the uttermost ends of the earth, affording shelter, and protection, and support to the other families and less favoured races of mankind. The Anglo-Saxons have been accomplishing their destiny. . . . The whole earth may be called the fatherland of the Anglo-Saxon race," &c. p. 4. A map was given in which the whole of North America, the whole of Hindostan, the whole of New Holland, was coloured as peopled by "the Anglo-Saxon race."

The doctrine taught concerning the Britons, as a matter of consistency, was the traditional one: "When the Saxons were the conquerors, they became so entirely masters and possessors of the land, that the ancient inhabitants were either banished to the mountains [the usual "of Wales" is omitted], or perished by the sword." p. 104. By one means or other we got rid of them entirely. This was bad enough as history. When speaking of the English language, the *Anglo-Saxon* was not over-learned, for it added on the same page: "If we trace it the English from its primitive, oral, and extemporaneous state, to the age of Alfred, when it assumed a written form, and from Alfred through Wickliffe and Chaucer to the reign of Elizabeth, when it put on a more classic and elegant dress, and even from Elizabeth to the present time, notwithstanding the corruptions which commerce or science, affectation or vanity, have introduced, the English language—simple, earnest, homely, expressive, is still substantially the same." This is certainly bold, especially when we remember that our present English, though more than ever "expressive," is not to half its extent derived from Anglo-Saxon, and that in grammatical inflection and construction it exhibits an almost total contrast to the language of Alfred. As to its being "simple," every Linguist will testify that there exists not in Europe or the world so complex and hetero-geneous a tongue.

The *Anglo-Saxon*, in truth, was simply the representative of a species of fanaticism, and, like all such productions, disdained the examination of facts, and the guidance of scientific induction. Its career, therefore, though doubtless "brilliant," was deservedly brief.

Now whatever may be thought of the existence in times past, and in other lands, of communities which might be correctly denominated Anglo-Saxon, it is manifest that in Britain no such community has been known since the period of the so-called Heptarchy. The "Saxon" and "Anglo-Saxon" people of England have, from the first establishment of their rule in this land, been blending themselves inextricably with the old British race, and have won many of their most valuable mental and moral characteristics through this very circumstance. The people of England to-day are possibly quite as little Anglo-Saxon as their speech. As to America, it is obvious that the great branch of the "Anglo-Saxon" race on that continent is still less Anglo-Saxon than their brethren of England. The first colonizers of North America were of the same ethnic mixture with our own ancestors; but for a hundred years and more the American people have been constantly receiving accessions of blood from all the nations of Europe—some from Asia and Africa, and some from the aborigines of America itself. They have already assumed a character in points strikingly differing from the parent stock in Britain, and in all these points they present a tendency to diverge from the "Saxon" type. It is a nice question, and one for which physiological science is scarcely as yet ripe, to determine how much of this differentia is owing to climate, food, and mode of life ; but it is not too much to say, that one of its chief causes is admixture of races. It is well that that great community, the inhabitants of the United States, should be called "Americans," for they are not English, and much less Anglo-Saxon in type. The study of anthropology and ethnology — young in England, has scarcely had its birth in America, but when it wakens and receives attention there, free from the partialities of race prejudice, and under guidance of that love of scientific truth which distinguishes Americans of culture, we shall hear no more of the "great Anglo-Saxon race" in America.

In fine, this people of England, so strong in mind, will, and hand, must learn to consider itself as something else than Anglo-Saxon ; for this it cannot in strictness be called, whatever style of loose nomenclature its humour may choose to adopt. Largely charged with ancient British blood, and formed on British ground, its proper designation is BRITISH. It is not Teuton, although it contains much Teutonic blood ; it is not Celtic, although it contains much Celtic blood. It is neither Anglican, Saxon, nor Cymri, but all these and more blended together. If it is more Teuton than Celtic, more Germanic than British, let proof thereof be given. Ever since the time of Gildas, the plea has been desultorily put in, and solely upon his worthless authority ; but the argument and the evidence have never been offered, and probably will long delay their appearance.

APPENDIX A.

Welsh Words Derived from the Latin and Other Languages.

The Welsh Orthography is that of Modern Welsh.

Welsh.	English.	Immed. Derivation and Cognates.
Achos,	Cause,	Lat. causa.
Actau,	Acts,	,, ago, actum.
Adail,	Building,	,, ædilis.
Addurn,	Ornament,	,, ad-orno.
Addurno,	Adorn	,, id.
Addysgu,	Instruct,	,, ad-disco; Gr. διδάσκω.
Adferu	Restore,	,, ad-fero.
Adnod,	Verse,	,, ad-nota.
Ais, asen,	A rib,	,, assis.
Allt, gallt,	Hill,	,, altus. (EBEL.)
Amddiffyn,	Defend,	,, defendo.
Aml,	Numerous,	,, amplus.
Amnhosibl,	Impossible,	English; Lat. impossibilis.
Angor,	Anchor,	Lat. anchora; Gr. ἄγκυρα.
Anifail,	Animal,	,, animale.
Anrheithio,	Devastate,	(See " rhaith.")
Antur,	Venture,	Fr. aventurer.
Anwiredd,	Falsehood,	(See " gwir.")
Appwyntio,	Appoint,	Fr. appointer.

[1] A few words added on the authority of Ebel (*Celtic Studies*—Prof. Sullivan's Ed.) are marked by the learned author's name.

Welsh.	*English.*	*Immed. Derivations and Cognates.*
Aradr,	Plough,	Lat. aratrum ; Gr. ἄροτρον. Name

of instrument, is clearly from Lat., but word for " act of ploughing "
belongs as clearly to Celtic, Gothic, Greek, &c. W. *aru,* to plough ;
Gael. *ar,* to plough ; Corn. *aras* ; A.-Sax. *erian,* to plough ; Gr. ἀρόω ;
&c. Eng. *ear* (of corn), earth ; W. *âr, daear* (earth) ; A.-Sax. *card ;*
Germ. *erde ;* &c. See "aru," Append. B.

Arch,	Chest,	Lat. arca ; Fr. arche.
Araeth,	Oration,	,, oratio, oro ; Ir. *oraid.*
Arf,	Weapon,	,, arma ; A.-Sax. *earm.*
Argyhoeddi,	Convince,	,, arguo.
Arian,	Silver,	,, argentum ; Ir. *airgiod.*
Arth,	A bear,	,, ursa.
Asen,	An ass,	,, asinus.
Assio,	Solder,	,, ad-suo.
Astud,	Attentive,	,, studio.
Astudio,	To study,	,, id.
Asyn,	Ass,	,, asinus. EBEL.
Athrist,	Sad,	,, tristis.
Astell,	A board,	,, assula.
Aur,	Gold,	,, aurum ; Ir. or.
Awch,	Edge,	,, acies.
Awdl,	An ode,	,, oda.
Awdwr,	Author,	Fr. *auteur ;* Lat. auctor.
Awdurdod,	Authority,	Lat. auctoritas.
Awgrym,	A sign,	,, augurium.
Awst,	August,	,, Augusti (mensis).
Awydd,	Desire,	,, avidus.
Bacsen,	Foot-covering,	,, baxea.
Bagl,	A crutch,	,, baculum.
Barf,	Beard,	,, barba (EBEL) ; but *barf* is

found in Corn. and Arm., and *bearble* in Ir. All, including Lat.,
probably derived from a common source.

Barwn,	Baron,	Lat. (late) baro ; or Fr. *baron.*
Bathu,	To coin,	,, batuo.
Bedydd,	Baptism,	,, baptizo ; Gr. βαπτίζω.
Bedyddio,	Baptize,	,, id.
Bendigaid,	Blessed,	,, benedictus.
Bendith,	Blessing,	,, benedictio.
Bendithio,	Bless,	,, benedico, benedictio.
Benthyg,	Loan,	,, benefactum, facio.
Benyw,	Woman,	,, fœmina ; but, Gael. *bean.*

Welsh.	English.	Immed. Derivations and Cognates.
Berf,	Verb,	Lat. verbum.
Berfa,	Barrow,	A.-Sax. *berewe.*
Berwi,	To boil,	Lat. ferveo ; Gael. *bruich.*
Bilwg,	Bill-hook,	English.
Bôch,	Cheek,	Lat. bucca.
Bollt,	Bolt,	English.
Bord,	Table,	A.-Sax. (See "*bwrdd.*")
Boreu,	Morning,	Gr. πρωί in the morning ; A.-Sax., *morne, morgen* ; Ger. *Morgen.*
Braich,	Arm, ·	Lat. brachium.
Brawd,	Brother	A.-Sax. *brother* ; Lat. frater.
Brefu,	To low,	Lat. fremo ; Gr. βρέμω.
Brwmstan,	Brimstone,	English. A.-Sax. *bryne,* a burning, and *stan,* a stone.
Budr,	Filthy,	Lat. puter, putris.
Bugail,	Shepherd,	„ vigilo.
Bresych,	Pot-herbs,	„ brassica.
Bwrdais,	Burgess,	English. A.-Sax. *burgh.*
Bwrdd,	Board, table	A.-Sax. *bord,* a plank.
Bwyst-fil,	Beast,	Lat. bestia. Last syll. from *mil,*

Celtic for animal. "Compounded like the German Maulthier, &c."—EBEL.

Bystach, ,	Steer,	Lat. bestia.
Cadair,	Chair,	Lat. cathedra ; Gr. καθέδρα.
Capten,	Captain,	Fr. *capitaine;* Lat. caput. The

Welsh spelling *cadben,* as if from *cad,* battle, and *pen,* a chief, is a fanciful adaptation.

Cadwyn,	Chain,	Lat. catena.
		„ captus.—EBEL. The root is in
Caeth,	Captive,	Celtic, as, W. *cae* enclosed field,
Caethiwed,	Captivity,	*cau,* to shut up ; Corn. *caid,* captive; Arm. *kez;* id.
Calan,	First day of month,	As *calan Mai, calanganaf, dydd, calan* ; Lat. calendæ.
Calenig,	New year's gift,	id.
Calch,	Lime (chalk),	Lat. calx.
Caled,	Hard,	„ calleo, callus.
Call,	Wise,	„ callidus.
Camp,	Exploit,	„ campus (Martius), Roman place of games.

Welsh.	*English.*	*Immed. Derivations and Cognates.*
Canu,	To sing,	Lat. cano. But both possibly from a common etymon.
Cantwr,	Singer,	„ cantator.
Cancr,	Cancer,	„ cancer.
Cant,	Hundred,	„ centum.

But the *hund*, in "hundred" (from A.-Sax. *hund*, 100) and Lat. *centum*, W. *cant*, Gael. *cend*, &c., are all from one etymon, the strong breathing represented in one by *h*, in the other by *c*.

Canwriad,	Centurion,	Lat. centurio.
Canwyll,	Candle,	„ candela.
Carchar,	Prison,	„ carcer.

The direct descent of the whole, *carchar*, is doubtless from Lat., but *car* or *caer* is common Celtic, as *caer*, a place of defence. The Lat. may be but a reduplication of the same archaic word, *car-cer.*

Cardod,	An alms,	Lat. caritas.

But the etymon, *car*, is common to Celtic, as W. *câr*, a friend; *cariad*, love, Gael. *car*, *caraid.*

Carrai,	Thong (of shoe),	Fr. *courroie*, Lat. corrigia.
Carw,	Stag,	Lat. cervus.
Castell,	Castle,	„ castellum.
Câth,	Cat,	„ (late) cattus.—EBEL.
Cawl,	Broth,	„ caulis (herbs).
Ceulad,	Runnet,	„ coagulo.
Cawn,	Reed-grass,	„ canna.
Caws,	Cheese,	„ caseus, or A.-Sax. *cese ;* Germ. *Käse.*
Cebystr,	Halter,	„ capistrum.
Cedrwydd,	Cedar,	„ cedrus.
Cegin,	Kitchen,	„ coquina, coquo.
Cengl, or Cingel,	Girth,	„ cingula, cingo.
Cerwyn,	Mash-tub,	„ car(o)enum, instead of car-(w)enaria.—EBEL.
Cessail,	Armpit,	Fr. *goussel*, Lat. axilla.
Cest,	Paunch,	Lat. cista ; Gael. *ciste*, likewise borrowed.
Cestog,	Large-bellied,	„ id.
Chwefror,	February,	„ Februarii (mensis).
Cingel,	Girth,	Fr. *sangle* , from Lat. cingo.
Ciniaw,	Dinner,	Lat. cœna.
Cist, as cist-faen,	Sepulchral chest,	„ id.
Ciwdawd,	Tribe, clan,	„ civitas.—EBEL.
Claddu,	To bury,	„ claudo, to shut up, inclose.

Welsh.	*English.*	*Immed. Derivations and Cognates.*
Clawdd,	A ditch,	Lat. id.
Cloddio,	To dig,	,, id.
Claer and clir,	Clear,	,, clarus.
Cleddyf,	Sword,	,, gladius, Fr. *glaive.*
Cler, as " Gwyr cler," literati,		Lat. clerus ; Gr. κλῆρος
Clo,	A lock,	,, clavis, claudo, Gr. κλείω.
Cloi,	To lock,	The same elements of the word,

c, or *k,* and *l,* transposed, are found in the A.-Sax. *loc,* a lock, *locian,* to lock. The Germ. *Schloss,* has the Latin order.

Clós,	A yard,	Lat. claudo.
Côch,	Red,	,, coccum.
Codwm,	A fall,	,, cado.
Cocth,	Purified,	,, coquo, coctus.
Côg,	A cook,	,, id.
Cogail,	Truncheon, staff,	,, (late) conucula—EBEL.
Cogi,	To cook,	,, coquo.
Coleddu,	To cherish,	,, colo.
Colofn,	Column,	,, columna.
Colomen,	Dove,	,, columba ; Fr. *colomb.*
Condemnio,	To condemn,	,, con-damno.
Congl,	Corner,	,, angulus.
Coron,	Crown,	,, corona ; Germ. *Kronc.* See
		" *cor,*" Append. B.
Corph,	Body,	,, corpus.
Coryn,	Top of the head,	,, corona.
Credo,	Belief, ·	,, credo.
Credu,	To believe,	,, id.
Crefft,	A trade,	Eng. craft ; A.-Sax. craeft. The

form *crefft* is borrowed ; but the Celtic, like the Teutonic tongues, have the etymon. Craeft, craft, and crefft alike indicate skill, manual and mental, but the former is the first and literal meaning —skill in using the hand, cutting, *carving.* Welsh *crafu, cerfio,* to scratch, carve. Ir. *sgrabam ;* Gael. *grabhal,* to carve ; Arm. *crava ;* Corn. *gravio ;* vide " *argraph*" and " *crafu,*" Append. B.

Creadur,	Creature,	,, creatura, creo.
Creu,	Create,	,, creo.
Creawdwr,	Creator,	Lat. creator.
Crefydd (cred-		
ffydd)	Religion,	,, credo and fides.
Croesaw,	To welcome,	,, recipio.
Croes-ffordd,	Cross-road,	,, crux ; and A.-Sax, *ford,* a

shallow to cross a river, then any road·

Welsh.	English.	Immed. Derivations and Cognates.
Crys,	Shirt,	Fr. creseau.
Cufydd,	Cubit,	Lat. cubitus.
Cûr,	Care, pain,	,, cura.
Cwcewll,	Cowl,	,, cucullus.

"According to Diefenbach, the Latin word had already been borrowed from the Celtic."—EBEL.

Cweryl,	Quarrel,	,, querela. In Pughe's Dict., but scarcely naturalized in W.
Cwestiwn,	Question,	From the English; scarcely naturalized in W., but in common use.
Cwlltwr,	Coulter,	Lat. culter, colo.
Cwnseri,	To conjure,	,, conjuro.
Cwmmwl,	Cloud,	,, cumulus.
Cwrw,	Ale,	,, cervisia.
Cwyr,	Wax,	,, cera; Gael. ceir, also borrowed.
Cybydd,	Miser,	,, cupidus, cupio. [rowed.
Cyffes,	Confession	,, confessio.
Cyllell,	Knife,	,, cultellus, dim. of culter.
Cymmar,	Partner,	,, com-par.
Cymharu,	To compare,	,, comparo.
Cymmell,	To compel,	,, compello.
Cymmwys,	Suitable,	,, commodus.
Cymmysg,	Mixed,	,, commisceo. See "Mysg."
Cyndyn,	Stubborn,	,, contendo.
Cynnwrf	Disturbance,	,, con-turba. But root of turba
(cyd and torf),		is frequent in the Celtic:

W. tor, a heap, tyrru, to crowd, tyrfa, a multitude (same as Lat. turba), Gael, torr, to heap up, &c.

Cystal, } Cystadl, }	As good, equal,	Lat. constatus.
Cysson,	Agreeing, consonant,	,, con-sono. But see "swn," "sain," in Append. B.
Cyssyl,	Council,	,, concilium, con-calo.
Cyssylltu,	To join,	,, con-solido, or sulo.
Cystudd,	Affliction,	,, castigo.
Dagrau,	Tears,	Gr. δάκρυα.
Damnio,	Condemn,	Lat. damno.
Dannod,	To cast in the teeth,	,, dens.
Dant,	Tooth,	Fr. dent; Lat. dens-tis.
Dâs,	Mow or stack,	,, tas.

Welsh.	English.	Immed. Derivations and Cognates.
Dawn,	A gift,	Lat. dono, donum.
Deddf,	Law,	„ datum.
Dedwydd,	Happy,	Fr. deduit.
Dewin,	Wizard,	Lat. divino.
Diafol,	Devil,	„ diabolus ; Gr. διάβολος.
Dibynu,	Depend,	„ dependo.
Difyr,	Amusing,	„ diverto.
Difyru,	To divert,	„ id.
Diffrwyth,	Fruitless,	„ de-fructus.
Diffyg,	Defect,	„ de-fectus, deficio.
Diffyn,	Defend,	„ de-fendo.
Dilëu.	Wipe out,	„ deleo.
Diliw,	Deluge,	„ diluvium.
Dimai,	Half-penny,	„ dimidium.
Diserth,	Desert,	„ deserta.
Disgyn,	Descend,	„ descendo.
Diwrnod,	Day,	„ diurnum.
Doctor,	Doctor,	English ; Lat. doctor.
Docth,	Wise,	Lat. doctus, doceo.
Dolur,	Pain,	Fr. douleur ; Lat. dolor. The

orthography and pronunciation of dolur favour its reception through the Norm.-French.

Dosparth,	A section,	Lat. dis-partio, pars.
Dosparthu,	To classify,	„ id.
Draig,	Dragon,	„ draco.
Dur,	Steel,	„ durus (hard).
Diwbl,	Double,	English, from Lat. duplex.
Dwl,	Dull,	„ „ A.-Sax. dol.
Dydd,	Day,	Lat. dies ; A.-Sax. daeg.
Dylifo,	To flow,	„ diluvio.
Dysgl,	A dish,	„ discus ; Gr. δίσκος,
Dysgu,	To learn, to teach	„ disco ; Gr. διδάσκω.
Dysgedig,	Learned,	„ id.
Dystryw,	Destruction,	„ destruo.
Dystrywio,	Destroy,	„ id.
Ebol,	Colt,	„ pullus ; Gr. πῶλος.
Ebrill,	April,	„ Aprilis (mensis).
Effaith,	Effect,	Prob. borrowed from English ; Lat. efficio, effectus.
Efyll,	Twins,	Lat. gemellus.
Eglur,	Clear,	„ clarus.
Eigion,	Ocean,	„ oceanus ; Gr. ὠκεανός.

Welsh.	English.	Immed. Derivations and Cognates.
Eiliad, as "eiliad llygad,"	A moment,"glance of an eye." "She gave strange eye-liads."—Shakesp.	Fr. oeillade, a glance.
Eistedd,	Sit,	Lat. assideo.
Elfen,	Element,	„ elementum.
Eli,	Ointment,	„ oleum ; Gr. ἄλειμμα.
Elusen,	An alms.	„ eleemosyna ; Gr. ἐλεημοσύνη.
Erthygl,	Article,	English, from Lat. articulus.
Esgus,	Excuse,	„ „ „ excuso.
Esgyd,	A shoe,	A.-Sax. gesceod, shod, from sceo, shoe ; Germ. Schuh.
Esponiad,	Exposition,	Lat. expositio, ex-pono.
Esponio,	To expound,	„ expono.
Estron,	Stranger,	„ extraneus.
Estyn,	To extend,	„ extendo.
Esgyn,	To ascend,	„ ascendo.
Ewyllys,	Will,	A.-Sax. willice, willingly ; willa, will ; Lat. voluntas.
Ffaelu,	To fail,	English ; A.-Sax. feallan, to fail ; Germ. fehlen.
Ffagl,	Torch,	Lat. facula.
Ffair,	A fair,	English. Germ. Feier (holiday, festival), and this from Lat. feriæ (Roman holidays), or from forum (market-place).
Ffaith,	A fact,	Lat. factum, facio.
Ffald,	A fold,	A.-Sax. fald.
Ffals,	Cunning,	English, false ; Lat. fallo, falsus.
Ffenestr,	Window,	Lat. fenestra.
Ffenigl,	Fennel,	„ fœniculum—EBEL.
Fferm,	A farm,	English. A.-Sax. feorm, food, support—hence the land which yielded support.
Ffarmwr,	Farmer,	English.
Fflàm.	Flame,	Lat. flamma.
Fflangell,	Scourge,	„ flagello ; Germ. Flegel, whence Engl. flail.
Ffoi,	To flee,	„ fugio.
Ffôl,	Foolish, fool,	Fr. fol, from late Latin, follis, a wind-bag, but this perhaps derived from old Celtic root. It is in Corn. and Arm.
Fforch,	Fork,	English. Lat. furca.
Ffordd,	Way, road,	A.-Sax. ford, a shallow in a stream, a ford.

Welsh.	_English._	_Immed. Derivations and Cognates._
Fforest,	Forest,	Engl.; from late Lat. foresta.
Ffortun,	Fortune,	Lat. fortuna.
Ffós,	A ditch,	,, fossa, fodio.
Ffrwyn,	Bridle,	Fr. _frein_; Lat. frœnum.
Ffrwyth,	Fruit,	English. Lat. fructus.
Ffugyr	Figure,	Lat. figura.
Ffumer,	Chimney,	Fr. _fumer_, to smoke; Lat. fuma-
Ffurf,	Form,	Lat. forma. [rium.
Ffurfio,	To shape,	,, formo.
Ffurfafen,	Firmament,	,, firmamentum.
Ffyrling,	Farthing,	A.-Sax. _feordhling_, from _feordha_, a
Ffyst,	Flail,	Lat. fustis. [fourth.
Ffwrn,	Furnace,	Fr. _fourne_, Lat. furnus.
Ffynon,	Fountain,	Lat. fons; late Latin, fontana.
Ffyrf,	Firm,	,, firmus.
Gafr,	A goat,	,, capra.
Gardd,	Garden,	A.-Sax. _geard_; Germ. _Garten._
Garth,	Inclosure,	id.
Gem,	A gem,	English, from Lat. gemma.
Golud,	Wealth,	A.-Sax. _geld_; Germ. _Geld._
Gonest,	Honest	English, from Lat. honestus.
Goreuro,	To gild,	See "_aur._"
Gormod,	Excess,	Lat. modus; and W. _gor_, extreme.
Grissill,	Gridiron,	,, craticula.
Grâdd,	Degree,	,, gradus.
Grammadeg,	Grammar,	,, grammatica; Gr. γράμμα,

(writing). From one etymon have sprung γράμμα, from γράφω, Welsh _crafu, cerfio_, Gael. _grabbal_, A.-Sax. _craeft_, also, perh. _writan_, to cut, write, Germ. _schreiben, Schrift._ The first part of the word "gram," therefore, may be considered pure Aryan.

Grawn,	Grapes,	Lat. granum.
Gronyn,	A grain,	,, granum.
Gwág,	Empty,	,, vacuus.
Gwael,	Vile,	,, vilis.
Gwain,	Scabbard,	Fr. _gaine_; Lat. vagina.
Gwâl,	A wall,	Lat. vallum. Corn. _gwal_; Ir. _gal_

and _bala_; Germ. _Wall_; Sansc. _valan._ The form in modern High-land Gael. is _balla_ and _balladh_, but that _gwal_, or _wal_, or _val_ was the earliest adopted form is evident from the well-known instance _Penfahel_, mentioned by Bede as a Pictish name of a place at the head or end of the _wall_ of Severus. Bede i. 12.

Welsh.	English.	Immed. Derivations and Cognates.
Gwastad,	A plain,	Lat. vasto, to waste, to level by cutting down trees, &c. A.-Sax. westan.
Gwastraff,	Waste,	{ Lat. vasto, or A.-Sax. westan, to
Gwastraffu,	To waste,	{ waste, and Welsh rhafu, to spread.
Gweddw,	Widow,	Lat. vidua.
Gwedyd,	To speak,	A.-Sax. cwedan. But conf. "gweyd," Append. B.
Gwener (dydd),	Friday,	Lat. Veneris (dies).
Gwenwyn,	Poison,	„ venenum.
Gwers,	Verse, lesson,	„ versus.
Gwersyll,	Camp,	Fr. guerre, war, and selle, seat.
Gwiber,	Viper,	Lat. vipera.
Gwilio,	To watch,	„ vigilo.
Gwin,	Wine,	„ vinum.
Gwisg,	Garment,	„ vestis.
Gwyrth,	Miracle,	„ virtus.
Gwydr,	Glass,	„ vitrum.
Gwyl,	Festival	„ vigil ; Fr. veille.
Gwyllt,	Wild,	A.-Sax. wild.
Gwynt,	Wind,	Lat. ventus, or A.-Sax. wind.
Gwyrdd,	Green,	„ viridis ; Gael. gorm; A.-Sax. grene; Germ. grün.
Gwyryf,	Virgin,	„ virgo.
Gwyrth,	A miracle,	„ virtus, power, strength.
Gyrru,	To drive,	„ curro.
Halin,	Spittle,	„ saliva—E.
Harnais,	Harness,	O. Fr. harnas, N. Fr. harnais.
Hat,	Hat,	A.-Sax. haet.
Heddyw,	To-day,	Lat. hodie.
Helyg,	Willow,	„ salix ; Gael. seileach, fr. same.
Hogi,	Sharpen,	„ acuo.
Hosan,	Hose,	„ A.-Sax. pl. hosan.
Hwyr,	Late,	„ sero, serus, late.
Hynod,	Notable,	„ notus ; W. hy, apt, giving emphasis.
Iau,	Jupiter,	„ Jovis.
Iau (dydd)	Thursday,	„ Jovis (dies).
Iau,	A yoke,	„ jugum.
Ionawr,	January,	„ Januarii (mensis).
Iuddew,	A Jew,	„ Judæus ; Gr. 'Ιουδαῖος.

Welsh.	*English.*	*Immed. Derivations and Cognates.*
Ieuangc,	Young,	Lat. juvencus.
Iwrch,	Roebuck,	,, hircus.
Llabyddio,	To stone,	,, lapido.
Llaes,	Loose,	,, laxus.
Llaeth,	Milk,	Fr. *lait*; Lat. lac-tis; Gr. γάλα,

gen, γάλακτος. Celtic and Teutonic cognates with this Gr. genitive, are Gael. *leig*, to milk; A.-Sax., *meolc;* Germ. *Milch;* Eng. *milk.* Prob. the Fr. *lait,* has descended from Belgic or Gallic. Ital. latte. All from Aryan root.

Llafur,	Labour,	Lat. labor.
Lle,	A place,	Fr. *lieu ;* Lat. locus.
Lledr,	Leather,	A.-Sax. *leder ;* Germ. *Leder.*
Lleidr,	Thief,	Lat. latro.
Lleisw,	Lye,	,, lixivium ; A.-Sax., laeg.
Lleng,	Legion.	,, legio.
Llesg,	Faint, feeble,	,, laxus.
Llew,	Lion,	,, leo.
Llewpard,	Leopard,	English. Lat, leo-pardus.
Lleyg,	Layman,	Lat. lay. Comp. Germ. *Leute.*
Llinell,	A line,	,, linea. See "*llin,*" App. B.
Llith,	A lesson,	,, litera.
Llong,	Ship,	,, longa (navis).—EBEL.
Llugorn,	A lantern,	,, lucerna.—EBEL. See "*lluscrn.*"

Llugorn *may* be from *lluab,* a light, and *Corn.* horn, the material of which the instrument was made.

Llun (dydd),	Monday,	Lat. luna (the moon).
Llun,	Figure,	,, lineo, delinio, to portray.
Llunio,	To shape,	
Llurig,	Coat of mail,	,, lorica.
Lluscrn,	Lantern,	,, lucerna, lux.
Llyfn,	Smooth,	,, lævis ; Gr. λεῖος.
Llyfr,	Book,	,, liber. But conf. "*llyfr.*" Append. B.
Llynges,	A fleet,	,, longa (navis).
Llythyr,	A letter,	,, litera.
Llythyrenog,	Learned,	,, id.
Llythyraeth,	Orthography,	,, id.
Llythyren,	Alphabetic letter,	,, id.
Machlyd,	Setting of sun,	,, occludo.
Maer,	Mayor,	Fr. *maire ;* Lat. major.

Welsh.	English.	Immed. Derivations and Cognates.
Magwr,	A wall,	Lat. maceria.
Mai,	May,	,, Maiæ (mensis).
Malais,	Malice,	English. Lat. malitia, malus.
Maneg,	A glove,	Fr. manique; Lat. manus, hand.
Mantais,	Advantage,	,, avantage.
Mantell,	Mantle,	A.-Sax., maentel; Germ. Mantel.
Marchnad,	Market,	English. Germ. Markt; Lat. mercor, mercator.
Maten,	A mat,	English. A.-Sax. meatte.
Mawrth (dydd)	Tuesday,	Lat. Mars, Martis (dies).
Mawrth (mis),	March,	,, ,, ,, (mensis).
Meidr,	Measure,	,, metrum; Gr. μέτρον.
Meddwi,	Get drunk,	Gr. μεθύω. But conf. " mêdd."
Meddyg,	Physician,	Lat. medicus. [Append. B.]
Medi,	To reap,	,, meto.
Medi (mis),	September,	,, id.
Meistr,	Master,	English. Lat. magister.
Melldigo,	To curse,	Lat. male-dico.
Melldith,	A curse,	,, male-dictum
Melldithio,	To curse,	,, id.
Melyn,	Yellow,	,, melinus; Gr. μήλινος; Ital. giallo, whence, yellow; Germ. gelb.
Memrwn,	Parchment,	,, membrana.
Mên, y fen,	Waggon, the wain,	A.-Sax., wacn; Gael. feun, id.
Mercher (dydd),	Wednesday,	Lat. Mercurii (dies).
Merthyr,	Martyr,	,, martyrus; Gr. μάρτυρ.
Mesur,	Measure,	English; or Fr. mesure.
Metel,	Metal,	Lat. metallum; Gr. μέταλλον.
Milwr,	Soldier,	,, miles.
Modd,	Manner,	,, modus.
Moes,	Behaviour,	,, mos, moris.
Moesol,	Moral,	,, ,, moralis.
Morthwyl,	A hammer,	,, martulus (martellus).—EBEL.
Morwyn,	Virgin,	,, virgo, vir-ginis.
Mud,	Mute,	,, mutus; Fr. muet.
Mur,	Wall,	,, murus.
Mwydo,	Moisten,	,, madeo.
Mydyr,	Metre,	English; or Fr. mètre.
Myfyrio,	Meditate,	Lat. memoro.
Mymryn,	A particle,	,, minima res.
Mynach,	A monk,	,, monachus; Gr. μοναχός.
Mynachdy,	Monastery,	,, id., and ty, a house.

Welsh.	*English.*	*Immed. Derivations and Cognates.*
Mynyd,	A minute,	English ; Fr. *minute ;* Lat minutus.
Mynwent,	Graveyard,	Lat. monumentum. Because erec

tions in memory of the dead were to *admonish* the living

Myrdd, ⎫ *Myrddiwn,* ⎬	A million,	Gr. μυριάς-άδος, pl. μυριαδῶν.
Mysg,	Among,	⎰ A.-Sax. *miscan ;* Germ. *mischen ;*
Cymmysgu,	To mix,	⎱ Lat. misceo.
Natur,	Nature,	Lat. natura.
Naturiol,	Natural,	„ id.
Neb,	None,	„ nemo.
Neges,	Errand,	Fr. *negoce ;* Lat. negotium.
Nifer,	Number,	Lat. numerus.
Nôd,	A mark,	„ nota.
Nocth,	Naked,	„ nudus.
Nwyfus,	Vigorous,	„ navus.
Odl,	An ode, ⎫	„ oda.
awdl,	rhyme, ⎭	
Oed,	Age,	„ aetas.
Oged,	Harrow,	„ occa.
Ogof,	A cave,	„ cavus. But see, "*cafn,*" "*ean,*" in Append. B.
Olew,	Oil,	„ oleum. See "*olew.*" Append.B.
Ongl,	A corner,	„ angulus.
Orgraph,	Orthography,	„ orthographia. See "*crafu,*" Append. B.
Orwyrain,	The east, quarter ⎱	„ orior, oriens.
dwyrain,	of sunrising, ⎰	
Pabell,	Pavilion,	Fr. *favillon ;* Lat. papilio.
Padell,	A pan,	Lat. patella.
Pâl,	Spade,	„ pala ; A.-Sax. *pal,* a stake.
Palas,	Palace,	Fr. *falais ;* Lat. palatium.
Palf,	Paw, palm of hand,	Lat. palma ; Fr. *palme.*
Pannu,	To full,	„ pannus, a cloth.
Papur,	Paper,	Fr. *papier ;* Gr. πάπυρος.
Pâr,	A pair,	Lat. par.
Parchell,	A small pig.	„ porcellus. See EBEL, "*porchell.*"
Pared,	A wall,	Span. *pared ;* Lat. parietes.
Parod,	Ready,	Lat. paro, paratus.

Welsh.	English.	Immed. Derivations and Cognates.
Parth,	Part,	Lat. pars, partis.
Pastwn,	Baton, staff,	O. Fr. baston.
Pau,	The country,	Fr. pays; Lat. pagus.
Pawl,	A pole,	Lat. palus.
Pen-elyn,	Elbow,	,, ulna.
Penyd,	Penance,	,, pœna, pœnitentia.
Pererin,	Pilgrim,	,, peregrinus (per-ager).
Perffaith,	Perfect,	Fr. parfait; Lat. perfectus.
Periglor,	A priest,	Lat. periculum. The Welsh viewed the priest as one averting " danger."
Peroriaeth,	Music,	Lat. os, oris. Prob. "per" from purus.
Person,	Person	,, persona, sono.
Perthyn,	Belonging to,	,, pertineo.
Perygl,	Danger,	,, periculum; Fr. péril.
Pescu,	To feed,	,, pasco; Gr. βόσκω.
Phiol,	A dish,	,, phiala—EBEL.
Pilio,	To peel,	,, pilo.
Pistyll,	Conduit,	,, fistula.
Plethu,	To plait,	,, plico; Germ. flechten. But, see "plygu," Append. B.
Plu, pluf,	Feathers,	,, pluma.
Pluawg,	Feathery,	,, id.
Plygu,	To bend,	,, id. But see Append. B.
Pocu,	Pain,	,, pœna; A.-Sax. pin.
Poenus,	Painful,	,, id.
Poenydio,	To impose pain,	,, pœniteo.
Pont,	A bridge,	,, pons, pontis.
Porchell,	A young pig, a pork,	,, porcellus.
Porphor,	Purple,	,, purpura, or Gr. πορφύρα.
Porth,	A gate,	,, porta.
Portreiadu,	To portray,	Fr. portraire.
Post,	A post,	,, poste; Lat. postis, pono.
Pothell,	Blister,	Lat. pustula.
Pottel,	Bottle,	Fr. bouteille; Ital. bottiglia.
Praidd,	A flock,	Lat. præda.
Prawf,	Proof,	,, probo.
Profi,	To prove,	,, id.
Profiad,	Experience,	,, id.
Preseb,	Manger,	,, præsepe.
Presenol,	Present,	,, præsens, præ-sum.

Welsh.	English.	Immed, Derivations and Cognates.
Preswylfa,	A habitation,	Lat. præsul. A man is "chief" in his own house.
Prif,	Chief,	„ primus.
Pris,	Price,	English; or Fr. *prix;* Lat. pretium.
Proffes,	Profession,	English. Lat. profiteor, professus.
Prudd,	Wise, thoughtful,	Fr. *prude;* Lat. prudens.
Punt,	A pound sterling; A.-Sax. *pund;* Germ. *Pfund,* a

weight of money (Lat. libra). The Norman pound was = 20
scillingas; the Saxon, 48; the Mercian, 60.

Pur,	Pure,	Lat. purus.
Pwdr,	Rotten,	„ putris.
Pwll,	A pit,	„ palus.
Pwnc,	Point,	„ punctum.
Pwrcas,	Purchase,	English; or Fr. *pourchasser,* to obtain by buying.
Pwys,	Weight,	Fr. *peser;* Lat. pendeo.
Pwyso,	To weigh,	„ id.
Pwyth,	Recompense,	Lat. pactum.
Pydew,	Pit,	„ puteus.
Pyg,	Pitch,	A.-Sax. *pic;* Lat. pix.
Pysg,	Fish,	„ *fisc;* Germ. *Fisch;* Lat. piscis.
Pysgotwr,	Fisherman,	Lat. piscator.
Rhaith,	Law, right,	A.-Sax. *reht, riht;* Germ. *Recht;* Lat. rectum.
Rhaith,	A jury,	A.-Sax. *raed,* Germ. *Rath,* counsel,

advice. "*Rhaith,*" law, and "*rhaith,*" a jury, seem to be related
to each other like A.-Sax. *riht* and *raed,* and Germ. *Recht* and *Rath.*

Rhadell,	A grater,	Lat. radula.
Rhamantus,	Romantic,	Fr. *romantique.* (Romanus.)
Rheibio,	To seize, bewitch, Lat. rapio.
Rhastel,	Hay rack,	Ital. *rastello,* palisades.
Rhaw,	A shovel,	Lat. rado.
Rhelyw,	Residue,	„ reliquiæ, Fr. *relique.*
Rheol,	Rule,	A.-Sax. *regol;* Lat. regula.
Rheswm,	Reason,	Fr. *raison;* Lat. ratio.
Rhesymu,	To reason,	„ id.
Rhialtwch,	Pomp, state,	Eng. royalty; Fr. *royauté.*
Rhidyll,	Riddle,	A.-Sax. *hriddel;* Germ. *Räder.*
Rhingcian,	To gnash,	Lat. ringor.
Rhôd,	A wheel,	„ rota.
Rhuo,	To roar,	„ rugio; Gr. ὠρύομαι.

Welsh.	*English.*	*Immed. Derivations and Cognates.*
Rhwyd,	A net,	Lat. rete.
Rhwyf,	An oar,	,, remus, Fr. *rame.*
Rhyfel,	War,	,, rebello, bellum.
Segru,	To set apart,	,, sacer, sacro.
Sadwrn (dydd),	Saturday,	,, Saturni (dies).
Saer,	Carpenter,	English saw-er, now sawyer, one who uses the saw.
Sail,	Foundation,	A.-Sax. *syl ;* Lat. solum.
Sarn,	A causeway, ⎫	Lat. sterno.
Sarnu,	To strew, ⎭	
Sarph,	Serpent,	,, serpens.
Sebon,	Soap,	Fr. *savon ;* Lat. sapo; Ital. *sapona ;* Gael. siabunn.
Segur,	Idle,	Lat. securus, sine-cura.
Senedd,	Senate,	,, senatus, senis.
Seneddwr,	Senator,	,, senator.
Serio,	To sear,	A.-Sax. *scoran.*
Siampl,	Example,	English. Lat. exemplum.
Sier,	Certain,	Germ. *sicher ;* Lat. securus.
Sierhau,	To assure,	,, id.
Siengl,	Single,	English. Lat. singulus.
Sill, ⎫	Syllable,	⎧ Engl. or Lat. syllaba; Gr. συλλαβή
Sillaf, ⎭		⎩ (taking together letters).

Uncert. from which of these the Welsh is borrowed.

Sionc,	Active,	Lat. juvencus, young.
Soddi, ⎫	To sink,	⎧ A.-Sax. *scothan,* to boil, seethe,
Suddo, ⎭		⎩ hence " sodden"; Lat. sido.
Sugno,	To suck,	Lat. sugo; A.-Sax. *sucan.*
Stigyl,	Stile,	A.-Sax. *stigel.*
Swch,	Ploughshare,	Fr. *soc ;* Lat. seco, to cut.
Swllt,	Shilling,	Lat. solidus ; late Lat. solta.
Swmbwl	A goad,	,, stimulus.
Sydyn,	Sudden,	English. A.-Sax. *soden.*
Symbylu,	To stimulate,	Lat. stimulus.
Swn,	Sound,	Fr. *son ;* Lat. sonus. Though a

common etymon exists, this particular form seems to be thus derived. See *swn, sain,* in Append. B.

Swydd,	Office,	Lat. situs.
Syber,	Sober, proper,	,, sobrius, or Fr. *sobre.*
Sych,	Dry,	,, siccus.
Sylfaen,	Foundation,	A.-Sax. *syl,* and W. *maen,* a stone.

Welsh.	English.	Immed. Derivations and Cognates.
Syml,	Simple,	Lat. simplex.
Symmud,	To remove,	„ se-moveo, motus.
Synio,	Perceive,	„ sentio.
Taenu,	To spread,	Sometimes der. from Lat. tendo. But see *taenu, tenen,* Append. B.
Tafarn,	Tavern,	English, from Lat. taberna,
Taradr,	Auger,	Fr. *touret;* Lat. terebra.
Tarfu,	To scare,	Lat. turbo.
Tasg,	Tax,	„ taxo; Gr. τάσσω.
Tewi,	To be silent,	„ taceo.
Terfyn,	End, bound,	„ terminus.
Terfysg,	Commotion,	„ misceo. *Terfysgu,* as if from *torf* (a crowd) or *twrw,* (noise , and *mysgu,* (to mingle.)
Terfysgu,	To make a com- motion,	„ id.
Teyrn,	A king,	„ tyrannus, Gr. τύραννος.
Teyrnas,	Kingdom,	„ id.
Teitl,	Title,	„ titulus; scarcely naturalized in Welsh, but in gen. use.
Tôn,	Tone,	„ tonus, prob. borrowed from English.
Traddodi,	To deliver,	„ trado, tradidi.
Traddodiad,	Tradition,	„ id.
Traeth,	A sand,	„ tractus.
Traethu,	Relate, treat of,	„ tracto, like *ffaith* from factum.
Trafael,	Travel, labor,	Fr. *travail* (s.), *travailler* (v.)
Trafaelu,	To travel,	„ id.
Trawst,	A beam,	Lat. transtrum.
Trebl,	Treble,	English. Not quite naturalized, but in common use. Lat. triplex.
Trist,	Sad,	Fr. *triste;* Lat. tristis.
Tristwch,	Sadness,	„ id.
Trosedd,	Transgression,	Lat. transeo-itum.
Trwsio,	Tie, or gird up,	Fr. *trousser.*
Trybedd,	Trivet,	English. Lat. tripes; Fr. *trépied.*
Trysor,	Treasure,	Fr. *tresor;* Lat. thesaurus; Gr.
Tymestl,	Tempest,	Lat. tempestas, tempus.
Tymer,	Temper,	English. Lat. tempero, id.
Tymmyg, (tymp-ig)	Timely,	English. A.-Sax. *tima,* time, has a common root with tempus

Welsh.	English.	Immed. Derivations and Cognates.
Tymp,	Time of child-birth.	Lat. tempus.
Tyner,	Tender,	,, tener.
Tyst,	Witness,	,, testis.
Tystio,	To bear witness,	.. id.
Tystiolaeth,	Evidence,	,, id.
Ufydd,	Obedient,	,, obedio ; f. substituted for b.
Uffern,	Hell,	., infernum.
Ugain, ⎫ Ugaint, ⎭	Twenty,	⎧ Lat. viginti; but a common root ⎨ is seen in Gr. είκοσι; Lat. viginti ; ⎩ W. ugain ; Gael. fichead.
Urdd, Urddas,	Order, ordination, ⎫ Dignity, ⎭	Lat. ordo.
Usuriaeth,	Usury	English. Lat. usura. Scarcely naturalized.
Uwd,	. . .	Lat. uvidus, spoon meat.
Ymbalfalu,	To grope,	,, palma.
Ymerawdwr,	Emperor,	., imperator.
Ymerodraeth,	Empire,	,, id. (Ymerawdwr-aeth.)
Ymgeleddu,	To cherish,	.. colo. Pref. ym, reflexive.
Ysgeler,	Wicked,	,, scelerosus.
Ysgol,	School,	,, schola ; Gk. σχολή.
Ysgol,	A ladder,	,, scala.
Ysgrin,	A chest,	., scrinium.
Ysgub,	A sheaf,	,, scopæ.
Ysgubell,	A broom,	,, scopula.
Yspaid,	A space of time,	,, spatium.
Ysplennydd,	Bright, splendid,	.. splendidus.
Yspryd,	Spirit,	., spiritus, spiro.
Yspytty,	Hospital,	,, hospitium.
Ystabal,	A stable,	,, stabulum.
Ystad,	Estate,	English. Fr. état ; Lat. statum "established possession."
Ystafell,	Chamber, a room,	Lat. stabulum.
Ystod,	Space, course,	,, stadium.
Ystôl,	A stool,	A.-Sax. stol.
Ystori,	History,	Lat. historia.
Ystorm,	A storm,	English. A.-Sax. storm.
Ystrad,	Vale, street,	Lat. stratum, sterno.

Welsh.	English.	Immed. Derivations and Cognates.
Ysu,	To eat, devour.	Lat, edo, esum
Yswain,[1]	Esquire, orig. a shieldbearer,	,, scutum (a shield), scutiger; Fr. *écuyer*.

ECCLESIASTICAL AND THEOLOGICAL.

Abad,	Abbot,	English. Lat. abbas-atis.
Aberth,	Sacrifice,	
Aberthu,	To sacrifice,	Lat. offero, offertorium (a place of sacrifice).
Aberthwr,	Sacrificer,	
Addoli,	To worship,	,, adoleo.
Adfent,	Advent,	,, advenio, adventus.
Allor,	Altar,	,, altare.
Angel,	Angel,	English. Lat. angelus; Gr. ἄγγελος.
Archesgob,	Archbishop,	Lat. archiepiscopus ; Gr. ἀρχιεπίσκοπος.
Bedydd,	Baptism,	,, baptizo; Gr. βαπτίζω; Gael.
Bedyddio,	To baptize,	*baisteadh* (same source).
Beibl,	Bible,	Prob. fr. English; Gr. Βίβλος.
Bendigaid,	Blessed,	
Bendigo,	To bless,	Lat. benedico, benedictus, benedictum.
Bendith,	Blessing,	
Calan (dydd),	First day,	,, calendæ.
Cangell,	Chancel,	,, cancelli.
Canghellwr,	Chancellor,	,, cancellarius.
Capel,	Chapel,	Fr. *chapelle ;* Lat. capella.
Clêr (as gwyr clêr. literati),	Literate,	,, Clerus ; Gr. κλῆρος.
Credo,	Creed,	
Credu,	Believe	Lat. credo.
Crefydd,	Religion,	,, credo, and fides (faith).
Creu,	To create,	,, creo.
Creadur,	Creature,	,, creatura.
Creawdwr,	Creator,	,, creator.
Creadigaeth,	Creation,	,, creatio,
Crist,	Christ	,, Christus ; Χριστός.

[1] When a word beginning with the letter *s*, followed by a consonant, is borrowed by a Celtic language, a vowel, generally the *y*, is prefixed. This is seen in all the words beginning with *Y*'s above.

Welsh.	English.	Immed. Derivations and Cognates.
Cristion,	Christian,	Lat. Christianus.
Cristionogaeth,	Christianity,	„ id,
Croes,	Cross,	„ Crux.
Croeshoelaid,	Crucifixion,	„ crux, and W. hoelio, to nail.
Cwcewll,	Monk's hood,	„ cucullus.
Cymmun,	Communion,	„ communio.
Cymmuno,	To communicate,	„ communico.
Cyffes,	Confession,	„ confessio, confiteo.
Cyffesu,	To confess,	„ id.
Cyssegr,	Holy place,	„ consecro.
Cyssegraid,	Consecration,	„ id.
Cyssegr-lân,	Holy,	Cyssegr, and glân, pure, holy.

Deddf, y ddeddf,	The law,	Lat. datum.
Deddf-roddwr,	Lawgiver,	Deddf, and rhoddi, to give.
Deddfol,	Legal,	Deddf, and adj. term. ol.
Degwm,	Tithe,	Lat. decem.
Degymmu,	To take a tenth.	„ decimo.
Diacon,	Deacon,	„ diaconus; Gr. διάκονος.
Diafol,	Devil,	„ diabolus; Gr. διάβολος.
Dieflyg,	Devilish,	Diafol, with adj. term. ig.
Diwinydd,	A divine,	Lat. divinus.
Diwinyddiaeth,	Divinity,	Diwinydd, and iaeth, or aeth, marking what belongs to the divine.
Duw,	God,	Lat. Deus; Gr. Θεός, Ζεύς, Δίς.
Duwdod,	Godhead,	„ divinitas.
Duwiol,	Godly,	Duw, and term. iol, indicating quality of likeness.
Duwioldeb,	Godliness,	Duwiol, and term. deb.
Dwyfol,	Divine,	Lat. divinus.

Efengyl,	Gospel,	„ evangelium; Gr. εὐαγγέλιον.
Efengylaidd,	Evangelical,	Efengyl, and adj. term. aidd.
Efengylu,	To evangelize,	Efengyl, and verb term. u.
Efengylwr,	Evangelist,	Efengyl, and term. wr, denoting, like Eng. er. a masculine agent.
Eglwys,	Church,	Fr. église; Lat. ecclesia; Gr.

ἐκκλησία. The W. word is used both for the building and the congregation of believers. Ἐκκλησία, by metonymy, came in like manner to have this twofold signification.

| Eglwyswr, | Churchman, | Eglwys, and gwr, man, |

Welsh.	English.	Immed. Derivations and Cognates.
Elfenau,	Elements (in the Sacrament),	Lat. elementa (ultimate derivation unknown).
Esgob,	Bishop,	„ episcopus ; Gr. ἐπίσκοπος.
Esgobaeth,	Diocese,	Esgob, and aeth, what belongs to.
Esgobyddiaeth,	Episcopacy,	Esgob-ydd-iaeth.
Ffydd,	Faith,	Lat. fides.
Ffyddlawn,	Faithful,	„ id. ffydd, and llawn, full.
Garawys,	Lent,	„ quadragesima.—E.
Gosper,	Vespers,	„ vesper.
Grâs,	Grace,	English. Lat. gratia.
Graslawn,	Gracious,	Gras, and llawn, full.
Grasusol,	Gracious,	Lat. gratiosus.
Gwener-y-	Good Friday,	Lat. Veneris (dies), crux, lectio.
Groglith,		The Friday on which a reading or service concerning the crucifixion was held.
Gwyl,	Festival,	Lat. vigiliæ ; Fr. veille, vigil.
Gwylnos,	Watch-night,	Gwyl, and nos, night—a night of watching over a corpse.
Llëyg (gwr),	Layman,	Fr. laique ; Lat. laicus.
Llith,	A lesson,	Lat. lectio.
Merthyr,	A martyr,	„ martyrus ; Gr. μάρτυρ.
Mynwent,	Grave-yard,	„ monumentum. Place of burial, and of erections to commemorate the dead and admonish or remind (moneo) the living.
Nadolig,	Christmas,	Lat. natalicia, a birthday festival.
Offeiriad,	A priest,	„ offero. A clergyman's chief function in the Roman Church was to offer the " sacrifice " of the mass.
Offeren,	The mass,	Lat. id.
Offerenu,	To perform mass	„ id.
Offrwm,	Sacrifice,	„ id.
Offrymu,	To sacrifice,	„ id.
Ordeinio,	Ordain,	English. Lat. ordo, ordinatio.
Ordinhâd,	Ordinance,	„ „ ordinatio.
Pabell,	Tabernacle,	Fr. pavillon ; Lat. papillio.

Welsh.	English.	Immed. Derivations and Cognates.
Pader,	Lord's prayer,	Lat. Pater (noster).
Pâb,	Pope,	Ital. papa.
Pabaidd,	Papal,	„ id.
Pabyddiaeth,	Popery,	„ id.
Pasg,	Easter,	Lat. pascha; Gr. πάσχω.
Pechadur,	Sinner,	„ peccator; Fr. pécheur.
Pechod,	Sin,	„ peccatum.
Pechu,	To sin,	„ pecco (root uncertain).
Periglor,	Priest, curate,	„ periculum (see p. 528).
Plygain,	Matins, cock-crowing.	„ pluma, cano.
Pregeth,	A sermon,	„ prædico, dictum.
Pregethwr,	Preacher,	„ prædicator.
Pregethiad,	A preaching,	„ prædicatio.
Prophwyd,	A prophet, ⎫	„ propheta; Gr. πρό, and φημί,
Prophwydo,	To foretell, ⎭	to foretell.
Prophwydoliaeth,	Prophecy,	„ propheta, and W. termns. ol-iaeth—the one adjectival, the other nominal.

Saboth,	Sabbath,	English. Heb. שַׁבָּת, rest.
Sabothol,	Belonging to the sabbath,	Saboth, an adj. term. ol.
Sanct,	A saint,	Lat. sanctus.
Sanctaidd,	Holy,	Sanct, and adj. termin. aidd.
Sancteiddio,	To sanctify,	Sanctaidd, and verb termin. io.
Sancteiddhâd,	Sanctification,	Id., and had, nominal term.
Sancteiddrwydd,	Holiness,	Id., and rwydd, nominal term.
Sect,	A sect,	English. Lat. seco, sectum. In common use, but scarcely naturalized.
Sectariaeth,	Sectarianism,	English, with W. termn.
Sul,	Sunday,	Lat. sol, solis (dies); A.-Sax, sunnan daeg; the sun's day. Germ. Sonntag. The Saxons worshipped the sun.
Sulgwyn,	Whit-Sunday.	Sul, and gwyn, white.

Teml,	Temple,	Lat. templum.
Trindod,	Trinity,	„ trinitas (post-class.).

Uffern,	Hell,	„ infernum.
Urdd,	Order,	„ ordo.
Urddas,	Dignity,	„ id.

Welsh.	English.	Immed. Derivation and Cognates.
Urddo,	To ordain, give	} Lat. ordo.
Urddasu,	dignity,	
Yscymmunedig,	Excommuni-cated,	
Yscymmuno,	To excommuni-cate,	} ,, excommunico.
Ystwyll,	Epiphany,	,, stella (the star of Bethlehem).
Ysgrythyr,	Scripture,	.. scriptura.
Ysgrythyrol,	Scriptural,	,, id.

It were easy to show that the Cymric is not the only Celtic tongue corrupted by contact with other languages. The Cornish contains much Latin, and is saturated with English. The Manx is not free from Danish. The French ingredients found in the Armoric are numbered by thousands. The Gaelic, by reason of its early separation and less frequent contact with English, might be supposed to have preserved its purity nearly intact, but a few examples will show how greatly it has borrowed: English, *master*; Gael., *maighster*; merchant, *marsanta*; mountain, *monadh*; honour, *onior*; common, *cumanta*; image, *iomhaigh*; figure, *fioghair*; feast, *feish*; failure, *faillinn*; draw, *dragh*; dozen, *dusan*; school, *sgoil*; scholar, *sgoilear*; devil, *diabhol*; save, *sabhail*; sacrament, *socramaid*; steer, v. *stiur*; sum, *suim*; board, *bord*; time, *tim*; pain, *pian*; reason, *reuson*; market, *margadh*. The Irish, though more separated, is scarcely less corrupted than the nearly identical Gaelic.

APPENDIX B.

———◆———

CYMRIC WORDS SOMETIMES DERIVED FROM LATIN, ETC.,
BUT WHICH SEEM TO PROCEED FROM ARYAN ETYMONS
WHICH HAVE BECOME THE COMMON PROPERTY OF
MANY EUROPEAN LANGUAGES, CLASSIC, CELTIC, AND
TEUTONIC.

Welsh.	*English.*	*Cognates.*
Afon,	A river,	Lat. amnis; Corn. *avon;* Arm. *avon;* Ir. *abhan;* Manx. *awin.*
Agos,	Near,	,, vicinus; Gr. ἐγγύς; Ir. *agus;* Corn. *agos; ogas;* Arm. *egos;* Gael. *fogus;* Germ. *enge;* Lith. *anksztas;* Slav. aza, azu, vazu (vinculum). Comp. Lat. angor, angustiæ—EBEL.
Ail,	Second, other,	Gr. αλλος; Lat. alius; Gael. *eill;* Corn. *eil;* Manx. *elley.*
Ar,	Earth,	Vide "*aru.*"
Argraph,	Imprint,	W. *ar,* upon and *crafu,* to scrape, scratch, cut; Gael. *grabhal,* to engrave; A.-Sax. *graef,* a graver; Gr. γράφω.
Aru,	To plough,	Gael. *ar,* to plough; Corn. *aras, aradar,* a plough; A.-Sax. *erian;* to plough; Gr. ἀρόω; Lat. aro : related to W. *âr, daear,* earth; A.-Sax. *eard;* Germ. *Erde,* earth; Engl. *ear* (of corn), and Old Engl. *ear,* to plough. "General in all European languages."—EBEL.
Aw,	A fluid	⎫ Lat. aër; Gr. ἀήρ, ἄελλα; Corn.
Awel,	A breath of air	⎪ *awel;* Arm. *awel;* Gael. *aile;*
Awen,	Poetic afflatus,	⎬ qu. Lat. *Aeolus?*
Awyr,	Air,	⎭
Awr,	Hour,	,, hora : Gr. ὥρα; Gael. *uair;* Germ. *Uhr;* Corn. *our;* Manx. *ovr.*

Welsh.	English.	Cognates.

Benyw, Woman, Lat. femina, venus; Gr. βανά, γυνή; O. Germ. winia (uxor); *ban*, Corn. *benow*; *benen* (spousa); Ir. *bainion*, *bean*, *ben*; Gael. *bean*; Sansc. *vanitá*; Arm. *gwam*; Fr. *femme*. Comp. BOPP, and EBEL.

Boreu, Morning, Gr. πρωΐ; A.-Sax. morn, morgan Germ. *Morgen*; Corn. *bore*; Arm. *beure*.

Bugail, A herdsman, Lat. vacca, pastor, bubulcus; Gr. Βοῦς.

Buwch, A cow, Lat. vacca; Gr. βοῦς; Gael. *bo*; Corn. *buch*; Arm. *bu*.

Brawd, pl. *brodyr*, Brother, Lat. frater; Gr. φράτηρ, φράτρα (clan); Goth. brothar; Germ. *Bruder*; Corn. *braud*; Ir. *brathair*; Arm. *breur*, pl. *bredeur*; Sansc. *brata*. Comp. EBEL.

Byw, Alive, to live, Lat. vivus, vivere; Gr. βίος; Goth. *quius*; Lith. *gyvas*: Slav. zivu; Corn. *bew*; Arm. *beva*, *buez* (life). Comp. EBEL.

Cae, An enclosure, ⎫ Lat. castrum, cavus. Not reducible
Caer, A city, fortress, ⎬ to any Latin roots. Related to W. *cau*, to close; Ir. *cathair*; Corn. *caer*. Comp. Pers. *car*; Syriac, *karac*; Arab. *carac*.

Caeth, Shut in, captive, Lat. capio. But whence "cap"? Cymbric has *cae*, an enclosure (as above); *cau*, to close, enclose; hence *caer*, a fortress; Gael. *comb*, a guard, defence; Corn. *caeth*; Arm. *kez*; Lat. cavus.

Cafn A hollow, W. *cau*, hollow; Lat. cavus, hollow; Gael. *uamh*, a cave; A.-Sax. *cafer-tun*, an enclosure before a dwelling. This "cafer" prob. same as W. *caer*.

Cain, ⎫ ⎧ Lat. candidus, candeo; W. *gwyn*,
⎪ ⎪ white. prob. same; Gael. *can*;
Can, ⎬ White, beautiful, ⎨ Ir. *fionn*: Corn. *can*: Arm. *can*.
⎪ ⎩ See, also, *Gwen*, *gwyn*.

Car A friend, Lat. carus; Gr. χαρίεις, χάρις; Gael. *cara*: Corn. *car*; Arm. *car*; Fr. *cher*; Sansc. *eriyas*.

Cariad, Love, Lat. caritas; Gr. χάρις-χάριτος, and χαίρω; Gael. *carantachd*; Corn. *carense*.

Can, Hollow. Lat. cavus: Gr. κοῖλος; Gael. *cuas*.

Carn, The end or haft ⎫ Lat. cornu, the projecting part; Ir.
of a thing, ⎬ and Gael. *uira*; W. *carn*, pro-
Corn, The horn, ⎭ minence, pile; Corn. *id.*, as of land, "Cornwall," the horn or premontor, of the Wealas, or Welsh.

Welsh.   *English.*   *Cognates.*

A.-Sax. *horn ;* Germ. *Horn.* The Teutonic differs from Celtic in
the rough breathing *h* being substituted for *c.*

Ceffyl,   Horse,   Gr. καβάλλης; Lat. caballus; Fr.
cheval ; Ir. *capall;* Corn. *cevil* (Corn. local name *Pen-cevil,* " horse's
head ") ; Manx. *cabbyl.* In use amongst peasantry in Yorkshire in
Welsh form *kevill.* " Slav. kobyla; Lith. kuméli, kumahikas."—EBEL.

Cell   A cell,   ⌐ Lat. cella, a cell ; celo ; Gr. κοῖλος,
Celu,   To conceal,   │ hollow ; Ir. and Gael. *cil, ceall;*
Cerfio,   To carve,   ⟩ Corn. *celes,* to hide : Sansc. *cal,*
Cil,   A corner, recess, │ to cover ; Gr. κλείω, to shut in.
Cilio,   To retreat,   ⌐ Vide "*crafu*" and " *argraph.*"
Ci,   A dog,   Lat. canis; Gr. κύων: Germ. *Hund;*
Ir. and Gael. *cu.* pl. *coin;* Corn. *ci,* pl. *ken, kuen :* Sansc. çvan, ç'un.
Clóch,   A bell,   A.-Sax. clucge; Germ. *Glocke ;* Fr.
cloche ; Gael. *clag ;* Corn. *cloch ;* Manx, *clagg.*
Cór,   A choir,   Lat. chorus ; Gr. χόρος ; Fr. *choeur ;*
Gael. *coisir ;* A.-Sax. *chor :* Germ. *Chor.* The first signif. of W. *cór,*
is a circle, which proves its affinity to Gr. χόρος, a dance in a ring.
Not improb. that W. *coron,* Lat. corona, Gr. κορώνη, Germ. *Krone,*
are from the same idea of a *circle*—surrounding the head.

Crafu,   To scrape, cut, Vide "*argraph*" and "*ysgrifio.*"
&c.,
Cynnwrf, or   Commotion,   ) W. *cyd,* together, *twrf,* a tumult;
Cynhwrf,   disturbance,) or *tyrfa,* a crowd, multitude ;
Lat. turba, a crowd ; turbo, to disturb; W. *twr,* a heap, tower ;
Gael. *tur,* id.; A.-Sax. *tor;* Germ. *Thurm ;* Lat. turris, &c. Vide
"*twr.*" W. *twrf,* is the tumult of a crowd, or *tyrfa;* and *tyrfa,*
like Lat. turba is a *twr, tor,* or *tur, i.e.,* a heap or accumulation (of
men). Vide "*torf.*"

Dagran,   Tears,   Gr. δάκρυα ; A.-Sax. *tächer,* tear;
Germ. *zähre ;* Gael. *deur :* Corn. *dager ;* Arm. *daer.*
Derw, derwen) Oak, an oak-tree (Gr. δρῦς, δόρυ ; Lat. quercus, quer-
(singular),)   (nus ; Goth. triu ; A.-Sax. treow,
a tree; Slav. drevo ; Ir. *dair, darach, duir ;* Corn. *dar,* pl. *derow ;*
Arm. *dero, derv.*
Dydd, pl. *dyddiau,* Day, Lat. dies ; Ir. *dia;* Corn. *dydh,*
dedh ; Arm. *dez, devez ;* Sansc. *dyu, divas ;* Slav. dini ; Lith. dëná.
Wanting with this meaning in Germ. and Gr.—EBEL.

Enw,   Name,   Gr. ὄνομα ; Lat. nomen ; Ir. *ainim*
Gael. *ainm ;* Corn. *anow ;* Sansc. *naman.*

Welsh.	*English.*	*Cognates.*

Galw, To call, Gr. καλέω; Lat. (archaic) calo; Gael. *glaodh;* Germ. *Schall,* a sound; Corn. *galow,* a call; Sansc. *cal,* to proclaim.

Genu, To give birth to, Gr. γίγνομαι, γίνος: Lat. gigno, geno, gens; Gael. *gin,* to procreate; *gincal,* offspring; Arm. *gana;* Corn. *geny;* Goth. *kuni;* Slav. *zenti;* Germ. *Kind;* A.-Sax. *cyn,* lineage, race; and prob. *cunnan,* to know, recognise. the nearly related, and, on this account, be *able, have power;* hence *cyn-ing,* a " king," either because a " power wielder," or one of the " race." Thus Engl. generate, genus; kin, kindred; king. know, are all of one root, the common property of most of the Celtic, Gothic, and other tongues of Europe.

Gwedyd, To speak, } Gr. αὐδάζω: A.-Sax. *cwyde,* a
Gweyd, Say, } speech, saying; *cwedan,* to speak;
Chwedl, A saying, } Corn. *gwesys.*

Gwèn, *f.,* White, fair, } Also applied as an epithet and
Gwyn, *m.,* Beautiful. } proper name to females. A.-Sax. *cwèn,* a queen, wife, woman. The Celtic adj. *gwèn,* white, fair, has a significance, when applied as an epithet of distinction, which the A.-Sax. *cwèn* has not. The latter is clearly borrowed from the former, as is proved by Cwensea, the Saxon name of the White Sea; Germ. *Weisse-meer;* Fr. *Merblanche.* The primitive sense of " white " is lost to the A.-Sax. cwen, and Eng. queen; and by this loss its use for a female ruler is simply arbitrary and technical. The W. *gwèn* retains the primitive signification, and explains the reason of the epithet. Gael. and Ir. *can* and *fionn;* Corn. *gwyn;* Arm. *gwenn.* The root is also seen in Lat. *candeo, candidus.* Comp. also, Gr. γυνή, γίγνομαι; Lat. Venus, cunnus; Goth. *quèns;* and Celtic, *benyw, bean,* as possibly all related.

Gwir, True, truth, Lat. verus; Gael. *fior;* Corn. *gwir;* Arm. *gwir;* Germ. *wahr;* Sansc. *varyas,* excellent; Engl. very— " the very man."

Gwin, Wine, This belongs to a class which from antecedent probability might be looked for in the primitive stage of most European languages. There can be no reason for deriving it into Welsh or Irish from Latin. It seems to be the property of all the Aryan tongues, with slight differences, initial and terminal, corresponding to the genius of each. Gr. οἶνος, Æol. γοῖνος (origin. Fίνος) Lat. vinum; Ir. and Gael. *fion;* Corn. and Arm., *gwin;* A.-Sax., *win;* Germ. *Wein;* Russ. *vino.* It is not absent from Semitic: Heb. ין, *ain.*

Gwlán, Wool, ? Gr. κάλον, beautiful, useful, good)

Welsh.	*English.*	*Cognates.*

Lat. lana ; Gael. *olann ;* A.-Sax. *wull ;* Germ. *Wolle.* The sheep is prevailingly white in all countries, and its covering, in W. *gwlân,* may owe its name to its pure and white appearance, from *glân,* pure, clean.

Gŵr, A man, Gr. γέρων, an *elder,* a *senator ;* Lat.
Gwron, A noble, brave vir, Gr. ἄρης ; Ir. and Gael. *fear ;*
man, A.-Sax. *wer ;* Corn. *gour ;* Goth.
vair ; Sansc. *varas,* from *var,* to defend.

Hafal, fel, mal, Like, similar, Gr. ὁμαλός ; Lat. similis ; Gael. adv. *amhuil ;* Corn. *haval ;* Arm. *hevel.*
Haul, The sun, Gr. ἥλιος ; Lat. sol ; Gael. and Ir. *soil ;* Corn. *heul ;* Arm. *heol ;* Goth. *sauil ;* Lith. *saule.*

Icuange, and Young, Lat. juvenis, juvencus ; Gr. ἥβη ;
Ifange, Corn. *yonc, iouenc ;* Arm. *iouanc*
Sansc. *yavan ;* Goth. *jungs ;* Lith. *jáunas ;* Slav. *junu.* Comp.—
EBEL. A.-Sax. *iung, iong, geong.*—BOPP.

Llab, llafn, Slab, blade, Lat. lamina, Gr. ἐλασμός, blade of a sword ; Gael. *lann ;* A.-Sax. *laef ;* Eng. *leaf ;* Germ. *Laub.*
Lled, llydan, Width, wide, Lat. latus ; Gr. πλάτος, πλατύς ; Ir.
Breadth, broad, *leathan ;* Corn. *ledan ;* Arm. *ledan ;*
Gael. *leud ;* Germ. *Platt,* a plain ; Lith. *platus ;* O. Norse, *flatr.*—
EBEL.
Llewyrch, Alight, a shining, Gr. λύχνος ; Lat. lux ; Gael. *lochran, soilcirich,* to lighten ; Corn. *lugarn ; luchas,* lightning.
Llin, Flax, Gr. λίνον ; Lat. linum ; Gael. *lion ;*
Llinyn, A string, Corn. *lin ;* Arm. *lin ;* Manx. *licen.*
Llu, lliaws, A multitude, Gr. λαός, λαϊκός ; Lat. laicus (hence Eng. *lay*-man) ; Gael. *lion,* to crowd ; A.-Sax. *leod,* people.
Lluchio, To lighten, Lat. luxeo ; Gr. λύχνος ; Gael. *lochran,* light ; Corn. *luchas,* lightning ; A.-Sax. *lihting.*
Llucheden, A flash of lightning Germ. *Licht, lichten,* &c.
Llyfr, A book, Lat. liber ; Ir. and Gael. *leabhar ;*
Corn. *lyvyr* and *levar ;* A.-Sax. *lar,* doctrine. Germ. *Lehre,* doctrine, *lehren,* to teach, &c., may be related.

Malu, To grind, Lat. molo ; Germ. *mahlen ;* Goth. *malan ;* Sansc. *mal ;* Ir. *meil ;* Corn. *melias ;* Arm, *mala.*

Welsh.	English.	Cognates.

Melin, A mill, Lat. mola : Arm. *melin ;* Gr. μύλη;
A.-Sax. *mylen ;* Germ. *Mühle ;* Goth. *moulin ;* Fr. *moulin ;* Arm.
melin ; Corn. *melin ;* Lith. *malunas ;* Sansc. *malanan.*

Marw, To die, Lat. morior; Ir. *merbh,* dead ;
Corn. *marwel,* to die ; Arm. *mervel.*

Mél, Honey, Lat. mel ; Gr. μέλι; Ir. *mil ;* Cor.
and Arm. *mel ;* Goth. *milith.*

Mis, Month, Lat. mensis; Gr. μήν, μεὶς ; Ir.
and Gael. *mios ;* Corn. *mis ;* Lith. *ménu ;* Sansc. *mas ;* Goth. *mena.*

Min, ffin, cyffi- Edge, bound, Lat. finis, confinis ;' Gael.' *finid ;*
niau, limits, Corn. and Arm. *min ;* also Corn.
mein, margin, lip, mouth. From these Fr. *mine,* whence Eng. *mien ;*
look, air, manner.

Môr, The sea, Lat. mare ; Ir. *muir ;* Corn. and
Arm. *mór ;* Anc. Gaulish, *mori ;* Germ. *Meer ;* Sansc. *miras.*

Mynydd, Mountain, Lat. mons; Fr. *mont* and *montagne ;*
Ir. and Gael. *monadh ;* Corn. *menedh ;* Arm. *menez.* Lat. mons is
referrable to no simple root in that language, unless it be the archaic
min, found in *emineo,* and this is none other than *myn* in W. *mynydd,*
men in Corn. *menedh,* and *mon* in Ir. *monadh.* Curiously enough,
mons and *mens* (mind) seem to have a common root, whose office is
to mark prominence, projection, in *mens* associated with the prominence of the *head,* the supposed seat of intelligence (hence also W.
menydd, brain), and in *mons* the prominence of the mountain.

Nef, Heaven, Lat. nubes ; Gr. νέφος; Ir. *neamh ;*
Corn. *nef ;* Arm. *env ;* Sansc. *navas, nabhas ;* Lett. *debbes,* for *dnebbes ;*
Slav. *nebo.*—BOPP.

Nigwl, niwl, Mist, Lat. nebula; Gr. νεφέλη ; Germ.
Nebel ; Ir. *neul ;* Corn. *niul.*

Nôs, Night, Lat. nox; Gr. νύξ; Ir. and Gael.
nocht ; Corn. *nôs ;* Arm. *nôs ;* Goth. *naht ;* A.-Sax. *niht ;* Germ.
Nacht ; Sansc. *nic, nakta ;* Russ. *noch ;* Slav. *nosch.* The word is
clearly from a common Aryan root. The history of its descent
offers no proof of its being a Latin or a Teutonic gift to Celtic.

Nyth, Nest, Lat. nidus ; Ir. and Gael. *nead ;*
Corn. *neid ;* Arm. *neiz ;* Sansc. *Nîda ;* A.-Sax. *nest ;* Germ. *Nest.*

Oes, An age, Lat. aetas; Gr. αἰών; Lat. aevum ;
O. H. Germ. *ewa ;* "is wanting in Slav. and Lith."—EDEL.

Olew, eli, Oil, ointment, Lat. oleum ; Gr. ἔλαιον; Gael. *ola,*
oladh ; A.-Sax. *ael ;* Germ. *Ael ;* Corn. *oleu ;* Arm. *oleon ;* Goth, *alev.*

Welsh.	English.	Cognates.

Plygu,   To bend,   Lat. plico, flecto; Gael. *pill;* Corn. *plegye, pleg,* a flexion ; Arm. *plega ;* Germ. *flechten.* Lat. plica, and Eng. "plait" and "ply" related.

Pobl,   People,   Lat. populus (rel. to which is *plebs) ;* Corn. *pobel ;* Arm. *pobl ;* Germ. *Pöbel ;* Gael. *poball.* Q. whether W. "*pobl*" is not of identical origin with W. "*pob,*" all, every ; or, whether *pobl,* and Lat. populus, are both derived from *pob. Populus,* sometimes contracted *poplus,* and *plebs, pleps, plebes,* are not reducible to Latin roots.

Rhi,   King,   Lat. rex; Gael. *righ;* A.-Sax. *rica ;* Germ. *Reich,* a kingdom ; Corn. *ruy,* and *ruif;* Arm. *roue :* Fr. *roi :* Goth. *reiks ;* Sansc. *raj.*

Swn, }   Sound.   Lat. sonus; perhaps akin to Gr.
Sain, }   στένω, to groan ; Gael. *son ;* Corn. and Arm. *son :* A.-Sax. *son ;* a sound, a song ; Sansc. *suaná.* There is no reason for deriving W. *swn* and *sain* from Lat. which is destitute of a root simpler than *sonus* itself.

Sédd, gorsedd,   A seat, throne,   Lat. sedeo, sedes; Gr. ἴζω; Corn. *sedhe, esedhe* (v.) ; Ir. *suidh ;* Arm. *aseza ;* Goth. *sitan ;* Slav. *sesti ;* Lith. *sésti.*—EBEL.

Sych,   Dry,   Lat. siccus: Gr, σαυκός; Fr. *sinc ;* Corn. *sych ;* Arm, *seach ;* Lith. *sansas ;* O. Slav. *suchu.*

Taenu,   To spread,   Lat. tendo, tenuis ; Gael. *tana,* thin ; Corn. *tanow ;* Arm. *tannaô.* The word *tin* seems to be from "*taenu,*" to spread (a coating) ; A.-Sax. *táu,* a spreading; Sansc. *tanu.* W. *teneu* is from same archaic root.

Taran,   Thunder,   Lat. tono, tonitrus Gr. στένω ; Gael. *torrun ;* Corn. *taran ;* Arm. *taran,* lightning. It is known that this word was in use amoung the Ancient Gauls, for Lucan informs us that Jupiter [Tonans] was called by them *Taranis.* See, also, p. 189. And so perh. TANARUS, Inscrip. Orell. No. 2054 ; A.-Sax. *thunder ;* Germ. *Donner.*

Tarw,   A bull,   Gr. ταῦρος ; Lat. taurus ; Umbr. *turu ;* Gael. *tarbh ;* Corn. *tarow ;* Anc. Gaul. *tarvos ;* Slav. *tour.* Conf. Max. Müller, Oxford Essays, 1856, p. 26.

Torch,   A ring, wreath, } Lat. torqueo. But torqueo is not
Torchi,   To coil, wreathe, } derivable from any Latin root ; tero, to rub, cannot be its origin. The idea of roundness, prominence, a bulging, or swelling, is expressed in Celtic by *tor, twr,* and

| *Welsh.* | *English.* | *Cognates.* |

the act of turning is expressed by *troi.* Big-bellied is *torrog,* in W. and Corn ; Arm. *torrec ;* Gael. *torrach.* The Gaulish and Briton princes wore as an ornament a gold ring or collar around the neck, in reference to which custom, Llywarch Hên, circ. A.D. 620, uses the word *eur-dorchawg,* golden-collared, or wreathed. See p. 69, ante. A.-Sax. *turnian,* to turn ; *tor,* a prominence, hill ; Germ. *Thurm ;* Eng. *torch,* because of the coiling action of flame.

Tir. dacar,   Land, earth,   Lat. terra ; Gael. Corn. Arm. *tir ;* Corn. *tir devrac,* watery ground ; *tir ha môr,* land and sea. Terra is not traceable to a Latin etymon simpler than itself. The word is not represented in the Teutonic tongues. Fr. *terre :* Ital. *terra.*

Torf   A crowd,   ⎫   Lat. turba ; Cymric *twr* is a
Tyrfa,   A crowd,   ⎬   heap, and *tor* means in Cymric,
Tyrru. v.   To crowd,   ⎭   Corn., Gael., and Arm. a rounded
prominence, a hill, a heap, an accumulation ; A.-Sax. *tor,* a hill, a peak, a tower ; Germ. *Thurm ;* Dan. *torm.*

Twr,   A tower,   Lat. turris. Same idea as in turba, and the Celtic and Gothic equivalents are the same as the cognates under " *torf ;* " Gael., Corn., and Arm. *tor;* A.-Sax. *tor* and *twr;* Germ. *Thurm ;* Dan. *torm :* Fr. *tour;* Gr. τύρσις.

Ty,   A house,   ⎱   Lat. tectum, tego, (to cover)
To.   Thatch,   ⎰   Gr. τέγος ; τοῖχος ; Ir. *teach, tigh ;* Corn. *ti ;* Arm. *ti ;* Germ. *dach ;* Lith. *stogas :* O. Norse, *thak ;* A.-Sax. *thace, theac ;* Icel. *thak,* thatch.

Ynys,   An island,   Lat. insula : Gr. νῆσος ἐνάλιος.— POTT. Ir. *inis ;* Arm. *enez ;* Germ. *Insel.*

Ysgrif,   A writing, ⎱   Lat. scribo, akin to Gr. γράφω ;
Ysgrifio.   To write, ⎰   Germ. *schreiben,* to write ; Corn. *scrifc,* to write ; *scrifen,* a writing : Ir. and Gael. *scriobh,* akin to W. *crafu,* to scrape, carve ; Ir. and Gael. *grabhal,* to engrave, and *grabhadh,* an engraving, a writing. A.-Sax. *writan* is not a very distant cognate, so that the words carve, engrave, groove, grave, gravel, write, are all from an archaic term meaning to scratch or cut. It is known that writing was at first effected by cutting or scratching a smooth surface.

APPENDIX C.

————◆————

SCHOOLS AND LEARNING AMONG THE CELTS.

REFERENCE has been made in preceding pages to the influence of Celtic thought and culture in the Middle Ages upon the literature of Europe, and to the deficiency of education among the Modern *Cymry* as compared with the state of things among their ancestors. (See pp. 483, 509.) The Celts of the British Isles have reason to remember with pride that, for many centuries, academic culture found among them an asylum when the Teutonic race, both in Britain and on the Continent, were principally concerned with war and conquest, and the feudal lords and even kings of England were so devoid of school knowledge as to be unable to write their own names.

Great as has been the change for good which has come over the quick and versatile intellect of Ireland, there has not been an age since Christian culture had its birth when the Irish were not votaries of learning. This is witnessed as to the Early Middle Ages by MS. treasures which have come down to our own time, many of which display an advanced intelligence and an artistic beauty unequalled by the productions of any other country of the same age. The higher education is represented among the Modern Irish by several diocesan and monastic schools, by the University and Trinity College, Dublin, and by the Queen's Colleges and University—the creation, indeed, of the English Government rather than of the Irish themselves. The reverence for learning and learned men inspiring all classes of Irishmen is an hereditary sentiment, the sign and memorial of ancient culture. The Scottish Celts give still greater proofs, if possible, of love for literary culture by the great universities of Edinburgh, Glasgow, Aberdeen, and St. Andrew's, which they took care to establish at an early period after the revival of learning, and which, in co-operation with numerous schools of a superior type, have raised the mind of Scotland to such a height of improvement.

The Welsh are now the only considerable section of the Celtic race not possessed of academic privileges; for even Brittany, longer than Wales a conquered and incorporated province, has several *lycées* and colleges of good standing affiliated to the University of France. And yet time was when the high schools of Britain—schools really high and distinguished for their period—were confined to that western region called *Wales*. To the Germanic clans who conquered what is now named England, schools were unknown, and some centuries had passed before Alfred the Great—in large degree through the aid of the Welshman Asser, whom he summoned for the purpose from St. David's[1]— succeeded in turning the minds of the Anglo-Britons (miscalled " Anglo-Saxons ") from the barbaric pursuit of the sword to mental culture and semi-civilized manners. Great schools at this time existed at Llanilltyd-fawr (now Lantwit-major) in Glamorgan, Bangor Iscoed, near Wrexham, and other places, to which the youth of Wales, and even of foreign countries, resorted by thousands. The site of the great monastery and school of Bangor is now covered by the green sward, and there exist but faint traces of the important institution of Llanill-tyd—once, it is said, possessed of not less than twenty " colleges." The domestic feuds of the Welsh in the early Middle Ages, and the desolating wars of the various invasions and conquests of Wales by English and Normans, totally annihilated, even to their last remains, these seats of learning, while concurrently with the growing power of the English arose by steady progress a taste for knowledge and great institutions of learning—of which Oxford was perhaps the first. Thus were the Welsh made to change positions with England.

The later Middle Ages, and the period of the Reformation, when thought and knowledge revived in Europe, found the Welsh at the lowest depth of humiliation and poverty, their country and race under ban, the wealth of their schools transferred to England, and a virtual veto put upon all intellectual culture. To this day nothing has been done by the State to repay this cruel injustice. But time will again come when Wales shall possess her schools, and the genius of her sons shall have free scope, and the stimulus of native culture, for the competitions of public life. Private benevolence has established many good seminaries. Education, by stealing marches, will still go on, creating its own opportunities and effecting its own deliverance. Statesmen will arise who, free from national prejudice, and capable of rational judgment, will discern and recognise the claims of *thirteen counties* of the realm, with a population of a million and three hundred thousand souls. Already a new life is being infused into the

---

[1] See Asser's *Life of Alfred*, A.D. 884.

older grammar schools, which, mainly through the pious liberality of individuals, had since the Reformation been established; and, in healthful competition with these, as population is increasing, middle-class schools of a superior kind, through the enterprise and ability of independent teachers, are arising. Under the new Education Act of 1870, with all its imperfections, a great impulse is being imparted to *elementary* education; and more pressing demands will be felt for a *higher* education midway between the common school and the university. The Oxford and Cambridge local examinations, along with other operations within the last ten years, have created a new educational period in Wales.

Before the Principality can attain to a proper intellectual status the description of schools just mentioned must be supplemented, or rather crowned, with an institution of a higher order, planned upon a basis strictly unsectarian, offering an education thorough and comprehensive, and adapted in its working to the circumstances of the country and the spirit of the age. The curriculum should be framed with the view of preparing young men for university graduation either at home or in England. Great efforts have been made to secure this object, and with hopes of ultimate success. The project was launched, and a scheme of Academic instruction drawn out, in 1862, by Dr. T. Nicholas, then of Carmarthen College,* in answer to whose appeals a large sum of money was subscribed, a magnificent building was purchased at Aberystwyth in 1867, for the cost of which (£10,000) the fund was more than adequate, and a basis was laid for an appeal to the Legislature for a Charter and a grant in aid. Though as yet unassisted by Government, the *University College of Wales* has had a beginning, and it is hoped will be fostered both by the people of Wales and by Parliament.

Although more fully developed than any other, this is by no means the first scheme proposed for academic culture for the Welsh. Under the Protectorate of Cromwell (himself descended from a [Cymric↑ ancestry), the eminent divine Richard Baxter, in 1657, made a definite proposal "for a College with Academic privileges for Wales," which it is believed only fell to the ground through the death of the Protector in the year following. But this was not the earliest attempt to resuscitate the spirit of learning in the Principality. When, in 1485, the Tudor line, in the person of Henry VII., ascended the English throne, we have clear intimations that the destitute condition of the country of his fathers touched the heart of that large-minded ruler, and that he granted the Abbot of Neath a Charter for a University of Wales. An intimation of the circumstance is given in Iolo Morganwg's *Cyfri-*

---

* See *Reports of Committee*, 1868, 1870, 1874.

nach y Beirdd, based on some ancient writings ; but a confirmation of a reliable kind is given to it by a passage in a poem by Lewys Morganwg, written in 1490, in praise of the same Abbot (Lleision). The passage may be rendered thus :—

> " A University at Neath ! A subject of celebration
> Through England ; a light for France and Ireland.
> A point of universal attraction to scholars
> As Zion is to pilgrims.
> Organs for choristers in white—
> The praise of competitions—
> Arithmetic, Music, shall in might contend
> With Rhetoric, Civil and Canon Law."

This was probably the poet's own idea of a university course for those days—a rather degraded modification, it must be confessed, of the recognised curriculum of study in the great schools of the Middle Ages. These schools taught the " Seven Sciences," the *Trivium* and *Quadrivium*, which were then held to embrace the whole circle of knowledge—grammar, rhetoric, dialectic, arithmetic, music, geometry, and astronomy, or in Latin verse :—

— " Lingua, tropus, ratio, numerus, tenor, angulus, astra."

The Abbot Lleision was descended from an ancient and honourable family in Glamorganshire, and a partisan of Henry as a man of Cymric lineage, in his efforts to obtain the throne. How this proposal failed of accomplishment is not known. But the Principality of Wales, after waiting nearly 500 years, is still without a " College with Academic privileges "—still without a shadow of compensation for ancient sequestration and pillage. The mind of the country is more than ever matured for high-class culture ; the population is vastly larger than in the time of Henry VII. and Cromwell ; wealth and industry, the demand for skilled labour and educated intelligence are rapidly augmenting, and every reason which favours the increase of knowledge and the elevation of a province, pleads for a High School for Wales. Men profess to be surprised at the intellectual inferiority of Wales to Scotland—not giving heed to the fact that Scotland, with only double the population of Wales, has several Universities, which for three or four centuries have been in operation for the culture of the Scottish mind. Men are surprised at the intellectual force and distinction of Germany, ignorant or oblivious of the fact that every petty German State, though not larger, perhaps, than a medium-sized English county, or a third part of Wales, possesses its well-equipped University.

The Celtic race in Britain, in one section of it, is thus depressed, intellectually, as a result of conquest, although that conquest in respect of liberty, law, and all political privilege, has been an unquestionable boon. The Celts of Wales, now far behind in literary attainments, are surpassed by none in a capacity and taste for knowledge. They maintain in this sense the reputation of the race which gave origin in Europe to the " University," as at Salerno, Bologna, Paris, and Padua—schools which arose after the decline of the great Monastic Schools of Wales, and had, as one of their chief originating causes, the romance literature, which has been already described as inspired by the Celtic genius of Wales and Brittany. It is curious to notice these alternations of Celtic learning and fortune, all of which, with many others, bring into strong relief the present and long past depression of education in Wales.

INDEX.

BY THE SAME AUTHOR.

Recently Published, in 2 vols., Super Royal 8vo., Embossed, Gilt, pp. 962.

Price £3 3s.

ANNALS AND ANTIQUITIES OF THE COUNTIES AND FAMILIES OF WALES.

Containing the Political History, Genealogy, and Heraldry of the whole Principality in separate Counties. With 180 *Illustrations* on wood, from photographs of Castles, Mansions, Arms, Seals, Tombs, &c.

By THOMAS NICHOLAS, M.A., Ph.D., F.G.S.

LONDON: LONGMANS, GREEN, READER & Co., PATERNOSTER ROW.

[*From the* ATHENÆUM.]

" This is one of the most valuable and useful historical works that we have seen for some time, and Dr. Nicholas deserves our thanks for the manner in which he has executed his task. . . . . Each county of the Principality is separately described. We have first its physical geography, and afterwards a careful description of its archæological remains, including notices of its ancient buildings, its castles, and abbeys. Then we have, in each county, an elaborate account of its old and extinct Families, as far as they can be traced, and this is followed by a history of the present County Families, and their pedigrees. We can recommend this book as one of great value as well as of authority; it is, in fact, the best and fullest History of Wales that we possess."

Milton Keynes UK
Ingram Content Group UK Ltd.
UKHW011534230124
436534UK00004B/226